TERRA USA

VERDICT

Boris Berezovsky vs. Russia's Oligarchs

TERRA USA

VERDICT
BORIS BEREZOVSKY VS. RUSSIA'S OLIGARCHS

Compiled and Edited by Yuri Felshtinsky

Publising House Terra-USA
46 Damon Drive, Falmouth, MA 02540
Tel.: (508) 540-6282
Fax: (617) 489-9814

E-mail: yuri.felshtinsky@verizon.net

ISBN 0-9787350-1-3

Printed in the United States of America

CONTENTS

APPENDICES

INTRODUCTORY NOTE

OVER THE YEARS, some famous Russian names have been featured in English libel cases. In 1933, Princess Irina Youssoupoff was awarded damages of £25,000, a record amount at that time; she had been depicted in a Hollywood film being ravished by Rasputin. Count Nikolai Tolstoy, a relative of the great Russian author, is the reluctant holder of the current English record; £1.5 million was awarded against him in 1989 for his part in the distribution of a pamphlet which accused the late Lord Aldington of complicity in the forcible return, at the end of the Second World War, of Cossacks to their fate at the hands of Stalin's Red Army.

The case of Boris Berezovsky v. Mikhail Fridman and *Alfa Bank* in May 2006 was never likely to set a new record. Indeed, long before the trial began, Mr. Berezovsky had offered to settle the case without payment of damages, provided that Mr. Fridman would withdraw his statement and apologize for the accusation.

Mr. Berezovsky took action over remarks made by Mr. Fridman on the popular Russian NTV program *The Duel*. The program takes its name from the traditional Russian challenge, which is particularly appropriate when discussing a libel claim. In the 16th century, attempts made by the Star Chamber to encourage the gentry to settle their disputes in matters of honor in court rather than on the duelling field played a part in the development of English libel law.

Many libel cases turn on the interpretation of the words spoken or written. Here there was no dispute over the meaning of the words Mr. Fridman used on the TV program. He stated on the program that Mr. Berezovsky had threatened him, and that he had threatened many other people along the way, as that was how Mr. Berezovsky worked. The case involved no complex legal issues. Mr. Berezovsky denied the allegation; Mr. Fridman claimed it was true. The simple question for the jury to decide, having heard all the evidence, was who to believe. On one side was Boris Berezovsky, who had held high office under President Yeltsin, and who had been forced to surrender his media interests and was driven into exile as a result of his opposition to the policies of President Putin. Pitted against him were Mikhail Fridman, the powerful chairman of *Alfa Bank*, who steadfastly refused to be drawn in to political issues; his partner, Peter Aven, who never shrank from criticizing the Russian government's treatment of the media baron Vladimir Gusinsky, who, like Mr. Berezovsky, had been forced out of Russia; and Boris Nemtsov, the suave politician and founder of the Union of Right Forces political party.

After a ten-day trial during which the witnesses were examined, cross-examined, and re-examined, the jury found in Mr. Berezovsky's favor and awarded him £50,000 in damages.

Andrew Stephenson
Carter-Ruck

Monday, May 15, 2006

JUSTICE EADY: Mr. Browne and Mr. Shields, I received a letter from one of the members of the jury panel, which you are welcome to see of course. But the thrust of it was that he or she, I am not sure which, knows Mr. Berezovsky. So therefore I will simply release that juror for other duties.

BROWNE: Yes.

SHIELDS: That is fine. My Lord, the only question we raise is whether that juror has had an opportunity to discuss that with any other jurors.

JUSTICE EADY: Discuss what?

SHIELDS: This case or his or her knowledge of Mr. Berezovsky. They are in the jury room together.

JUSTICE EADY: Yes.

SHIELDS: That could be a problem, my Lord.

JUSTICE EADY: I do not suppose—it is a careful letter. I do not suppose the person concerned would be that—perhaps we had better have the individual...

SHIELDS: I am just being cautious, that is all.

JUSTICE EADY: Do you want to see the letter?

SHIELDS: Would that be all right, my Lord? (*Handed*).

JUSTICE EADY: Needless to say, the letter is confidential; it is addressed to me.

SHIELDS: Yes, my instructing solicitors—of course, my Lord in the context of that letter, it is highly unlikely …

JUSTICE EADY: I mean, I will have the juror or panel member in to check whether he or she has in fact discussed it with anybody else, but it seems pretty unlikely in the light of the contents of that letter. So what would you like me to do, Mr. Browne and Mr. Shields?

BROWNE: If Mr. Shields has misgivings about what I think in some Crown Courts they call "taint," then of course his proposal seems sensible.

SHIELDS: No, my Lord. My instructing solicitor, having seen the letter, has decided not to pursue it. I think plainly he understands the position.

JUSTICE EADY: Then that particular juror—I take it, madam, you know who the juror is? Is it a woman or a man? A man. Can you tell him he will be released for other duties and will not be needed for this case. Thank you very much. We can now have the other panel in.

OPENING REMARKS BY JUSTICE EADY

Now, members of the jury, may I just say a few words by way of introduction. As I have already indicated to you, this is a libel action which you are about to try, which will probably conclude by the end of next week.

May I mention one matter at this stage which applies throughout the case, although I shall only say it once? Please do not discuss the evidence in the case with anyone outside your own number. And if you are discussing it amongst yourselves, please be sure to do so only in circumstances where you cannot be overheard by anyone else; I hope that is for obvious reasons.

Now, the acoustics in this room are, I am afraid, notoriously bad; sometimes it is quite difficult to hear what people are saying. So, if somebody is nervous and speaking quickly and quietly and you cannot hear what is being said, do not hesitate to let me know so we can have the evidence again, because it is very important that you hear all the evidence because you are the people who are going to be making the important decisions at the end of the day. So, do not hesitate to pass a note through the usher or put a hand up or anything of that sort. If in the course of the trial in any way a matter causes you concern, any of you, for whatever reasons, please do not hesitate to make contact with me through a note through the usher, either during the case or before the case begins on any particular day. So do not worry about that. Please let me have a note if there is anything concerning you at all.

Now, it has been agreed between the parties that I should introduce the case to you very briefly before either party's counsel says anything at all. And that is very unusual, but I will explain why.

This is a claim, as I have said, for libel, which means it is a claim for damage to reputation, brought by the claimant, who is Mr. Boris Berezovsky, against the defendants, who are Mr. Mikhail Fridman and the *Alfa Bank*. Mr. Berezovsky is a Russian businessman and a political campaigner who has lived in England now since 2001. Until recently, he controlled a newspaper in Russia which is called *Kommersant*. Mr. Fridman, the defendant, is a Russian also who lives in Russia, and he is Chairman of the Board of Directors of the *Alfa Bank*, which is one of the largest privately owned banks in Russia.

In October 2004, Mr. Fridman, the defendant, and the then editor of *Kommersant*, Mr. Andrei Vasiliev, appeared on a topical television show in Russia, known in English as *The Duel*, or *En Garde*, which is hosted by a man called Vladimir Soloviov. The subject matter of the program was a recent decision of the Moscow court awarding US $11 million to the *Alfa Bank* over an article published in *Kommersant*. The article related to a crisis in the Russian banking sector in the summer of 2004.

Now, the program was broadcast in Russia on October 28th 2004, on a station which is known as NTV. It was also broadcast on that same date via a satellite service which is known as NTV Mir or NTV World in English, and that was at 7:35 pm English time.

Now, viewers in England and Wales who had a subscription to the NTV World service would have been able to see the program here in various parts of England and Wales.

In the course of the program, Mr. Fridman made reference to Mr. Berezovsky, and those remarks, which are relatively brief, are the subject matter of this libel action.

Now, before Mr. Browne QC opens the case on behalf of Mr. Berezovsky, it has been agreed between the parties that the sensible thing is for you and I to watch a video of the whole program before anybody says anything about it. Just to reassure you, the part which you are directly concerned with is relatively short, as I have said, only a few minutes, but in order to give a proper context of what was said, it has been agreed that you should see the whole of the program.

One of your roles in this trial, as any jury in any libel action, is to put yourselves in the position of the viewer at the time of the broadcast to see what impression the program will have made on you as ordinary viewers.

A slight drawback in this case is that the program is in Russian. Therefore for our benefit, yours and mine, it has been agreed that there should be added some subtitles in English. In a sense, that is artificial, but it is for obvious reasons. What I must say to you is that as far as possible you are to try throughout the case to put yourselves in the shoes of ordinary viewers of the program, the ordinary Russian speaker. So try to get rid of that barrier, so far as you can, of the subtitles. That is the object of the exercise.

Now, before we proceed any further, you will be invited to watch the program. May I just say this before we do that, purely a matter of administration. Many juries find it, I think, convenient to start the court day at 10:15 and then have a quarter-of-an-hour break for tea or coffee at some convenient moment during the morning, about halfway through, and then have another break in the afternoon, and generally finish—depending on how the evidence is going—at 4:30; very rarely after 4:30, but sometimes before.

If we were to adopt that practice in this case and start every morning at 10:15, would that cause major inconvenience to any of you or would that suit you?

All right, shall we proceed on that basis tomorrow? We will sit at 10:15 every morning unless I say anything to the contrary because of changed circumstances. Having said that, members of the jury, may we now watch the program.

(*Television program played to the court.*)

Opening Statement
by Mr. Browne, Attorney for Mr. Berezovsky

Well, members of the jury, if, as I imagine is the case, that was your first exposure to Russian state-run television, I guess that your heads must still be spinning, so it is my job on behalf of Mr. Berezovsky, the claimant in this action, to try to tell you what this case is all about. Try, from the start, to focus your minds on the issues that you are going to have to decide in this action. I, as I say, appear for Mr. Berezovsky, who sits in front of me, with Mr. Matthew Nicklin. And the defendants—Mr. Mikhail Fridman who you saw on the television program—are represented by Mr. Shields and Mr. Eardley, who sits behind him.

Mr. Fridman is not in court at the moment; the gentlemen who sit in front of Mr. Shields are his solicitors, in case you are wondering.

I do not know whether any of you, before you came to this case, had ever heard the name Boris Berezovsky. I see one member of the jury nodding. There is of course a well-known Russian pianist called Boris Berezovsky, but he is not to be confused with him.

If you have not heard his name, then performing that very difficult task that the judge mentioned to you of imagining how a Russian or a Russian speaking viewer of the program would have understood it, you have to bear in mind that they—I suggest—would all have heard of Mr. Berezovsky. And when his name is dragged into the program by Mr. Fridman, about a third of the way through, it would have made them sit up.

Now, Mr. Berezovsky is one of a number of Russian businessmen who have become extremely wealthy as a result of the business opportunities that have arisen in Russia since the fall of Communism at the end of the 1980s. Most of them, like the absent Mr. Fridman, continue to live and thrive in President Putin's Russia.

Mr. Fridman, as is clear from the program you watched, is the chairman of *Alfa Bank*, the second defendant in this case. *Alfa Bank* is Russia's largest privately owned bank, with assets of billions of dollars and over 100 branches in Russia and the former Soviet Union. It is known in this country not least because it has a subsidiary here in London.

But, members of the jury, those whose businesses thrive in Russia today have learned that they must stay silent and turn a blind eye to the manifest human rights abuses of President Putin's government. Those abuses, you will hear, are universally acknowledged. You may have read about them. Political opposition has been crushed. The criminal justice system has been abused for purely political ends, to crush opposition, and there is no longer a truly free or independent press.

So the price of continuing commercial success for businessmen who remain in Russia today is silence. And of course they know they must keep their lips sealed; they know that if they publicly criticize Mr. Putin's dictatorial regime, let alone demonstrate any political ambitions themselves, they will be forced to choose between becoming a political prisoner and becoming a political exile.

In Russia today, playing no part in politics is itself a political act. Mr. Berezovsky, sitting in front of me, is one of those who have had to face the stark choice between prison and exile. He chose exile. And in October 2001, he came to live in this country. Just under two years later in September 2003, he was granted refugee status in this country, what we sometimes call "political asylum." He was granted refugee status on the basis that the government was satisfied that he had a well-founded fear of political persecution back home in Russia.

So why, you may ask, did Mr. Berezovsky have a fear of political persecution? And more significantly, why did the British government regard that fear as well founded? Let me give you the answer in a nutshell.

Mr. Berezovsky, before his arrival in this country, had been publicly pressing for greater democracy and more freedom of the press than Mr. Putin was prepared to tolerate. In order to retaliate against Mr. Berezovsky, the Putin government launched baseless criminal charges against Mr. Berezovsky and then later tried to extradite him from London back to Russia to face a criminal trial.

I said "baseless criminal charges"; let me explain why I did. We can be quite sure that the criminal charges were without foundation for two reasons. Firstly, the British government would not have granted Mr. Berezovsky political asylum in the autumn of 2003, if they had thought he was guilty of a serious criminal offense as the Russians were alleging. As I say, the extradition proceedings failed in the court hearing in London.

The second reason that we can be sure the charges were baseless was that in November 2005, the supreme arbitration court, the highest

Russian appeal court, upheld a number of previous appeal court rulings, that what was said by the Russian prosecutor to be Mr. Berezovsky's crime was not even civilly unlawful, let alone a crime. So London and Moscow courts combine to show that the criminal charges that the Russian government brought against Mr. Berezovsky to try to get him back to Russia were without foundation.

But because he did not wish to become effectively a political prisoner in Russia, Mr. Berezovsky was forced to become a political exile. Sadly, he is not the only member of the business community who has had to face such a choice. Mr. Vladimir Gusinsky, whose independent television channel NTV had consistently expressed opposition to Mr. Putin, was charged with fraud and thrown into jail back in June 2000. At that stage, President Putin had been in power for a matter of months. But Mr. Gusinsky, having crossed Mr. Putin's tracks, was only allowed to leave the country after he had signed an agreement surrendering his interest in NTV to Gazprom, the state-owned gas company. NTV of course was the channel on which this program was broadcast and is now effectively an arm of the Russian state, being owned, as I say, by Gazprom, who got hold of it in the way that I have just described; Mr. Putin throws him inside until he signs an agreement surrendering his interest.

What could possibly be a starker abuse of human rights than the arrest of a man to intimidate him into handing over his property?

Another successful businessman, Mikhail Khodorkovsky, who was mentioned on the program, also tried to mount political opposition to Mr. Putin. You will have recognized if you picked up the name "Khodorkovsky," that the Russian audience all knew the story of Mr. Khodorkovsky; it was notorious. He had been tried in Russia, and his business—which was called Yukos—was effectively seized by the Russian government.

Mr. Khodorkovsky's "sin" was to indicate, not just political opposition to Mr. Putin's government, but to hint that in the future he might well run for president himself. So he too was named the subject of criminal charges. And whereas Mr. Berezovsky and Mr. Gusinsky chose to become political exiles, Mr. Khodorkovsky became a political prisoner. In October 2003, he was arrested, he was held in custody until his trial in May of last year. He was duly convicted and, perhaps as some of you will know, is now serving an eight-year sentence in the dreadful conditions of a Siberian prison camp 4,000 miles from Moscow.

There is absolutely no doubt, we say, members of the jury, that the charges against Mr. Khodorkovsky were politically motivated like those against Mr. Gusinsky and Mr. Berezovsky. In Mr. Khodorkovsky's case, it was to allow the state to grab Yukos, just like it had grabbed NTV from Mr. Gusinsky.

Well, let us now just think about those who have thrived under Mr. Putin. Those who have remained in Russia and thrown in their lot by keeping silent have done very well. Mr. Fridman is one such businessman.

One of his witnesses, a Vladimir Potanin, is another. They are both multimillionaires.

So that is the contrast. Let me tell you now a little more about Mr. Berezovsky. He has just turned 60. He was born in Moscow in 1946. He did a degree in engineering. He became a Doctor of Science and ultimately the head of the Department of Computer Design at the Institute of Control Sciences. Then he became a Corresponding Member of the Russian Academy of Sciences. Prior to the fall of Communism in 1989, he set up one of the first private companies in Russia, called LogoVAZ.

Initially, LogoVAZ sold software, which was Mr. Berezovsky's area of specialization, but in 1991 it began to distribute foreign cars in Russia: Mercedes, Volvos, Chryslers, Hondas and so on. And it soon proved, in the burgeoning Russian economy, very successful.

In November 1994, a consortium in which LogoVAZ played a leading role acquired 49 percent of ORT, the major Russian TV channel. *Alfa Bank*, Mr. Fridman's privately owned bank, is another shareholder in ORT, and Mr. Berezovsky and Mr. Fridman have known each other since that time. Not only were their respective businesses shareholders at ORT but they were actually each directors of ORT, so they sat on the same board.

Now, having played a role in dismantling the old Communist system, Mr. Berezovsky was naturally keen to ensure that what was substituted in its place was truly democratic and worked; that it should have none of the inefficiency of the old Communist regime. He naturally began to take an interest in politics. In those days, as you will recall, Russia was under the presidency of Boris Yeltsin. In October

1996, Mr. Berezovsky was appointed Deputy Secretary of the Security Council of the Russian Federation; an important post that he held for about a year.

Members of the jury, just pausing there and seeing that one of your numbers has the packet open; there is a packet in front of you. Normally we share them one for every two, but unless the judge has any objections, we will try over lunch to get one for each of you. You will see, if you have poked a nose inside already, that there is a cast list and also a chronology.

It would be natural if at this stage you were wondering: will I ever get on top of all these different names I have never heard of and all these different events over a ten-year history? Well, I will show you, you will; partly because barristers repeat everything about six or seven times, and partly because there is that crib that you can use in the packet.

Now, I was telling you about the time that Mr. Berezovsky was Deputy Secretary of the Russian Security Council. During that time, he played an important role in negotiating the peace treaty between Russia and Chechnya, which ended the first Chechen war in May 1997. You will remember, I am sure, the shots on television of the appalling conditions in Grozny as a result of the fighting that had gone on. Mr. Berezovsky was involved in initially bringing that to an end in May 1997. And also involved in the negotiations was a Mr. Boris Nemtsov, then first Deputy Prime Minister, and a witness for the defendants in this action.

In April 1998, Mr. Berezovsky was made Executive Secretary of the Commonwealth of Independent States. As you will recall, Russia, the old Russia, broke up into a number of independent states, and it was important for the Russian government of the new Russia—not the Soviet Union—to have a body which ensured some degree of coordination between the old states of the former Soviet Union. That was an important post. And in December 1999, Mr. Berezovsky stood for the Russian House of Commons, the Russian Parliament, which is called, as you may well know, the Duma.

Now, Mr. Yeltsin's term as president came to an end on the eve of the Millennium. He chose December 31st 1999, to resign as president, and Mr. Putin—then the Prime Minister—replaced him.

Mr. Putin had been a KGB Colonel before the fall of Communism; indeed he had been stationed in Dresden in East Germany. Before becoming Prime Minister in August 1999, he was head of the FSB, the body which was the successor to the KGB. When he was made Prime Minister, he was little known to the Russian public. The Russian public, as you can imagine, were not too keen to make acquaintance with the head of the FSB. But he made them sit up with a start the following month when—using coarse Russian criminal slang, which is not easy to translate—he said that he would "waste" the Chechen terrorists, wherever they were found.

It was surprising language for the president to use. It surprised those who heard it, as you will hear in evidence, and it has significance in this case which will become apparent later.

Initially, Mr. Berezovsky believed that Mr. Putin would continue Mr. Yeltsin's policy of liberal political and economic reforms. Indeed, Mr. Berezovsky had played a part in suggesting Mr. Putin for the post of Prime Minister. But Mr. Berezovsky, to his cost, found out that he was wrong. The new president rapidly began to show that he wanted to concentrate all political power in his own hands in the Kremlin.

I will explain very shortly how he did that, and just give a few examples. Firstly, in mid 2000—in May of that year—he passed a decree that abolished the democratically elected governors of the regions and put in their place seven officials who answered to the Kremlin in Moscow.

Mr. Berezovsky was fervently against that antidemocratic force and publicly spoke out against it.

The following month, June 2000, was the month—just to remind you and give you the chronological sequence—that Mr. Putin moved against Mr. Gusinsky. It was the month in which Mr. Gusinsky was put in jail and only released after surrendering NTV to the state.

Mr. Putin, to Mr. Gusinsky's distress, aggressively continued the war in Chechnya. Mr. Berezovsky, who, as I have said, had negotiated the peace there back in 1997, publicly criticized what Mr. Putin was doing in Chechnya.

Mr. Berezovsky's concern about the new Russia under President Putin was so great that in July 2000, he became the first person in Russia in the post-Soviet era to resign voluntarily from the Duma in protest against Mr. Putin's policies. And as he did so, he announced that he would attempt to consolidate the political opposition to Mr. Putin.

Well, having done that, by now the writing was on the wall for Mr. Berezovsky. In late July 2000, there was a meeting at the Kremlin organized by Mr. Nemtsov, the former Deputy Prime Minister. Mr. Nemtsov organized a meeting between Mr. Putin and a small group of businessmen, hardly more than 20 if I am right, who included both Mr. Fridman and Mr. Potanin, the witness that I have told you about.

The purpose of the meeting was effectively to call a truce in what was seen as the contest between the Kremlin and businessmen. Well, it will not surprise you to hear that Mr. Berezovsky and Mr. Gusinsky were not invited to that meeting.

The upshot of the meeting was quite simple. Mr. Putin indicated that he would agree not to pursue any other businessmen just so long as they kept their noses out of politics. So it was a significant meeting; a truce, if you like: Mr. Putin saying, "I will lay off, none of you will go the way of Mr. Berezovsky or Mr. Gusinsky just so long as you do not go into politics."

The following month, August 2000, something I am sure you will all remember, the ghastly tragedy of the sunken Russian submarine Kursk in which all the crew died of slow suffocation underwater. You may remember, too, the press, both Russian and international, were highly critical of President Putin's slow reaction to that human disaster. Mr. Putin was on holiday in the Black Sea. He initially declined either to return to Moscow or to visit the scene of the tragedy in northern Russia. The press coverage was extremely hostile and it made Mr. Putin extremely angry. He appears to have gotten particularly angry about that on ORT, the television station in which Mr. Berezovsky had an interest.

Mr. Putin blamed Mr. Berezovsky for this hostile coverage and he summoned him to the Kremlin; not, you can imagine, an invitation that Mr. Berezovsky would have welcomed. You would be right, because when he got there he was told that unless he surrendered his share in ORT to the state he would go the same way as Mr. Gusinsky.

Mr. Berezovsky was made of relatively stern stuff under the circumstances; he refused to do as Mr. Putin demanded, and he publicly exposed and denounced what he regarded as nothing less than blackmail.

So, in Russia today it is President Putin who always tries to have the last word. In the autumn of 2000, the government got its own back on Mr. Berezovsky and Mr. Gusinsky, who were then abroad paying visits outside Russia. It was announced that they were both to be charged with separate criminal offenses the following month. That was the turning point at which Mr. Berezovsky was forced to choose between, as I say, being a political prisoner or a political exile. He chose the latter, and ever since has of course been unable to return to his native land.

In October 2001, he came to England and applied for political asylum. 18 months later in March 2003, the Russians sought to extradite him on baseless charges of fraud and theft, and I have already explained why you can be sure that they were baseless. And in the autumn of 2003, he was granted political asylum and the court refused the request for extradition.

Well, let me tell you next a little about *Alfa Bank's* libel action against *Kommersant*, which was the subject of *The Duel*, the debate, on NTV. Back in September 1999, Mr. Berezovsky had bought ownership of *Kommersant*. It is, and was, a popular and then independent business newspaper. Its very independence was to prove a thorn in Mr. Putin's side. Mr. Berezovsky managed to hang on to the ownership of *Kommersant* even when he went into exile. And by 2004, when the events that were discussed on the program took place, *Kommersant* was one of the very few opposition newspapers left in Russia. It was all the more authoritative for being a specialist business newspaper.

In the summer of that year, several Russian banks ceased payments to depositors and went into liquidation. In May and June, banks closed their doors and, as you heard on the program, the very day before the publication of the article in *Kommersant* that led to the libel action, another bank called Guta Bank closed its doors.

These events had been going on since May. As you can imagine, it made the public very nervous. There was a run on other banks; rumors ran rife. The run on the banks included *Alfa Bank* as, naturally, frightened customers queued to withdraw their money. On July 6, *Alfa Bank* put out a statement trying to reassure its depositors. You would not expect a business newspaper not to cover the details of such a serious banking crisis. And on July 7, the day after Guta Bank closed its doors, *Kommersant* published an article where they described long queues at the cash machines and extra cash having to be brought in, in special vehicles. You will recall those are matters that are discussed on the program.

Mr. Fridman and *Alfa Bank* took great offense at this article, as you know. They sued for libel. The case was heard with great speed, and within a matter of two or three months on October 20, 2004, the Moscow court ruled against *Kommersant*.

When Mr. Putin read his copy of *Izvestia* or whatever it is he reads in the Kremlin the following morning, the news of the verdict must surely have gladdened his heart; because the Moscow court awarded *Alfa Bank* 320 million roubles. Now, that is approximately US $11 million, or £ 6.5 million.

Of that truly colossal award, only a mere 20 million roubles, one 16th, was for actual proven financial loss; in other words, for what the court had found the libel had caused *Alfa Bank* in actual financial loss. The rest, 300 million roubles, well over £6 million, was for supposed injury to reputation; non-financial loss; nothing to do with actual financial losses in the balance sheet, but merely for supposed injury to reputation. You, on hearing those figures, will surely react, as many did even in Russia, that the amount of the award was plainly ridiculous. It led to much controversy. That is how the program on NTV came about.

The 300 million roubles for non-financial loss naturally struck many people in Russia as being designed to teach a lesson to *Kommersant* for being such a thorn in the Kremlin's side. In other words it looked like a gigantic fine and a signal to other newspapers who might be tempted to criticize the Kremlin or its allies.

So NTV, the state-controlled TV channel by now, arranged a debate on the issues. The program, which I have called *The Duel* or *En Garde*, which I may say is more like the three musketeers—you have the idea of the program. And the presenter, Mr. Vladimir Soloviov, was very well known to Mr. Fridman because the two of them had studied together at university.

Mr. Fridman, as you will have seen from the early part of the program, had effectively thrown down the challenge, and it was the chief editor of *Kommersant*, Mr. Vasiliev, who was the other duelist, the respondent to the challenge.

The debate was recorded in the studio on October 27, 2004, and broadcast the following day.

Now, before we look in more detail at what Mr. Berezovsky says is seriously libelous, let me explain, as the last thing before lunch, what exactly is libel. Libel, members of the jury, are words which are defamatory and which the defendant cannot show to be true. "Defamatory" means that it makes you think, when you read the words, or when you hear them, the worst of the person concerned. It is the defendant, if the words are defamatory, who has to show that they are true. It is not for the claimant in the situation of Mr. Berezovsky to show that they are untrue.

Now, we will look at the words, because we have them transcribed, immediately after lunch. But when we do, I suggest to you that you will be in no doubt that they are defamatory. And when you hear the evidence, you will equally be in no doubt that they are untrue. If that is right, Mr. Berezovsky has established that he has been seriously libeled.

Objection by Mr. Shields,
Attorney for Mikhail Fridman *(In the absence of the jury)*

One matter, my Lord. When we came before your Lordship on Tuesday, your Lordship made certain observations about how this case was to be opened and how the political line was to be drawn. And I just raise this now, my Lord, I know the opening has not concluded yet, but the opening ten minutes of that was directed towards establishing the simple proposition that anyone who stayed in Russia in the light of the persecution of Mr. Gusinsky and others was in effect a lackey of Mr. Putin, because that was the only way you could thrive.

Maybe I misunderstood the way your Lordship was putting it on Tuesday. I can refer your Lordship to the transcript. What your Lordship said was that you had no problem with evidence being given in accordance with Mr. Berezovsky's witness statement paragraphs 3 to 6—which I have re-read—but you were not going to have this becoming as it were a political trial of a friendly state, or as I understood it—maybe I have got this wrong—that if he should be so starkly defined, that in other words anyone who stayed in Russia is per se a "toady," is per se a beneficiary of largesse as a result.

That is a line I have argued before to your Lordship. I thought your Lordship defined it on Tuesday; maybe I am wrong. Obviously I will look at the transcript again. But when one dovetails that with my learned friend's rendition of the *Kommersant* story—and I have re-read the statement, which is very short on *Kommersant*, narrowly short—and then says that that would have given some sort of cheer to Mr. Putin when he read the verdict the next day; the web is being weaved very cunningly and very obviously. And I do not want to be the fly in that web in particular because I would like to try this on the issues.

At the moment, the way this has been opened, and I put my marker down, we would say is quite contrary to how your Lordship defined it on Tuesday. An opening is a very damaging and powerful vehicle in setting a scene. And my position I would say is more and more difficult, because, am I to cross-examine in relation to those matters in the opening? I will not hear from Putin. And that has been said, and your Lordship foresaw it.

Can I say, just to give you an example, as your Lordship will recall, my learned friend in opening, in addition to *Kommersant* he mentioned a meeting summoned by Mr. Putin. Does your Lordship recall that? That is not in any witness statement I can find; I have been trawling through it, and am happy to be corrected.

There is no witness statement of that particular meeting. It has been mentioned for the first time, involving Mr. Nemtsov and the threat to the businessmen. I cannot find it.

Well, my Lord, I understood that to be your Lordship firmly directing that he could open in relation to the four paragraphs of Mr. Berezovsky's witness statement, which had been subject to scrutiny with your Lordship early in the year, and which, although I objected to, your Lordship with some diffidence allowed in, because you said this was not Purley; therefore they had to have some understanding why he had left Russia. It is a fair leap from that to what I say he has now chosen to do.

This is a tactical maneuver, my Lord. We did not hear anything about Mr. Berezovsky really in the first ten minutes. What we heard about was this—the lack of rule of law, the lack of a free press in Russia. And then—this is the killer bit—we are effectively lackeys who—you only thrive if you stay in Russia and blindly follow Mr. Putin, and that is how you get very rich. That is a pretty big task, a pretty major statement of evidence, I respectfully say, from counsel. What is the base for that? It is counsel giving evidence in this court.

And I respectfully ask your Lordship: how do I deal with that? I say, "Oh no, of course Mr. Putin is not on trial in this courtroom." You must not have a value judgment about Putin. It is about my clients and the issues; and it is a big task for a jury to make that divorce within their minds.

JUSTICE EADY: So, what are you actually asking me to do at this stage?

SHIELDS: Take it out—on that. He has taken the risk. He cannot do it. Your Lordship said on Tuesday: that is why we have these hearings.

JUSTICE EADY: Are you asking me to discharge the jury?

SHIELDS: Yes, if that is the way he wants to play it. He has opened on that basis. I do not like the idea of it.

On top of that, my Lord, just to show, we have had two additional areas not within Mr. Berezovsky's statement. I may be corrected because I read it quickly; but there is no reference in that to this famous meeting of the 15 Russian businessmen set up by Mr. Nemtsov and Mr. Potanin, to which Mr. Berezovsky was not invited and to which Putin said: keep out of politics. I cannot possibly deal with that. You could say that is one for my client, but at least I am entitled to know about it beforehand if it is part of his case. I cannot see how it is part of his case.

Secondly, in relation to the *Kommersant* libel action, which was fairly neutrally dealt with in respect to Mr. Berezovsky in his witness statement and in the pleadings, but then we have this aside as to how Mr. Putin must be pleased.

REPLY BY MR. BROWNE

Well, my Lord, what Mr. Shields has not done is to go back to the ground rules that were originally set by your Lordship in the judgment you gave at the PTR on the 1st of March. On that occasion, you accepted that the effective key to the resolution of the issues between Mr. Berezovsky and the defendant and his witnesses was the fact that there were two different political camps; one owing allegiance to Mr. Putin and the other, like Mr. Berezovsky, firmly opposed and by their records shown to be firmly opposed to Mr. Putin.

Now, can I say just before we look at this that I have not referred, as your Lordship indicated the other day that I should not, nor do I intend to refer—unless it be necessary in cross-examination—either to the ECHR judgment in the Gusinsky case or to the judgments of District Judge Workman in the cases, in which he refused to extradite Khodorkovsky's associates and Yukos subordinates to Russia, having found that the prosecution of Mr. Khodorkovsky was politically instigated by Mr. Putin.

My Lord, it is not simply because Russia is not Purley, as Mr. Shields suggests, that your Lordship let this material in.

There were, as you made clear, not just one but two justifications for going into this. One, the need for Mr. Berezovsky to introduce himself and his history and why he is here, which inevitably necessitates going over the proceedings that were brought against him in Russia and the failure of extradition and the granting of political asylum.

But the other is that, to use your Lordship's words, it is important for the jury to have as much background as possible in determining who is likely to be telling the truth in relation to the central issues in this case.

So as you said, the relevance of the two camps has a significant role potentially to play in the jurors' decision-making process. Mr. Shields overlooks all of that in his remarks to your Lordship now.

Equally, he overlooks a point that we went into in some considerable detail at the PTR on May 1st; namely that in addition to Mr. Berezovsky's own witness statement and the contents thereof, the witness statements of Mr. Fridman and his sub-witnesses—both before he had seen Mr. Berezovsky's witness statement and afterwards, the responsive witness statements—went hammer and tongs at Mr. Berezovsky.

Now, obviously I have to guard against that. Your Lordship may recall that in Mr. Fridman's witness statement, even before he had seen Mr. Berezovsky's and replied to it, as he did in his third witness statement, he was dealing with the suggestion that the libel action had been politically motivated.

The politics of all of this are inescapable, regrettably…

JUSTICE EADY: Show me the passage you are referring to.

BROWNE: My Lord, yes. It is at 259B.

JUSTICE EADY: Yes, *The Moscow Times.*

BROWNE: One sees there the interview with Mr. Berezovsky, and quotes from an *Alfa Bank* spokesman and the Vice President, Alexander Gafin. And the two other clippings, which we do not need to look at in any real detail, also quote Mr. Berezovsky as saying that he believed the legal action had been instigated by Mikhail Fridman, the principal owner of *Alfa*, partly for personal reasons and partly as a sign of loyalty to the Kremlin.

Back on 259B, something rather similar is said in *The Moscow Times.* About halfway down, does your Lordship see a sentence that begins, "Berezovsky said that the lawsuit was probably prompted by factors such as a desire to curry favor with the Kremlin."

Now, my Lord, that is—as I say—before he has seen Mr. Berezovsky's witness statement. After he had done so, he put in a third witness statement which your Lordship has in 9C, page 264, suggesting that he was a businessman pure and simple, not interested in politics, paragraph 6:

"I have always deliberately avoided becoming involved in politics, and do not consider myself to be in any political camp."

And also, I think, saying possibly in his earlier witness statement that he was not interested in the media or any role in the media.

When your Lordship looks at Mr. Fridman's third witness statement, one sees why you use the phrase that the defendants were "going hammer and tongs at Mr. Berezovsky." There is more of it in Mr. Aven's witness statement, and more of it in both Mr. Nemtsov's first witness statement and his second one. Just looking at his second one in 9F, page 280, paragraph 2:

"I understand that it is being suggested that Mr. Fridman has invented the matters pleaded in relation to the sale of *Kommersant*, because he is in the opposite political camp to Mr. Berezovsky. If the same suggestion is to be made concerning my evidence as to Mr. Berezovsky's approach to Gazprom, I reject such a situation."

And then he says it is well known he is an opponent of Mr. Putin. Well, Mr. Shields will have to wait and see how we challenge Mr.

Nemtsov's credibility. But what is clear is that all of these witnesses are putting into play the issue of the two camps, because they rightly see—and the legal advisers on each side rightly see—that that is the key to the resolution of the issues as to whether or not it is true that Mr. Berezovsky made the threat to Mr. Fridman over *Kommersant*, and then the threats over Gazprom.

So nothing that I have opened with went further than was justified by your Lordship's ruling. I carefully avoided saying anything about the court proceedings. My reference to how Mr. Putin must have heard the news and reacted to the news of the *Kommersant* verdict was entirely legitimate forensic rhetoric. The reference to the meeting at the Kremlin is a matter of record, which we will be able to put to Mr. Nemtsov, Mr. Fridman and Mr. Potanin who were all there.

JUSTICE EADY: Who is the third one?

BROWNE: Potanin.

JUSTICE EADY: Mr. Potanin?

BROWNE: Yes. I had a firm and proper basis for making that allegation, and it is fairly and squarely relevant to the history of the dealings between Mr. Putin and his opponents, and those whom he has brought on-side, by the means that I have been describing to the jury.

My Lord, politics is at the heart of this action; it is the key to resolving the issues. And in my respectful submission, nothing that I have said is open to objection at all, let alone the kind of high-pitched objection that Mr. Shields advances.

SHIELDS: He would say that, would he not, my Lord?

My Lord, can I deal with the *Kommersant* aspect too, my Lord. My objection to *Kommersant* was not that it would not come in; because it is referred to in the program. My objection to *Kommersant* was how he used it to adapt it to Mr. Putin's remarks.

As regards the statements which have been lodged by my clients, your Lordship will recall what happened was this. Your Lordship gave me leave to put further statements in, in relation to the political side, because your Lordship said: if it was going to be argued that there was a political angle, then we should counter it, if we were so minded.

Your Lordship had this before you on Tuesday because that was what led your Lordship, as I understand it, to take the view that politics was not out but they have been more on the touchlines because we were not taking direct issue on politics.

That is quite a leap from that position to how it was opened today, opened today with the suggestion that if anyone stays in Russia under this present regime, that thereby makes them a lackey in effect; that they condone that conduct.

That is my objection, my Lord. I accept that Mr. Berezovsky is going to portray himself as someone who does not like the present regime, but there is a large inference, a large leap then to be invited for the jury to take, to say that anyone who stays there must in itself have therefore tied themselves firmly to Mr. Putin's mast. If they take that leap, you see where it would lead against my clients; not a determination on the issues. Because the issues are actually fairly polarized. The issue relates to what happened prior to 1999, as in three specific instances which have been particularized.

As I understand it, and I will be corrected if I have got this wrong, your Lordship was not saying they are going to make a valued judgment on individuals as to whether they stayed in Russia or not; as to whether that means that they are telling the truth about those issues. That is the danger, that is the danger as I understand it.

JUSTICE EADY: There are a number of things obviously which are important. One is the political background, and in particular the political differences between the parties, are part of the background of the case.

Secondly, equally importantly, the jury cannot be asked to resolve questions of the merits of particular political activities or parties in Russia. We have to be careful about that; they must focus on the parties in this litigation.

And thirdly, the justification for the political matters being introduced into the case in the first place was, as I described it on the 1st of March, twofold. One, it is background CV material and the other is to show that they are—if it be the case, it is a matter on which they will no doubt give conflicting evidence—whether they are in different political camps.

It seems to me it is a very fine line to draw. But what I was dealing with on the 9th of May was, I think, that Mr. Browne should not introduce evidence dealing with matters purely of credit. That is not to say that he could not introduce matters of that kind in cross-examination on credit; if it genuinely went to credit. And it would follow that if he were not allowed to introduce evidence on credit, such as for example the various court proceedings which were before the court on that occasion, then he should not refer to them in opening. I think he has tried to adhere to that, as far as I can tell.

But what you are objecting to really is his going to adopt that phrase once again, "Hammer and tongs of Mr. Fridman" in order to demonstrate to the jury that he is in an opposite political camp.

That is part of this case; but it seems to be primarily dealing with an allegation introduced originally by Mr. Fridman, seeking to distance himself from Mr. Putin. If that is a genuine dispute between the parties, then I do not think it can be disguised or hidden.

SHIELDS: You then gave me leave to serve a supplemental statement. The supplemental statement was not seeking to go into the pros and cons of the Putin regime. All it stated was, "I am in business, I am a businessman, I am not in politics." Which, as I understand it, it is now open to my learned friend to say that: anyone who stays in Russia and makes money like you, must therefore be taken to be a lackey of Mr. Putin. That is what worries me.

JUSTICE EADY: That is a generalization of course, which is probably outside the scope of this litigation. But so far as Mr. Fridman is concerned, he has made it clear I think in his witness statement that he meets head-on any allegations to the effect that he was in Mr. Putin's camp. And secondly, that being in Mr. Putin's camp motivated him to tell a lie, which is the issue in the case, on the television program.

Now, it is Mr. Berezovsky's case—and Mr. Browne will obviously be advancing that case—that what Mr. Fridman said on the television program about the threats in 1999, and it is also relevant to the earlier alleged threats, was a lie. There is no dispute about that; it is not a shade of meaning. One person is lying and the other person is not. Therefore they have to be open to cross-examination vigorously on credit on these matters. And it may very well be part—and Mr. Browne has signaled it in the course of his opening, if not earlier—that it is part of the attack he is going to make on Mr. Fridman that in telling a lie on the television program about Mr. Berezovsky, he was, at any rate in part, politically motivated.

Now, if he is going to put that to Mr. Fridman, of course Mr. Fridman is fully entitled to deny it. That is what he has done by way of anticipation in his statement. It is very difficult to exclude those issues, it seems to me, from the central dispute in this case as to who is telling the truth.

SHIELDS: I do not want to argue with my Lord, I am not. Actually I am with your Lordship on that. My objection—obviously I have not made it very clear—is this.

If you start with the proposition that anyone who stays in Russia is a lackey, you can only make riches by being a lackey and agreeing with Mr. Putin as to what Mr. Putin has done, that has nothing to do with the cross-examination as to, "You wish to stay in Russia, that is what suits you. That is your life." That is my objection, because the first part is not tied in. I do not know if it is tied in at the end. The first bleak picture is of a universal darkness. When your Lordship sees the transcript, one will see it is a universal darkness which shadows everyone who has made money who has stayed in Russia. How can I answer that general proposition?

JUSTICE EADY: That is a generalization which as I suggested a moment ago is probably unnecessary to and extraneous to the true issues in this case. Whether it is a matter, by way of advocates' license, which justifies me in discharging the jury is of course another question.

SHIELDS: I can see which way your Lordship is moving, and I obviously respect that. But whether it does is still, I would say, a monumental question, whether it is part of an advocate's license to make such a generalization as the opening part. I will invite your Lordship and your Lordship will see the transcript, to see the effect. In fact, it is making a stance for the juror, "Do you approve what is happening in Russia? Only someone who behaves badly would stay in Russia." That is how it started. If it had come at the end, in the context, "I would put forward a motive why he may not be telling the truth, because he wants to keep with Mr. Putin," that is different. But that is not how it has been opened.

BROWNE: Well, my Lord, first of all, the way in which Mr. Shields puts our approach is an oversimplification. Can I just indicate what I intended to say in opening about the motivation for what has been, as your Lordship has pointed out, so far as we are concerned, a case that Mr. Fridman's account of events back in 1999 is invented; and the witnesses' accounts of events back in 1997 also so. I was just going to summarize it by saying that it was an invention for a variety of motives. Firstly, hostility to Mr. Berezovsky and his democratic politics. Secondly, the desire to keep in with the Kremlin, not to step out of line. And thirdly, loyalty or obligation to the defendants.

Now, so far as the second is concerned—it is the second that seems to cause Mr. Shields problems—the issue of "Currying favor with the Kremlin," to use the quote in the first page of MF1, has been there from the beginning, introduced by Mr. Fridman in his first witness statement. And your Lordship on that occasion, when we were before you on March 1st, said that it was Mr. Fridman and his witnesses who were going hammer and tongs at Mr. Berezovsky.

Now of course, as you summarized Mr. Shields' arguments, he is complaining about me going hammer and tongs at Mr. Fridman. And the "hammer and tongs" remark was very revealing because your Lordship had spotted that Mr. Fridman was going hammer and tongs at Mr. Berezovsky, even before the second round of witness statements which came later that month.

Mr. Shields cannot possibly complain about me responding in that way; and so far as his point that this all goes back to 1999 is concerned, before Mr. Putin came into power, that is really by the way. Because one is not concerned with that and what happened in 1999; when one is considering what is the motivation for witnesses not telling the truth today.

My Lord, nothing, in my respectful submission, that your Lordship said on the most recent occasion when we were before you when you ruled on the ECHR judgment and District Judge Workman's judgments, in any way modified the approach which you have set out in your judgment of the 1st of March. And I have tried loyally to follow that.

So far as Mr. Shields' other complaints are concerned, I do not know, I am obviously concerned about any application to discharge the jury. If your Lordship is with me, then I will not go on. But if your Lordship is even minded to consider that, then your Lordship should also take into account the fact that you are of course the judge. A judge will always remind the jury in his summing up that it is the evidence they have heard from the witnesses, rather than the assertions of counsel.

But it is counsel's duty to make assertions about the evidence that will be called. And if the assertions that I have made are not, in the event, substantiated by the evidence as it comes out, well then that will doubtless be a matter for comment; not just by Mr. Shields but by your Lordship as well.

So we say that this is a matter which will come out in the evidence. The witnesses will be the ultimate determination of this argument. It may prove that I have opened this case too high, given the way in which the evidence pans out. We will just have to see.

But the jury decides cases not on counsel's opening, but on the evidence that is given. And your Lordship, I am sure, will remind them of that. In our respectful submission, Mr. Shields really has no basis whatsoever for any complaint about the way it was done. All I have done is to cover ground which I inevitably had to, was duty bound to cover, and Mr. Shields will—in turn—have his opportunity to respond.

Ruling

Justice Eady: Well, I will make it fairly brief because of the time. But nothing that has happened so far has persuaded me that I ought to discharge the jury yet. What I do urge upon counsel, and in particular Mr. Browne in the light of Mr. Shields' complaint, is so far as possible to avoid generalization. Because we all agree that this is not a Chatham House seminar about politics in Russia; it is primarily about the issues between the parties; although politics comes into it by way of background. But I urge upon counsel to avoid, so far as possible, generalizations about Russia, to focus so far as possible on the narrowly pleaded issues between the parties. And in particular, when opening the case, not to refer to evidence which is not reflected in a witness statement or witness statements. You must have some regard to what the jury is going to hear from the witnesses and not be drawn into general political discussion of, as I say, a Chatham House nature. But subject to that general urging and warning, it does not seem to me there is anything to justify discharging the jury at this stage; but obviously I shall have to keep it closely monitored.

Opening Statement by Mr. Browne *(continued)*

Browne: Members of the jury, apologies to those who are having to share. Can we have a quick look through this packet. The passage complained of, as I say, is on page 1. Perhaps you could just go to that, because I wanted to look at this now in some detail. You will remember what I said, that defamatory means whether it makes you think the worst of the person who is described. And you will notice that the mention of Mr. Berezovsky that is complained about in this action is the first mention in the program. Mr. Berezovsky is dragged into this by Mr. Fridman, who volunteers, as you will see in the sixth or seventh line, "In 1999 when everyone knew that Boris Berezovsky was going to buy *Kommersant*." And that, as I say, is Mr. Berezovsky being brought in. No previous mention of him in the program.

And Mr. Fridman, after interruptions from both Mr. Vasiliev and the host, ploughs on. He goes on: "The newspaper founder, Yakovlev."

It was Mr. Yakovlev who was wishing to dispose of his shares in *Kommersant*. Mr. Fridman goes on: "The *Kommersant* shareholders, Yakovlev's partners, came to us and requested a loan so that they would be able to reacquire this publication."

It seems to be being suggested that they were trying to get a loan from *Alfa Bank* in order to mount a management buy-out and prevent Berezovsky from buying it. I will remind you that in 1999, Berezovsky controlled the all-Russian TV channel, that is what I called "ORT," where Mr. Vasiliev was working as head of information and programming.

And that was apparently wrong, and Mr. Vasiliev says that, protesting. But Mr. Fridman is still determined to plough on with what he wants to say about Mr. Berezovsky—and that is important because he is clearly determined to get this out. It is not in any way a throwaway remark. It is a stiletto attack, we say, of a deliberate nature by Mr. Fridman on Mr. Berezovsky. It does not just slip out. He brings it up and he ploughs on with it over all these interruptions from the host and Mr. Vasiliev, and he keeps going. And after Mr. Vasiliev has rebuked him for saying that Mr. Vasiliev was working at ORT at the time, he continues on and says:

"And we told them at that moment that if they want to buy shares in order to keep the newspaper really independent we are ready to give them a loan."

And the question was discussed.

"Moreover, even Berezovsky called me with regard to this matter. He was very displeased."

Now, you can imagine how Russian viewers and Russian-speaking viewers of this program would have perked up at this stage, because here is someone who is a very, very well known figure in Russia over the past decade being brought into this discussion.

And what is it therefore that Mr. Fridman says about him? Mr. Berezovsky is very displeased. Mr. Vasiliev says:

"Did he give you a piece of advice?"

Mr. Fridman says:

"No. He threatened as usual. He said that …"

Again Mr. Vasiliev cuts across him, and again Mr. Fridman ploughs on: "He even threatened me. He threatened everybody."

Presumably, that is everybody, he is suggesting, involved in the *Kommersant* deal: "That is how he works."

Now, members of the jury, our contention to you is that what Mr. Fridman said in that passage clearly suggested that Mr. Berezovsky threatened him with violence, and that that was Mr. Berezovsky's normal way of operating.

Now, the translation into English has been agreed to between the parties. So in a sense you can forget that they were spoken in Russian to a Russian audience when considering what they convey. You have got to do the best you can with the English, and construe that. But as I say, bear in mind that they were spoken in Russian to a Russian audience. We can only deal with the English. And of course, when someone in English claims that a threat has been made and the nature of the threat is not specified, it suggests to the listener that it must be a threat of violence.

If I come in, run into court and say, "I have just been threatened outside in the corridor," that plainly in context implies, "I have been threatened with violence." It is only when, in English, we qualify or explain the words that the implication of violence disappears. If you say, "I threatened to go home if the weather did not improve," then we all understand that the threat is not a threat of violence, but merely a statement of what the speaker will do in certain circumstances. And one can think of many other examples. But if you simply say, "I was threatened," or "he threatened me," the blatant, and we say clear-cut, implication is that the threat is one of violence. In this context, that inference is all the greater, for these particular reasons. Firstly, the reference to the threat comes directly in answer to Mr. Vasiliev's question whether Mr. Berezovsky had given Mr. Fridman a piece of advice. "Did he give you a piece of advice?" says Mr. Vasiliev. Mr. Fridman replied: "No, he threatened as usual."

In other words the response was not merely a verbal response; it was not giving advice or making a statement of future intentions, it was more than that; it was, in contrast to a piece of advice, a threat of violence.

And the words go on with Mr. Fridman emphasizing the threat, emphasizing that even he had been threatened—which suggests violence, does it not, that Mr. Berezovsky had the barefaced impudence even to threaten him with violence; to say then "He threatened everybody," which makes matters worse.

As I say, presumably it must be understood as meaning "everybody involved in trying to acquire *Kommersant* was threatened." And then finally it is said that the use of threats was how Mr. Berezovsky operated, "That is how he worked," in other words he is a man used to making threats of violence and that is how he conducts his business operations.

The program went out at about 7:35 our time on *NTV World.* It was 10:35 by now in Russia. But we are not concerned with the publication in Russia; this is an English court, we are concerned with those who viewed it in England and Wales. It could be viewed on satellite in this country by those who had purchased the necessary subscription. And you will hear in the course of this case from a number of viewers who watched the program.

Mr. Berezovsky himself knew that the program was coming on because Mr. Vasiliev had told him. The program was in fact recorded the previous day, the 27th. He watched it at his home in Surrey, together with his partner, who is the mother of his two youngest children. Not surprisingly, his reaction to Mr. Fridman's gratuitous allegation was one of shock and anger; not only because it was a serious allegation, but also because it was quite untrue, and worse, Mr. Fridman must have known it was quite untrue.

Mr. Berezovsky had never spoken to Mr. Fridman at all at this time when the *Kommersant* shares were up for sale in mid 1999. He left all the negotiations over the purchase of the *Kommersant* shares to his partner, Mr. Badri Patarkatsishvili, which is so difficult to pronounce that he is always referred to as "Mr. Badri." From now on, I will too.

So Mr. Badri goes over to California where the founder of *Kommersant* resides, that is Mr. Yakovlev. The negotiations go on with them, and Mr. Berezovsky just waits to hear the news when there is a result.

I repeat, there was no question of Mr. Berezovsky speaking or ringing up Mr. Fridman at this time, and Mr. Fridman surely knows that.

Mr. Berezovsky started by, naturally, asking Mr. Fridman to withdraw the allegation. And when Mr. Fridman refused, he had no choice but to start court proceedings.

Can I now ask you to look at that correspondence between the solicitors. It is at tab 5, starting on page 36, with the first letter from a firm called Carter Ruck who are the solicitors for Mr. Berezovsky. It is addressed to Mr. Fridman at the office of *Alfa Bank* in Moscow. It says:

"Dear Sir, we have been consulted by our client, Mr. Boris Berezovsky …"

I will stop because, unless I am mistaken, the final three packets have just come into court.

Members of the jury, nobody is going to look at these packets, and of course you are free to mark them as you wish. They are yours. I will start again. Page 36, tab 5, the first solicitors' letter on Mr. Berezovsky's behalf:

"Dear Sir, we have been consulted by our client, Mr. Boris Berezovsky, who as you know is resident in this country where he was granted refugee status in September last year."

That of course is September 2003.

"It is a matter of serious concern to our client that in a program broadcast in this country by NTV on the 28th of October you alleged that he had called up and threatened you while you were discussing with *Kommersant* shareholders the possibility of your bank lending money to them in order to prevent him from taking control of the publication.

In context, the specific Russian word you used, *ugroza* meant, and would have been understood by Russian speaking viewers to mean, that you were accusing our client of threatening you with violence. Further, you went on to allege that this was Mr. Berezovsky's usual approach.

Our client denies that he ever threatened you with violence. Indeed, he denies even speaking with you at the time concerning his acquisition of *Kommersant*, and is deeply offended that you have chosen to make this false statement against him. Whilst we do not presently have precise viewing figures for NTV in this country, our understanding is that there are several hundred subscribers, and the program on which you appeared is popular.

Our client's reputation amongst the Russian community in this country, likely to form the bulk of the audience, is important to him, and he is not prepared to allow your allegation to pass unchallenged.

Accordingly, the purpose of this letter is to invite you to agree at the earliest opportunity to issue to our client a public apology withdrawing the allegation you have made, which we would then propose to invite NTV to broadcast to its subscribers in this country.

Our client will also require you to reimburse the legal costs which it has been necessary for him to incur. Our client will review his entitlement to seek damages for libel in the light of your response to this letter.

We should make clear that in the absence of prompt and satisfactory proposals from you, we have instructions to commence proceedings for libel in this country, naming both you and *Alfa Bank* as defendants.

We trust accordingly that we shall hear from you within ten days of the date of this letter."

So it was not a demand for 320 million roubles in damages for libel; it was a letter which quite clearly asked for a public apology. And that, you may think, was a very reasonable stance, under the circumstances, for Mr. Berezovsky to adopt. But the response was not so reasonable.

Three weeks later, on page 38, the firm of solicitors, Herbert Smith, acting for Mr. Fridman, respond:

"We have been instructed by Mr. Mikhail Fridman and *Alfa Bank* in respect of the complaint of your client Mr. Berezovsky, set out in your letter to Mr. Fridman dated November 18, 2004. We have now had an opportunity to investigate this complaint with our clients. Our clients deny any liability to your client in respect of the statements made by Mr. Fridman in the course of the NTV television program, *To the Barrier*, or *En Garde* or *The Duel*, translated as you wish, broadcast on October 28, 2004.

We note that you have not provided the transcript of the program or the part of the program in respect of which your client complains. The program consisted of a lengthy debate between Mr. Fridman and Andrei Vasiliev, General Director of the publishing house *Kommersant*, and was chaired by Vladimir Soloviov.

The subject of the debate was *Alfa Bank's* recent successful libel action against *Kommersant*. In the course of the debate Mr. Fridman referred to the fact that in 1999 he had discussed with the then shareholders of *Kommersant* the prospect of *Alfa Bank* loaning them money. He further stated that your client called him in respect of these discussions and threatened him.

Mr. Fridman informs us that your client did telephone him at the relevant time and made threats *(ugrozy)* that he would use his influence by virtue of his ownership of certain media entities to bring commercial pressure to bear upon Mr. Fridman and *Alfa Bank* if *Alfa Bank* loaned money to the then shareholders of *Kommersant*. It was threats of this nature that Mr. Fridman was referring to when he used the word *ugroza* and not threats of violence as you suggest in your letter."

Well, you may be surprised by what the solicitors are saying in the context of what Mr. Fridman had said in the program. But they plough on:

"In context, the viewers of the program in this country would have clearly understood the use of the word *ugroza* in these terms. Accordingly, our clients deny publishing any statements that are capable of being defamatory of your client."

So it is the brush-off. Mr. Berezovsky offers the easy way out, "Apologize and withdraw," and has that offer thrust back in his teeth.

His solicitors respond on what is practically Christmas Eve 2004:

"Whether viewers of the program would have understood your client to be alleging that our client had threatened him with violence or that he had made other improper threats as you assert in your letter,

Mr. Fridman's words spoken in his capacity as chairman of *Alfa Bank* are defamatory of Mr. Berezovsky.

There is also a direct conflict of evidence between our respective clients. As we have made clear, Mr. Berezovsky denies ever discussing the matter with your client. If, as it appears, your clients are not prepared to apologize, we must ask you to confirm that you have instructions on behalf of Mr. Fridman and *Alfa Bank* to accept service of proceedings in this country."

Then the New Year starts on this surprising note. Herbert Smith returns to the attack, and on January 14, 2005, we see this. After taking Mr. Fridman and *Alfa Bank's* instructions following the Russian New Year holiday, they respond:

"We have made our client's position clear. Mr. Fridman's statements referred to threats of a commercial nature, and this is how they would have been understood by the audience of the broadcast. We note that in your letter, you seek to characterize threats of this nature as 'improper.'

We understand that in the context of Russian business, threats to exert commercial pressure are relatively commonplace. We are instructed that this was particularly true of the period in question. Accordingly, statements that your client made threats of a commercial nature in 1999 are not capable of being defamatory of him."

Well, members of the jury, just let that sink in for a moment. It is a pretty extraordinary letter. First of all, it is being said that nobody would have thought the worse of Mr. Berezovsky as a result of what Mr. Fridman said on the program; indeed, the words were not even capable of defaming Mr. Berezovsky.

Secondly, it is being asserted on Mr. Fridman's behalf, by solicitors who have just taken his express instructions, that threats to exert commercial pressure in the context of Russian business were, to use the words of this letter, "Relatively commonplace." And hence they go on to argue, nobody would think the allegation of any significance.

Well, I say it is a pretty extraordinary letter, is it not? It reveals worlds about the way in which Mr. Fridman approaches business, but you will hear from Mr. Berezovsky that it is certainly not the way in which he goes about things; still less is it his habitual way of operating. As I say, it is a valuable early insight in this case into the world of Mr. Mikhail Fridman and the manner in which he operates.

Now, that is the last of the solicitors' letters.

But you need to know that the correspondence between the solicitors went on for another six months. Mercifully, we have spared you all the correspondence; it is not in the file and I am not going to read it. The important thing though is this. On-and-on the solicitors went, letters going to and fro. But never once was it suggested in all those letters that there had been threats of any kind whatever by Mr. Berezovsky on any other occasion. It was only when, after some months had gone by, on June 16, 2005, when the defendants had to file their defense documents with the court, that they suggested for the very first time that there had been threats on two previous occasions. Nothing, not a whiff of this, in the correspondence in the preceding six-month period.

Just touching on this very briefly for the moment, because we will have to go into this later with the defendants' witnesses, the threats on the two previous occasions were, firstly, it was said that in June 1997, Mr. Berezovsky wanted to become chairman of Gazprom, the state-owned energy company, and that he threatened Mr. Nemtsov if he opposed Mr. Berezovsky's appointment. That is the first threat.

The second threat is said to have been the month after that in July 1997. In that month, the Russian government put up for auction 25 percent of the shares in a Russian telecommunications company called Svyazinvest. There were two groups competing in the auction, and one of them was Mr. Potanin, of whom I have already made reference. And it is alleged that Mr. Berezovsky threatened Mr. Potanin if he continued with his bid in the auction for the Svyazinvest shares.

Mr. Berezovsky says that this is all a fabrication. He does not just say that it is nonsense: that it is a fabrication. So the question is, why, if Mr. Fridman was telling the truth in saying that Mr. Berezovsky habitually made threats, and why if these incidents now alleged by the defense are true, were they not mentioned by his solicitors from the outset in early December 2004?

Just reflect for a moment. The allegation is that Mr. Berezovsky does this the all the time. If that were true, and if Mr. Fridman knew it were true, it must surely have emerged in response to the very first solicitor's complaint from Mr. Berezovsky's solicitors. But it takes six months to emerge. Regrettably, members of the jury, I have to say that these other incidents, not just the allegation by Mr. Fridman of the threat over *Kommersant* but these two other incidents, have been invented by people out of a variety of motives.

I will go into this in more detail at the end of the evidence, but firstly there is hostility amongst them to Mr. Berezovsky and to the role he has played in Russian politics both before and since he has left the country.

The second factor is the desire to keep in with the Kremlin. I am sure you understand what I mean by that; if you like, curry favor; but at any rate to ingratiate himself with the Kremlin and to ensure in that way that all goes smoothly in Russian business.

And the third motive is out of loyalty or a misguided sense of obligation to the defendants.

So you will want to consider the evidence called by the defendants very carefully. Ask yourselves, as it comes out from the witness box on the other side of the court: can Mr. Fridman prove to your satisfaction that Mr. Berezovsky made threats? In any event, was that what he actually said on the program? Because what he said on the program is naturally the starting point for your deliberations.

Ask yourself: does the evidence which appears for the first time six months into the action fill the holes in Mr. Fridman's case which have been apparent right from the start, with the letter from the end of November 2004? Or is it, as I suggest, and as often happens in libel actions, an attempt by the defendant to prove some other allegation, one not involving threats of violence, because he realizes that he should never have said what he did on the broadcast, and he is trying to cover his tracks?

Members of the jury, I have practically finished my opening. I ought, though, just to say a word or two about damages, about compensation. The English court cannot order anyone to apologize; it is not in the legal armory of judges in this court. You can ask for an apology from someone but if they are obstinate and refuse to give it, the only thing that a claimant in those circumstances can do is to come to this court and ask for damages.

You cannot order Mr. Fridman to apologize. All you can do is to award a sum of money which will make the public realize that he should have apologized.

Now, plainly, when we consider damages, the audience in England and Wales for this broadcast is, by comparison with a number of people reading *The Sun* or *The Mirror*, relatively small. Perhaps one could even say very small. But—and this is the important "but"—for Mr. Berezovsky, it is the audience that mattered because they are the people who know him, who are familiar with his reputation.

If you are libeled in *The Sun*, the chances are that it would be read by hundreds of thousands, if not millions, of people who have never heard of you before. That is not the case with Mr. Berezovsky here. The libel hits home amongst the very audience for whom his reputation is most important.

Now, that Mr. Fridman should have chosen to make these remarks is particularly damaging, we say, because it is well known that Mr. Fridman and Mr. Berezovsky have done business in the past. And they will therefore assume that when Mr. Fridman speaks from what appears to be direct experience of his dealings with Mr. Berezovsky, he knows what he is talking about. In other words, they will not at once discount him, saying, "Well, he is just shooting his mouth off, he does not know what he is talking about." On the contrary, they will remind themselves that Mr. Berezovsky and Mr. Fridman have had dealings together and therefore say, "Well, if anyone knows about the way in which Mr. Berezovsky operates, it is Mr. Fridman." They will believe it.

Of course, if that is what the world ends up believing about Mr. Berezovsky, that will suit everyone in the Kremlin very nicely because it undermines the credibility of Mr. Berezovsky's opposition to the present regime.

I have shown you the solicitors' correspondence. I remind you that the defendants have to prove to your satisfaction that the words are true. At the end of the trial, when it comes to damages, you will have to take into account the gravity of the libel—which is obviously a serious one—the damage it has done to Mr. Berezovsky's reputation, amongst a small audience but a very precious and significant one for him, and finally the injury to his feelings at being treated like this, being put through the mangle of a public trial with all the allegations that will doubtless be made against him, when a simple apology at the beginning would have sufficed, if Mr. Fridman had not been too proud to climb down and apologize.

Ultimately, what Mr. Berezovsky is entitled to do is what lawyers call "vindication." In other words, the amount you award by way of damages has to be large enough to send out a signal to the world at large that Mr. Fridman's allegation is completely false. In England, that does not mean thinking in the size of figures that they apparently think of in Moscow, but it does have to be enough to convince even the most cynical doubter who thinks that there is no smoke without fire; in other words it must be enough to signal to such people that the allegation Mr. Fridman made is utterly untrue.

EXAMINATION-IN-CHIEF BY MR. BROWNE

JUSTICE EADY: Yes, Mr. Berezovsky. Either sit or stand as you prefer.

BEREZOVSKY: If you do not mind, I will stand.

JUSTICE EADY: Yes, certainly.

BROWNE: Mr. Berezovsky, can you please keep your voice up and speak slowly.

BEREZOVSKY: I hope that you will hear me at the same level that I hear you.

BROWNE: Good. Now, you are Boris Abramovich Berezovsky. I do not imagine your Lordship needs his address heard in open court?

JUSTICE EADY: No.

BROWNE: You are the claimant in these proceedings, and—I think I can lead on this—you have been resident in England since October 2001, when you applied for political asylum; is that correct?

BEREZOVSKY: Yes, yes, it is correct.

BROWNE: And you were granted refugee status and indefinite leave to remain in this country on September 10, 2003.

BEREZOVSKY: That is correct.

BROWNE: Now, just so far as your name is concerned; when you were granted political asylum did you keep the name that you had always been known by, Boris Berezovsky?

BEREZOVSKY: No, this is not the case. Because of security precautions, the need for more protection, I asked the Home Office to give me, in my travel documents, another name. But nevertheless there is a reference in this travel document, under some page, as "Known as Boris Berezovsky."

BROWNE: And what was the name that you were given for your protection?

BEREZOVSKY: Platon Elenin.

BROWNE: Platon, as in Plato, and then Elenin. Mr. Berezovsky, what was the reason that the British Government decided you had a well-founded fear of political persecution in Russia?

BEREZOVSKY: As I understand, it was the final conclusion of the court that was the basis of the reason—there were two steps. The first step was to grant—to refuse a warrant to extradite me, and the second step was to grant me political asylum. And the first step was done with the understanding that all accusations against me, all charges against me, were politically motivated and that I had not been involved in anything illegal in Russia, ever. And what is perhaps important, that after two years of this British court—London court decision, the Russian highest arbitrage court made the same decision. And this is the reason why I was granted—the extradition warrant was refused. And after that came the absolutely logical next step by the Home Office to grant me political asylum.

BROWNE: If the British Government had thought that you might be guilty of a crime in Russia, would they have granted you political asylum?

BEREZOVSKY: It is very clear in the statement, in the conclusion of the court, that the basis—there were two reasons to grant me political asylum, because first the charges were politically motivated, and the second, that I did not do anything criminal according to the understanding of the London court.

BROWNE: And you have referred to the ruling of the highest appeal court in Russia, the supreme arbitration court. Do you remember the date of that ruling?

BEREZOVSKY: I think that the final decision was made on the—in the previous year.

BROWNE: 2005?

BEREZOVSKY: 2005.

BROWNE: And in a nutshell, what did they say about the lawfulness or criminality of your alleged conduct? What did the Russian highest court decide about whether your alleged conduct was criminal?

BEREZOVSKY: Their final decision was that nothing at all was done criminal in the deal, which they initially described as a criminal case, and which they presented as arguments in Great Britain to extradite me. And the final decision was that it had been an absolutely proper deal, with no illegal activity in terms of Russian law.

BROWNE: Now, let us wind the clock back. You were born in Moscow in 1946. Where did you work in your early adult years?

BEREZOVSKY: I was born in Moscow in 1946. My father was an engineer; my mother was a nurse in the Institute for Children. I was—I had an absolutely typical Soviet life. School, university, and then for 28 years I was in the Applied Mathematics section in the Institute of Control Sciences in the Academy of Sciences of the Soviet Union.

BROWNE: Was that in Moscow?

BEREZOVSKY: It was in Moscow.

BROWNE: And what position did you ultimately hold at the Institute of Control Sciences?

BEREZOVSKY: As I told you, I spent 28 years there. And I started as a low level assistant. I got a Ph.D. I became a professor. I got a laboratory; no—I created a laboratory of computer aided design systems. And finally, I became Corresponding Member of the Academy of Sciences, at that time of Russia, because the Soviet Union had just collapsed.

BROWNE: And during your career in academic life did you write any papers?

BEREZOVSKY: Yes, I wrote more than 100 articles on my theory of optimization, multi-criteria optimization. And I wrote two books in this area, and I presented lectures at numerous conferences in the United States, Europe, Japan, all over the world.

BROWNE: Now, when you were at the institute, did you work with any industrial enterprise?

BEREZOVSKY: Yes, as I told you, I was in applied mathematics. This means that I needed practical results. For the last 10 years, when I worked in the Institute of Control Sciences, I also applied my theory with the largest car manufacturing company in the Soviet Union, AvtoVAZ.

BROWNE: AvtoVAZ?

BEREZOVSKY: AvtoVAZ.

BROWNE: And what did you do for them?

BEREZOVSKY: For them, I developed software for, as I told you, a computer aided design system which helped a designer to computerize his work.

BROWNE: Did there come a time when you set up your own company?

BEREZOVSKY: This happened in 1989, in April, because at that time I already had the feeling that a new time was coming. Perhaps you remember Gorbachev and Perestroika. And so it opened up a new field for activity.

I had spent a lot of time with mathematical theories and I decided to move into the world of business because it had become legal. In the Soviet Union, all business was illegal. Gorbachev opened up countless new opportunities, and later on Yeltsin. And I moved into this new area.

BROWNE: And what did your new company do?

BEREZOVSKY: My company, first of all the name of the company which I gave was LogoVAZ; LogoVAZ because it was a partnership with an Italian company, a joint venture. The Italian company's name was Logo System; and we took the first part from the Italian company and the second part from AvtoVAZ. Initially the partnership was between AvtoVAZ, my institute, the Institute of Control Sciences, and this Italian company. And this Italian company specialized in software, in the production of software; also for computer aided design systems. And they had contracts with AvtoVAZ. And the first step was to develop software and to sell software.

BROWNE: Now, the Berlin Wall came down in November 1989, and revolutionary changes followed. How did LogoVAZ develop its business in the years after the fall of Communism?

BEREZOVSKY: It is a very—when I moved into the business world, I recognized that professional knowledge is not enough to make money. You need to feel the market, you need to feel what people want. And every Soviet had two dreams; a car and an apartment. And maybe even in this order of priority, the car first, the apartment second. And in the Soviet Union, we deal and produce enough cars for the market. And maybe you know that we did not have even a market for the cars, because the state split the cars, among different kinds of professionals.

Yes, yes. You could not just go to a shop and buy a car. You had to be somebody exceptional to have the right to buy a car.

And for sure, there was a black market where cars sold for ten times more than the state price. And as I was familiar with the car production company and knew the realities of this field, I decided to start to collaborate with foreign companies. And in one year, LogoVAZ increased their area of activity from software to car sales and workshops to repair shops. And after one year, I made history with the first Russian contract with Mercedes, with Volvo, and later on with General Motors and then Chrysler. At that time, the companies were split.

BROWNE: Any Japanese?

BEREZOVSKY: And with Honda, and with the Korean company, Daewoo.

BROWNE: Now, was LogoVAZ successful in this enterprise of importing and selling foreign cars?

BEREZOVSKY: Yes, LogoVAZ became # 1 in the post-Soviet arena. Not only because we bought and sold cars, but because we started to develop an infrastructure to repair the cars. And we built an enormous network all over Russia to repair the cars and to sell the cars.

BROWNE: Now, in November 1994, did you consider the question of going into television?

BEREZOVSKY: Yes, it was maybe not only television; I also began thinking about going into politics. Because as maybe you know, the reforms were passed with a lot of difficulties and there were many mistakes, and a lot of people who initially supported democracy in Russia started to think in a different way. Because life did not become immediately better; life became worse for the majority of the population, compared with Soviet times. It was very complicated to understand that this was a necessary result of any revolutionary transformation. And many people were disappointed by Yeltsin, by rich people at that time in Russia. And I recognized that there would be a big battle in the new presidential elections between new and old, let us say, between Russian Democracy and Communism. And it is for this reason that I decided to move into television and politics, because I understood that the mass media would play the decisive role in the new elections.

BROWNE: And so what did you do to become involved in the mass media?

BEREZOVSKY: At that time, I became a member of the Presidential Club, at the recommendation of Peter Aven, who also is mentioned here and is a witness for Mr. Fridman.

BROWNE: Just pausing there; I think Mr. Aven is also one of the directors of *Alfa Bank*?

BEREZOVSKY: Correct. He introduced me to a person who was very close to Yeltsin, Mr. Yumashev. Later on he became the head of Mr. Yeltsin's administration. This was in 1994, and we became very close friends. Yumashev then introduced me to Yeltsin, who was at that time the President of Russia. And we discussed a lot about the coming elections and I had just begun to develop the idea for transforming the most powerful TV channel to private from state control; because at that time the state was not able or ready to bankroll this channel, which spent approximately $250 million per year.

BROWNE: What was the name of this TV channel that you have been talking about?

BEREZOVSKY: Well, we called it Central TV, a typical Soviet name, Central TV. We changed it to ORT, in translation—roughly in English—"Public TV." Public, not in the sense of the BBC, which is subsidized by subscribers, but in the sense that we were trying to present the general point of view of the Russian public.

BROWNE: So the initials, just in case anybody did not catch it, are ORT?

BEREZOVSKY: ORT.

BROWNE: Thank you. And did LogoVAZ buy into ORT?

BEREZOVSKY: Yes, LogoVAZ—again, it was my initiative to create a consortium of leading businessmen and to buy shares of the state under the name of this consortium. And it was my initiative; but this initiative was supported by leading Russian businessmen, including Mr. Fridman, including Mr. Potanin. And including other businessmen. And we created a group of businessmen who bought 49 percent of the shares from the state, who held onto 51 percent of shares—in other words, the majority belonged to the state.

BROWNE: Now, did *Alfa Bank* have shares in ORT?

BEREZOVSKY: Yes, correct.

BROWNE: Did you become a director of ORT?

BEREZOVSKY: No, I have never been the director of ORT. Moreover, we—our problem was to collect money to organize its operation. As I mentioned, ORT was just draining money from the state, $250 million per year. Yeltsin's condition for converting 49 percent into private shares was that the state would stop financing ORT.

BROWNE: What role did Mr. Fridman play in ORT?

BEREZOVSKY: The same—at the beginning, the same as me; but later on, because it was not profitable, as I told you, ORT was supplying money without an equal return. And not everybody, even the rich in Russia, were prepared only to spend money as a long-term strategy. And Mr. Fridman was one of them. Moreover, after three years, in 1996, I think already—no one wanted to pay out just to spend money. And step by step they sold their shares to my company. But at the beginning it was—I do not remember exactly, five or six different banks and different companies who bought the state shares. Not equally. Let us say my company bought 8 percent, Fridman bought 5 percent, Potanin bought 5 percent, but there were several shareholders.

BROWNE: When did President Yeltsin assume the presidency of Russia? When did he become President of Russia?

BEREZOVSKY: He became the President of Russia in 1991, for the first time. In 1996, for the second time.

BROWNE: And did you occupy any political office during President Yeltsin's second term, starting in 1996?

BEREZOVSKY: Yes, after Yeltsin became president. I believed that one of the biggest problems for the stabilization of the political situation in Russia was the war in Chechnya, which Yeltsin started in 1994. Mr. Rybkin became, in the Yeltsin administration, the Secretary of the Security Council of Russia, who was responsible for the, let us say, control and preparation of decisions for all Russian power ministries. Mr. Rybkin proposed that I try to help to build peace in Chechnya.

BROWNE: So what position were you given?

BEREZOVSKY: I was given the position of Deputy Secretary of the Security Council. As I remember, there were four or five deputies on this council.

BROWNE: And just roughly, how long did you remain Deputy Secretary of the Security Council?

BEREZOVSKY: As I remember, only a little bit over a year. But I think the most important problem was solved during this time, because we had normalized our relations with Chechnya; for the first time in the history of Russian and Chechen relations for more than two centuries, we signed a peace agreement between Russia and Chechnya.

BROWNE: Do you remember when that agreement was signed?

BEREZOVSKY: This I remember well. It was May 12, 1997.

BROWNE: Was there anyone involved with you in the negotiations with the Chechens?

BEREZOVSKY: Certainly. Mr. Rybkin, as I told you, who was the Secretary of the Security Council. And some others—on the lower level, who were professionals with an understanding of the Caucasus region. But because of Yeltsin's decree, I was the responsible, let us say, executor for this region.

BROWNE: Who was the first Deputy Prime Minister of Russia at this time?

BEREZOVSKY: The first—Nemtsov was the first Deputy Prime Minister? I do not remember. Did we have at that time one or two first deputies?

BROWNE: I am told I can lead. Is it right that Mr. Nemtsov and you were involved in negotiations which led to an agreement for transporting Azerbaijan's oil through Chechnya to a Russian port on the Black Sea?

BEREZOVSKY: Yes, absolutely correct, that is absolutely correct. Because after we agreed on a political basis for peace in Chechnya, we took the next economic step to help the countries recover from the war. And I asked Nemtsov to help broker this deal, together with travel to Azerbaijan, because this was Azerbaijani oil which could be transported to Russia.

BROWNE: So in the months leading up to the Chechen peace treaty in 1997, what were your relations like with Mr. Nemtsov?

BEREZOVSKY: You see, my relations with Nemtsov—I am really surprised because my relations with him at that time were quite good. Moreover, when I was moved from Russia to Great Britain, to London, Nemtsov many times visited London and many times visited me at my home in the English countryside. I was absolutely surprised by his affidavit.

BROWNE: When did you last see Mr. Nemtsov in London?

BEREZOVSKY: The last time I saw him, I think, was one and a half years ago.

BROWNE: What did the two of you do in London?

BEREZOVSKY: It is usual for us to discuss Russian political life, because, as you know, Nemtsov is a well-known politician in Russia, and still now politically active, and his opinion was very important. And—besides being in touch with him here in London, I had met with him several times in Israel while I was traveling there, in Eilat, because we have a common friend, Mr. Prokhorov, who is a colleague of Potanin. Prokhorov likes to celebrate his birthday in Israel and Nemtsov always accompanied him.

BROWNE: During these recent meetings with Mr. Nemtsov, did he ever complain that you had threatened him in the past?

BEREZOVSKY: Not at all.

BROWNE: Mr. Berezovsky, you have described how you held office as Deputy Secretary of the Security Council for a year or so from October 1996. Were you again given high office in 1998?

BEREZOVSKY: First of all, would you allow me to make some corrections to my previous answer?

JUSTICE EADY: Yes.

BEREZOVSKY: I just ask permission to make a correction to my previous answer because I did not catch correctly your question: have you been involved with the directors—the directors of ORT? And the problem is that, again, there are some problems with my English because "directors" in Russia has an executive power. And members of directors, members of boards, are a legitimate power, not an executive power. And I was a member of the board of ORT. I was never part of the executive power, but I was included, I was part of the board of ORT.

JUSTICE EADY: I understand. So you were a member of the board of ORT, the television company.

BEREZOVSKY: Correct.

JUSTICE EADY: But did not have any executive function.

BEREZOVSKY: Absolutely correct.

BROWNE: And just to complete the picture, was Mr. Fridman a director of ORT?

BEREZOVSKY: No, I do not remember. I think that in the initial phases, all of us who had become shareholders had been members of the board. Later on, as I told you, one by one, they sold the shares to me. But during that phase, I do not remember. It is not a problem to reconstruct that, but I do not remember right now ...

BROWNE: Sorry, can we now go back. I was asking you about the office that you took up in April 1998. What was that?

BEREZOVSKY: It was when the Soviet Union collapsed, at that time 15 new countries appeared. 15. Three Baltic republics, Estonia, Latvia and Lithuania, and they immediately moved to the west. But all the rest, well, including Russia, tried to create some common economic space, on a new basis where every country was independent. And the so-called CIS was created, Commonwealth of Independent States, which included Russia, Ukraine, Belarus, the Middle East countries and the countries of the Caucasus. And Central Asia, yes, Central Asia, and Uzbekistan, Turkmenistan, and so on.

And according to the decisions of the leaders of these countries, they created a special organization that was to manage these new unions. And according to the status of this organization, they were to elect a chairman and executive secretary. The chairman was to be chosen from among the presidents, and Yeltsin was to become the chairman of this organization. They then elected me as the executive secretary. They voted from amongst themselves. I received 12 votes.

BROWNE: Were these offices, as Deputy Secretary of the Security Council and the Executive Secretary of the Commonwealth of Independent States, full time jobs for you?

BEREZOVSKY: Yes, full time jobs.

BROWNE: So what happened to your business career during this time?

BEREZOVSKY: According to Russian law, when I became Deputy Secretary of the Security Council, I had to follow rules similar to other countries. I transferred all my business activities to my partners and did not actively participate in any of these businesses. And I did just this, including with my western company in Switzerland, and so on. I removed myself from all posts that I had been holding in these private companies.

BROWNE: Now—I think I can lead on this—did you remain as an Executive Secretary of the Commonwealth of Independent States for about a year until April 1999?

BEREZOVSKY: Yes, correct.

BROWNE: And did you subsequently stand for the Russian Parliament, the Duma?

BEREZOVSKY: Yes, that is correct. I just want to tell the jury, just to be clear, it was never my desire to leave this post—the post of Deputy of the Security Council or Executive Secretary of the CIS. Yeltsin fired me, twice. And in autumn 1999 we began to run for the new parliamentary elections, and I put my name in for one of the regions of the Caucasus—Karachaevo-Cherkessia—to become a member of the lower chamber of the Russian Parliament, the Duma. And I was elected in December 1999, as a member of the Russian Parliament.

BROWNE: Where was your constituency? What part of Russia were you …

BEREZOVSKY: I mentioned this, it was in the Caucasus in Karachaevo-Cherkessia.

BROWNE: Now, in December 1999, the same month that you became a member of the Duma, Mr. Yeltsin resigned as president, and was succeeded by the then Prime Minister Mr. Putin. What was your position in relation to Mr. Putin? Did you support him?

BEREZOVSKY: At that time, I had already known Putin for ten years. Mr. Aven first reintroduced me to Mr. Putin in St. Petersburg in 1991, I think. At that time, he was deputy mayor of St. Petersburg. We got on well. It might be important for you to know that I was completely surprised that he was—maybe the first bureaucrat I had ever met in this revolutionary time who was not accepting bribes. He never asked for anything. And we became friendly, not close friends, but we got along well. We even traveled abroad together to ski, in Switzerland and in other countries. I have known him fairly well all these years. Again, we were not that close, not best friends, but friendly, particularly when he moved to Moscow after the Mayor of St. Petersburg lost the election. Putin was his deputy. Putin refused the new mayor's proposal for him to stay on, which also reflected on him positively. He then moved to Moscow and I supported him as a candidate for Prime Minister. At that time I was close to Yeltsin and I had, let us say, chances to present my opinion. Later on, I supported him in the presidential elections.

BROWNE: Yes. So, Mr. Putin becomes Prime Minister in August 1999, steps into President Yeltsin's shoes when he resigns on New Year's Eve 1999. When were the presidential elections in 2000?

BEREZOVSKY: It was in March.

BROWNE: And did you support Mr. Putin as a candidate for the election?

BEREZOVSKY: Yes, correct. I supported him 100 percent.

BROWNE: And after the election, did he act as you had expected?

BEREZOVSKY: No, the first—in general, the first problem of my understanding of him appeared before he even became president, when he started the second Chechen war. As I told you, I participated directly in stopping the first Chechen war. I was certainly disappointed by him. I met with him many times to explain my position, my understanding, that a military solution was not the answer to keeping this region inside of Russia part of Russia.

BROWNE: When you say he started the second Chechen war, what precisely did he do?

BEREZOVSKY: This is the subject of numerous questions, because even now it is not known who precisely gave the order to start the bombings, to bomb Chechnya again—him or Yeltsin.

BROWNE: But at any rate, the war started again, and you were not happy with that?

BEREZOVSKY: No, and as I mentioned, I met with Putin many times, trying to explain to him that this was not the way to manage Chechnya.

BROWNE: In a couple of sentences, what did you think was the best way to deal with the problems in Chechnya?

BEREZOVSKY: Well, not only—not just what I thought, but my actions as well, what we had done under Yeltsin; we had created a peaceful political platform. But it is not enough just to find peace. The republic had been completely destroyed, and we needed to invest a lot to help rebuild the country. And even the Prime Minister at that time of Russia, Mr. Chernomyrdin, did not want to take part in that reconstruction. There were discussions. I think the reason why the second war started was because they did not—on the one hand—have jobs and the fighting continued inside the republic. On the other hand, there were numerous groups inside of Russia and Chechnya that wanted to continue the fight. But you put forth the question about how my view of

Putin changed. As I told you, the first message, the first signal came before he became president. And when he became president in March 2000, he immediately started to initiate a set of laws which worked against the basic conditions for democracy in Russia. And one of these basic steps was to give himself the right to fire the elected governors. Perhaps you know that Russia is a federation, which means that based on the constitution, we elect the governors. And if I get to elect someone, why should someone else be able to fire him? It is not logical. This was the first thing. And I met with Putin and I spoke to him about this. And when we could not find a common language, I told him that I would be running for an open public position. I then wrote an open letter addressed to Putin, May 31, 2000, where I criticized this new law and laid out my position concerning this new law.

BROWNE: Was that open letter published in the Russian press?

BEREZOVSKY: It was published in the *Kommersant* newspaper on May 31.

BROWNE: And was there any reaction from Mr. Putin to that?

BEREZOVSKY: Yes, he called me, we met and he said, "Are you sure you want to fight against me?" But this was not the decisive break in our friendship.

BROWNE: Now, it is a matter of record that Mr. Gusinsky was held in prison from, I think, the 10th to the 13th of June 2000. What was your public reaction to his arrest and imprisonment?

BEREZOVSKY: The entire time I was certain that this was not the way for a government to interact with the mass media. Because it is absolutely clear that Gusinsky was arrested just because of his position during the parliamentary and presidential elections. And I would like to stress that my position had been in favor of Putin; and Gusinsky's position was opposed to Putin, in favor of Putin's opponents. But as far as Putin's acts after he became president, I was completely opposed to them. I officially expressed my position against the dismantling of NTV as a company, in the possession of Gusinsky.

BROWNE: What was the position of NTV while it was in Mr. Gusinsky's hands? What was its political stance?

BEREZOVSKY: No, what I'm trying to explain to you is that I think that Gusinsky, for the first time in Russian history, had truly created a section of the mass media that was independent from the state. I'm trying to explain my view, that it is not possible to discuss independence as an abstract form of journalism. Certainly every company belongs to some state or to some private concern. And this private entity at least nominates a general manager. Let us say that I am a powerful force in ORT, I will never nominate a Communist as the general manager. This is a political privilege, a political preference of mine. Gusinsky created the most powerful—one of the three most powerful—channels, and it was completely independent of the state. And all the journalists, up until now, have been the most professional in Russia. Even the new NTV, which you can watch, and which is very much under the control of the Kremlin, still has the best journalists in Russia.

BROWNE: What happened to the independence of NTV after Mr. Gusinsky was forced to surrender it to Gazprom, the state-owned energy company?

BEREZOVSKY: After that, everything happened very logically from Putin's point of view. They fought for shareholder control. I mean, the state fought for shareholder control over NTV, and very soon Gazprom, the largest Russian monopoly, bought Gusinsky's shares because he was squeezed into prison and forced to sign a letter giving up his control. But the main reason was to bring it under state control. And Gusinsky signed this letter, and after that came Gazprom Media, a subsidiary of Gazprom. They took control of NTV. Gazprom itself is controlled by the state.

BROWNE: Now, you had been elected to the Duma in December 1999. How long did you remain a member?

BEREZOVSKY: Until I recognized that the parliament had become more and more of a puppet.

BROWNE: Puppet?

BEREZOVSKY: Puppet, because—the puppet of the Kremlin. And step-by-step, my, let us say, personal opinion does not mean anything at all. And as a member of the Duma, I had obligations to the people who elected me in Karachaevo-Cherkessia. And at that time, it was a very complicated situation in that region. I was not able to do anything, and in July, I think, I simply gave back my mandate in Parliament.

BROWNE: When you resigned your seat in the Duma, what public statement did you make about the reasons for that action?

BEREZOVSKY: Exactly what I just said; that Putin, step-by-step, had put under control more than—the Parliament is 450 members. And there is a simple majority, 226. And a constitutional majority, 300 or more. And when Putin took the step that even the independent deputies were under his control, that they created a majority, more than 300, which is a constitutional majority, then everyone else, the150, does not mean anything.

BROWNE: Did you make any public statement about your future political intentions?

BEREZOVSKY: Yes, I made a statement that the most important act was to create a real opposition to the existing power. And I decreed officially that I would try to do that.

BROWNE: In August 2000, the submarine Kursk sank in the Northern Sea around Russia. How did the Russian media respond to that tragedy?

BEREZOVSKY: At that time, even though NTV was no longer owned by Gusinsky, their journalists still responded as objective journalists. And ORT, which I had 49 percent of, had an enormous amount of influence. The other channels also criticized Putin strongly because he remained on the beach, in the south of Russia, and the sailors remained in the submarine, dying. There was a great amount of pressure on him.

BROWNE: What did ORT say about President Putin remaining on the beach?

BEREZOVSKY: ORT was also very critical of him. And moreover, ORT ran interviews with wives and sisters of soldiers who had sunk on the submarine. And at that time, Putin called me and asked me to meet with him in Moscow after he returned from Sochi. This was our last meeting. And he was very angry. He accused me and ORT of running a smear campaign against him. And after he said, "I will personally control and manage all the TV channels." I responded, "That's not very likely." This was our last meeting. After that, I never saw him again, except on TV.

BROWNE: I am sorry, I just want to be clear that I caught what you were saying. What did he say about the control of ORT in the future?

BEREZOVSKY: He said that, "I will control it myself."

BROWNE: I, Putin?

Berezovsky: Me, Putin, "You should return to the state the shares which belong to you." I said, "I will never do this voluntarily." And that was that.

Browne: And after that demand by Mr. Putin for you to surrender your shares in ORT, did you make any public statement about the meeting you had had with him in the Kremlin?

Berezovsky: No, I did not make any public statement about my meeting. But later on, I commented about that meeting.

Browne: And what did you comment?

Berezovsky: I said exactly what I have just reported to you. That I met the president. The president requested that I return my shares, and that I had refused his request. That is all.

Browne: Now, moving forward to October 2000. When you were in France, did the Russian Public Prosecutor make an announcement?

Berezovsky: No, it was a little bit different. They just—it was announced that they had opened a criminal case against me in Russia. At that time, I was in France, but I was still able to travel around Europe, around the world, to the United States. And I traveled also to Great Britain. And when I was in Great Britain, I got a message that they had issued a warrant against me. And after that, I decided to stay in London, and I asked for political asylum.

Browne: When was the last time you were in Russia, Mr. Berezovsky?

Berezovsky: Autumn 2000.

Browne: In December 2000, did anything happen to a business colleague and close friend of yours named Nikolai Glushkov?

Berezovsky: Yes, in December 2000. He is my friend. He was my business partner and what is also important, Mr. Putin also knew him very well; he was the deputy of—the CEO of Aeroflot. He was arrested. And the general prosecutor put him in jail. And this was in December, and he spent three and a half years in jail.

Browne: What was Mr. Glushkov's state of health?

Berezovsky: He is extremely infirmed according to Russian standards, part of the so-called first group, because he has a blood disease—not exactly cancer, but a similar problem.

Browne: What were the conditions like that he was held in?

Berezovsky: In conditions like everybody else.

Browne: Just explain to us what those are like.

BEREZOVSKY: Well, it is well known, there are numerous reports of human rights organizations, that conditions in Russian prisons are more than terrible. And you already mentioned Khodorkovsky, who is the most, let us say, visible case in Russia; he has been imprisoned for the last few years, and he owned the largest Russian oil company. But this is not what's important. The point is that he is the focus of attention. And recently in jail he was injured by another prisoner during the night, while sleeping.

BROWNE: Well, let us just go back to Mr. Glushkov. He was put in prison. Did anyone approach you about Mr. Glushkov's predicament?

BEREZOVSKY: No, when they put Glushkov in jail, I was visited by Abramovich, my former oil partner. And he came in the name of Putin, saying that I should sell immediately my shares in ORT, and that if I sell them, Glushkov would be released. And under this pressure, I sold my shares to Abramovich; but Glushkov was not released.

BROWNE: Was Mr. Abramovich acting on his own behalf in demanding the sale of the ORT shares, or was he acting on behalf of someone else?

BEREZOVSKY: No, he mentioned to me that he was acting on behalf of Putin and Voloshin. Voloshin at that time was head of the presidential administration.

BROWNE: So you sold the shares, but the other part of the deal was not done and Mr. Glushkov remained in jail. What happened to Mr. Glushkov subsequently?

BEREZOVSKY: He was charged with three offenses: money laundering, fraud, and that he had misappropriated funds—office abuses. And when already in jail, he received the added charge that he had tried to escape from jail. And the result of this hearing was that he was not involved with money laundering, he was not involved in any type of fraud, but that he had tried to flee jail. In other words, no single financial accusation against him was proven in court. And after that they released him, calculating three and a half years, which he had spent as a result of the two other charges. But the general prosecutor's office appealed, and now his case is again being heard in Russian court.

BROWNE: Now, you came to England, you told us, in October 2001. And subsequently the Prosecutor General announced that you were wanted for arrest, and you applied for political asylum. None of this, I think, is in dispute but just so that we have the chronology. In March 2003, an official request was made for your extradition. What were the charges upon which the Russian government sought your extradition?

BEREZOVSKY: The charge was not the same one they had initially charged me with when I fled Russia. They opened a new case related to 1994–1995 as I remember, saying that it was a sham deal between LogoVAZ, AvtoVAZ and the regional administration. If you want, I can go through the details of this deal, but as I told you, as a result, the final result—the London court did not find that there were sufficient facts to prove that I had done anything against Russian law. And two years later the supreme arbitrage court of Russia made the same decision.

BROWNE: So can we just summarize the position. What is the position of those who publicly disagree with Mr. Putin's political stance?

BEREZOVSKY: It depends—it depends on do you want to be public against, or not public? If you run a large company, a nationwide company, you do not have a choice. You do not have a choice, because you must be loyal to Putin, and moreover Putin made his position absolutely clear in this meeting which you refer to with 15 businessmen. He said, "You want to run a business? Stay out of politics, don't get involved in this field." And this is the principal position. For those who share this position, everything works extremely well. There are no problems. But those who do not share this position, have no chance to do business in Russia, and moreover there is a 100 percent chance that their business will be destroyed.

BROWNE: You are quite right to reprove me for making a general statement, and perhaps Mr. Shields was as well. But what I was simply driving at was, what lesson do we deduce from the experience of Mr. Khodorkovsky, Mr. Gusinsky and yourself?

BEREZOVSKY: If you do not mind—it is perhaps not polite—but I will start with myself, and then move on to Khodorkovsky, Gusinsky, and so on, because maybe I have the most, how do I say, the most visible experience? Because, as I mentioned to you, Mr. Abramovich and I were partners 50/50 in our oil, aluminum, and various businesses. And when Putin was elected, I started, as I told you before, to present my oppositional stance to Putin's steps. And I had discussions about this with Abramovich, who said, "Boris, it is your choice; my choice is different. I will stay with Putin." And finally, today we are in two different camps: objective, or subjective, if you like. That is why—all the stories are different; maybe the key point is that all these people want to be independent, or they want not to be Putin clones. They truly want to be independent. As far as Gusinsky is concerned, he wants to be independent with his NTV channel; as far as Khodorkovsky is concerned, he wants to be independent in his business affairs and to make personal decisions as to whom to sell oil to or which pipeline he should build and so on. And those who accepted the new rules, they are very successful in Russia.

BROWNE: Mr. Berezovsky, I want to move on now to the broadcast on NTV on October 28, 2004. Could you explain to the jury the popularity of this program hosted by Mr. Soloviov. Is it a popular program for Russian speakers?

BEREZOVSKY: It is very popular, and he is a very popular journalist; well known; for a very long time he has worked in the top levels of various TV channels. And he is particularly important now when discussions, real discussions, real differing points of view are so rare on today's Russian TV. And even this program, which I watched, I do not want to comment on because I want you to have your own understanding, but even this program is now attractive because it has different points of view and people really try to prove their arguments. And it really is very interesting to watch how Fridman and Vasiliev argue. And Soloviov, there is no doubt that he is one of the best Russian anchors today.

BROWNE: Now, we know that on October 20th, that is to say seven days before recording the program and eight days before it was broadcast, the Moscow court had awarded *Kommersant* (sic) 320 million roubles in damages. Are you able to tell the jury how that award was composed? How much of the 320 million roubles was for actual financial loss?

BEREZOVSKY: First of all, I want—please understand, this is not a professional comment because it has been a long time since I was involved in *Kommersant* operations, even financial; because first of all they do not need my financial support, they are an absolutely profitable company, and this year I was told they generated $50 million in profit. As far as what I know about this 11 million, which was absolutely ridiculous, not because it is too much in general, but because I know of no precedent in world journalist history where this amount of money has been fined. It does not mean that it does not exist, it is that I personally do not know …

BROWNE: How much of this 320 million roubles actually represented a loss caused to *Alfa Bank* by *Kommersant.*

BEREZOVSKY: It was a little bit more than 10 percent, I think. Around 12 percent. 88 percent was compensation of the reputation of the bank. It means that from this 348, whatever, only 40 million cover losses and 300 is image damage.

BROWNE: Damage to reputation?

BEREZOVSKY: Yes, damage to reputation. And it is strange, because even in the Russian law it is very strange. Damage of whose reputation? It is impossible to—to represent the damage of the reputation of a legal entity. In Russian law, it is—the individual's reputation must be damaged, not a legal entity.

JUSTICE EADY: Not a company.

BEREZOVSKY: Correct.

BROWNE: In the week following the court's award on October 20th, what reaction was there in the media to this enormous award?

BEREZOVSKY: My God, for one, I want to be precise with my answer. It is my understanding that there is no Russian law which allows you to fight for the reputation of a company. Please excuse me.

BROWNE: In the week following the award by the Moscow court on October 20, 2004, what was the reaction in the media to the award?

BEREZOVSKY: It was—the reaction was predictable. No doubt if you opened up a newspaper or watched TV, in spite of—how do you say—in spite of some concern that *Kommersant* belonged to me and concern over the support of journalists for *Kommersant*, it was common opinion that it was all a very odd game. A very strange game. It is true that many people perceived this game as being led by the Kremlin and Fridman; that Fridman wanted to appear loyal to the Kremlin. I do not know. I do not know the reasons behind this game, but in general, most people were unable to come up with a reasonable argument for the court's decision. Later on *Kommersant* appealed this decision in Russia. And the final decision included just compensation to

Alfa Bank, not damages, but simply losses. And the final payment from *Kommersant* was around 40 million roubles. All the rest was returned, obviously.

BROWNE: About US $1.5 million.

BEREZOVSKY: Correct.

BROWNE: So that is about £800,000.

BEREZOVSKY: Well, it is still an enormous amount.

BROWNE: Yes. Just the last question perhaps for tonight. Subsequently, has *Kommersant* appealed to the European Court of Human Rights?

BEREZOVSKY: Yes, that is correct.

BROWNE: And is that application…

BEREZOVSKY: Presented.

BROWNE: Presented, but not yet heard.

BEREZOVSKY: Correct.

BROWNE: My Lord, that might be a convenient moment. I was going to come to his reaction to the broadcast.

Tuesday, May 16, 2006

EXAMINATION-IN-CHIEF BY MR. BROWNE *(continued)*

BROWNE: Mr. Berezovsky, when we broke off last night I was about to ask you about the night of the broadcast, October 28, 2004. Did you watch the program when it was broadcast on NTV? Did you watch the television program?

BEREZOVSKY: Yes, I was at my home in Wentworth Park in Surrey.

BROWNE: Wentworth Park?

BEREZOVSKY: Because I was informed by Mr. Vasiliev that he had decided to participate in this TV show.

BROWNE: Did you watch the whole of the program?

BEREZOVSKY: Yes, I watched the whole program from the beginning to the end.

BROWNE: And when Mr. Fridman mentioned you, how did you react?

BEREZOVSKY: I was very surprised, and my wife, my partner, who watched with me, because she also still pays a lot of attention to events in Russia, in spite of the fact that we left together five years ago. She also was completely surprised. And you know, I was surprised because I did not have any particular problem with Fridman before. I certainly understood that they were all trying to be nice to Putin, but not on this level. I have never before seen anything like this happen among the top-level business community.

BROWNE: What was your reaction to the suggestion that your habitual way of working with people was to use threats?

BEREZOVSKY: You see, there is a basic problem. This is the basic problem, because—I am sorry—I should explain something else first, because unfortunately this was not the first time, though the first time involving people from the Russian business community. For six years I was involved in a legal case in London, the *Forbes* case. The magazine had published an article by Mr. Khlebnikov, a *Forbes* journalist, who said that I was involved in murder, violence, and so on, and it took me six and a half years here in London to prove that he was wrong. And *Forbes* eventually made a statement that this information was false. But this had a lot of—there was a lot of discussion about this case in Russia. And not just in Russia; it also took time to prove that the London courts should take this case and investigate it in London. And this is the main reason why I was so disappointed, because Fridman made statements that were directly opposed to what I had spent six and a half years proving in London.

BROWNE: How long had you had business dealings with Mr. Fridman?

BEREZOVSKY: We began working together on ORT, and Fridman, as I mentioned, was one of the partners of ORT TV, which was the privatized version of Central TV. I mentioned yesterday about the 49 percent that several of the most powerful groups shared. This is when I began to work with him. Moreover, he introduced me to Mr. Abramovich.

JUSTICE EADY: The evidence yesterday was since 1994.

BEREZOVSKY: From the end of 1994. If you calculate up until today, we still have some joint business interests.

BROWNE: Yes. When your name was introduced into the program, what was the reaction to being raised in the context of a debate about the verdict against *Kommersant*? How did you feel when your name was mentioned in the context of the libel verdict?

BEREZOVSKY: I was not surprised that my name was mentioned in the context of *Kommersant* because it is a well-known fact that I, along with my partner Badri, were *Kommersant* shareholders. It was not a surprise to me on the one hand. On the other hand, I was surprised by the statement which Fridman made, and that he made them repeatedly. He said that I threatened him and that I routinely threatened other people. At first I was more disappointed than shocked.

BROWNE: So what action did you take?

BEREZOVSKY: I first discussed the issue with my wife because, to tell you the truth, I was a bit exhausted from all the different court cases in London. As I mentioned, there was the six and a half years dealing with *Forbes*, then an extradition request, then political asylum, then a case against the *Sunday Times* and another newspaper, which we won. Nevertheless, after I thought about it some more, I came to understand that it was already a story, it was already spread all over the Russian business community. There are businessmen who are prepared to serve whoever is in power, to serve the Kremlin in such an absolutely dirty manner, and I unfortunately had no choice but to go to court.

BROWNE: Mr. Berezovsky, I do not know whether you have a copy of the file that the jury has up in the witness box. I think you may not. I will just ask for one to be handed up. Members of the jury, could you go to tab 5 in that file, page 36. I read this letter to the jury yesterday. The question I want to ask you, Mr. Berezovsky, is this. That letter at the foot of page 36 asks for a public apology withdrawing the allegation Mr. Fridman had made. If he had given you a public apology would you have brought these proceedings?

BEREZOVSKY: Yes, I formulated, along with my lawyers, an absolutely clear position. I was not asking for any money, any compensation, because the principle of the case was what was important. My reputation was at stake, and not only my reputation as, unfortunately, I had become a symbol of all those rich individuals who had left Russia, not voluntarily, but because we were in a situation where we are not able to remain in Russia or to go abroad and ask for political asylum; like me, like Gusinsky, like Nevzlin, like hundreds today, Russian businessmen. I had no choice. And so far as I became the focus of these events, I was fighting not just for my personal reputation. I was of course fighting for that, because I have children, I have a mother. But I was also fighting for all these people who are today under immense political pressure, which they try to transform into criminal pressure. And Fridman, unfortunately, being from the same part of society, played an absolutely dirty trick. And it is not a problem of money, it is simply a problem of reputation, and not just mine, as I understand it.

BROWNE: Now, Mr. Berezovsky, we know that the program was broadcast via satellite. Do you have a satellite subscription to NTV in this country? Is it possible to watch NTV in this country without being a subscriber to NTV?

BEREZOVSKY: Before I answer that question, my Lord, could I go back to a previous question?

JUSTICE EADY: You want to go back and correct something?

BEREZOVSKY: Yes, sometimes I overestimate my English and do not properly understand the questions, so if you do not mind, I propose that all questions be translated by the interpreter and I will try to respond in English.

JUSTICE EADY: Certainly. Take your time.

BEREZOVSKY: To return to the previous point, I recognize that the question as I understand it was if Fridman apologized would I go to court or not. My answer is absolutely clear that if he had apologized publicly, I would not have gone to court. Because for me what was important was my public position, that he was wrong; nothing more. Now, about...

BROWNE: About the satellite subscriptions. Is it possible to watch NTV in this country without having a subscription?

BEREZOVSKY: You know, I heard that there is a black market for the—a scam which allows one to pirate—and I know that now a lot of Russian speaking people have moved here and not all of them are rich. There are many people who simply can't afford it. But I do not know anyone in particular who has done this.

BROWNE: Since you have mentioned that many Russians have come to this country, including from Ukraine, can I just ask the jury to look at one thing which I did not mention in the opening. In your file you will see the control of immigration statistics provided by the Home Office in 2003. I just want to look at one part of these figures. "Grants of settlement by nationality in the years between 1993 and 2003." If you look two thirds of the way down the page you will see "Former

USSR" and then it is broken down, the Baltic republics, Russia, Ukraine and the other republics of the former Soviet Union. If one looks at the last four years, one sees that in 2000 there were altogether 2095 settlers from the former Soviet Union; 2000 again the following year, 2001; just over 2,500 in 2002, and then a big jump in 2003, 4,145. Anyway, I hope you can see those figures. Now, given the size of the Russian community now in London, are you able to tell the jury how many such individuals would be likely to subscribe to NTV?

BEREZOVSKY: I want to be very precise as I was involved in TV in Russia and I understand that there are different levels of society, and traditionally NTV served the more intellectual part of society—as opposed to ORT, for example, and the other state channels. And what is clear to me is that people who move abroad prefer NTV to the other channels, because moving abroad is a difficult step in life and those people who take this step are either very strong internally, or are pushed out of the country, like me. I think that—I do not want to be incorrect, so I will simply say that this TV channel is the most popular amongst the most active and intellectual part of society.

BROWNE: Mr. Berezovsky, English people may or may not have heard of you. How well known are you to Russian speakers in England?

BEREZOVSKY: I think that it is a tradition that when Russians move abroad they pay more attention to Russia and to political life in Russia because maybe they have more time to think about it. It has turned out that I have been involved in almost all the major political events in Russia over the past decade, which is why many people who I do not know come up to me on the street and shake my hand. This is one reason. The second reason is that the Abramovich and Chelsea case brought a lot of attention to the entire Russian community, and particularly to Abramovich and to me as his former partner. The current case is much more personal to me.

BROWNE: Now, I want to turn to the subject of your purchase of shares in *Kommersant* in September 1999. That is by way of an introduction. The question is this: Mr. Yakovlev was the founder and the majority shareholder in *Kommersant*. When did you first learn that Mr. Yakovlev wished to sell his shares in the paper?

BEREZOVSKY: Very briefly, Yakovlev moved from Russia not in 1999, but, I think, two or three years before that. In 1999, at the very beginning of 1999, I started to discuss this with my partner Badri, because Yakovlev's other partner, Mr. Miloslavsky, had come to see me. Everyone knows everyone else in the Russian mass media community. He came to me and said that he thought that Yakovlev was looking to sell *Kommersant.* And I replied that it was a very interesting proposition. He also mentioned that he had told others about the possible sale. After speaking with Badri, who was also very interested in the deal, a meeting was organized with Miloslavsky and Yakovlev in Amsterdam. It was the very beginning, I think, spring, maybe even the end of—winter, 1999. No, winter 2000—winter 1999, yes, or the very beginning of spring in 1999.

BROWNE: And what was the political stance of *Kommersant* at this time?

BEREZOVSKY: The political position of *Kommersant* changed little from what Yakovlev had originally constructed. It was the first independent newspaper, free from the government. It is possible to compare it to what Gusinsky did with NTV. They always tried to present an objective position with different opinions. They followed the western tradition of letting both sides have an opportunity to make their points. Yakovlev created this, and it remained this way.

BROWNE: What were Mr. Yakovlev's concerns about a purchaser of *Kommersant?*

BEREZOVSKY: I only had one meeting with Yakovlev in Amsterdam. We spent two days in Amsterdam going over things, and he, of course, was interested in getting the best price possible. But on the other hand, he was extremely concerned about maintaining *Kommersant's* reputation. His reputation and *Kommersant's* reputation were very important to him—and not just market reputation, but the general public's opinion of the company. From the very beginning I said, "The price is not my main concern, you can discuss that with Badri." Yakovlev spoke mainly about his concern that *Kommersant* remain independent, and he wanted to know what sort of influence I planned on exerting over *Kommersant's* policy.

BROWNE: Did you plan to influence the policy of *Kommersant?*

BEREZOVSKY: You see, today we have a very clear answer to this question, which is based on reality. *Kommersant* is the number one newspaper in Russia. Everybody accepts that *Kommersant* is the absolute leader among newspapers in Russia, and not in the sense of circulation, but as a power that continues to support democracy. As I just mentioned, two or three months ago I had a meeting with the entire *Kommersant* team in London where they all confirmed that I have never given any instructions to a journalist about what to do, what to write, what not to write.

BROWNE: You had your meeting with Mr. Yakovlev as winter turned into spring in the early part of 1999. Did you meet Mr. Yakovlev again?

BEREZOVSKY: I do not remember any meetings with him at all.

BROWNE: So how did the negotiations progress after that?

BEREZOVSKY: After we came back to Moscow, Badri and I decided to go forward with the deal, and after that Badri flew to the United States, because at that time Yakovlev was mainly based in the United States. And after that Badri spent—with some interruptions—returning for a few days to Moscow here and there—three or four months together with Yakovlev trying to make this deal happen.

BROWNE: Were you involved in making this deal happen?

BEREZOVSKY: Initially there was an agreement in principle between me and Yakovlev, but after that I never spoke with him about it. Later when I did speak with Miloslavsky and the minority shareholders, the negotiations in Moscow had been finalized. We were already thinking about a new general manager for *Kommersant*. I was never involved in the technical negotiations, about how to make it all happen.

BROWNE: Was there anyone else interested in buying *Kommersant* at this time?

BEREZOVSKY: Yes, as said earlier, when Miloslavsky made the proposal to me he had mentioned that he had discussed it with other people too. And later on it became clear that there were several groups interested in the purchase: Chubais himself wanted in. Fridman also wanted to buy it. And later on I heard that another group—led by Potanin—was interested in the purchase. Potanin already controlled different newspapers and other forms of the mass media, and there were several groups interested in working with him.

BROWNE: When did you learn that Mr. Fridman might have an interest?

BEREZOVSKY: It was the spring, the beginning of spring, almost the same time that I met—just after I met Yakovlev.

BROWNE: Can you give us an idea of the month?

BEREZOVSKY: April, May.

BROWNE: Now, did you ever speak to Mr. Fridman about his intentions in relation to *Kommersant*?

BEREZOVSKY: Not at all. I never spoke to anyone, not to Fridman, not to Chubais, not to Potanin, and it was—moreover, so that I'm absolutely clear, it is common practice between, let us say, top level businessmen in Russia, to never discuss a proposal with a competitor, because if one does, it would give the impression of wanting to form a partnership, and I was not prepared to go into a partnership, similar to what was created with ORT, for example, in 1994. I didn't think such a partnership would work in this case. As you know, ORT's owners quickly changed and everyone ended up selling their shares to me. This was a pretty clear statement that a partnership with different people wouldn't work.

BROWNE: Did you ever threaten Mr. Fridman?

BEREZOVSKY: I have already tried to give an answer to this question. I never threatened Mr. Fridman; and moreover, as far as *Kommersant* is concerned, I never called Mr. Fridman to discuss any aspect of the deal.

BROWNE: Mr. Berezovsky, it is said by Mr. Fridman that in the course of a telephone conversation which he cannot precisely date, you used the words "my vas zamochim" in the course of threatening him. Now, first of all, did you use those words?

BEREZOVSKY: I would be very surprised if anyone who knows me well could give an example of a time that I've used this type of language. I don't use this type of slang.

BROWNE: Can you translate for us what "*my vas zamochim*" means?

BEREZOVSKY: I think that the best translation of that word was given by President Putin in autumn 1999. This word is pure criminal slang—from the streets. Criminal argot. And I was absolutely surprised when the President of Russia used this word on TV, when he announced his fight against terrorists, meaning the Chechen terrorists, and he said that we would "zamochim" the Chechens, or terrorists, even if they were in the toilet. This word has other meanings too. It has a much stronger connotation than "threaten." It means to "kill" or do physical violence. But again—and I am familiar with Fridman's statement—I absolutely disagree that this word is used widely among the Russian business community.

BROWNE: I just want to take this in stages because it is important. It is suggested by the defendants that the equivalent English phrase is, "We will waste you."

BEREZOVSKY: Again, maybe I am wrong about the Russian president's understanding of the language, but it seems absolutely clear to me that there was no reason for him to use this word. This is not language fit for a president. But what is even more shocking is the wide range of the population, who believe that we should be in Chechnya, that he was justified in using this word. "We will kill you even if we find you on the toilet." This was the clear interpretation of the statement by the President of Russia.

BROWNE: Now, that is the interpretation. What I want to ask you about now is whether that language, what the interpreter calls argot, or slang, is common in business usage in Russia?

BEREZOVSKY: Again, I want to be very precise with my explanation. The business community is not united in Russia. There are various levels of business in Russia—businesses at the top, in the middle, and then very small businesses. And I do not really think—at least five years ago, because I left Russia five years ago. At least five years ago this language was not commonly used among the top level of Russian businessmen.

BROWNE: Who did use this sort of language?

BEREZOVSKY: As I told you, it is used mainly by criminals. It is argot.

BROWNE: And what the defendant Mr. Fridman says is that not only is it widely used in the Russian business community, but it means that someone is proposing to damage the business interests of another?

BEREZOVSKY: First of all, I disagree that it is used widely among businessmen, at least on the level of Fridman's scale of business. And second, I absolutely disagree with the interpretation because, as I mentioned to you, the President of Russia spoke the best interpretation.

BROWNE: Now, I want just to ask you one last thing about this issue of purchasing *Kommersant*. Did you gather from speaking to Mr. Badri how it was that Mr. Fridman intended to acquire *Kommersant*?

BEREZOVSKY: Not at all. I was confident that the deal would happen because Badri stayed in L.A. with Yakovlev, and everyone else was in

Moscow deciding how to buy *Kommersant.* Yakovlev was the sole decision maker about what to do. Later on I did hear that some of the other interested groups had made the mistake of approaching the managers as a way of buying *Kommersant,* but the owner of *Kommersant* was the one who was making the decisions. As I understand it, Badri didn't feel like there was any real competition for *Kommersant.*

BROWNE: But was Mr. Fridman's intention to purchase the shares in *Kommersant* directly from Mr. Yakovlev or was his intention different?

BEREZOVSKY: As I understand it, Fridman did not speak directly to Yakovlev. Though I never asked Yakovlev if he had spoken with Fridman . . .

BROWNE: Did Fridman?

BEREZOVSKY: Just a moment. I did not answer the question. As I understand it, Fridman communicated with managers of *Kommersant.*

BROWNE: Yes. And what was his proposal, as you understood it?

BEREZOVSKY: I do not know the details of that proposal, but I was aware that it was common for *Alfa Group* to propose to buy debts. At that time *Kommersant* did have a debt. This was how the *Alfa Group* regularly operated. I have numerous examples of that, of them buying debts or giving credit.

BROWNE: Mr. Berezovsky, was it your understanding at that time that Mr. Fridman was considering making a loan to the managers of *Kommersant* so that they could buy out the shares themselves?

BEREZOVSKY: What do you mean by "that time?"

BROWNE: Well, prior to your buying *Kommersant.*

BEREZOVSKY: As I told you, the last time I was actually involved in discussions about *Kommersant* was in the spring of 2000, or maybe the spring of 1999, and at that time I knew about the different plans, how other groups were planning to buy *Kommersant.* I want to stress again that at that time Badri was working directly with Yakovlev and I did not pay any attention to the other groups.

BROWNE: What I wanted to ask you, which I think you may not have picked up, was simply this. Answer this, please, yes or no. Did you discover whether there was a proposal by Mr. Fridman to loan money to the managers of *Kommersant*?

BEREZOVSKY: I did not know the exact details of this proposal but I did know that a proposal existed.

BROWNE: Could the managers have afforded to pay the interest on a loan?

BEREZOVSKY: You see, I never discussed that with the managers of *Kommersant* and I do not know if they would have been able to do that or not. The only thing that I'm aware of is that *Kommersant* had a debt.

BROWNE: Now, moving on, what would have happened—perhaps this is obvious—if the managers had not been able to pay the interest back on the loan?

BEREZOVSKY: I should say that this scheme is used not only by *Alfa Bank*.

BROWNE: I just want you to focus, please, on the proposal to loan money to the managers. Just confine your answer to this question. If the managers had been unable to repay the interest on the loan, what would have been the result?

BEREZOVSKY: It is absolutely clear, the result would have been that *Kommersant* would end up under the control of the *Alfa Group*.

BROWNE: Let me move on. The defendant's case, Mr. Berezovsky, is not simply that you threatened Mr. Fridman over the *Kommersant* deal in 1999; they also say that you are used to making threats in business dealings. And they rely on two incidents two years earlier in the summer of 1997, which I am going to ask you about. First of all, a general question. Do you habitually make threats in business? All I want to know is, is the way you operate to make threats?

BEREZOVSKY: I really do not understand how three people who know me well—Fridman, Potanin, and Nemtsov—could make the statement that I have threatened them. Furthermore, I find it quite strange that we've been able to continue our friendships for such a long time if they truly believed that I had treated them this way. And these are friendships that existed in Russia and now outside of Russia. Even now, when they visit London, they call and meet with me, or come over to my home.

BROWNE: Who are you talking about when you say "they?"

BEREZOVSKY: I mean Nemtsov and Peter Aven. I have never met with Potanin—but as far as Nemtsov and Aven are concerned, I see them at least once a year, perhaps two times a year, and not only as I mentioned in London, but in Israel; Nemtsov personally invited me to celebrate his birthday.

BROWNE: I want to go through this quite quickly. Gazprom, first of all. In June 1997, were you interested in becoming chairman of Gazprom, which was the state-owned monopoly gas supply?

BEREZOVSKY: Absolutely correct, yes.

BROWNE: At that time, was Mr. Nemtsov the First Deputy Prime Minister responsible for state monopolies such as Gazprom?

BEREZOVSKY: Yes, correct.

BROWNE: What is suggested by Mr. Nemtsov is that some time in June 1997, at the Russian Embassy in Beijing, you threatened to destroy Mr. Nemtsov's political career if he opposed you becoming chairman of Gazprom. Is that true?

BEREZOVSKY: It is not true at all. It is not true. I read Mr. Nemtsov's statement and I really—I really do not understand how he could say this. There were only two individuals with real power—first, the Prime Minister and then the president. Of course the president wasn't paying that much attention to this issue at that time. I understood that I needed the support of Mr. Viakhirev, first of all, who was the chairman of Gazprom, and then Prime Minister Chernomyrdin. I asked them very directly, and Viakhirev signed his name. As for Mr. Chernomyrdin, I flew to China to get his signature. I do not understand why Nemtsov, in his statement, said that I had come to convince him to support me, because I did not have the signature of Mr. Chernomyrdin and I came to discuss the matter with Mr. Chernomyrdin, not with Nemtsov. I understood that there was no chance of this happening without Mr. Chernomyrdin's signature. Even with Mr. Nemtsov's support, without Chernomyrdin's signature it would have meant nothing. Mr. Chernomyrdin was the deciding factor. Furthermore, you have the conclusion of a lawyer in Russia…

BROWNE: Just pause there. Mr. Berezovsky, if there was a conflict between Mr. Chernomyrdin wanting you as chairman and Mr. Nemtsov not wanting you as chairman, whose will would have prevailed?

BEREZOVSKY: First of all, I am not familiar with this conflict. I do not know anything…

BROWNE: It is a hypothetical question.

Berezovsky: If this conflict had existed, there is no question that I would have spoken with Prime Minister Chernomyrdin. The government is built vertically, and Chernomyrdin's decision would have been final. It was 100 percent his authority to make this decision, and if he would have decided not to support me, then there's nothing I could have done.

Browne: Mr. Berezovsky, I want to move from Gazprom to Svyazinvest. In July 1997, were 25 percent of the shares in Svyazinvest, the state-owned telecommunications company, put up for auction?

Berezovsky: Correct.

Browne: Were there two groups of bidders for those shares?

Berezovsky: I only knew about two groups.

Browne: Was one group led by Mr. Gusinsky?

Berezovsky: Correct.

Browne: And did that group include Mr. Fridman?

Berezovsky: Correct.

Browne: Was the other group led by Mr. Potanin?

Berezovsky: Correct.

Browne: And was Mr. Potanin ultimately successful in purchasing the shares?

Berezovsky: Correct.

Browne: At this time, in the middle of 1997, you were Deputy Secretary of the Security Council. Did you have any commercial involvement in either of these bids?

Berezovsky: No.

Browne: What is suggested by Mr. Fridman is that prior to the auction you promised to exert commercial pressure on Mr. Potanin if his bid went ahead. Is that the case?

Berezovsky: Not at all.

Browne: Finally, I just want to ask you about Mr. Fridman. You have told the jury something about your own reputation. Could you tell us how Mr. Fridman is perceived amongst Russians in this country?

Berezovsky: I have never spoken about Fridman in this country.

Browne: I am sorry, I fear my question may not have been understood. Is Mr. Fridman well known amongst Russians in this country?

Berezovsky: There are many successful Russians who have moved to this country, most of them concentrated in London. They all certainly know who Mr. Fridman is. But I've never had reason to talk about Fridman here. Many Russians who live here pay a lot of attention to the Russian business community, particularly to Abramovich and the people around him.

BROWNE: If someone in the Russian community in London is watching television and sees Mr. Fridman saying something on television, would he think that it was the truth?

BEREZOVSKY: I think that everyone—well, not everyone, but a majority of the people who have moved here—cast a critical eye on Russian TV. They would certainly be forced to ask themselves if it is or is not true.

CROSS-EXAMINATION BY MR. SHIELDS, ATTORNEY FOR MIKHAIL FRIDMAN

SHIELDS: Mr. Berezovsky, I need to ask you a number of questions over the next couple of hours. So none of us are under any illusion, Mr. Berezovsky, your case is that my client Mr. Fridman, Mr. Nemtsov, Mr. Aven and Mr. Potanin are liars?

BEREZOVSKY: This is absolutely correct.

SHIELDS: I want to start by asking you a few questions about *Kommersant* and the program. Now, in 2004, is it correct that Mr. Vasiliev was chief executive and editor of *Kommersant*?

BEREZOVSKY: Yes.

SHIELDS: And is it correct that Mr. Dubov was chairman of the board?

BEREZOVSKY: This is also correct.

SHIELDS: And Mr. Dubov had worked for you for many years?

BEREZOVSKY: I was also familiar with Mr. Dubov's scientific research from my involvement in the science department, and I knew Dubov, I think…

SHIELDS: In 1972?

BEREZOVSKY: Yes, sir, approximately then. When I moved to London—and then when I left—I should confirm—when I left the Institute of Control Sciences and created LogoVAZ, Dubov joined LogoVAZ a couple of years after that and worked for LogoVAZ. And when I moved to London he also was forced to leave Russia because of a book he put out that the Kremlin did not like. He moved to London and was also granted political asylum in this country. He is present in this room.

SHIELDS: You had effective control of *Kommersant*, did you not, in 2004?

BEREZOVSKY: I would like to be precise about this point. What do you mean by "effective control?" We have a law in Russia that clearly divides the powers that an owner does and does not have over a company. An owner has control within the strict framework of Russian law.

SHIELDS: I am just reading from your own claim. Your own claim says: "You also are widely known to have effective control of the company that publishes the leading independent Russian daily newspaper, *Kommersant*."

BEREZOVSKY: It means that, again to be precise, effective control means that me and my partner Badri owned 100 percent of the *Kommersant* shares.

SHIELDS: Yes, you owned them?

BEREZOVSKY: Correct.

SHIELDS: That is what effective control means and that is something you say was widely known in Russia and no doubt among the Russian community in England?

BEREZOVSKY: As far as Russia is concerned, there is no doubt. I'm also fairly certain that this is the case in terms of the majority of the Russian community in London—in this country, let us say.

SHIELDS: So references to *Kommersant* would in many ways be taken as references to you?

BEREZOVSKY: This is not absolutely correct because, as I told you, the most important problem when we took over control of *Kommersant* was to demonstrate that I did not have any influence over *Kommersant* policy. My only power was the ability to call shareholder meetings, to change the general manager, and nothing more. What I would like to stress—and it was absolutely clear from the TV show which you watched—and even Fridman confirms today that, after 1999—after approximately six years—*Kommersant* is—in the minds of Russian-speaking people who read *Kommersant*—the most independent entity within the mass media. It does not depend on the government or on me.

SHIELDS: Let me just ask you this question: does that mean you would never interfere in any media organization which you own?

BEREZOVSKY: No—that is not correct. I had a great deal of influence over ORT.

SHIELDS: That is right. So you are quite happy to interfere in ORT, are you not, Mr. Berezovsky?

BEREZOVSKY: No, no. I stated openly that I was actively managing ORT's policy, even though I had hired a manager. I own 49 percent of ORT and I made it absolutely clear to society that I was attempting to influence the policy of ORT.

SHIELDS: Thank you. So that is a message you sent to society: everyone in Russia knew that you could influence the editorial content of ORT television programs?

BEREZOVSKY: That is absolutely correct.

SHIELDS: Good. Now, going on to the program, I think we heard yesterday that the program was actually pre-recorded the day before?

BEREZOVSKY: This is absolutely correct.

BROWNE: I think it was shown on October 28th but pre-recorded on the 27th.

BEREZOVSKY: This is absolutely correct.

BROWNE: Thank you. Now, the *Kommersant* verdict was on October 20th. We heard that yesterday.

BEREZOVSKY: I do not remember exactly, but maybe.

SHIELDS: When did you first discover that Mr. Vasiliev had agreed to appear on it?

BEREZOVSKY: He called me one or two days before recording and informed me that he—that he had decided to accept the challenge, and he said that it would air on the 28th.I then asked him a question: tell me, please, will it be live or will it be pre-recorded?" He responded that, "We don't have live programs in Russia anymore. It will be pre-recorded."

SHIELDS: You knew it was going to be pre-recorded. Did you ask him when it was going to be pre-recorded?

BEREZOVSKY: No, I did not ask him that question.

SHIELDS: Did you have any more conversations after it was recorded and before it was shown?

BEREZOVSKY: I do not remember exactly, but it seems that after he—just a moment, I am trying to remember. Yes, I spoke to him midday of the 28th at which point I asked him for his take on it and he said, "I do not know."

SHIELDS: Did he say to you that Mr. Fridman had made some awfully defamatory remarks about you, for example?

BEREZOVSKY: He just told me—he just told me that he thought that Fridman was not correct "as far as you are concerned"—about me personally.

SHIELDS: Not correct about you?

BEREZOVSKY: Yes.

SHIELDS: So did you not then say: "What did he say about me?"

BEREZOVSKY: No, I did not ask him to go into details; I just asked him to confirm when it would be aired.

SHIELDS: So, when you sat down to watch that evening with your wife in your home in Surrey, did you expect that something was going to be broadcast that would be quite horrible about you or might upset you?

BEREZOVSKY: I did not have any particular feeling about it. Perhaps I've lost some feeling because every day on Russian TV, particularly Russian TV, something more and more terrible is said about me—that I organized terrorists in Russia, that I am preparing other such terrible things, and so on. I've lost a certain sensitivity to all of it.

SHIELDS: I think it is right that you subscribe to the package which includes this as part of its satellite programs.

BEREZOVSKY: Absolutely correct.

SHIELDS: And I think it is right that subscribers to those packages get about nine other programs.

BEREZOVSKY: I do not remember exactly how many stations in Russian, but somewhere around nine. I subscribe not just to Russian TV but also to channels from Ukraine and the Baltic Republics

SHIELDS: Just as a matter of interest while we are on the subject, do you subscribe to any other TV packages?

BEREZOVSKY: Sky.

SHIELDS: You may or may not know this: do a lot of Russians, do you think, watch Sky?

BEREZOVSKY: It depends on how well they know—how well they know English. What I do know is that Russians love to watch Russian TV in this country. They prefer it.

SHIELDS: I think it is right that other than you and people who may have worked with you, no one knew what was going to be on that night on this particular program, did they?

BEREZOVSKY: I think you are absolutely correct.

SHIELDS: I am correct, thank you, Mr. Berezovsky. So you had a reason to watch it?

BEREZOVSKY: I have a favorite set of programs, and, as I've mentioned before, this program is one of the most popular because it allows people in Russia, which is now very rare, to present independent positions and fight it out in public. In this sense the program is unique.

SHIELDS: Now, Mr. Berezovsky, can I just have a look at the program? Do not worry, I am not going to show it again. Can we just look at the transcript? We have the transcript in the packet. Could I just take you to the transcript, which is at tab 2, members of the jury. The actual words come, I think, on page 13 in that transcript. Internally it says 12. Mr. Berezovsky, you watched the program along with the rest of us and you will no doubt accept that by then there had been frequent references to *Kommersant*?

BEREZOVSKY: I do not remember, up to this point, how many times *Kommersant* had been mentioned, but the basic conflict was around *Kommersant*.

SHIELDS: And as you told us already, you were widely known to be the person in control of *Kommersant*?

BEREZOVSKY: As an owner of *Kommersant*, correct.

SHIELDS: Mr. Vasiliev is the person who brings up: "In 1999 you were trying to buy *Kommersant* together with Chubais. Is that right?"

Mr. Vasiliev brings up the subject of *Kommersant* and Mr. Fridman says: "We never tried to buy *Kommersant*."

The host says: "Why would he need Chubais? You are friends with Chubais."

Mr. Fridman: "Being friends with Chubais is definitely one of the gravest sins you can commit in this life. I would like to clarify the situation just mentioned by the respected editor-in-chief. In 1999, when everyone knew that Boris Berezovsky was going to buy *Kommersant* … "

Then Vasiliev says: "You decided to save it."

The host says: "Save it from Boris Berezovsky."

And Andrei Vasiliev says: "Well, I do not know."

Then Mr. Fridman says: "The newspaper founder, Yakovlev, *Kommersant*'s shareholders, Yakovlev's partners, came to us and requested a loan so that they would be able to acquire this publication and prevent Berezovsky from buying it. I remind you that in 1999, Berezovsky controlled the Russian public television station." That is right, is it not? You did at that stage?

BEREZOVSKY: 1999, yes, that is correct.

SHIELDS: You did, you controlled ORT: "where Mr. Andrei Vasiliev was working as the head of the information program." Just pausing here, this is a program called *The Duel*, is it not? That is what it is called?

BEREZOVSKY: Yes, correct.

SHIELDS: And people are pretty frank with each other.

BEREZOVSKY: Yes.

SHIELDS: And Mr. Vasiliev then is not one to hold back, is he? Look at what he says here: "Now you are lying again."

BEREZOVSKY: Just a moment.

SHIELDS: He is abusing Mr. Fridman, is he not?

BEREZOVSKY: This is up to Mr. Fridman. It depends on how sensitive he is.

SHIELDS: "I was not working there in 1999. I quit in 1998."

Host: "Well, at least you were working."

Vasiliev: "It is good that you are not a journalist, you would be sued at every turn."

Mr. Fridman: "We told him at the moment that if he really wants to buy shares in order to keep the newspaper truly independent, you are ready to give them a loan and the question was discussed. Moreover, even Berezovsky formally regarded this matter. He was very displeased."

And Mr. Vasiliev: "Did he give you a piece of advice?"

Mr. Fridman: "No, he threatened, as usual. He said that ..."

Mr. Vasiliev is now quoted as saying: "And you too."

I am putting this to you because I just want to try and clarify it. Do you think actually, if you can recall, that Mr. Vasiliev says that? This is an accepted transcript, but I am trying to be fair here. We have had another listen to this and is it possible that it is the host who says: "And you too?"

BEREZOVSKY: You see, I do not remember.

BROWNE: You do not remember? But you see, it would appear on its face that Mr. Vasiliev is saying, "And you too," there, is he not?

BEREZOVSKY: Again, I understand your question, but I can't exactly tell if it is stated by Vasiliev. It could also be Soloviov. We should first clarify this matter before discussing it further.

SHIELDS: That is why I am trying to be fair about this. I do not want to take a false point because your counsel opened it on the basis—I am not criticizing it—it was Mr. Soloviov. As I understand it, you say Mr. Soloviov is one of the best Russian anchors. Is he someone whom you have respect for?

BEREZOVSKY: Correct.

SHIELDS: So it is Mr. Soloviov or Mr. Vasiliev who says, "And you too." And then Mr. Fridman says: "He even threatened me. He threatened everyone. That is how he works."

I just want to put that in context. I just want to get this clear: your case, as I understand it, is that this would have suggested to anyone viewing the program that you made physical threats?

BEREZOVSKY: Correct.

SHIELDS: Am I not right in this, that you regard it as equally serious if what that meant was that you threatened to damage another man's business or to ruin a politician's career?

BEREZOVSKY: Certainly there is a big difference between them but neither of them is acceptable.

SHIELDS: Well, you say there is a big difference, but it is a pretty serious matter either way, if you said to someone, "I will destroy your business," or, "I will destroy your political career?"

BEREZOVSKY: Absolutely correct, and this is the reason why I said that—you asked me to compare them and I gave you a comparison. The other question is, are either of these acceptable, and I don't believe that they are.

SHIELDS: Yes, neither is acceptable because you have told us, his Lordship and the jury, that you are a man who does not make threats.

BEREZOVSKY: Absolutely correct.

SHIELDS: Thank you. Now, Mr. Fridman is referring to an event which occurred in 1999, is he not, when you sought to buy *Kommersant*?

BEREZOVSKY: Yes.

SHIELDS: That was in June 1999?

BEREZOVSKY: As I remember, the deal was finalized in August or September 1999.

SHIELDS: Help me here: Mr. Putin became Prime Minister in August 1999.

BEREZOVSKY: As I remember, August or September.

SHIELDS: Yes. I think you will find I am quite good on my dates: in August 1999.

BEREZOVSKY: Unfortunately I am not.

SHIELDS: I will do my best and if I am wrong, I will stand corrected.

BEREZOVSKY: You will help me?

SHIELDS: Yes.

BEREZOVSKY: Thank you.

SHIELDS: You have told this court a lot about your opposition to Mr. Putin since he became president but I want to focus on your position, just take now an example, in June 1999. Mr. Yeltsin, as president, was very, very powerful, was he not?

BEREZOVSKY: As you know, Russia is now a presidential republic. This means that the president has a lot of power.

SHIELDS: I would like you to set aside your modesty, Mr. Berezovsky, and just tell the jury how powerful you were in June 1999?

BEREZOVSKY: You mean what people knew about me in Russia?

SHIELDS: Yes, that will do.

BEREZOVSKY: They knew that I was one of several people who helped Yeltsin get re-elected in 1996. At the same time they knew that this was a fairly small group, which included Mr. Fridman and Mr. Potanin. They also knew that I tried to rally them together to once again support Yeltsin in 1996 against the Communists. They also understood that Mr. Fridman, Mr. Potanin, Mr. Gusinsky, and I had a great deal of power in Russia. This is absolutely correct.

SHIELDS: I am asking about you. Would it not be right to say that in June 1999, your power was such that you could almost decide who would be the next President of Russia?

BEREZOVSKY: That is absolutely wrong.

SHIELDS: Absolutely wrong?

BEREZOVSKY: And it is quite simple to explain why this is not so. I will give you a single example. The only man who truly had the power to influence the position was the President of Russia, Yeltsin. I spent a great deal of time working together with him and I am familiar with all the principal decisions, and with no exceptions, he made all the decisions himself. Moreover, if you read his memoirs, when he wrote about me, you will see that he said, "I never liked Berezovsky." But there is no doubt that he was a real person who supported democracy.

SHIELDS: While I am just on this for a moment—we will come back to this later—did you give an interview to a television program called "How Putin came to power?"

BEREZOVSKY: I gave many interviews and I cannot refute that I gave an interview to this program.

SHIELDS: But you might have given an interview to a television program broadcast earlier this year. I believe it was called "How Putin came to power."

BEREZOVSKY: Again, I give interviews to TV outlets and newspapers almost every day. I did not refute your statement. I just said it is possible.

SHIELDS: I just want to look at your position in June 1999, Mr. Berezovsky, so we can have a feel of just how powerful you were. You had become one of the richest men in Russia by that time, had you not?

BEREZOVSKY: Correct.

SHIELDS: I think the population of Russia at that stage would have been about 170 million people?

BEREZOVSKY: 150—20 million more, 20 million less, numbers don't really matter to you.

SHIELDS: I will always gladly stand corrected. You had developed substantial interests in the automotive industry through LogoVAZ?

BEREZOVSKY: Absolutely correct.

SHIELDS: You had dealerships with Mercedes Benz, Volvo?

BEREZOVSKY: This is how I started my business career.

SHIELDS: General Motors?

BEREZOVSKY: Correct.

SHIELDS: I am just taking you through the 90s. You had launched a thing called AVVA Investment Fund? Is that right, AVVA?

BEREZOVSKY: Correct.

SHIELDS: And you had raised substantial sums of money from the Russian public?

BEREZOVSKY: Correct.

SHIELDS: You had become the owner or part owner of the AvtoVAZ factory in Togliatti?

BEREZOVSKY: Correct.

SHIELDS: I think that was named after the Italian country's Communist leader, was it not?

BEREZOVSKY: Yes, correct.

SHIELDS: And they made Russia's most popular car, which I will now mispronounce. Is that called...

BEREZOVSKY: The *Zhiguli*. We simplified it for the West—Lada.

SHIELDS: I hear that answer with feeling. You owned Sibneft, one of Russia's richest oil companies?

BEREZOVSKY: Correct.

SHIELDS: And you acquired that from the government in late 1995?

BEREZOVSKY: From the state, absolutely right.

SHIELDS: From the state, that is right, and Sibneft was a merger of the most modern refinery in Omsk...

BEREZOVSKY: Correct.

SHIELDS:—with a Siberian oil production company called Noyabrskneftegaz. And you bought that in an auction, did you not?

BEREZOVSKY: Correct.

SHIELDS: How many people took part in that auction?

BEREZOVSKY: Three groups.

SHIELDS: Who was the auctioneer?

BEREZOVSKY: The state committee for privatization.

SHIELDS: And you won it?

BEREZOVSKY: Correct.

SHIELDS: Was that auction organized by Mr. Chubais?

BEREZOVSKY: Chubais was a minister—I do not remember, no, not him, it was organized by Mr. Kokh.

SHIELDS: Because Mr. Chubais is going to be featured in this case, Mr. Chubais was the minister who was essentially in charge of privatization, was he not?

BEREZOVSKY: Absolutely correct, but also Mr. Kokh, who was in charge of technology. Chubais was not directly in charge, which is why I mentioned Mr. Kokh.

SHIELDS: Mr. Kokh was directly in charge?

BEREZOVSKY: Absolutely correct.

SHIELDS: It was all Mr. Chubais's brainchild? Would it be right that you had an airline called Transaero?

BEREZOVSKY: A minority share.

SHIELDS: Minority, and you had a substantial interest in the revenue of Aeroflot, the Russian airline?

BEREZOVSKY: This is not correct.

SHIELDS: Not correct?

BEREZOVSKY: Not correct.

SHIELDS: Did you have an insubstantial interest in Aeroflot?

BEREZOVSKY: As far as shareholding is concerned, nothing at all. As far as management control, a person from our group, Mr. Glushkov, whom I mentioned already, was deputy general manager of Aeroflot.

SHIELDS: Do you have a substantial financial interest in the monies generated by Aeroflot?

BEREZOVSKY: Not at all, not substantial. We created a partnership with Aeroflot but it was not substantial. Again, what do you mean by "substantial." It depends on which kind of business you are involved in. It was not a billion dollars, it was not $100 million. It was maybe a $10 million investment.

SHIELDS: $10 million, well, I suppose the average wage in Russia at that stage was what?

BEREZOVSKY: Very low.

SHIELDS: Very low. We have already detailed your wealth. Now I am going to come to your interest in the media.

BEREZOVSKY: Because you mentioned Sibneft, Aeroflot, AvtoVAZ, and ORT, I just wanted to mention I only had effective control over one company. This was LogoVAZ. I did not have effective control of the other companies, not in ORT, where the state owned 51 percent, not in Sibneft, where my share was just 25 percent and 50 percent belonged to Abramovich and all management control, not in Aeroflot, where I do not have any shares at all, only a connection with the deputy general manager. And AvtoVAZ was absolutely being controlled by a group of managers. We had a percentage of shares, I believe it was around 30 percent.

SHIELDS: Now, in addition to your business interests, you also gained control in the 1990s of large sections of the media, did you not?

BEREZOVSKY: We already discussed ORT and by the end of the 1990s, I also owned the channel TV6. It is not a nationwide channel. Together with Badri we had, I think, I do not remember exactly, maybe 70 percent...

SHIELDS: Can I just start with ORT? ORT is pretty unique in Russian broadcasting, is it not, because it has a signal which reaches 98 percent of the Russian population?

BEREZOVSKY: You are absolutely correct, it is an absolutely unique channel.

SHIELDS: It has a tower, I think, in Moscow, is it, called Ostankino, which is 1,771 feet high and is Europe's tallest structure?

BEREZOVSKY: But ORT isn't the only one to use this tower. All the nationwide channels of Russia use it.

SHIELDS: And the charm of ORT, Mr. Berezovsky, is that ORT reaches everyone in Russia?

BEREZOVSKY: This is absolutely correct; 98 percent of the population.

SHIELDS: So your desire, as you told us in evidence yesterday, to use the media for political ends was very well satisfied by your interest in ORT?

BEREZOVSKY: This was my goal in 1994. My goal was not to allow the communists to take power in Russia and this is the reason why I insisted, in front of the president, that ORT should be privatized. That is absolutely correct.

SHIELDS: So you had real power through the media?

BEREZOVSKY: Absolutely correct.

SHIELDS: You had the power to make or break reputations?

BEREZOVSKY: Absolutely correct.

SHIELDS: You had the power to influence the way people would vote?

BEREZOVSKY: This is how ORT used its power. Absolutely correct. You are absolutely correct about how ORT used its influence.

SHIELDS: Yes. You bought out the other ORT shareholders so at the end you had effective control. That is right, is it not?

BEREZOVSKY: We should again, to be precise, agree on a definition because you continue to use the phrase "effective control," and I've already stated several times that I had only 49 percent. Do you mean effective control in terms of shares, or as something that is less than 50 percent, or control over management, or all of these? What do you mean in this case by "effective control?"

SHIELDS: Let us put it like this. I want to ask you this in terms of public influence, using it as a means of communication. The state, you say, owns 51 percent?

BEREZOVSKY: Correct.

SHIELDS: And you own 49 percent?

BEREZOVSKY: Correct.

SHIELDS: Who decided editorial policy, you or the state?

BEREZOVSKY: The editorial policy was decided completely by the company itself, and again I want to say that I only used my power to help convince the president to hire a proper general manager because, as I've said, the state had 51 percent and it was the president's job to nominate a general manager. After that the general manager made all the decisions.

SHIELDS: But your interests and the state were one and the same, were they not, in the 1990s?

BEREZOVSKY: Absolutely correct.

SHIELDS: Thank you. Just to complete the picture on your media interests—you may have mentioned this already—TV6?

BEREZOVSKY: Correct.

SHIELDS: The newspaper, *Nezavisimaya Gazeta*?

BEREZOVSKY: Correct. Also there are two magazines within the *Kommersant* publishing house.

SHIELDS: What are they called?

BEREZOVSKY: One is *Money* and the second is *Power*. There was also a magazine called something like *Autopilot* for car enthusiasts and a home magazine, I forget its exact name. But when Yakovlev sold *Kommersant*, it went to another group.

SHIELDS: So just two magazines, *Money* and *Power*?

BEREZOVSKY: Correct.

SHIELDS: And in June 1999, you sought to buy control of *Kommersant*. Is that right?

BEREZOVSKY: We started the purchase that spring and finally made the purchase at the beginning of August.

SHIELDS: We have covered the money, we have covered the media. Now I am going to come to your political influence, the third leg.

BEREZOVSKY: No problem.

SHIELDS: In 1994, I think, as you have told us, you became close to President Yeltsin?

BEREZOVSKY: Correct.

SHIELDS: So, to get this in context, as you said, the president has immense power, he hires and fires prime ministers and their deputies.

BEREZOVSKY: This is not correct. A president may not simply nominate a prime minister. He needs the approval of parliament. He has—he may propose a candidate to the parliament, and if they cannot agree on a candidate after three votes then the president does have the authority to disband parliament. However, this has never happened in Russian history, despite the fact that there have been numerous times when parliament did not vote to approve the candidate put forth by President Yeltsin. One instance was with Chernomyrdin, when he was attempting a second term as Prime Minister.

SHIELDS: Am I right in thinking it is the president who fires prime ministers?

BEREZOVSKY: This is absolutely correct. The president is able to fire a prime minister, but the president cannot individually hire a prime minister.

SHIELDS: It is Mr. Yeltsin who would decide ultimately on what and how many Russian companies would be privatized?

BEREZOVSKY: Not only Yeltsin. There were an enormous number of companies within Russia and previously within the Soviet Union. Certainly all the main, principal decisions concerning the top-level companies were under the scrutiny of Yeltsin, but the key person in terms of privatization was Chubais.

SHIELDS: We will come back to Mr. Chubais later. In about that time in the early 1990s, you became a friend of Mr. Yumashev? You mentioned his name yesterday, Valentin Yumashev?

BEREZOVSKY: Yes, this is absolutely correct, I was introduced to Yumashev by Mr. Aven, who is also your client.

SHIELDS: Mr. Yumashev, I think, used to be a journalist and he ghost wrote Mr. Yeltsin's first book of memoirs. Would that be right?

BEREZOVSKY: This is absolutely correct. This is how Mr. Aven introduced me to Mr. Yumashev.

SHIELDS: I think it is right that when the president, Mr. Yeltsin, wrote a second volume of memoirs—perhaps they called it *Notes of a President*—you became the publisher of those memoirs?

BEREZOVSKY: This was the first time that I had met the president, after first meeting Yumashev through Aven. Aven explained to me that

Yeltsin wanted to know if AvtoVAZ would be interested in the rights to his book, and I was invited to meet with him. I met with Yeltsin together with the general manager of AvtoVAZ, Mr. Kadannikov. That is absolutely correct.

SHIELDS: That is correct, and you became part of Mr. Yeltsin's inner circle. Would that not be right?

BEREZOVSKY: You should define what you mean by "inner circle."

SHIELDS: Let us put it like this…

BEREZOVSKY: I just explained—I understand—who I became. Yes?

SHIELDS: Of course.

BEREZOVSKY: At that time Yeltsin had decided to create the first—in the history of Russia—presidential club, because Yeltsin loved to play tennis. I was the first businessman invited to this club because I also played tennis, but certainly not only because of that. I was delighted to have the opportunity to discuss matters directly with the president, as far as my understanding of the Russian business community, which was starting to grow at that time. You are absolutely correct about this.

SHIELDS: Thank you. You became friendly with his daughter. Is that Tatiana Dyachenko?

BEREZOVSKY: Yes, maybe six months later he invited me to celebrate a Russian holiday with them—all of the members of the presidential club were invited, along with his family.

SHIELDS: Fine. Would it be right, at the end of 1995 you, among others, were concerned with Mr. Yeltsin's health and his failing popularity?

BEREZOVSKY: You are absolutely correct.

SHIELDS: Because you saw that he was in danger of losing to a Communist rival. Was this Mr. Zyuganov?

BEREZOVSKY: Zyuganov, you are absolutely correct.

SHIELDS: And the presidential elections were coming in 1996, were they not?

BEREZOVSKY: The presidential elections happened—there were two rounds. The first round was in June 1997—1996, and the second round was on July 3, 1996.

SHIELDS: Would it be right that you and other people bankrolled the electoral campaign for Mr. Yeltsin?

BEREZOVSKY: Yes and no. As far as I am concerned, I used, as I told you, ORT as political leverage to help Yeltsin get re-elected. As far as money is concerned, I did not put one penny into his campaign.

SHIELDS: Fine. Was Mr. Chubais actively involved in that campaign?

BEREZOVSKY: He led a committee for the electoral campaign, and if you allow me, I just want maybe two minutes of your time to better explain this to everyone, because it touches on a number of important questions. Do you mind?

SHIELDS: Of course not.

BEREZOVSKY: Thank you. You are absolutely correct. At the end of 1995, Yeltsin became very sick and his popularity was at 5 percent, and not only because he was sick but because, as I have said before, he had not been able to deliver, to satisfy the expectations of the people who had trusted him. In 1990, many people thought that democracy would make them fantastically rich the very next day. Of course this was not realistic, and Yeltsin was in a very dangerous position. As I mentioned before, I stopped all my business activities at that time just to concentrate on the campaign. I called every top-level businessman—in Davos and in Switzerland, including Potanin, including Fridman, including Aven, including Gusinsky, and so on. This group had previously been in direct and serious competition with each other, but I worked to explain to them that we needed to, for the time being, unite, and I proposed that Chubais should lead this group as he had a firm grasp of the technical issues.

SHIELDS: You see, this is Chubais, was it not? You wanted to lead the election campaign?

BEREZOVSKY: Not only me. I initiated that idea but it was supported by Potanin, Fridman, by all these people, and it was absolutely supported by President Yeltsin.

SHIELDS: I mentioned Chubais—I am going to come back to this later—because when it came to the auction of Svyazinvest, it is your view that Mr. Chubais behaved in a corrupt manner, is it not?

BEREZOVSKY: I never said that he was corrupt. His actions in this instance created some doubt in my mind as to if he was using fair tactics. Was he really being fair?

SHIELDS: I am going to come back to that but I suggest to you that your accusation against Mr. Chubais is that he was acting in what would be regarded as a corrupt manner.

BEREZOVSKY: Again, let me explain the situation to you. Some facts came to light that Mr. Chubais was not as clean, in terms of his business practices, as I had originally thought. And in order to win the campaign we needed someone who was beyond reproach. Originally I had thought that Mr. Chubais was 100 percent clean, but then later I realized that he had used some unscrupulous practices.

SHIELDS: Fine. We will come back to that later because I want to add him to the list of people whom you say are corrupt or that my clients are liars. Now, Mr. Yeltsin was re-elected, as you said, in July and would it be right that you used ORT to support him and to discredit his Communist rival?

BEREZOVSKY: You are absolutely correct.

SHIELDS: Thank you, Mr. Berezovsky. Would it be right that in October you became Deputy Secretary of the Security Council of the Russian Federation?

BEREZOVSKY: That is absolutely correct.

SHIELDS: I think that is the position you would regard as high political office?

BEREZOVSKY: No doubt.

SHIELDS: It was a recognition, was it not, of the powerful position you had reached in Russian society?

BEREZOVSKY: Among the other hundreds of people who had the same level and higher.

SHIELDS: And in 1997, your wealth, your power, had reached such dizzying heights, Mr. Berezovsky, that *Forbes* magazine, in a list of the world's richest individuals, described you in these terms as: "Perhaps the most powerful man in Russia, financial backer and adviser to Boris Yeltsin."

BEREZOVSKY: I have already dealt with *Forbes*.

SHIELDS: I am asking you—I put it badly. That is how *Forbes* described you?

BEREZOVSKY: Is that a question or an answer?

SHIELDS: On the pleadings you have accepted that they did describe you in that way?

BEREZOVSKY: What do you mean that I accepted it? I read that. Does it mean that I accepted it?

SHIELDS: No. I put the question perhaps badly. That is how you were described. Is that a description you would agree with?

BEREZOVSKY: No.

SHIELDS: No. You did not ask for a correction, I suppose.

BEREZOVSKY: Okay, just once…

SHIELDS: Let me ask again because we are at cross purposes and we want to get this right. In 1997, I said that your wealth and your power had reached such dizzying heights that *Forbes*, an American magazine, in the list of the world's richest individuals, described you as: "Perhaps the most powerful man in Russia, financial backer and adviser to Boris Yeltsin." So there are two questions here: do you recall that that is how they described you?

BEREZOVSKY: I do not remember exactly, but I will accept that you are correct in how you read that section in *Forbes*.

SHIELDS: Second question: would you have agreed with that description?

BEREZOVSKY: No.

SHIELDS: But would I not be right in saying that is how everyone else in Russia saw you?

BEREZOVSKY: Certainly not.

SHIELDS: This morning in your evidence I asked you questions about your rise to power in the 1990s. I am now going to come to 1999. So everyone knows where we are going, I am just going to deal with Mr. Putin's election and then I am going to take you to three specific incidents where we say you made threats. Now, in 1999, I think it is right that the Prime Minister was Yevgeny Primakov.

BEREZOVSKY: Yes, just a moment. He became, I think, in 1998 he became Prime Minister, after the crisis, the economic crisis in Russia, and it was for a very short time in 1999, correct, 1998 or 1999.

SHIELDS: I think it is right Mr. Primakov was showing very dangerous symptoms of being very sympathetic to the Communists?

BEREZOVSKY: Correct.

SHIELDS: And on March 4th, you lost your position as Executive Secretary of the Commonwealth of Independent States?

BEREZOVSKY: Absolutely correct.

SHIELDS: And in May, I think it is right, the Communists in the Duma tried to impeach Mr. Yeltsin?

BEREZOVSKY: I am generally good with dates, like you, but I am not able to remember if it was exactly in May. It certainly happened around that time.

SHIELDS: I think the position was that in May 2004, you were concerned, were you not, as to who might succeed Mr. Yeltsin? I meant 2000. In May 2000, you were concerned as to who might succeed Mr. Yeltsin.

BROWNE: It was 1999.

SHIELDS: I mean 1999.

BEREZOVSKY: Correct.

SHIELDS: And it therefore became imperative to find a suitable successor.

BEREZOVSKY: You see, everybody in Russia who was directly involved in politics understood that Russia was still not at the final stage of democracy, and we all wondered what would be next?

SHIELDS: I asked you this morning, Mr. Berezovsky, I said, "Your power was such you could almost make presidents." Do you remember me asking you that question?

BEREZOVSKY: You put forth the question and I gave you an answer.

SHIELDS: You did. And therefore I suggest that what happened in June, it was very much that you were part of a group who decided that Mr. Putin was the man to become Prime Minister?

BEREZOVSKY: I do not refute that, it is correct.

SHIELDS: You do not refute that, do you? At that time, Mr. Putin was described by your counsel in his opening—day 1, line 18, 19 in the transcript, my Lord—that he had been a KGB colonel and that he had become head of the FSB, the body which is successor to the KGB. The impression that I got—I do not know what other people got—from that was that it was being portrayed that he was the kind of man no one would want to do business with because of his background?

BEREZOVSKY: Is that a question?

SHIELDS: Yes.

BEREZOVSKY: You see, the problem is that you don't always have a choice between good and bad. At that time we had to choose between bad and worse. And the "worse" was Primakov, the "bad" was Putin.

SHIELDS: The bad was Putin?

BEREZOVSKY: Yes. Just a moment. Let me—I understood the problem with Putin, that he had been in the KGB. I understood this and his mindset. But unfortunately—I don't mean to be impolite, but it really was not how you describe it, that I had "the power to make presidents." I never made this choice. And the choice didn't belong to me, but to President Yeltsin, and the main problem was that he had tried many people in the roll of his successor. If you remember, after Chernomyrdin was fired in 1998, he put in Kirienko. I was completely against that. I was against the move. But in spite of being against it, he put him in office. Then three months later he put in another person. My point is that I did not have the power to choose presidents. I did have power, and a considerable amount, but it was restricted to giving recommendations, to explaining my vision for things, and not even directly to Yeltsin, unfortunately.

SHIELDS: I suggest to you that you are understating your power, Mr. Berezovsky. Your power is very important in this case. Is it not right that you went down and saw Mr. Putin on vacation in the South of France?

BEREZOVSKY: Absolutely correct.

SHIELDS: And you spent the entire day talking with him?

BEREZOVSKY: Absolutely correct.

SHIELDS: And at the end of the day—and these are your own words—"Putin accepted our offer." That being an…

BEREZOVSKY: Absolutely correct.

SHIELDS: …Offer to become Prime Minister.

BEREZOVSKY: Absolutely wrong.

SHIELDS: So it was an offer from you to make Mr. Putin Prime Minister?

BEREZOVSKY: Absolutely wrong.

SHIELDS: Absolutely wrong?

BEREZOVSKY: Can I correct you? Not an offer from me, an offer from President Yeltsin to take this position. The message was delivered to Putin through me because I had already known him for ten years; that is the point. It was not my offer, it was an offer from President Yeltsin.

SHIELDS: I will show it to you, I am quoting from your words on the television program, "Our offer."

BEREZOVSKY: That is also correct.

SHIELDS: And when Mr. Putin became Prime Minister in June 1999, it would also be right that he had no party?

BEREZOVSKY: When Putin became Prime Minister, he was not a member of a party.

SHIELDS: He was a political nobody?

BEREZOVSKY: If head of the FSB is nobody, then he was a nobody.

SHIELDS: Then you, Mr. Berezovsky, decided that the only way to get him to stay in power and help him become president was to create a party which backed him?

BEREZOVSKY: Unfortunately, according to Russian laws, it is not possible to create a political party, because a political party needs at least one year to form. And that is the reason why I proposed to create not a political party but a movement of people who would support him.

SHIELDS: Was that called "Unity," "Yedinstvo?"

BEREZOVSKY: It was at that time—yes, initially—"Interregional Movement Unity."

SHIELDS: Unity?

BEREZOVSKY: Then it was shortened to just "Unity."

SHIELDS: I can show you the clipping from the TV program, but you say: "I remember that meeting at the country house ... Putin was there, Yeltsin's daughter Tatyana and her husband. I said that we needed to create a political party that would concentrate the power of the state machine. They said I was crazy."

BEREZOVSKY: That translation is not correct because again I proposed to create not a political party, because according to Russian law this is impossible; I created a political movement. In the way that you put the question to me it does matter.

SHIELDS: Thank you. I just want to ask you this question because your counsel opened with it. "You did not agree, would that be right, with Mr. Putin's attitude towards Chechnya?"

BEREZOVSKY: That is correct.

SHIELDS: And you thought it was wrong to invade Chechnya in October 1999?

BEREZOVSKY: You are absolutely correct.

SHIELDS: And you stood as a Unity candidate, did you not, in the election for the Duma?

BEREZOVSKY: No, absolutely wrong. I was an independent candidate. I was never a candidate for any party.

SHIELDS: Do you remember whether the party which supported Mr. Putin took a line in relation to Chechnya?

BEREZOVSKY: You know, at that time, as I already told you—you are confusing the words. It was not a party, it was a movement, which was created for a couple of months. A movement does not have any ideology. The ideology of this movement was only "Putin, our President." That is it. To continue to answer your question, as far as Chechnya was concerned, this movement also did not have—because it did not have a unified vision, some people supported what Putin was doing, other people were completely against it, even inside the movement.

SHIELDS: I may be putting this badly. My suggestion to you is as follows. You set about consolidating Mr. Putin's position as Prime Minister?

BEREZOVSKY: You are absolutely correct.

SHIELDS: You knew that the person that was prime minister was most likely to become president?

BEREZOVSKY: You are absolutely correct.

SHIELDS: You created a party called Unity, or financed the party or a movement called Unity, which backed Mr. Putin?

BEREZOVSKY: Absolutely wrong. I created the idea to do that. And I created the idea for how to consolidate people around Putin. That is correct. I never paid anyone a dollar or penny to support this party—this movement.

SHIELDS: You created the movement which supported Mr. Putin?

BEREZOVSKY: Again, I initiated this idea and I was one of the key persons who created the idea.

SHIELDS: Would I be right in saying that movement believed in the continuance of the war in Chechnya?

BEREZOVSKY: Certainly not. And I explained to you why. Perhaps I am presenting the issue poorly, or you are just not understanding me. I said that there was no unified vision for the party, which meant that some people inside of this movement supported the idea to fight in Chechnya and there were other people who were completely against it. This was absolutely clear from the newspapers at that time. And so you found different points of view of people around Putin as to what to do with Chechnya. I am a good example of this today. I supported Putin as president and I was completely against the war in Chechnya. I presented my position openly to Putin.

SHIELDS: The point I am making is this. You knew full well that Russian voters admired Mr. Putin because he was in favor of tough action within Chechnya.

BEREZOVSKY: You are absolutely correct, but—just a moment—you are absolutely correct, but what set me apart from other people is that I knew that Putin could win the election without his support for the war in Chechnya. And—give me one minute, because when you asked me the question, do you remember what was written in *Forbes*—the phrase about me being the most powerful man in Russia. And I put the question to you, "In the public's view, or in public opinion?" And you said, "Yes." These were completely correct responses, because Russia is very different from this country. Having a seat at the table in Russian politics means fantastic power, just a seat, no matter who this person is. I can give you an example—when Yeltsin fired Chernomyrdin and put in Kirienko. Kirienko had a rating of zero; no one knew who this guy was. After two months his approval rating was at 20 percent. He fired Kirienko after three months and put in Primakov, no, put—yes, put in Primakov and Primakov, at that time, had an approval rating of one percent because he had been the minister of foreign affairs, and after two months his ratings were at 40 percent, then 50, just because he was occupying the position of Prime Minister. The same thing happened with Stepashin, the next prime minister, and then Putin. And this was my conflict with people who supported Chechnya and thought that we could only win if we continued the war. My position was that it does not mean that much at all. We will win because Putin is the Prime Minister. That was enough.

SHIELDS: So at the end of that, you wanted Putin to be elected Prime Minister, you supported Putin in the elections for the Duma and you knew full well that the person who was prime minister was best placed to succeed Yeltsin as president?

BEREZOVSKY: Absolutely correct.

SHIELDS: The position is this, is it not, Mr. Berezovsky, because I am now going to come to the three instances. In 1997, and again, as we have seen, in 1999, you were a man of immense power?

BEREZOVSKY: This is your definition.

SHIELDS: You had a grip on the media.

BEREZOVSKY: I do not know what you mean by "grip."

SHIELDS: You had control—I will simplify it. You had control...

BEREZOVSKY: I understand, I just wanted to confirm...

SHIELDS: You had control of ORT?

BEREZOVSKY: You are putting the same question to me and so I will give you the same answer. What do you mean by control? I told you that the state controlled 51 percent. I that time I had 49 percent of the shares. The president nominated the general manager. What do you mean by control?

SHIELDS: Is it right that ORT supported Mr. Putin between June and December 1999?

BEREZOVSKY: No. I will explain why. Because when Putin was—between June and August, the station did not support him because there were a lot of voices on ORT against the general position of the FSB over many points, including the situation in Chechnya. And moreover, when Putin started the war—after he had become Prime Minister of Russia—ORT had a very diversified position concerning the war in Chechnya. There were voices for the Chechen war and there were voices against the Chechen war. Moreover, to be precise, to answer to your question: until I left Russia, ORT was very critical of Putin, for the entire time.

SHIELDS: I must have phrased it badly. I am asking you, am I not right that in that period, the end of 1999, he was supported by ORT, he regularly appeared on the ORT television program hosted by Mr. Dorenko?

BEREZOVSKY: You are absolutely correct, in comparison to Primakov.

SHIELDS: You put your political muscle and media muscle behind Mr. Putin?

BEREZOVSKY: You are absolutely correct.

SHIELDS: Thank you. Because you see, Mr. Berezovsky, you are a man who is to be feared, because you are a man who likes to get his way, are you not?

BEREZOVSKY: Is that a question or statement?

SHIELDS: Yes. I am putting it to you: you are a man who likes to get his way?

BEREZOVSKY: You know what, my way is described in the manifesto of Russian liberalism. This is my way, and you are absolutely correct that I follow my way.

SHIELDS: But your way, for example, which is why I have looked at Mr. Putin's rise to power, you wanted Mr. Putin to become President of Russia; you were party to his selection; you put the force of a media organization behind him and you were quite happy for him to support the violence in Chechnya?

BEREZOVSKY: The first three points are absolutely correct. The fourth one is absolutely false.

SHIELDS: But would you accept that the Unity party was in favor of continuing the war in Chechnya?

BEREZOVSKY: Certainly not. I will try to explain this again. The Unity party never existed—ever. It was a movement. Different people inside the movement had different opinions. Today this Unity refers to the unification of all people, because Putin destroyed the political opposition in Russia, and all the people inside of Unity today certainly support every step of Putin, but when we started to build the movement it was a completely different situation. There were many different views about the issue, and many people inside of Unity were not against the war in Chechnya.

SHIELDS: But this movement had a manifesto, did it not? It had plans?

BEREZOVSKY: Again, I never participated in a Unity manifesto because my position was very simple—I needed to create some power behind Putin at a very complicated time where we were forced to choose between bad and worse. And for me Putin was better than Primakov; that is the point.

SHIELDS: So you are quite happy to turn a blind eye to things you do not like in order to get Mr. Putin elected?

BEREZOVSKY: What do you mean by ignore? For example, I do not like needing to appear in this court. I preferred that Fridman apologize so that we wouldn't need to be in this court. I am not happy being here, but I will stay here.

SHIELDS: I am asking you a question: you are quite happy for Mr. Putin to advance the destruction of Chechnya or the destruction of the terrorists in Chechnya, even though you do not agree with it, if that can get him elected?

BEREZOVSKY: This question is very simple to answer. You can look back at all my statements concerning Chechnya and see that I maintained an absolutely clear position: I was absolutely against the war in Chechnya. And moreover, I should say that the other candidate—and we are not speaking abstractly about "If Putin. Or Putin." Putin was not the sole candidate. Primakov and Luzhkov had created a great deal of opposition to Putin. And as you know, the position of Primakov as regards the war in Chechnya was more dangerous than the position of Putin.

SHIELDS: Mr. Berezovsky, I will ask my question one more time and then I will move on. Mr. Putin was in favor—and your counsel has referred to it and you have referred to it—in taking very strong action against Chechnya, was he not?

BEREZOVSKY: You are absolutely correct.

SHIELDS: The party or the movement which you created was called "Unity," and I am putting it to you that Unity believed in the pursuit of that war?

BEREZOVSKY: No. There were people who believed in it and there were people who did not believe in it.

SHIELDS: I have obtained the manifesto, which we have disclosed to the other side. If you do not agree, but I will put it to you, the translation….

BEREZOVSKY: I agree with almost everything that is written here, except the last sentence. And the last sentence is: "First we should act and then we should negotiate." The last sentence.

SHIELDS: Can I…

BEREZOVSKY: Just a moment. In answer to your question, I agree with almost everything that is written here except for the last sentence. And I have stated this position a number of times.

SHIELDS: Can I just read it and then I will move on. "Yedinstvo" it says at the top, which I think is the name of Unity:

"Thesis of the electoral block … November 22, 1999. Today we see the grief and suffering of civilians in the north Caucasus. The flood of refugees … There should be no place for terrorism, the threat of which is on the rise today, primarily from Chechnya on Russian soil. Its breeding grounds should be destroyed ... of force and, where possible, political methods. We are for the annihilation of militants ... blockaded zones. Maximum care must be taken with children, women and the elderly ... a demand must be made to the Chechen authorities, first to hand over terrorists, free hostages ... only then can there be talks on the political order and future status of Chechnya within Russia."

BEREZOVSKY: Absolutely correct, yes, I agree, except with the last sentence. In December 1999, when Yedinstvo had already won the parliamentary elections, and it was clear that Putin would become president, I had a very important meeting with Putin, because at that time our military had worked themselves into a special formation inside of Chechnya.I met with Putin and presented to him a very simple idea. I said, "The goal which you have set"—and which is wrong from my point of view—"has already been accomplished because the Chechens now think that they have lost the war and that Russia has won the war." And told him that he should cease any further military operations and switch the priority to political negotiations. He did not agree with this proposal. And again, if you refer to the mass media at that time, I openly stated my position—that we should halt all military action and begin to negotiate. This was December 1999.

SHIELDS: I want to ask you some questions about Gazprom...

BEREZOVSKY: Before Putin was president.

SHIELDS: There are three things I am going to ask you about: Gazprom, Svyazinvest and the purchase of *Kommersant*. I just want to put this in some context in terms of a timetable. It is going to be in 1997, and I think I would be right in saying in July 1996, that Mr. Yeltsin had been re-elected President of Russia?

BEREZOVSKY: Correct.

SHIELDS: And he was meant to take up the presidency in December but he was too ill to do so?

BEREZOVSKY: I have a different recollection, that he was elected for the second time around July 3, 1996, and according to our constitution—I do not remember exactly when the inauguration was. But as he had already been the president, his term automatically continued up to the inauguration.

SHIELDS: I think he returned to power effectively in March 1997. Because that coincided with your appointment as Deputy Secretary of the Security Council. So in March 1997, you became Deputy Secretary of the Security Council?

BEREZOVSKY: Yes. I was nominated as Deputy Secretary of the Security Council in 1996, not 1997. And I think in autumn 1996, not 1997.

SHIELDS: Thank you, I might have made a mistake and I apologize for that. Mr. Chernomyrdin—he was Prime Minister…

BEREZOVSKY: In 1996 he was Prime Minister.

SHIELDS: Yes, in 1996, 1997. Mr. Chubais was the First Deputy Prime Minister?

BEREZOVSKY: Yes.

SHIELDS: Mr. Boris Nemtsov was at that time First Deputy Prime Minister?

BEREZOVSKY: I do not remember the First Deputy Prime Minister but I remember he was in the top position in the government.

SHIELDS: And most importantly he was also appointed minister of fuel and energy?

BEREZOVSKY: You are absolutely correct. The minister or the head of the committee of energy and oil, one of them.

SHIELDS: Just so we understand who Mr. Nemtsov was, he had been governor of a province called Nizhny Novgorod?

BEREZOVSKY: Correct.

SHIELDS: And you had met him possibly some years before?

BEREZOVSKY: Yes, I had met him—I do not remember the exact event when I met him but I met him maybe two or three years before this time.

SHIELDS: And he stood with you as a candidate I think in the December 1999 elections. He was also a candidate for the Duma in the 1999 elections?

BEREZOVSKY: Not just him; there were two types of elections. You may be elected as a private citizen, without representing a party. And a representative party may elect you. And Mr. Nemtsov fought for this parliamentary election, being one of the leaders of the so-called SBS party. And the party lost the elections.

SHIELDS: And one of Mr. Nemtsov's responsibilities, was it not, was to reform the energy sector?

BEREZOVSKY: Just a moment, what we have been discussing about 1999 is incorrect. He was elected. He was elected to the parliament, not him, the party was elected to the parliament, and I think that he did not join the parliament because he wanted to be in the executive branch.

SHIELDS: Going back to 1997, one of his responsibilities as minister of fuel and energy was to reform the Russian energy sector?

BEREZOVSKY: You are correct.

SHIELDS: And Russia of course had vast resources of oil and gas?

BEREZOVSKY: That is well known.

SHIELDS: And the greatest national monopoly of all at that stage was Gazprom?

BEREZOVSKY: Correct.

SHIELDS: And just so we have an idea about Gazprom, I think Mr. Chernomyrdin had at one stage been the chairman of Gazprom?

BEREZOVSKY: Correct.

SHIELDS: And in 1989, he had brought the whole gas industry into one company, namely Gazprom?

BEREZOVSKY: I do not remember that exactly, but I do know that he was the first person to lead all the Russian gas companies.

SHIELDS: Just so we can get some idea of the size of Gazprom, I think it had 360,000 employees. Does that sound about right to you?

BEREZOVSKY: I do not know about then, but I do know that Gazprom's current capitalization is around $300 billion.

SHIELDS: I am trying to look back at 1997, when you wanted to become chairman of Gazprom. It was huge, was it not?

BEREZOVSKY: Gazprom at that time was one of the leading monopolies in Russia.

SHIELDS: It controlled 30 percent of the world's known gas reserves and it counted for about 8 to 10 percent of the Russian GDP?

BEREZOVSKY: I think that is close to reality.

SHIELDS: It was Russia's biggest hard currency earner?

BEREZOVSKY: I am not sure about that, because there were already private companies which—like Yukos for example, were comparable in size.

SHIELDS: In 1997, I think it was said about Gazprom that it "heated and fed all Russia." In other words it was a massive corporation?

BEREZOVSKY: Again, we may discuss this emotionally or rationally. If we discuss it rationally, it was not only Gazprom that heated all of Russia. But Gazprom was one of the biggest monopolies in Russia, there is no doubt about that, and one of the most powerful and influential.

SHIELDS: Had you any experience in the gas business up to then?

BEREZOVSKY: I had experience, as you know, in the oil business.

SHIELDS: In Sibneft?

BEREZOVSKY: Yes, which is similar in terms of dealing with energy resources.

SHIELDS: In 1997, when you already had an appointment in the government, you suddenly decided that you wanted to be the chair of Gazprom?

BEREZOVSKY: No, it didn't happen suddenly or occasionally, and this was also the case with Chechnya. I didn't wake up one day and decide that I wanted to make peace in Chechnya. Because in 1996, after the Yeltsin election, I understood that the most sensitive, the most painful issue for Russia was Chechnya; because without political stability…

SHIELDS: Can I ask about Gazprom—sorry, I apologize, sorry.

BEREZOVSKY: No, I am sorry. Because without political stability we are not able to move forward in terms of the Russian economy. And I was delighted to be able to participate in the Chechen negotiations on the federation's side. As I mentioned before, I was the one who reached a peaceful agreement with Chechnya in May 1997. After that I began thinking about what to do next, what the next step was. And after putting an end to the war in Chechnya, I came to the realization that Gazprom was the next biggest issue, because Gazprom, as you accurately described it, was one of the biggest monopolies. And on the other hand, as far as my experience in Sibneft and my interest in this sector, I understood that Gazprom was not working effectively. This is why I decided that I would be able to make a difference in Gazprom, along with certain individuals that I had worked with in AvtoVAZ and Aeroflot.

SHIELDS: So you decided that you were the right man, then, to become chairman?

BEREZOVSKY: Absolutely correct.

SHIELDS: And did it have a chairman at the time?

BEREZOVSKY: Yes. I just want to clarify one point. There is a chairman, and there is a CEO. OK? We are currently discussing the chairman and not the person who has executive power; the person who participates in the construction of laws for the company. At that time, as I remember—but you may correct me—the same person, the very same person, Mr. Viakhirev, was both chairman of the company and CEO of the company, as I remember; you may correct me.

SHIELDS: That is the man whose name we find three up from the bottom on the cast list?

BEREZOVSKY: Just a moment. Yes, exactly. Just a moment. It is very important what I have to say. Viakhirev, who was only one person, held all the power of Gazprom, being both chairman and executive manager.

SHIELDS: And how long had he held that position for?

BEREZOVSKY: From the very beginning, when Chernomyrdin left his position to—from Gazprom to the government.

SHIELDS: So you decided one day in 1997, that the man who had had the job for 10 or so years had to go and you had take his place?

JUSTICE EADY: He does draw a distinction between two things: being chairman and being executive…

BEREZOVSKY: Absolutely correct.

SHIELDS: So he should not go on as chairman but as the chief executive.

BEREZOVSKY: Certainly. Correct.

SHIELDS: So he should step down as chairman?

BEREZOVSKY: Absolutely correct—no, no, he should be CEO, maintain executive power; and I wished to become chairman of the board.

SHIELDS: Chairman of the board. That is a powerful position, is it not?

BEREZOVSKY: Again it is not an executive position. It is very powerful, it contains a lot of power, but it is not executive power. And what is also very important, it was absolutely logical to split this position between two people, not to keep it all in the hands of one.

SHIELDS: How many directors were there on the board then?

BEREZOVSKY: I do not remember.

SHIELDS: There must have been directors, must there not?

BEREZOVSKY: Certainly. They—as with any similar company, there was certainly a board, they had a large managerial staff, and so on.

SHIELDS: If I suggested to you that there were eleven directors then on the board, would that be something you would accept?

BEREZOVSKY: Maybe there were 11, I do not remember the exact number, maybe 11, maybe 15, maybe fewer.

SHIELDS: Can you remember the names of any of them at this stage?

BEREZOVSKY: I do not remember.

SHIELDS: Mr. Nemtsov, was he a director?

BEREZOVSKY: Of Gazprom? I do not remember.

SHIELDS: Mr. Nilov?

BEREZOVSKY: I remember this name, but I do not know whether—was he a member of—chairman of the board or not.

SHIELDS: And Mr. Dinkov, is that name familiar?

BEREZOVSKY: I also know the name.

SHIELDS: Presumably you would want to consult with the board before you became chairman, because the board would have to vote you in as chairman. That would be normal, would it not?

BEREZOVSKY: No, unfortunately it is completely different, the reality is completely different. The reality at that time was—maybe it is the same now, maybe now it is different—but the reality then was, that first of all I needed the joint support of whoever was the former or existing chairman, Mr. Viakhirev, because you are absolutely correct, as you said, I was not in a position to simply fire someone and put me in their place. Yes? And this is why I began speaking with Mr. Viakhirev, and eventually reached an agreement with Mr. Viakhirev. As you know, Mr. Viakhirev came to this position through the post of Chernomyrdin's deputy, when Chernomyrdin was head of Gazprom. In other words, they were very close. After I received Viakhirev's support, I asked him to call Chernomyrdin to speak to him about it because two different people needed to agree to the proposal. So Viakhirev called Chernomyrdin and Chernomyrdin did not have time to discuss it, so then I talked to—three days later Viakhirev called me and said, "You know, he is in China now, and he is prepared to speak to you but you will need to fly to China." This is how it happened.

SHIELDS: I want to ask you about this: did Mr. Viakhirev draw up any draft of any documents setting out your appointment?

BEREZOVSKY: Viakhirev signed—not signed, how do you say, initialed the document, the project, the draft of the document, with my appointment as chairman of the board.

SHIELDS: Who drew up the draft, yourself or Mr. Viakhirev?

BEREZOVSKY: It was prepared in the office of Mr. Viakhirev, because I am not familiar with the bureaucratic necessities of such a document.

SHIELDS: And was the board consulted at that stage or not?

BEREZOVSKY: Not at all.

SHIELDS: Not at all?

BEREZOVSKY: About me, no. About Viakhirev, I do not know.

SHIELDS: Not at all. Now, I just want to ask you so I get this correct, because we have two versions of this and I just want to make it clear. In your witness statement—paragraph 17, my Lord, page 1236. This is a statement you signed on February 22, 2006, as being true. If you would like to be handed a copy, that would be proper.

BEREZOVSKY: Could I have that.

SHIELDS: Yes. You said in this: "It is true that I put myself forward as a suitable person to be chairman of Gazprom."

BEREZOVSKY: This is true.

SHIELDS: "I recall that I spoke to the chief executive officer of Gazprom, Mr. Viakhirev, and he in general terms agreed to my appointment. "Mr. Viakhirev drew up a draft of a document setting out my proposed appointment."

BEREZOVSKY: Correct. Everything that you have just repeated is the same.

SHIELDS: You want me to repeat it?

BEREZOVSKY: You have just repeated what we were discussing.

SHIELDS: I understand your answer now, that was not a document that was drawn up by the board, Mr. Viakhirev drew it up?

BEREZOVSKY: Yes.

SHIELDS: That is right. Good. Now, in your…

BEREZOVSKY: Again, let us—after we discussed it with Viakhirev, Viakhirev said that he was in agreement. Nothing happened immediately after that. First Viakhirev's office had to prepare the document, and then when I came back the next day the document was ready, including his initials on the proposal.

SHIELDS: Now, in your legal document file in this case, in the reply—that is at page 35, my Lord—we are just dealing with a document, and I know it is disputed you ever showed any document from Mr. Nemtsov, but you say here: "It is not admitted that the document setting out his appointment as chairman of Gazprom, which to the best of his recollection was drawn up . . . was signed by Mr. Viakhirev." I just want to make it clear, do you think it was or was not signed by Mr. Viakhirev? And was it or was it not drawn up by the company's board?

BEREZOVSKY: As far as the board, again I do not know. As far as Viakhirev's signature, yes. Mr. Viakhirev's signature was on this paper.

SHIELDS: So in short...

BEREZOVSKY: And no other signatures.

SHIELDS: You go to Mr. Viakhirev saying you want to become chairman of Gazprom, replacing him as chairman?

BEREZOVSKY: Correct.

SHIELDS: You do not talk to any members of the board?

BEREZOVSKY: Correct.

SHIELDS: You impose yourself as chairman of Gazprom by getting his signature?

BEREZOVSKY: Certainly not. Let me give you an example, so that you will understand it better. This is my personal experience, okay? Just my personal experience. I was Deputy Secretary of the Russian Security Council, and shortly after I took over this position, I began to negotiate with the Chechens, who put forth the condition that before we could go any farther in our negotiations, Russia must withdraw two of its military detachments from Chechnya. The decision to place troops in Chechnya was made by the Security Council. It was not just the decision of the president; he needed the support of the Security Council. And I went to him, to the president, and said that we needed to withdraw the troops if we really wanted peace. There was a great deal of arguing over this issue—among Yeltsin, Chernomyrdin, me, and the Minister and Secretary of the Security Council, Mr. Rybkin. Finally Yeltsin accepted this condition and the appropriate documents were prepared in a couple hours. The very next day we returned to Chechnya with this decree to withdraw the troops, and began the process of withdrawal.

Why give you this example? According to the rules, Yeltsin should have called the entire Security Council to discuss the issue. But he did not want to do that. I think that basically the same thing has happened in this instance. You are absolutely correct to point out that this is a vital part of the Russian economy. It is a very important sector of the economy. And certainly not just anyone could have stepped in and filled this post. Both Chernomyrdin and Viakhirev knew me well, so when I went to Viakhirev with my proposal, he responded by saying that in general he was in agreement that the two positions should be split, and that he was in favor of my appointment, but that he could not make the decision himself. He then said that he would prepare and initial the necessary document. I then took this document to the chairman without a signature. I do not understand why anyone present would suggest that I already had Chernomyrdin's signature. If I had the signature of Chernomyrdin, I would not have flown to China to discuss the matter with Nemtsov.

SHIELDS: I am coming to that now. Mr. Nemtsov was minister for fuel and energy, and he was responsible for the reform of Russia's natural resources; you have agreed to that, have you not?

BEREZOVSKY: Yes.

SHIELDS: Thank you. So, to be absolutely clear about this, it is your account of what happened that you did not need, nor did you ever seek, Mr. Nemtsov's support as the minister for fuel and energy for your appointment as chairman of the biggest company in Russia?

BEREZOVSKY: You see, I made things a bit difficult for him. I first wanted to get approval from the top and then discuss it with the next level. And for this—I am sorry. This is why I first spoke to Viakhirev and then Chernomyrdin. And after that I was planning on discussing the matter with Nemtsov, and with hundreds of others. But you should know that the signature of Nemtsov, his support, was not mandatory for this decision.

SHIELDS: The question was fairly simple. You never sought, and you never needed, as far as you were concerned, the consent of Mr. Nemtsov for your appointment.

BEREZOVSKY: Yes and no. I will explain to you why yes, and why no. Yes, because it is better to have that. No, because it was not necessary. It was possible to do it without Nemtsov, but it was simpler to do it with Nemtsov.

SHIELDS: Right. Let me put to you what our case is on this: Mr. Nemtsov, as I have said, was minister for fuel and energy. And he was responsible for Gazprom. He sat on the Gazprom board, and three other directors as well as him represented the state's panel, a panel of state representatives, because the state had a large interest, did it not, in Gazprom?

BEREZOVSKY: Correct.

SHIELDS: Mr. Nemtsov was the chairman of the state panel, and that was by state decree. Do you accept that?

BEREZOVSKY: Absolutely.

SHIELDS: Thank you. So on the board of 11 people, four would vote as one, so that would require two others on that—six others on that board to vote against the minister for fuel and the state representatives. Correct?

BEREZOVSKY: Correct.

SHIELDS: And the reality is, is it not, Mr. Berezovsky, that that was very unlikely to happen?

BEREZOVSKY: What was the question?

SHIELDS: If Mr. Nemtsov did not want you to become chairman then it was very unlikely that the board would outvote him for you to become chairman?

BEREZOVSKY: Is that a question?

SHIELDS: Yes.

BEREZOVSKY: It is unlikely, but it is not the deciding point. Again, the prime minister has the ultimate say, and I hope you also have in your file the conclusion of the Russian lawyer, Mr. Ariya, which clearly explains their legal…

BROWNE: We must not go into that. He is referring to a document which is privileged.

JUSTICE EADY: Is it? The document is privileged and therefore you should not go into it.

BEREZOVSKY: I am sorry.

SHIELDS: Right. Now, the meeting of the board, the June meeting, Mr. Berezovsky, was fixed for June 28, 1997.

BEREZOVSKY: I am sorry.

SHIELDS: The meeting of the board of Gazprom was fixed for June 28th. It is not in the document; I am just putting it to you; all right?

BEREZOVSKY: I do not remember that.

SHIELDS: I will tell you what our case is, so everyone knows. I will do it slowly. Prior to that, you visited Mr. Nemtsov at his offices in the

White House. The White House is the seat of power in the Kremlin, as well as in Washington.

BEREZOVSKY: I visited Nemtsov in the White House, okay.

SHIELDS: Yes, that is what I am saying to you. You are saying that this is all a pack of lies. But I have to put it to you so you can say it is a pack of lies. You brought with you a draft of a document which set out your appointment as chairman of Gazprom. Chernomyrdin signed that document?

BROWNE: Do you mean Mr. Chernomyrdin?

SHIELDS: Mr. Chernomyrdin, I apologize. And by the current chairman, Mr. Viakhirev.

BEREZOVSKY: The question?

SHIELDS: That is untrue?

BEREZOVSKY: Absolutely not true.

SHIELDS: Okay. Mr. Nemtsov is rather surprised to see this document, and in your presence he made two telephone calls, one to Mr. Chernomyrdin and the other to the existing chairman?

BEREZOVSKY: Does he remember the order of his calls?

SHIELDS: Yes, he did. He phoned Mr. Chernomyrdin first, and then he phoned the chairman second?

BEREZOVSKY: And Viakhirev second?

SHIELDS: Yes?

BEREZOVSKY: Good.

SHIELDS: And after those telephone conversations he refused to sign the document, Mr. Berezovsky. I will tell you why—but you did not hear this conversation—because neither gentleman told him that they wanted you to become chairman of Gazprom. And then you made this remark—or a remark to this effect, rather—that there was no escape from this.

BEREZOVSKY: Yes.

SHIELDS: That is a lie, is it?

BEREZOVSKY: 100 percent a lie. Do I now comment or will you continue to question me?

SHIELDS: In June—and you agree with this—you went to Beijing, did you not?

BEREZOVSKY: Absolutely true.

SHIELDS: And Mr. Chernomyrdin was on state business.

BEREZOVSKY: Absolutely correct.

SHIELDS: And along with Mr. Chernomyrdin was Mr. Nemtsov, who was coordinating the trip?

BEREZOVSKY: I do not know his function on this trip, but he was in China at the same time.

SHIELDS: And you telephoned and asked to meet them at the Russian Embassy in Beijing?

BEREZOVSKY: Absolutely wrong. I only called Chernomyrdin and asked to meet only with Chernomyrdin. It is true that I met him at the Russian Embassy.

SHIELDS: And this is what Mr. Nemtsov remembers very clearly, that you tried to persuade Mr. Chernomyrdin, in his presence, to exert pressure on him to sign that document?

BEREZOVSKY: Absolutely a lie.

SHIELDS: And you were quite rude about Mr. Nemtsov in the presence of Mr. Chernomyrdin?

BEREZOVSKY: Absolutely wrong, because there was no discussion in the presence of Nemtsov about Gazprom with Chernomyrdin, between Chernomyrdin and me. I never discussed the issue of Gazprom in the presence of Nemtsov in China.

SHIELDS: Well, you discussed Gazprom with Chernomyrdin in Beijing?

BEREZOVSKY: In Beijing, directly with Mr. Chernomyrdin, without the presence of Nemtsov.

SHIELDS: Presumably you flew to Beijing because you were that keen to have him confirm your appointment?

BEREZOVSKY: Because I wanted to get his signature, Chernomyrdin.

SHIELDS: You were desperate to become chairman of Gazprom, were you not?

BEREZOVSKY: You know—again it is—if—we may discuss this in terms of emotions, and we may discuss in terms of reality, the facts. I wanted to be chairman of Gazprom, true. I needed to have the signature of Chernomyrdin, true. I got the signature of Viakhirev, true. I called Chernomyrdin to meet with him, true. Did I ever ask Nemtsov to participate in that? That is a lie.

SHIELDS: Because I am Boris Berezovsky and I get what I want. That is what it is about.

BEREZOVSKY: And what? Where is the contradiction—am I telling you the truth or am I lying?

SHIELDS: Let me just finish. It will not take long, I have one more bit of information about this. He said...

BEREZOVSKY: He? Who?

SHIELDS: Mr. Nemtsov was saying that you chided Mr. Chernomyrdin for allowing him to be disrespectful to him by not agreeing?

BEREZOVSKY: Could you please ...

SHIELDS: You chided Mr. Chernomyrdin for allowing Mr. Nemtsov to behave this way.

BEREZOVSKY: Okay, but I have already told you, Nemtsov was not present at this meeting with Chernomyrdin. This means that Nemtsov—everything that he—you want me to confirm what exactly? I cannot confirm something that never happened.

SHIELDS: I know what your answer is, but it is my obligation as counsel that I put to you what our case is. I will go on. You referred to Mr. Nemtsov as "this boy," and suggested that he was being disrespectful to Mr. Chernomyrdin by refusing to listen. You then told Mr. Nemtsov that if he continued to refuse your proposal, you would do everything in your power to destroy him as a politician.

BEREZOVSKY: This never happened, this conversation.

SHIELDS: And Nemtsov said he did not sign.

BEREZOVSKY: You see, this is all a lie, and I understand that there is a different mindset in this room, and it is good that it is not the same. But if you were to tell this story in Russia, everybody would laugh. That Nemtsov actually took an oppositional stance to Chernomyrdin? It never happened.

SHIELDS: Well, your counsel will no doubt call him Mr. Chernomyrdin's poodle to his face when he gives evidence.

BEREZOVSKY: Sorry?

SHIELDS: Your counsel will no doubt call him Mr. Chernomyrdin's poodle when he gives evidence.

BEREZOVSKY: Unfortunately, Nemtsov has this name because of his hair and not because of his economic policies. He has this—I am sorry.

BROWNE: I did not know that; which only goes to show how perceptive the comment of Mr. Shields was.

SHIELDS: Actually, it is quite a serious matter because you are suggesting that the Deputy Prime Minister, then the minister in charge of fuel and energy, was basically a nobody who just did what he was told to do.

BEREZOVSKY: No. What I said was that Nemtsov certainly had power. He did not have the power to reverse a prime minister's decision, but he had a significant amount of influence. But knowing the decision-making mechanisms in the Russian government—you may like them, you may hate them—but they are a reality. I knew that the first thing I had to do was get the permission of the person at the top, Mr. Viakhirev. Then I understood that I needed the support of the person on the next level, and after that it wouldn't be a problem to get everyone else's support. This is the, I am sorry to say, way it works.

SHIELDS: So if that formula works, were you appointed chairman of Gazprom?

BEREZOVSKY: If Chernomyrdin signed, yes.

SHIELDS: Were you appointed?

BEREZOVSKY: No, because Chernomyrdin disagreed with the appointment. This is the other point, completely different from what Nemtsov discussed.

SHIELDS: Did you, when you were in China, see Mr. Nemtsov at all?

BEREZOVSKY: Certainly. I met with him. And not just once. The first time he saw me he asked: "What are you doing here?" I said: "I am going to meet Mr. Chernomyrdin."

SHIELDS: Do you recall traveling with him along the Yangtze River?

BEREZOVSKY: It wasn't a trip along the Yangtze. We were traveling to where China had built the most powerful hydroelectric station in the world. It was not a trip by river; it was a voyage to this site. Moreover, at that time the river was all but dried up.

SHIELDS: Mr. Berezovsky, now I am going to come to the privatization of Svyazinvest. This is in 1997.

BEREZOVSKY: Correct.

SHIELDS: I think it would be right that at that stage the Russian telephone system was slightly outdated compared with, say, America or this country?

BEREZOVSKY: It is difficult to say because I am not an expert in that area. I do know that it was not, let us say, sufficient. And like all companies within the post-Soviet Union, they needed to be improved because they had been built on a model that didn't include competition. And from my perspective, Mr. Gusinsky was exactly the right person to build this company because in Soviet times it was split into...

SHIELDS: I will deal with that, because there were 88 regional telephone companies?

BEREZOVSKY: Perhaps.

SHIELDS: And they were joined into the single company called Svyazinvest?

BEREZOVSKY: You are absolutely correct.

SHIELDS: And "Svyaz" means "link" or "communication," and the object was to auction 25 percent of that company, together with Rostelkom, which was the long distance provider?

BEREZOVSKY: In general, I think you are correct.

SHIELDS: And a date was fixed for the auction of July 25th?

BEREZOVSKY: Yes, it was July 25th. I remember that it was not the 26th because it was, as I remember, Friday. That is the reason I remember.

SHIELDS: The purpose of the auction was presumably to try to get more than one bidder?

BEREZOVSKY: That is correct.

SHIELDS: So, to get the highest price for the Russian people?

BEREZOVSKY: You are absolutely correct.

SHIELDS: And the person in charge of overseeing the auction was Mr. Chubais?

BEREZOVSKY: Yes, I told you, he was the person in charge of privatization in Russia at that time.

SHIELDS: And he was overseeing the auction?

BEREZOVSKY: You are absolutely correct.

SHIELDS: And there were two consortia who had emerged as potential bidders at the auction.

BEREZOVSKY: Initially as I remember, there were even more but eventually, by that time, there were just two.

SHIELDS: One headed by Mr. Gusinsky?

BEREZOVSKY: Correct.

SHIELDS: And one headed by Mr. Potanin?

BEREZOVSKY: Correct.

SHIELDS: And you were not part of either?

BEREZOVSKY: No, I did not have any business interest in either of them.

SHIELDS: I suggest to you that you were in fact supportive of Mr. Gusinsky?

BEREZOVSKY: This is completely wrong and I want to—though perhaps you are correct, could you please explain what you mean by "support."

SHIELDS: You wanted Mr. Gusinsky to win. That is what supportive means?

BEREZOVSKY: This is not so.

SHIELDS: Was a member of Mr. Gusinsky's consortium *Alfa Bank*, for whom I act in this case?

BEREZOVSKY: Yes, there were, as I remember, four parties of this consortium, which were led by Gusinsky: Gusinsky, Fridman, Telefonica, a Spanish company, and the Swiss Bank.

SHIELDS: That is a good memory. Is it right that you attended meetings of the consortium when the auction was discussed?

BEREZOVSKY: This is not at all true. I was invited by Gusinsky and Potanin and the meeting happened in Gusinsky's office at the stage when it had become absolutely clear that there was going to be a serious conflict between these two groups.

SHIELDS: Were you present at a number of meetings attended by both Mr. Gusinsky and Mr. Potanin, when the auction was discussed?

BEREZOVSKY: I remember, as I told you, one, and it was not a discussion about the auction itself; it was a discussion about a conflict between Gusinsky and Potanin. I was present at this meeting because of a request by Mr. Yumashev, who at the time was the head of the presidential administration.

SHIELDS: Were you not present at at least two of these meetings where the auction was discussed?

BEREZOVSKY: Again, I remember one meeting. I cannot rule out that there was another meeting at which I was present, but I clearly remember this meeting because it was the one where a solution to the problem was found. Gusinsky and Potanin invited me to meet with Mr. Chubais, who at that time was in the south of France.

SHIELDS: That is what I am going to come to, that meeting. Would it not be right that, as you said, there was a meeting in the south of France a few days before the auction?

BEREZOVSKY: Absolutely correct.

SHIELDS: Mr. Chubais was on holiday in the south of France.

BEREZOVSKY: As I understand it, that is correct.

SHIELDS: And I put it to you that it was you who, with Mr. Gusinsky, invited Mr. Potanin to go down to that meeting to see Mr. Chubais?

BEREZOVSKY: This is wrong. Mr. Gusinsky and Potanin invited me to meet, referring to Mr. Yumashev's request. I even called Mr. Yumashev to verify, and he confirmed that he had already spoken to Chubais about the meeting and that Chubais was prepared to meet. But again, the initial invitation for this meeting came directly from Gusinsky and Potanin.

SHIELDS: And at that meeting Mr. Chubais made it clear that the auction was going to be open and fair and that no exceptions would be made for anyone, including those present?

BEREZOVSKY: This is absolutely correct.

SHIELDS: And I suggest that you did not like hearing that because you wanted Mr. Gusinsky to win.

BEREZOVSKY: This is completely wrong. I understood that the conflict between them was very dangerous, by what was confirmed later, because Yeltsin had just been re-elected and there were many fights going on concerning other companies, especially the oil companies. My concern was that it would create a new, let us say, war and that this was also the concern of Mr. Yumashev. This is why Mr. Yumashev organized the meeting, knowing that, on the one hand, Chubais was favorably disposed to Potanin, and as I already mentioned to you, this was because Chubais, before the presidential elections, was hired by Potanin to be a member of the Onexim group. Yumashev told me that he had some doubts—and earlier you asked me a question about Chubais: do I think that he is corrupt? This was one of the instances where I began to have second thoughts about him. When we asked him in 1996 to lead the electoral campaign, I had no doubts about him, but this event changed that. But regardless, you are absolutely correct, that was Chubais's exact formula, in terms of what you said. He wanted to have absolutely fair and free competition.

SHIELDS: This was an auction, and the person who makes the highest bid wins the auction. That is how an auction works.

BEREZOVSKY: You are correct.

SHIELDS: And Mr. Chubais was overseeing the auction and you became involved in this because, as I understand it, you were concerned—I am going to read from your witness statement—paragraph 19, my Lord: "I felt that Mr. Chubais, who, along with Mr. Nemtsov, was at that time First Deputy Prime Minister in charge of the ... state industries was showing favoritism to Mr. Potanin possibly because, before entering government, he had been invited by Mr. Potanin to work for him at Onexim Group."

BEREZOVSKY: Correct.

SHIELDS: That is a pretty straightforward allegation of Mr. Chubais in fact being corrupt, is it not, because he is going to show favor to one party in the auction process—there are two bidders and he is going to show favoritism to one because he had a prior business relationship...

BEREZOVSKY: This is not corrupt; it shows the possibility that he might be corrupt. I am not able to confirm this, and Mr. Yumashev had the same concern. Again, I want to stress, I was not there upon my own initiative; I was invited by Gusinsky and Potanin, which was later confirmed by Yumashev. He also had doubts that Chubais was going to be equally balanced between the two groups.

SHIELDS: You were worried that Mr. Potanin's syndicate, consortium, might win, were you not, Mr. Berezovsky?

BEREZOVSKY: I was worried not about that, as I told you, I was worried that Chubais—as you mentioned, he was a key person in the auction—might use his influential power to skew this bid in the favor of Potanin.

SHIELDS: I am going to put to you, Mr. Berezovsky, that you did get involved in this auction process, that in your meetings with Mr. Potanin, you made it quite clear that you wanted Mr. Gusinsky to win.

BEREZOVSKY: Again, as I already told you, I did not have any separate meetings with Mr. Potanin about this auction. I had a meeting with Mr. Gusinsky and Potanin together.

SHIELDS: Yes, that was right, when they were all present, and that you made it clear that if he went ahead, he would be going against your wishes, and that you would use your political power and media resources to inflict harm on him as a businessman.

BEREZOVSKY: This is a lie.

SHIELDS: It is a lie?

BEREZOVSKY: Correct.

SHIELDS: You see, this is another example Mr. Berezovsky of you trying to get your own way.

BEREZOVSKY: It is true that I always follow my own way. Perhaps this is not correct, but it is the way that I work.

SHIELDS: Mr. Chubais was a minister—Deputy Prime Minister, the minister in charge of privatization. This was a major auction, was it not?

BEREZOVSKY: Up to this point it was the most important of all auctions.

SHIELDS: Yes, an opportunity for someone possibly to make large profits?

BEREZOVSKY: Yes, because if the person would be able to improve the company, he would certainly make a profit.

SHIELDS: And you formed the view that that minister, that Deputy Prime Minister, was favoring one side?

BEREZOVSKY: Again, I am not able to say that I was certain he was on the side of Potanin, but I certainly had my doubts because, as I told you before, Potanin had hired him. But it is also important that, when Chubais did not have a job and Potanin hired him, Chubais was also receiving job offers from numerous other companies. There was a great deal of discussion about why ultimately he had chosen to work for Potanin. Because of this they already had an established business relationship, which is why we both had our doubts.

SHIELDS: I think the result of the auction was that Mr. Potanin won with a bid of about 1.8 billion to 1.7 billion bid by Mr. Gusinsky.

BEREZOVSKY: It was very close, but Potanin put 100—100, I think—100 million more than Gusinsky.

SHIELDS: Did you ever confront Mr. Chubais with your suspicions about his possible favoritism?

BEREZOVSKY: When we all met together, I said precisely that. Before the auction—when we met in France, this is exactly what I said to Chubais, that it was not proper for him to be the arbiter in this specific case because it was well known that he already had a business relationship with Potanin.

SHIELDS: Did you report him to anyone afterwards?

BEREZOVSKY: Certainly, to Yumashev.

SHIELDS: Did you sever all contact with him yourself?

BEREZOVSKY: With Chubais?

SHIELDS: Yes.

BEREZOVSKY: Good question. Because after the auction, there were many questions about the connection between Chubais and Potanin. It was unclear how it had happened that the amount bid by Potanin was just slightly over the bid of Gusinsky. There was a good deal of discussion about the fact that it had not been done properly, so I went to Mr. Kokh, who was minister at that time—who at that time was Minister of Privatization, on the Committee of Privatization, and a very close friend of Chubais because Chubais had nominated him to this position. We have already mentioned his name in relation to Sibneft. I went to his office after the auction. This was in the morning. I remember it clearly because he was already a little bit drunk. I started to explain to him that there was already a lot of discussion about the fact that the auction had not been run properly, and he answered: "Boris, I am Onexim. I am Onexim. Me, Mr. Kokh, I am Onexim." Onexim is the group who won the auction. I was absolutely shocked, absolutely shocked, and after leaving his office I went directly to Chubais at the White House and reported to him what had happened, and Chubais said, "No, impossible, it cannot be." I said, "You are lying. I spoke to Kokh. I just came from his office." And he said, "I will speak to him later."

SHIELDS: I am going to ask you this question, a simple question: in an auction, as this was, there were sealed bids, were there not?

BEREZOVSKY: I did not participate in this auction. As far as I understand the rules, which were used when I bid on Sibneft, the bids should be sealed.

SHIELDS: So there are sealed bids. So how does someone, when there are sealed bids, favor one party over the other?

BEREZOVSKY: This is a question for the head of security. You surely know that all groups in Russia have ways of getting inside information. This is not a question for me. If you are asking me, is it possible that the other side got this information, my answer would be, certainly, yes.

SHIELDS: I am asking you in relation to Mr. Chubais. Are you suggesting therefore that Mr. Chubais discovered the amount Mr. Gusinsky was going to bid and told Mr. Potanin?

BEREZOVSKY: Again, I do not know the technical aspects, how it came to happen. I could describe to you a thousand different ways that it could have happened, but I do not know. First and foremost if it actually happened. I do not know. I said that there were doubts about it, but my conversation with Mr. Kokh confirmed any doubts, any of my personal doubts.

SHIELDS: The point of my question is this: if you say in broad terms someone has favored someone, one then asks how could they possibly have favored someone where you have sealed bids in an auction?

BEREZOVSKY: Again, do you want me to explain technically how it could be done, do you want an example? It is very simple.

SHIELDS: There is only one way...

BEREZOVSKY: No, it is very simple. All you need is one spy from Potanin's camp. Should I continue?

SHIELDS: No, you said, "Mr. Chubais favored."

BEREZOVSKY: I did not make an accusation. I said I had serious doubts. That is completely different than accusing him of something.

SHIELDS: If you say you have doubts that someone favored someone in an auction process, if you analyze it, the only way you can favor someone in an auction process is if you tell them what the other person is going to bid?

BEREZOVSKY: Again, I gave you a clear answer. And I still have many doubts; but my conversation with Kokh confirmed my doubts because he said very clearly to me that "I am Onexim" and that this was the reason why Onexim had won the bid.

SHIELDS: So in other words, just so I get this right, it is your suspicion that Mr. Chubais discovered what Mr. Gusinsky was going to bid and told Mr. Potanin?

BEREZOVSKY: You see, I do not know—Chubais, Kokh, or some other officer of the ministry, it could be, again—I said to you that I still have doubts. That is the point. I never gave a statement that Chubais was behind Potanin and that he organized—that he had information; I do not know that. But what happened after, particularly after meeting Kokh, confirmed my doubts.

SHIELDS: Right, can we move on? Before we move on there is one thing I missed out asking you in relation to Gazprom. It is a brief question. When this all occurred in Gazprom in June 1997, would it be right that Mr. Nemtsov was widely regarded as the likely successor—and I will get the name right—to Mr. Chernomyrdin—to Mr. Yeltsin, rather?

BEREZOVSKY: Nemtsov himself spread many rumors that he would be the successor. But as far as everyone else was concerned, society wasn't paying that much attention to who would be next—only the next three years. And as far as the political elite of Russia, no one took him seriously. Nemtsov thought he would be next because on one occasion Yeltsin made a comment that he would be next. But that wouldn't have been the first time that Yeltsin had said something similar and then forgotten about it. He said the same thing about Kirienko. Nemtsov was of course delighted to spread the news that he would be the next.

SHIELDS: So this was all Mr. Nemtsov's doing, was it?

BEREZOVSKY: Not only him, because as I told you Yeltsin said this publicly, which means that it wasn't only Nemtsov, a lot of people thought that he would be, and just as many people had already forgotten that just two months before Yeltsin had said something completely different.

SHIELDS: Let us go forward now to June 1999, to *Kommersant*. Again to put this in perspective. At that stage, you had already owned *Kommersant* since June 1999, or controlled rather, 49 percent of ORT, the television company?

BEREZOVSKY: In June 1999? Correct.

SHIELDS: 25 percent of TV6?

BEREZOVSKY: I do not remember exactly, perhaps even more, but at least 25 percent.

SHIELDS: And you owned another newspaper called *Nezavisimaya Gazeta*?

BEREZOVSKY: Correct.

SHIELDS: So you had a substantial interest in the Russian media already?

BEREZOVSKY: That is correct.

SHIELDS: And you freely admit, as I understand it, that you were quite happy to use that media to further your political beliefs?

BEREZOVSKY: No, that is not so. I disagree with that. I said that it is absolutely correct that as far as ORT is concerned, yes, you are correct, but it wasn't about my political interest, it had to do with my understanding of Russia's future. My understanding certainly coincided with the interest—but again it was my understanding of Russia's future that led me to use ORT as political leverage, you are correct. As far as *Kommersant* is concerned, never. As far as *Nezavisimaya Gazeta* is concerned, never. As far as TV6 is concerned, never.

SHIELDS: You were approached, was it by Mr. Yakovlev, who was one of the shareholder owners of *Kommersant,* who wished to sell his shares?

BEREZOVSKY: Again, I met Yakovlev once in Amsterdam, as I have already told you. As far as *Kommersant* is concerned, it was the very beginning of spring of 1999, maybe the end of winter 1999. This meeting was a continuation of a previous discussion—the previous meeting was with—the other partner, I mentioned his name, Miloslavsky, and at this meeting he said, "Boris, I know that you are interested in the mass media and I think that Yakovlev is looking to sell *Kommersant*." He initiated the contact. And I said, "Yes, we would be interested in buying it." And after that I met Yakovlev.

SHIELDS: Would it be right that Mr. Yakovlev had other shareholder partners, one of whom was a Mr. Kaskov?

BEREZOVSKY: As I remember, he had two other partners—Mr. Miloslavsky and Kaskov, but he was definitely the major shareholder...

SHIELDS: The majority shareholder. And your partner was dealing with Mr. Yakovlev. That is right, is it not? Badri.

BEREZOVSKY: Yes, Badri was communicating with Mr. Yakovlev, but not only with him; he was also communicating with Mr. Miloslavsky at the same time.

SHIELDS: Were you aware that Mr. Kaskov had approached *Alfa Bank* and Mr. Fridman with a proposal to either selling his shares or obtaining a loan to fund the purchase of Mr. Yakovlev's shares?

BEREZOVSKY: I did not know anything about that.

SHIELDS: Are you sure?

BEREZOVSKY: 100 percent.

SHIELDS: Because I put it to you that you did find that out?

BEREZOVSKY: No, again, I told you that I only got my information from Badri.

SHIELDS: And that you did not like the idea of your desire to buy *Kommersant* being thwarted?

BEREZOVSKY: Of course I would not like the idea of someone else buying *Kommersant*, when I was working on a deal to purchase it. This is absolutely natural. But as far as I know, Mr. Kaskov played no role in this matter, at this stage at least. The deciding voice was Mr. Yakovlev.

SHIELDS: *Kommersant* was a very important paper at that stage, was it not?

BEREZOVSKY: Not just "was," is now still.

SHIELDS: You wanted to own it. What I suggest to you is what happened was as follows. You telephoned my client Mr. Fridman at his offices and you told him that you understood that he was in discussions regarding the ownership of *Kommersant*, that you were in negotiations with Mr. Yakovlev, and close to a deal, but that my client's actions were restricting him—you—and that if he continued to make the acquisition difficult, there would be consequences?

BEREZOVSKY: I never discussed *Kommersant* with Fridman; not by telephone, not privately, never.

SHIELDS: And you never used the expression as Mr. Fridman remembers you using, "my vas zamochim?"

BEREZOVSKY: I never spoke to Mr. Fridman about *Kommersant*. I never used that expression, not with Fridman, not with anyone.

SHIELDS: You never put pressure on Mr. Nemtsov to ratify or agree to your appointment as chairman of Gazprom?

BEREZOVSKY: I never even discussed Gazprom with Mr. Nemtsov.

SHIELDS: And Mr. Nemtsov has made this all up. You never needed to consult him at all about Gazprom?

BEREZOVSKY: You should put this question to Mr. Nemtsov. You have my answer.

SHIELDS: You did not favor Mr. Gusinsky in the Svyazinvest auction and make it clear to Mr. Potanin?

BEREZOVSKY: You are absolutely correct; I never took Gusinsky's side. If you want to know my opinion, my personal opinion, I have a great deal of respect for Gusinsky because he created the company

Svyazinvest. And I never spoke with Potanin as a favor to Gusinsky. Moreover, I was invited by Gusinsky and Potanin to voice my concerns, and at the same time at the request of Mr. Yumashev.

SHIELDS: Even though it was an auction, as you have told us, where you feared that Mr. Chubais was favoring Mr. Potanin?

BEREZOVSKY: That is correct, but it does not matter, after the fact, that I threw my support behind Gusinsky. I spoke with Chubais only to ask him to remain truly neutral.

SHIELDS: And you never phoned my client when you knew he might be a competitor in relation to *Kommersant*?

BEREZOVSKY: I never called your client and never spoke to him about this matter.

SHIELDS: You see, I put it to you, Mr. Berezovsky, that the real truth of your character is that you like to get what you want?

BEREZOVSKY: I think that every independent person needs to have such a goal, to constantly be working towards a goal.

SHIELDS: But you are—and have achieved enormous power in Russia. As I said, you had the power almost to make presidents, just as you did with Mr. Putin?

BEREZOVSKY: Is this a statement or is it a question?

SHIELDS: That is a question. That is what I am suggesting to you: that was the extent of your power, how powerful you were.

BEREZOVSKY: My big problem seems to be one of mindset. I truly believe in a liberal Russia. And again, if you want to better understand what I believe, you can refer to the manifesto of Russian liberalism that I wrote in 2000. I have done everything I can to move the country in that direction. This necessarily means that I have often times had to be not a nice guy because many people were against democracy. Almost half the population of Russia was against it—they did not want to move towards democracy. And I absolutely used my personal influence, my power, my investments—such as ORT—and I never concealed that I was using these tools to move Russia towards democracy.

My big problem is that if you are involved in real politics, you of course want official political power. I hate power in itself. This is the problem. This is the contradiction within me. I took the position of Deputy Secretary of the Security Council simply because I understood that perhaps no one else at that time would have been able to bring peace to Chechnya.

SHIELDS: You do not like the abuse of power?

BEREZOVSKY: I hate the abuse…

SHIELDS: You hate it. And you believe in liberal government?

BEREZOVSKY: Absolutely.

SHIELDS: You believe in democracy?

BEREZOVSKY: Democracy as in a realization of liberal ideas, yes.

SHIELDS: How come then in June 1997, you decided that you should become chairman of Gazprom without even bothering to ask any of the other directors, any of the board?

BEREZOVSKY: In absolutely the same way that I decided to use ORT in support of Yeltsin against Zyuganov, understanding that it was not a game anymore. I did everything I could to avoid the use of tanks, guns, and soldiers in deciding who would prevail. This is the sole reason why I used ORT as an instrument of support for Yeltsin. It is not the best example in terms of Gazprom, but at that time I really was convinced that Gazprom was the key to a stable economy and a stable political situation. And I understood that I needed the support of two individuals. Again, I do not at all understand why anyone would insist that I had Chernomyrdin's signature. I never had the signature of Chernomyrdin. This is a precise example of the sort of power that I did not have. Chernomyrdin refused my proposal to become chairman of Gazprom. He refused it. This is the end of the story. Chernomyrdin was much more powerful.

SHIELDS: Now, you have brought these proceedings to vindicate your reputation; is that right?

BEREZOVSKY: Absolutely correct.

SHIELDS: You saw the program that night with your partner and you were shocked and angry?

BEREZOVSKY: You are absolutely correct. And the basic reason for this shock was that never before had people from this circle of society—and I mean people who have a clear understanding of today's Russia—decided to start a fight with me as a way of showing their loyalty to Putin. I am referring to Fridman, Nemtsov, and later Potanin. This really was a shock to me because it was the first time I had been attacked in this way. I had been through plenty of previous battles, including with Gusinsky when were competing for the TV market. And I battled Fridman in competition for—no, against Potanin in competition for Sibneft. But that is completely different, that is a story concerning business competition.

SHIELDS: And the people who would have seen that program that night could only have been people who subscribe to that channel; is that right?

BEREZOVSKY: You see, this is not a question for me. There are a lot of other shows to watch. Though certainly any number of Russians could have seen the show on tape. But you are correct that the main audience would have been people who had subscriptions to NTV.

SHIELDS: And people who chose to watch it that night in preference to all the other programs available?

BEREZOVSKY: You are correct.

SHIELDS: As I understand it, it is your case that this program has caused serious or substantial injury to your reputation?

BEREZOVSKY: I am sure that is the case. One's reputation is vital to anyone who is interested in working in politics and the economy. I am sure that it has already created numerous problems for me.

SHIELDS: You are sure? Give me some examples of how this program, you say, has caused you a lot of problems?

BEREZOVSKY: I will give you a simple example. I have a friend here who is not Russian. He is an investment banker and a British citizen. His wife is Russian. The very next day he called me and said, "Boris, I could not believe, I could not believe what—how could people, even in this small circle, how could they be so arrogant?" And he said, "I've heard a lot about Mr. Fridman, but I never imagined that he would use his influence in such a way." And then he said, "I do not—I cannot understand how he could dare to suggest that you ever used that phrase."

SHIELDS: Oh really? You are suggesting this person saw the program, are you? Did this person see the program?

BEREZOVSKY: Yes.

SHIELDS: What is his name, then, because we have never heard of this person?

BEREZOVSKY: His name is Jonathan. I do not know his last name...

SHIELDS: We have asked you to give us the names of all the people you know who saw this program. We asked you that last year, so that we could know who they are. And you have never mentioned this person's name before?

BEREZOVSKY: And?

SHIELDS: Well, why not? When you were asked who has seen this program?

BEREZOVSKY: Because there are people who I want to be involved and there are people I do not want to be involved in this matter.

SHIELDS: So you pick and choose who is involved?

BEREZOVSKY: No, because not every person wants to be present here. And you understand why. Because people who have business interests in Russia are afraid that their involvement in this case will end up destroying their businesses. Sometimes I have trouble finding lawyers, because they're also afraid. They work in firms in Moscow, and they understand perfectly well that if they take me on as a client, they might never work in Russia again. What we are discussing today is not a game.

SHIELDS: Well, Mr. Berezovsky, I suggest you suffered no damage whatsoever to your reputation…

BEREZOVSKY: It could not have been any worse.

SHIELDS: As a result of this program, and if you suffered any damage, it is deserved.

BEREZOVSKY: Okay, that is your conclusion.

SHIELDS: That is a conclusion?

BEREZOVSKY: I hope that the jury will come to a different conclusion.

RE-EXAMINATION BY MR. BROWNE

BROWNE: Mr. Berezovsky, you have just said that there are people whose names you have been prepared to involve in this case and other names that you have not.

BEREZOVSKY: Correct.

BROWNE: In relation to those that you have decided not to involve, what is the reason for that?

BEREZOVSKY: I just mentioned that because these people have business in Russia they are afraid to support me here, understanding that this business would be under attack by the Russian government.

BROWNE: And have there been people that you have tried to approach who have refused to assist you?

BEREZOVSKY: No, I have enough experience not to make a proposal that will be refused.

BROWNE: Mr. Shields put to you that you like to get what you want. Are you a man who is prepared to do anything to get what you want?

BEREZOVSKY: My life is a perfect example of the fact that I have never done anything against the law in Russia. No single court in the world has ever proved that I have done something illegal. I have a clear understanding of my goals in life, and at the same time I have a clear understanding of what it means to stay in harmony with yourself—with yourself, with your soul, with your heart—and within the frame of law.

BROWNE: It has been suggested that you had immense power through the media and it was put that you had effective control of *Kommersant*, the independent business newspaper. Did you have, to use Mr. Shields's words, "effective control" of the journalism in *Kommersant*?

BEREZOVSKY: The wife of one of my friends is a journalist at *Kommersant*, and because—and this is absolutely true, Mr. Shields—because of the power I have at ORT, and the way that I used this leverage to crush communism, I have tried to be absolutely, how do you say, Kosher, in my relations to the rest of the mass media. And I read the statement of Mr. Fridman where he says that he was concerned about Berezovsky taking control of *Kommersant*, that *Kommersant* would lose its independence. And I was very happy that Fridman, in his duel with Mr. Vasiliev, stated that *Kommersant* is the number one newspaper in Russia. This shows that Fridman is not very good at predicting things. And I am delighted that Mr. Fridman admits that *Kommersant* is still the number one newspaper in Russia, in spite of the fact that I have been the owner of *Kommersant* since 1999.

BROWNE: And of course Mr. Fridman was speaking five years later in 2004?

BEREZOVSKY: This was in 2005, as I understand.

BROWNE: No, four.

BEREZOVSKY: No, this is NTV.

BROWNE: It was October 2004. The chronology of all of this...

BEREZOVSKY: 2004, I am sorry.

BROWNE: Is a bit complicated, all of this, and I just wanted to put it into... You have just mentioned ORT and said that your influence over

ORT was designed to oppose the Communists taking back power. Can I just ask you, in relation to the appointment of the general manager who you said made all the decisions, whose was the power to appoint the general manager?

BEREZOVSKY: Only the president. It was solely his choice. The board of ORT had no power to refuse, and the board was also not able to propose another candidate.

BROWNE: Mr. Shields…

BEREZOVSKY: And moreover, the board of ORT was not able to fire the manager. Only the president had the ability to fire the general manager.

BROWNE: Mr. Berezovsky, Mr. Shields put to you what he said was the manifesto of "Yedinstvo," Unity. Did you have any hand in drafting this document?

BEREZOVSKY: You may or may not believe me, but this was the first time I've ever seen it. And again because I want to stress, it was—it is—again, it is complicated to understand. The basic idea for this movement was not to present any ideology. This was very important. Because at that time people already did not believe in ideologies, because that mindset had been destroyed. And to be completely honest, I was surprised that this manifesto existed because I was against any documents that presented a position, because my idea was: Putin, and that is all. You may believe him, you may not believe him, but do not discuss ideology. That was my position. And I am really surprised…

BROWNE: Mr. Berezovsky, you were asked about paragraph 12 of this manifesto. Perhaps if you still have it there, you can have a look at it. You may prefer to look at it in Russian.

BEREZOVSKY: Okay.

BROWNE: Does this document talk about opposition to terrorism?

BEREZOVSKY: Yes, it is written clearly that terrorism is dangerous, and so on. And I said that in general I accept everything except for the last sentence.

BROWNE: Well, before we get to the last sentence, does it say, "There should be no place for terrorism?"

BEREZOVSKY: Yes, correct.

BROWNE: Does it say, "We are for the annihilation of militants?" Is that a correct translation?

BEREZOVSKY: Yes, correct.

BROWNE: Are you in any way in disagreement with those proposals?

BEREZOVSKY: No, not at all.

BROWNE: And then it goes on: "A demand must be made of the Chechen authorities first to hand over terrorists, free hostages, fully disarm armed gangs, and only then can there be talks on the political order and future status of Chechnya within Russia."

BEREZOVSKY: This is in a sense where I disagree, because it is not realistic.

BROWNE: You say it is not realistic?

BEREZOVSKY: It is not realistic, and that is exactly the point of our disagreement with Mr. Putin, because I constantly insisted that we should negotiate without any conditions.

BROWNE: The sentence refers to the freeing of hostages. Have you had experience seeking the freedom of hostages in Chechnya?

BEREZOVSKY: This may be the reason why I said that we should accept a negotiation without conditions, because I was with Mr. Rybkin, who was Secretary of the Security Council, who was responsible for the release of hostages. Yes, I have had a great deal of experience with this. I even personally obtained the release of two British citizens, at the request of British Ambassador Mr. Andrew Wood. He even presented me with a letter addressed to the Security Council thanking me for my efforts.

BROWNE: When was that? When you were Deputy Secretary…

BEREZOVSKY: When I was Deputy Secretary of the Security Council. All told, we obtained the release of 1,546 refugees—hostages.

BROWNE: So is it right, when Mr. Shields says that this document was advocating a renewed war against Chechnya and that you supported it?

BEREZOVSKY: That is absolutely wrong. This document does not advocate it. I ought to repeat again, only the last sentence is—for me, incorrect. For me. For the others it is debatable, but based on my experience, there is no chance to stop this war without negotiating—without negotiating with so-called separatists. And I am 100 percent certain that the current tactic is absolutely the wrong way to proceed—not to speak—not to speak to them.

BROWNE: Now, I want to turn to Gazprom. Mr. Viakhirev was, as you have said, the chairman and the chief executive officer, simultaneously, of Gazprom?

BEREZOVSKY: Yes.

BROWNE: What was Mr. Viakhirev's attitude to you becoming chairman in his place?

BEREZOVSKY: Complicated. On the one hand he was already, at that time, not a young man. He was extremely professional and at first my request was difficult for him. It is difficult for people to share power, so at first Viakhirev was not that happy with my request. But, being very professional, Viakhirev also understood that Gazprom had reached a dead end, that they needed to find new solutions for the company. And he was very familiar with all the companies—I want to stress—with all the companies that we had created and managed in different ways. AvtoVAZ, for example, is the only automobile company that still produces cars in Russia; not great cars, but nevertheless they are competitive on the market, because they are very cheap. All the other car companies shut down. All of them, without exception. This is the only car company to survive because of the professionalism—first and foremost of my friend, Mr. Glushkov. The same thing happened with Aeroflot. When we came to Aeroflot it was almost dead. I can give you figures as an example. The price for one share was $7, and when we left—when Glushkov left—the price for one share was $200. And I was absolutely certain that Viakhirev knew about these examples, so even though he was not exactly happy, he eventually accepted the proposal.

BROWNE: And was it intended that he would continue as chief executive officer?

BEREZOVSKY: Correct.

BROWNE: Now, the jury will appreciate that there is a dispute between you and Mr. Nemtsov, with you saying that you never got Chernomyrdin's support and that was why you flew to China to try to persuade him?

BEREZOVSKY: Correct.

BROWNE: Your evidence is as I have just described. But let us assume a hypothetical situation. If, as Mr. Nemtsov suggests, the board of Gazprom was faced with Mr. Viakhirev and Mr. Chernomyrdin wanting your appointment and Mr. Nemtsov opposing it, would Mr. Nemtsov's views have prevailed?

BEREZOVSKY: That is certainly a very hypothetical situation, but I will answer it again anyway—no. There is no chance. No chance that Nemtsov's position—I want to make this perfectly clear. All committees that exist at the top level of government—working with the prime minister or president—are there to be consulted, to present a position, and then to sign off on a decision. They may accept or refuse the proposal, but the president and the prime minister make the final decision. That is that. And if, let us say, Chernomyrdin had signed this document, and I had been appointed chairman of Gazprom, and if I would have been successful in that post, then Chernomyrdin would have been pleased. And nobody else would have been able to say or do anything against Chernomyrdin. If I had been unsuccessful, then Chernomyrdin would have taken a risk, certain people would have reacted negatively to him and said, "You are incompetent; you made a bad decision." And that would have been that, nothing more.

BROWNE: You see, Mr. Shields put this question to you. He suggested that if Mr. Nemtsov did not want you as chairman, it would be very unlikely that the board would overrule him. But would the board be likely to overrule him if you had, as Mr. Nemtsov claims you had, the support of Mr. Viakhirev and Mr. Chernomyrdin?

BEREZOVSKY: Not a chance, there is no chance. They would have absolutely backed the decision of Viakhirev and Chernomyrdin. Again, I want to explain to you how the board works. They are, in general, professional people. Nemtsov is not a professional at Gazprom, not in the sense of Viakhirev and Chernomyrdin. He has never served in this capacity in the company.

BROWNE: Mr. Shields put to you that you had said to Mr. Nemtsov that there was no escape from you becoming chairman of Gazprom. And you said that it was a one 100 percent lie. And you wanted to add a comment, but then matters passed on. Do you recall now what the comment was you wanted to add?

BEREZOVSKY: I've forgotten, I do not remember because this conversation did not take place.

BROWNE: It is said that not only did you threaten Mr. Nemtsov but in addition to that you insulted him in the presence of Mr. Chernomyrdin by referring to him as "this boy."

BEREZOVSKY: This never happened.

BROWNE: That is the preface to my question. My question is this. Mr. Nemtsov agrees that the two of you spoke together at the end of last year, 2005. How often have you recently had dealings with Mr. Nemtsov?

BEREZOVSKY: We had many discussions in the past, particularly when I was working on creating a liberal party, Liberal Russia. This party was attempting to create an opposition to Putin. And, as is well known, Nemtsov is opposed politically to Putin. He was involved for several years with another democracy party, the so-called SPS. And at that time, when I had decided to create another party, we discussed various ways of cooperating. In other words, I had the ultimate goal of integrating all the democrats together, but instead, as usual, they started fighting amongst themselves. I began to build a new party as a favor to one of them to show that I was truly interested in cooperating. But unfortunately it never happened because the two founders of this party were murdered. There were three of us who came up with the idea to build this party: Mr. Yushenkov, Mr. Golovlyov, and me. And Mr. Golovlyov and Mr. Yushenkov were killed. And after that the Kremlin started to play games inside of the party and ultimately never allowed the registration of the party. Back then I often times spoke with Mr. Nemtsov about these issues.

BROWNE: And Mr. Nemtsov says that at the end of last year, in other words after this action had been ongoing, the two of you spoke about Ukraine. Is he right about that?

BEREZOVSKY: This is absolutely correct because at that time it was—perhaps you know, there was a revolution, the so-called Orange Revolution, and I supported a lot of its ideas, and Nemtsov also was a supporter of the revolution. He traveled to Ukraine. I was not able to travel because I was still wanted by the Russian authorities. We did cooperate quite a bit. No, we didn't actually cooperate, but we did have many discussions about the revolution.

BROWNE: Over the past three years have you met with Mr. Nemtsov in London?

BEREZOVSKY: I believe that I have met with him in London over the past three years. And I am 100 percent certain that I met with him last year in Israel, and also the year before last in Israel. He had invited me to celebrate Mr. Prokhorov's birthday. He owns 50 percent of Mr. Potanin's share. We spent quite a bit of time together there.

BROWNE: Was Mr. Potanin at that birthday party?

BEREZOVSKY: No, Potanin was not.

BROWNE: Has Mr. Nemtsov visited your offices in London?

BEREZOVSKY: I seem to remember that he has, but I'm not sure. All visitors must register in the office. It is not a problem to check.

BROWNE: Have you ever entertained?...

BEREZOVSKY: Nemtsov was at my home...

BROWNE: I was going to ask—that is my next question. Have you ever invited him to your home in Surrey?

BEREZOVSKY: Yes, that is correct. And not just once. One time he even visited me with a group of friends.

BROWNE: How often have you entertained Mr. Nemtsov at your home in Surrey?

BEREZOVSKY: I remember at least two occasions, but maybe more. I definitely remember two.

BROWNE: In what, the last two years?

BEREZOVSKY: The last two years—two years ago and three years ago.

BROWNE: My Lord, I am not going to finish in five minutes but I might finish in fifteen?

JUSTICE EADY: I think it is probably better to finish at 4:30.

BROWNE: Very well. Can I just go on and see how far we get. I want to move on to Svyazinvest now. You said that Mr. Gusinsky created Svyazinvest. How did he do that?

BEREZOVSKY: First of all what do you mean by "created" and "how?"

BROWNE: Yes.

BEREZOVSKY: To create means what Mr. Shields mentioned when he started to question me. As he correctly stated previously, in the Soviet era, there were many separate companies, regional companies. It was Gusinsky's idea to build a united company because it immediately became more effective. Moreover, he combined—again I am not that clear on the details, but as I understand it, he combined their land service with their satellite service. NTV was the first Russian TV company to create satellite broadcasting in Russia.

BROWNE: Now, you told us that there were two consortia bidding for Svyazinvest, the Gusinsky consortium, which included Mr. Fridman and *Alfa Bank*, and Telefonica?

BEREZOVSKY: Yes, as I remember...

BROWNE: What was Telefonica? What is Telefonica?

BEREZOVSKY: As I understand it, Telefonica is a Spanish company which—I do not remember exactly—operates in the field of telecommunications or mobile phones. I do not remember exactly.

BROWNE: Did the competing consortium of Mr. Potanin have amongst its members a company which had any experience in the world of telecommunications?

BEREZOVSKY: It was not clear at that time because the West's interest was presented by Mr. Soros. Mr. Soros is known as a financial speculator, not a strategic investor. And as I understand it—as I remember, one of the reasons that Gusinsky won, in spite of Chubais, was that he brought along their strategic investor, not their speculator, simply to buy and sell a company. I remember this was one of Mr. Gusinsky's arguments.

BROWNE: What is Mr. Soros best known for?

BEREZOVSKY: This is a very tricky question because he is well known in this country. He was once responsible for destroying the financial markets in this country. And not only in this country, but also the markets in Malaysia, as I remember it. But he is a uniquely talented financier, well-known in the world, and he made many gains in Russia and—I am reminded of one very important thing, that Mr. Soros, when he started moving in to Russia, to the Russian market, was constantly asking me about what would be more or less profitable in this market. And I remember that he started to take an interest in telecommunications, approximately a year after this bid.

BROWNE: But just answering my question yes or no, did the Potanin/Soros consortium have a member with any experience in telecommunications?

BEREZOVSKY: I do not remember.

Wednesday, May 17, 2006

Examination-in-chief by Mr. Browne

Justice Eady: Mr. Voronkov, do sit down if you would like to.

Browne: Mr. Voronkov, what is your full name?

Voronkov: Vladimir Voronkov.

Browne: Are you happy giving evidence in English?

Voronkov: Of course.

Browne: How long have you worked for Mr. Berezovsky?

Voronkov: I have worked for Mr. Berezovsky since early 1996.

Browne: And what do you do for him?

Voronkov: I am managing his office here in London.

Browne: When did he first set up an office in this country?

Voronkov: It was in the middle of April of 1996.

Browne: How long have you been resident in this country?

Voronkov: Since September 1991.

Browne: And prior to working for Mr. Berezovsky in 1996 what was your occupation?

Voronkov: I have a journalistic background and I have worked for 18 years in one of the world's leading news agencies, ITAR-TASS.

BROWNE: Could you just tell us something now about NTV World or NTV Mir, as it is referred to in Russian? First of all, who in October 2004 was running the NTV channel?

VORONKOV: Well, I understand that that year the NTV channel went into the hands of the Russian state, probably prior to that, sometime prior to that.

BROWNE: Are you aware of the way in which satellite cards for NTV Mir were sold to people who wished to watch the channel in this country?

VORONKOV: Yes, basically I think it is the same principle as for instance Sky TV here in this country. So you can do it in two ways. You can either apply to your local dealer, who in our case was the company called Vitex, with Mr. Burkin. They normally install the necessary equipment, which is a satellite dish and a receiver, and they can also provide you with a card, meaning a subscription. The second way is you can call directly the NTV World center in Germany, which you mentioned before.

BROWNE: In Frankfurt?

VORONKOV: In Frankfurt. And buy the services over the phone. And they will send you a card which you can use with the existing equipment. So both options are registered either by the dealer or the call center and then are transferred into their database. And after the subscription has expired it is an automated system which actually enables them to send you a reminder that you have to either extend the subscription or cancel it.

BROWNE: When you say "for them," who do you mean, NTV or Vitex?

VORONKOV: I mean NTV.

BROWNE: Thank you. So there were four separate cards. Why was it necessary to have four?

VORONKOV: In the office we have two Russian satellite receivers, who are autonomous and work separately; one for Mr. Berezovsky and the other for the rest of the office, and the other two were actually supplied for his home at Wentworth Park in Surrey. We have been subscribers to NTV Mir, although with different providers, since 2001. Sometimes it happens that a card which was provided before does not work for some technical reason, and in this case we normally call the NTV center in Germany, in Frankfurt, and ask them either to replace the card or to fix the problem. So that might be the case, that the original card has become invalid due to some technical reason, and we received a new card.

BROWNE: Now, the new card that you get has an expiration date of February 28, 2005, although, as a sort of goodwill gesture, it seems that the company gave you another month. The company has extended the term of your subscriber agreement for another month. If one looks at the subscriber agreement, the jury will see the date of deactivation, March 30, 2005. So that is the extra month…

VORONKOV: That confirms that we have been loyal customers of NTV, so to speak, for quite a long time. So they allocated one month free of charge.

BROWNE: Mr. Voronkov, does the fact that the new card runs until February 28, extended to the end of March, enable you to say when the old card was acquired by you?

VORONKOV: Yes, normally it is either a six-month or 12-month contract. In our case it was always 12 months.

BROWNE: Now, what follows here are similar documents, members of the jury, to the ones that we have just been looking at. There are three pages relating to, I think, four or five cards. There is a similar group to the ones we have just been looking at sent to Mr. Sapounov at Wentworth Park. Who is Mr. Sapounov, Mr. Voronkov?

VORONKOV: Mr. Sapounov is the manager of Wentworth Park, which is Mr. Berezovsky's house in Surrey.

BROWNE: Mr. Voronkov, do you recognize what this document is a copy of?

VORONKOV: Yes, it is a television program for Russian channels. It is the Russian London Info, probably weekly. I think it is a weekly newspaper for the Russian speaking audience, for the Russian speaking readers in England. And this is the name of the program, the television program that is being discussed here in this court.

BROWNE: Are you able to say what the weekly circulation of London Info is?

VORONKOV: I would estimate something around 2,000 copies.

BROWNE: How long have you personally subscribed to NTV Mir?

VORONKOV: I would probably say now for more than four years; four and a half years.

BROWNE: Have you watched the program *The Duel* before?

VORONKOV: Yes, I have.

BROWNE: How popular is it amongst Russians both in Russia and in this country?

VORONKOV: It is quite a popular, I would say. The program used to be live at some point, which added some more spice to it, so to speak.

BROWNE: Why is it so popular?

VORONKOV: Because the people who actually take part in it, they—or at least they were able to express their views quite openly and confront each other in quite interesting dialogues.

BROWNE: What subjects were picked for these "duels" or debates?

VORONKOV: Different; mostly political, some of them economic, some of them just day-to-day life; but mostly politics.

BROWNE: And how do you assess the interest to the viewer of the subjects that the program dealt with?

VORONKOV: I would think it is more or less on a par with the English program *Question Time*.

BROWNE: In the summer of 2004, there was a crisis in the Russian banking system; that is not in dispute. How closely did Russians here follow the progress of that crisis?

VORONKOV: I think very closely because most people still have their bank accounts back in Russia and they have families, they have relatives, and they are quite interested in what is happening with their money.

BROWNE: We have some evidence on this subject already but could you just explain to the jury the extent of the reputation—how widely Mr. Berezovsky is known amongst Russian language speakers in this country?

VORONKOV: Well, I think he is very well known here in this country. I cannot say anything precisely about the extent, but I would probably think that there is—it is—it would be easier probably to name people who do not know him rather than the other way round.

BROWNE: Did you watch the broadcast on the evening of October 28?

VORONKOV: I did.

BROWNE: Did you watch it with anyone?

VORONKOV: Yes, I watched it with my family.

BROWNE: Could you just give us the details: your wife?

VORONKOV: My wife.

BROWNE: Anyone else?

VORONKOV: No.

BROWNE: Did you speak to Mr. Berezovsky about the program?

VORONKOV: Yes, I called him immediately after the program on his mobile and I actually asked him whether he watched the program or not. He said that he did and we actually exchanged some opinions on it, especially the segment which is being discussed here in this court.

BROWNE: What was the state of mind of Mr. Berezovsky after having seen the program?

VORONKOV: I think he was both outraged and upset for the reasons he gave already to these courts yesterday.

BROWNE: If you were in court yesterday, you will have heard me asking about the words that Mr. Fridman claims Mr. Berezovsky used to him on the telephone: "my vas zamochim." As a Russian speaker, can you tell the jury what sort of language that is?

VORONKOV: I can say not only as a Russian speaker but as a linguist by education. I have a degree in linguistics. Moreover, my previous journalistic background—my latest position in the news agency was Chief Commissioning Editor on the foreign desk—allow me to say that this is language, to put it mildly, inappropriate for somebody who is actually, you know, conducting a normal conversation.

BROWNE: But who does use this language?

VORONKOV: The criminal fraternity in Russia normally uses it, I would say, and it is a special slang language, probably not even very easy to understand for normal people. So it is kind of a coded language in a way.

BROWNE: Insofar as it can be translated into English, are you able to do so for the jury?

VORONKOV: It is very difficult because it is slang.

BROWNE: Yes.

VORONKOV: I can try and translate it as close as I can. So I would describe it as—if you translate it literally, the meaning, it is just to soak somebody down.

BROWNE: Soak?

VORONKOV: Soak. It is like when you pre-wash clothes or something. You soak clothes before you start washing but in this particular context it means, "We will wash you down the toilet." This is the meaning, but I am trying to be as close as possible.

BROWNE: Mr. Fridman says—and I am reading from his further information—the phrase—that is, "my vas zamochim"—is widely used in the Russian business community and means that a party proposes to damage the business interests or defeat another party?

VORONKOV: It might be widely used in the, I would say, criminal section of the business community rather than under normal circumstances.

BROWNE: The question I wanted to ask you is, is it widely used, as Mr. Fridman now claims, in the Russian business community?

VORONKOV: I do not know.

BROWNE: What was the reaction of Russians and Russian speakers when Mr. Putin used the phrase in September 1999?

VORONKOV: Well, Mr. Putin is notoriously known for his catchphrases, in inverted commas. I would say that this particular expression, which he used in public, on public television, would be seen as inappropriate for a common viewer or listener.

BROWNE: Do you remember, Mr. Voronkov, how Mr. Berezovsky reacted when Mr. Putin used this phrase in 1999?

VORONKOV: Yes, I do, he was quite appalled by the fact that, you know, the highest leader of a major country is using such language in public.

BROWNE: Have you ever heard Mr. Berezovsky use such language?

VORONKOV: No.

BROWNE: Have you ever heard him threaten anyone?

VORONKOV: No.

BROWNE: When Mr. Berezovsky is of a different opinion to somebody else, how does he treat that other person?

VORONKOV: Well, as he is obviously quite often of a different opinion than certain people, he maintains it as a conversation—it is an exchange of opinions and nothing else. So he is normally very articulate, well balanced. He tries to convince you of his argument, but there is no aggression in it.

Cross-examination by Mr. Shields

SHIELDS: As I understand it, you have been working for Mr. Berezovsky since 1996?

VORONKOV: Yes, correct.

SHIELDS: And you gave a witness statement in this case. Do you remember giving that statement?

VORONKOV: Of course.

SHIELDS: Of course. February 13, 2006. And in it you said you had been managing his affairs generally?

VORONKOV: Yes.

SHIELDS: Just tell his Lordship and the court, what does that actually mean, managing his affairs generally?

VORONKOV: That I am the manager of his office. I am his office director.

SHIELDS: Does that mean you run his businesses in London?

VORONKOV: No, not businesses, office.

SHIELDS: Office. Purely his office?

VORONKOV: Yes.

SHIELDS: Therefore you do not have a chance to see him conducting his business?

VORONKOV: What do you mean by conducting?

SHIELDS: You are present with him in his business meetings?

VORONKOV: Sometimes.

SHIELDS: Sometimes here, yes?

VORONKOV: Yes.

SHIELDS: But when he was in Russia were you present with him then?

VORONKOV: No.

SHIELDS: No. Never?

VORONKOV: In Russia not in business meetings.

SHIELDS: Or in political—meetings with other politicians?

VORONKOV: No.

SHIELDS: Before you joined Mr. Berezovsky, as I understand it you were a journalist?

VORONKOV: Yes, used to be.

SHIELDS: And you worked for a news agency?

VORONKOV: Yes.

SHIELDS: Is that a news agency called ITAR-TASS?

VORONKOV: It is.

SHIELDS: When did you work for them?

VORONKOV: From 1987 until 1995.

SHIELDS: Who owned that agency?

VORONKOV: It is a state-run agency, governmental agency.

SHIELDS: It was the agency of the old Soviet Union, was it not?

VORONKOV: It is, which acquired a new name after the collapse of the Soviet Union.

SHIELDS: So you were, in a sense, a servant of the government when you were working for TASS?

VORONKOV: No, I was not a civil servant; I was a journalist.

SHIELDS: But it was owned by the state?

VORONKOV: Well, it is a state-run agency, a governmental organization by its status. If I remember correctly, the initial question was how the Russian community living in England regards this particular program. This is what I am actually trying to convey.

SHIELDS: I did not ask that question, as I recall. Your counsel asked that question.

VORONKOV: We are in the same court.

SHIELDS: Now, you said in response to Mr. Browne that many people in this country in the Russian community would obviously have followed what was happening in the Russian banking crisis.

VORONKOV: Yes.

SHIELDS: Presumably those people would have been extremely worried if they had read in the newspaper, for example, that one bank was unable to pay out money owed?

VORONKOV: That is what actually happened.

SHIELDS: And that would be a very serious allegation to make, if one made that allegation against the bank?

VORONKOV: Well, people are trying to take care of their money. It is not an allegation. It is real life.

SHIELDS: Presumably you have had an opportunity over the last few years to observe Mr. Berezovsky's character?

VORONKOV: Yes.

SHIELDS: And you heard me yesterday suggest to him that he was an incredibly powerful person. Would that be right?

VORONKOV: "Powerful" meaning what?

SHIELDS: A very powerful person in Russia?

VORONKOV: In Russia, now?

SHIELDS: In the 1990s when you started working for him?

VORONKOV: He was powerful to a certain extent.

SHIELDS: When he said yesterday that he had enough life experience not to make proposals that would be refused, would you say that that accurately defines him as a person, that when he makes a proposal he expects to get his way?

BROWNE: No, that is a gloss, and very misleading. Are you referring to Frank Sinatra's song?

SHIELDS: No, I was referring to something else, which I will refer to later. The words he said: "I have enough life experience not to make a proposal that will be refused." The context was how many witnesses he could get a hold of. He made a general statement: "I do not make proposals that will be refused."

VORONKOV: Mr. Berezovsky has not made any proposal to me, that is for sure!

SHIELDS: If he did, you would refuse him?

VORONKOV: That is why I am here.

SHIELDS: You continue to work for Mr. Berezovsky?

VORONKOV: I do.

SHIELDS: And you have told us that you are not involved with him in his business affairs, you do not attend his business meetings?

VORONKOV: No.

SHIELDS: So you would not necessarily know what language he may use when conducting his business affairs, would you?

VORONKOV: I would, because before he opened what I would call a proper office, when he settled down in England in 2001, he was a frequent visitor to this country. He was still living in Russia. And when he visited this country I accompanied him all the time.

SHIELDS: When he was coming over in 1996 and 1997, was he conducting business over here?

VORONKOV: No, he was basically coming for, as far as I remember, for meeting different, I would say, people representing a different strata of English society, the City, lawyers and things like that.

SHIELDS: So he was meeting people in the City?

VORONKOV: Yes.

SHIELDS: That would be for the purpose of doing business, would it not?

VORONKOV: No. He actually was—telling him what was happening in Russia. He was kind of a—I would describe it as a consultancy rather than business.

SHIELDS: So you did not see him in a business context?

VORONKOV: No.

EXAMINATION-IN-CHIEF BY MR. BROWNE

BROWNE: Mr. Dubov, what is your full name?

DUBOV: My full name is Yuli Dubov. Yuli is the first name and Dubov is the family name.

BROWNE: Were you born in Moscow in 1948?

DUBOV: I was.

BROWNE: Have you been living in London since October 2002?

DUBOV: Since September.

BROWNE: Did you apply for political asylum in this country?

DUBOV: I did.

BROWNE: Were you given it that month, September 2002?

DUBOV: Yes, I applied for political asylum in October 2002, at the end of October 2002, and I was granted political asylum here I think early in October 2003.

BROWNE: How long have you known Mr. Berezovsky?

DUBOV: Beginning in May 1972.

BROWNE: Where were you when the two of you first met?

DUBOV: Well, it was my first day at the Institute of Control Sciences and Mr. Berezovsky was the second man I met there.

JUSTICE EADY: Sorry, I missed that—for which subject?

DUBOV: Control Sciences.

BROWNE: How long have you been working with him in business.

DUBOV: Well, he invited me to join LogoVAZ in, I would say, in May 1992, and since then until I came here, up to the period when I came here.

BROWNE: Were you LogoVAZ's general director?

DUBOV: Yes, I was general director of LogoVAZ beginning in March 1995, until October 1999.

BROWNE: What did the general director do at LogoVAZ?

DUBOV: Well, managing the company. I was responsible to the owners for the company operations.

BROWNE: And now do you work with Mr. Berezovsky?

DUBOV: Well, I do something for him. Sometimes he asks me to participate in certain political projects.

BROWNE: Are they solely political or are they something else as well?

DUBOV: Well, it is not something else because I used to be the chairman of *Kommersant*'s board, either from the spring of 2001 or 2002. I do not remember exactly. But I stopped last summer.

BROWNE: Do you subscribe to NTV World?

DUBOV: I do now.

BROWNE: Did you back in October 2004?

DUBOV: No.

BROWNE: Did you watch the program which is the subject of this action?

DUBOV: I did.

BROWNE: Did you have advance notice of what was going to be shown?

DUBOV: Yes.

BROWNE: And who gave you that notice?

DUBOV: I think that earlier that day I got a phone call from Mr. Vasiliev, who told me that he was going to appear that night with Mr. Fridman on the program.

BROWNE: So did you watch it?

DUBOV: I did.

BROWNE: Where?

DUBOV: At the office.

BROWNE: And did you watch the whole of the program?

DUBOV: Yes, to the very end.

BROWNE: Did you speak to Mr. Berezovsky after it was over?

DUBOV: Not immediately. He called me the next day.

BROWNE: Did he talk to you about the program?

DUBOV: Well, he asked whether I watched it the night before. I said yes, and he told me that he was absolutely distressed about what he had heard from Mr. Fridman, these allegations, and he would like to talk to me about it in more detail when he comes to the office, which he did later.

BROWNE: Did you then discuss it again later?

DUBOV: Yes.

BROWNE: What state was Mr. Berezovsky in?

DUBOV: Well, he was—when he called me in the morning, he was furious. When he came into the office, say two or three hours later, he was much more calm and he said that he wanted to go to court and he asked me what I thought about this idea. Well, I agreed.

BROWNE: Now, some time after the broadcast did you make inquiries about how widely the program may have been viewed in this country?

DUBOV: No.

BROWNE: Did you ask any acquaintances of yours whether they had watched the program?

DUBOV: I think that I asked a dentist to whom I go from time to time. And other people just came up to me in church or in other places where we meet, just to say that they had watched the program.

BROWNE: Were these all Russian acquaintances? A Russian dentist?

DUBOV: All Russians.

BROWNE: How many people, either because you approached them or because they approached you, mentioned to you that they had seen the program?

DUBOV: Well, it was the dentist, it was another person who lived not far from the place which I was renting at that time, and two or three people at church.

BROWNE: Did they say to you whether they were subscribers to NTV World?

DUBOV: I know that my—that the dentist and my neighbor, they subscribe to NTV World. I do not know about the people in church. They just told me that they had watched the program.

BROWNE: Were any of those people willing to be identified or to help in these proceedings?

DUBOV: I asked two of them. Unfortunately people in the church, we come and go, it's not the same people now as they have been two or three years ago. I asked the dentist and I asked this neighbor of mine who have been very unhappy with the idea of going to court.

BROWNE: Why was that? Did they say?

DUBOV: As far as I understand, they still have very close connections with Russia, and for some reason they did not like the idea of being associated with Mr. Berezovsky.

BROWNE: Why did they not want to be associated with Mr. Berezovsky?

DUBOV: Well, as far as I know—if you want my opinion, there is nothing really dangerous in being associated with Mr. Berezovsky on such a minor case. This is not important. But many people, they tend to think that even this connection could give them some problems when they go back.

BROWNE: Did you subsequently speak to Mr. Alexander Litvinenko?

DUBOV: Yes, I did.

BROWNE: Why did you speak to him?

DUBOV: Well, because we were preparing for court. Mr. Berezovsky was preparing to go to court and I understood that we needed witnesses, people who had watched the program, and so I asked Mr. Alexander Litvinenko whether he knew of anyone who had actually watched the program and was ready to give evidence in court.

BROWNE: You said a moment ago this case is not important. What did you mean by saying that? Important to whom?

DUBOV: Excuse me, I am not saying that this case is not important. What I was saying is that the connection to Mr. Berezovsky, which could be established during this case, is not important, is not really dangerous for people who have become associated as witnesses giving statements in the court. I do not think that is really dangerous for anyone. But people tend to think that the further they are from this case the better.

CROSS-EXAMINATION BY MR. SHIELDS

SHIELDS: Can I turn your attention back to October 2004? At that stage, I think, you were chairman of *Kommersant.*

DUBOV: At that time I was.

SHIELDS: Am I right, having heard your evidence, that you could not travel to Russia at that stage?

DUBOV: Yes.

SHIELDS: So you performed your duties as chairman from this country?

DUBOV: I did.

SHIELDS: Did the chief executive or editor report to you, Mr. Vasiliev?

DUBOV: Of course.

SHIELDS: So he reports to you from Russia to this country?

DUBOV: Yes.

SHIELDS: And you were based at the offices of Mr. Berezovsky; is that right?

DUBOV: Yes, that is right.

SHIELDS: And is it Mr. Berezovsky who had appointed you chairman?

DUBOV: No, I was appointed by Mr. Berezovsky and his partner Mr. Badri Patarkatsishvili.

SHIELDS: It is Mr. Berezovsky's case in this court that he is regarded as having effective control of *Kommersant*, or at that time he did?

DUBOV: Yes.

SHIELDS: That would be right, would it not? So Mr. Berezovsky and Mr. Badri appointed you chairman, and you were carrying out your duties from Mr. Berezovsky's office in London?

DUBOV: That is right.

SHIELDS: At that stage of course there had been the libel action between my client *Alfa Bank* and *Kommersant*. That had already taken place?

DUBOV: Yes.

SHIELDS: You were not happy about the verdict, the size of damages?

DUBOV: Absolutely.

SHIELDS: Therefore when Mr. Vasiliev was asked to take part in this program against Mr. Fridman, did he not seek your permission first or have a word with you about it?

DUBOV: No, he did not.

SHIELDS: He did not, and you did not see him at all beforehand?

DUBOV: No.

SHIELDS: You did not talk to him?

DUBOV: No, he called me on the day of the program and said that he was going to be on the air.

SHIELDS: We now know that the program was recorded the day before. So do you think he would have phoned you the day before, before it was recorded?

DUBOV: No, I think the first time that I'd I heard that it was pre-recorded was yesterday.

SHIELDS: You yourself do not subscribe to NTV?

DUBOV: No, I do.

SHIELDS: You did not then?

DUBOV: No.

SHIELDS: Did you have a television then?

DUBOV: Yes, I did.

SHIELDS: What channels did you have on your television then?

DUBOV: From first to fifth.

SHIELDS: Just terrestrial?

DUBOV: Yes.

SHIELDS: English programs?

DUBOV: Yes.

SHIELDS: This was a program which was called *The Duel*, is it not?

DUBOV: That is right.

SHIELDS: Where people express quite strong sentiments and words about each other?

DUBOV: Yes.

SHIELDS: And when you watched it, you probably recall Mr. Vasiliev accusing Mr. Fridman of being a liar?

DUBOV: I remember that.

SHIELDS: You remember Mr. Bashmet making some quite tough remarks about your newspaper?

DUBOV: No, I do not.

SHIELDS: You know who he is?

DUBOV: He is a musician.

SHIELDS: A very famous one?

DUBOV: Yes, a famous one.

SHIELDS: A viola player?

DUBOV: No, it is alto violin.

SHIELDS: It is the same thing. Did you record the program?

DUBOV: No.

SHIELDS: Were you shown a recording of it subsequently?

DUBOV: No.

SHIELDS: Or a transcript of it?

DUBOV: Yes, I have seen the transcript.

SHIELDS: When were you first shown a transcript of it?

DUBOV: I think it was one week after the program.

SHIELDS: One week after the program?

DUBOV: Yes, because I made a special call to Moscow, called *Kommersant* and asked them to provide me with a transcript of the program.

SHIELDS: And you say in your witness statement that some time after the broadcast you talked to other Russians who had seen the program?

DUBOV: That is right.

SHIELDS: Just pausing there, would these Russians have known that you had a connection with *Kommersant*?

DUBOV: These people knew that I had a connection with Boris.

SHIELDS: Did they know you were chairman of *Kommersant*?

DUBOV: No. Nobody knew that.

SHIELDS: You said they talked about the program. What did they say, "Yes, we have seen the program"?

DUBOV: Yes, "We have seen the program. What do you think about the words which Mr. Fridman used about Mr. Berezovsky?"

SHIELDS: That is what they said to you, did they?

DUBOV: Yes.

SHIELDS: When you gave your statement, you might recall, in April 2006, you did not mention they said anything about "what do you think of the words they said about Mr. Berezovsky?"

DUBOV: I did not think it was important to put it in the statement.

SHIELDS: I see.

DUBOV: Since I discussed it with them, what else would they discuss?

SHIELDS: When did you tell them, then; because you have known Mr. Berezovsky a long time, have you not?

DUBOV: Yes.

SHIELDS: Many, many years. What did you say, "It is all untrue?"

DUBOV: Yes, that is exactly what I said.

SHIELDS: So you told them straight away they did not have to believe what they had seen?

DUBOV: Yes, I did.

SHIELDS: Did some of these people see you afterwards? You saw them again?

DUBOV: I have not seen my neighbor for maybe half a year. I do not know even whether he is in England right now or not because he was working for some United States company. I am not sure whether he is still here or not. I am in touch, of course, with my dentist.

SHIELDS: I was going to ask you that.

DUBOV: But unfortunately I do not ever see these people from the church who I met.

SHIELDS: Now, but you see your dentist?

DUBOV: Yes.

SHIELDS: And the dentist knew you worked for Mr. Berezovsky?

DUBOV: Of course.

SHIELDS: And your dentist, you say, is one of these people who raised the remarks made in the program?

DUBOV: No, I discussed it with him. It was my initiative.

SHIELDS: Your initiative?

DUBOV: Yes.

SHIELDS: So you said to him: "Did you see the program?"

DUBOV: Yes.

SHIELDS: Did you say to him: "Did you see what they said about Mr. Berezovsky"?

DUBOV: No, I asked him whether he had seen the program. Then we exchanged opinions about this libel case, *Kommersant* vs. *Alfa Bank* or vice versa, and after that he asked me: "What about these threats made by Mr. Berezovsky to Mr. Fridman?"

SHIELDS: So do you remember when you had seen your dentist? How long after the program?

DUBOV: No.

SHIELDS: You do not?

DUBOV: I do not.

SHIELDS: You said to him it is all untrue?

DUBOV: Yes.

SHIELDS: And he knows you work with Mr. Berezovsky?

DUBOV: Of course.

SHIELDS: And he has not refused to do your teeth or anything, has he?

DUBOV: No. You know, pulling teeth is a very private thing. It is not a public affair, like court hearings. So he is not afraid of pulling my teeth.

SHIELDS: Now, you have also told his Lordship and the jury that you approached a Mr. Litvinenko.

DUBOV: Yes.

SHIELDS: I want to ask about the circumstances of this. Somebody asked you to go and approach Mr. Litvinenko?

DUBOV: No, nobody did.

SHIELDS: Were you not prompted by Mr. Berezovsky's lawyer?

DUBOV: No.

SHIELDS: You were not?

DUBOV: No.

SHIELDS: Are you sure about that?

DUBOV: Absolutely.

SHIELDS: Would you have a look at your witness statement, please, which is signed in April 2006? Look at that statement. It is a statement prepared for the purposes of this action. Do you see what you say: "I confirm the facts stated in this witness statement are true." And it is signed by you?

DUBOV: Of course.

SHIELDS: Let us read together: "I confirm that, prompted by Mr. Berezovsky's lawyer, Clare Gill, I asked a mutual friend of myself and Mr. Berezovsky." So is it right or is it wrong?

DUBOV: This is right. What I said—let me explain. Of course, when we started preparing the case, I was asked by Clare Gill and by other lawyers whether I do know any witnesses who watched the program and are prepared to give evidence in court. But nobody prompted me to ask Mr. Litvinenko about that. I did it on my own initiative. Nobody asked me to prompt Mr. Litvinenko.

SHIELDS: When she asked you that, was that in about July last year?

DUBOV: I do not know.

SHIELDS: Let us try and think about it. Would you accept it may well have been in July of last year?

DUBOV: It could be, I do not remember.

SHIELDS: The reason I am asking you that is because the program was broadcast in October 2004 and you were being asked, I suggest to you, in about July, about nine months later.

DUBOV: I do not remember. You know, I think that I got involved in this case several days after the broadcast and I don't think that such an important issue as a witness statement could have been postponed for nine months. I am not sure about July or how late after the broadcast it happened but I do not think that it took nine months.

SHIELDS: You cannot remember when it was. Was it several months afterwards, do you think?

DUBOV: I do not remember, I just really do not remember.

SHIELDS: I will suggest to you it may well have been around July 2005, about nine months after the program was broadcast?

DUBOV: Is this a question?

SHIELDS: Yes.

DUBOV: I do not remember.

SHIELDS: And you, prompted by Clare Gill to find witnesses, of your own accord asked Mr. Litvinenko?

DUBOV: Yes.

SHIELDS: Why did you choose Mr. Litvinenko to go out and do this exercise?

DUBOV: It was just an idea because Mr. Litvinenko comes to the office from time to time. We discuss different issues and somehow the—this particular topic of the NTV broadcast came up into our discussion and then I said to Mr. Litvinenko: "Do you know anyone who actually watched the program and is prepared to give evidence in court?"

SHIELDS: Did he know about the program?

DUBOV: Yes he did.

SHIELDS: How did he know about the program?

DUBOV: I do not know.

SHIELDS: You do not know?

DUBOV: I do not.

SHIELDS: Did he know what you were talking about?

DUBOV: Yes.

SHIELDS: Did he say "I remember that program?"

DUBOV: Yes, he did. This is the impression I got.

SHIELDS: So what were your instructions to Mr. Litvinenko? Did you give him a transcript or a video of the program?

DUBOV: I do not remember.

SHIELDS: You do not remember?

DUBOV: I do not remember.

SHIELDS: Do you think you might have done?

DUBOV: Could be but I do not remember.

SHIELDS: Did you have one in your possession at that stage, either a video or the transcript?

DUBOV: It was in my files.

SHIELDS: A transcript?

DUBOV: The transcript and the tape recording.

SHIELDS: And the tape recording?

DUBOV: Yes.

SHIELDS: When did you get the tape recording?

DUBOV: It was sent to me from Moscow.

SHIELDS: So you had a tape recording from Moscow and you had a transcript?

DUBOV: That is right.

SHIELDS: Try and think about this: Did you give either or both to Mr. Litvinenko?

DUBOV: I do not remember.

SHIELDS: But you might have done?

DUBOV: Of course. It was not classified information so there was nothing to keep me from that. I just do not remember whether I did or not.

SHIELDS: So you said to Mr. Litvinenko: "Would you go out and try and find people who may have seen this program."

DUBOV: Yes, that is right, some words to this effect.

SHIELDS: That was what you had been asked to do by the claimant's, Mr. Berezovsky's, solicitors to try to find witnesses?

DUBOV: Yes.

SHIELDS: Did you give Mr. Berezovsky's lawyer the name of the dentist or anything like that?

DUBOV: No, because, before mentioning anything to anybody, I called him and asked whether he would be a witness in court, to give evidence in court, and he told me that he goes to Moscow every month, he has some important clients there, he would not like to be associated with Mr. Berezovsky. He agreed with me that what was said by Mr. Fridman could possibly be wrong but that he was not prepared to be a witness in court.

SHIELDS: So you left it to Mr. Litvinenko to try to find the witnesses?

DUBOV: Yes.

SHIELDS: Did he report back to you?

DUBOV: Yes, he did.

SHIELDS: And did you ask him how he was going to find them?

DUBOV: He called me several days later after I asked him to do it and said that he was going to visit Russian shops here because he knows some managers in Russian shops and he would ask the Russian customers who visit these shops, and this is what he was going to do. I said, "That is fine."

SHIELDS: He was going to do it as a favor to you?

DUBOV: Yes.

SHIELDS: He was not going to be paid or anything like that?

DUBOV: By me?

SHIELDS: No, by anybody. He was going to go around and try and find people who had seen the program?

DUBOV: As far as I know.

SHIELDS: Because, other than those people you have told us about, the dentist and one or two people in the church, you knew no one else yourself?

DUBOV: No.

EXAMINATION-IN-CHIEF BY MR. BROWNE

BROWNE: My Lord, for this witness we require an interpreter. Mr. Litvinenko, what is your full name?

LITVINENKO: My name is Alexander Litvinenko. Litvinenko is my surname, Alexander is my first name.

BROWNE: How well do you speak English?

LITVINENKO: My English is good enough. I can hold simple conversations. I need a translator here. I would like to both receive questions and answer questions through the interpreter. To avoid any ambiguity.

BROWNE: I quite understand, that is perfectly reasonable. Were you born in Russia, Mr. Litvinenko?

LITVINENKO: Yes.

BROWNE: How old are you now?

LITVINENKO: 43.

BROWNE: How long have you been living in the United Kingdom?

LITVINENKO: Five years and about four months.

BROWNE: When you came to this country, did you apply for political asylum?

LITVINENKO: Yes, I was granted political asylum in 2001, it was granted to me by the Home Office.

BROWNE: Prior to that have you served in the counter intelligence agencies of the KGB?

LITVINENKO: Yes, I worked for the KGB for almost 20 years. I was lieutenant colonel and deputy head of the most covert department of the FSB.

BROWNE: Is the FSB the successor to the KGB?

LITVINENKO: Basically, yes, it was the same organization, just under a different name.

BROWNE: In October 2004 did you have a subscription to NTV World?

LITVINENKO: Yes, I did have a satellite dish.

BROWNE: But I think it is right you did not watch the program.

LITVINENKO: No, I did not. I do not particularly like watching Russian programs.

BROWNE: In the course of last year were you approached by Mr. Dubov about this court case?

LITVINENKO: Yes, Mr. Dubov spoke to me and asked me if I knew anybody who had watched this program.

BROWNE: Do you remember, Mr. Litvinenko, when Mr. Dubov approached you with that question?

LITVINENKO: Some time in summer, last year, I believe.

BROWNE: What did you do in response to Mr. Dubov's question?

LITVINENKO: I did ask people, and they were visibly shaken by it. And whenever I asked anyone about appearing in court, they became frightened.

BROWNE: Do you remember what sort of people you made inquiries with?

LITVINENKO: I would not like to mention them because I am 100 percent certain that the minutes of this hearing will end up on the table of the Russian special intelligence services and if you are interested to know why I am so sure or why I would not like to mention it, I can explain. I could explain in some detail if you are interested. I can only give you the name of one lady who lives here in London, as an example. This lady came to see us. She is a friend of my wife. And I asked her if she had seen the program. She said, yes, she had seen the program because she was visiting another house where it was on—she is Russian as well. So I asked her to come to the solicitors and give testimony—to tell them that she had seen the program. She agreed at first, but the next morning, after she had left, I found a note from her. I can produce this note. The note said: "Sasha, I am sorry but I am too scared." And I can understand because I can give examples of Russian citizens who have taken their cases to Strasbourg, to the court, and they end up murdered. I can give you the names of those people. If you are interested in hearing those names and the details of who, when, and where they were killed.

CROSS-EXAMINATION BY MR. SHIELDS

SHIELDS: Mr. Litvinenko, could you have a look at your witness statement we saw this morning. You see that statement, Mr. Litvinenko, is in English.

LITVINENKO: Yes.

SHIELDS: You see it has your signature, "Alexander Litvinenko" and it says: "I confirm the facts stated in this witness statement are true." It is right, Mr. Litvinenko, that you cannot write in English?

LITVINENKO: No, I do not do it very well.

SHIELDS: Thank you. Therefore I just want to clarify a question I asked you this morning. Did you make this statement in Russian?

LITVINENKO: Yes, I did.

SHIELDS: A written statement?

LITVINENKO: Yes, in writing.

SHIELDS: In writing. In manuscript or was it typed?

LITVINENKO: In manuscript.

SHIELDS: In manuscript. Was anyone with you when you made that statement?

LITVINENKO: No.

SHIELDS: Who did you give that statement to?

LITVINENKO: To Mr. Dubov.

SHIELDS: And when did you see this statement, which you signed, for the first time?

LITVINENKO: Shortly after I actually handed in the statement in Russian.

SHIELDS: Did you check this statement against an original statement you gave in Russian?

LITVINENKO: To the extent my English enabled me to do that.

SHIELDS: That is all?

LITVINENKO: It is not difficult; it is a rather simple text, so I just looked over it and I thought that it was all correct. I am not a professional translator so it is possible that some of the words have alternate meanings.

SHIELDS: Do you remember what happened to the statement you made in Russian?

LITVINENKO: What do you mean, "happened?"

SHIELDS: Where is it?

LITVINENKO: As I told you, I gave it to Mr. Dubov.

SHIELDS: My Lord, the only matter that is outstanding is whether I would be entitled to ask to see the statement of Mr. Dubov, which he apparently has possession of, or may have possession of.

I am calling Mr. Fridman tomorrow and I assume he will be cross-examined for the entire day. Mr. Aven is arriving tomorrow and then Mr. Nemtsov is here and then—I was hoping to get through those then—we can resolve this—we would like to have Mr. Potanin in last and we have asked him to stand by, we will notify him and he will be ready in Russia.

BROWNE: I think I have said already to my learned friend that I cannot possibly guarantee that we will have finished Nemtsov by the weekend.

SHIELDS: We have accepted that but what we have decided to do is—we do not want to upset the logical running order as far as we are concerned, and Mr. Potanin, as I understand, has agreed to make himself available provided we can give him some form of reasonable notice.

Thursday, May 18, 2006

FURTHER EXAMINATION-IN-CHIEF BY MR. BROWNE

BROWNE: My Lord, on day 2, the 16th, in the course of his cross-examination, Mr. Berezovsky told Mr. Shields that he thought that the same person, Mr. Viakhirev, was chairman and CEO of Gazprom. What he actually said was: "At that time, as I remember, but you may correct me, the same person, Mr. Viakhirev was chairman of the company and CEO, as I remember. You may correct me." Since May 16th, Mr. Berezovsky has recalled that in fact Mr. Viakhirev was only deputy chairman. He was anxious that that should be put right.

JUSTICE EADY: Members of the jury, just before Mr. Shields does open his case, which I indicated to you yesterday was next in the program, Mr. Berezovsky wishes to clarify or correct one part of his evidence, which will not take very long but he is going back into the witness box for that purpose now.

BROWNE: Mr. Berezovsky, you and the interpreter are still under oath, of course. Mr. Berezovsky, the matter I wanted to correct was this: on May 16, the second day of this trial, in the course of your cross-examination you referred to a Mr. Viakhirev and you said this:

"At that time, as I remember, but you [addressing Mr. Shields] may correct me, the same person, Mr. Viakhirev was chairman of the company and CEO, as I remember. You may correct me."

JUSTICE EADY: Meaning chief executive officer?

BROWNE: Yes. Meaning chief executive officer, yes. Now, Mr. Berezovsky, since you gave that evidence two days ago, have you considered again the question of whether Mr. Viakhirev was simultaneously chairman of Gazprom and its chief executive officer?

BEREZOVSKY: Yes, you are absolutely correct. I'm constantly going back over the information that is presented to the jury and to your Lordship. Yesterday evening I took information from the Internet, which was published July 1, 1997, and if this information is correct, I made a mistake. Viakhirev at that time was CEO and at the same time deputy chairman of the board, and Mr. Kazakov, who at that time was the First Deputy of the administration of the President of Russia, was chairman of the board. He was nominated in 1996 and was re-elected in 1998. This means that—we were discussing 1997—I was mistaken, it is my fault, I was not sure of the positions. This is why I included, "please correct me if I am wrong," and I wanted to mention that.

FURTHER CROSS-EXAMINATION BY MR. SHIELDS

SHIELDS: Briefly so I can get this absolutely clear, Mr. Berezovsky, Mr. Kazakov was chairman of the board.

BEREZOVSKY: Correct.

SHIELDS: He had been appointed in 1996?

BEREZOVSKY: Yes, correct.

SHIELDS: And he was the person who you wanted replaced by Mr. Berezovsky.

BEREZOVSKY: Correct.

SHIELDS: Mr. Viakhirev—would that be right—he was chairman of the executive board of Gazprom, the management board?

BEREZOVSKY: Absolutely correct.

SHIELDS: That is where we might be confused. He was chairman of the management board?

BEREZOVSKY: That is correct.

SHIELDS: But it was Mr. Kazakov, appointed in 1996, whom you wanted replaced by you in 1997?

BEREZOVSKY: Absolutely correct.

OPENING SUBMISSIONS BY MR. SHIELDS

SHIELDS: May it please your Lordship, members of the jury, the first act you undertook as a juror when you came into this court was to take an oath, an oath that you would well and truly try this case, and a true verdict give, according to the evidence. I stress that word "evidence," and I stress it to you now because there is an obvious temptation to succumb to the emotional appeal which has been made to you by those acting on behalf of Mr. Berezovsky to paint a picture of Russia under President Putin, which leads to the simplistic conclusion that Mr. Berezovsky is good, because he is a political exile, and that Mr. Fridman, who now sits here in front of you, is bad because he continues to carry out business there.

It was not by chance that the opening speech was so heavily slanted toward events which have occurred since Mr. Putin was formally elected president in March 2000, and that Mr. Berezovsky is portrayed to you as a solitary and almost saintly figure set against such a desolate political background. Members of the jury, I invite you now to resist such a temptation; to resist that appeal and to approach the defense, the defense case, which is now being put before you with the objectivity and dispassion which is the hallmark of English justice.

There are, I suggest to you, both unreal and real elements of this case. Let me start with the unreal, namely the strained meaning which the claimant seeks to put on the words of which he complains. Lasting but a few seconds, they must be judged in the context of this hour-long program, aptly entitled *The Duel*, and characterized, you might think, by ferocious, emotional thrusts and parries on both sides. In one second Mr. Vasiliev is calling my client a liar, and minutes later, Mr. Bashmet, a famous musician, is attacking the integrity of *Kommersant* and by implication the man who is effectively known to control that newspaper.

When you come, as you must do, to ask yourself what impression would this program have made on a viewer watching it throughout, and only once—you will remember this, members of the jury, that that viewer, that Russian viewer, did not have the benefit of having Mr.

Browne sitting beside him in his sitting room with possibly one hand on the pause button and the other holding a transcript.

Now, members of the jury, I suggest to you that no sensible viewer watching those words lasting but a few seconds would ever have thought that the remark, the "threats," would have conveyed the suggestion that Mr. Berezovsky was threatening physical violence. In that context, and at best fleetingly, the suggestion of threats would have been limited to threats, I will suggest to you, of mainly a commercial nature of the way he conducts his business.

What then is unreal? As I said, there are several unreal elements to this. In an action for defamation to libel for damage to reputation the claimant must establish the publication of the words, because unless the words are published to third parties your character or your reputation cannot be forfeit.

Now, let us take the claimant's case at its highest. At its highest, there are about 500 known subscribers to this channel. 500 known subscribers. And what we also know and we will explore further in this case is that many, and I would suggest to you possibly all, of those subscribers receive this channel as part of a package, a package offering them 10 channels.

Now, it may also be—we know in Mr. Berezovsky's case it is—that a viewer will subscribe to more than just Russian channels, he will receive other channels: maybe Sky, maybe, obviously, terrestrial channels. So the choice on any given night will be enormous. So you are being asked to make this leap, that on that night that subscriber was watching television, and on that night that subscriber chose that channel.

Two leaps which you are being invited to take. And that is why the claimant has strained to try to find people who actually saw this program. We know three people who saw it, Mr. Berezovsky and two people who worked for him, Mr. Voronkov and Mr. Dubov, but he would not be bringing his action because he has been lowered in his reputation to those people; they continue to work for him. So they sent out Mr. Litvinenko, himself apparently a former KGB colonel, to round up some viewers. As we know, there were viewers from Bognor to Gravesend. You have to ask yourselves, "Are there really this few?" And I suggest to you that they are a small number. Very few people watched it.

And the rationale behind the cause of action in defamation is that the claimant's reputation has been damaged, his business reputation damaged. And I would suggest to you that there is not a scintilla of evidence of any damage whatsoever to Mr. Berezovsky or in reality any hurt to the feelings of this man.

But, members of the jury, there was one element in this case which is starkly real. I suggested, you may recall, to Mr. Berezovsky, that if he had suffered any damage to his reputation—and I suggest to you it is a big if—that the damage was fully deserved. To understand that, members of the jury, you must turn your minds away from Russia under President Putin at the moment, and go to the Russia which existed back in the 90s, right up to 1999, when Mr. Putin came to power. That is a time, members of the jury, when Mr. Berezovsky, I would suggest to you—and it is pretty clear, I suggest, from cross-examination—aptly lived up to *Forbes*'s description of him as perhaps the most powerful man in Russia; financial backer and adviser to Boris Yeltsin. He was a man, you will have realized by now, who almost had the power to make presidents. And indeed you will recall when I took him through the rise to power of Mr. Putin, there was no doubt whose hand was in the glove which helped him put him in that office. When I make my closing speech to you after my evidence I will remind you of the very words which he himself said on television, boastfully, about his power.

Now, members of the jury, it is the defendant's case, and we do not shrink from this, that Mr. Berezovsky was a man whose political muscle and media strength meant that he liked to get his own way; a man who in his own words does not make proposals which are likely to be refused. This is the man who candidly admitted before you, almost unashamedly, that he bought ORT in effect to influence public thinking; that he had—and this he answered under cross-examination—the power to make and break reputations and to influence the way people thought.

This is the man, members of the jury, who having been appointed to high political office in October 1996, suddenly decides that in 1997, he should become the chairman of Gazprom, Russia's largest public company. "Move over, the chairman. Here comes Mr. Berezovsky." The man, we have heard, who had just been appointed the year before. This is the same man, Mr. Berezovsky, who we say decided that because he did not like Mr. Potanin's syndicate possibly being the winner in the auction—members of the jury what is an auction? An auction is an offer to sell which is won by the highest bidder, and the highest bidder in this case would be the bid that benefits the Russian people most, because the state is selling off 25 percent of its telephone company. He was a man who had a view about who should view (sic) it, and who made his feelings very clear, we would say, to Mr. Potanin the message was that he regretted going ahead with his bid. This was the man, members of the jury, who, already rich in media assets, in June 1999, wanted to buy *Kommersant* and found that someone else concerned at the concentration of ownership in his hands was interested in keeping ownership independent.

Members of the jury, what we say to you is this—when Mr. Berezovsky meets such opposition, when faced with not getting his own way, what does he do? He makes his displeasure very, very clear.

Now, members of the jury, you are going to hear from four witnesses called on behalf of the defendants. You will hear from Mr. Nemtsov. He was Deputy Prime Minister, you will recall, and the minister specifically charged with reforming the fuel and gas industry, a man whom you might recall whom Mr. Berezovsky dismissed in evidence as if he had no more authority than someone who read the meter. You will hear from Mr. Potanin of how it was made clear to him that his business would suffer if he continued to maintain his interest in bidding for Svyazinvest. You will hear from my client and you will hear from Mr. Aven, who, together with Mr. Fridman, is a substantial shareholder in *Alfa Bank*.

Now, members of the jury, what do all these men have in common? The easy retort would be, "They are all liars." Well, members of the jury, we will suggest to you, and you will judge them, you will see them, that they are not liars. What they have in common is that they have the courage to stand up to a man who has fallen in love with power, who now wishes to romance his past in Russia in the 90s, when capitalism and politics were finding their feet and when he had possibly his strongest pair of legs.

I will now call Mr. Fridman.

EXAMINATION-IN-CHIEF BY MR. SHIELDS

SHIELDS: Mr. Fridman, would you like to try to give your evidence in English?

FRIDMAN: Yes, I will try to do my best to speak in English but just in case maybe it would be better to have the interpreter.

SHIELDS: Mr. Fridman, that is not a microphone, therefore it is important that the juror at the back can hear you. Mr. Fridman, you are the first defendant in this action, and what is your position in relation to the second defendant, *Alfa Bank*?

FRIDMAN: I am the chairman of the board of *Alfa Bank*.

SHIELDS: And are you one of the co-founders of the *Alfa Group* consortium?

FRIDMAN: Correct.

SHIELDS: Would you describe what the *Alfa Group* consortium is?

FRIDMAN: It is for the time being one of the leading financial/industrial groups in Russia and we actively participate in the oil and gas business, telecommunications, financial services, retail and so on and so forth. So for the time being we are the largest privately owned group in Russia.

SHIELDS: How old are you, Mr. Fridman?

FRIDMAN: I am 43 years old.

SHIELDS: And you were born on April 21st 1964. Where were you born?

FRIDMAN: I was born in Lvov. It is the western part of the Ukraine. It is the former Soviet Union.

SHIELDS: Are you a Russian citizen?

FRIDMAN: Yes.

SHIELDS: And where do you live?

FRIDMAN: I am living in Moscow.

SHIELDS: And are you a married man?

FRIDMAN: I am currently divorced.

SHIELDS: Do you have children?

FRIDMAN: Yes.

SHIELDS: I will just ask you a few questions. Where did you go to university?

FRIDMAN: I entered the university in 1981. I went to the Moscow Institute of Steel and Alloys. That is the name of the university.

SHIELDS: What happened following graduation from that institute?

FRIDMAN: I graduated from university in 1986, and then I briefly worked as a metallurgical engineer in a metallurgical plant called Electrostal.

SHIELDS: Where is Electrostal?

FRIDMAN: It was in the Moscow region, a city called Electrostal.

SHIELDS: In 1988, did you found a cooperative, and what was that called?

FRIDMAN: We established First Cooperative, which was a private legal entity, in 1988.

SHIELDS: And what was that trying to do?

FRIDMAN: We started from, you know, very simple things like—because we had just recently graduated university—we hired students, we cleaned windows, we traded in certain consumer goods, and when development of the private sector happened in our country, we started to develop our business.

SHIELDS: Did that involve new technologies?

FRIDMAN: Yes. One of our first businesses was to implement new technology for the photo industry of the Soviet Union.

SHIELDS: Could you just tell us briefly how the business developed over the next few years?

FRIDMAN: It is a long story, but at that time it was pretty easy, let us say, to do business because there were few competitors. So we traded computers, we traded copy machines, fax machines. Then we started to import certain consumer goods from different countries. After a while we decided to invest our money in banking because we wanted to develop a banking business, and *Alfa Bank* was established in 1991. We also, in that period of time, started to export certain goods, such as oil, coal, and then we invested the money in other areas. *Alfa Bank* is the largest private bank in the country; we are in partnership with BP in a joint venture for oil and gas. We also have heavily invested in the telecommunications industry. So we are a fairly diversified group.

SHIELDS: Is there a Mr. Aven involved in the group? Just tell us briefly about Mr. Aven.

FRIDMAN: Mr. Aven was a well-known person in the country because in 1991 he was appointed as a member of the government of the first democratic government of Mr. Gaidar. When he resigned from his position at the end of 1992, he started his own private business.

SHIELDS: Just to interrupt you there; did he become a partner with you?

FRIDMAN: Yes, we met each other in the middle of 1993, and we started to work together then. We have been partners since 1994.

SHIELDS: I just want to ask you some questions related to your knowledge of Mr. Berezovsky, and we will turn later to the program. When did you first meet Mr. Berezovsky?

FRIDMAN: As far as I can recall, the first time we met was in 1994, the summer of 1994. So Mr. Aven introduced me to Mr. Berezovsky.

SHIELDS: Were they friends?

FRIDMAN: They had been friends—Mr. Aven and Mr. Berezovsky were friends since the 1970s.

SHIELDS: At that stage in 1994, was Mr. Berezovsky a well-known businessman?

FRIDMAN: Yes, he was already a quite well known businessman because he was the largest trader of Russian cars, and his company LogoVAZ was well known in the country.

SHIELDS: How would you describe your relationship with Mr. Berezovsky at that time?

FRIDMAN: We were not friends but we were, you know, familiar with each other.

SHIELDS: Did you have any direct business dealings with Mr. Berezovsky at that period in the mid 1990s?

FRIDMAN: Not much, actually. As I already mentioned, I used to work exclusively for *Alfa Bank*, and Mr. Berezovsky's group of companies from time to time worked with *Alfa Bank* as a client of the bank.

SHIELDS: At the time, in the 1990s, were you aware of what interests Mr. Berezovsky had? For example, other than LogoVAZ, were there any other companies which you knew of which he was involved in?

FRIDMAN: Yes, he also was—I mean, in the middle of the 1990s he also was involved in the auction for Sibneft, which was the oil company.

SHIELDS: Was that a big oil company?

FRIDMAN: Yes, it is a very big oil company.

SHIELDS: Did he win that auction?

FRIDMAN: Yes, he won that auction.

SHIELDS: What other interests did you understand he had?

FRIDMAN: He also actively participated in Aeroflot, which was the state-owned Russian airlines company. I was also one of the principal shareholders of ORT, which was the state run Russian TV channel.

SHIELDS: I want to ask you a bit about ORT. We have heard evidence about ORT. I understand that 49 percent of ORT was privatized by the government?

FRIDMAN: Yes, 49 percent was made private, and Mr. Berezovsky headed a group of the private investors.

SHIELDS: Were you one of those investors, your company?

FRIDMAN: Correct. We owned 5 percent of the stock.

SHIELDS: What happened to that 5 percent?

FRIDMAN: After a few years I sold this stock to Mr. Berezovsky.

SHIELDS: As far as you were concerned, who was it that controlled ORT?

FRIDMAN: At the management level I think Mr. Berezovsky and his partner, Mr. Patarkatsishvili, controlled that because Mr. Patarkatsishvili was the executive—chief executive officer of ORT at that time.

JUSTICE EADY: He is the one we are referring to as Mr. Badri.

SHIELDS: Correct. He is the one we have been referring to as Mr. Badri because no one can pronounce his name properly. I am asking your opinion here: how did you see Mr. Berezovsky using his media interests?

FRIDMAN: It is probably common knowledge that in 1996, Mr. Berezovsky was very actively involved—through his support of ORT and other media sources that he controlled, such as NTV, which was the other important and very influential TV channel owned by Mr. Gusinsky. It took a lot to support the re-election of Mr. Yeltsin in the election. Therefore his influence was huge because obviously together with Mr. Gusinsky they controlled, I would say, a significant part of the media market.

SHIELDS: Now, at that time—and we know from evidence that Mr. Berezovsky was also politically active?

FRIDMAN: Yes.

SHIELDS: Can you remember back in the middle of the 1990s what post he held, or you were aware of him holding?

FRIDMAN: Yes. After the re-election of Mr. Yeltsin in 1996, Mr. Berezovsky—it seems to me it was in 1997, if I recall it properly—was appointed Deputy Chief of the Security Council of Russia, and after some time he was appointed Executive Secretary of the CIS, which is the interstate organization.

SHIELDS: Is that the Commonwealth of Independent States?

FRIDMAN: Correct, the Commonwealth of Independent States, yes.

SHIELDS: Now, if you had to ask the question as to what Mr. Berezovsky's influence was with Mr. Yeltsin at that time, what would your response be?

FRIDMAN: He was an extremely influential person both as a businessman and as a politician. I would say that he was by far the most influential businessman in Russia.

SHIELDS: If someone said to you, "How powerful would you consider Mr. Berezovsky in the 1990s in terms of Russia," how high would you put him up the list?

FRIDMAN: Of course, Mr. Yeltsin was president—but among the other people, he probably was the most influential person in the country. Of course there were others, but taking into consideration his combined force within the media, certain capital access, and his political position, Mr. Berezovsky was a very strong political and economic force in the country.

SHIELDS: I am going to take you now to the program—and ask you some background questions before the program itself, briefly, about the program itself, *The Duel*. Is that a weekly television program?

FRIDMAN: Yes.

SHIELDS: Is it well known in Russia?

FRIDMAN: Yes.

SHIELDS: As we have seen—you were not in court when we have seen this—two individuals debate a topic of popular interest. Is that right?

FRIDMAN: Correct.

SHIELDS: And that debate is termed a "duel?"

FRIDMAN: Yes.

SHIELDS: Am I right in thinking that what happens is popular celebrities give their views on the debate at various points during the program?

FRIDMAN: Yes.

SHIELDS: Is it right—and I think this is agreed—that the program is broadcast as if it is live but it is actually broadcast the day before?

FRIDMAN: Yes.

SHIELDS: As we have seen, viewers who are watching it as if it was broadcast live can telephone in and express their support?

FRIDMAN: Yes.

SHIELDS: And someone called Vladimir Soloviov hosts the program?

FRIDMAN: Yes.

SHIELDS: Now, we all know that was shown on October 28. Before that program was shown—and we know the program was about the *Kommersant* libel action—could you just tell us briefly about that libel action where I believe *Alfa Bank* was the person bringing the complaint?

FRIDMAN: Yes. We had a problem with *Kommersant*, with articles which appeared in the summer of 2004, which consisted of certain accusations that *Alfa Bank* was in financial trouble, which inevitably caused a large number of customers to pull their money from the bank. Those articles were completely false. At that time *Alfa Bank* was in good financial shape, and we were fully meeting all of our clients' demands. But of course, for any bank, losing customers is a painful thing. So when all this trouble was over we decided to take *Kommersant* to court. We won every stage of the hearing according to Russian legislation and we received a certain amount of damages from the newspapers. And that TV program, which you mentioned, was devoted to the results of the court hearings.

SHIELDS: Were you invited to go on the program?

FRIDMAN: Yes, I was invited by Mr. Soloviov.

SHIELDS: What was your initial reaction?

FRIDMAN: My first reaction was that I wouldn't do it. I do not want—I usually do not participate in public spectacles. I am not a public figure. I am a well-known businessman in the country, but I generally try to stay off of TV and the radio. But because there had been so many accusations against us, brought out in this court case, claiming that we were simply following Kremlin orders, I decided to participate in the discussion.

SHIELDS: You said that—I think I got your answer right—there had been a lot of, was it, publicity to that effect? Was that in the media or what?

FRIDMAN: That was very broadly reflected in the Russian media and there was of course a very strong reaction within the media, because it was quite unprecedented for a large commercial entity to take an influential business newspaper to court.

SHIELDS: And was Mr. Vasiliev quoted in the papers?

FRIDMAN: Yes, he was quoted in the newspapers. He also gave an interview on the radio, on a very famous radio station called *Radio Ekho Moskvy*, where he accused me of being a tool for Kremlin policies, which is not true.

SHIELDS: Was there an article, of which you were aware, in *The Moscow Times*?

FRIDMAN: Yes, of course.

SHIELDS: "*Kommersant* ordered to pay $11 million." Is that one of the articles?

FRIDMAN: Yes.

SHIELDS: Then there is another article: "Director of Berezovsky's newspaper, *Kommersant*, says Kremlin behind $11 million libel suit." Was it well known that Mr. Berezovsky was the man behind *Kommersant*?

FRIDMAN: Yes, it was a well-known fact.

SHIELDS: Finally, as we know, this was in the *FT*, written by Andrew Jack. Do you get the *FT*?

FRIDMAN: Yes.

SHIELDS: They are the articles there, and as I understand your evidence you initially refused to go on the program, but what was the effect of those articles which you read?

FRIDMAN: Yes, just that I decided to participate in this program because I wanted to clarify our position. There was no political reason for going to court. Our bank had been seriously damaged, because when the story appeared, we were forced to put up more than US $1 billion of our own cash reserves to support the bank community. It was very damaging for us and the shareholders—for the customers, because it severely damaged the bank's reputation. That was the only reason why we went to the court. And we were delighted that the court supported our position. That all the "facts" published in the *Kommersant* article were untrue. And then came all of the allegations that we were being directed by Kremlin policy, that we were attempting to destroy the independent media, which is in direct opposition to my personal beliefs. So that is why, despite the fact that I am not a public person, I decided to go on the TV show and take part in a direct discussion with the chief editor of *Kommersant*. And again I was delighted that the jury, which consists of well-known figures in Russia and, of even more importance, public opinion, were on my side. The majority of voters who called supported me, which is quite an unusual thing because generally public opinion falls in favor of the media and not big business.

SHIELDS: We have reached the program now, Mr. Fridman, and do you have a recollection of the program now, two or so years later?

FRIDMAN: Yes.

SHIELDS: Fine. The jury has seen, as we know, that you stand in this room and you are called to duel. And it is, as it were, a duel between two contestants. And just to add a little bit more color to it I think each contestant is allowed to have two supporters, is it, for the duel?

FRIDMAN: Yes.

SHIELDS: That is what they used to have in the old days in a duel. And there are a panel of judges as well?

FRIDMAN: Yes.

SHIELDS: And you do not have any say in the choice of the panel of judges?

FRIDMAN: No, that is—it is the responsibility of Mr. Soloviov as the head of …

SHIELDS: Do you remember who your two supporters were?

FRIDMAN: Yes, of course. I had two supporters. First a very well-known violin player, Mr. Bashmet, and the other one was the famous rock musician, Mr. Makarevich. He is sort of the Paul McCartney of Russia.

SHIELDS: Who were Mr. Vasiliev's supporters?

FRIDMAN: As far as I can recall, it was former governor of the Central Bank of Russia, Mr. Geraschenko, and the advocate, Mr. Astakhov.

SHIELDS: Now, Mr. Fridman, as you well know, the action here is brought by the complaint of Mr. Berezovsky to you in relation to *Kommersant*, and in particular what he complains of are the words at the top of page 14:

"No, he threatened as usual. He said that." "He even threatened me; he threatened everyone. That is how he works."

Now, as everyone knows, that is an allegation which you stand by.

I am now going to ask you about the sale of *Kommersant*. Now, it is knowledge and accepted I think in this court that in 1999, Mr. Berezovsky was offered the opportunity to buy control or ownership of *Kommersant*. You knew of *Kommersant* at that stage obviously, the newspaper. Would you describe to us what you knew about *Kommersant* in 1999?

FRIDMAN: At that time it was, as it probably is now, the most influential business newspaper—daily newspaper—in the country.

SHIELDS: Can you remember, or do you know, when it had been founded?

FRIDMAN: It was founded by Mr. Yakovlev and also by a couple of his partners.

SHIELDS: And it was influential, you say, in 1999?

FRIDMAN: Yes, this was a very influential newspaper, especially in business circles.

SHIELDS: Did there come a time when you became aware that the newspaper might be up for sale?

FRIDMAN: Yes, I had heard rumors in probably spring of 1999, and I was approached by one of the partners of Mr. Yakovlev, Mr. Boris Kaskov.

SHIELDS: He was a partner of Mr. Yakovlev?

FRIDMAN: Yes.

SHIELDS: A partner in the sense that he owned shares in *Kommersant*?

FRIDMAN: Yes.

SHIELDS: What did Mr. Kaskov say to you?

FRIDMAN: Mr. Kaskov came to us and told us that according to his sources, Mr. Berezovsky had approached Mr. Yakovlev and was negotiating with him to buy *Kommersant*, and he was quite worried about that because, as you know, *Kommersant* shareholders wanted to retain their newspaper's independence. As I already mentioned, Mr. Berezovsky at that time controlled ...

SHIELDS: Would you slow down? At that stage you said Mr. Berezovsky controlled what?

FRIDMAN: He controlled two media channels. ORT, which was the main TV channel in the country, and also TV6.

SHIELDS: What was TV6?

FRIDMAN: TV6 was the fourth largest TV channel in the country. And also he controlled a few influential newspapers. He owned *Nezavisimaya Gazeta*, an independent newspaper. He also owned the *Novaya Izvestia* newspaper. So altogether—and as I already mentioned, he was a very influential businessman/politician.

SHIELDS: What was your reaction?

FRIDMAN: My reaction was—actually, the initial idea of Mr. Kaskov was to provide a financial loan to the *Kommersant* journalists, to *Kommersant* itself, to buy back shares from Mr. Yakovlev, effectively to provide financing for a management buyout of the company.

SHIELDS: What was your purpose in providing that loan?

FRIDMAN: We used to work with *Kommersant*, as a client of *Alfa Bank*, over quite a long period of time. So we were very familiar with the journalists and we respected the quality of the newspaper and its influence. We wanted to assist the reporters so that they could remain independent from any influence of Mr. Berezovsky.

SHIELDS: Now, did you meet with Mr. Kaskov to pursue the proposals?

FRIDMAN: Yes, I met with him a few times.

SHIELDS: When would that have been?

FRIDMAN: It was, I believe, May—April or May of 1999.

SHIELDS: As a result of those meetings, did you reach any kind of agreement?

FRIDMAN: We did not reach any formal agreement. We only discussed general conditions of the deal. This agreement depended on Mr. Yakovlev selling his shares to the journalists.

SHIELDS: Apart from providing a loan to the management of *Kommersant* as you told us, was there any other proposal on the table?

FRIDMAN: We also discussed with Mr. Chubais an idea to arrange a certain group of businessmen to buy shares from Mr. Yakovlev. The initial idea was to find a group of four to six businessmen, and then to distribute a small portion of *Kommersant* shares, which would alleviate any personal influence over the editorial policy of the newspaper.

SHIELDS: Can you remember the names of those businessmen?

FRIDMAN: We discussed the participation of Mr. Potanin, Mr. Chubais, *Alfa Bank* and, you know, a few others, but unfortunately because we did not issue any formal agreement we did not make any more details.

SHIELDS: If it is suggested that your purpose in lending money to *Kommersant* was ultimately to acquire it for *Alfa Bank*. What is your reaction to such a suggestion?

FRIDMAN: That is not true at all. We just wanted to provide a loan to them. We would make money on the loan and *Kommersant* would remain an independent newspaper.

SHIELDS: What is your view about businessmen being involved in politics and the media. What was your view at that stage?

FRIDMAN: No, I am not seriously involved in politics. I usually try to stay away from political intrigue. I do believe that business inevitably must cooperate with politics, but in a well-established system such as the United Kingdom, this relationship is already set. In a country like Russia, it sometimes creates a certain, let's say, volatility. I would prefer to keep my focus purely on the business issue. And that has always been my philosophy.

SHIELDS: Does *Alfa* have any interest in any television stations or other media? I am talking about at that stage.

FRIDMAN: Yes, we are currently the owner of the flagship TV channel STS. This week STS will have an IPO on the Stock Exchange.

SHIELDS: Is that an entertainment channel?

FRIDMAN: That is purely an entertainment channel, and according to our decision as the shareholders, since establishing the channel in 1999, as far as I can recall, we decided to include no politics—no informational programming on this channel. The channel is strictly for families—movies, sitcoms, and so on. It is purely an entertainment channel.

SHIELDS: This is not, I think, in dispute: Mr. Yakovlev sold his interest in *Kommersant* to Mr. Berezovsky, or Mr. Berezovsky and his partners. What happened to Mr. Kaskov's shares, which you have told us about just now?

FRIDMAN: As far as I know, Mr. Kaskov, after Mr. Yakovlev concluded a deal with Mr. Berezovsky, also sold his shares to Mr. Berezovsky because he was the minor owner of the shares. This was the natural thing to do.

SHIELDS: I am going to ask questions about which you have direct personal knowledge. I am going to be calling on Mr. Nemtsov about other issues. What was this threat to which you were referring on that TV program? Please tell his Lordship and the jury.

FRIDMAN: As far as I can remember, it was actually around June 1999. I received a telephone call from Mr. Berezovsky. I was in my office. He asked me whether we would be interested in buying shares of *Kommersant* from Mr. Yakovlev, or to provide certain financial support to individuals to buy their shares. I confirmed that this was true. He then asked me why we were doing this, to which I answered: "Because we would like this newspaper to stay independent, and for it to continue to be an objective and reliable source of information."

Then Mr. Berezovsky said to me, you know, "I should inform you that we are working on buying these shares from Mr. Yakovlev, and your involvement is getting in the way of my plans." I knew this was the case. I said: "Yes, I have heard."

He then told me that if we continued to stand in his way, he would—what is the word? Waste you. I do not know what it is in English.

SHIELDS: What is it in Russian?

FRIDMAN: "My vas zamochim."

SHIELDS: And how did you understand that?

FRIDMAN: It was quite clear. Of course it does not mean that Mr. Berezovsky threatened me physically but it was clear that he was explaining to me that if we got in his way he would work to damage our business.

SHIELDS: Did you take that threat seriously?

FRIDMAN: Yes, of course. Mr. Berezovsky was, as I already said, a quite influential person and of course I took this threat seriously.

SHIELDS: Did you talk to anyone at *Alfa Bank* about what Mr. Berezovsky had said to you?

FRIDMAN: Yes, I shared this information with my partner, Mr. Aven, who had known Mr. Berezovsky for a long time. We decided to continue meeting with Mr. Kaskov and talking with him about the loan. But eventually Mr. Berezovsky, as you know, reached an agreement and bought the newspaper.

SHIELDS: I want to ask you about another matter which is part of your defense of the truth in this case. I think it is right, in 1997 the

Russian government decided to privatize 25 percent of the telephone industry?

FRIDMAN: Yes.

SHIELDS: And I think the companies, the many Russian telephone companies, had been brought together in a single company called Svyazinvest?

FRIDMAN: Yes.

SHIELDS: Do you recall that?

FRIDMAN: Sure.

SHIELDS: Did you become involved in the auction for Svyazinvest, which was to take place on July 25, 1997?

FRIDMAN: Yes, I was involved in that. I was a part of the consortium which tried to buy this in the privatization auction.

SHIELDS: Can you remember who else was in the consortium and who ran it?

FRIDMAN: It was a consortium, including the—the main participant was the Spanish telecom company Telefonica. It also included *Alfa* and Mr. Gusinsky' entity called Most Bank. And Mr. Berezovsky was also part of the consortium. He did not participate formally as a person but he had struck a deal with Mr. Gusinsky to participate in that bidding.

SHIELDS: And who was part of the rival consortium?

FRIDMAN: The rival consortium included Mr. Potanin as the head of the consortium, and his entity Oneximbank, and Mr. Soros, who was a well-known financier from the United States; Deutsche Bank, and a couple of other portfolio investors.

SHIELDS: I think I am right in this, that the bidding was going to be by way of sealed bids?

FRIDMAN: Yes, that was—actually the way it worked is that we all sat in the commision's room, they opened the envelope that contained everyone's bids, and the highest bidder won the company.

SHIELDS: Was Mr. Chubais involved in the organization of the auction?

FRIDMAN: Yes, because he was the Deputy Prime Minister at that time.

SHIELDS: Can you remember any meetings of Mr. Gusinsky's consortium where Mr. Berezovsky might have been present?

FRIDMAN: Yes, I remember a few meetings where Mr. Gusinsky and Mr. Berezovsky, me and other, you know, people, participated and discussed conditions and terms of the auction.

SHIELDS: If someone asked you whose side Mr. Berezovsky was on, what would your response have been?

FRIDMAN: Mr. Berezovsky obviously was supportive of our side.

CROSS-EXAMINATION BY MR. BROWNE

BROWNE: Mr. Fridman, if you do not understand my questions, tell us and either I will repeat them or they will be interpreted for you. Similarly, if you want to answer in Russian and have it translated into English, ask the interpreter.

FRIDMAN: Thank you.

BROWNE: Mr. Fridman, you said a moment ago that you had always tried to stay out of politics. Is that really the truth?

FRIDMAN: Yes.

BROWNE: Is the reason you are saying that to contradict the assertion that you have invented these allegations against Mr. Berezovsky because you are in the opposite political camp?

FRIDMAN: No, that is—I have always had the same personal philosophy towards business.

BROWNE: Are you telling the jury that you always tried to stay out of politics because the suggestion is that you and Mr. Berezovsky are in opposite political camps?

FRIDMAN: No, I stay out of politics because it follows my own ideology, that is all.

BROWNE: So throughout your career, you have always stayed out of politics?

FRIDMAN: As far as it is possible for me as a well-known businessman in Russia.

BROWNE: Do you want to qualify this in any way and tell the jury now about any experience in politics that you have had or are you saying you have had no experience in politics?

FRIDMAN: It depends on what you define as politics because, for instance, I am an active member of the Russian Jewish Congress—if this is considered politics?

BROWNE: The Russian Jewish?

FRIDMAN: Congress, yes.

BROWNE: I see?

FRIDMAN: I am also an active member of the Russian Union of Industrialists and Entrepreneurs, where we discuss questions of legislation, economic legislation, first and foremost; we provide certain initiatives for economic law and so on. I do not know how to define this, whether it is out of the sphere of politics—it is in part connected with politics.

BROWNE: So apart from bodies like the Jewish forum and the Russian Union of Industrialists, which is presumably like our—have you heard of our CBI? You have heard of the Confederation of British Industrialists, CBI?

FRIDMAN: Yes, I have heard something about it.

BROWNE: It is a bit like that?

FRIDMAN: Something like that, yes.

BROWNE: I suppose people would have different views about whether they were politics or not, but apart from that you have had nothing to do with politics.

FRIDMAN: No, I was recently elected to the so-called Public Chamber as a businessman.

BROWNE: You see, you told the jury nothing about that originally, did you?

FRIDMAN: Yes.

BROWNE: And you did not mention it in your witness statements, did you either?

FRIDMAN: Yes, correct.

BROWNE: You see, in your third witness statement you said: "I have always deliberately avoided becoming involved in politics." That is what you said, is it not?

FRIDMAN: Yes.

BROWNE: And you said in no uncertain terms that you had not sought election to the Duma, the Russian parliament?

FRIDMAN: Yes, I am not participating in Duma elections.

BROWNE: But what you did not say in your witness statement and what you did not tell this jury when you were giving evidence earlier this morning was that you were actually a member of the public chamber…

FRIDMAN: Yes, I just mentioned that.

BROWNE:—when I pressed you about it. The public chamber was created by President Putin, was it not?

FRIDMAN: No, that was created according to legislation adopted by the Russian parliament. The initiative, as far as I understand, was created in the presidential administration, but it is a special law that describes the function and, you know ...

BROWNE: Does *Alfa Bank* have a website?

FRIDMAN: Yes.

BROWNE: In English?

FRIDMAN: Yes.

BROWNE: I imagine you browse it just as you would read the *Financial Times*?

FRIDMAN: Yes.

BROWNE: "In November 2005, Mikhail Fridman was elected to Russia's public chamber." The chamber was created by President Vladimir Putin. That was just what I was putting to you?

FRIDMAN: That is probably a mistake because it was created by the initiative of President Putin, but according to the law of the Russian Federation.

BROWNE: I see, but in Russia what Mr. Putin says goes, at the moment, does it not?

FRIDMAN: I would not like to comment too much about the political system of Russia, but as far as I understand, the President of Russia has a lot of influence over the country.

BROWNE: Yes, and the purpose of the chamber is to act as a kind of legislative reviewing body?

FRIDMAN: Yes, correct.

BROWNE: It is perhaps not a very apt analogy but it is a bit like our House of Lords reviewing legislation in the House of Commons?

FRIDMAN: I am not that familiar with the working system of the House of Lords and House of Commons, but in principle it is a consultancy body for reviewing certain legislation and providing certain advice.

BROWNE: It is in effect a second legislative chamber?

FRIDMAN: I am not a lawyer, but as far as I know—it is not a legislative chamber; it is not—we have two chambers of the parliament. One is the lower chamber of the parliament and the second is the upper, higher chamber of parliament, called the senate, and that is not part of the legislative procedure; that is just a group of influential and well-known Russian people, Russian citizens, who can advise legislators in making certain comments about legislation which takes place.

BROWNE: So being a member of the public chamber and commenting on legislation would clearly, by anyone's definition, be involvement in politics, would it not?

FRIDMAN: I do not think so because a lot of—the majority of the members are not politicians. For instance, we have a few businessmen there, we have a very famous sportsman there, an Olympic champion, we have a writer, poets, so on and so forth. So there are representatives of different groups of society who achieve significant results through their participation.

BROWNE: Everything you say, describing the membership, makes it sound like our House of Lords?

FRIDMAN: Maybe. Maybe this is true, I do not know.

BROWNE: We see on the *Alfa* website: "The chamber oversees official bodies and reviews and advises on legislative initiatives undertaken by the government."

FRIDMAN: Yes, undertaken. It is also probably a mistake, not only by the government but also by the parliament. I was elected by a charitable organization—a non-governmental organization—the Military Officer Family Members Society, which elected me to…

BROWNE: Officers' wives?

FRIDMAN: Officers' wives and relatives.

BROWNE: We will come back and deal with that in just a moment. The way in which the members of the public chamber take their places is as follows, is it not: first of all, there are in total 126 members?

FRIDMAN: Yes.

BROWNE: President Putin nominates the first 42?

FRIDMAN: Yes.

BROWNE: Those 42 nominees of Putin select the next 42 from names advanced by various organizations, including the one which is known as "Officers' Wives?"

FRIDMAN: Yes.

BROWNE: The 84 that we then have select the final 42. So the position with the Public Chamber is that the stamp of President Putin is put upon it because he selects the first 42. Do you agree?

FRIDMAN: Of course, Mr. Putin impacts his nominees.

BROWNE: Now, there has been for a very long time an association in Russia called "Soldiers' Mothers?"

FRIDMAN: Yes.

BROWNE: If you want the Russian, Mr. Berezovsky will supply it. Soldiers' Wives is a very influential lobbying group, is it not?

FRIDMAN: No, it is not a very influential lobbying group. It is just a charitable organization for which I provide certain financial support.

BROWNE: It has been a thorn in the side of the Putin government because they have constantly protested about the appalling conditions under which young conscripts serve in the military?

FRIDMAN: This organization which I was elected by?

BROWNE: No, I am sorry. I am talking about Soldiers' Mothers?

FRIDMAN: You said, probably, Military Wives.

BROWNE: I am sorry, I should have said Soldiers' Mothers. Soldiers' Mothers has been a thorn in the side of the government because of the appalling conditions under which young conscripts serve?

FRIDMAN: Yes, that is true.

BROWNE: So I suggest that the body known as "Officers' Wives" was brought into being in order to try and reduce the public effect of Soldiers' Mothers?

FRIDMAN: That is a completely wrong perception.

BROWNE: And you, as you have said, were a delegate of Officers' Wives. That is right, is it not?

FRIDMAN: Yes, I was a delegate of the Officers' Wives organization.

BROWNE: But you have never been a professional soldier, have you?

FRIDMAN: I am an officer of the Russian army.

BROWNE: A professional soldier?

FRIDMAN: Not professional. I am a reserve officer.

BROWNE: Of the reserves, but you have never been a professional soldier?

FRIDMAN: No.

BROWNE: And, of course, I do not want to make a flippant point, you are not an officer's wife either, are you?

FRIDMAN: No, I am not an officer's wife. According to Russian law, it is impossible for me to be a wife.

BROWNE: So not surprisingly your election caused a massive protest, did it not?

FRIDMAN: No, that is not true.

BROWNE: It caused protest, did it not?

FRIDMAN: No, there was a public event that was initiated by our competitors as a way of attacking me.

BROWNE: Sorry, who did you say was responsible for instigating this public event?

FRIDMAN: I do not know. I have certain suspicions but I would not like to state these suspicions without confirmation.

BROWNE: Could there not have been legitimate concern about somebody in your position being a delegate of Officers' Wives?

FRIDMAN: No, there was no concern. I have provided more than $1 million of financial support for the widows of the officers and soldiers who were killed across Russia and the Caucasus, and also for the relatives of policemen killed by criminals. So, therefore, that was the main reason why this organization elected me to the Public Chamber.

BROWNE: Was there no petition against your election to the Public Chamber?

FRIDMAN: There was no opposition to that.

BROWNE: Sorry, was there a petition or was there not?

FRIDMAN: Again, I would like to repeat what I said before: there was a particular public event that opposed my election to the public chamber, which I believe was connected with the activity of my, let's call them, rivals and competitors.

BROWNE: And you are not prepared to accept, are you, Mr. Fridman, that there might have been legitimate cause for regarding you as an inappropriate delegate to the public chamber in that capacity?

FRIDMAN: No, I do not think so.

BROWNE: The 1990s were a tumultuous period in Russia, were they not?

FRIDMAN: Yes.

BROWNE: And during this period people became very wealthy, particularly by making loans to the government in return for shares in what had formerly been state-run businesses?

FRIDMAN: Yes, part of the—people made money this way, that is right.

BROWNE: And you were one of them.

FRIDMAN: No, I am not. Mr. Berezovsky is one of that group. I never provided loans to the government for company shares.

BROWNE: Would Mr. Potanin count as one of those people?

FRIDMAN: Yes, Mr. Potanin was one of the participants of so-called loan for shares.

BROWNE: And Mr. Potanin, of course, is another member of the Public Chamber, is he not?

FRIDMAN: Yes, as I already mentioned, a few well-known businessmen became public chamber members.

BROWNE: But you are not being elected as a businessman, are you, you were elected as a delegate of the Officers' Wives?

FRIDMAN: Correct, but I was elected as a distributor of funds to that charitable organization.

BROWNE: Do you see, Mr. Fridman: "During the tumultuous period of the 1990s, Fridman was a close adviser to President Boris Yeltsin." Do you see that?

FRIDMAN: Yes.

BROWNE: That is involvement in politics all right, is it not?

FRIDMAN: No, I do not think so. I think "close adviser" is too strong of a description. I met with a group of—I have never met Mr. Yeltsin one-on-one. By the way, I have never met Mr. Putin one-on-one. I always met Mr. Yeltsin as part of a group of businessmen, including Mr. Berezovsky and a few other people with whom we discussed certain important questions of the country's economic and business climate.

BROWNE: You see, Mr. Fridman, this is the second, if not the third, sentence on this single page which you say is not quite correct, yet it is *Alfa Bank's* website, is it not?

FRIDMAN: Yes, that is true.

BROWNE: I suggest you were a close adviser to President Yeltsin and that amounts to involvement in politics?

FRIDMAN: I think it depends on the definition. I think if I met three or four times with Mr. Yeltsin together with a group of businessmen, which is a well-known fact in Russia, and we discussed certain questions of legislation or privatization of development of the banking and business in the country, whether it is possible to count me as a close adviser or not I do not know.

BROWNE: Well, *Alfa Bank*, your bank, the defendants in this action, would not want to deceive the public, would they?

FRIDMAN: We do not want to lie to our customers.

BROWNE: Or anyone else, I suppose?

FRIDMAN: No one else.

BROWNE: You say that you have never met Mr. Putin one-on-one. Do you mean just the two of you?

FRIDMAN: Yes.

BROWNE: You mean, you have met Mr. Putin any number of times, have you not?

FRIDMAN: Yes, I also met with him as part of a group of businessmen a few times.

BROWNE: And, indeed, your relationship with Mr. Putin was so close that when TNK, *Alfa's* oil company, signed a partnership agreement with British Petroleum, you actually managed to persuade Mr. Putin to come to London to be present when you signed the agreement?

FRIDMAN: He did come but I was not responsible for convincing him. That was the achievement of Her Majesty. She invited him for a state visit to the United Kingdom. And, by the way, if you are following this logic, I probably also have very close ties with Prime Minister Blair because he also participated in that event.

BROWNE: I know that, but the fact is that this shows, does it not, that Mr. Putin looks very favorably on *Alfa Bank*?

FRIDMAN: No, that is not the case. Because it was the largest foreign direct investment in the Russian economy it warranted an official visit by Mr. Putin, as president of the country. It was a good opportunity for us to sign the deal together with Prime Minister Blair and with Lord Browne as head of BP. So it was a chance for us to underline how important that event for the Russian economy and for Russian/British relations. So that was the reason why Mr. Putin and Mr. Blair participated there.

BROWNE: But when a head of state comes to this country on a state visit, there are any number of things that they can do potentially, are there not?

FRIDMAN: Yes.

BROWNE: From inspecting the Brigade of Guards to visiting a children's hospital?

FRIDMAN: True, but probably among all the other very important issues, participating in the signing ceremony of the largest British investment in Russia was also quite important.

BROWNE: But it was not simply the largest British investment in Russia, it was a joint venture with *Alfa Bank's* subsidiary, TNK?

FRIDMAN: Yes, it was a joint venture between BP and a group of Russian shareholders headed by me, including *Alfa Bank*.

BROWNE: And the reason that Mr. Putin smiled so favorably on you was that you are in effect his favorite oligarch?

FRIDMAN: That is completely untrue. I have never had a personal relationship with Mr. Putin. I never—again, I will repeat: I never met with him one-on-one. I respected him, obviously, as President of the Russian Federation, but I do not have any special relationship with him.

BROWNE: You see, you told the jury that businessmen, in your view, should cooperate with politicians?

FRIDMAN: Of course.

BROWNE: The truth is that in Russia today successful businessmen have to cooperate with politicians in order to survive?

FRIDMAN: What do you mean, "to survive?"

BROWNE: To continue making money?

FRIDMAN: I know thousands of businessmen who do their jobs and run their businesses on a much smaller level and are never in contact with the Kremlin authorities, such as the owner of a boutique.

BROWNE: You know very well that I am not talking about Muscovite grocers; I am talking about businessmen at your level of business, of whom there are probably not more than a dozen.

FRIDMAN: Yes, but I think for businessmen like me it is absolutely normal to be in contact with the political authorities because our business obviously touches on the interest of the state as a whole. I mean, first of all, its economic interest. So, therefore, it is absolutely logical to be in touch. If you recall this event, where Mr. Browne signed the agreement with *Alfa*, I would like to point out that, before we finalized the agreement, Mr. Browne contacted the Prime Minister and consulted with him about this transaction as well, from what I can remember. So it seems to me very common practice for big business to be in regular contact with the political authorities, to follow certain, let us say, general lines of the country.

BROWNE: Are you suggesting, Mr. Fridman, that Mr. Blair runs this country like President Putin runs Russia?

FRIDMAN: I do not know. I am not familiar with Mr. Blair's style of management. I am not well prepared for a discussion of that. I think, of course, Russia has its own traditions and its own form of legislation. However, I believe that its managerial system is, in general, a very similar system. Of course, there are many differences, but generally, conceptually it is very similar.

BROWNE: When you are talking about Russia's traditions, are you talking about the period going back to Peter the Great or a more recent period?

FRIDMAN: When I talk about Russian traditions, I am talking about the fact that the history of democracy in our country is very brief. So, therefore, the institution of democracy is not nearly so well established as it is here in the United Kingdom.

BROWNE: You have told the jury that you do not have a special relationship with Mr. Putin?

FRIDMAN: Yes.

BROWNE: That is your evidence. Mr. Fridman, we agreed a moment ago that *Alfa Bank* would not want to post anything on its website which misled the public. This is an article which appeared in a journal called *Institutional Investor* on September 1, 2003. Have you read it before? Is it familiar?

FRIDMAN: It seems to me, yes. It is one of the articles published about us.

BROWNE: Yes. And you put them there in order to promote the business reputation of *Alfa Bank*.

FRIDMAN: No, I think we just put it there because we wanted to have—to represent a different view of *Alfa* activities from different you know…

BROWNE: You are promoting *Alfa Bank* and I suggest—and I will make this good as we go through this article—what you are doing is trying to promote it by telling people how closely you are allied with President Putin?

FRIDMAN: No.

BROWNE: That is the purpose of it being there, is it not?

FRIDMAN: No, that is not the purpose of this interview at all. Some journalist requested an interview with me, so I answered his questions.

BROWNE: You do not have to put an article in a journal written by some completely independent American journalist on your website, do you?

FRIDMAN: No we don't necessarily have to do it, but we wanted to have opinions that differed from ours.

BROWNE: And you put it there because you hoped that people who want to do business in Russia will say, looking at your website: "*Alfa Bank* are the right people because they are close to President Putin."

FRIDMAN: I do not think so.

BROWNE: Now, this is an interview with you. Do you remember the name of the journalist?

FRIDMAN: No, I do not remember who the journalist was.

BROWNE: "We looked for really big businesses like banking and oil." That is true, is it not? Your enormous wealth has been based on banking and oil?

FRIDMAN: Yes, that is quite simple to explain because when we started our business it was almost an empty playing field for investments. There were few competitors, which allowed us to choose the direction of our investments. From the beginning we had decided not to get involved in any business that could be potentially limited by size. We chose to invest in businesses that had infinite possibilities. So that was probably the right choice for us.

BROWNE: "Eventually everything we own is for sale probably to foreign investors." Now, you hope to make yet further wealth, do you not, by selling off *Alfa's* assets to foreign investors?

FRIDMAN: If you have a reliable proposal we will of course seriously consider that proposal.

BROWNE: I will not although my namesake did. My name is Browne and you are saying whether I have a reliable proposal but Lord Browne did, did he not?

FRIDMAN: Yes, correct.

BROWNE: And that is an example of *Alfa Bank* making an enormous amount of money as a result of selling a share in its oil business to British Petroleum?

FRIDMAN: Yes, that was one of our transactions. Maybe one of the more successful but not the only.

BROWNE: And the point about this website, I put it to you again, is that you have put this article on your website so that potential foreign investors will think to themselves: "*Alfa Bank* are the people for me because they are a safe investment in Russia because they are closely tied to President Putin."

FRIDMAN: I'm sorry, I don't see it that way. We are involved in a lot of businesses that we constructed from scratch, such as the banking business. As I already mentioned to the jury, we established that business in 1991. Now it is the largest private bank in the country. We are the largest retail network, which we started from scratch. We are involved in a telecommunications industry that was started from scratch because mobile communication did not exist in the country. So we invested our money properly and what I mentioned there is that I am actively inviting foreign investors to participate in the development of the Russian economy together with us.

BROWNE: I am sorry, and I appreciate that this is not easy for you, but the point I was making was this: the reason that you made these remarks to the journalist and the reason that you placed the resulting article on *Alfa Bank's* website, is to advertise that *Alfa Bank* is a safe investment for foreign investors because they have a close relationship with the government of President Putin.

FRIDMAN: It seems to me I did not mention that. Where do you see that we have a close relationship with the government?

BROWNE: We will get to that in just a moment. "No matter how much wealth you amass, stick to business and leave politics to the professionals." That sounds like the Fridman philosophy, does it not?

FRIDMAN: Yes, I repeat it quite often.

BROWNE: "Mikhail Khodorkovsky appears to have gotten himself into deep trouble by breaching that barrier." We can agree on that, can we not?

FRIDMAN: That is not my point. That is probably the opinion of the journalist but it is widely spread…

BROWNE: It is not an opinion; it is a statement of fact and an accurate statement of fact, is it not?

FRIDMAN: Yes.

BROWNE: Mr. Khodorkovsky was thrown into jail for 18 months before coming to trial and was then given an eight-year prison sentence.

FRIDMAN: Yes.

BROWNE: So the statement that he got himself into deep trouble by breaching the barrier of intervening in politics is correct?

FRIDMAN: I do not know, I am not a lawyer. He was sentenced according to the decision of the Russian court and of course I am not a lawyer.

BROWNE: What I am suggesting Mr. Fridman, and we will deal with this in more detail later—is that his prosecution was the most blatantly politically motivated prosecution there could ever have been in Russia.

FRIDMAN: Maybe it is more obvious for you as a lawyer, not for me as a businessman.

BROWNE: Are you saying it was a perfectly legitimate use of the criminal justice system?

FRIDMAN: No, I did not say that, I said I do not know, I am not a lawyer. So I cannot make a fair judgment about the quality of the court decision.

BROWNE: So if I were to indicate what court decisions had been taken, would you accept that?

FRIDMAN: Sorry, say it again?

BROWNE: If I were to indicate to you the judgment of the British courts in this matter, would you accept it?

JUSTICE EADY: Sorry, in which matter?

BROWNE: In the matter of whether Mr. Khodorkovsky's prosecution was politically motivated.

FRIDMAN: It would be a very serious matter if the British court, which I respect, had a different legal position towards Mr. Khodorkovsky's trial. It would be very important for me as a citizen to know about this.

JUSTICE EADY: Can we just establish exactly why you say that the plight of Mr. Khodorkovsky is relevant to the issues in the case?

BROWNE: My Lord, because everyone in Russia knows that the Kremlin has only to mention the example of Mr. Khodorkovsky to bring people into line. You will remember the question that Mr. Soloviov made on the program. He says that the Kremlin can always ask, "Do you know Khodorkovsky? You are next." The ever-present example of Khodorkovsky is what keeps businessmen in line, toeing the Kremlin line and your Lordship may recall the judgment of District Judge Workman on March 18, 2005. The judge actually has evidence on the initiation of the prosecution of Mr. Khodorkovsky and Natalia Chernyshova, who is one of the two people sought to be extradited in the hearing before him. He says: "Some eight years later it seems that President Putin became involved and I have seen a report prepared by the prosecutor..." The prosecution of Khodorkovsky and his minions was not only politically motivated but also personally directed by President Putin.

JUSTICE EADY: I have read to the end. He comes to the conclusion that "there is cogent evidence that the prosecution was politically motivated but it could not be regarded as conclusive. It is necessary to examine the background." Is that what he goes on to do?

BROWNE: He then goes on to say: "I am satisfied with the evidence ... that the prosecution of Mr. Khodorkovsky was politically motivated." So the answer to your Lordship's question is, yes: "As the allegation against these defendants is on the basis of a conspiracy with Mr. Khodorkovsky, in my view it is the inevitable conclusion that the prosecution of these two defendants is also politically motivated." Then he goes on to deal with concerns about the independence of the judiciary in Moscow and something called the existence of a no-acquittals policy, which cannot have been a cause for much optimism for Mr. Khodorkovsky. Then he concludes: "However in respect of this particular case I am satisfied that it is so politically motivated that there is a substantial risk that the judges of the Moscow court would succumb to interference."

The contrast is between Khodorkovsky and what the journalist describes as the man who believes that he will stick to business and leave politics to the professionals, who is described as more prudent and has emerged as President Putin's favorite oligarch. This is absolutely at the heart of our case, in what your Lordship has called the opposing political camp. People know that they must keep in line with Mr. Putin because there are these examples of politically motivated prosecutions: Gusinsky, Berezovsky, Khodorkovsky, which—it is *pour encourager les autres* and they know it.

JUSTICE EADY: The burden of Mr. Browne's cross-examination so far to the witness has been to this effect: namely that it shows that Mr. Fridman and the *Alfa Bank* are keen to put on their website documents which show them to be advantageous as potential partners or as targets for investment from foreign investors because, it is said, the content of the website shows a desire to be closely associated with Mr. Putin and therefore to reassure such foreign investors as to *Alfa Bank's* influence within Russia. And the subject of Mr. Mikhail Khodorkovsky arose because there is a passage which says:

"No matter how much wealth you amass, stick to business and leave politics to the professionals. Mikhail Khodorkovsky, Russia's richest oligarch, appears to have got himself into real trouble by breaching that barrier. After hinting at presidential ambitions he and his Yukos oil company recently came under criminal investigation. On the other hand, the more prudent Fridman, a 39-year-old with an impish grin, who is Russia's third richest man, has emerged as President Putin's favorite oligarch …"

Now it seems to me that in view of the answers which Mr. Fridman has given so far, it is legitimate in exploring this theme for Mr. Browne to challenge the way in which this came into the website and the version of Mr. Khodorkovsky's fate which appears on the website. The conclusions in relation to Mr. Khodorkovsky of the district judge were that Mr. Khodorkovsky's prosecution was politically motivated.

BROWNE: I was suggesting to Mr. Fridman that the prosecution of Mr. Khodorkovsky was plainly politically motivated, and you were not willing to accept that?

FRIDMAN: Yes.

BROWNE: But you said, very fairly, that you would respect the opinion of a British court?

FRIDMAN: Of course.

BROWNE: Can I therefore tell you about the decision of a British court in 2005? In March of that year the district judge at Bow Street Magistrates' Court had to decide an application for the extradition of two associates of Mr. Khodorkovsky in Yukos, whose names were Dmitry Maruyev and Natalia Chernyshova. Do the names mean anything to you?

FRIDMAN: No.

BROWNE: But Mr. Khodorkovsky's name means a lot, does it not?

FRIDMAN: Of course, I am familiar with him.

BROWNE: The two individuals were accused by the Russian government of having conspired together with Mr. Khodorkovsky to defraud the government of Russia. The district judge refused the Russian government's application for their extradition. The judgment of the district judge first said this:

"It was some eight years later that it seems that President Putin became involved, and I have seen a report prepared by the Prosecutor and dated April 2003, advising the president that there were no grounds for taking action. Despite that decision, a prosecution was launched two months later. I have not been advised of any new evidence that had come to light between April 2003 and June 2003, and I have reached the inevitable conclusion that President Putin directed that Miss Chernyshova and Mr. Khodorkovsky should be prosecuted. Although this finding would amount to cogent evidence that the prosecution was politically motivated, it could not be regarded as conclusive, and it is necessary to examine the background to the events leading to the liquidation of the Yukos company."

He then proceeds to do that before reaching a conclusion about whether the prosecution was politically motivated:

"I am satisfied on the evidence of Professor Bowring and the evidence of Dr. Gladyshev that Mr. Khodorkovsky was seen as a powerful political opponent of Mr. Putin. In view of the facts that I have outlined, I am satisfied that it is more likely than not that the prosecution of Mr. Khodorkovsky is politically motivated. As the allegation against these defendants ... (that is Mr. Maruyev and Miss Chernyshova) in my view it is the inevitable conclusion that the prosecution of these two defendants is also politically motivated."

Now, that is the judgment of the senior district judge who deals in London with applications for extradition. Will you accept now that, as I suggested to you earlier, the prosecution of Mr. Khodorkovsky was first of all directed by President Putin?

FRIDMAN: I of course would like to say that I respect the judgment of the British lawyers and British judge about that, and I would like to underline that it simply contradicts the official legal position of the Russian authority, and as I am not a professional lawyer, I could not make my own judgment from the legal point of view whether it was politically motivated or for some other reason.

BROWNE: Well, the grounds that the district judge gives for suggesting that President Putin had directed the prosecution are that he had been told by the Prosecutor in April 2003 that there were no grounds for taking action, but nevertheless—and with no new evidence appearing in the meantime—the prosecution was launched in June 2003. Now, does that not sound like a politically motivated prosecution directed by President Putin?

FRIDMAN: Again, with all my respect for the opinion of the British judge, it is a completely contradictory opinion to the Russian court. How can I decide whose opinion is more professional? I am not a lawyer, I cannot tell you which side I prefer.

BROWNE: Do you feel embarrassed there, knowing that your evidence is reported, in criticizing in any way the stance by President Putin and the Russian government?

FRIDMAN: First of all, I have my own position. Mr. Putin's opinion and position do not matter. I have my own judgment about a lot of different things. I am not a public figure. I am focused on my own job. I think that I have a responsibility to my partners, to my shareholders, to my clients, creditors and so forth, and so I will repeat my formal position, I am not a lawyer. I am unable to make a fair and professional judgment about the merit of this court case.

BROWNE: But those responsibilities that you have just mentioned require you to keep in step with President Putin, do they not?

FRIDMAN: It does not mean that I must behave according to certain appointments by Mr. Putin. It just means that I must behave in the interests of my investors, of my shareholders, clients, and the interests of my business.

BROWNE: And the point I am making to you is that those interests are precisely what makes it necessary for you to be in the good books of President Putin—I am sorry, do you understand what I mean by "good books?"

FRIDMAN: My business interests require actually not to get involved in political life, because I think for business purposes it is not useful to get deeply involved in political issues.

BROWNE: Over lunch, Mr. Fridman, I discovered the name of the journalist that I had forgotten this morning, to whom you gave an interview. The name is Mr. Jonathan Kandell. Do you remember the interview now?

FRIDMAN: Yes, I remember that I gave the interview to the *Institutional Investor* journal.

BROWNE: And was it in August 2003?

FRIDMAN: Probably, yes. You know, I normally give a couple of interviews every week.

BROWNE: Yes. So you are a public figure to some extent, are you not? You said you were not a public figure but you give interviews, do you not?

FRIDMAN: Yes, that is true, but I give interviews as a businessman, and I try to share my point of view about certain business issues. But when I mentioned that I am not a public figure, what I mean is that I don't regularly make public appearances, such as appearing on TV shows as part of public entertainment. It was very uncharacteristic of me to have taken part in this TV show.

BROWNE: You regarded it as public entertainment, did you, rather than as a serious debate on a matter of important topical interest to Russians?

FRIDMAN: Of course it was a serious debate. That is why I participated in the debate. But generally it is a TV show for a very wide range of Russian spectators, so therefore it is entertainment.

BROWNE: It was a serious matter, was it not?

FRIDMAN: For me, of course it was very serious. That is why I finally decided to participate.

BROWNE: Now, Mr. Khodorkovsky had indicated, had he not, that he was—might be interested in running for president?

FRIDMAN: He never mentioned that he wanted to become President of Russia, as far as I know.

BROWNE: He indicated, I suggest, at this period with the presidential elections due in March 2004, that he might be a candidate against Mr. Putin?

FRIDMAN: No, as far as I remember, no.

BROWNE: Did he hint at such ambitions, as Mr. Kandell suggests?

FRIDMAN: As far as I am aware, he declared a certain ambition to become a political figure. He announced that he had left the business world and was attempting a life in politics.

BROWNE: Yes. In other words it was clear that he wanted to go into politics, and the natural course would be to run against Mr. Putin, would it not?

FRIDMAN: Not necessarily, you know, that is up to his personal position.

BROWNE: And very shortly after this article was published he was arrested. Indeed, it was the following month. So Mr. Kandell was being pretty perceptive, was he not?

FRIDMAN: Yes, he was arrested as far as I can recall in October of 2003.

BROWNE: And then kept in jail until his trial in May last year, May 2005?

FRIDMAN: Yes.

BROWNE: Now, Mr. Kandell goes on: "On the other hand, the more prudent Fridman, a tall, burly 39-year-old with an impish grin, who is Russia's third richest man, has emerged as President Vladimir Putin's favorite oligarch." Do you accept that?

FRIDMAN: No, he made the same conclusion as you did, because the presence of Mr. Putin for the signing ceremony was interpreted by him as a sort of special relationship with Mr. Putin, which is not the case at all.

BROWNE: I suggest that is exactly what it was. And when he refers to you as being more prudent than Mr. Khodorkovsky, it is because you do not present any threat to President Putin because you go around saying: "I am not interested in politics."

FRIDMAN: Possibly, yes, because for the whole of my business career I have tried to steer clear of political issues.

BROWNE: Let us just now go on, if we may: "Aside from Boris Berezovsky and Vladimir Gusinsky, who were forced abroad after clashing with Putin, the new President allowed the oligarchs free rein until recently." Do you agree with Mr. Kandell that Mr. Berezovsky and Mr. Gusinsky were forced abroad after clashing with Putin?

FRIDMAN: Yes, it is widely believed that one of the reasons why Mr. Berezovsky and Gusinsky left the country was because of certain political conflicts.

BROWNE: So would you accept that it was true? It is more than just widely believed, it is actually true, is it not?

FRIDMAN: I do not know. Mr. Berezovsky and Mr. Gusinsky probably know that better. There are numerous publications that have attempted to explain the situation surrounding their departure from the country.

BROWNE: There are now 17 known Russian billionaires, of whom you and Mr. Aven would be one and two, and Mr. Potanin would be a third?

FRIDMAN: I am not number 1. First of all, I doubt the accuracy of certain types of ratings. Of course, as you know, I am one of the most well-known businessmen in Russia—Mr. Potanin as well, but I do not know where we both fall in these ratings. I doubt that we are number 2 and 3. We aren't nearly that ambitious.

BROWNE: Then he mentions a number of incidents, searches by the police of the Yukos offices. Then: "The incidents come ... after he announced his financial support for several political parties that opposed Putin." Now, you, far from having no interest in politics and keeping well out of politics, have in fact been a heavy contributor to the United Russia Party, have you not?

FRIDMAN: No.

BROWNE: Through *Alfa Bank*?

FRIDMAN: No, I have never been a contributor to the United Russia Party.

BROWNE: Are you sure of that?

FRIDMAN: Yes.

BROWNE: *Alfa Bank* has never contributed? No company in the vast empire under your control has ever contributed?

FRIDMAN: As far as I recall, no, we have never been a contributor to the United Russia Party.

BROWNE: What on earth, in that case, are you doing posting on *Alfa Bank's* website this article with that statement?

FRIDMAN: We are merely clipping and posting the article that appeared in the media. I would like to clarify that I am not responsible for *Alfa Bank's* website. I am the chairman of the board. Our press service is probably responsible for that. If they made a mistake, that is not my fault. If a journalist has printed a fact that is not true, that does not make it my fault. That makes it their fault.

Browne: If someone says something that is untrue and it is published in a magazine which is sold at the railway station, that is one thing; but if you then choose or if *Alfa Bank* chooses to place this on its own website, does it not thereby represent to the public that the contents of the article are true?

Fridman: Of course not. What would you recommend that we do? Change the words in the article? Or take Mr. Kandell for making wrong…

Browne: Well, I know you are very quick to bring libel proceedings, but you could, could you not, very simply have added a note to the website, saying: "This is quite untrue. Neither Mr. Fridman nor any part of the *Alfa Group* has ever contributed a rouble to the United Russia Party?"

Fridman: I think that probably for our customers and for our clients it is probably not so important, but I would follow your advice.

Browne: I suggest that from somewhere in the enormous financial empire of *Alfa Bank*, contributions were indeed made to the United Russia Party and you acknowledged the fact to Mr. Kandell?

Fridman: I did not mention this fact because it did not exist, as far as I remember. That is completely untrue.

Browne: "The political entity most closely linked to Putin." That is completely true, is it not?

Fridman: That is completely untrue.

Browne: No, forgive me, it is my fault. It is completely true that the United Russia Party is the political entity most closely linked to Putin?

Fridman: Yes, that is true.

Browne: "Who remains highly popular and heavily favored to win a second term? Fridman leaves no doubt that he will support Putin and the United Russia Party."

Fridman: This is simply incorrect information. We have never been contributors to the United Russia Party.

Browne: I am now reading on after the words "second term": "Fridman leaves no doubt that he will support Putin and the United Russia Party." That is plainly the impression you made on Mr. Kandell by what you said to him?

Fridman: Again, my position always was the following. I respect the choices of the Russian people. I respect the United Russian Party because the majority of the Russian population chose them. I respect Mr. Putin as president because he was elected by a wide majority of Russian votes. I am personally not involved in political things; I do not contribute money to them. I do try to remain loyal to the Russian authorities because I am a citizen of the country.

BROWNE: You try to be loyal to Mr. Putin?

FRIDMAN: Well, I try to be loyal not personally to Mr. Putin but to the President of the Russian Federation, as a businessman at least.

BROWNE: You will see that Mr. Kandell then quotes you as saying: "'Under Putin, the right of business to exist is no longer in question,' says Fridman, who points out that threats to businesses and their owners were commonplace during the Yeltsin era." Did you say that to Mr. Kandell?

FRIDMAN: Probably yes, if he quoted me; I do not know, I do not remember exactly. I trusted Mr. Kandell. Mr. Putin, by the way, mentioned the question of property many times. And I welcome this approach—as a businessman.

BROWNE: Has *Alfa Bank* or yourself or any company within the *Alfa Bank* group ever provided money to the Union of Right Forces, also known as SPS?

FRIDMAN: As far as I know, *Alfa Bank* as an entity has never provided any money to the Union of Right Forces. I am aware of the fact that a few people, including my partner, provided certain financial support to the Union of Right Forces; which is by the way an opposition party.

BROWNE: I am going to come back to that later. Its Mr. Nemtsov's party, is it not?

FRIDMAN: Yes.

BROWNE: So Mr. Aven provided financial support to Mr. Nemtsov?

FRIDMAN: I do not know.

BROWNE: What Mr. Kandell was referring to in his article, I suggest, was a meeting at the Kremlin on Friday, July 28, 2000, that Mr. Nemtsov organized. Do you remember that?

FRIDMAN: No, I do not remember a meeting organized by Mr. Nemtsov.

BROWNE: Is *The Moscow Times* a reliable journal, Mr. Fridman?

FRIDMAN: Under certain—you know—yes.

BROWNE: You would certainly accept, I think, that the *Financial Times* is reliable?

FRIDMAN: I would say that, if you are talking about specific Kremlin news, that there are few sources of reliable information, either in *The Moscow Times* or *Financial Times*. If they wrote that Mr. Nemtsov arranged a meeting with the president, it is probably misinformation, because meetings with the president are usually arranged by the president.

BROWNE: What I am suggesting is that it was at the initiative and suggestion of Mr. Nemtsov?

FRIDMAN: That is very different, that according to his initiative or arrangement. Maybe he was one of the initiators of the meeting.

BROWNE: That is what I am suggesting. Mr. Fridman, do you accept now, first of all that you attended a meeting with Mr. Putin at the Kremlin on Friday, July 28?

FRIDMAN: Probably, yes. I do not remember the exact date, but I met Mr. Putin a couple of times, as I said, with a group of businessmen.

BROWNE: And the meeting was the initiative of Mr. Nemtsov?

FRIDMAN: Probably, yes.

BROWNE: And that there were about 18 of you wealthy Russian businessmen present including Mr. Potanin?

FRIDMAN: I do not remember exactly how many people were there but probably you are right.

BROWNE: And was Mr. Aven also there?

FRIDMAN: No, he was not there.

BROWNE: Mr. Nemtsov's purpose in calling the meeting was to try to secure an understanding between Russian businessmen and Mr. Putin, was it not?

FRIDMAN: I do not know.

BROWNE: Was not Mr. Nemtsov's idea in calling the meeting to try to procure from Mr. Putin a promise not to use governmental powers to do battle with business groups?

FRIDMAN: Yes, I read this paragraph.

BROWNE: Do you agree with me that that was why you attended the meeting; it was in effect to call a truce?

FRIDMAN: No, I attended that meeting because I received an invitation from Mr. Putin, who was the President of the Russian Federation.

Mr. Nemtsov's reasoning, perhaps one of the reasons why he initiated the meeting, has some basis in what is written here, but I was not aware of this motive when I participated in that meeting.

BROWNE: Yes, and I suggest that at this stage Russian businessmen were very keen to call a truce in the war that Mr. Putin was seen as waging against them. You all feared you might be next?

FRIDMAN: I never felt threatened—that I would be next. I am hopeful that what I am doing as a businessman is useful for Russia, useful for our economy, for our people. A lot of people have worked for our companies. I have generated a lot of profit, created a working structure, so I doubt that any reasonable political leader would choose to punish me just because I am successful as a businessman.

BROWNE: But, as Mr. Soloviov said, Mr. Putin could say at any time to any one of you, "You know what happened to Mr. Khodorkovsky? You are next."

FRIDMAN: I never heard that from Mr. Putin. I never heard it.

BROWNE: No, but that is the fear, is it not, and Mr. Soloviov on the program expresses that fear?

FRIDMAN: I do not know what Mr. Soloviov is fearful of. Is Mr. Soloviov a witness here—he probably could deliver his own view about that. But as a businessman I never received, personally or indirectly, threats from Mr. Putin.

BROWNE: You see the chronology of all this is a bit complicated to keep in the mind, but this meeting was at the end of July 2000, and in June Mr. Gusinsky had been arrested and held in jail until he surrendered NTV, had he not?

FRIDMAN: No, as far as I remember, Mr. Gusinsky was jailed for three days for some reason, again I do not know what it was, and I am not a lawyer. I believe it was connected with an allegation against him that he was planning to strip certain assets that were part of Gazprom.

BROWNE: So you are saying, are you, Mr. Fridman, that the Soviet criminal justice system was properly employed against Mr. Gusinsky? Are you saying that?

FRIDMAN: I did not say that. I said it was a specific legal decision. And again, you know my position on that. I would not like to comment. I do not have the professional ability to make fair and serious judgment about whether it was politically motivated or legally motivated.

BROWNE: You know, do you not, that very shortly after his arrest and imprisonment, he relinquished NTV, the station on which you appeared, to Gazprom, a state-owned energy supplier. You know that, do you not?

FRIDMAN: Yes, but the situation was very different. NTV had borrowed money from Gazprom, more than $1 million. And of course NTV could not pay back this loan because it was a huge loan for NTV. And effectively what happened was that Gazprom, as the lender, instigated bankruptcy proceedings, and inevitably the assets were withdrawn from Mr. Gusinsky in favor of Gazprom as the lender—as a lender to NTV.

BROWNE: But that is not a reason, is it, to throw Mr. Gusinsky into a criminal jail until he relinquishes NTV to Gazprom?

FRIDMAN: I do not know the reasons. From what I can remember, there was an allegation against him that he tried to strip these assets, I mean NTV, from their collateral for the Gazprom loan. That was their explanation for why he was put in jail for three days.

BROWNE: I suggest that it was to put pressure upon him, to intimidate him, to surrender NTV to Gazprom. You do not accept that?

FRIDMAN: I do not think so. I think there were enough, you know, financial reasons in regards to the bankrupt company, and therefore to withdraw that asset from Mr. Gusinsky.

BROWNE: Do you regard the judgments of the European Court of Human Rights in Strasbourg with as much respect as the judgment of this court?

FRIDMAN: Of course.

BROWNE: Then unless there is an objection, I would like to move to the next step. Were you aware that Mr. Gusinsky brought an appeal against his treatment in Russia to the European Court of Human Rights?

FRIDMAN: Okay.

BROWNE: Did you know that?

FRIDMAN: Yes, I have heard about that.

BROWNE: And were you aware of what the European Court said in their judgment of May 19, 2004?

FRIDMAN: No.

BROWNE: Is it that you have heard about it and forgotten or just never been interested?

FRIDMAN: I actually—I have never paid much attention to the decision of European Courts, but generally it is important information. So maybe I simply forgot.

BROWNE: This is a Court of Human Rights. Are you interested in human rights, Mr. Fridman?

FRIDMAN: Yes.

BROWNE: Mr. Gusinsky's complaint was that his detention in prison in June 2000 represented an abuse of power. He claimed that, by detaining him, the authorities intended to force him to sell his media business to Gazprom on unfavorable terms and conditions. Then the judgment says which article of the convention is the relevant one which was said to have been breached, which of his human rights was breached. You knew that Mr. Gusinsky had been imprisoned?

FRIDMAN: Yes.

BROWNE: Is it right you are saying he was properly imprisoned because he was guilty of criminal offenses?

FRIDMAN: I did not say it.

BROWNE: Is that your stance?

FRIDMAN: My position is I am not a lawyer; I could not make a judgment. I in principle respect the decision of the Russian court. So I assume that the decision of Russian courts are made on a legal basis.

BROWNE: Are you also assuming that the Russian prosecuting authorities behaved fairly, and properly respected Mr. Gusinsky's human rights?

FRIDMAN: Yes.

BROWNE: Did you know, Mr. Fridman, that in July 2000, Mr. Gusinsky had surrendered NTV to Gazprom? I think you knew that, did you not?

FRIDMAN: Yes, I read in the newspaper that Mr. Gusinsky had decided to settle the problem with the law, with Gazprom, by transferring assets to Gazprom.

BROWNE: Did it ever occur to you that there might be a connection between the two, the imprisonment and the surrender of NTV?

FRIDMAN: I do not know. I just do not know about that.

JUSTICE EADY: His previous answer, according to my note was: "I knew that he had settled the problem with the law by transferring NTV to Gazprom."

FRIDMAN: Correct.

JUSTICE EADY: The previous answer I have noted was from the witness, that he knew he had settled the problem with the law by handing over NTV to Gazprom. I think the witness is confirming that is what he has said. So he is accepting, to that extent, there was a link. That is my understanding of the evidence so far.

BROWNE: What I suggest Mr. Fridman is that these two were plainly linked and that Mr. Gusinsky made an enormous protest at that time in 2000. Do you not remember his complaints to the press about the way he had been treated?

FRIDMAN: Sorry, would you repeat the question?

BROWNE: Yes, of course. Do you not recall that in the late summer of 2000, after Mr. Gusinsky had surrendered NTV to Gazprom, he complained to the press about the way in which his human rights had been infringed?

FRIDMAN: Yes, I remember that. I remember it.

BROWNE: Did it not occur to you that he might be right?

FRIDMAN: Of course he might be right, he might be wrong. That was his position.

BROWNE: Did the circumstances not seem to you to indicate that he was right?

FRIDMAN: Not necessarily. I was aware of the serious debt of Mr. Gusinsky to Gazprom and it was clear to me that according to the normal procedure that exists in any civilized country, the borrower can undertake action to protect their interest as a financial lender—the lender can undertake steps to protect their rights and Gazprom obviously wanted a return on their loan. So one of the obvious steps to retrieve that loan was the withdrawal of the assets from the borrower.

BROWNE: That would not justify putting Mr. Gusinsky in prison for three days, would it?

FRIDMAN: If it was proven that Mr. Gusinsky tried to strip the assets, that probably was the right step. Again, I am not a lawyer. By the way, I signed a letter to the general prosecutor, immediately after Mr. Gusinsky was imprisoned, that asked to release him, and that volunteered to provide personal guarantees that he would not leave the country because I know him, and I believe he is an honest businessman.

BROWNE: But he was released on, I think, June 13, was he not? He was only held in prison for three days but during that time he signed the agreement?

FRIDMAN: As far as I remember, as far as I read in the newspaper, this agreement was signed later on, like in July, according to...

BROWNE: Yes, he had agreed to sign it and it was finalized in July?

FRIDMAN: According to your information. I do not remember the exact date but I believe that after he was released, he started negotiations with Gazprom on how to settle the problem with the debt, and then in July he probably signed the agreement as a settlement.

BROWNE: And Gazprom asked him to sign the agreement that he ultimately signed in July when he was in prison, did they not?

FRIDMAN: No, it seems to me, as far as I remember, he was in prison before. I do not know what Gazprom asked him to sign when he was in prison. I was not fortunately his neighbor in prison.

BROWNE: That was fortunate for you, was it not?

FRIDMAN: Yes, that is fortunate for me.

BROWNE: Do you remember the name of the acting press minister, Mr. Lesin, Mikhail Lesin?

FRIDMAN: Yes.

BROWNE: He was involved in negotiating with Mr. Gusinsky, was he not?

FRIDMAN: I do not know. Probably, yes.

BROWNE: Do you remember him being upbraided publicly for going to see Mr. Gusinsky and asking him—forcing him, I would suggest—to sign the July agreement. Do you remember that?

FRIDMAN: I remember a publication that said something about that. So the media describes the participation of Mr. Lesin, or certain negotiations with Mr. Gusinsky. That is my only source of information.

BROWNE: It was suggested that he had infringed on Mr. Gusinsky's human rights by visiting him in prison and securing his agreement to signing a formal agreement of his release.

FRIDMAN: I never heard through the press that Mr. Lesin visited Mr. Gusinsky in prison.

BROWNE: But at any rate Mr. Lesin's role in securing the surrender of NTV to Gazprom was the subject of criticism in the press, was it not?

FRIDMAN: Yes, it was—that after Mr. Gusinsky was released from prison Mr. Lesin tried to force him to sign an agreement with Gazprom.

BROWNE: That, I suggest, is exactly what happened, and Mr. Gusinsky's human rights were thereby infringed?

JUSTICE EADY: I think there may be a misunderstanding between you, because I think what the witness said, and it is not always easy, but I think what the witness said was that according to his recollection he remembered Mr. Lesin being criticized for approaching Mr. Gusinsky after he left prison.

BROWNE: Oh, after.

FRIDMAN: Exactly. I never heard that Mr. Lesin was in prison and met Mr. Gusinsky while he was there.

BROWNE: Whilst he was in prison, I suggest, Mr. Gusinsky had agreed to sign the agreement when he got out?

FRIDMAN: I do not know about that. I have never heard that.

BROWNE: All right. Now, can we go back to the Kremlin meeting of July 28, 2000? I was just setting the scene. The problems with Mr. Gusinsky had been in June and July. Mr. Berezovsky had resigned from the Duma, had he not, on July 17, 2000?

FRIDMAN: You could ask him. I do not remember, frankly.

BROWNE: At any rate it sounds right, does it not?

FRIDMAN: Yes.

BROWNE: And he had publicly announced his intention to consolidate political opposition to Mr. Putin?

FRIDMAN: Yes, probably, yes, maybe not immediately but sometime around then.

BROWNE: And 11 days after his publicized resignation from the Duma, this meeting takes place. Before you went into the Kremlin you had a pretty good idea, did you not, of what the objective of the meeting was?

FRIDMAN: Yes, again I participated a few times in meetings with President Yeltsin, and it was probably not the first meeting with Mr.

Putin as president. I also had probably met with him when he was prime minister or acting president. And in general, as far as I understand, it is normal for a president to meet with groups of the most, you know…

BROWNE: It was not a run-of-the-mill meeting, was it, Mr. Fridman? It was a very important meeting, because what Mr. Nemtsov wanted to secure at it was a moratorium on any investigations into the legitimacy of privatization over the previous decade.

FRIDMAN: Maybe that was Mr. Nemtsov's agenda.

BROWNE: It was the agenda of you all?

FRIDMAN: No, that is not true. I had no agenda. I would like to repeat, that when I receive an invitation from the President of the Russian Federation, I usually agree to this invitation. I don't have any precise agenda for such meetings. We of course discuss numerous hot topics in the business community.

BROWNE: But the agenda was a hot topic for the business community, a scalding hot topic in the context of what had happened to Mr. Gusinsky in June and Mr. Berezovsky's resignation in July, 11days before?

FRIDMAN: No, Mr. Berezovsky's resignation was not a public event for the business community. Mr. Berezovsky thought of himself as a politician at that time. He did not think of himself as a businessman any more because he was a Duma member and a well-positioned political bureaucrat.

JUSTICE EADY: There may be a misunderstanding. I thought you asked a question about Mr. Gusinsky. The witness is answering about Mr. Berezovsky.

BROWNE: I think the question was about both. You see, it was precisely because Mr. Berezovsky had publicly announced his political ambitions that he was not invited to this meeting.

FRIDMAN: Mr. Berezovsky publicly announced his political ambitions in the early 1990s. So it was not a new agenda for him.

BROWNE: But the fact that he had resigned from the Duma 11 days before this meeting and said that he was interested in running and helping the opposition against Putin made it all the more important for Mr. Putin to consolidate his position, did it not?

FRIDMAN: I do not think so. Mr. Berezovsky had been a close friend of Mr. Putin for a long time and he was one of the, you know, authors of the idea to create a United Russia. He was one of the persons behind the proposal for Mr. Putin to become president.

BROWNE: We know that, Mr. Fridman.

FRIDMAN: So I would say that he had made a number of different political statements within that period of time.

BROWNE: If you had been here for the earlier part of this trial, you would have known that Mr. Berezovsky was completely candid about that, indeed that he told the jury that he had played a part in selecting Mr. Putin to be Prime Minister in August 1999, but that Mr. Putin did a series of things in 2000, which Mr. Berezovsky thought were very wrong, and which he publicly stated were wrong. That is right, is it not?

FRIDMAN: As far as that report, yes, he made certain statements, and maybe he was opposed to certain decisions of Mr. Putin. But none of this had anything to do with why I met with President Putin.

BROWNE: What I suggest therefore happened at this meeting was that it all went very well for both the businessmen and Mr. Putin. Mr. Putin, I suggest, told the businessmen, of whom you were one, that there would be no further review of the privatizations that had taken place.

FRIDMAN: Mr. Putin made a number of statements, such as what you were just saying. He mentioned many times that he did not want to revisit the privatization process that had taken place in Russia in the 1990s.

BROWNE: Because there was great controversy, was there not, about whether fair prices had been paid for the state assets that had been privatized?

FRIDMAN: That is a good question for Mr. Berezovsky.

BROWNE: And to others as well, Mr. Fridman?

FRIDMAN: And to others, of course, and actually I think in general for the development of the Russian economy it was a smart decision not to review it because, of course, I would like to repeat that our history of capitalism is relatively short. There were many contradictions in our legislation and many mistakes were made during the privatization. And it seems to me that it was a wise decision by our authorities not to revisit it, because any privatization process normally contains numerous mistakes. To go back over everything would be a never ending circle. I fully support the idea of not reviewing privatization.

BROWNE: Just have a look, please, at the second paragraph of this *Financial Times* article of July 29, which I am now going to hand up. There are two *Financial Times* articles. Mr. Nemtsov says what he is going to do before the meeting on the 27th, and then on the 29th he says how it went. Just look at the second paragraph, would you, please, Mr. Fridman. Does that accurately reflect how the meeting had gone?

FRIDMAN: I do not remember exactly, but again our president repeated this many times. So it was probably repeated in the same meeting—and that meeting as well.

BROWNE: Perhaps I can then read it, if you think it is probably what Putin said: "The president clearly and concisely said that there had been no review of the outcome of privatization. Today's meetings, said Mr. Nemtsov, draws a line under 10 years of the initial accumulation of capital. The era of the oligarchs is over." Does that seem right?

FRIDMAN: Probably, yes.

BROWNE: I suggest that, in exchange for Mr. Putin in effect saying, "Well, none of the rest of you will go the way of Mr. Gusinsky or Mr. Berezovsky," you all agreed to keep out of politics. That was the bargain, I suggest?

FRIDMAN: You are absolutely wrong. We never discussed that we would keep out of politics. The president never proposed that we must stay away from politics. I think the message that privatization would not be reviewed is fairly clear. He repeated it a number of times and again I am fully supportive of this idea.

So if we understand the meaning of the word "oligarchs" as a kind of businessmen who, on one hand owns significant assets, and on the other hand tries to impact the political life of the country, from that point I would rather agree with Mr. Putin's statement—or Mr. Nemtsov's statement that the era of the oligarchs is over. But frankly, for me, this was not the case because I had never tried to be politically influential. Maybe Mr. Gusinsky and Mr. Berezovsky were simply upset, as they had been the king makers, deciding who would become Prime Minister, who would be appointed as a minister and what party will win—or will participate in the election. But not for me.

BROWNE: Mr. Fridman, I want to move on now and deal with *Kommersant*. But before I do, can I ask you about your evidence that you strongly believe that businessmen should stay out of the media? Is that an accurate summary of your evidence?

FRIDMAN: Yes.

BROWNE: So not only do business and politics not mix but business and the media do not mix either?

FRIDMAN: You know, it is a question—it is a question of definitions. As I already mentioned, we invest money in a TV channel. We own 30 percent of the shares of the fourth largest TV channel in Russia, called STS, which is purely an entertainment channel, which airs family shows, movies, some reality shows, serials, sitcoms. And I believe that to invest money in that kind of media is okay. I also believe that for certain people it is also proper to invest money in more politicized media channels, such as in an informational channel. I have no interest in that. I always try to stay away from that.

BROWNE: But ORT was perhaps the most influential television channel of all in Russia, was it not?

FRIDMAN: Of course.

BROWNE: Particularly in 1995?

FRIDMAN: Yes.

BROWNE: When you were a director and *Alfa Bank* a shareholder?

FRIDMAN: Yes, we owned 5 percent of that, and, by the way, we were involved at the request of Mr. Berezovsky, who was the head of the group of businessmen.

BROWNE: I know that, but Mr. Berezovsky, again, if you had been in court and heard his evidence, explained all that. And you sat on the board with Mr. Berezovsky, did you not?

FRIDMAN: Yes.

BROWNE: And at that early stage he had 5 percent, and *Alfa Bank* had 5 percent, in 1995?

FRIDMAN: I do not know how much Mr. Berezovsky owned. As far as I remember he owned more than 5 percent.

BROWNE: I think it may have been 8, I am sorry.

FRIDMAN: Yes.

BROWNE: But that surely counts as involvement in the media, does it not?

FRIDMAN: Yes, but there were a few reasons why we invested. First, at that time ORT was in a very difficult financial situation; it was effectively bankrupt. Second, we believed, when we made this investment, in the financial prospectives of those shares. We believed that to invest money in those shares would be potentially quite profitable for us as investors.

BROWNE: But you either believe in keeping out of the media or you do not. And I suggest, Mr. Fridman, that your effective control of Novi Canal in Ukraine is another example of the fact that you are quite willing to get involved in both the business and political media?

FRIDMAN: Yes, that is a good example. We invested in Novi Canal, which was transmitting as a new channel. We helped to establish that channel, and later when it became an important player in the political arena, before the election in Ukraine, before the parliamentary election, before the presidential election, which took place a couple of years ago, we sold those shares for exactly the same reason—because we understood that it had become a factor of political influence in Ukraine.

BROWNE: It always had political influence in Ukraine, I suggest, and you went into it, I accept, to make money, but it plainly shows that you are not someone who consistently keeps out of the media?

FRIDMAN: No, it was not influential in political terms because it had been started from scratch. It could not, at first, be an important political player in Ukraine. And I do not live in Ukraine. I have no impact on the Ukrainian political situation. I have no interest in that. For me it was purely a financial investment.

BROWNE: But the Ukraine was your birthplace, was it not?

FRIDMAN: So what?

BROWNE: I am suggesting that you always remain interested in the politics of your birthplace?

FRIDMAN: I'm not that interested in the politics of where I live; why should I be interested in the politics of the place where I was born?

BROWNE: And I suggest too, Mr. Fridman, that in the new political life of Ukraine, a channel like Novi Canal, once it's started up, will become of immense political influence?

FRIDMAN: That is why I sold it three years ago.

BROWNE: And you sold it when, having started it up, you could make a healthy profit?

FRIDMAN: Yes, we made a good profit.

BROWNE: Exactly.

FRIDMAN: Not because of political influence.

BROWNE: It is the profits which interest you, just as you said a moment ago you went into ORT for profit as well?

FRIDMAN: Yes, exactly.

BROWNE: And you saw that as a profit?

FRIDMAN: Yes, we went into ORT for the profit as well, not for the political influence, and that is why when Mr. Berezovsky started to use ORT as his political tool, we decided to sell these shares.

BROWNE: It is seeking to make profits out of political influence, is it not?

FRIDMAN: For us it is not a profit, political influence. I believe it is potentially damaging for our financial interests, political influence.

BROWNE: You see, I have given you two examples of instances where you have gone into the political media?

FRIDMAN: Sorry, if you do believe that political influence is a profit, why did we sell Novi Canal before the election? This was precisely when the TV channel was of most importance politically.

BROWNE: Mr. Fridman, I am saying that you were seeking to make a profit out of ventures that were peddling political influence, the two are not exclusive.

FRIDMAN: Yes, these are examples of times when we invested money in media outlets that became involved in the political life of a country, whether in Russia when we owned the shares of ORT, or in Ukraine. But when it became a situation where things had become too political, issues were too hot, before the election, or when somebody like Mr. Berezovsky had started to seriously impact political life—and he was a partner in ORT—in those cases we immediately decided to sell our shares.

BROWNE: You all went into ORT for a political purpose in 1995, and that was to promote the re-election of President Yeltsin in the presidential elections of 1996. That is right, is it not?

FRIDMAN: I never invested money in ORT or Novi Canal for certain political reasons. The only purpose of our investment was to make a profit from the investment.

BROWNE: But you all—Mr. Berezovsky, Mr. Potanin...

FRIDMAN: Mr. Potanin was not a part of ORT.

BROWNE: Was he not in ORT?

FRIDMAN: No.

BROWNE: Does Microdin have nothing to do with?...

FRIDMAN: As far as I remember, he is not.

BROWNE: Are you sure?

FRIDMAN: Yes.

BROWNE: At any rate, Mr. Berezovsky, yourself, all went into ORT in 1995, in order to be sure that you could promote the interests of President Yeltsin in the election the following year, 1996?

FRIDMAN: That is not true. I never was involved personally in the activity of ORT. Mr. Berezovsky was deeply involved in that. We bought this 5 percent of the largest Russian channel for a token amount. It was something around $100,000, which was quite a good price for 5 percent of ORT. Of course, during that time ORT was in trouble and heavily in debt, but I believed that sooner or later the largest TV channel in the country would become profitable. Unfortunately in a very short period of time it became a leverage of political influence for Mr. Berezovsky, and we decided to leave that channel and so we sold our shares.

BROWNE: Could you—we have quite a bit of ground to cover and I know that this is obviously important to you, as it is to Mr. Berezovsky, but could you just keep your answers quite short and avoid the temptation to make cracks? Do you understand what I mean?

FRIDMAN: Sorry, my English is not that strong, so I will try to do my best.

BROWNE: So another instance, I suggest, of your being quite willing to go into the media if it had turned out right, was *Kommersant*. You, Mr. Aven and Mr. Potanin all considered, did you not, as a consortium, buying *Kommersant*?

FRIDMAN: You are mistaken about something. Mr. Aven is a partner of mine. So effectively if you are talking about that, you are talking about an entity rather than about an individual. *Alfa Bank* and Mr. Chubais, who is head of the United Energy System, and Mr. Potanin, who was head of the InterRos group of companies, briefly discussed, on a preliminary basis, this opportunity.

BROWNE: What you were discussing was a consortium to purchase *Kommersant*, involving these individuals: yourself, Mr. Aven, Mr. Potanin and Mr. Chubais?

FRIDMAN: No, we discussed—as I would like to repeat my point. We discussed, with the shareholders of *Kommersant*, providing a loan for management to buy out shares from other shareholders of *Kommersant*.

BROWNE: That is simply not right. You yourself say in your witness statement that there were two possible proposals. One was a loan, which of course, if they had defaulted on would have meant *Kommersant* falling into your hands. But what I am asking you about—and if you have forgotten about this part of your evidence, I can show you—was the informal discussions with a view to putting together a consortium to buy *Kommersant*; in other words, to own *Kommersant*; and that consortium consisted of the individuals I have just listed?

FRIDMAN: I just—I have not forgotten. I have just not finished. So as an alternative approach, we discussed very preliminarily that in the case that management would not want to borrow money from the bank to buy shares back, to fund the management buyout, we would attempt to build a consortium of investors who would invest money in *Kommersant*. And the initial condition would be that all of those investors could not own more than 15 to 20 percent of the shares, so as not to impact the editorial policy of the newspaper.

BROWNE: But do you think, you being a reader of the *Financial Times*, that people would still respect the editorial integrity of the *Financial Times* if it were owned by half a dozen big city businessmen in London?

FRIDMAN: I think it is much better for it to be owned by five, six, or seven independent business entities rather than to belong to someone who already controls the two most influential TV channels and a couple of other very influential media sources.

BROWNE: But nobody would trust the *Financial Times* under those circumstances. They would all think it was simply a mouthpiece for the half dozen wealthy businessmen who owned it, would they not?

FRIDMAN: Sorry, repeat that again?

BROWNE: If half a dozen wealthy British businessmen from London took over the *Financial Times*, nobody would think that it was an independent and objective newspaper?

FRIDMAN: That is why a first priority for us was to provide a loan for the management of the newspaper, to allow them to buy back their shares.

BROWNE: Because, you see, "independent" is a tendentious word, is it not?

FRIDMAN: Correct.

BROWNE: It merely means "you are independent, you agree with me. You are not independent, you disagree with me."

FRIDMAN: Okay, you are absolutely right. It of course would not be the best choice for the newspaper to be owned by six or seven or eight wealthy businessmen in Russia. But it would be—it would be a much better choice than for it to belong to Mr. Berezovsky or to belong to some other individual.

BROWNE: But you see, you criticize Mr. Berezovsky and suggest in effect that if *Kommersant* fell into his hands, he would manipulate its editorial policy. That is what you are suggesting, is it not?

FRIDMAN: No, but I do believe that if a single individual owns the paper, they would have a much deeper influence on the newspaper than if six or seven or eight businessmen owned it.

BROWNE: What you mean by "independent and objective" is that it agrees with you. Shall I put it again? When you say that you want the newspaper to be independent and objective, what you are saying is that it should have a political stance which is the same as your own and not Mr. Berezovsky's?

FRIDMAN: No, that is not the case. When I say that the editorial policy should be independent, it means that it should reflect the position of the editor and its journalists—a collective of journalists' minds in the newspaper, not reflect the opinion of the shareholders. Because the shareholders, as businessmen, might have very different opinions or specific political or economic concerns.

BROWNE: But you see, your attack on Mr. Berezovsky as the owner of *Kommersant* is completely misconceived, is it not? You yourself on the program referred to your great respect for the newspaper and the fact that it was an epoch in the history of Russian journalism, and that was after Mr. Berezovsky had owned it for five years?

FRIDMAN: Yes, that is true. I would like to remind you that Mr. Berezovsky bought *Kommersant* in the middle of 1999, and as you just mentioned, Mr. Berezovsky left the country in 2000. Of course, for the time being, journalists at *Kommersant* behave according to—rather according to their own vision than according to certain requests by Mr. Berezovsky, for the obvious reason: because he is here in London and they are there in Moscow.

BROWNE: You see, again, if you had been here for the earlier part of the trial you would have heard your counsel putting to Mr. Berezovsky and Mr. Dubov that they were controlling *Kommersant* from London. That was the subject of the complaint, not, as you have just suggested, a subject of congratulations?

FRIDMAN: Yes, that is good. I am happy that it was done properly. The newspaper's policy should not be influenced from London, because I believe that newspaper journalists should work without any strong influence from shareholders.

BROWNE: So the point I am making is that your entire criticism of Mr. Berezovsky as a proprietor of *Kommersant* was completely misconceived because his record in the period of five years between his acquisition of ownership in September 1999 and the broadcast of *The Duel* in October 2004 was one of complete editorial independence?

FRIDMAN: No, that is not the case. Mr. Berezovsky demonstrated numerous times how he could personally impact the editorial policy of ORT, TV6 and the other media.

BROWNE: I am asking—he accepts—and again if you had been willing to come to this case earlier, you would have heard his evidence. He accepts that when he went into ORT it was for the political purpose in which you joined him, of promoting President Yeltsin's re-election. He then pointed out the distinction between that and *Kommersant*, which he regarded as editorially independent and in which he had no influence. Now, you yourself are praising *Kommersant* for which you said you had great respect under Mr. Berezovsky's ownership?

FRIDMAN: Yes, that is true.

BROWNE: "*Kommersant* is an epoch in the history of Russian journalism." Agreed?

FRIDMAN: Yes.

BROWNE: You were only speaking the truth, were you not?

FRIDMAN: Of course, I completely support this view.

BROWNE: "The golden quills of Russian journalism are working for *Kommersant*." In other words, Mr. Berezovsky does not employ mere hacks to do his bidding? Agreed?

FRIDMAN: Yes.

BROWNE: And then we return to the subject of the objectivity of *Kommersant* when Mr. Soloviov intervenes. You say: "An independent press is an objective press."

FRIDMAN: Yes, correct, that is exactly my view.

BROWNE: Then Mr. Soloviov says: "According to that definition, *Kommersant* is unquestionably independent." Do you agree with that?

FRIDMAN: Correct, yes.

BROWNE: So, far from Mr. Berezovsky corrupting the editorial independence of these golden quills of Russian journalism, he is in fact leaving them to create an epoch in Russian journalism. And no less a person than Mr. Soloviov says that *Kommersant* is unquestionably independent?

FRIDMAN: Yes.

BROWNE: Do you not think, in the light of that, Mr. Fridman, that your attack on Mr. Berezovsky for having corrupted or being liable to corrupt *Kommersant* was completely baseless?

FRIDMAN: No. First of all I was not attacking Mr. Berezovsky when he intended to buy *Kommersant*. I was just doing my best to provide a loan for the shareholders. I would like to remind the jury that Mr. Berezovsky, not just once, used his political force, muscles, to chase his own goals. I would like to recall that in 1997, after a very severe attack on Mr. Berezovsky's control of ORT, both Deputy Prime Minister, Mr. Chubais, and Mr. Nemtsov effectively lost their positions in the government.

BROWNE: Now, the *Kommersant* libel action. Are you aware that *Kommersant* has appealed to the European Court of Human Rights?

FRIDMAN: Yes.

BROWNE: Now, by 2004 *Kommersant* was one of the very few independent newspapers left in Russia, was it not?

FRIDMAN: Now? Yes.

BROWNE: Let us just focus on October 2004, at the time of the program and the libel action?

FRIDMAN: Yes.

BROWNE: One of the very few independent newspapers left and a thorn in the side of President Putin, I suggest.

FRIDMAN: Yes.

BROWNE: You have heard, of course, the concern expressed by people interested in human rights about the lack of a free press in Russia today?

FRIDMAN: Yes.

BROWNE: And those concerns have a real foundation, do they not?

FRIDMAN: I do not know.

BROWNE: Just think about it. They have a real foundation, do they not? You might be embarrassed to admit it, but they do, I suggest?

FRIDMAN: They probably do a good job. Human rights organizations. They probably are trustworthy. So probably they are right.

BROWNE: Now, the article in *Kommersant* which led to the libel action was published on July 7, 2004, by which time the banking crisis in Russia had been going on for several months, had it not?

FRIDMAN: That was in July 2004.

BROWNE: The article?

FRIDMAN: The article and the crisis were in July 2004.

BROWNE: No, it began earlier than that, I suggest. As early as in May the Central Bank had revoked the license of one of the banks, had it not?

FRIDMAN: It seems to me, yes.

BROWNE: So I was right, was I not, when I was putting to you that by July a major banking crisis had been in progress for some months?

FRIDMAN: Yes.

BROWNE: And it had completely undermined the confidence of ordinary depositors and the investing community?

FRIDMAN: May I clarify this issue? The Central Bank withdrew the license for two small banks in May of 2004, as far as I recall, in part because of allegations of money laundering. One of these banks was also announced as having been on the so-called blacklist of the Central

Bank. I think it was a mistake by the authorities of the Central Bank to mention this blacklist because rumors immediately started circulating as to who was on the list. Many smaller banks were destroyed by this rumor as customers started pulling out their deposits.

BROWNE: What that means is that customers wanted their money back, did they not?

FRIDMAN: Yes, they wanted to withdraw all their money, but no single bank in the world could immediately satisfy all of these demands.

BROWNE: That I can understand, but when you talk about having to inject money into *Alfa Bank*, what you mean is that you had to put back the money that customers had put in?

FRIDMAN: Yes, that is true. I do not want to blame our customers. It is a normal reaction to such rumors, that something was wrong with *Alfa Bank*—especially when the rumors appear in an article—a front-page article in the leading business newspaper.

BROWNE: I will come to that but, before I do, it is very important to establish what you did not initially agree with, which was that the banking crisis had started as early as May?

FRIDMAN: The banking crisis began in a small bank in May, but it started at *Alfa Bank* after the publication of the article in *Kommersant*.

BROWNE: I know you say that, and I promise you I will come to that, but what you say in your witness statement is that between May and July 2004, Russia was hit by a banking crisis that paralyzed a number of Russian banks.

FRIDMAN: Yes.

BROWNE: You agree with that?

FRIDMAN: Yes.

BROWNE: And as early as May there were widespread rumors going around as to which banks might be next?

FRIDMAN: Yes.

BROWNE: Not least, as you pointed out, because the Central Bank had made public statements about this.

FRIDMAN: Yes.

BROWNE: So there were loads of rumors about all sorts of banks, including *Alfa Bank*?

FRIDMAN: Yes.

BROWNE: Even before the *Kommersant* article on July 7?

FRIDMAN: I think so because there were rumors about all the banks in the country.

BROWNE: And those rumors led, obviously, to a lot of depositors trying to withdraw their money?

FRIDMAN: No, not at first, because at that time it only impacted one small bank. Perhaps you are not aware that we have more than 1,000 banks in the country, which is quite different to your practice in the United Kingdom. What happens to a small bank doesn't concern people in terms of *Alfa Bank* because *Alfa Bank* is one of the largest banks in the country.

BROWNE: But after Sod Business Bank—I am sure I have mispronounced its name?

FRIDMAN: You are right.

BROWNE: I am sure I should not put the emphasis on "sod"—on May 12th went under. On June 3rd Credit Trust went bust, closed its doors, other banks that month as well?

FRIDMAN: Yes.

BROWNE: And there were many newspaper articles about the banking crisis around that time?

FRIDMAN: I do not remember any articles mentioning *Alfa Bank*.

BROWNE: On July 5th there was a television program suggesting that Guta Bank and *Alfa Bank* might be in trouble?

FRIDMAN: That TV program was, it seems to me, after the publication.

BROWNE: I suggest it was on July 5th and that on July 6th a Mr. Kristyuk of *Alfa Bank* made a public statement.

FRIDMAN: Yes.

BROWNE: Do you remember that?

FRIDMAN: Yes, probably, yes.

BROWNE: It is actually referred to, I think, by Mr. Vasiliev. Mr. Kristyuk was the bank's vice president?

FRIDMAN: Yes.

BROWNE: If we look at that long chunk of Mr. Vasiliev we see at the end of it: "What should our journalists do when they receive so much information and moreover there was a press release from your bank's

Vice President Kristyuk, who was desperately calling on clients not to worry." Mr. Vasiliev is right about that, is he not?

FRIDMAN: Yes, probably he mentioned that.

BROWNE: And, of course, in a panic there is nothing worse than telling people not to panic?

FRIDMAN: I don't think this is the case, because *Alfa Bank* is a very trustworthy bank. In the deep financial crisis of 1998, it was the only large bank in the country that fully met all the demands of its creditors and customers.

BROWNE: This two-month long banking crisis in Russia had undermined trust in all banks, including *Alfa Bank*?

FRIDMAN: Not at all.

BROWNE: Why then did Mr. Kristyuk need to make a statement on July 6th if there was no concern about a lack of confidence in *Alfa Bank*?

FRIDMAN: Exactly because of the reason you already mentioned, because a lot of rumors were circulating and he was just making a public statement on behalf of *Alfa Bank*, that we were having no problem with liquidity and we are ready to satisfy all the requests of our clients.

BROWNE: But you were not ready, were you, because, as you yourself say on the program, the demands to withdraw money were so great you had to bring in extra cash in transit vehicles?

FRIDMAN: But that happened after this publication.

BROWNE: I suggest it was already happening on July 6.

FRIDMAN: No. There is a big difference between rumors and a front-page story in the leading newspaper. Can you imagine what would happen if rumors started circling about NatWest Bank, if *FT* published a front-page article that NatWest was under threat? Is there a difference between the two events.

BROWNE: You see, you are wrong about the chronology, are you not, because in fact the ordering of the vehicles to bring in more cash was one day before the article was published. Just look on page 6. It will not do to suggest that the run was caused by *Kommersant*'s article of the 7th because one day before the story was published, namely on July 6th, when Mr. Kristyuk put out his statement, you were already having to bring in vehicles with extra cash.

FRIDMAN: Yes, of course I do not remember exactly when we required extra cash. There were already rumors, which of course impacted cash withdrawals from the bank. This increased demand was very different compared to the increased demand after publication of the article. This was just a small shower and after it came a downpour.

BROWNE: A moment ago you were saying this did not even happen until after the article. Now you are accepting, in the light of what I pointed out to you about what you said on the program, that the vehicles were actually ordered before the article of the 7th?

FRIDMAN: Yes, I did not state that nothing had happened, I mentioned that there were rumors, but there is a big difference between rumors and the rumors being confirmed by an article in the most respectable newspaper in the country.

BROWNE: Let us just look at what happened at this point in the broadcast. Mr. Vasiliev says: "This is why you have ordered these vehicles, cash in transit vehicles, one day before the story was published." You do not challenge that. You say: "We ordered the vehicles because the market was in an uproar." The truth is, the market was in an uproar before the *Kommersant* article. *Kommersant* did not create the uproar.

FRIDMAN: Yes, but *Kommersant* created a hurricane for *Alfa Bank*.

BROWNE: And what contributed to the uproar the day before the article was that Guta Bank had declared itself bankrupt; it had shut its doors.

FRIDMAN: Yes.

BROWNE: And as you say, the inevitable result of that was massive pressure on all private banks, which, of course, included *Alfa Bank*?

FRIDMAN: Yes.

BROWNE: All before anyone opened *Kommersant* on the morning of July 7th.

FRIDMAN: Yes, but in that particular case, due to this publication, demand from the *Alfa Bank* clients became enormous.

BROWNE: There were lines for ATMs.

FRIDMAN: Yes.

BROWNE: Including *Alfa Bank* ATMs?

FRIDMAN: Yes, and inside the banks as well.

BROWNE: So these were pre-existing problems, which were known to all Muscovites?

FRIDMAN: Yes.

BROWNE: On the evening of July 6th, there were lines, including at the Sokol branch of *Alfa Bank*. Do you know the Sokol branch?

FRIDMAN: Yes, we have many branches.

BROWNE: And that was the branch that the journalist from *Kommersant* referred to in her article of the 7th?

FRIDMAN: Yes.

BROWNE: Now, the article on July 7th. A month later *Alfa Bank* issues proceedings, on August 8th, does it not?

FRIDMAN: Say it again, please?

BROWNE: Forgive me. On August 8, 2004 *Alfa Bank* issues libel proceedings against *Kommersant*?

FRIDMAN: Yes.

BROWNE: A month after the article?

FRIDMAN: Yes.

BROWNE: And in those proceedings you claimed that, as a result of the run on the bank, allegedly attributable to the article, you had lost 20 million roubles?

FRIDMAN: Yes.

BROWNE: But that you also wanted 300 million roubles for non-specific financial loss, damage to mere reputation?

FRIDMAN: Yes.

BROWNE: You are the banker, I am not: 300 million roubles is well over £6 million, is it not?

FRIDMAN: Something like that, probably.

BROWNE: At least US $11 million?

FRIDMAN: Yes.

BROWNE: It certainly does not happen as quickly here, but do libel actions normally get tried within two months in Russia?

FRIDMAN: Yes, it is absolutely normal.

BROWNE: Two months?

FRIDMAN: Two months is a normal timetable for issuing arbitrage.

BROWNE: I suggest that it went through the court system at exceptional speed and, when the news came out on October 20th that the damages were of the figures that I have just mentioned, there was amazement?

FRIDMAN: Yes, of course, because it was strange that we went to court because it was obvious for us that it was not a question of money; we went to court just to prove that *Kommersant* should report more accurately when they are dealing with issues that impact the interests of millions of customers. They published information that we were not fulfilling our obligations, that we were not paying money back to customers, which was completely false, and this caused an untold amount of damage to our material assets and reputation.

BROWNE: I know you say that, but for the moment, because we cannot try the merits of that action, I just want to concentrate on the enormous award of non-financial damage, 300 million roubles.

FRIDMAN: It is not enormous. I have read a lot of examples in Western business practice—by the way in the U.K. and the U.S.—where the claim for defending one's image and reputation was even more than…

BROWNE: But Mr. Fridman, not only are you wrong about U.K. damages, a moment ago you were telling this jury you were not a lawyer. Now you are lecturing them not just on Russian law but U.S. and U.K. law as well.

FRIDMAN: I am sorry, I don't mean to lecture you, it's just that I recently read something in a newspaper about the question of reputation and business in the U.K. and the U.S. I do not think it is a question of my legal education, it is a question simply of my understanding of how the business system works here.

BROWNE: I do not know what you have read about the U.K. The damages awarded were not, as you have said, to recover the losses suffered by *Alfa*, were they? The truth is that the award of 300 million roubles was quite simply to punish *Kommersant*?

FRIDMAN: No, it was not to punish *Kommersant*, the idea was to create a precedent that the leading business newspaper, with whom we have worked for many years, should report their information more accurately. We are regularly in contact with the chief editor of *Kommersant*. He could just as simply have called me and asked whether everything was okay with *Alfa Bank*. We have worked with them for a long time. We have provided help and assistance over many years. And they published completely false information, which damaged our material assets and image.

BROWNE: I am going to leave it, but they published no more, I suggest, than what was going through the minds of everyone affected by the Russian banking crisis?

FRIDMAN: No, they were not publishing a story about the general problem of the Russian banking system. They were publishing concrete allegations against *Alfa Bank*. They wrote that we were not fulfilling our obligations; that we were not releasing money to our customers. And this never happened. So it was very painful for us, for the management, for the shareholders, and for the clients of the bank.

BROWNE: They did not say that you had defaulted, they merely said there were long lines at cash machines.

FRIDMAN: No, that is not true, they mentioned that we were not releasing funds to our clients.

BROWNE: And whether you are right or I am right, the award of £6 million damages was, I suggest, perceived by everybody as a lesson to *Kommersant* and any other part of the independent Russian press not to wrestle with *Alfa Bank* again.

FRIDMAN: Yes, I think it was a lesson to *Kommersant* to be more accurate and very careful about providing information about a company that could damage public interest, I mean, thousands and millions of customers.

BROWNE: But it was a ridiculous sum, was it not?

FRIDMAN: You know, first of all, for the sake of the jury, I should note that at the end of the day the sum was decreased to $1 million.

BROWNE: I was going to say it was reduced to one tenth on appeal, but that of course was after the program?

FRIDMAN: It was two months after the program. The program took place immediately after the decision on the first. At the first hearing our request was something like $10 million. But for us, as I have already mentioned here today, and also on the TV program, money was not the objective. The point was to show journalists that they needed to behave differently if they truly wanted to be objective and professional in their work.

BROWNE: But the money awarded was the sum that *Alfa Bank* had claimed. To you, money was all important to teach *Kommersant* and other newspapers a lesson?

FRIDMAN: Yes, if after the *Kommersant* case journalists from other newspapers are more careful with what they publish, then a lesson was learned

BROWNE: I think you have agreed with me that *Kommersant* was regarded by President Putin as a thorn in his side?

FRIDMAN: I don't think there is any connection between President Putin and our situation with *Kommersant.*

BROWNE: Just let me ask my question. He must have read of this award with delight, do you not think?

FRIDMAN: I do not know.

BROWNE: Let us just use our imagination. Mr. Putin opens his morning newspaper on October 21st, sees that *Kommersant*, this thorn in his side, has been the subject of a verdict for over £6 million damages. He must have been extremely pleased?

FRIDMAN: I do not know about that. I am not a close friend of Mr. Putin, so I do not know what his personal feelings are towards *Kommersant.*

BROWNE: And that is really the point that Mr. Vasiliev was making, was it not, not that this was all a Kremlin plot, this libel action, but Mr. Vasiliev says that you, Mr. Fridman, have decided to trade your loyalty to the Kremlin?

FRIDMAN: Yes, just—sorry, it is just completely untrue. These are all lies. And I mentioned the same thing on this TV show, according to my source, Mr. Vasiliev is lying.

BROWNE: Now, during this show you were quick, were you not, to threaten to sue *Kommersant* again? You wanted to teach them a lesson and rub it in, did you not?

FRIDMAN: No, I just mentioned that if Mr. Vasiliev was going to continue to lie, I would sue him again.

BROWNE: Yes. And you said with glee, "I am afraid you will lose more money."

FRIDMAN: Meaning that it wouldn't take much of a lie.

BROWNE: If he says something you do not like, there is going to be another £6 million bill. Is that what you are saying?

FRIDMAN: First of all, this $6 million figure you keep mentioning was ultimately only $1 million. And again, if he lies, as a citizen, there is little damage involved; but if he lies as the chief editor of the main newspaper in the country, he should be responsible for his actions.

BROWNE: You keep on talking about only $1 million or whatever; the fact is the court initially awarded what you asked for and that was the size of the award at the time of the program, was it not?

FRIDMAN: Yes.

BROWNE: No one could see into the future?

FRIDMAN: Yes.

BROWNE: Now, *The Moscow Times* was among the papers to express concern, was it not?

FRIDMAN: Yes.

BROWNE: Do you know Mr. Reznik, the deputy chairman of the Duma's information committee?

FRIDMAN: I do not know him.

BROWNE: He is not somebody who could be said to be party political, is he? He is a perfectly neutral observer?

FRIDMAN: I do not know him.

BROWNE: He called, as you will see: "The ruling an absolutely wrong decision. I think it is just an attempt to destroy an unwanted brand, he said. Even if *Kommersant* is guilty of something, which I strongly doubt, the amount of the award is too large."

FRIDMAN: Yes, but maybe—that is his opinion, but it somehow contradicts your previous point that all authority in Russia behaves according to President Putin's orders.

BROWNE: I am saying here is somebody who is a neutral observer commenting on the size of the award?

FRIDMAN: But why did you decide that the court was not neutral and the chief of the committee of the state Duma was independent and neutral?

BROWNE: I am asking you.

FRIDMAN: I do not know him, so I do not know. I assume that all these people should be neutral, including the court judge.

BROWNE: I am putting to you, this was somebody who was a neutral observer of the press, who was extremely concerned about the size of the award, and he was only one of many, was he not? You see if you look on page 111, this is in the *Financial Times*.

FRIDMAN: Okay.

BROWNE: Halfway down Mr. Oleg Panfilov, head of the Center for Journalism in Extreme Situations said: "This is a political Act. *Kommersant* is not a paper of opposition but with an independent stance. The authorities could not use the police, so it was easier to use a legal action."

FRIDMAN: That is his opinion, so I respect it.

BROWNE: These clippings, which we have just been looking at and Mr. Shields spent rather long on, were only part of a considerable volume of bad publicity that this libel action brought *Alfa Bank*?

FRIDMAN: Yes, of course, media in society was against this wording, for the obvious reasons. In Russia we have a tradition of journalists publishing articles for very small bribes.

BROWNE: You are not suggesting that *Kommersant* published this article because they were bribed, are you?

FRIDMAN: I do not know.

BROWNE: Why do you suggest that it might even have been a possibility, because you yourself have said they were an epoch in Russian journalism?

FRIDMAN: Because they published incorrect facts.

BROWNE: Why would you so casually blacken their name by suggesting that they might have been bribed?

FRIDMAN: I do not want to blame them. I am just wondering why they did not call us at some point to ask what was going on with *Alfa Bank*, if they had this type of information about *Alfa Bank*. It is the obligation of a journalist to verify information with the people who are involved in the story. It seems to me that this is a norm for journalists all over the world.

BROWNE: If you are right about that, it does not follow, does it, that they were bribed?

FRIDMAN: I did not say that they had been bribed; I just said that I do not know that they weren't.

BROWNE: Or might have been bribed. What I suggest is that you were so concerned about the bad publicity that you decided to deal with it by challenging Mr. Vasiliev to a duel. You were the challenger, were you not?

FRIDMAN: No, I decided to go to the TV show because Mr. Vasiliev accused me of exactly what you are saying, that I bargained with the Kremlin over *Kommersant*. I am not a Kremlin loyalist; I am an independent businessman. I do not appreciate being labeled as politically committed to the authorities. That was the only reason why I decided to go to court—sorry, to the TV show.

BROWNE: And although you did not mention it in your evidence this morning, in fact you and Mr. Soloviov were close friends, were you not, dating back to university times?

FRIDMAN: I would not say that we are close friends, but we know each other quite well. We studied at the same university.

BROWNE: "I know Soloviov well," you said?

FRIDMAN: You know him—sorry, yes, I know him quite well.

BROWNE: Yes, you do know him quite well, do you not, because the two of you had been at university for five years in the 1980s.

FRIDMAN: Yes.

BROWNE: Can I just ask a bit about the program? It is of course a very well known program, is it not?

FRIDMAN: Yes, you are right.

BROWNE: The reason for that is that Russians are interested in it because it always chooses to debate a controversial topical subject?

FRIDMAN: Yes.

BROWNE: And furthermore, celebrities appear and give their views?

FRIDMAN: Yes.

BROWNE: And you took, as your champions or allies, two musicians. Is that right?

FRIDMAN: My assistants? Yes, two musicians. They are very different, but they are musicians.

BROWNE: And their complaint is not that *Kommersant* had libeled *Alfa Bank* but that their musical critics did not know their Rostropovich from their Shostakovich?

FRIDMAN: Say that again.

BROWNE: The complaint of those who appeared with you on the program was that *Kommersant*'s musical critics were ignorant?

FRIDMAN: Yes—no, no, they did complain to *Kommersant* about an article that reported on a concert—the way that *Kommersant* had covered the performance, which they saw as completely unfair.

BROWNE: And you see, Mr. Fridman, that shows, does it not, the way that Russian libel law operates, does it not, because opinions are stamped on in Russia, there is no right to comment honestly?

FRIDMAN: Why do you make this conclusion?

BROWNE: Well, I will get to this very shortly as it is the end of the day. What I am suggesting is that nobody here would sue or be able sue on the basis of criticism of a performance of a concert artist. We are allowed to express an honest opinion. In Russia it would appear that you think that is not the case.

FRIDMAN: As far as I can remember, they criticized *Kommersant* not because they were critical of the quality of their concert but because they had published incorrect facts. For instance, Mr. Makarevich, who is as I have already mentioned a very famous rock musician in the country, said that the *Kommersant* article pointed out the concert hall was empty. But the hall was overflowing with people. Again, this was not a claim against the quality of the concert, but simply misinformation.

BROWNE: But all of this is quite inconsistent with your own paean of praise to the excellence of the journalism?

FRIDMAN: It is not to contradict that. It seems to me that it is not uncommon to have brilliant journalists and bad editors that allow false facts to slip in.

BROWNE: Now, Mr. Fridman, just before we end this evening, in your witness statement you said that the program was filmed live on October 28th. That is not right; I think that is agreed.

FRIDMAN: Yes, it was recorded one day before they aired it.

BROWNE: It is a small point, but how could your recollection have been so mistaken?

FRIDMAN: Sorry?

BROWNE: How could you have forgotten something as simple as that, that it is recorded on one day …

FRIDMAN: I did not forget it. I mentioned that it was taped one day before it aired on TV.

BROWNE: I am thinking about your witness statement, because you said, "the program is filmed live and viewers have the opportunity to telephone the program and vote?"

FRIDMAN: Can I explain? It was taped before but when it was shown on TV it was in the TV show, in the live show, people could call in and vote for one of two participants. So it was taped before, but the voting was live during the airing of the show. Am I clear?

BROWNE: The voting takes place on the 28th, does it?

FRIDMAN: Yes.

BROWNE: Exactly.

FRIDMAN: So the voting was live.

BROWNE: Could you explain something for me? Why does the voting start on the screen even before anyone has said anything in the debate?

FRIDMAN: Because I would say that people who watch this TV show have a preliminary take on the participants.

BROWNE: So they do not wait, do they? They start voting even before they have heard anything?

FRIDMAN: They start voting immediately after the number of the telephone appears on the TV.

BROWNE: It certainly sounds as though the voting is something one can attach real weight to?

FRIDMAN: By the way, the score did not start in my favor.

BROWNE: We have noticed that.

FRIDMAN: Because a lot of people do not like businessmen in our country.

Friday, May 19, 2006

BROWNE: Mr. Fridman, yesterday the gist of your evidence to the jury was that you have never, never tried to be influential politically; that is correct?

FRIDMAN: Yes.

BROWNE: Can we just test that with one example? Going back to 1996, were you one of the authors of an open letter in *Izvestia*?

FRIDMAN: Yes.

BROWNE: Could you just look at the end at the signatories to that letter?

FRIDMAN: Yes.

BROWNE: You were one of them, were you not?

FRIDMAN: Correct.

BROWNE: Would you agree with me, Mr. Fridman, this letter was the most blatant attempt to influence the political course of Russia on the eve of the presidential election in June 1996?

FRIDMAN: Yes. That was the position of the people who signed this letter. All of those people were well-known businessman, and among them, you can analyze it yourself—except for a couple of people like Mr. Berezovsky and Mr. Gusinsky—nobody else really was involved in politics.

BROWNE: Mr. Potanin was, was he not? We see his name.

FRIDMAN: No, he did sign the document, but as far as I know, he was acting just as a businessman.

BROWNE: You are not trying, are you, to disown your signature of this letter because it conflicts with your evidence that you have never sought to be politically influential?

FRIDMAN: From my point of view it is not in conflict because I do believe that as a businessman—and as a business society—we have to express our position towards important events that take place. As I already mentioned to you yesterday, I am a member of the Russian Union of Industrialists and Entrepreneurs, and we send letters like that very often concerning hot political and economic topics. And I do not believe that the position of big business should be counted as a political activity, as my own personal political activity.

BROWNE: This letter was an attempt by businessmen to exercise political influence in relation to the forthcoming presidential election, was it not?

FRIDMAN: No, that was just our request to find a peaceful solution, because, I would like to remind the jury and you, that in 1996, Russia was more or less at the beginning of civil war.

BROWNE: Russia at this time was on the eve of a presidential election?

FRIDMAN: Correct.

BROWNE: Now can we look at the letter? It contains pretty lurid terms, does it not?

FRIDMAN: Sorry?

BROWNE: Pretty lurid terms.

FRIDMAN: Yes, yes. Yes.

BROWNE: "Society is falling apart. With each new day, its disintegration becomes more and more catastrophic and the crack that splits us into Reds and Whites and to 'us' and 'them' runs through the heart of Russia… At this critical hour." Critical, I suggest—do you agree—because of the imminent election; is that right? It was a critical hour because the presidential election was imminent?

FRIDMAN: Yes.

BROWNE: This was an attempt, was it not, to influence Russian politicians?

FRIDMAN: I would like to underline that we made this attempt purely as entrepreneurs, and we underlined a couple of times that it was the responsibility of politicians to make a decision. This is always the position I take as a businessman.

BROWNE: You were trying to use the influence that you and your fellow businessman could exert to influence Russian politics; that is what you are saying, is it not?

FRIDMAN: Not influence. Influence it seems to me is the wrong word. It seems to me the right word is our position.

BROWNE: "The serious political threat consists in the fact that if the Communists win the presidential election they can realistically attempt to extract ideological retribution. This once again compels us to regard them as a force that wishes to make final and grave decisions as if they were making them in the name of society as a whole." What you were seeking to do in this letter was to ensure that the Communists did not win the presidential election?

FRIDMAN: Yes, as a capitalist I am strictly against the concept of communism, as it anticipates the expropriation of property.

BROWNE: You were seeking to make a political intervention in order to ensure that Communists did not win the election who might expropriate all your property; is that what you are saying?

FRIDMAN: No, I think "influence" is not the right word. I would say I wished to express our position, because it is effectively impossible to influence the peoples of Russia, as far as I understand. So from my point of view it is difficult to say that we were using influence to bring about a certain result.

BROWNE: You are saying you were not seeking to exercise influence on politicians?

FRIDMAN: It is—how to define it, where is the influence, where is the announcement of our own position? As a big businessman it seems to me we are obliged from time to time, if a topic is of great interest, either economic or political, to take a certain position. I would like to remind you, if possible, that when Mr. Gusinsky was in prison for three days, a fact that you mentioned yesterday, we, a group of businessman, including a couple of businessman on that list, also sent a letter to the general prosecutor with a request to release him from jail and provide certain guarantees that he would not leave the country.

BROWNE: That, I suggest, was an intervention prompted by a blatant disregard of Mr. Gusinsky's human rights?

FRIDMAN: No, that was just our approach to the authorities to avoid a certain kind of, you know, strong—cruel approach towards Mr. Gusinsky who was a representative of the media and big business. We were opposed to the authorities using this case as an example of what could happen to other members of the media. By the way, Mr. Berezovsky did not sign this letter. He refused to sign it.

BROWNE: Can we look at the last main paragraph: "Those who seek to undermine Russian civil society, gambling on a desire to ideological revenge and social confrontation." That is a reference to the Communists, is it not?

FRIDMAN: Not necessarily to the Communists; there are many extremists in the country.

BROWNE: "Must understand that Russian entrepreneurs ..." That includes you?

FRIDMAN: Yes.

BROWNE: "... possess the necessary resources and willpower to exert their influence on politicians who are either too unprincipled or too uncompromising." What could be clearer than that as an admission that this letter was an attempt by you and your fellow entrepreneurs to use the precise words of this letter to exert their influence on politicians?

FRIDMAN: Yes, I fully agree with what you are saying, but you asked me before about our influence over voting results, which is different. Of course we have a certain influence over politicians as businessmen because we cooperate with them, we talk with them, we represent certain economical and political platforms in the parliament. In this way we might have some impact, on a personal level, but we had no impact on the voting results; that is what I meant to say.

BROWNE: I would remind you, Mr. Fridman, that yesterday you told this jury, "I never tried to be politically influential."

FRIDMAN: That is exactly the case.

BROWNE: Nothing could be more of an attempt to be politically influential than this letter?

FRIDMAN: What does this mean, "politically influential?" If I am on the list of big businessman who signed this letter, which is asking people to find a compromise between different parties when the country is effectively at the beginning of civil war, between the pro-Communist and anti-Communist groups. I don't think this means that I am trying to achieve certain political influence. Maybe I am wrong, but this is how I understand my obligation as a citizen of the country and as a member of big business.

BROWNE: Mr. Fridman, yesterday—and I summarize—you also told the jury that you had no special relationship with Mr. Putin?

FRIDMAN: Correct.

BROWNE: That you had not met him one-on-one.

FRIDMAN: Yes.

BROWNE: That you had met him on a couple of occasions.

FRIDMAN: Yes.

BROWNE: And that when you went to see him it was essentially out of politeness because he was the President of the Republic; is that a fair summary?

FRIDMAN: Yes.

BROWNE: You also told the jury that you were an ordinary businessman, not a public figure.

FRIDMAN: Yes.

BROWNE: And that you tried not to appear on television or chat shows?

FRIDMAN: Or where?

BROWNE: Well, do you know the expression "chat shows," where people are interviewed in studio?

FRIDMAN: Yes, I understand. Yes.

BROWNE: That is a fair summary?

FRIDMAN: Yes.

BROWNE: Do you remember giving an interview in 2002 on the TV show *Breakfast with Soloviov*?

FRIDMAN: Yes.

BROWNE: So that was one occasion when you decided to participate on TV?

FRIDMAN: Yes.

BROWNE: And of course, as we learned yesterday, Mr. Soloviov is your old friend back from university days?

FRIDMAN: Yes, that is why, in part, it was difficult to refuse his invitation.

BROWNE: I will ask now if you can be handed a copy of the transcript of this interview on July 28, 2002. Mr. Voloshin is the head of Mr. Putin's administration, is he not?

FRIDMAN: Not now.

BROWNE: He was then?

FRIDMAN: He was then, yes.

BROWNE: A sort of cabinet secretary?

FRIDMAN: I do not—I do not know exactly what the position is in the United Kingdom.

BROWNE: Well, we will stick with "head of administration?"

FRIDMAN: Head of administration.

BROWNE: Mr. Soloviov asks you: "When does the government start soliciting a businessman." And you reply: "If I am not mistaken, the first time we were gathered together was in 1993, just before the October coup. The situation was rather tense then, so the soon-to-be regulars of the oligarchic get-togethers were invited to come to the Kremlin by Gaidar." Gaidar was then the Prime Minister, was he not?

FRIDMAN: No, he was deputy Prime Minister.

BROWNE: This was three years before Mr. Putin became Prime Minister?

FRIDMAN: No, nine years—six years before Mr. Putin.

BROWNE: 1993—yes, Mr. Putin takes over in August 1999.

FRIDMAN: As Prime Minister.

BROWNE: Thank you for correcting me. So this is six years before. Now, what I suggest was that the Kremlin has established regular get-togethers of businessmen such as yourself.

FRIDMAN: Yes.

BROWNE: Which have been ongoing since at least 1993.

FRIDMAN: Yes.

BROWNE: Regular meetings with the president, whoever it may be.

FRIDMAN: Yes, for—to a certain degree, yes.

BROWNE: Mr. Soloviov enquires, "For a chat?" And you reply: "Well, to sort of discuss some issues. I do not even know which criteria they used to invite us at that time. Well, sort of a publicly recognized group." When you refer to a "publicly recognized group," what I suggest you are saying is that these meetings between businessmen and the president were so regular, to use your word, that they became known to the public, and the businessmen were a publicly recognized group. That is right, is it not? You became a publicly known group?

FRIDMAN: Yes, we became a publicly known group of businessmen, correct.

BROWNE: "Since then I have been a pretty regular participant of these pow-wows. Some of the people left for certain objective reasons. New ones have appeared." Then Mr. Soloviov says: "A pow-wow? Is it just a slip of the tongue, or your real attitude? ...Mr. Fridman: No, it is only an ironic name for that." Did you use the word pow-wow when you were speaking in Russian?

FRIDMAN: Pow-wow? I have never heard this word before. What does pow-wow mean?

BROWNE: Pow-wow is a chat?

FRIDMAN: The interpreter does not know this word.

BROWNE: Let me interpret for the interpreter. A pow-wow is a get-together—a group of people who get together and chat.

FRIDMAN: Okay, so it is a group of people, a kind of club?

BROWNE: Yes, a cabal; do you know that word?

FRIDMAN: No, I do not know.

BROWNE: A little group. It does not matter.

FRIDMAN: The right word, sorry, is like a club of businessmen who sometimes meet regularly with the authorities.

BROWNE: Do you happen to remember now that your memory has been jogged what word you used in Russian?

FRIDMAN: No, I do not remember. It was three years ago.

BROWNE: But anyway, these little groups, you have been a regular participant at?

FRIDMAN: Yes, yes.

BROWNE: So far as the membership of the group is concerned, you say some of the people left for certain objective reasons. Now, that of course would include Mr. Berezovsky and Mr. Gusinsky, would it not?

FRIDMAN: Not necessarily. As you probably have heard, there were a number of crises in Russia, for instance in 1998, many successful businessmen suddenly found themselves in bankruptcy. Businessmen who had signed this letter found themselves in situations where they were no longer able to attend.

BROWNE: Yes, but my question was: I am not suggesting that it was Mr. Berezovsky and Mr. Gusinsky alone that you were referring to, but they were amongst the people who left…

FRIDMAN: Of course, yes, because they live in London right now.

BROWNE: Mr. Soloviov's remarks: "Obviously your company has to take part in the regional elections. I think it often happens that your personal political views come into conflict with your company's interests. One should support those who will guarantee stability, not necessarily a pro-market person."

You reply: "I would say an open non-supporter of a market economy will never have our votes because he will eventually become a threat to us. If we elect someone as a citizen and an individual, we would probably support more liberal kinds of politicians and so on."

FRIDMAN: Yes.

BROWNE: Are you not saying there that your company takes part in regional elections and—sorry, let me finish—and supports those who will not eventually be a threat to your commercial interests?

FRIDMAN: It seems to me very clearly underlined that we participated in that as individuals and citizens.

BROWNE: But you see, Mr. Soloviov has said, "Your company has to take part in the regional elections."

FRIDMAN: When he asked me about the company, I told you yesterday, that we as citizens had tried to create a partnership in response to certain political situations that were taking place in Russia. But as a company we tried to be as neutral as possible. By the way, in the same interview I also expressed the position that: "We subscribe and have been subscribing in all the years of our business's existence to the concept of the non-association of ourselves and our business to any political figures or public officials."

BROWNE: "We as a bank assume a very passive role."

FRIDMAN: "We as a bank assume a very passive role," yes.

BROWNE: "… and try to be loyal to all the candidates because I have said before it is most important for us to be left well alone so that we would not have to deal with the tax police all the time." Now, it was the tax police who were the downfall of Mr. Khodorkovsky, was it not?

FRIDMAN: Yes.

BROWNE: And Yukos.

FRIDMAN: As far as I remember that is true.

BROWNE: You did not want to go the way of Mr. Khodorkovsky, did you?

FRIDMAN: I for sure did not want to go the way of Mr. Khodorkovsky, for the time being.

BROWNE: And *Alfa Bank* does not want to go the way of Yukos, does it?

FRIDMAN: Yes, that is absolutely true.

BROWNE: So what you do, I suggest, is, with the exception of the Communists, you back all the horses in the race?

FRIDMAN: No, that is not true. I would like to repeat again, we tried to be as passive as possible. And you quoted, exactly, my thoughts.

BROWNE: The article on your website was accurate in saying that you had financed the United Russia Party, and you said it was not.

FRIDMAN: Yes.

BROWNE: But what I am suggesting is that in addition to the United Russia Party, which we will leave because we have dealt with that, you also supported Mr. Nemtsov's Union of Right Forces or SPS?

FRIDMAN: Yes, I told you yesterday that certain individuals, and my partner, supported different political parties, but I would like to clarify our position. I would like to clarify our view towards politics in relation to business and personal interests. As a citizen and individual, we have the right to support anyone. And I, of course, could not confirm that no one from *Alfa Bank* has provided financial assistance to any party. But as a businessman, as an entity, we prefer not to participate in political activities.

BROWNE: You keep on making that distinction, but I suggest it is completely at odds with how you express yourself in the passage I have just read where you say: "We as a bank assume a very passive role and try to be loyal to all the candidates."

FRIDMAN: Exactly, exactly, because we do not want to make a choice, as an entity. As a bank we are interested in maintaining a stable and sustainable set of rules for, which is called business.

BROWNE: Let us go on. "Mikhail Fridman: First, the issues that need the support of the deputies." The "deputies" are the deputies of the Duma, are they? Members of Parliament?

FRIDMAN: Yes.

BROWNE: "...are as a rule issues to be dealt with from the standpoint of an ideology of a political force, for example SPS or Yabloko." Let us leave Yabloko to one side. The SPS or Union of Right Forces was a political movement founded by Mr. Nemtsov, was it not?

FRIDMAN: Not just him personally, he was among the founders of this movement.

BROWNE: And among the leaders of the movement?

FRIDMAN: Yes, right.

BROWNE: So Mr. Soloviov says: "So you place a call to the boss?" And you reply: "I can easily meet them and explain that there is a certain issue and I would like their support on that." So you are able to ring up Mr. Nemtsov to place a call to the boss of the SPS and explain that there is an issue on which you would like their support?

FRIDMAN: Yes, of course, I know him quite well, since the early 90s, and we are the same age, so I would go so far as to say that we are friends.

BROWNE: Mr. Soloviov goes on: "Will they ask you for money?" "Well, I would say they will ask for support for their activities in some form." Now we know that money was provided to SPS; you have said that, have you not?

FRIDMAN: No. First of all I did not say that here. I just underlined that we—for support and—were "activities in some form," which does not mean necessarily only money. We always—we are very often asked for our advice and our expertise.

BROWNE: I suggest—this is a question I shall be putting to Mr. Aven—that *Alfa Bank* has financed the Union of Right Forces.

FRIDMAN: Again, I would like to express very clearly that some people who used to work for *Alfa Bank* or still work for *Alfa Bank* could be supporters of the Union of Right Forces, including myself, but this is separate from our business activities at *Alfa Bank*.

BROWNE: Can we go on down this page to just by the second punch hole: "Moderator: Do you have to spend a lot of money on direct political support to the same parties during election campaigns?"

You reply: "I would say that what we spend is normal by Russian standards but can be considered a lot by Western standards."

We know that by Western standards loans of £1 million or so and gifts are made to political parties; what is normal by Russian standards?

FRIDMAN: It is probably, you know, dozens of thousands of dollars.

BROWNE: Dozens of thousands of dollars? I suggest it is millions and millions of dollars.

FRIDMAN: We never spend that much money on political activities. Again, we did this as individuals, I've repeated this a number of times.

BROWNE: Then, if we skip to Mr. Soloviov's question: "Do you give equal amounts to all the parties?"

You reply: "No, absolutely not; for example we would never fund the Communists."

So what I suggest to you is that you and *Alfa Bank*, through its hundreds of different subsidiaries, do distribute large sums of money to nearly all the parties, and certainly Putin's party and the SPS, but you draw the line at the Communists?

FRIDMAN: That is completely not true.

BROWNE: Mr. Fridman, have you ever made a political contribution, personally, to the Union of Right Forces?

FRIDMAN: Yes.

BROWNE: How much?

FRIDMAN: It was—I do not remember, but it was a relatively small amount.

BROWNE: Tens of thousands of dollars?

FRIDMAN: Correct.

BROWNE: $100,000? More?

FRIDMAN: As far as I remember it was less than $100,000.

BROWNE: That was when Mr. Nemtsov was the leader of the party?

FRIDMAN: No, it was before—I always support—was supportive of that party; even now.

BROWNE: Is the answer to my question "yes?"

FRIDMAN: Yes.

BROWNE: I will not ask you about the United Russia Party or we will be going over the same ground we covered yesterday. Now, what about *Alfa Bank*? There are hundreds of companies, are there not, under the *Alfa Bank* umbrella?

FRIDMAN: Yes.

BROWNE: So far as you know, have any companies in the *Alfa Bank* group paid money to the Union of Right Forces?

FRIDMAN: As far as I know—as far as I can recall, no.

BROWNE: I will pursue that with Mr. Aven; I do not want to take up time now. Have any companies in the *Alfa* group given money to Mr. Putin's party?

FRIDMAN: As far as I remember, no.

BROWNE: Why do you say "as far as I remember?" Why do you qualify it in that way?

FRIDMAN: Because I do not sign any of the invoices in our group of companies.

BROWNE: Do you think it is possible that in what I accept is a very large group some part of it is subscribed to Mr. Putin's party?

FRIDMAN: Of course, it is possible. For instance, I am the chairman of the board of the TNK/BP venture, which has an annual revenue of $25 billion. We have a certain amount of flexibility to provide assistance. But I never ordered this assistance. And I do not know about these facts. That is why I answer, "According to my knowledge, no."

BROWNE: So it is possible, and if it happened that might explain what was written on the *Alfa Bank* website, would it not?

FRIDMAN: It is not connected. It is not *Alfa Bank*, it is a different company.

BROWNE: What, what is there on the *Alfa Bank* website?

FRIDMAN: Yes, for *Alfa Bank*, as far as I know, management never provided any financial assistance to any political party.

BROWNE: Now, can we go on, Mr. Fridman? Mr. Soloviov says: "The presidential elections are looming ahead. Have you already decided which of the candidates you are going to support or is it the money issue you have to decide when you have to financially commit yourself?" So Mr. Soloviov clearly believes, does he not, that in addition to you deciding who you are going to support you also have to decide who to put your money on; who to financially support?

FRIDMAN: Yes, that was a joke. That was a very ironic question.

BROWNE: The jury will judge whether it was ironic. This is a man who has known you since you were both students?

FRIDMAN: Correct, that is why…

BROWNE: This is what he thinks, that you have to decide whom you are going to financially support.

FRIDMAN: Yes, and my answer is very clear and I would like to remind you that Mr. Putin won this election and took more than 80 percent of the votes. It was absolutely clear to everybody when we discussed this issue that there were no competitors for Mr. Putin; it was not necessary to fund Mr. Putin because he was the obvious winner in the election. That is why my answer at that time was largely rhetorical.

BROWNE: Well, Mr. Fridman, that is all very ingenious what you have said, but you did not have a crystal ball in July 2002, that would enable you to know the result of the election in 2004, did you?

FRIDMAN: As far as I can remember, it took place in 2003.

BROWNE: No, 2002.

FRIDMAN: Okay, but even in 2002, the popularity of Mr. Putin, which is still at the same level, if you analyze the popularity of this entire period. His support never fell below 70 percent, so it was quite obvious that Mr. Putin would be the next president.

BROWNE: I want to ask you now about what you said about your personal experience of dealing with the president. Do you remember yesterday you told the jury that you had never met Mr. Putin one-on-one?

FRIDMAN: One-on-one; correct.

BROWNE: Let us just read what you say just below the first punch hole? Do you see the passage beginning, "I would say from my personal experience?"

FRIDMAN: Mm-hmm.

BROWNE: "I would say from my personal experience of dealing with the president I see that, despite his way of expressing emotions, which can indeed be singled out, he is a living person, and this probably accounts for his being such a popular and successful politician." When you referred to "expressing emotions," were you thinking of such matters as his emotional outburst in September 1999, about the Chechen terrorists?

FRIDMAN: Yes, I am talking just about my personal experience. So during my meetings, I mean, when I participated in meetings with the president, he was emotionally very balanced.

BROWNE: "He remains a rational, well-balanced, and serious man. I believe that what is important is not how a politician expresses their emotions but rather whether or not they understand the necessity and possibility of interacting with the entrepreneurial community, and I have no concerns in this department."

FRIDMAN: Correct.

BROWNE: Then Mr. Soloviov says: "When you communicate with the president, do you have a sense of his personal attitude to you?"

You reply: "Good question. I would say, as I have seen it, to give the president his due, everybody who communicates with him has a good idea of his attitude to them. I do not know if it is only a feeling on an emotional level."

So, regardless of whether the two of you meet on your own, or perhaps more likely with civil servants in the Kremlin being there, the fact is that you are able to personally communicate in the literal sense face to face with Mr. Putin.

FRIDMAN: No, that is—I mean, first of all in the Russian language the word "you" means, you know, a group of people. So "you" means a group of people.

BROWNE: It is the same in English, is it not? "You" can mean "you, singular, "you, Mr. Fridman," or it could mean "you, *Alfa Bank*." But you see, what Mr. Soloviov is asking about is personal attitudes?

FRIDMAN: Correct.

BROWNE: He is asking about your personal experience. And therefore, I suggest, Mr. Fridman, quite contrary to what you are suggesting...

FRIDMAN: Absolutely not from my point of view...

BROWNE: Let me finish. When he says, "Do you feel his personal attitude to you?" he means "you," singular, Mr. Fridman.

FRIDMAN: May I answer?

BROWNE: Yes, of course, sorry.

FRIDMAN: If you read the article before, all of Mr. Soloviov's questions were dedicated to the relationship between the group of so-called oligarchs. He mentioned a lot of different names. And when he asked about that he asked, as far as I recall, exactly the relationship of Mr. Putin to you, to the group of oligarchs; because it was a pretty hot topic of discussion, the relationship between the president and the business community as a whole. And my answer was completely honest because I said that my personal take from all of these meetings was that—and I would like to repeat again—only in groups of significant Russian businessmen—that he was generally positive towards us, and to me personally.

BROWNE: I will just put it again so you are quite clear what I am suggesting. This is clearly a part of the discussion dealing with your personal relationship: you have a sense of his personal attitude to you when you communicate with the president?

FRIDMAN: Exactly.

BROWNE: And you are seeking to minimize your personal relationship with Mr. Putin by pretending it is all to do with the bank?

FRIDMAN: Yes, that is why I just took the time to explain that the expression "you" means "you group of businessmen," and if you analyze it, there are a lot of names who belong to the same group of businessmen that we are talking about. Mr. Deripaska, Mr. Potanin, Mr. Mordashov, Mr. Vakselberg; all these names are mentioned in this interview. So, in other words I will repeat again that I have never met President Putin one-on-one. I do meet with him several times a year as part of a group of big businessmen that represents leading business groups in the country.

BROWNE: So, it is now a few times a year that you meet him?

FRIDMAN: It is—this happens on a regular basis. We usually meet with the president two, three, or four times a year; depending on his schedule. Since 1999, when he came to power, we have probably met with him 12-14 times.

BROWNE: We have now found the Russian. And I am instructed that in fact this article is on the *Alfa Bank* website.

FRIDMAN: Great.

BROWNE: My last questions about this are linked to something earlier on. You see, I suggest not only do you have these regular meetings with Mr. Putin, but in addition you have the great advantage that there are a number of former *Alfa* employees actually employed in the Kremlin.

FRIDMAN: Yes.

BROWNE: Mr. Soloviov says: "But there are certain names directly linked to yours; they are even called *Alfa* people. You are sure to know the names very well; for example Mr. Surkov."

FRIDMAN: Yes.

BROWNE: You reply: "This collective name is in a way justified; it simply means that these people had worked with us before they came to the Kremlin. Besides speaking about Mr. Surkov, I do not deny we have known each other for many years, just like you and I." Mr. Surkov had been first deputy chairman of *Alfa* in the 1990s, had he not?

FRIDMAN: Yes, correct, 1996.

BROWNE: And since March 2004, he has been deputy chief of the presidential administration.

FRIDMAN: Since—those dates are wrong. He worked at *Alfa Bank* between probably 1996-1999. Since 2000, he has worked for the Kremlin administration, yes.

BROWNE: And most recently he has been, I think, deputy chief of the presidential administration.

FRIDMAN: Yes.

BROWNE: That is what I was putting forth, yes, sorry. So he is a powerful friend in the Kremlin, is he not?

FRIDMAN: Correct. He is my friend because I studied together with him at the same university as Mr. Soloviov; as I mentioned in this interview. The next question Mr. Soloviov asked me: "He comes to you for advice?" So we discussed exactly, you know, a very broad issue, but we never ask him for special favors.

BROWNE: You lobby him? Do you know that word?

FRIDMAN: No, that is not the right word. He is just a friend because we lived in the same hostel when we were 17-year-old boys.

BROWNE: Well, I am glad the Russians have—do you know the English expression an "old boy network?"

FRIDMAN: We probably do have a special relationship after living together in the hostel, playing soccer, hanging out, that is true.

BROWNE: There are others, are there not? Mr. Soloviov asks: "Who else is close to you in the government?" "There are several other people who came to the Kremlin from our firm—Abramov, Alexander Sergeyevich, Popov and some others I know."

FRIDMAN: All these people used to work for Mr. Surkov and when he came to the Kremlin they joined him. They were previously employed by *Alfa Bank*, so of course I was familiar with them.

BROWNE: Mr. Soloviov says: "How come people leave your bank, a place where they get good salaries and where they are doing things they like, and take jobs in the government where the remuneration is not comparable to what they used to earn in the business structures; it is not at all easy?"

Over the page, you say: "I do agree with you, even though this move is a wise and justified thing to do. By the way, this happens not only in Russia, it happens in all countries in the world; in America for instance."

Of course it is true that in America this has led to all sorts of allegations of conflicts of interest and corruption, has it not? Think of Mr. Cheney…

SHIELDS: That is a pretty bold statement to make.

FRIDMAN: So you blame me that I corrupted these people?

BROWNE: No, I am not; I am saying that this kind of—I was going to put that what I am saying is that it leads to conflicts of interest, does it not?

FRIDMAN: No, I think our relationship is strictly friendly, but we do continue to look out for our own interests as businessmen.

BROWNE: And Alexander Sergeyevich Abramov has been assistant to Mr. Putin?

FRIDMAN: Yes.

BROWNE: And is now acting Secretary of the Russian State Council. A very powerful figure in Russian life. Is that not right?

FRIDMAN: Yes, that is true. Can I just quote from the same interview a few paragraphs below?

BROWNE: Of course.

FRIDMAN: Mr. Soloviov asked me if we would gain anything by them leaving for the Kremlin. And I answer: "I do not think we gain anything, because we lose a qualified professional."

BROWNE: Mr. Soloviov says that in addition to *Alfa's* people in the Kremlin, there are in effect the Kremlin's people in *Alfa*. He says: "There is a reverse tendency, as far as I understand. Are there not many former public officials now working in *Alfa*?"

You reply: "Yes, certainly there are: Sysuev and Mr. Aven if anyone remembers that he used to be a public official, and others. I believe it is a totally normal transition."

Then if I just skip to Mr. Soloviov's next question: "How does such a move take place, and people go from you to the Kremlin? Do they phone you and say, 'Look, Mikhail, I got this job offer and want your advice."' So the Kremlin feels that they are able, when they want to fill a post, to ring you up and say, "Have you got somebody at *Alfa* who might be suitable?"

FRIDMAN: No, no. That is, it seems to me, a misinterpretation. I said originally—if they had already reached an agreement they would probably call me and ask a rhetorical question, "Are you opposed to somebody from your staff, from *Alfa Bank*, leaving for, let's say, the presidential administration?" And my answer is, if they already have reached an agreement, "Good luck to them."

BROWNE: But you would welcome it because it is a way in which you could ensure that *Alfa Bank* has friends in high places.

FRIDMAN: That is exactly contradictory to what I answered. I am okay with that but I do not think we gain anything because we lose a qualified professional. For us it is not a gain, it is actually damaging.

BROWNE: I want to look now, Mr. Fridman, at the broadcast that is the subject of this action. This was a program obviously about the banking crisis of 2004, and you refer back to 1998, do you not, to the banking crisis then? You are turning the clock back six years to 1998, and that provokes Mr. Vasiliev into saying that in 1999, you had tried to buy *Kommersant* together with Chubais.

FRIDMAN: Yes.

BROWNE: That was right in this qualified sense that purchasing *Kommersant* with Chubais and Potanin and others was one option you had considered. Could you just say yes so we have it on the transcript?

FRIDMAN: Yes.

BROWNE: The other option was of course the management buy-out?

FRIDMAN: Yes.

BROWNE: That would have involved the managers personally taking out a loan in order to buy Mr. Yakovlev's shares.

FRIDMAN: Yes.

BROWNE: How many people would have been involved in such a buy-out? Half a dozen?

FRIDMAN: I mean, we discussed with the shareholders of *Kommersant*, which you mentioned Mr. Kaskov yesterday, providing a loan to *Kommersant*, to the company, to the entity, to buy back shares from Mr. Yakovlev.

BROWNE: I see. It was not a management buy-out in the sense that the individual managers…

FRIDMAN: No, it was—if you provide a loan to a company and the company buys their shares back, according to financial terminology;

it is called a management buy-out. Because management makes the decision to buy the shares; it does not mean it belongs to the management, it just means that these shares become so-called treasury stock.

BROWNE: I am not going to debate it with you but that is not the English understanding. But at any rate, you have made clear what the Russian is. So the money would have been loaned to *Kommersant* by its own shares?

FRIDMAN: Yes.

BROWNE: If *Kommersant* had defaulted on the loan, then the shares would have been surrendered to *Alfa Bank*, the lender, would they not?

FRIDMAN: Yes.

BROWNE: In that way, you would have taken over a very valuable asset?

FRIDMAN: That is not the case because, if they were to default, we would put it up for auction, according to legislation, as collateral. And if the collateral for this loan happened to be shares of *Kommersant*, we would auction off the shares in order to pay back the bank's loan.

BROWNE: Just as the situation in relation to a company buying its own shares is different in this country, my memory is that it is actually unlawful to do it. A management buy-out means a buy-out by managers. There is a difference between English and Russian bankruptcy laws.

FRIDMAN: Let us assume that there were 10,000 people in the company. So we estimate that the loan must be provided to 10,000 owners. This is not the case. A management buy-out means that we are providing a loan to the company and the company buys their shares back.

BROWNE: I am not challenging what you say is the position in Russia; I am merely saying it is different in this country, as I understand it, and I am suggesting too that Russian bankruptcy laws have peculiarities and contradictions which are different from English bankruptcy laws. And one British company that criticized Russian bankruptcy laws was British Petroleum, was it not?

FRIDMAN: Yes.

BROWNE: They were livid about what your subsidiary, TNK, had done in seizing a company called Chernogorneft?

FRIDMAN: Yes, British Petroleum...

BROWNE: My learned friend will see what the relevance is. Your Lordship will recall what Mr. Berezovsky said about the planned loan merely being a way in which it was anticipated that Mr. Fridman and his allies, if it went ahead, might get their hands on *Kommersant.* I am suggesting, by reference to one example, one document, that if that had gone ahead it would not have been the first time. My Lord, we do have what was said on the *Alfa Bank* website about this, and indeed by Mr. Fridman, and I was just going to come to this: "Legally, we acted properly. True our bankruptcy laws can be contradictory, even our judges do not always understand them."

FRIDMAN: Yes. You did not quote that I said, "Legally we acted properly, says Fridman, through our bank."

BROWNE: I am going to come to that. I am not suggesting you did anything illegal. What I am suggesting is that, because Russian bankruptcy laws are very different, and to use your words, contradictory, you have exploited that position very skillfully to make large sums of money for *Alfa Bank*, or TNK, in this case at the expense of British Petroleum.

FRIDMAN: What was the question?

BROWNE: That is the question: have you not exploited opportunities?

FRIDMAN: No, we have exploited—we have exploited situations where we have been the creditors of a company and we used bankruptcy law in the interest of our business, but this was all done absolutely legally.

BROWNE: And at the cost of BP and its shareholders, who had paid close to half a billion dollars for this Chernogorneft field, which was next door to the TNK oil field in Siberia; that is what happened. They lost half a billion dollars.

FRIDMAN: They did not lose, they gained a lot. If you are so certain that we stole something from BP, why did they decide to establish an exclusive joint venture with us?

BROWNE: That is subsequently. Subsequently, I accept the hatchet was buried at the meeting blessed by Mr. Putin's presence, but what I am talking to you about is the use to which you put Russian bankruptcy laws at this earlier period, in 1997.

JUSTICE EADY: What I am not for the moment seeing, Mr. Browne, is how this BP exercise relates to the *Kommersant* matter.

BROWNE: Well, my Lord, Mr. Berezovsky's case is that if the *Kommersant* loan had gone ahead, what Mr. Fridman had in mind was a cheap way of getting his hands on *Kommersant* by exploitation of the idiosyncrasies, the peculiarities, of Russian law. Now, Mr. Fridman will not accept that from me and very shortly, although it has been extended by the need to deal with Mr. Shields' interruptions, I am just trying to say that that tests the credit of this denial; that would have been consistent with what happened with the Chernogorneft field in 1997.

FRIDMAN: I would like to just point out that we have the portfolio of the *Alfa Bank* loan for over $8 billion. So I do believe that the allegation that we used—we attempted to use the loan as a tool for absorbing this property, is completely false. And *Alfa Bank* did not provide the loan to TNK. This is a separate issue. We began the bankruptcy procedure because they were not paying back our money.

BROWNE: A loan for the *Kommersant* shares would have involved a loan of $35 to $40 million, would it not?

FRIDMAN: I do not know, it depends on the price.

BROWNE: That is what the price was in my instructions. Let us move on. Can we go to the transcript of the words which are complained of, which is on the first page of this packet? Just looking at the last half a dozen lines or so, which are the crux of the matter, you refer to Mr. Berezovsky having called you. Mr. Vasiliev says: "Did he give you a piece of advice?" You say: "He threatened as usual. "He even threatened me," you say. Obviously you mean he even threatened you in relation to the sale of *Kommersant*. Because you do not suggest he threatened you in any other context, do you?

FRIDMAN: Yes, we just discussed this implication.

BROWNE: Then you say, using the past tense, "he threatened everybody." That must mean, must it not, it can only mean, he threatened everybody in relation to the sale of *Kommersant*?

FRIDMAN: No, of course not.

BROWNE: How do you explain it? If what you meant was that he is always threatening people, you would have said, "He threatens everybody" (present tense)?

FRIDMAN: I do not know what it is in translation, but what I meant to say in Russian is that he threatens everybody. In Russian it means not in relation to this case but as a general way of doing business.

BROWNE: Do you understand the point I am putting to you?

FRIDMAN: No.

BROWNE: I will put it again. The words "he even threatened me" plainly mean he threatened you in relation to *Kommersant.*

FRIDMAN: Yes, correct.

BROWNE: The words "he threatened everybody" must mean he threatened everybody in relation to the sale of *Kommersant.*

FRIDMAN: No, that is—that is a logical mistake. Mr. Soloviov said, "And you too?" Means he also threatened him, because Mr. Berezovsky threatened Mr. Soloviov as well, for a different reason, and I then remarked that he had also threatened me.

BROWNE: You are saying he even...

FRIDMAN: Mr. Soloviov, both of us, for different reasons, were the subject of threats made by Mr. Berezovsky.

BROWNE: This has never been alleged before, you are just making this up as you go along, are you not? An allegation is now made from the witness box that Mr. Berezovsky threatened Mr. Soloviov; you have never said that before now and I suggest it is an untrue invention.

FRIDMAN: No, that is the information that I received from Mr. Soloviov personally.

BROWNE: Mr. Soloviov of course remains a good friend of yours?

FRIDMAN: Yes, we studied together.

BROWNE: And is in very good health as we speak?

FRIDMAN: Hopefully, yes.

BROWNE: Yes, good. Let us go on. You received this letter some time in November at your offices in Moscow, did you not? You instructed your solicitors to say that what you had said was true and you were not going to apologize.

FRIDMAN: Yes.

BROWNE: You realize that Mr. Berezovsky was essentially only asking for an apology at that stage?

FRIDMAN: Yes.

BROWNE: You made it clear that you were not alleging that Mr. Berezovsky had threatened anyone with violence but, as we see: "Mr. Fridman informs us that your client did telephone him and made threats that he would use his influence by virtue of his ownership of certain media entities to bring commercial pressure to bear upon Mr. Fridman and *Alfa Bank* if *Alfa Bank* loaned them money."

FRIDMAN: Yes.

Browne: I suggest that at this stage you were in some difficulty. Firstly, you could not claim that you had been threatened with violence because you had not been, had you?

Fridman: Yes, I had not been threatened by personal violence, physical violence.

Browne: Of course, depending obviously on what the jury makes of the meaning of your words, you could not substantiate the allegation that Mr. Berezovsky had threatened anyone else in relation to the sale of *Kommersant*, could you?

Fridman: Yes. I do not know any other people who have suffered from this kind of threat concerning *Kommersant*.

Browne: I suggest your solicitors were pretending that this was all a lot of fuss about nothing.

Fridman: Yes. Frankly speaking, I believe that I have spent two days here over a relatively small matter—in terms of the business that I am not able to work on back in my office. Of course I would prefer not to be here, but I have great respect for British law and the British criminal system.

Browne: You do not see it at all from Mr. Berezovsky's point of view, do you not?

Fridman: What is his point?

Browne: This letter was written after taking your instructions after the Russian New Year holiday.

Fridman: Yes. So what?

Browne: I just wanted to confirm that was so. What is being said in this letter is that threats of a commercial nature are relatively commonplace in the context of Russian business. Do you see that?

Fridman: Yes.

Browne: "Threats to exert commercial pressure are relatively commonplace." So the implication is no one would think the allegation that you had made of any significance. Nor would anyone think it was discreditable or defamatory of Mr. Berezovsky.

Fridman: My point was that I would never—I would never make something like this up. He is an emotional person. I have heard many examples of his temper getting the best of him, which is why perhaps I didn't think that much about my comments.

BROWNE: You hoped you could brush it off, did you not? There was a lot of fuss about nothing.

FRIDMAN: No. At that time, when it was made, I took the threat quite seriously. But I—because of Mr. Berezovsky's current situation, I did not want to raise this issue.

BROWNE: What you were saying was: nobody would think this was defamatory because threats to exert commercial pressure are relatively commonplace? That is what the letter says, does it not, Mr. Fridman?

FRIDMAN: Yes. That is, first of all, not me; that is Herbert Smith.

BROWNE: Yes, on your instructions. That is why it is so important.

FRIDMAN: No, I did not instruct them precisely about how to deal with...

BROWNE: Are you really saying that when Herbert Smith writes a letter saying, "We have now had an opportunity to take our client's instruction following the Russian New Year holiday," that is not true; is that what you are saying?

FRIDMAN: No, we talked about that with the lawyers and I told them the whole story, about what had happened with Mr. Berezovsky. We described all the circumstances of the conversation and then asked them to take the necessary steps—I told them that it was a very important matter to me.

BROWNE: Did you tell them that, in your view, in Russian business, threats to assert commercial pressure were relatively commonplace?

FRIDMAN: I would say that there is a different way of doing business in Russia. It is more emotional sometimes. I would make a distinction between threats from Mr. Berezovsky, who was the most influential businessman in the country, and general business practices in Russia. On the one hand you are right: it is quite common practice, especially in a low level Russian business, to make certain threats—by the way, in the interview which you mentioned before, I said that violence is an absolutely unacceptable way to do business, but it unfortunately still exists in Russia...

BROWNE: Could you answer my question yes or no? I suspect you have forgotten what it was.

FRIDMAN: Your question was: is it commonplace? Yes, it was sometimes—I would not call it common, but it did occasionally happen.

BROWNE: My question was: did you instruct Herbert Smith to write saying that threats to exert commercial pressure are relatively commonplace?

FRIDMAN: I did not instruct him to write those precise words.

BROWNE: So they just made this up, did they?

FRIDMAN: Yes, they did it according to the best of their knowledge, how they should answer it.

BROWNE: The reason you are trying to disclaim this is that it shows your attitude to Russian business conduct in a pretty extraordinary light, does it not? It shows you as believing that all is fair in business and war and that threats to exert commercial pressure are commonplace and therefore in no way discreditable.

FRIDMAN: No, that is—it seems that my view is not being understood. It shows that I did not want to go forward with this case against Mr. Berezovsky, who is an exile and not in the best of situations.

BROWNE: Mr. Fridman, when you are conducting Russian business, do you regard threats to exert commercial pressure as being legitimate weapons?

FRIDMAN: Of course not.

BROWNE: Then why do you say such threats are relatively commonplace?

FRIDMAN: I did not say that.

BROWNE: And therefore to make an allegation that someone has made such a threat is not capable of being defamatory?

FRIDMAN: I did not say, never said, that threats are common business practice in Russia.

BROWNE: You see, I am suggesting that, far from Herbert Smith having misunderstood your instructions, they had taken your instructions and this reflects your attitude to the way in which business is conducted in Russia?

FRIDMAN: It is not my—there was no personal instruction given to Herbert Smith to write the expression "common practice" or "commonplace." My understanding of this situation is that threats unfortunately still exist in Russian business practice. Threats from Mr. Berezovsky, I took quite seriously, at that time. For him, it was pretty common practice, for him personally. I have heard countless stories of people suffering at the hands of his threats.

BROWNE: If that is really your evidence, let us see how this case developed because I suggest this is, again, all invention. Between January 14th, the letter that we have just been looking at, and June 16, 2005, when you served your defense for the court, take it from me your solicitors, Herbert Smith, wrote no less than seven letters. All right?

FRIDMAN: Yes, I think so.

BROWNE: Take it from me too: never once was it suggested during that six month period, in which they wrote no less than seven letters, that there had been threats on any other occasion.

FRIDMAN: That is the case—the only case which we put to your attention.

BROWNE: Exactly. Then lo and behold, when you have to file your defense document with the court on June 16th, for the very first time, without any previous mention, it is said that there had been threats on two previous occasions. That is right, is it not? I think it is not in dispute.

FRIDMAN: I just mentioned the one occasion concerning *Kommersant*, I did not mention...

BROWNE: I am asking you about the correspondence. The point I am putting to you is that it was not until this action had been going for six months that for the very first time you alleged that there had been threats on two previous occasions. I suggest that the reason that this only emerged after six months is that this evidence is all untrue. And that if it had been true, if you had known that Mr. Berezovsky had threatened people on other occasions, as you alleged on the program, then it would have been mentioned by your solicitors in these letters; that is my suggestion.

FRIDMAN: I think you are completely wrong. Mr. Berezovsky had a great deal of power in the country. He appointed ministers, the Prime Minister, he actually created the party that became the leading party in the elections, and he found Mr. Putin, who became the president. Now he is in exile, in a fairly difficult situation.

BROWNE: Would you answer my question, please, Mr. Fridman?

FRIDMAN: Early on he threatened countless people, and I hope the witnesses will confirm this. I think it is very unfair to label us liars.

BROWNE: I am suggesting that these are plainly lies because if at the time you made this original allegation you had known about the matters that were first mentioned nine months later, it would have been mentioned in the correspondence, and it was not.

FRIDMAN: You can confirm with our lawyers that at our first meeting I made mention of numerous examples of threats made by Mr. Berezovsky during his period of power in the country.

BROWNE: You see, I suggest that in your case the motive for not telling the truth about Mr. Berezovsky is twofold. Firstly, I suggest, as you have made clear in your evidence, you have a very deep personal hostility to Mr. Berezovsky.

FRIDMAN: Not at all. I am not hostile towards him. It just seems odd to me that Mr. Berezovsky is using this court as a way of promoting his personal, political and personal agenda and...

BROWNE: That is the slant you put on it. What I suggest is that, in addition to the deep hostility at a personal level to Mr. Berezovsky, you do not like his democratic politics, and that was shown by your last answer.

FRIDMAN: No, that is not true at all. Mr. Berezovsky's ideals are quite far from democratic, believe me. If you had any awareness of the Russian situation you would share my point of view about Mr. Berezovsky. But I am not his judge. That is up to him. I am unhappy with him only because I've had to leave my office to deal with this problem. I am forced to spend time away, and I don't want to be used as a tool for his popularization, or for promoting Mr. Berezovsky's political view. Generally I am quite tolerant of him.

BROWNE: You want to make it quite clear that your politics are fundamentally different from Mr. Berezovsky's so that you keep your relationship with those in the Kremlin; that is the position, is it not?

FRIDMAN: No, I am quite different from Mr. Berezovsky because Mr. Berezovsky has always tried to play political games, he has always tried to be the most influential appointer of political figures, in establishing political movements, and so on. My response to him was always that I did not want to be involved. On occasion I was forced to get involved because I am part of big business, and responsible for many employees, so sometimes I had to get involved. But I always have attempted to minimize my influence if possible because I believe that my goal is to engage in business. That is what I like to do, it is what I have a knack for. This is what I prefer to focus on. He has a very different style, and for a period of time he had an enormous amount of power because he was the guy who made kings, the puppet maker. He is currently in a very difficult situation. I am distressed that his personal situation has been so changed. But it is perhaps an inevitable outcome based on his previous career.

BROWNE: I want to move now to the telephone call you say you received from Mr. Berezovsky. You understand that I am suggesting to you that your account of this call is a complete invention.

FRIDMAN: Yes, I strongly reject your point.

BROWNE: We will just go into the detail of this now. Did you say yesterday that you had a clear recollection of this conversation?

FRIDMAN: Yes.

BROWNE: Clear recollection?

FRIDMAN: Relatively clear. It did happen seven years ago.

BROWNE: Let us just look and see what has been said over the months that this action had been going on. In your second witness statement, dated March 23, 2006, you said that you could remember neither the exact time nor even the date of this telephone conversation, did you not?

FRIDMAN: Yes.

BROWNE: You also said that you could not recall where Mr. Berezovsky was telephoning from.

FRIDMAN: I do not know, that is made by phone so—I could not know.

BROWNE: In a court document on March 2006, you said that you could not recall the precise words you used in response to the threat. Do you want to see it?

FRIDMAN: Yes.

BROWNE: "In response to the threat made to him by the claimant, the first defendant cannot recall the precise words that he used but he made it clear he did not propose to withdraw from his discussions with the then shareholder of *Kommersant*." Now, Mr. Fridman, you are saying that you were seriously threatened by Mr. Berezovsky but you cannot recall the precise words that you used in response. Does that remain your evidence?

FRIDMAN: Yes, I very clearly remember the meaning of my response. I told him that I would ignore his threats and form my own plan for *Kommersant*.

BROWNE: You cannot recall the precise words of your reaction to the threat, nor can you recall, it would seem, any other details of a conversation that lasted five whole minutes?

FRIDMAN: Yes, I do not remember the precise words.

BROWNE: But this is a call that lasted five minutes?

FRIDMAN: Approximately five minutes. It was a short call.

BROWNE: Five minutes is rather a long time depending on what you are doing. If we were to stand here silent for five minutes it would seem a very long time and I am suggesting that this was a fairly lengthy telephone conversation and it is most remarkable that you cannot remember any details of it.

FRIDMAN: First of all I am not convinced that you will necessarily find—maybe it was only three or four minutes. It was around five minutes. In Russian the expression five minutes means a small amount of time. In English you say "a couple of minutes," and Russians usually say "five minutes." It is an expression to show that a brief period of time has passed.

BROWNE: What you in fact said was, on March 23rd of this year, the telephone call lasted for no more than five minutes.

FRIDMAN: Exactly. No more than five minutes, that is what I meant.

BROWNE: I suggest that whereas, when you were being asked about this in the court documents, you said you could not recall the precise words, you are now claiming to have a clear memory and, in a nutshell, are embellishing the story, embroidering the story.

FRIDMAN: What do you mean? From the beginning, I said to you—to our lawyers—that Mr. Berezovsky had threatened me and I responded, though I did not remember precisely what I said. I ignored his threat and continued with the plan to provide a loan to *Kommersant*.

BROWNE: You made no note at the time of this serious threat, as you suggest, did you? You did not make a note recording the threat?

FRIDMAN: No.

BROWNE: You did not write to Mr. Berezovsky saying, "Dear Boris, we have known each other for many years now. I cannot believe you have acted in this way?"

FRIDMAN: No, we did not do that.

BROWNE: Apart from Mr. Aven, did you complain to anyone else. You did not actually complain to him but…

FRIDMAN: I told Mr. Aven about it just a few minutes after the conversation because he has a neighboring office.

BROWNE: I challenge that but I will deal with the details of that in just a moment.

FRIDMAN: But I shared this information later on with a number of people.

BROWNE: You see, Mr. Fridman, again I am suggesting that this is all an invention. The jury can be certain that this is all made up because the negotiations for the purchase of *Kommersant* were all being conducted by Mr. Badri? You knew that, did you not?

FRIDMAN: By whom?

BROWNE: Mr. Badri was conducting the negotiations…

FRIDMAN: I was not aware of that.

BROWNE: I want to ask you about the use of these words "my vas zamochim," forgive my Russian pronunciation. In your defense on June 16th, you said on your behalf: Mr. Berezovsky then made it clear through the use of his language that the defendants would suffer commercial consequences if you, Mr. Fridman, continued to make the purchase of *Kommersant* difficult for him. That is all that you said.

FRIDMAN: Yes.

BROWNE: That Mr. Berezovsky had made it clear through his words. You did not say, did you, what those words were? You did not specify the words? It is only on March 14, 2006, that you claim, for the very first time, that Mr. Berezovsky used the phrase "my vas zamochim?"

FRIDMAN: Okay.

BROWNE: So that is three months after the defense, when you claim for the very first time that Mr. Berezovsky had used the phrase "my vas zamochim." And you say that this is a phrase widely used in the Russian business community as a slang term and carries the meaning that a party proposes to damage the business interests of or defeat another party. Now that, I suggest, is completely wrong; the words are in fact very uncouth criminal slang.

FRIDMAN: It is not criminal slang because I have heard Mr. Berezovsky mention that this expression is used by politicians, for instance Mr. Putin used this expression. I would call it an arrogant expression. It is not very polite conversation but it is not criminal. It is just a vulgar expression.

BROWNE: Vulgar. I suggest that it is criminal slang and that when Mr. Putin used it on September 1999, everyone was astonished that he could be so coarse.

FRIDMAN: I would disagree with you. It's not an uncommon expression and it was even, to some extent, welcomed by the people of Russia when Putin used it. But all this really doesn't matter. It is, in general, a vulgar expression.

BROWNE: Mr. Putin himself, when he made the remark, apologized for his language, did he not?

FRIDMAN: Yes, Mr. Berezovsky did not do that.

JUSTICE EADY: When Mr. Putin used it in relation to the Chechens, it plainly would not mean commercial pressure there, would it?

FRIDMAN: No, that means physical pressure because he was referring to the separatists and extremists, to the terrorists.

BROWNE: What he said was: "We shall pursue them everywhere and if, pardon my language, we catch them in the toilet, we shall finish them off right there in the water closet." Now, there are variations in the translation obviously but that is the substance of what he said, was it not?

FRIDMAN: Yes.

BROWNE: Are you familiar with a newspaper called *Vedomosti*?

FRIDMAN: Yes.

BROWNE: Do you read it regularly?

FRIDMAN: Yes.

BROWNE: *Vedomosti* was taken aback, was it not, by Mr. Putin's use of this language? Do you remember reading this?

FRIDMAN: Probably, yes.

BROWNE: Mr. Fridman, Mr. Putin's use of this language was so extraordinary that *Vedomosti* made it the quote of the week, did they not? You see where this is headed?

FRIDMAN: Yes.

BROWNE: It is a highly reputable Russian daily newspaper. Mr. Berezovsky tells me it is of the status of the *Wall Street Journal* or the *Financial Times*. Is that right?

FRIDMAN: It is a joint venture between the *Wall Street Journal* and the *Financial Times*.

BROWNE: Clearly a highly reputable paper, which is required reading. And their quote of the week was Mr. Putin's remarks at the press conference on the question of Chechen paramilitaries. Then it says this:

"Sergei Dovlatov, a former Gulag guard has noted that long serving labor camp guards gradually began to resemble the people they were guarding, began to speak the same language and began to live in accordance with the same simple rules. Now the Kremlin (that is, of course, Mr. Putin) has started to speak like a long serving convicted criminal of a modest rank."

Now, that is completely inconsistent with your suggestion that in 1999, "my vas zamochim" was a commonplace phrase in business use, is it not?

FRIDMAN: I never mentioned that it was commonplace in the business world. I said that sometimes it was used.

BROWNE: Here is a well-known journalist, Mr. Bershidsky, complaining that the Prime Minister of a great nation has begun to speak like a long serving convicted criminal of modest rank.

FRIDMAN: That is probably the influence of Mr. Berezovsky on him, because Mr. Berezovsky said this exact phrase to me three months before Mr. Putin used the same expression.

BROWNE: You see, that is another of your completely irrelevant personal digs at Mr. Berezovsky...

FRIDMAN: I said probably.

BROWNE: Was what you have just said a joke?

FRIDMAN: Yes, that was an assumption.

BROWNE: A joke?

FRIDMAN: Yes, not a joke. I said probably.

BROWNE: Is it what the American journalist called your gallows humor?

FRIDMAN: I do not know.

BROWNE: You see, it is nonsense, because it was not three months before. You claim that—well, the sale of *Kommersant* was in 1999, was it not?

FRIDMAN: Correct.

BROWNE: In September, ultimately?

FRIDMAN: Yes. That is when it happened—Mr. Putin's quote was from September of 1999.

BROWNE: So what are you saying? Mr. Berezovsky uses these words "my vas zamochim" sometime in the summer of 1999, but unfortunately I cannot remember the date. And I am so appalled by this that I will go up to Mr. Putin and say, "Goodness gracious me. Mr. Berezovsky has threatened me using the words "my vas zamochim" and lo and behold, three months later, Mr. Putin uses the words on television." Is that what you are saying, Mr. Fridman?

FRIDMAN: I am saying it is absolutely the same expression as Mr. Putin used three months later and at that time Mr. Berezovsky was very often in contact with Mr. Putin, as you are probably aware of.

BROWNE: You allege that these words were used three months before Mr. Putin did. Now, there cannot possibly therefore be any connection, can there? Can there?

JUSTICE EADY: What he is suggesting, I think, is that Mr. Putin picked up the expression from Mr. Berezovsky.

FRIDMAN: That is exactly what I said.

BROWNE: And that, I suggest, is completely absurd and typical of your no-holds barred "anything will go" attitude towards Mr. Berezovsky.

FRIDMAN: Yes, that is my—you know, that is my assumption. He used exactly the same phrase which Mr. Putin used three months later.

BROWNE: The reason that you have made this absurd and irrelevant charge against Mr. Berezovsky...

FRIDMAN: I did not make any charge.

BROWNE: ...Is to distract attention from the fact that this article plainly shows that the assertion you have made that "my vas zamochim" is a phrase used in business to suggest commercial damage is absurd.

FRIDMAN: Why?

BROWNE: For the very simple reason that my Lord pointed out a moment ago. Mr. Putin was not suggesting, was he, that he was going to go around and if he found Chechens on the lavatory damage their commercial interests?

FRIDMAN: Of course not.

BROWNE: Sorry to steal your Lordship's joke.

JUSTICE EADY: It was not intended as a joke.

BROWNE: There is a serious point about it, is there not, Mr. Fridman?

FRIDMAN: Yes, but the expression has a lot of different meanings, depending on the context.

BROWNE: Nonsense. Nonsense. *Vedomosti* plainly shows that it is the language of long serving convicted criminals of modest rank.

FRIDMAN: That is absolutely not the case. And you can refer to experts in the Russian language. It could mean either physical or material or any other form of damage, this expression—that is what I would like to explain to the jury. It does not necessarily mean to physically destroy. It means to damage your business, or to damage your interests, or whatever.

BROWNE: Let us just consider that in the light of the reminder of this section of *Vedomosti*. Mr. Putin then had to apologize because his language was so foul, did he not?

FRIDMAN: Yes.

BROWNE: Putin apologized for this unpremeditated use of prison slang, saying that he was not yet an experienced public speaker. He had then been Prime Minister a month, had he not?

FRIDMAN: Something like that.

BROWNE: Then the columnist goes on: "Primakov, with his educated highbrow vocabulary, can forget all about it. Now the Prime Minister's political opponents will have to urgently hire speech writers from street gangs, or at the very least they would have to study the very modest, in terms of its lexicology, dictionary of Russian prison slang." It could not be clearer, could it, that this is solely a Russian criminal or prison expression?

FRIDMAN: So what is the question?

BROWNE: The question is that it could not be clearer that in the estimation of Mr. Bershidsky of *Vedomosti* this was, and was only, Russian prison slang.

FRIDMAN: Yes, it is, according to his view. According to my understanding of Russian language, it is of course sometimes used for criminal means, sometimes used for more, let us say, vulgar discussion on a social level. For instance, when one soccer team beats another team, sometimes people say one team cheated the other team. It is a pretty widespread expression. Originally it probably came from street gangs, and it is certainly common street language.

BROWNE: Now I want to—and I think I am going to be able to finish in five minutes with your cooperation—just to deal with what you said about the report of the conversation to Mr. Aven, who will be giving evidence next. In your witness statement of February 21, 2006, you mentioned for the very first time that you had informed Mr. Aven about this alleged threat?

FRIDMAN: Yes.

BROWNE: This was the first time, February of this year, and again, like the other matters that I have been dealing with, you had never claimed before, either in solicitors' letters or in court documents, that you had mentioned this to Mr. Aven?

FRIDMAN: I would like to repeat again: I mentioned the entire conversation with Mr. Berezovsky, the precise expression he used, on the first day I spoke with the lawyers. And I shared the incident with Mr. Aven on the same day that Mr. Berezovsky used those words.

BROWNE: I suggest that cannot be true, or it would have been mentioned at some stage between October 2004 and February 2006. Do you understand?

FRIDMAN: Yes. I do not know why it appears as first being written down only in February 2006, I cannot answer that question. My understanding is that it was always there.

BROWNE: Furthermore, Mr. Fridman, when your solicitors were asked in July last year to name their witnesses, Mr. Aven was not given as one of them. The witnesses who they said they would be calling were yourself, Mr. Nemtsov and Mr. Potanin but, very significantly I suggest, not Mr. Aven.

FRIDMAN: I do not know why that is. Mr. Aven was aware of the threats on the day that they happened.

BROWNE: You see, there was no reason for you to mention this to Mr. Aven because, as you say, in your opinion, threats of this sort are relatively commonplace.

FRIDMAN: I did not mean that they are relatively commonplace in my life. I—what I said was that sometimes one hears this expression. Secondly, I did not want to raise this issue because I was being quite, let us say, patient with Mr. Berezovsky, taking into consideration his current circumstances.

BROWNE: Mr. Fridman, you said, or your solicitors said, having taken your instructions, threats to exert commercial pressure are relatively commonplace. If it was simply a commonplace event, there was no reason for you to mention it to Mr. Aven, was there?

FRIDMAN: No, I took this threat quite seriously, because I would like to remind you that Mr. Berezovsky had a good deal of power and the ability to impact businesses through his influence, through TV channels, political circles, and so on. He was also close to President Yeltsin at that time.

BROWNE: Your evidence, that you have just given to the jury, is not consistent with what was said in your letter of January 14. Therefore, you are forced to say that it was written without your explicit instructions.

SHIELDS: I now call Mr. Aven, my Lord.

EXAMINATION-IN-CHIEF BY MR. SHIELDS

SHIELDS: Your full name, please, Mr. Aven.

AVEN: My name is Peter Olegovich Aven.

SHIELDS: Would you like to answer questions in English or through the Russian interpreter?

AVEN: I will try English and, if necessary, I will enlist help.

SHIELDS: Your position within the *Alfa Bank*, please, Mr. Aven.

AVEN: I am a shareholder of the bank and I am president of *Alfa Bank*.

SHIELDS: And *Alfa Bank* is the second defendant in this action. Apart from being president of *Alfa Bank*, are you on the board of any other companies?

AVEN: I am on the board of several companies in Russia; some of them are *Alfa Group* companies and some of them are other companies.

SHIELDS: Are you a member of the board of trustees of the Russian Economic School?

AVEN: Yes, I am a member of the board of trustees of the Russian Economic School, as well as the Bolshoy Theatre.

SHIELDS: That is dance; is that right?

AVEN: Yes, that is dance and opera.

SHIELDS: Dance and opera in Moscow. And your background is as an economist?

AVEN: I am by training, and a good deal of my career has been spent in an academic setting.

SHIELDS: First I want to ask you some questions in relation to Mr. Berezovsky. How long have you known Mr. Berezovsky?

AVEN: I have known Mr. Berezovsky for almost 30 years.

SHIELDS: When did you first meet him?

AVEN: We met through common friends in—about 30 years ago.

SHIELDS: And did you become a close personal friend of his?

AVEN: We were close personal friends, as I would characterize it, for many years.

SHIELDS: And did that friendship come to an end?

AVEN: Not completely, but we are not as close as before, definitely.

SHIELDS: And were there differences between you and Mr. Berezovsky?

AVEN: We had no serious personal differences but for a while we definitely did not share the same political views. We believed in different political goals and we are very different in our assessment of what is going on in Russia.

SHIELDS: When you say you believed in different political goals, what is your political goal or view as an economist?

AVEN: Well, I am a liberal economist. I was a member of the first post-Communist government and was always a proponent of liberal values, civil society, and a free economy.

SHIELDS: You said you were a member of the first Russian government?

AVEN: Yes.

SHIELDS: Who was Prime Minister then?

AVEN: Acting Prime Minister was Gaidar.

SHIELDS: We have had his name before; that is Gaidar. You said that you did not share the same views as Mr. Berezovsky. What was your understanding of Mr. Berezovsky's views?

AVEN: I believe that the main belief of Boris Berezovsky is that the western states are mainly managed by a small group of wealthy individuals. That was he openly stated this a number of times, and many times in fact in my presence, that he believes that the wealthy part of society and a small group of the wealthiest part of society *de facto* are the most influential and *de facto* are crucial for the management of the country, which I strongly disagree with.

SHIELDS: You know a newspaper called *Kommersant*; is that right?

AVEN: Yes.

SHIELDS: You know what this trial is about of course. I would like to ask you some questions about the sale of *Kommersant* in 1999. Did there come a time that you recall when your bank or Mr. Fridman became involved in that sale?

AVEN: Yes, I remember the story very well.

SHIELDS: Would you tell us what interest *Alfa Bank* may have had in relation to that sale?

AVEN: Well, *Alfa Bank* definitely wanted one simple thing, to obtain real independence for *Kommersant*. And at that time *Kommersant* was by far the most popular and the most influential newspaper in the country. At that time we had already experienced a number of cases where the media—TV channels or newspapers—had been bought by a so-called oligarch, and then became much less independent as they started to reflect the opinion of people who owned them and not of society as a whole. So we wanted *Kommersant* to be independent, as it was before. That was our position. So when we found out that *Kommersant* was for sale, our idea was to somehow find a way to protect its independence. And as far as I can remember, I was told by Mikhail Fridman that one of *Kommersant*'s shareholders called him and that they had started to discuss options and one option was that if one of them—the major shareholder, Mr. Yakovlev wanted to sell, that they needed money to buy his share—then other shareholders would stay in the newspaper and the newspaper would have then stayed independent.

So they wanted money, and we were able to provide this financing. And I heard here discussions about our intention to buy *Kommersant*. We could easily have done so. We had the money for that. We were very friendly with the *Kommersant* shareholders; Mr. Miloslavsky especially, and we could easily have bought *Kommersant* if we had wanted to; within a single day. We did not want it because we never wanted to buy our way into the media—newspapers and TV channels—but we also did not want *Kommersant* to be bought either by Boris Berezovsky or somebody else. So our intention was to provide financing for *Kommersant* shareholders to stay independent; that is all.

SHIELDS: Was there any other proposal in relation to *Kommersant*, other than lending money?

AVEN: I do not—I do not think so. In fact the proof that we did not want to buy it ourselves was that we started to discuss it openly with different groups of people, with the business world, with other business people, such as Mr. Chubais and Mr. Potanin. We did this precisely because we believed that even if we were to provide just the loan it might go wrong, we might end up being somehow too influential. We only wanted to build a foundation so that the money was coming not only from us, but from others. Not only from us but from other banks and other groups. So the idea was that we would find other investors, so that a group of us would be able to ensure the paper's independence. That was the discussion about *Kommersant* at that time.

SHIELDS: Did you have any discussions with Mr. Fridman at this time in relation to Mr. Berezovsky's desire to purchase *Kommersant*?

AVEN: Yes.

SHIELDS: Could you tell the court what those discussions were or what Mr. Fridman may have told you?

AVEN: We spoke—I spoke with Miloslavsky about *Kommersant*, as one of the shareholders. Mikhail Fridman spoke with Mr. Kaskov about that, and we exchanged information, of course. We all knew that Mr. Berezovsky was interested in purchasing the newspaper. Secondly, Mikhail Fridman contacted me immediately after Boris Berezovsky called him. This incident is at the center of this discussion.

SHIELDS: Where is your office in relation to that of Mr. Fridman?

AVEN: Our offices are on the same floor, in neighboring rooms. There is one room in between these two rooms. Our offices are about 10 meters apart.

SHIELDS: You were going to tell us what Mr. Fridman told you.

AVEN: Mr. Fridman told me that he had received a call from Mr. Berezovsky, who wanted us to step aside, "Do not touch *Kommersant*," and he told me that Boris Berezovsky was threatening him and threatening our joint business.

SHIELDS: You told me Mr. Berezovsky was threatening him and then something about business? Could you just repeat the last bit?

AVEN: Mr. Fridman told me that he had received a threat from Mr. Berezovsky, and the threat was concerning our business.

SHIELDS: And what was, as you understood it, the threat as regards to your business?

AVEN: We knew very well that Mr. Berezovsky was the most influential, I would say "business politician," in the country, and we knew about his ability to make life difficult for businesses. That is what Mr. Fridman had in mind. Because Mr. Berezovsky controlled a TV channel, it would have been simple for him to spoil our image. Unfortunately there is a lot of yellow press in Russia. Mr. Berezovsky was a media tycoon at that time, and he knew how to damage someone's image. We had already had this problem in Russia several times.

SHIELDS: Could you say that again, please.

AVEN: I understood that the problems would focus on our business and our image.

SHIELDS: You have told his Lordship and the jury of the conversation in your room. Would you tell us again your recollection of that conversation.

AVEN: I remember Mr. Fridman came to my room and told me that he had just received a call from Mr. Berezovsky and that Mr. Berezovsky wanted us to stay away from *Kommersant*; that is number 1. And then he told me that if we did not he might make trouble for us. And I am not sure that Mr. Fridman specified exactly what problems, but we understood the concept. The problems would have concerned our business and our public image.

SHIELDS: Your public image. Right. Now, what did you decide to do, if anything, in the light of that threat?

AVEN: We decided to continue in spite of all the threats.

CROSS-EXAMINATION BY MR. BROWNE

BROWNE: Mr. Aven, you, as we heard this morning, are someone who has mixed politics and business, have you not?

AVEN: Not really. I was a member, briefly, of the government, that is right, but I never mixed the two. When I left the government I no longer dabbled in politics.

BROWNE: Well, can I just ask about that? You were in Mr. Gaidar's government, were you not?

AVEN: I was.

BROWNE: And in January 1992, you were the Russian minister of foreign trade?

AVEN: It was called foreign economic relations.

BROWNE: But does that mean, in effect, foreign trade?

AVEN: It is wider than just trade. I was responsible for foreign debt and several other issues.

BROWNE: And you remained in that post for about a year, did you not?

AVEN: I did.

BROWNE: And the following year were you a help to Mr. Berezovsky over LogoVAZ, as an adviser?

AVEN: Yes.

BROWNE: As you say, you have known Mr. Berezovsky for at least 30 years, have you not?

AVEN: Exactly.

BROWNE: And you stood for the Russian parliament, the Duma, in 1993, did you not?

AVEN: I was elected to parliament but I decided not to join parliament and to stay in business.

BROWNE: Exactly. I was going to put to you what in fact happened. Three months afterwards the central election commission pronounced your election invalid because you had not given up your business dealings. Is that not right?

AVEN: That is wrong. It was my decision. They gave a chance to everyone to choose. We were elected on party lists. I was on Yegor Gaidar's party. So then after the elections everyone had to choose either to leave business or to go into the parliament; parliament or business. Everyone had a choice and I chose to stay in business.

BROWNE: Having made that choice, your election was, as I have suggested, invalid?

AVEN: Not really. That is a party list. So somebody else from this list could take my position. There were a number of people elected by party lists. So the number of these people elected for Gaidar's party did not decrease. It was a substitution. Somebody took my place.

BROWNE: So your place in the Duma was invalidated because you would not give up business, is that right?

AVEN: No, it was not invalidated.

BROWNE: Your personal seat?

AVEN: No, it was not a personal seat; it is a party seat. So it went to another member of the party.

JUSTICE EADY: Can you just say what the party was? I did not quite catch it.

AVEN: It was called Democratic Choice.

BROWNE: Why, Mr. Aven, had you not thought of it before the election? Would that not all have avoided a great deal of fuss and bother?

AVEN: Very simple. I thought about it before the elections, but the party needed my name for the election. It helped Mr. Gaidar and his government—for his party to be elected. That is the usual story, not only in Russia. I was on the list. I had a chance to take part in political campaigns for the party. They wanted my voice and my name, and my speeches. So I was prepared to leave and they knew that I would leave even before the election.

BROWNE: So the whole thing, you are saying, is a complete sham…

AVEN: Absolutely not.

BROWNE: Just let me ask the question. You decided it would be to the benefit of the party to have your speeches in the election, but the moment you were elected you were going to step down?

AVEN: It was for the benefit of the party, not for myself.

BROWNE: I suggest it was a complete sham, and what happened shows how business and politics at that level can never be separated in Russian life?

AVEN: Completely wrong. In every party, which we had in Russia, in every party during the elections there were many people who were on the party lists and who resigned after the election. There were dozens or hundreds of such examples. And the list of people who helped their parties was not only from business; they are from very different groups. For example, Moscow Mayor, Mr. Luzhkov, has been elected several times and then he resigned. That had absolutely nothing to do with business at all.

BROWNE: You do not believe, Mr. Aven, do you, for one moment that a man you have known for 30 years has gone through his life constantly threatening people. You do not believe that, do you?

AVEN: I think that is a different—well, I do believe that he did. That is what you meant by threaten once again. I'm not referring to personal harm or criminal affairs but to the use of political power to make life more difficult for his rivals. That was common for Boris Berezovsky. Yes, I have known him for 30 years.

BROWNE: You are not suggesting that threats of this nature were not serious. On the contrary you are saying they were very serious, are you not?

AVEN: They could be serious.

BROWNE: Yes. And your evidence and Mr. Fridman's was that these were serious threats, which you took seriously?

AVEN: Unfortunately that was not the only example I was familiar with; that was only one story. I have known Mr. Berezovsky for many years and have been present many times in the room when he has used threats to get his way—using the same threats.

BROWNE: You see, none of this has ever been suggested before. You and Mr. Fridman have come to this court in London to make up your evidence as you go along and to make allegations about Mr. Berezovsky threatening people, which 18 months previously had never been made before? The reason that I suggest that you do not believe these charges is that for 30 years you have had a cordial relationship with Mr. Berezovsky, and that relationship has continued right up to 2006, has it not, Mr. Aven?

AVEN: No, because of all our differences and the pressures of life now, we are definitely much less close than before.

BROWNE: Let us test that out. Mr. Berezovsky, as I told the jury in opening, was 60 in January, was he not?

AVEN: He was, yes.

BROWNE: You knew that?

AVEN: I did know that, I congratulated him through *Kommersant*.

BROWNE: I am going to ask you to show the jury what you said about Mr. Berezovsky in *Kommersant*?

AVEN: Shall I read it?

BROWNE: Do you actually have it there?

AVEN: No, I do not know where it is.

BROWNE: I will hand it to you. You placed this birthday message for Mr. Berezovsky, did you not?

AVEN: Yes.

BROWNE: And it started with an affectionate nickname. You did not call him Boris you called him "Boria?"

AVEN: Yes.

BROWNE: A bit like calling Peter "Pete," something you only do if you are affectionately disposed towards someone. The point is that you only do it if you are close to somebody?

AVEN: Yes.

BROWNE: "Many happy returns of the day. You are having a fantastic, interesting life, so rich in extraordinary events. Impossible to forecast anything like that about 30 years ago when we first met. And indeed you are happy. I suppose I have never met a person who is as happy as you are, though not everyone believes it is true. In spite of the fact that we have almost never agreed on anything and we are not doing it now, I wish you all the best."

Just pausing there, of course what you are referring to about never agreeing about anything is politics?

AVEN: No, not only.

BROWNE: Well, I suggest it is politics.

AVEN: It is not only. The second thing on which we never agreed was business style, the means used as part of a business strategy.

BROWNE: I suggest that that is what you are saying now to minimize the effect of this message in *Kommersant.*

AVEN: Not at all.

BROWNE: Let me read on: "I wish you love. I remember you tried to convince me once that unlike... once in half a year. I wish you health and happiness. The latter, as I have already said, is always with you; it simply cannot abandon you."

Now, Mr. Aven, that expression of affectionate wishes for his birthday, love, health and happiness, is not something that any human being would wish for somebody who went through life threatening other people, is it?

AVEN: No, not that—I would disagree. Human beings are complicated animals and if somebody in his business strategy uses political threats—unfortunately it was, as you discussed in the morning, relatively common in Russia. I do not like it, but they are not sufficient grounds to start hating my former friend, Berezovsky.

BROWNE: So you are saying, are you, that these sorts of threats are run of the mill or commonplace in Russia?

AVEN: They were not exactly common, but they were used.

BROWNE: Was it right when Herbert Smith said it was commonplace?

AVEN: It is a question of the definition. It was used. And I would like to stress that our major difference, whether you believe it or not, from Mr. Berezovsky was that in *Alfa* we always tried to pursue a different strategy, without threats, without using the government, wherever it was possible not to, simply to build businesses. This was exactly not what Mr. Berezovsky was trying to do.

BROWNE: But Mr. Aven, you know perfectly well that a man who had gone through 30 years habitually threatening people, which is your allegation and that of Mr. Fridman, could not possibly be so happy, and to whom you would wish on his 60th birthday, love, health and happiness?

AVEN: Again, my attitude towards Mr. Berezovsky is complex, and I remember different episodes—30 years of history is a complicated, not a black-and-white picture. That is all what I want to say. And the reason why we are no longer close is because of his attitude towards political priorities and towards business, and the use of threats, for example, as well.

BROWNE: You did not believe, I suggest, a word of what is contained in the defendants' defense, namely that Mr. Berezovsky is somebody who issues habitual threats. If you had done so, you would have never wished him this message?

AVEN: I disagree.

BROWNE: And it is not just birthday wishes, is it? This threat is alleged to have been in 1999?

AVEN: Mm-hmm.

BROWNE: And you claim that you were told about it right away in 1999, do you not?

AVEN: No. It was in fact—it is difficult to say whether threats are that common in Russian economic reality, but it was common for Mr. Berezovsky. We were used to him threatening people, for him it was commonplace. Mr. Berezovsky, in my presence, for example, threatened the finance minister with his resignation, if he did not follow his advice. Telling people that Berezovsky had threatened us would have done nothing for his reputation in Moscow.

BROWNE: Again you are just making this up as you go along. None of this that comes from the mouths of you and Mr. Fridman has ever been mentioned before. You knew, did you not, perfectly well, that you had to set out the incidents alleged to be threats in *Alfa Bank's* defense; you knew that, did you not?

AVEN: I knew just that I have to tell the story which I am telling here.

BROWNE: You say that you were informed of this threat made by Mr. Berezovsky to Mr. Fridman…

AVEN: Yes.

BROWNE: …In 1999 at the time it was allegedly made?

AVEN: The same day.

BROWNE: The same. Now, after that period Mr. Berezovsky came to London and we all know that he was given political asylum. Now, you have said you are an economist and you come over for meetings in economic forums?

AVEN: Yes.

BROWNE: And during that time you have made a point of meeting Mr. Berezovsky, have you not?

AVEN: I guess we met once or twice.

BROWNE: Twice. Let us not minimize it. Twice, I would suggest. In 2003, you came over here and he took you out to dinner at a Chinese restaurant called Hakkasan, do you remember that?

AVEN: I went with my friend, Farkhad Akhmetov, who invited Mr. Berezovsky.

BROWNE: Indeed, and his wife Gillian, and your wife too. And Mr. Berezovsky was the host at this dinner?

AVEN: I am not sure that he was the host, but he was in the restaurant.

BROWNE: When I say "the host," that is a genteel way of saying he paid the bill. You accepted his hospitality, did you not?

AVEN: I am not sure that Mr. Berezovsky paid the bill. We'd have to go back and check credit card statements.

BROWNE: You did not pay the bill, that is clear, is it not, or you would remember?

AVEN: I do not remember.

BROWNE: And it happened again in 2004, when he repeated the Hakkasan dining experience in June or July of that year?

AVEN: Maybe.

BROWNE: And again he paid; yes?

AVEN: Maybe.

BROWNE: And this time Mrs. Berezovsky was in the party, so it was a sort of family gathering?

AVEN: This might be the case.

BROWNE: A thoroughly friendly social occasion, was it not?

AVEN: Yes.

BROWNE: Repeating what had happened a year before?

AVEN: Yes.

BROWNE: When your wife had been present?

AVEN: Yes.

BROWNE: So friendly and agreeable was the dinner and the socializing that went with it that you then all went back to the bar at the Lanesborough Hotel?

AVEN: This also is quite possible.

BROWNE: All of that is quite inconsistent, is it not, with believing Mr. Berezovsky to be a man who went through life threatening people as opposed to paying for their dinners?

AVEN: Well, again, I think that you do not completely understand Russian reality. If Mr. Berezovsky was a criminal personality and he regularly threatened people with force, personal violence, it would be unacceptable to shake his hand.

BROWNE: Sorry, you would shake hands?

AVEN: I would not shake his hand. But in Russian political and business reality, unfortunately, for a segment of our businessmen, to use their political influence—and to use political influence is *de facto* to set up your rivals with your political influence—was usual and was not—was something which *de facto* does not make you closer with your former friends but at the same time is not sufficient to completely destroy relations.

For many years, five or six, I met Mr. Berezovsky every day. We had—he used to live close to me in Moscow and he used to come to my apartment for breakfast or for dinner almost every day. Now we meet once a year. And the reason is exactly what you stated, that his business practice and his business more or less is different from us. That is the difference. You meet either every day or you meet once a year. That is a big gap. And unfortunately maybe what you are advising—for me to be tougher with my former friends—perhaps is good advice, but the result that we are not as close as before is exactly because of his business tactics. That is my assessment.

BROWNE: The simple reason you are unable to be as close as before is that Mr. Berezovsky has been chased out of Russia, is it not?

AVEN: I am in London every month.

BROWNE: And the fact is that when you had these regular, almost daily meetings, that was well before 1999, was it not?

AVEN: Sure.

BROWNE: And in 1999, if you are right, there was a watershed when Mr. Berezovsky seriously threatened your partner, Mr. Fridman?

AVEN: Unfortunately sometimes you have to partially forgive your former friends for what they do. Sometimes you forgive your friends when they have been friends for 30 years, even if you do not like what they are doing to you, you still meet them and shake their hand, and even sometimes drink whisky in a bar.

BROWNE: You have never raised this matter with Mr. Berezovsky and said, "Well, what you did in 1999 was simply awful. I am amazed that you did it, in view of our friendship. But in view of our long friendship of 25 years let us kiss and make up"; you never said that, did you?

AVEN: We had several discussions with Mr. Berezovsky about politics.

BROWNE: Just answer the question.

AVEN: I never mentioned this exact story.

BROWNE: Exactly. Why not, if it was as serious as you say and you were told about it in 1999?

AVEN: Because for him it was natural. It was just the way he behaved. And to persuade Mr. Berezovsky that it had been completely wrong was simply impossible. That is part of his belief system. That is his religion. That is how he thinks. He behaves in a certain way and he makes money, and to discuss this issue with him, just like trying to talk politics with him, would result in the friendship being severed permanently. That is how it is with him.

BROWNE: You never mentioned it because it never happened?

Aven: It happened, I have already sworn that it happened, so what else can I add?

Browne: I suggest the reason that you have to be circumspect about your meetings in London with Boris is that if it was known that every month you were having meetings with Mr. Berezovsky in London, that would not exactly please Mr. Putin, would it?

Aven: Do you think my congratulations to Mr. Berezovsky in *Kommersant* pleased Mr. Putin or not?

Browne: What would be the effect of the…

Aven: Mr. Browne, I have survived the Soviet Union. I met many dissidents who were not allowed—who underwent serious KGB threats. I was not allowed to leave the country because of that. For three years I could not go to Vienna just because I had certain connections in Russia. My father had the same problem. Mr. Berezovsky would know that. But I would never compromise my meetings with my friends in London, no matter what Mr. Putin likes. That is what I am saying; I do not care about that, I do not care what Mr. Putin thinks about me visiting my friends here.

Browne: I want to ask you about something different now, the financing of political parties. *The Moscow Times* is another reputable Russian newspaper, is it not?

Aven: Yes.

Browne: And I imagine you read it?

Aven: Sometimes.

Browne: From time to time you give interviews to their reporters. Is that right?

Aven: Yes.

Browne: Could I just ask you to look at this clipping from *The Moscow Times* on April 22, 2005? This is two and a half pages, but you may recognize it, Mr. Aven, because I suggest you are quoted at the very end of the article.

Aven: The very end? Yes. (*Pause*). Okay.

Browne: Do you recognize the article now?

Aven: Absolutely.

Browne: This article came at a time when TNK/BP had just received a back tax claim for nearly $1 billion. Yes?

Aven: Maybe. I do not remember.

BROWNE: Concentrate please. The fourth paragraph: "Aven's comments about the liberalization of economic life ... on businesses owned by *Alfa Bank's* parent company, the multi-billion-dollar oil and telecom holding *Alfa Group*. TNK/BP, the 50/50 ... last week said it received a back tax claim for nearly $1 billion. BP president Lord Brown is to meet with President Vladimir Putin on Friday ..." That is the 23rd of April: "... together with Aven's partner, *Alfa Group* founder Mikhail Fridman, to discuss the tax claim and the country's overall investment climate." You knew that TNK/BP had received this whopping back tax demand, had you not?

AVEN: I did.

BROWNE: And it must have been a matter of very considerable concern because these were the sort of tactics that were applied to Mr. Khodorkovsky, were they not, and Yukos?

AVEN: I do not think so.

BROWNE: They also received an enormous tax claim?

AVEN: Not at all. 1 billion for TNK was much less than for Yukos—this amount wouldn't put the company under. These are different circumstances.

BROWNE: It is not small change, is it?

AVEN: It is not small change.

BROWNE: And indeed it appears that Mr. Fridman went with Lord Brown to discuss it with Mr. Putin?

AVEN: Yes.

BROWNE: If I get a brown envelope from the Inland Revenue, I do not immediately go to 10 Downing Street, do I?

AVEN: I am not familiar with British practice, but I think that Mr. Browne is speaking of Downing Street, 10, I would suspect.

BROWNE: This, I suggest, is all part of the tactics in Russian life today: serve an enormous tax demand on a large commercial enterprise and use it as a way of ensuring that they stay in line. That is what happens in Russia today, is it not?

AVEN: I could not find many examples of that.

BROWNE: Well, was not Mr. Khodorkovsky one?

AVEN: Yes, Khodorkovsky was definitely an example when the tax claims were used to destroy the company; that is right. But I could not find many other examples of this sort.

BROWNE: But it is a way for Mr. Putin to wave his big stick, is it not?

AVEN: I do not think so.

BROWNE: Let us now just look at what you say at the end of this article. I think you have confirmed that you did give this interview. Could you just confirm that you have been accurately quoted?

AVEN: Everything except one thing. I see here in quotation: we give funding to the Union of Right Forces. By "we," I mean shareholders of *Alfa Bank* and not *Alfa* as an institution because one, just above, is that *Alfa* was prepared to support. When I say "we," I mean individuals from *Alfa Group* partners.

BROWNE: At any rate, those under the *Alfa* umbrella gave funding to the Union of Right Forces, which is Mr. Nemtsov?

AVEN: I did personally.

BROWNE: And on a scale which would have given him cause for great gratitude to *Alfa* shareholders?

AVEN: Not at all. We gave, as far as I can remember, as myself and Mikhail Fridman or whoever else from *Alfa*, we gave not more not less than other businessmen in Russia. It was nothing major. And just to come back to your question, Mr. Putin was definitely not pleased with that.

BROWNE: What I am suggesting is that you back all the horses in the race except the Communists, and that is why we saw on the *Alfa Bank* website the article that we were looking at yesterday, which seems to show that *Alfa* had contributed to the United Russia Party of Mr. Putin?

AVEN: I think you have a high assessment of our moral qualities, but we support only those who we believe are politically right. And I gave money personally only to my former friends, my former party and to Mr. Nemtsov, who is here in the room, and to Mr. Chubais. We never gave a single penny to anyone else.

BROWNE: This was posted on *Alfa Bank's* website. "Like most oligarchs, however, Fridman is a heavy contributor to the United Russia Party, the political entity most closely linked to Putin. Fridman leaves no doubt that he will support Putin and the United Russia Party." What I am suggesting to you is that it would be simply inconceivable, you being the president of *Alfa Bank*, to put that on your website if it was not true?

AVEN: No, you are wrong. We are not responsible for all the material in all the papers that you can find on our website. And if journalists make mistakes, they are their mistakes, that is all.

BROWNE: If the journalist has made a mistake, would it not be very easy to add a note saying, "We publish this article as it was originally printed but it is not correct that Mr. Fridman is a heavy contributor to Mr. Putin's party"?

AVEN: Thank you for your advice. Maybe we will do it in the future, but we never thought it was that important.

BROWNE: It would have been a very simple step to take, would it not?

AVEN: Mr. Fridman already mentioned in the morning that Mr. Putin does not need our financial support.

BROWNE: Please answer my question. It would have been a very simple step to add a note correcting it, would it not?

AVEN: We are—a big organization, and sometimes mistakes are made within the organization.

BROWNE: It would have been a very simple step to add a correction?

AVEN: For whom? I do not read our website. I do not read every newspaper article about *Alfa Bank*.

BROWNE: Are you going to answer my question? It would have been a very simple step?

AVEN: If I had read that, it would have been a simple step. I've never seen this article before.

BROWNE: It would have been a very simple step for anyone in your press department, for example, would it not?

AVEN: Maybe.

BROWNE: Just going back to the article of April 22nd in *The Moscow Times*, where you talk about giving funding to the Union of Right Forces, you say: "This is not because Chubais and Nemtsov are our friends but because this right wing ideology is clear to us." "This is because they are our natural ideological allies and we are prepared to support the right wing somehow in the future." Have I understood you correctly? What you are saying there is this: Chubais and Nemtsov are your friends but it is not on that account that you are funding the Union of Right Forces?

AVEN: Yes.

BROWNE: *Alfa Bank* wishes to see Mr. Putin given a third term if the constitution can be changed, does it not?

AVEN: Not at all.

BROWNE: Can we just pursue this in a little more detail? *Alfa Bank* has a chief strategist whose name, I think, is Chris Weafer?

AVEN: He published the article, well he proposed that Putin—that it would be good for investors if Putin stayed for a third term.

BROWNE: Indeed. We are talking about the same thing. That was on September 12, 2005, was it not?

AVEN: Exactly.

BROWNE: Just as there is a White House in Moscow there is a White House in Washington, the Russian constitution, like the United States constitution, does not allow the president to serve more than two, four-year terms, is that correct?

AVEN: Yes.

BROWNE: So Mr. Putin will be out for good in 2008 unless the Russian constitution is changed?

AVEN: Yes.

BROWNE: There is a great deal of speculation about whether Mr. Putin will try to change the constitution, is there not?

AVEN: Some people discuss that.

BROWNE: I suggest that the contribution to the debate of *Alfa Bank* and of Mr. Weafer is to create a favorable climate for Mr. Putin to change the constitution by saying that it would be good for business.

AVEN: This is completely wrong. Mr. Weafer, who is an American, as far as I remember—or British—is an analyst hired by *Alfa Bank*, who does not listen to any advice from myself or Mr. Fridman. He is an absolutely independent analyst in the bank. That is number one. When he expresses his views, it is absolutely independent from the opinion of shareholders. That is completely independent. And then what he says, that it is not good for the country, that Mr. Putin should stay, he says that the investment community prefers stability and if Mr. Putin stays, the investors will like it—and, believe me—once again you do not have a very high opinion of our moral standards—we did not like this article. We think this article, in principle, was a mistake for Mr. Weafer, but it was his business. I personally do not think that it would be good for the country if Mr. Putin stays for a third term.

BROWNE: This again is something you have to disown in order to maintain the pretence of yourself and Mr. Fridman that *Alfa Bank* is not mixed up in politics. That is what I suggest.

AVEN: No, when I say that Mr. Putin—that I would prefer not to change the constitution, I am saying this as a private Russian citizen. It has nothing to do with our business. It would not be good for the country if Mr. Putin stays and the constitution is changed.

BROWNE: This was a report put out on *Alfa Bank's* behalf by no less than its chief strategist Mr. Weaver, was it not?

AVEN: That is right.

BROWNE: And what it said was that Mr. Putin remaining in office beyond 2008 would be the most favorable scenario for the business.

AVEN: For investors.

BROWNE: I am reading from the newspaper. I do not think it matters. That, I suggest, was the plainest possible indication that *Alfa Bank* were preparing the ground for Mr. Putin to change the constitution and plough on as president regardless.

AVEN: You are wrong.

BROWNE: Mr. Aven, I do not want to go over recent political developments in Russia like I did with Mr. Fridman but there is just one matter I want to ask you about and that is the treatment of Mr. Gusinsky. Now, you are certainly aware that Mr. Gusinsky was arrested and put in jail for three days during June 2000?

AVEN: Yes.

BROWNE: All of this was a matter of enormous publicity in the Russian press, was it not?

AVEN: Yes.

BROWNE: You would have followed it in *The Moscow Times*, presumably?

AVEN: It was in all the newspapers.

BROWNE: *The Moscow Times* and *Financial Times*?

AVEN: Maybe.

BROWNE: And by September had you, following it in the press, reached the conclusion that it was clear that Mr. Gusinsky had been put in jail and charged with criminal offenses in order to ensure that he give up NTV to Gazprom?

AVEN: I do not know all the details of Mr. Gusinsky's case, but I do know that it was related to his deep financial troubles, his sizable loan with Gazprom. That was the basis of the case. I do not know whether there were political reasons behind it, but I am aware of the enormous debt of Mr. Gusinsky's company to Gazprom for about $1 billion, as far as I can remember. That is what I am aware of.

BROWNE: Do you remember Mr. Lesin, the press minister, getting into terrible trouble and conceding that he had made a mistake by putting his signature on the deal whereby Mr. Gusinsky surrendered NTV to Gazprom?

AVEN: I know that from the newspapers.

BROWNE: Can we just look at how it was reported in *The Moscow Times* and *Financial Times*? I am going to take just one day, September 21, 2000, when the statement by Mr. Lesin that he had made a mistake was publicized. As you rightly say, there is a mass of clippings one could rely on. It was abundantly clear from all the press publicity over this period, but particularly on this day, September 21, 2000, that Mr. Gusinsky had only been put in jail to get him to surrender his share of NTV. I will be saying to this witness, anyone like him reading *The Moscow Times* and the *FT* on this day, let alone all the preceding days, could have been in no doubt, if they were independently minded, that Mr. Gusinsky had been thrown into jail in order to get him to surrender NTV. Now, what caused all the publicity at this time were Mr. Gusinsky's protests about the way in which he had been treated. Is that not right?

AVEN: Yes.

BROWNE: He had been put in jail in June. He was forced to sign an agreement in July surrendering his interest in NTV. He was then permitted to leave the country as part of that agreement and in September he publicized his treatment, did he not?

AVEN: I think so.

BROWNE: After he had done so, there was enormous pressure on the press minister, whose name was Mikhail Lesin. "In the clearest sign yet … fate of Media MOST, Mikhail Lesin said that he had approved a contract between Mr. Gusinsky and Alfred Kokh, the head of Gazprom's media arm, and acknowledged that he had made a serious mistake in doing so." The serious mistake was Mr. Lesin taking part in this agreement whereby Mr. Gusinsky had to surrender the Media MOST Company, including NTV, to Gazprom. That was the mistake, was it not?

AVEN: Yes.

BROWNE: Yes, it was. The two were plainly linked; yes?

AVEN: Yes.

BROWNE: And one sees how they were, if one just looks at *The Moscow Times* now. There is Mr. Lesin. The article begins: "Press minister Mikhail Lesin conceded Wednesday that as a minister he had made a mistake by putting his signature on a deal selling Vladimir Gusinsky's … controlled Gazprom." He says it is true he did not have the right to put his signature on the document and so on: "The disputed deal, known as appendix 6, in a document signed by Gusinsky and Gazprom media head, Alfred Kokh …" Had he previously been the privatization minister, Mr. Kokh?

AVEN: Yes.

BROWNE: Back in the days of Svyazinvest?

AVEN: Yes.

BROWNE: "… links the sale of … shortly after signing the appendix." Nobody reading this could be in the slightest doubt that he was imprisoned and kept in the country until he had surrendered his commercial interests, could they?

AVEN: It might be the case.

BROWNE: Then, if one looks at the agreement, which no doubt everyone was very keen to see, that is set out in *The Moscow Times*. This is the July agreement. This is the document signed by Mr. Lesin:

"The parties understand that the successful implementation of the agreement is possible only when citizens and legal entities acquire and realize their civil rights by their own volition and in their own interest without coercion on the part of anyone to perform any actions, which at present requires the fulfillment of particular mutually binding conditions, specifically termination of the criminal investigation against Citizen Gusinsky Vladimir Alexandrovich under the criminal case brought against him on June 13th … "

That, just to interrupt, was when he was imprisoned: "… transferring him to the status of witness in respect of the case, termination of measures taken by prosecutors that forbid his leaving the country."

Then turn over the page, the last main paragraph: "Everyone hoped that this deal would be kept strictly confidential." Is that right?

AVEN: I read it as you gave me.

BROWNE: So there it was down in writing: "The criminal investigation will be terminated so long as you surrender the shares in NTV, Media MOST." Agreed?

AVEN: Agreed, that is what the newspaper says.

BROWNE: That is what the newspaper said. They published the agreement, Mr. Lesin apologized and in the light of that nobody reading the newspapers could have been in the slightest doubt that he had been compelled to surrender his commercial interest in Media MOST as the price of leaving the country and being let out of jail?

AVEN: This could be the case but just let me remind you that immediately after Mr. Gusinsky had been arrested, the same day, Mr. Fridman and myself arranged—a letter, signing a letter by many prominent businessmen in the country against this action of the government and requested that Mr. Gusinsky be released immediately.

BROWNE: Yes, because the breach of human rights was so flagrant. That was why you wrote, was it not?

AVEN: No, it was just because we believed that in that case the government was completely wrong because the entire story was absolutely wrong and we had to defend Gusinsky. That is the whole story.

BROWNE: And the result of the press publicity was to leave nobody in any doubt that Mr. Gusinsky had been compelled under this agreement to give us his commercial empire?

AVEN: No, that is only the partial truth. Mr. Gusinsky definitely had political problems with the authorities but at the same time he had a debt of $1 billion to Gazprom; you also had to take that into consideration and you also had to take into consideration that Mr. Gusinsky, similar to Mr. Berezovsky, had built his empire through his relationship with the state and by money extorted through his political influence. So, he took $1 billion. He had to pay the price.

BROWNE: But that price, that debt, did not entitle the Russian state to throw him into jail and draw up criminal charges?

AVEN: I do not want to comment on that because I am not aware of all the details. I only know that there was a $1 billion debt—$1 billion is a lot of money. And this money was obtained by Mr. Gusinsky only because of his close political relationship and his friendship with some top authorities of the country. That I know.

BROWNE: Mr. Aven, I want now to ask you about the report, the evidence that you have given about Mr. Fridman telling you of the conversation that he said he had had with Mr. Berezovsky. That, I have to put to you, is a complete invention. Is it an invention, as I suggest?

AVEN: No.

BROWNE: You are under oath.

AVEN: Everything that I've told you is completely true.

BROWNE: I suggest regrettably that it is an invention at a late stage out of loyalty to Mr. Fridman?

AVEN: Absolutely wrong.

BROWNE: The first that any mention was made of Mr. Fridman telling you of the alleged threat by Mr. Berezovsky was in the witness statement served by him and you on February 21st of this year, 2006.

AVEN: Again, it is difficult for me to comment on timing again. Mr. Fridman informed me immediately about the story and again when we started, when we found out about Berezovsky's invitation to the court, I immediately told our lawyers (*inaudible*) that is absolutely the case, that is all.

BROWNE: Mr. Aven, the question I put to you—and if I got it wrong I would have been corrected—the first time that it was ever mentioned by you and Mr. Fridman that he had told you about the supposed threat was February 21st this year, something like 17-18 months after the broadcast on NTV; all right? It was never mentioned, was it, in either solicitor's letters, was it? No, it was not, it was never mentioned in any court documents either, was it? It was never mentioned until February 21st. And when *Alfa Bank's* solicitors were asked to say in July last year who their witnesses would be, they simply named Mr. Fridman, Mr. Nemtsov and Mr. Potanin, and your name was singularly absent. Is that not indicative that this is a very recent invention to try to assist Mr. Fridman?

AVEN: I do not think so.

BROWNE: Could you just look at the letter that we were looking at this morning, when you were in court, the letter of Herbert Smith? What this letter is saying is: "This is so commonplace that it is not improper." In other words, it is not discreditable. If that were the case, as this letter suggests, there would be no reason for Mr. Fridman to have mentioned this matter to you, would there?

AVEN: Completely wrong. Drugs, prostitution, and alcoholism are also common in our life, but it does not mean that it is proper. If it happens among our friends, we definitely discuss it. Unfortunately Russian business standards, business morals, are not as lofty as in the United Kingdom, and we speak out when some of our former friends use threats as an instrument of influence, we certainly discuss this among ourselves.

BROWNE: But if Russian conduct of business life is of a lower standard than in the United Kingdom, that would be even less reason for Mr. Fridman to mention it, would it not?

AVEN: Absolutely wrong. Mr. Fridman and I both believe that our main target as a business structure is to try to implement Western business standards, and we hope that our friends, our partners, will do the same. So when it does not happen, we definitely speak up, we do not like it, and we discuss it.

BROWNE: Could you, please, be given the Russian version of your witness statement? And also the English version.

AVEN: Okay.

BROWNE: In the English version you say this—and I will just read the sentence: "Mr. Fridman told me that Berezovsky promised to destroy us." Do you see that?

AVEN: Yes.

BROWNE: Now, in the Russian version you use the word "unichtozhit" for what is translated into English as "destroy" do you not?

AVEN: Yes.

BROWNE: You do not use the phrase "my vas zamochim," do you?

AVEN: I did not.

BROWNE: That, I suggest, is because Mr. Fridman never told you what Mr. Berezovsky had said to him, or allegedly said to him?

AVEN: What I am telling you is exactly what Mr. Fridman told me. Mr. Fridman used the word "destroy" with me.

BROWNE: Mr. Fridman and you have got your stories wrong, have you not?

AVEN: No, not exactly. In fact we have known Mr. Berezovsky so well that these minor changes in his wording do not really matter.

BROWNE: It is not a minor change. You were in court this morning, were you not, Mr. Aven, when we went through the significance of the phrase "my vas zamochim?"

AVEN: I can tell you more, that in my presence, Mr. Berezovsky...

BROWNE: Could you just answer my question.

AVEN: When we spoke with Mr. Fridman...

BROWNE: You were in court this morning when I went through the article from *Vedomosti*, and *Vedomosti* said in the plainest terms that this was criminals' language?

AVEN: I have a PhD in economics, not in linguistics and for me it is difficult to comment on exact meaning. But in Russian, to destroy "zamochim," or as Mr. Berezovsky used to say in English, "We shall tear them to pieces," that is what he likes to say, is more or less the same.

BROWNE: Let us just concentrate on the questions, Mr. Aven, rather than taking the opportunity to make digs at Mr. Berezovsky. Are we agreed that when President Putin used the phrase "my vas zamochim" in September 1999, everyone was astonished at the coarseness of his language?

AVEN: No, the majority of the population was not astonished.

BROWNE: Just look at *Vedomosti*. Is that not indicative?

AVEN: Mr. Bershidsky represents a very small part of Russian society, and definitely not the Russian people.

BROWNE: You have seen, have you not, what he was saying, that in the future if people were to join the political debate they would have to get a dictionary of Russian criminal slang. That is what he was saying, was it not?

AVEN: Again, I do not have a degree in linguistics.

BROWNE: Well, a degree in linguistics is not necessary. Let us not fence about this, Mr. Aven. It is simply that if you are right, if it is commonly used in every day language; if you are right, which I suggest you are not. It is not exactly linguistics, is it?

AVEN: I believe that it does involve linguistics.

BROWNE: You see, Mr. Putin apologizes before he uses the phrase, does he not?

AVEN: I do not remember exactly... I guess it sometimes is a problem when the president of the country uses vulgar language.

BROWNE: He says: "Pardon my language, if we catch them in the toilet we will finish them off right there. We will rub them out." Kill them, in other words. That is what "my vas zamochim" means, is it not?

AVEN: Not exactly, it has a lot of different meanings within different contexts.

BROWNE: I suggest it has only one meaning and that is why Mr. Putin had to apologize, as *Vedomosti* shows, the following day for the use of his language?

AVEN: Maybe you've learned something else about Russian, but for me it definitely has many meanings. It certainly does not mean killing or anything like that. For me, "destroy," "zamochit" in Russian, or to "tear into pieces" is more or less the same in Russian everyday language.

BROWNE: You see, I am going to put this one last time. You and Mr. Fridman have been caught because you have failed to match your stories. He says that Mr. Berezovsky threatened him by saying that he would kill him, "my vas zamochim"; you say that Mr. Fridman told you that Mr. Berezovsky would destroy him using the much less unpleasant word, the ordinary word for destroy, "unichtozhit."

AVEN: I did not mean and I did not intend to make an investigation of what exact wording Mr. Berezovsky used speaking with Mr. Fridman. For me it was sufficient just to know that we had received a threat from Mr. Berezovsky. What he said exactly had absolutely—was absolutely not important. I did not ask him for the exact wording because it was absolutely irrelevant. It is irrelevant.

BROWNE: If Mr. Berezovsky had threatened to "my vas zamochim" Mr. Fridman, Mr. Fridman would surely have told you and you would not in your witness statement have used the different, much less strong, word "unichtozhit."

AVEN: Mr. Browne, if you are accusing me of lying it would be much easier for me to say that Mr. Fridman told me exactly what he told the court, "my vas zamochim." I am telling the truth. He never used the word "my vas zamochim," he just told me that Mr. Berezovsky was threatening us.

BROWNE: Mr. Aven, sometimes liars are caught because they do not both get their lies straight.

SHIELDS: Mr. Nemtsov, please.

Examination-in-chief by Mr. Shields

Shields: Mr. Nemtsov, would you like to give your evidence in English or have my questions translated by the interpreter.

Nemtsov: I could try to speak English, but unfortunately I don't have that much practice. That is why I need some translation. I will try my best, because this is a great opportunity for me to improve. Okay, but I will need some translation.

Shields: Your full name, please, Mr. Nemtsov?

Nemtsov: Boris Yefimovich Nemtsov.

Shields: You live in Moscow, is that right?

Nemtsov: Yes.

Shields: Mr. Nemtsov, are you a politician?

Nemtsov: Yes, I am a politician.

Shields: Are you a member of the Federal Political Council of the Union of Right Forces Party?

Nemtsov: Yes.

Shields: And co-chairman of the 2008 Committee?

Nemtsov: Yes, I am a member of the 2008 Committee.

Shields: Would you just tell the jury—they have to hear your voice over there—what is the 2008 Committee?

Nemtsov: Well, this is an organization which was founded a few years ago by the old chess champion Mr. Kasparov, me and some other opposition political leaders. Also by some independent journalists, including journalists who lost their jobs at NTV, and some other independent TV companies. The main goal of the organization is to protect the Russian constitution and to thwart a third term for President Putin. And the next task is how to organize transparent, honest and competitive elections in Russia. Of course the main elections will be 2008, I hope, and the parliamentary elections and regional elections.

Shields: So you do not want—as one of the aims—Mr. Putin to have a third term in office?

Nemtsov: This is one of the biggest dangers for Russia and, I believe, one of the biggest dangers for the world. That is why I am opposed to this, and that is why I am a member of the committee of 2008. Of course we have problems in Russia because public opinion in the country—unfortunately—but this is true—public opinion in the country supports Putin for a third term, which is a problem.

SHIELDS: I understand. So no one could accuse you, would that be right, of being a supporter of Mr. Putin?

NEMTSOV: Never, never.

SHIELDS: You told us you are involved with the Federal Political Council of the Union of Right Forces Party. What does that stand for?

NEMTSOV: My existing position…

SHIELDS: No, what are the aims of the council?

NEMTSOV: This is a council that formulated our policy—both domestic and international affairs. I was a leader of this party for four years from 1999 up to—the end of 1999 up to the beginning of 2004. Now I am a member of the council. The council is the highest organization for promoting the policies of our party. The party is a liberal democratic organization. Liberal and democratic. This is not Zhirinovsky's party, which has the same title; this is a real liberal democratic party.

SHIELDS: Were you an active supporter of the Ukrainian Orange Revolution in November and December 2004?

NEMTSOV: Yes, I took part in the revolution. I supported Mr. Yuschenko.

SHIELDS: Was he elected—he is the current president?

NEMTSOV: Yes, he is the reigning president now. I have known him for eight years. We have very, very similar political views on the development of our countries. We want Russia to become part of Europe, and he wants the same thing for Ukraine. That is why I supported him during the Orange Revolution, and support him now. I am an adviser to the President of Ukraine; I am economic adviser to the president.

SHIELDS: Was Mr. Putin in favor of the election of Mr. Yuschenko or was he opposed to it.

NEMTSOV: Completely against it. He was completely against the Orange Revolution. He was completely against Yuschenko. He tried to pressure the Ukrainian authorities, for example, through Gazprom fuel prices.

SHIELDS: I am going to ask you very briefly a bit about yourself. It is right you were born on October 9, 1959. Were you born in 1959?

NEMTSOV: Exactly.

SHIELDS: It is all right, we are not going to have your full life story. In the city of Sochi, is that right?

NEMTSOV: Yes. This is in the south of Russia.

SHIELDS: You are a married man?

NEMTSOV: Yes.

SHIELDS: You have four children?

NEMTSOV: Absolutely.

SHIELDS: In 1981, you graduated from the Gorkovsky State University with a degree in radio physics, and after university you worked as a scholar in the Research Institute until 1990?

NEMTSOV: Yes.

SHIELDS: In 1990, you started becoming involved in politics?

NEMTSOV: Exactly.

SHIELDS: Would you tell us what happened in 1990, in relation to your political involvement?

NEMTSOV: I became a member of the Democratic Movement of Russia, an anticommunist organization. I took part in the election campaign, parliamentary election campaign, in 1990. This was still during the Communist era in the Soviet Union.

SHIELDS: Mr. Gorbachev was in power then?

NEMTSOV: Yes, it was his last year.

SHIELDS: That is what I thought.

NEMTSOV: After the October Revolution they were the first free elections in Russia. And I took part in these elections. I won from among 11 candidates. That is why I became a member of the parliament.

SHIELDS: Mr. Yeltsin became president in 1990. In August 1991, were you appointed by Mr. Yeltsin to be his representative in one of the Russian regions?

NEMTSOV: Yes, I became his representative in the Nizhny Novgorod region at the end of August 1991, immediately after the August coup, after the collapse of the Soviet Union.

SHIELDS: Did you become governor of that region?

NEMTSOV: Yes, in the beginning of December I became a governor of the Nizhny Novgorod region.

SHIELDS: And were you, in December, elected to the Federation Council, which is the upper house of the Russian parliament?

NEMTSOV: Yes, I was elected at the end of 1993, as a member of the upper house.

SHIELDS: Just to get that chronologically straight. Mr. Yeltsin was re-elected as president in 1996. Do you recall that? Obviously you do.

NEMTSOV: I supported him.

SHIELDS: You supported him?

NEMTSOV: Of course. What was our choice? Between communism and Yeltsin. Of course...

SHIELDS: Did Mr. Yeltsin invite you to take up political office, high political office? Were you then appointed First Deputy Prime Minister?

NEMTSOV: In March 1997, I was appointed a First Deputy Prime Minister in the Russian government, and at the same time I was appointed Minister of Fuel and Energy.

SHIELDS: You were appointed First Deputy Prime Minister. Who was the Prime Minister at that time?

NEMTSOV: Mr. Chernomyrdin.

SHIELDS: Was there another first deputy?

NEMTSOV: Yes, Mr. Chubais.

SHIELDS: Two firsts?

NEMTSOV: Yes, we have two firsts. This is a very complicated structure.

SHIELDS: We will not go down that one. But you had two firsts. You were also, you told us, appointed to a position of responsibility for fuel and energy, or fuel and gas, was it?

NEMTSOV: Yes. I had two positions in the government. First Deputy Prime Minister and Minister of Fuel and Energy.

SHIELDS: What was your role as Minister for Fuel and Energy? What were your duties?

NEMTSOV: I was responsible for reconstructing the energy sector, which was the main problem. First of all, the coal sector, oil, business and the gas business. I was responsible for the fuel supply of the country and international trade. We established transparent rules for the Russian pipeline system, and other regulations.

SHIELDS: Thank you. Did that involve restructuring the national monopolies?

NEMTSOV: Yes, it was my responsibility.

SHIELDS: What was the biggest monopoly in Russia at that stage in energy terms?

NEMTSOV: The biggest monopoly, not only in Russia but in the world, was Gazprom.

SHIELDS: I think it is right that Gazprom is Russia's largest national gas company?

NEMTSOV: Gazprom is the third largest company in the world, and the biggest gas company in the world, with a capitalization of more than $300 billion.

SHIELDS: That is the day—my learned friend said. What was it in 1996, or 1997 when you became minister?

NEMTSOV: The biggest company in the country, the company generates about 10 percent of Russia's GDP and the role of this company has increased each year. The company was under state control at the time. At that time the state controlled 38 percent of the shares. That is why the state was the biggest shareholder of the company.

SHIELDS: Now, in June 1997, cast your mind back then, did Gazprom have a board of directors?

NEMTSOV: Yes, of course, 11 members.

SHIELDS: Were you one of those directors?

NEMTSOV: Me, no. I was a chairman of a collegium of state representatives in Gazprom. I will explain…

SHIELDS: We will come back to that in a minute. Who was the chairman of that?

NEMTSOV: At that time?

SHIELDS: Sorry, of Gazprom itself. Can you remember?

NEMTSOV: The chairman of the board was Mr. Kazakov and the executive manager was Mr. Viakhirev.

SHIELDS: Can you remember when Mr. Kazakov was appointed?

NEMTSOV: That is a good question. It seems to me that was in 1996.

SHIELDS: In 1996. Now, of the 11 directors of the board, did any of that number represent another state body?

NEMTSOV: We had four representatives from the state, who were members of my commission, and seven members who represented the management of the company and several independent individuals, such as the governor of the Yamalo-Nenetsky region, Mr. Neyelov.

SHIELDS: Now, do you remember who had appointed the then chairman, Mr. Kazakov?

NEMTSOV: The board.

SHIELDS: The board?

NEMTSOV: Yes, this is board's responsibility. The chairman called this meeting to appoint the board. After that the board appointed the chairman.

SHIELDS: At that stage, did you know a Mr. Boris Berezovsky?

NEMTSOV: Yes, I knew him.

SHIELDS: Did you know him in 1997?

NEMTSOV: Well, I have known him for 10 years. Of course I knew him in 1997.

SHIELDS: At that stage was Mr. Berezovsky in the government or in a government position that you can recall?

NEMTSOV: In 1997, he was Deputy Secretary of the Security Council of the Russian Federation, which is not a member of the government. This is a member of the Kremlin administration.

SHIELDS: Did you see much of Mr. Berezovsky at that time through your government work?

NEMTSOV: Yes, of course—he worked in the Kremlin and I worked in the White House, in the government building, and we were in touch with each other.

SHIELDS: Did there come a time when you encountered Mr. Berezovsky in relation to Gazprom?

NEMTSOV: Yes, we met for the first time in June of 1997. It was a discussion about Gazprom.

SHIELDS: Would you tell us about that discussion?

NEMTSOV: Yes, he told me that he wanted to be chairman of the board.

SHIELDS: Can we do this slowly? The jury has to hear this.

NEMTSOV: He told me that he wanted to be the chairman of the board of Gazprom.

SHIELDS: Where did you have this discussion?

NEMTSOV: As far as I can remember, at the beginning of June.

SHIELDS: Do you remember where it took place?

NEMTSOV: In my office, in the White House.

SHIELDS: And Mr. Berezovsky came to see you?

NEMTSOV: Yes.

SHIELDS: And tell us what happened then?

NEMTSOV: Well, he showed me a draft document that contained a proposal for him to be appointed the chairman of the board of Gazprom, and he said that Mr. Viakhirev, who at that time was the executive manager of Gazprom, had drafted and signed it, the draft, and Mr. Chernomyrdin, he told me, had also agreed.

SHIELDS: Can you stop there? What was your reaction when you say that, I think, you called it a draft document?

NEMTSOV: I was completely surprised by it because, you know, he had no real connection with Gazprom, and Gazprom was the biggest company. And I was completely against this idea because the consolidation of political and economic power in one set of hands would be disastrous for Russia and, it seems to me, for every country in the world. That is why I was against it.

SHIELDS: Just pausing there, did you take any steps when you saw that document?

NEMTSOV: I called Mr. Viakhirev, who was the executive manager of Gazprom, and asked him, "Do you really think that Berezovsky should be the chairman of Gazprom?" He said, very dejectedly, "Yes, I do, but I hope that you will be able to make the correct decision."

SHIELDS: What did he say to you, or you say to him?

NEMTSOV: He said, "I signed this draft, but I hope that you will be able to make the correct decision." That is what he said.

SHIELDS: What did you understand by that?

NEMTSOV: Well, he then said one more thing, that "Boris, you understand that Berezovsky controls the country, that is why, as a manager, I cannot be against this proposal. That is why I signed." He was a very powerful man and I was very surprised that he had signed this draft, but he had. And I asked him if he was against the idea, and he said, "Well, it's your choice; you can do what you want because you are a state representative of the company, within the company." Next I called Mr. Chernomyrdin, the Prime Minister of the Russian Federation, and asked him the same thing.

SHIELDS: That is Chernomyrdin?

NEMTSOV: Mr. Chernomyrdin, yes, the Prime Minister of the Russian government, and I asked him the same question: "Are you ready to appoint Mr. Berezovsky as chairman?"

He said: "Well, it is an idea, I know about that idea, maybe I support it, maybe not. I still have to think about it; I'm somewhat supportive of the idea, but perhaps I will change my mind."

He was in a very confused state, and then he said: "You are responsible for this decision and you are responsible for this decision because I am a chairman of the state representative. Of course you have to think more carefully about this proposal." I asked that—my opinion is absolutely clear. I am 100 percent against, that is it, and I explained to him why. He said: "Okay, I understand." And after that we continued discussions with the Prime Minister and Mr. Berezovsky in China when we were reviewing...

SHIELDS: I want to pause there.

NEMTSOV: ...In the middle of June.

BROWNE: Sorry, "we continued discussions," means that he continued the discussion.

SHIELDS: Were you going on ahead in time when you said, "We continued the discussion"? I am asking about what happened that day.

NEMTSOV: Oh, yes, there were two calls, one to Viakhirev and one to Chernomyrdin. Viakhirev said he had signed that document and Chernomyrdin had said that he was still deciding whether to support it, but he had not made a final decision yet.

SHIELDS: Now, what did you say, if anything, to Mr. Berezovsky?

NEMTSOV: I said that I am completely against it.

SHIELDS: What was Mr. Berezovsky's reaction to that?

NEMTSOV: In my office the reaction was—"Let's discuss this further, and I'm certain that in the end you will make the right decision. I am certain because the Prime Minister will explain to you what is right and what is wrong." But, frankly speaking, it was my responsibility, it was my responsibility to make the decision about the state representatives on the board. That is why, without my support, it was completely impossible for him to become chairman of the board. That is why he was in my office.

Monday, May 22, 2006

SHIELDS: I was asking on Friday about the meeting with Mr. Berezovsky and I asked you about the board of Gazprom.

NEMTSOV: Yes.

SHIELDS: Can you recall how many members there were on the board in 1997?

NEMTSOV: Eleven.

SHIELDS: Of that—those 11, how many, if any, represented what you call the Collegium of Representatives?

NEMTSOV: Four.

SHIELDS: Can you remember who those four were?

NEMTSOV: Well, I remember Mr. Kazakov.

SHIELDS: Was he the chairman?

NEMTSOV: Yes, he was the chairman at the time.

SHIELDS: Of the board?

NEMTSOV: Yes.

SHIELDS: Who else can you recall?

NEMTSOV: Kazakov, Kudrin.

SHIELDS: Kudrin?

NEMTSOV: Well, Belousov, so far as I know he was a representative from a property fund.

SHIELDS: But there were four representatives of the collegium?

NEMTSOV: Yes.

SHIELDS: Could you tell us something about the collegium? When was the collegium set up and how?

NEMTSOV: Well, it was a special presidential decree which was published on May 12, 1997. Mr. Yeltsin signed it because we wanted to increase the role of the state in the largest Russian company. At that time, the state had 38 percent of the shares and the state was the biggest shareholder of the company. The idea was to establish a joint and united decision from the state representatives on the board, and if you look at this decree and the charter numbers 4 and 5, you will notice that the decision of this collegium has to vote on the board of Gazprom, and that all four members from the board have to vote based on our decision. The last representative on the board was Mr. Kutovoy.

SHIELDS: "Decree of the President of the Russian Federation."

NEMTSOV: Yes.

SHIELDS: That would be Mr. Yeltsin?

NEMTSOV: Yes.

SHIELDS: Number 478, May 12th?

NEMTSOV: Yes.

SHIELDS: "For the purpose of ensuring state management of the shares of the Russian joint stock company Gazprom."

NEMTSOV: Yes.

SHIELDS: He therefore resolves: " …to form a collegium of state representatives of … hereinafter referred to as the collegium, in the following composition." If you look at the names, there is yours at the top, Nemtsov.

NEMTSOV: Yes.

SHIELDS: And it says: "First Deputy Chairman of the Government of the Russian Federation, Fuel and Energy Minister of the Russian Federation, Chairman of the Collegium." So that is where you were appointed chairman. And the names down there, I think you told us that, of those ten, four of them were directors. One was Mr. Belousov—deputy chairman of the state property management committee…

NEMTSOV: Yes.

SHIELDS: ...Kazakov, First Deputy Head of the Administration of the President of the Russian Federation. Kazhirev, Deputy Fuel and Energy Minister of the Russian Federation, and Mr. Kudrin. So they were the four who were the directors representing the collegium on the board?

NEMTSOV: Yes.

SHIELDS: You yourself were not a director of Gazprom?

NEMTSOV: No.

SHIELDS: "To establish that state representatives of the Russian Joint Stock Company, including those representing the state under the contract, shall act in accordance with the policy determined by the majority of votes of the collegium's members and drawn up in the form of the collegium's decision protocol." What is the effect of that particular paragraph then?

NEMTSOV: Well, for example, here we are discussing a concrete problem, who will be chairman of the board of Gazprom. This decision has to be discussed in the collegium, and if the collegium makes the decision that, for example, Mr. Kazakov should be chairman, the four members of the board of Gazprom have to vote, unanimously. Here we are discussing the problem: should Boris Berezovsky become chairman of the board of Gazprom. And the collegium decides that "no." Then nobody from the board, I mean the four representatives from the list, would vote for this gentleman.

SHIELDS: So, if the board wanted to vote Mr. Berezovsky in as chairman, and these four voted against, would that require therefore the seven other people on the board to vote in favor?

NEMTSOV: Well, we have this list of four. And seven other individuals represent the management of Gazprom and the governor of the Yamal-Nenetsky region.

SHIELDS: Who was that?

NEMTSOV: Mr. Neyelov. And one individual who was chairman of the tender commission for construction of pipelines in Siberia, Mr. Dinkov. Unfortunately, he died.

SHIELDS: Mr. Neyelov and Mr. Dinkov were therefore directors.

NEMTSOV: They are not members of Gazprom. Neyelov was elected—which is very important—he was elected governor of the Yamal-Nenetsky region and he was an independent representative on the board of Gazprom. And I know his position and knew his position about Berezovsky; he was completely against this decision. And Mr. Dinkov, he was against it too. We had six representatives on the board of Gazprom who were against Berezovsky as chairman of Gazprom, and this was enough to reject him as a candidate.

SHIELDS: You say you had six out of the 11 votes?

NEMTSOV: Yes.

SHIELDS: Did you go to Beijing in June 1997?

NEMTSOV: Yes.

SHIELDS: Who did you travel with to Beijing?

NEMTSOV: Well, I was a co-chairman of a Russian/Chinese intergovernmental commission. It was my responsibility. And the main goal was to prepare a visit by Mr. Chernomyrdin to China. That is why I flew to Beijing myself before Chernomyrdin's visit.

SHIELDS: When you were in Beijing, did you meet with Mr. Chernomyrdin?

NEMTSOV: Yes, I met with him. I prepared his visit.

SHIELDS: When you were in Beijing, did you have any contact with Mr. Berezovsky?

NEMTSOV: Yes, Berezovsky flew independently to Beijing, and I met him in Beijing. We visited one hydroelectric station in the middle of the country and we spent maybe one day together. And the main purpose of his visit to China was to discuss Gazprom?

SHIELDS: You said "the main purpose"; how do you know that and how did that take shape?

NEMTSOV: We discussed this issue once again. The first time we had discussed it in my office in the White House in Moscow.

SHIELDS: This was the second time?

NEMTSOV: Yes, this was the second time—

SHIELDS: Where did you discuss it the second time?

NEMTSOV: In Beijing. We visited the Three Gorges hydroelectric station together. We discussed this topic during our trip from Beijing to the Three Gorges. We spent, I do not know how many hours—several hours together discussing it. Finally, we decided that…

SHIELDS: Just tell me what happened. Was anyone else present in your discussion with Mr. Berezovsky?

NEMTSOV: There were some advisers, my advisers, with me during this trip. But we discussed it separately; we did not involve anyone else in the discussion.

SHIELDS: When you discussed it with Mr. Berezovsky, what was the purpose of that discussion?

NEMTSOV: He insisted once again that he should be chairman of Gazprom.

SHIELDS: What was his attitude towards that?

NEMTSOV: Well, frankly speaking, I do not know. You know, he had already concentrated a lot of power at that time. He was a Deputy Secretary of the Security Council. He had interest in many businesses, including oil, automobiles, and aluminum. And from my point of view, to control Gazprom would have meant the privatization of Russia, and that is why I was completely against it. And I repeated again and again that it was absolutely impossible, and that I would do everything in my power to avoid such an outcome.

SHIELDS: When you were in Beijing did you see Mr. Chernomyrdin at all?

NEMTSOV: Yes, Chernomyrdin traveled to China a little bit later, a day later than me. I met him in the airport. We discussed the details of the visit. And after that, Mr. Berezovsky suggested that we discuss Gazprom one more time.

SHIELDS: Where did that discussion take place?

NEMTSOV: The discussion took place in the Russian Embassy in Beijing.

SHIELDS: What happened during that discussion?

NEMTSOV: Well, Berezovsky insisted that Chernomyrdin should appoint him as chairman. Chernomyrdin said that there were people for and against this idea, but what is most important is the opinion of Mr. Nemtsov, because I was responsible for Gazprom and I was the chairman of the State Representative Committee. That is why to adopt a decision without my support would be impossible. I can say that—and this is very important—that our views differed from Chernomyrdin's concerning Gazprom. And this is one of the—we had a certain amount of conflict in the government over Gazprom. I will explain what I mean by conflict. I was against the so-called trust agreement between CEO Mr. Viakhirev and the government, which would have put up

38 percent of Gazprom for auction for only six million dollars. At that time, 38 percent of Gazprom, whose price at that time was $20 billion, due to this trust agreement, would have been sold for only $6 million. I was completely against this idea, and Chernomyrdin supported it. That is why we had different views concerning Gazprom, not only because of Berezovsky but because of the so-called privatization of Gazprom.

SHIELDS: In this meeting with Mr. Berezovsky and Mr. Chernomyrdin, how did Mr. Berezovsky react to your decision?

NEMTSOV: Well he tried to explain to Chernomyrdin that Chernomyrdin was my boss and that Chernomyrdin had to explain to me that we should support this idea. And Chernomyrdin said that, yes, I am Prime Minister and he is First Deputy Prime Minister, but first of all he is responsible for Gazprom and secondly he has a very good relationship with Yeltsin. And finally, he will be the one with the opportunity to go to the Kremlin and explain to Yeltsin that it is unwise to appoint Berezovsky as the chairman of Gazprom. That is why, without his agreement, it is impossible. "It is impossible to appoint you as chairman," he tried to explain to him.

SHIELDS: How did Mr. Berezovsky react to your refusal to agree to the proposition?

NEMTSOV: Of course he was very angry about it. He repeated once again, "You are the boss, you have to explain to him, you have to put pressure on him, you have to do something to change his decision" et cetera.

SHIELDS: How did you feel Mr. Berezovsky would behave towards you if you did not agree?

NEMTSOV: Well, when our discussion finally ended, and we were out on the street, he said to me, "I will destroy you as a politician." Well, I took this very, very seriously. I will explain to you why, because he controls the biggest and the most influential television channel in Russia, Channel 1. At that time, Channel 1, and even now, plays an unbelievably huge role in public opinion, and to destroy somebody using blackmail PR techniques was not that difficult; not only in the past but even now. I will give you one example.

SHIELDS: Just stop there.

Cross-examination by Mr. Browne

Browne: Mr. Nemtsov, you were in court on Friday, were you not?

Nemtsov: Yes, yes.

Browne: Were you also here on Thursday?

Nemtsov: No, I was not.

Browne: At any rate, you were in court on Friday when Mr. Aven gave his evidence?

Nemtsov: Yes. Maybe for the last part of his testimony.

Browne: You see, I suggest that, like Mr. Aven, you are another witness who knows perfectly well that Mr. Berezovsky does not go through life habitually threatening people. You know that perfectly well, do you not?

Nemtsov: What do you mean?

Browne: I will put a slightly different question to you. Like Mr. Aven, you show by your continuing friendly relationship with Mr. Berezovsky that he is not a person who goes around threatening people.

Nemtsov: Well, I have known Berezovsky for ten years. I do not think that—we are friendly, but of course we have a relationship because he was in the power structure and he was one of the biggest tycoons within the Russian economy, the Russian business world. But we never became friends. Anyway, I know that he threatened me and I have a very concrete case. That is why I am trying to describe this instance to you. I can repeat once again.

Browne: No, just please answer my questions. My questions are directed at the fact that I am suggesting that even after Mr. Berezovsky left Russia you continued to maintain friendly relations with him, did you not?

Nemtsov: Well, first of all…

Browne: Yes or no, Mr. Nemtsov?

Nemtsov: Well, I want to tell you very frankly. I was completely against Putin's political pressure on Berezovsky, or on Khodorkovsky, or on anyone, including the Russian opposition, and that is true. That is why I was against his immigration and the attempts by Russia's Kremlin to extradite him. That is absolutely true.

Browne: Please answer my question.

Nemtsov: And I have a relationship with him, but on the other hand the last time I talked with him was in 2005. This is not exactly a friendship. Sometimes we have a common understanding of what is happening in Russia, and outside, and sometimes we have differing views. We are independent persons.

BROWNE: So you do not have a friendly relationship with Mr. Berezovsky? You simply from time to time discuss matters of mutual interest; is that your testimony?

NEMTSOV: We discussed Russian politics, and international politics. The last time we spoke was in 2005.

BROWNE: Right at the very end of 2005, was it not?

NEMTSOV: Yes, the latter half of 2005.

BROWNE: Your testimony is that, apart from that, you do not maintain a friendly relationship?

NEMTSOV: Well, frankly I have friends, but Berezovsky is not among them.

BROWNE: So it is not a friendly relationship, it is a relationship?

NEMTSOV: What I am saying—we had a relationship. And I mentioned that maybe six months ago we talked on the telephone about Ukraine and the Orange Revolution, and Yuschenko, et cetera.

BROWNE: You see, Mr. Nemtsov, you claim that Mr. Berezovsky made a serious threat to you and insulted you in front of Mr. Chernomyrdin. That is your testimony, is it not?

NEMTSOV: I just said that he, after our discussion with Chernomyrdin, said that "I will destroy you as a politician." That is it.

BROWNE: Before that, you were implying that he had insulted you by telling Chernomyrdin that he was the boss and that he should insist on him putting his foot down and insisting that you should go along with the proposal, that Mr. Berezovsky should become chairman. That was insulting, was it not?

NEMTSOV: Berezovsky insisted that Chernomyrdin should pressure me to agree with the idea of his position in Gazprom.

BROWNE: Did you not feel insulted by the way Mr. Berezovsky was treating you in front of Mr. Chernomyrdin?

NEMTSOV: Well, you know, I think that this is his style. Everybody knows about it. Not only me, but many individuals in our government.

BROWNE: Is the answer to my question yes or no, that you felt insulted by the way he treated you?

NEMTSOV: I said that it was a very serious matter. He did say, "destroy you as a politician."

BROWNE: Did you feel insulted by the way he spoke about you in front of Mr. Chernomyrdin; yes or no?

NEMTSOV: You know, it's difficult for me to say.

BROWNE: Very well. You see, I suggest that over recent years, even after this action, you continued to have many conversations on the telephone about Ukraine with Mr. Berezovsky.

NEMTSOV: Well, during the Orange Revolution, we talked a lot about what is happening in Kiev and with Chernomyrdin and in Independence Square, but frankly we have differing positions...

BROWNE: I know you do, and I will...

NEMTSOV: —at that time, but we discussed what was happening...

BROWNE: I will come back and explore that in a moment. Can we agree for the moment that, to use your words, you talked a lot to Mr. Berezovsky about these matters?

NEMTSOV: We spoke several times.

BROWNE: I see.

NEMTSOV: Several times.

BROWNE: I suggest that there were many conversations, particularly at the time of the so-called Orange Revolution in Kiev?

NEMTSOV: We had maybe 3 or 4 discussions about that. It happened at the end of 2004.

BROWNE: Yes, just before Christmas 2004?

NEMTSOV: 2004, November and December.

BROWNE: Since then you have discussed matters such as the roles played by the former woman Prime Minister, Mrs. Timoshenko, and President Yuschenko?

NEMTSOV: I supported Yuschenko, the politician, and now, as the president of the country. I am his adviser. And I was against Timoshenko, because she is the Ukrainian Che Guevara—she destroyed the country's economy. And Berezovsky supported Timoshenko; that is the point.

BROWNE: Since we have gotten to that, let me just ask you a few questions about it. Mr. Berezovsky believes that what is needed in Ukraine is an alliance between Mrs. Timoshenko and Mr. Yuschenko, does he not?

NEMTSOV: There is this view.

BROWNE: It is Mr. Berezovsky's view, is it not?

NEMTSOV: Yes. As far as I know, he has reported—he supported this idea.

BROWNE: Yes. The reason he supported it was this. In the Ukrainian election in March this year, Mr. Yanukovich, the pro-Russian candidate, was the overall holder of the most votes. He had 32 percent of the electorate, did he not?

NEMTSOV: Yes.

BROWNE: Mrs. Timoshenko had 22 percent. And the person you support, Mr. Yuschenko, had 14 percent. Is not the point that Mr. Berezovsky has made to you on numerous occasions is that it suits the Russians and Mr. Putin to have a divided opposition to Mr. Yanukovich, who has the largest proportion of the vote at 32 percent. That is Mr. Berezovsky's point, is it not?

NEMTSOV: Well, first of all, Yanukovich is not a pro-Russian candidate. During his campaign, only American advisers were around him and Yanukovich voted for Ukrainian troops to be sent to Iraq. And the Russian government was completely against this idea. That is why he has the image of being pro-Russia, but he is not. That is the first point.

Second point. A coalition with Timoshenko already existed. It happened immediately after the Orange Revolution, and we know the results. Timoshenko destroyed the Ukrainian economy. During seven months, she reduced the GDP from 12 percent of growth to minus 2 percent. She destroyed the economy. And that is why I am against her. She destroyed the financial system of the country; she decided to re-privatize all of the Ukrainian industries. She organized a disaster in the investment climate. Capital has come out of the country; no investment in to the country. That is why I, as an economic adviser, of course am against her. I explained that she is not an Orange Princess; she is a Red Manager, a Soviet-style Red Manager. That is the point. That is why I was against it.

On the other hand, if you look more carefully at who is behind everything, you will see that it is Ukrainian business. And I think that a coalition with Ukrainian business and Yuschenko is a real opportunity to move the country forward into the European arena. My last point. If you look at the program of Mr. Yanukovich, he declared that they should join the European Union. This is in his program. He is pro-Russian but he said that Ukraine wants, at some point—maybe not now—to be a member of the European Union.

BROWNE: Sir, can we leave it at this: you said in that long answer that Mr. Yanukovich is pro-Russian and has an image of being pro-Russian?

NEMTSOV: Yes, he has that image.

BROWNE: And we agreed, did we not, that only by Mrs. Timoshenko and Mr. Yuschenko combining their percentage of the vote, of respectively 22 percent and 14 percent, that they can constitute a plausible opposition to Mr. Yanukovich?

NEMTSOV: Well, all of the Oranges have more than Yanukovich. That is basic arithmetic. But we are talking about the future of the country. We are talking about the economic development of the country. And if you want Timoshenko to be Prime Minister of this country it means that you want to destroy the results of the Orange Revolution. When she was Prime Minister, she ravaged the economy for seven months. Do you want to repeat that once again with this lady? I do not.

BROWNE: Would you accept this, Mr. Nemtsov: your view of Mrs. Timoshenko's economic record, it comes from the mouth of someone who is an adviser to her bitter opponent, Mr. Yuschenko, does it not?

NEMTSOV: No, no, of course not. Of course not. These are official statistics, economic statistics of the country, which are well known, not only in Ukraine but throughout the world. And if you look at the results of Timoshenko's policy, I once again want to tell you that she started from 12 percent of economic growth in February 2005. By the end of August, when she was fired, we were at minus 2 percent. These are the official statistics of the country. Do you need some other proof to understand what this means in terms of Timoshenko? I think it is enough for me. These are the statistics, these are the official results of her policy.

BROWNE: Well, we are going to leave, regrettable though it may be, the subject of Ukrainian politics. But I want to ask you this: you have told the jury that you had phone conversations with Mr. Berezovsky. You have told them nothing, have you, about your visits to him in London?

NEMTSOV: Well...

BROWNE: Why is that?

NEMTSOV: I met with him in London several times. That is true.

BROWNE: Yes, and why is it that you said nothing in your witness statement and nothing in your evidence about that?

NEMTSOV: Do you think that this is that important? I mentioned that I have a relationship with him. That is enough.

BROWNE: Can I suggest that the reason that you have suppressed this important evidence from the jury until now is that you think the jury will not believe that Mr. Berezovsky is a man who threatened you if they know what a close social relationship you have had with him.

NEMTSOV: If you look more carefully at my witness statement, I mention that I have known Berezovsky for ten years, and I had a relationship with him.

BROWNE: You say nothing in your witness statement, Mr. Nemtsov, about having been entertained by Mr. Berezovsky in London, do you? Nothing. Look at your witness statement as long as you want…

NEMTSOV: Well, I can say that I met him in London, that is true.

BROWNE: And you say that now because I am asking you about it. You did not mention it in your witness statement, did you?

NEMTSOV: I did not think that it was very important.

BROWNE: Let us just see how important it is. It is ultimately a matter for the jury. You visited Mr. Berezovsky in his offices in London in April 2004, did you not?

NEMTSOV: April—I do not remember the exact date. I do not know. I visited his office, yes, that is correct. But I do not remember when this happened. A few years ago, yes, you are right.

BROWNE: That was a meeting in Mr. Berezovsky's office with a gentleman called Mr. Malashenko, who was the former manager of NTV, from Mr. Gusinsky's days?

NEMTSOV: Yes.

BROWNE: Please just look at this photograph.

NEMTSOV: Yes.

BROWNE: That shows, does it not, Mr. Nemtsov, just how friendly your relationship was with you and Mr. Berezovsky?

NEMTSOV: Do you think that a picture is enough to characterize a relationship?

BROWNE: Was that photograph taken of you and Mr. Berezovsky in his office on your visit on April 20, 2004?

NEMTSOV: Maybe. Maybe.

BROWNE: No "maybe" about it. You know perfectly well it was. Why are you so unwilling to admit it, Mr. Nemtsov?

NEMTSOV: Well I—no, no, no, I do not remember what—when this happened. But I agree that this picture was taken when I was in his office, that is true.

BROWNE: It does not look as though Mr. Berezovsky is threatening you there, does it?

NEMTSOV: Look, this happened seven years after our discussion in the Russian Embassy in Beijing. Time sometimes means a lot.

BROWNE: You are not saying you have forgotten all about it, are you? You are saying it was a serious threat and you have come to this court to give evidence...

NEMTSOV: I will explain why this has happened. I was the most popular politician at that time, I mean in 1997, and there were a number of discussions about me possibly being the next President of the Russian Federation. And of course at that time I was very disappointed when Berezovsky said that, "You will be destroyed as a politician," and he did his best to destroy me. And finally we end up with Putin as president. After all of his policies, we end up with Putin. That is why at that time, of course I took the threat very seriously. That is true. Now I am a free person. I resigned as chairman of the SPS party. I was not in business at that time. It was 2004. Well, we failed, unfortunately—we failed in the election in 2003. At that time I became a free person, like Berezovsky. Of course in 1997, it was an absolutely different story, absolutely different. We had a liberal democratic government with Mr. Chubais, and we had a real chance to move the country in a democratic direction. And when he decided to destroy our government, and he succeeded in doing this, what do we get? We get a KGB government.

BROWNE: Please just answer my questions, Mr. Nemtsov. The jury may think that instead of doing that you are making speeches. Please look at these photographs, which I suggest were taken on the same occasion and show you and Mr. Berezovsky with Mr. Malashenko. These last two photographs show a cordial discussion, do they not, with yourself, Mr. Berezovsky and Mr. Malashenko?

NEMTSOV: Yes. This picture was taken at the same time as the first.

BROWNE: Is there any other social connection between you and Mr. Berezovsky, that you have not told the jury, that you now want to tell them about? You did not tell the jury about the meeting on April 20, 2004; are there any other meetings with Mr. Berezovsky that you want to tell them about now?

NEMTSOV: Well, I repeat once again, we met several times.

BROWNE: Yes. Another one of those occasions was in the autumn of 2004, when you went to his office? Do you remember that?

NEMTSOV: Autumn 2004.

BROWNE: October or November of that year?

NEMTSOV: I do not remember the exact dates, but yes, I was at his office.

BROWNE: Can I just see if I can jog your memory? The meeting went so well that when you left you forgot to take your papers. Do you remember that?

NEMTSOV: I do not remember that.

BROWNE: You forgot to take your papers. Were you staying at the Lanesborough Hotel? Is that where you were staying, at Hyde Park Corner?

NEMTSOV: Sometimes I stayed in this hotel, yes.

BROWNE: The reason I can put that to you is because the papers you left behind after this cordial meeting were sent to your hotel, the Lanesborough?

NEMTSOV: Maybe.

BROWNE: Do you really not remember?

NEMTSOV: No, it wasn't an important thing.

BROWNE: And it was not just a discussion in his office on either of these occasions, was it? You were actually entertained at dinner by Mr. and Mrs. Berezovsky at his home in Surrey on both occasions in 2004, were you not?

NEMTSOV: I was at his home, that is true.

BROWNE: Twice?

NEMTSOV: Twice.

BROWNE: And served dinner by Mr. and Mrs. Berezovsky?

NEMTSOV: Yes. We had dinner.

BROWNE: You were happy to accept his hospitality, were you not?

NEMTSOV: You know, after—you know, after our resignation we had no real conflict with each other. We had conflict when I was in the government and I was responsible for key Russian issues. Now we are free individuals, so we can do what we want. It was different in 1997 and 2004.

BROWNE: You were happy to accept his hospitality, were you not? At his home?

NEMTSOV: It was—it was a nice dinner.

BROWNE: Around the time of that meeting in London in autumn 2004, Mr. Berezovsky also entertained you on his boat off the coast of Eilat in Israel, did he not?

NEMTSOV: We met in Israel.

BROWNE: He entertained you on his boat?

NEMTSOV: I do not know what you mean by "entertained." We met on his boat in Israel, yes, that is true.

BROWNE: And he provided you with more hospitality on his boat in Israel?

NEMTSOV: We had dinner—I do not know what—maybe drinks after.

BROWNE: Why have you never mentioned that before, Mr. Nemtsov?

NEMTSOV: Because it does not matter. We are independent; we can do what we want. The most important issue happened not now and not two years ago but in 1997. At that time Mr. Putin appeared on the scene. Nobody knew his name at that time. But Berezovsky's policy to destroy democrats ended up leading to the KGB taking power in the future. That is why 1997 was important. 2004/5 is nothing. We are private individuals, we can do what we want, to discuss... Berezovsky—well, my relationship—relationship with him is not a relationship between Berezovsky and Putin, you know, it is not. It all happened back in 1997.

BROWNE: Please look at this photograph which has been taken from a video.

NEMTSOV: It is a good picture.

BROWNE: Does it look to you as if that is part of a video shot on Mr. Berezovsky's boat in the autumn of 2004?

NEMTSOV: (*Pause*).

BROWNE: Again I suggest the photograph shows a very cordial relationship with Mr. Berezovsky, does it not?

NEMTSOV: I was on his boat, that is true.

BROWNE: And when you were back on shore after the trip on his boat, he took you to a restaurant and gave you dinner. And the restaurant was called "The Last Refuge?"

NEMTSOV: No, no, that is not true. We invited him to be a guest at our restaurant. We invited him. It was Mr. Prokhorov, who is my friend, who invited this gentleman with his friends, invited him to our restaurant, and he decided to join us. Boris, explain.

BROWNE: Correct. It seems I have muddled up two occasions. Let me see if I have this right?

NEMTSOV: Mr. Browne, I will explain these invitations. We invited Mr. Berezovsky several times to the restaurant and he always agreed, always at our invitation.

BROWNE: Again, I suggest that this is not something you do to somebody who has seriously threatened you: voluntarily invite them out to dinner on several occasions?

NEMTSOV: Well, as I've explained to you, everything is long in the past. We lost the country. That is the problem and we cannot change the situation. This gentleman is responsible for that. For destroying me, destroying everybody. Threatening me and threatening any number of people in our government. All of these things lead to our current KGB government.

BROWNE: Mr. Nemtsov, another occasion which you have not so far told the jury about, when you partied with Mr. Berezovsky in Israel, was in May of last year, was it not?

NEMTSOV: In May of last year? Maybe.

BROWNE: Yes. I think around May 3rd, when you and he partied together at a 40th birthday celebration for Mr. Michael Prokhorov, who is the partner of Mr. Potanin in Norilsk Nickel?

NEMTSOV: Mr. Prokhorov had a birthday at the beginning of May, that is true. We celebrated his birthday in Israel, in Eilat. And as far as I know, Mr. Prokhorov invited Mr. Berezovsky to take part; that is true.

BROWNE: You were a fellow guest, and you met and talked with him during the celebrations, did you not, in a friendly fashion?

NEMTSOV: Well, we were sitting at the table all together. Of course everybody talked with each other. But Mr. Prokhorov invited me and he invited—he invited me to Israel and he invited Berezovsky to the birthday, that is true. It happened last year.

BROWNE: As Mr. Fridman said in testimony on Friday, you and he have known each other well for going on 15 years, have you not?

NEMTSOV: I have known him very well; for more than ten years, yes.

BROWNE: He said, I think, since the early 1990s. You would not disagree with that, would you?

NEMTSOV: Maybe we had met then, but we were not that close at the beginning of 1990; but in the middle of the 1990s, when I was a governor of the Nizhny Novgorod region, he visited my region to discuss an investment opportunity in the Nizhny Novgorod region. From 1995-96 we became closer.

BROWNE: What Mr. Fridman said—I do not suppose you disagree with it: "I have known him [that is you] quite well since the early 1990s."

NEMTSOV: We had a close relationship beginning in the middle of the 90s. Maybe we had met each other before, but it was not a close relationship. We might have met on occasion.

BROWNE: The two of you are the same age, Mr. Fridman said.

NEMTSOV: He is younger. Five years younger.

BROWNE: Mr. Nemtsov, the fact is that he describes you as a friend. You have been close friends all this time, have you not?

NEMTSOV: We have a very good relationship.

BROWNE: Yes.

NEMTSOV: A very good relationship.

BROWNE: And part of the reason for that very good relationship, I suggest, is that *Alfa* and those associated with *Alfa* have funded your political party, Union of Right Forces.

NEMTSOV: I should say first of all that they did give us money for our campaign and for the political party when I was party chairman. Second, which is very important, according to party rules it is strictly forbidden—it is strictly forbidden to take more than five percent of the party's budget from a single sponsor, because the party has to be independent and the party shouldn't be privatized. I implemented these party rules when I was chairman, and this is very, very important. That is why nobody, including Mr. Fridman and Mr. Aven, has the power to pressure us into doing things within the party. Moreover, for example, Mr. Khodorkovsky was one of the sponsors of our party, and he never had the opportunity to pressure us into voting one way or the other. One example: all these individuals have an interest in the oil business, and when there was discussion about taxation for the oil industry, our party—SPS—voted for an increase in taxes because profits in the oil industry were huge compared to the Russian economy. Our donors were 100 percent against it, but we made this decision because we understood that teachers, kindergarten workers, soldiers, officers needed a stable salary. But because of our rule that nobody can give us more than five percent of the budget, we were able to maintain an independent position.

BROWNE: That is a matter for the jury to determine, Mr. Nemtsov. Five percent of the total budget of a political party could be a very large sum of money indeed, could it not?

NEMTSOV: Yes. Of course, this is significant money, but this is not enough to control the party.

BROWNE: Can you explain why—until I started asking you about it now—you have told the jury nothing nor said anything in your witness statement about the funding which the Union of Right Forces has received from *Alfa Bank*, nothing at all. Why is that?

NEMTSOV: Because there is no connection between what is our—what is under discussion today and my past political career.

BROWNE: Can I just suggest what the jury may think the connection is, so that you can address it? You decided to omit this just as you decided to omit all reference to your cordial relationship with Mr. Berezovsky because you thought that if the jury knew they would be less likely to believe your evidence?

NEMTSOV: This is your opinion.

BROWNE: It is not my opinion; it is what I am going to be suggesting to the jury.

NEMTSOV: Well, I—I believe that for this case it does not matter what my relationship is—what my relationship was with Fridman, and when I was chairman of the party. And we discussed an absolutely concrete instance, which happened in 1997, when I was in the government, when I was First Deputy Prime Minister and Mr. Berezovsky was in Russia, and had a very strong position in business and politics.

BROWNE: Mr. Nemtsov, Mr. Fridman told the court that he was always able to call on you and explain that there was an issue on which he would like your support. Do you remember that?

NEMTSOV: Well, we have a very good relationship, and of course he can ask me questions as he wants, and if I agree with him I will support him. So far as the Berezovsky case is concerned, yes, he asked me the question: do I remember when Mr. Berezovsky threatened me? And I answered, "yes."

BROWNE: Okay. Mr. Nemtsov, what Mr. Fridman said about his friendship with you was derived from the interview that he gave to Mr. Soloviov. What Mr. Fridman was explaining to Mr. Soloviov was that he could place a call to the boss of the Union of Right Forces—otherwise known as SPS, and that was—and that was you, was it not?

NEMTSOV: Yes, I was a leader of SPS.

BROWNE: And Mr. Fridman says, "I can easily meet them ..." That is in the context of someone like you. " ...and explain that there is a certain issue and I would like their support." Now, that happened frequently with Mr. Fridman, did it not: he called you and asked for your support?

NEMTSOV: Well, he called very often, of course. And he can ask whatever he wants. But as for my response—this depends on my view of the situation. If I were in favor of his idea I would of course support it. If—for example, when he called and asked me to vote against tax increases, I answered, that we would not vote for that. That is it. And if he asks, "We want you to protect private business from Putin's influence," of course I will support him because I am against KGB influence in Russian business.

BROWNE: And as Mr. Soloviov says, the response then is that the political party may ask for money. "Will they ask you for money?" says Mr. Soloviov. Mr. Fridman said, "Well, I would say they will ask for support for their activities in some form." Do you see that?

NEMTSOV: I do not know what Mr. Fridman was responding to, but I can say that Mr. Fridman supported our party.

BROWNE: Financially?

NEMTSOV: Financially. With limitations, of course.

BROWNE: Just moving from Mr. Fridman to Mr. Aven. Were you in court when Mr. Aven accepted that you and Mr. Anatoly Chubais were friends of *Alfa Bank*? Do you remember that?

NEMTSOV: Maybe—I was absent that day. Because I was here on Friday, but only for the second part of the day. I think that he said that before. But anyway, he said that we had a friendly relationship, which is true.

BROWNE: What Mr. Aven said was that, although it was true that you and Mr. Chubais were *Alfa's* friends, that that was not the reason they supported you with money. The reason that they gave funding to the Union of Right Forces was because they liked your right-wing ideology, which would defend the interests of business?

NEMTSOV: Yes.

BROWNE: In other words it was a self-interested gesture, was it not?

NEMTSOV: They represent Russian private business, and of course, like every business in the world, they support the protection of private property, rules of law, real—rules of law not only for ordinary people but for the president and for others. That is why, of course, they supported parties who proclaimed this idea.

BROWNE: Just going back to your relationship with Mr. Berezovsky, when you were one of the two First Deputy Prime Ministers in the first half of 1997, Mr. Berezovsky was Deputy Secretary of the Security Council, was he not?

NEMTSOV: Yes.

BROWNE: But in November 1997, you and Mr. Chubais persuaded President Yeltsin to sack Mr. Berezovsky?

NEMTSOV: Yes, it was my idea. It was my idea, and I will explain why. Because it was a typical conflict of interest. He had a lot of business interests. I mentioned the oil industry, automobiles, Aeroflot, the aluminum business. On the other hand he was a bureaucrat. This is clearly a conflict of interest. So that is why I explained to Yeltsin that to continue such a combination of business and state was completely impossible. And Mr. Yeltsin…

BROWNE: Mr. Nemtsov, you know perfectly well that during the period that Mr. Berezovsky held this office his considerable business interests were put in trust and handled by other people?

NEMTSOV: Well, I know plenty of examples when he—when he had a state position and tried to change things to support his businesses. For example—only one—if you want, only one…

BROWNE: Despite what you say about Mr. Berezovsky, the fact is that in April 1998, he was brought back into government service as Executive Secretary of the Commonwealth of Independent States?

NEMTSOV: This is not a governmental position. This is not—this is a position within the Commonwealth of Independent States. He was not a member of the government at that time.

BROWNE: He was elected unanimously to that position by the twelve state presidents of the independent states?

NEMTSOV: That is true, that is true.

BROWNE: So they did not hold your hostile view about his business interests, did they?

NEMTSOV: I do not know. I do not know. I was very concerned about a conflict of interest. Maybe Nazarbayev and somebody else was not concerned, but this is their view.

BROWNE: It is clear, Mr. Nemtsov, that those twelve state presidents who unanimously elected Mr. Berezovsky to this important post did not share your views about his business interests?

NEMTSOV: Well, I have an independent view of this subject, which is very clear. A conflict of interest finally leads to corruption and a conflict of interest spells disaster for the Russian economy and for Russian political life. Maybe somebody like the last dictator of Europe, Mr. Lukashenko, thinks of it another way. But this is his choice; it is not my choice. I had my own view of this subject. We have had many problems with corruption. One of the reasons is conflict of interest. That is why people who potentially have this conflict of interest should never receive a position in the government and in the Kremlin. This is my view.

BROWNE: You would not accept the hospitality of someone whose wealth was born of corruption, would you?

NEMTSOV: I already said that conflict of interest is a reason why corruption happens. I did not say that Berezovsky was corrupted, because I do not think that he made his money when he was in office. He made his money before that, of course. But I do think that conflict of interest is a real phenomenon, it is a serious problem in Russia. And finally we have to solve this problem and that is why I support—I explained to Yeltsin, that this is a real danger for the Russian economy and for Russian liberal and democratic development.

BROWNE: Can I ask you now about the meeting that you organized at the Kremlin on Friday, July 28, 2000, between a small group of businessmen and Mr. Putin? You organized that meeting, did you not?

NEMTSOV: Well, I made the arrangements for this meeting, and this is not—it was not a small group of businessmen. It was maybe more than 20 people around a table.

BROWNE: I think 18 to 20 is the figure that we see in the press at the time, would that be about right?

NEMTSOV: Well, around the table were people who controlled about 50 percent of the Russian economy. I will explain to you why I decided to do this…

BROWNE: This was not the first meeting between businessmen in the Kremlin which you had organized, was it?

NEMTSOV: Unfortunately I was only able to do this once, in 2000, when Putin was pressuring the business community in Russia. I tried to put together another meeting after that, but it never worked out.

BROWNE: Do you remember, not a meeting with President Putin, but that you helped to arrange a meeting between business leaders and President Yeltsin in September 1997? Do you remember that?

NEMTSOV: When I was in the government? Of course I was—well I was the First Deputy Prime Minister and I was connected with the business community for several reasons. That is why; it was my job. 2000 is a little bit different of a case because I was a member of the parliament and I was—there was no opportunity to influence the Kremlin because Putin had become president, and the only opportunity for me was to explain to the Kremlin that it was necessary to create a relationship with the business community that was based on the rule of law, not on—what they call "po ponyatiyam," I do not know how to translate that—but by rule of law. My main task was to explain that we needed to follow rules of law in the Kremlin and not put pressure on the business community, because this is against Russian interests.

BROWNE: I just want to ask you first about an earlier meeting you helped to arrange in September 1997, between businessmen and Mr. Yeltsin. Can I deal with it in this way: are you a reader of *The Moscow Times*? A regular reader of *The Moscow Times*?

NEMTSOV: Sometimes.

BROWNE: Please look at this clipping from *The Moscow Times* of Wednesday, July 26, 2000. This is a clipping from *The Moscow Times* of that Wednesday, 48 hours before the meeting on July 28, 2000, on that Friday. Do you remember there was a lot of newspaper publicity about the meeting? Do you remember reading this?

NEMTSOV: Well, this happened six years ago, but anyway…

BROWNE: Do you agree that you helped arrange a meeting in September 1997, between business leaders and President Yeltsin in the aftermath of the Svyazinvest auction?

NEMTSOV: I organized maybe ten, maybe more, meetings between the business community and Yeltsin when I was in the government. In particular, a meeting in 1997. Of course the meeting was organized by the Kremlin administration, but I helped.

BROWNE: What I am talking about is this particular meeting in September 1997, in the aftermath of the Svyazinvest auction?

NEMTSOV: It was a very, very difficult time for the government and for Russia because of the Svyazinvest privatization project. Maybe you know that certain oligarchs, two of them, Gusinsky and Berezovsky, wanted to destroy the government. So it was absolutely necessary for us to organize a discussion.

BROWNE: Please, we know that you are extremely hostile to Mr. Berezovsky…

NEMTSOV: No, no. This is true.

BROWNE: Was one of the reasons for that meeting public controversy over the fact that it came to light that Mr. Potanin's bank, Oneximbank, had made payments to Mr. Chubais and Mr. Kokh, supposedly for advances on a book? Do you remember that controversy?

NEMTSOV: It was a huge scandal, the so-called writer's scandal, in Russia, and several members of the government were involved in this scandal, including Chubais.

BROWNE: And Mr. Kokh, Alfred Kokh, was someone else who received these scandalous royalties?

NEMTSOV: Yes, he was involved, yes.

BROWNE: Let us go back in your evidence—to the meeting on Friday, July 28th. Do you remember giving an interview to the *Financial Times* about this meeting?

NEMTSOV: When?

BROWNE: July 24, 2000.

NEMTSOV: I do not remember. I have given so many interviews, including to the *Financial Times*. I do not remember what happened six years ago in these interviews. It may be—can you show me the interview?

BROWNE: Yes, I am going to. Sorry.

NEMTSOV: Great.

BROWNE: Do you know Mr. Arkady Ostrovsky, or did you in 2000?

NEMTSOV: Yes, he is a journalist at the *FT*.

BROWNE: Do you remember now giving this interview to Mr. Ostrovsky? I just want to ask you about two particular matters which you appear to have said to Mr. Ostrovsky. "Mr. Nemtsov said the business leaders would present a three-point declaration to the government." So you were very much in touch with the business leaders, were you not?

NEMTSOV: Yes.

BROWNE: "Firstly they would call on the Kremlin to declare a moratorium on any investigations into the legitimacy of privatization over the past decade and not initiate any redistribution of former state property." Now, is it fair to say that in the middle of 2000, there were many Russian businessmen who were concerned that the state might take back what they had gained during the shares for privatization loans in the mid 1990s?

NEMTSOV: Well, even now a lot of businessmen are concerned about what has happened with private property in the country. Even now, not only in 2000. As for the second point, fortunately I was not involved in the loans for privatization shares.

BROWNE: I am not suggesting that you were, so we need not go down that route.

NEMTSOV: Because I was a governor of Nizhny Novgorod.

BROWNE: Then you mentioned the second point, but it is the third point I want to ask you about: "'Thirdly, the government must rid itself of corrupt bureaucrats, starting with the prosecutor's office, said Mr. Nemtsov." You said that, did you not?

NEMTSOV: Yes.

BROWNE: You regarded the prosecutors' office as corrupt. And I suggest that one of the reasons you did so was because Mr. Gusinsky had recently been arrested, held in jail in June and forced to relinquish NTV to Gazprom?

NEMTSOV: Gusinsky was arrested for political reasons. It is trivial; everybody knows that. Of course, Putin used the financial problems of Mr. Gusinsky. For example, his debt to Gazprom, but Mr. Putin's main goal was to take the independent and very influential NTV company into Kremlin hands. And he used the financial problems of Gusinsky to put him in jail.

BROWNE: And the person who signed the agreement whereby Mr. Gusinsky relinquished NTV to Gazprom was no less than Mr. Kokh, was it not? He was the head of the media part of Gazprom.

NEMTSOV: Well, frankly speaking I do not—I do not know about this. I never saw this document. As far as I know the document was signed by Mr. Lesin, so far as I can remember.

BROWNE: Mr. Lesin signed it on behalf of the government. What I suggest happened was that "Citizen Gusinsky," as one can see, was one party to the agreement to transfer NTV shares?

NEMTSOV: Yes, that is right.

BROWNE: And the other party was, of course, Gazprom Media. And the head of Gazprom Media was no less than Mr. Kokh, recovered from the scandal over the bogus book royalties. I am right, am I not?

NEMTSOV: I have never seen this document and I do not know about the signature of Mr. Kokh under the sixth paragraph of this agreement. I do not know about that.

BROWNE: At any rate, it was signed by Mr. Lesin.

NEMTSOV: Yes, yes. I know that because Lesin one time told me about that. But Kokh never told me about it.

BROWNE: Not surprisingly, neither Mr. Berezovsky nor Mr. Gusinsky were on the guest list for this meeting, were they?

NEMTSOV: Well, for me it was not surprising because the Kremlin had problems with these two gentlemen. That is the reason why Putin did not want to invite them.

BROWNE: And you thought it was regrettable that they had not been invited?

NEMTSOV: Well, I think that that...

BROWNE: Please answer yes or no?

NEMTSOV: My view at that time, I believed that to talk was better than to shout at each other; you know. That is why from my point of view it was better if everyone seated at the table could talk civilly.

BROWNE: After the meeting, did you speak to *The Moscow Times* and tell them that it would have been better if Gusinsky and Berezovsky had attended?

NEMTSOV: I have already answered this question.

BROWNE: You agree that was your view: better if they attended?

NEMTSOV: Of course. I do not think that the relationship between the president and specific businessmen should be reason to invite or not invite someone to a meeting. What we should be focusing on is running the country.

BROWNE: Well, it may have been regrettable, but it was inevitable, was it not, given the stance of Mr. Putin?

NEMTSOV: Well, what—I had no choice at that time, or we—Putin was responsible for the invitations. I did not invite people; Putin invited them. If he wanted to invite some people and not others, what was I to do? To say that "Okay, we will never speak with you," this is crazy.

BROWNE: Mr. Nemtsov, I am not criticizing you; I am simply saying that it was not surprising that they were not invited?

NEMTSOV: It was surprising, of course.

BROWNE: Well, first of all, Mr. Gusinsky had left Russia for the last time and flown to Spain on Wednesday, July 26th, had he not?

NEMTSOV: You know better than me the dates, but I think, yes—in the summer, yes, you are right.

BROWNE: He had finally managed to make a deal whereby he was allowed to leave the country the moment he signed over NTV to Gazprom?

NEMTSOV: As far as I know, yes.

BROWNE: As for Mr. Berezovsky, just ten or 11 days—11 days before this meeting—he had resigned from the Duma, had he not, in protest of Mr. Putin's policies?

NEMTSOV: Yes, that is right.

BROWNE: And he had indicated his intention to consolidate opposition to Mr. Putin; in other words, to be a political rival of Mr. Putin?

NEMTSOV: Russia's main problem is that everybody wants to consolidate the opposition, everybody, including Berezovsky. What we have now is a split, and that is all.

BROWNE: Now, at the time, your Union of Right Forces was continuing to support Mr. Putin, was it not?

NEMTSOV: No. Why do you think so?

BROWNE: Well, I suggest that was the case.

NEMTSOV: Well, let me give some explanation for that.

BROWNE: Well, was it the case or not?

NEMTSOV: No, no. No. What we had during the election of 2000 was a heated discussion inside the SPS. There were four or five party chairman: Irina Khakamada, Chubais, Gaidar, Kirienko, and me. Decisions had to be made—and they had to be made by these five members of the SPS board. We had very heated discussions. Khakamada and I were against Putin, and we voted against his support during the campaign. Chubais, Gaidar and Kirienko supported Putin, and that is why the vote was 3:2 in favor. So far as my opinion is concerned, I was against him.

BROWNE: Forgive me, I was simply asking you about the Union of Right Forces and I think the truth is that we agree that by three to two the Union of Right Forces supported Putin.

NEMTSOV: Well, unfortunately our party was divided on this subject.

BROWNE: The result of the meeting was effectively a truce, was it not, between the businessmen and Mr. Putin?

NEMTSOV: What do you mean? Meeting of 2000?

BROWNE: Yes.

NEMTSOV: Oh, yes. I do not think that it was—I do not think that it was us signing a peace treaty. I do not think so. Maybe he—Putin I mean—was preparing other attacks, I do not know, but he never stopped putting pressure on the business community, not only in 2000, but also in 2003. Do you remember the Khodorkovsky case, for example, and others—my friend Mr. Lifshits? That is why he never stopped. Maybe he stopped for a few days…

BROWNE: Please have a look at this clipping from the *Financial Times* of July 29, 2000. Now, Mr. Nemtsov, this again is a story which is partly written by Mr. Ostrovsky and you are quoted in the second paragraph as describing the meeting of the previous day: "The president clearly and concisely said that there would be no review of the outcome of privatization." "Today's meeting draws a line under ten years of the initial accumulation of capital. The era of the oligarchs is over." Can I suggest to you that this was a truce whereby President Putin promised to let the businessmen keep their assets safe from the State and in return the businessmen agreed to keep out of politics.

NEMTSOV: He said so. He said that: I do not want to initiate a repatriation campaign in the country; I understand the meaning of the rule of law, I understand property rights, the economy, et cetera. But his words and his actions are not the same.

BROWNE: That may well be so, but I just want to ask you about what was being said at the time in 2000. The position effectively was that businessmen like Mr. Potanin, who had only that month been in dispute with the Prosecutor General over Norilsk Nickel, were very relieved were they not?

NEMTSOV: Well, I mean, Putin's speech looked very promising for the business community and some people believed him, some did not. But the next events showed that all of his promises were a bad joke.

BROWNE: Well, Mr. Nemtsov, one of the people at this meeting—one of the 18 or 20 whichever it is—was Mr. Potanin was it not?

NEMTSOV: Yes.

BROWNE: And Mr. Potanin that very month had been embroiled in a dispute with the prosecutor general, who you called corrupt, over Norilsk Nickel, which was one of the great nickel mines that he had acquired in the privatization.

NEMTSOV: A lot of companies have a problem with the tax administration, the prosecutor's office, maybe Potanin was involved—I do not know—everybody. This is the reason why I decided to help to organize the meeting. Everybody had a problem with Putin.

BROWNE: I know this. The point I was making to you is that Mr. Potanin's problem was particularly acute over Norilsk Nickel because it was actually happening that month?

NEMTSOV: So far as I know we did not discuss Potanin's case in the Kremlin, we did not discuss this particular case.

BROWNE: I am not suggesting that you did. Please look at *The Moscow Times* of July 29th, which you were looking at a moment ago.

NEMTSOV: Where is Mr. Potanin?

BROWNE: It is probably a loose page.

NEMTSOV: We have Mr. Abramovich and Berezovsky, who had not paid taxes, yes.

BROWNE: Hang on, Mr. Nemtsov. Can you find *The Moscow Times* of Saturday, July 29th. If you just cast an eye over this, it looks as if you and Mr. Potanin together gave an interview to *The Moscow Times*.

NEMTSOV: Together, no, never. I think that it was separate, you know. I gave an interview independently from him.

BROWNE: Please look halfway down page 153, the first page in this article, to the right of the box saying "The Beat": "'The meeting was very successful,' added Vladimir Potanin, whose Norilsk Nickel was at the center of a dispute over privatization with the prosecutor general's office this month." So do you think I am right about there having been a dispute between Mr. Potanin and the prosecutor general only that month.

NEMTSOV: Well, a lot of people were very lucky during this meeting, that is true, including Potanin.

BROWNE: When you say "very lucky" you mean were very relieved at the result of this meeting?

NEMTSOV: Yes.

BROWNE: They went away from the Kremlin thinking "phew?"

NEMTSOV: It is difficult to understand what happened in Potanin's soul, frankly speaking. I do not know whether he believed Putin or not. He said so, and I cannot comment on that.

BROWNE: Looking further down, do you see a sentence about two thirds of the way down which begins, "In return, the oligarchs promised to obey the laws and play on a level field."? Do you see that? "'The oligarchy is over in Russia,' Nemtsov quipped, 'Ask Potanin.' Potanin smirked in reply." It looks as though you and Mr. Potanin were giving a joint interview to the newspaper, does it not?

NEMTSOV: Well, I never gave an interview together with Potanin. I can say, "Ask Potanin," or say, "Ask Fridman," or somebody else but we never sat down at the table with a journalist from *FT* or *The Moscow Times* to give an interview, never.

BROWNE: Finally, just three lines between the sentence, "Potanin smirked in reply," you are quoted as saying, "Everyone agreed that business has to turn away from political power and the authorities cannot ask anything of business."

NEMTSOV: Well, I will explain: I gave an interview maybe, but I never gave an interview with somebody else. This is very unusual, this you know.

BROWNE: Of course.

NEMTSOV: Of course journalists can combine answers and can organize such an article to explain what I asked to him—and after they assemble the article.

Browne: I just want to ask you about this quote: "Everybody agreed that business has to turn away from political power and the authorities cannot ask anything of business."

Nemtsov: That is true, yes.

Browne: That is true?

Nemtsov: This is our dream.

Browne: Thank you. Now I want to move on to the business of the day which is the issue about the chairmanship of Gazprom. Gazprom in 1997 had its annual general meeting of shareholders due on Saturday, June 28, 1997, did it not?

Nemtsov: Yes.

Browne: This is not in dispute—so I will just prepare the grounds—that Mr. Berezovsky in that month wished to be appointed chairman, are we agreed on that?

Nemtsov: Yes.

Browne: Are we also agreed that the approval of the Prime Minister, Mr. Chernomyrdin, was a precondition—an essential condition—of Mr. Berezovsky being appointed?

Nemtsov: No, no. According to our rules, governmental rules, we need an agreement on two sides, from Mr. Chernomyrdin and from the chairman of the state of representatives in Gazprom. This is how it is decreed. This is a presidential decree.

Browne: Yes, I think it may be my question, or you are failing to understand it.

Nemtsov: This is a so-called two keys problem.

Browne: Two keys.

Nemtsov: Two keys.

Browne: One key was Mr. Chernomyrdin?

Nemtsov: Yes.

Browne: That is all I was putting to you. Not the only key but one key?

Nemtsov: One key.

Browne: And in the week beginning Monday, June 23, 1997, Mr. Chernomyrdin was part of a Russian delegation on state business in China?

Nemtsov: Yes.

BROWNE: So that we have it all fresh in our minds, what you said on Friday afternoon was this: Mr. Viakhirev had agreed to the appointment of Mr. Berezovsky as chairman?

NEMTSOV: Yes.

BROWNE: And had actually signed a draft appointment or agreement?

NEMTSOV: Yes.

BROWNE: But that Mr. Chernomyrdin had not made up his mind and was very confused about what to do?

NEMTSOV: Well, he was in a very difficult situation and he—when I talked with him by telephone in the office, he was in a difficult situation and he said that: from one side it is okay, and from another side I am not so sure. That is why we decided to talk in the future about the subject.

BROWNE: You see, what you said on Friday was that Mr. Chernomyrdin had not made up his mind; that he had said, "Maybe I support it, maybe not." He was very confused.

NEMTSOV: No, no. You think that this was confused—he did not—at that time he had not make a decision. He had not made a decision, that is true. But he had some reasons to support it and some reasons against it. From my point of view he was generally ready to support it, but he was not 100 percent convinced. This was Chernomyrdin. This is how he worked. Sometimes this and sometimes that.

BROWNE: We can agree that he had not made a decision: maybe I support it, maybe not. That is what you said on Friday?

NEMTSOV: Yes, yes. He had not made a decision at that time.

BROWNE: Could you please, Mr. Nemtsov, now be given your witness statement of February 21, 2006. That witness statement ended with you confirming.

NEMTSOV: "I believe that the facts stated . . ." Yes. "I believe that the facts stated in this witness . . . are true."

BROWNE: Yes.

NEMTSOV: Okay.

BROWNE: Was that true on February 21st, that you believed the contents of your witness statement were true?

NEMTSOV: Yes.

BROWNE: Is it still true?

NEMTSOV: I hope so.

Browne: Well, just think, because hopes are not good enough. Are you saying today to this jury that what you said in your witness statement on February 21st of this year was true? Because if any part of it was not, will you please tell us now.

Nemtsov: I hope that I was truthful.

Browne: I imagine you have read it in the last 24 hours, have you not? Your witness statement?

Nemtsov: Frankly speaking, no.

Browne: When did you last read it?

Nemtsov: Maybe five—five days ago.

Browne: When you read it five days ago, was there anything in it that struck you as being untrue?

Nemtsov: Well, I explained that I talked on Friday about our telephone calls with Chernomyrdin—about our telephone calls with Chernomyrdin—during these telephone calls I understood that he had not made a final decision. On the other hand, when Berezovsky came in to my office and said that everybody was in agreement with this idea, including Chernomyrdin, he showed me this draft and I then and there saw that the draft existed with signatures. But I did not believe it. That is why I decided to call Chernomyrdin. And I described my call with Chernomyrdin, my discussion with Chernomyrdin, which is true. He had not made a decision. If at that time he had already made a decision there would have been no point in discussing the subject in China, in Beijing, if the decision had already been made. One more point. Why did I call him? Because Berezovsky had said that Chernomyrdin agreed to everything, basically; that is why I called.

Browne: Mr. Nemtsov, is there any part of this witness statement which you now want to change? Tell me now, please.

Nemtsov: Maybe. Maybe it will be better if I add this statement about my discussion with Chernomyrdin in my office, because unfortunately there is no information about these talks, no. What we had there was a document already signed by Viakhirev, chairman of the board, and Chernomyrdin, the Prime Minister of Russia.

Browne: You see, Mr. Nemtsov, let me state my point: your story has completely changed.

Nemtsov: No, no, you are not right.

Browne: Just look at it.

NEMTSOV: Mmm-hmm.

BROWNE: I will read the account you give of Mr. Berezovsky visiting your office in the White House.

NEMTSOV: Yes.

BROWNE: In June 1997.

NEMTSOV: Mmm-hmm.

BROWNE: When he informed you that he wanted to be appointed chairman of the board of directors of Gazprom. You say this, do you not?

NEMTSOV: Yes.

BROWNE: "Mr. Berezovsky had brought with him the draft of a document which set out his appointment as chairman of Gazprom ... This document had already been signed by Mr. Viakhirev, the chairman of the board of directors of Gazprom, and by Mr. Victor Chernomyrdin, the Prime Minister of Russia. The document only needed my signature in order to have Mr. Berezovsky's candidature finally approved for consideration by the board."

NEMTSOV: Yes.

BROWNE: So you were saying there that Mr. Chernomyrdin had already signed the agreement confirming his approval for Mr. Berezovsky being made chairman. Now, is that true or is it not?

NEMTSOV: I believe that. That is why I called.

BROWNE: And what?

NEMTSOV: I did not believe at that time, because it was absolutely impossible, you know, to give control to Berezovsky of the biggest company in the world. I did not believe that, that is why, yes, he gave me this document with these draft signatures, et cetera, and I did not believe it, that is why I called. And I then responded to his answer, which is different than a signature, as you know. An answer is a little bit different.

BROWNE: Mr. Nemtsov, you are not saying that Mr. Berezovsky claimed he had a document signed by Mr. Viakhirev and Mr. Chernomyrdin. You are saying in this witness statement that he had actually brought with him such a document?

NEMTSOV: Yes, he gave me a document. That is true.

BROWNE: And that document was signed by Mr. Viakhirev and Mr. Chernomyrdin?

NEMTSOV: Yes.

BROWNE: Yes?

NEMTSOV: Yes. But what—it does not matter. It does not matter in Russia. You know, we sign a lot of things in the country. That is why I called and tried to check: "Is it true or not?" and I recognized that Chernomyrdin was not ready to support it completely. He was in a—a difficult situation, and that is why we decided to continue our discussion in the future.

BROWNE: You see, Mr. Nemtsov, I suggest that the account that you are now giving of Mr. Chernomyrdin having actually signed this agreement is totally at odds with his having said to you that he was undecided: maybe I support it, maybe not.

NEMTSOV: Well, you know—there is one very interesting thing: do you know what Mr. Viakhirev's first response was about the same subject?

BROWNE: Please answer my question.

NEMTSOV: He said: "Yes, I signed. But I signed because I read this document. I do not agree with the document but I read it and like a lot of people in the world I sign what I read. That is it." That is why I needed to check to see what was happening in reality. That is why I called.

BROWNE: Mr. Nemtsov, you know perfectly well that what you are now telling this jury is that Mr. Chernomyrdin's having signed the agreement is wholly inconsistent with him being undecided as to whether to support Mr. Berezovsky. They cannot be made consistent, can they?

NEMTSOV: Well, this is a draft. This is not a final document. And signatures were not—on this page, you know—Mr. Browne, look for a moment. A document to appoint Mr. Berezovsky as chairman of Gazprom. After that, the decision of the board of directors. Signatures were here, Mr. Browne. Look—here, these are not signatures. Only here. That is it. That is why I called: "What does it mean?"

BROWNE: You have never said any of this before, have you, Mr. Nemtsov, this is just…

NEMTSOV: I will tell you why…

BROWNE: Just let me put the question to you. It is a desperate attempt to lie your way out of a glaring inconsistency in your evidence.

NEMTSOV: Unfortunately—unfortunately, Mr. Browne, this is the truth. Unfortunately. The document was signed on a different page and I explained to you why, because Chernomyrdin and even Viakhirev had no authority to sign this document. The document has to be signed by the board of directors, not by the Prime Minister and not by CEO Mr. Viakhirev. That is why they signed the document just here. That is why I was verifying.

BROWNE: We have agreed that Mr. Chernomyrdin's approval was a condition of Mr. Berezovsky being appointed and that, I suggest, was what he had done in signing the agreement as you have described.

NEMTSOV: Chernomyrdin signed the document—draft, signed the draft—on a different page but he had not made a final decision. This is true, unfortunately. That is why Berezovsky decided to visit China to talk with Chernomyrdin once again, to try to reach an agreement. Do you think that he would fly to China only?...

BROWNE: Mr. Nemtsov, what you have just said is very revealing. That is precisely my point. You have had to change your story between your witness statement and your evidence today because you realize that Mr. Berezovsky would have had no reason to fly to China, if Mr. Chernomyrdin had already signed the agreement. In other words, you realized how you were going to be caught in your original story and you have changed it.

NEMTSOV: No, no, no. I just add—I just added and I gave new information about my talks with the Prime Minister and with the CEO. It was really very important to understand what was really happening. It was really very important. That is why the discussions continued in China, because a decision—a final decision—had not yet been made in Moscow, in the White House.

BROWNE: Mr. Nemtsov, we can agree it is new information but it is also completely different information that you are now giving, is it not?

NEMTSOV: No, no. It gives a clearer picture of what happened, that is true. Maybe it would have been better to give this information in these previous statements, I agree. Maybe it would have been better. But that is why we are here, to discuss...

BROWNE: Where in your witness statement do you say that Mr. Chernomyrdin told you "Maybe I'll sign it, maybe not"; where do you say that?

NEMTSOV: No, no, no, no. He said that this is a complicated situation and there are some reasons why I support it and some reasons why I am against it.

BROWNE: Please answer my question. I will put it to you again: on Friday you said that you called Mr. Chernomyrdin and he responded, well, it is a proposal. I know about the proposal and maybe I will support it, maybe not?

NEMTSOV: Yes, exactly.

BROWNE: Very well. Where in your witness statement do you recite those words of Mr. Chernomyrdin?

NEMTSOV: I have already explained to you that there is no information about my calls in the statement…

BROWNE: Exactly. I suggest that you are making this up as you go along in order that it should appear that Mr. Berezovsky had a reason for flying to Peking, to Beijing.

NEMTSOV: This is your opinion.

BROWNE: Whereas on your account he would have had no reason because Mr. Chernomyrdin had already signed.

NEMTSOV: I repeat once again. Any information about my talks—my calls to Chernomyrdin and to Viakhirev really did not—is not contained in the statement. That is why I am explaining, now what really happened. Maybe it would have been better if I had put this information in the statement, but I want to explain to the jury what really happened. I have a draft; I did not believe the draft. That is why I called and got an answer. That is it.

BROWNE: All right. Now please look at your witness statement. We have already agreed that nowhere did you say that Mr. Chernomyrdin said, "Maybe I'll support it, maybe not." Does this appear in your witness statement?

NEMTSOV: A moment, please. Well…

BROWNE: Let me read it to you because the jury does not have it: "With Mr. Berezovsky still in the room I telephoned Mr. Chernomyrdin in order to check the position … Mr. Chernomyrdin confirmed that he had signed the agreement but asked if I could do something to prevent Mr. Berezovsky's appointment." Now, what could be more different, Mr. Nemtsov, from your account of him—of Mr. Chernomyrdin—saying "maybe I support it, maybe not," than what you say in this witness statement, which is that Mr. Chernomyrdin confirmed that he had signed the document?

NEMTSOV: Okay, let me read the entire sentence, all right? "Mr. Chernomyrdin confirmed that he had signed the document but asked if I could do something to prevent Berezovsky's appointment." This is a statement, you know. This is a sentence. That is why it showed that he was not able to, that he had made no real final decision at that time and the statement which I have already read shows that: "Boris [Nemtsov], can you do something to prevent Berezovsky's appointment?" What does it mean?

BROWNE: The point that I am putting to you is that in this conversation Mr. Chernomyrdin confirmed signing the document. He did not say to you, as you now claim to this jury he did, "Maybe I support it, maybe not." They are irreconcilable are they not, your two accounts?

NEMTSOV: Well, maybe if I read this sentence one more time. Will that be enough: "Could I do something to prevent Berezovsky's appointment." What does it mean? Could I do something—me, I mean.

BROWNE: I have read that to the jury. The point I am making is that, far from appearing indecisive, he told you that he had indeed signed the document.

NEMTSOV: He signed the document and after that, the next sentence: " ...confirmed that he had signed the document. Asked if I could do something to prevent Berezovsky's appointment." If he were to make the decision, do you think that such a discussion would happen: Boris, I made the decision, Berezovsky has to be appointed. The end, discussion over.

BROWNE: It is very simple, Mr. Nemtsov, as you yourself have pointed out: if Mr. Berezovsky had Mr. Chernomyrdin's signature on an agreement, there was no reason to fly to Peking. That is why you had to change your story. You yourself have revealed the underlying reason.

NEMTSOV: No, no, I already explained to you that to make the decision we need two signatures from the government—two: from the Prime Minister and from me. At that time he only had one. That is why he needed a second signature and after he had one, I checked on Chernomyrdin's decision. This was not a final decision.

BROWNE: He did not fly to Beijing to get your signature. You are saying that he flew to get Mr. Chernomyrdin's consent?

NEMTSOV: I do not know what his real purpose was, but we discussed the agreement and we discussed why I was against this decision, et cetera. He talked with me. After that he talked with Chernomyrdin and explained to him that he is my boss, he is the Prime Minister and he should explain to me why I am wrong. That was the reason for his visit. That is the reason for Berezovsky's visit. If I agree with this appointment in the White House, he will be appointed. He will be appointed immediately.

BROWNE: Mr. Nemtsov, my suggestion is that some time between the date of your witness statement—which was February 21st of this year—and giving an interview to *Komsomolskaya Pravda* some time in March, you realized that the details of your story were quite implausible and you therefore changed them so as to make it appear that Mr. Chernomyrdin had not signed the agreement, as you twice said in your witness statement, but was indecisive. That is my suggestion. Do you remember giving an interview to a Mr. Alexander Gamov of *Komsomolskaya Pravda*?

NEMTSOV: I remember this interview, yes.

BROWNE: *Pravda* means "truth," does it not?

NEMTSOV: What?

BROWNE: Does *Pravda* mean "truth" in Russian?

NEMTSOV: Newspaper? No.

BROWNE: But that is what the word means. Were you telling the newspaper the truth, Mr. Nemtsov?

NEMTSOV: Yes.

BROWNE: Let us just look at this. "Boris Nemtsov" it is headlined. "If I had given Gazprom to Berezovsky I would have become President of Russia." Is that a serious statement by you?

NEMTSOV: This is not my statement. This is a journalist's statement. I did not say this in the article and in the interview. The title was prepared by a journalist, Mr. Gamov.

BROWNE: Mr. Gamov had apparently interviewed you during a session in the steam room, is that right? In the sauna?

NEMTSOV: We spent some time in the sauna; after that I gave him an interview.

BROWNE: The record of this interview is set out over these half a dozen pages, is it not?

NEMTSOV: I gave this interview not that long ago. And we really, before the interview, we used the sauna, that is true.

BROWNE: Yes. So all this business about offering Mr. Gamov "a pair of pants with girlies," he is right about all of that, is he not?

NEMTSOV: Well, this is, you know, this is a typical style for this type of journalist. This is a very particular type of newspaper—similar to *The Sun* in this country. Well, he was at my home and he said that—and he said that he wanted to take this—this underwear. Well, what should I do in this situation? I can respond, "Okay, if you want to take them, take them; no problem."

BROWNE: And you also discussed your three wives and children and so on.

NEMTSOV: You think that this is important?

BROWNE: I just want to enable the jury to get a flavor of the sort of man you are.

NEMTSOV: I am very proud that I have four kids and three wives. I am very proud of that.

BROWNE: Yes. Let us just look at the passage in which you, I suggest, practice your new account of your evidence. We are agreed, are we not, Mr. Nemtsov, that in your witness statement you said that not only had Mr. Chernomyrdin signed the agreement, but on the telephone he had confirmed to you that he had signed the agreement? Now, where do you say that Mr. Chernomyrdin had signed the agreement and confirmed to you that he had done so?

NEMTSOV: Yes, I understand. This is not—you know, this is an interview to a newspaper; this is not a witness statement, and that is why I describe what has happened and ask: who supports this idea? And I get the answer that Viakhirev and Chernomyrdin supported this idea. That is it.

BROWNE: Where in this account to the journalist of *Pravda* do you say that Mr. Chernomyrdin had signed the agreement and confirmed to you that he had?

NEMTSOV: Well, this is not a witness statement. This is an interview and I—I am only saying that Berezovsky told Viakhirev and Chernomyrdin that they should agree with this draft. That is why I called and talked with Chernomyrdin and Viakhirev. This is an interview, you know. I have no ideas to describe all the details, because this is an interview in—not in a business newspaper, you understand, this is—I should say, entertainment. This is a newspaper which is not taken very seriously; maybe like *The Sun*, maybe a little bit different, but this is not a serious newspaper.

BROWNE: I suggest that it was serious for you because you were effectively practicing your evidence for this court, were you not?

NEMTSOV: No. No, that is not right. This is an interview to *Komsomolskaya Pravda*, which is not what we are doing here in the Royal Court. This is a completely different thing, completely.

BROWNE: You knew, Mr. Nemtsov, when you gave this interview to Mr. Gamov that you would be shortly coming to London to give evidence?

NEMTSOV: Yes, I knew about that of course, but this is absolutely a different thing. An interview and a court discussion.

BROWNE: Let us just look at what you say. Far from telling Mr. Gamov that Mr. Chernomyrdin had signed the agreement and confirmed he had, you told Mr. Gamov that Mr. Chernomyrdin had "mumbled and had avoided the answer." "More or less." Do you see that? The journalist says, "He avoided the answer?" and you respond, "More or less?"

NEMTSOV: Yes.

BROWNE: That is completely inconsistent, is it not, with Mr. Chernomyrdin having signed the agreement and confirmed that he had?

NEMTSOV: You are not right. You do not know Chernomyrdin. Sometimes it is impossible to understand what he is talking about. Mr. Yeltsin one time asked me, "Boris, do you understand what this gentleman is talking about?" I asked: What you mean? You have worked with him for five years. Frankly speaking, I did not understand what he wanted to do. That is the point. This is my understanding of what he was talking about. On one side he supported it, on another side, he did not support the draft. That is the point.

BROWNE: Mr. Nemtsov, all we are doing at this stage is comparing the accounts you gave in your witness statement with what you said about a month later. Now, in addition to changing the story about whether Mr. Chernomyrdin supported Mr. Berezovsky, I suggest that there are a number of other details of your story which show that you are not telling the truth and making it up as you go along. I am going to list four.

NEMTSOV: Four in this interview?

BROWNE: Four matters which show that you are not telling the truth. The first, Mr. Nemtsov, relates to the order in which you called Mr. Viakhirev and Mr. Chernomyrdin on the phone. Who did you call first?

NEMTSOV: I do not remember. It does not matter. It absolutely does not matter. I called both of these gentlemen, Viakhirev and Chernomyrdin. This is a very important issue. Who I called first or second does not matter.

BROWNE: It is a matter for the jury whether it matters.

NEMTSOV: Maybe.

BROWNE: You are now saying you cannot remember, are you? You are now saying you cannot recall who you called first?

NEMTSOV: I cannot remember who was the first or the second...

BROWNE: On Friday, you quite clearly told the jury that you called Viakhirev first and then Chernomyrdin. Now you cannot remember, is that right?

NEMTSOV: Well, I do not think that this is important. The important thing is that I talked with both gentlemen, Chernomyrdin and Viakhirev. This is important. It does not matter who was the first and who was the second because they were absolutely separate discussions with Viakhirev and with Chernomyrdin. The discussion happened during, maybe, I do not know how many minutes, a few minutes, that is why I really do not remember. This happened nine years ago.

BROWNE: So you do not remember—your memory is not clear about this?

NEMTSOV: About who was the first and who was the second? Yes.

BROWNE: You see in your witness statement, you said you first phoned Chernomyrdin and then Viakhirev, did you not?

NEMTSOV: Well, in my witness statement, yes. Here it is—well, the first was Chernomyrdin, second Viakhirev—I do not remember; I do not remember.

BROWNE: I asked you at the beginning whether there was anything in your witness statement which was not true and you wanted to change. And we were not told this, that you did not remember, were we?

NEMTSOV: Because it does not matter to me.

BROWNE: So let us just see how again the story changes. We are agreed that in your witness statement it is first phoning Chernomyrdin and then phoning Viakhirev. In *Komsomolskaya Pravda*, it is the other way round, is it not?

NEMTSOV: Well, I can repeat once again, I do not care about who was the first and who was the second.

BROWNE: In your evidence on Friday you said it was Viakhirev followed by Chernomyrdin, and now you say you cannot remember. Is that right?

NEMTSOV: Well, it does not matter.

BROWNE: Now, let us look at another detail of the story, to see how truthful you have been. You remember on Friday, you said twice that Mr. Viakhirev had said to you, "I hope you will make the right decision." Do you remember that?

NEMTSOV: Yes, Viakhirev hoped that I would ultimately make the right decision.

BROWNE: Yes?

NEMTSOV: And he adds that, you know, Berezovsky is such a powerful and strong man that he—that he runs Russia. And now I can protect my own view of the subject; that is why I hope the government will finally make—will make the right decision. That is true.

BROWNE: Now, where is that in your witness statement of February 21st? Those words of Mr. Viakhirev are not there at all, are they? In your witness statement, does Mr. Viakhirev say, "I hope you make the right decision?"

NEMTSOV: Well, wait a second. "Mr. Viakhirev confirmed that he had signed the document and said that he had little choice as Berezovsky ran the country. 'Again, Viakhirev expressed hope that I could do something to prevent Berezovsky's appointment.'"

BROWNE: Where does Mr. Viakhirev say in your witness statement, "I hope you will make the right decision?" He does not, does he, anywhere?

NEMTSOV: Well, if I describe all of our talks, including talks with Chernomyrdin, I am afraid that some ladies will be forced to leave the discussion, you know, because we sometimes use very particular words. It is very difficult to translate it in English and it is very difficult to explain. I can give you my general conclusions on the subject, that Viakhirev said: "Berezovsky is powerful and I cannot protect my own interests." And Chernomyrdin on one side was for; on another was against. That is the point. But they use a specific type of slang, and even in the Russian court it will be difficult for me to explain, and impossible for me to explain in English. That is why, when you ask me, "Why you do not mention this sentence and that sentence?" I'm giving you the general picture of the subject, and the real position of Mr. Viakhirev, and the real position of Mr. Chernomyrdin.

BROWNE: It does not require any skill in the English language to know the difference between Mr. Chernomyrdin and Mr. Viakhirev, does it?

NEMTSOV: Of course, Viakhirev signed this draft and he said that I hope that you will do something. You know, Chernomyrdin, like any prime minister, had an undecided view of the subject: on one side he was for, and another was against. That is the difference.

BROWNE: Can I take you through how this story that Viakhirev said, "I hope you will make the right decision," has developed. We are agreed, are we not, Mr. Nemtsov, that the words of Mr. Viakhirev, "I hope you will make the right decision," do not appear in your witness statement.

NEMTSOV: Viakhirev expressed hope that I could do something to prevent Berezovsky's appointment. This is not his direct speech, but it is his hope and his main point. I am not here to recreate his exact words. We talked about many things, and I'm only mentioning his concluding point. The conclusion. And the conclusion was that: Boris, I hope that you will do something to prevent. That is it. Why should I be responsible for transcribing the entire discussion—why, why do you think that I should be doing this? What is important is a real conclusion, a real statement.

BROWNE: Now let us look at what you told Mr. Gamov in the *Komsomolskaya Pravda* interview.

NEMTSOV: Yes.

BROWNE: Do you see there, first of all you telephoned Viakhirev, who does not say anything about, "I hope you will make the right decision." Then you say: I called Mr. Chernomyrdin. He mumbled, "I know that you will make the right decision." Can I suggest what has happened here? This account of either Viakhirev or Chernomyrdin saying, "I know that you will make the right decision," is invented for the first time in your *Komsomolskaya Pravda* interview, having not appeared in your witness statement, is it not?

NEMTSOV: No. You know, an interview and a witness statement is a different subject. The main statement is that Viakhirev supported this idea but he hoped that I would be against it. This is the main statement which we will find in the interview and in the witness statement here. Absolutely the same. Of course, the answer which I used may be different. But this is absolutely a different instance, you know, to be in the Royal Court and to give an interview to a Russian newspaper, but the main message and main conclusion is absolutely the same, one hundred percent the same. Should I be retelling absolutely everything I've said in popular Russian newspapers? And what if I've used archaic Russian words…

BROWNE: Mr. Nemtsov, please do not ask me questions, otherwise you may find me answering them. Which was it who said to you, "I hope you will make the right decision": Mr. Chernomyrdin, as you said to *Komsomolskaya Pravda*, or Mr. Viakhirev, as you told this jury? Or did it never happen at all, as in your witness statement?

NEMTSOV: Viakhirev.

BROWNE: It was Viakhirev?

NEMTSOV: Viakhirev.

BROWNE: So you were wrong about saying it was Chernomyrdin to the journalist?

NEMTSOV: No, Chernomyrdin—I repeat I do not know how many times once again—Chernomyrdin had not made a decision during our calls and our discussion. Finally he made a decision against. But at that time, when I called him, he had not made a decision. And I repeated several times once again, because this is true. 100 percent true. I think that the exact words do not matter; the most important thing is the real conclusion. The conclusion is crucial. And if you look at the witness statement and in my interview you immediately recognize that this is absolutely the same position, one hundred percent the same position.

BROWNE: Are you seriously telling the jury, in the light of what I have just been putting to you, that the evidence that you have given in this court and your account in *Komsomolskaya Pravda* is 100 percent the same?

NEMTSOV: The conclusion is completely the same.

BROWNE: Now let us just consider some further details. I have said there were four matters. Item 3 is this: where in your witness statement do you say that you discussed the chairmanship of Gazprom with Mr. Berezovsky on the visit that you paid to the Three Gorges?

NEMTSOV: Well, I did not mention this.

BROWNE: No?

NEMTSOV: No, this is a different story. I did not mention that we visited the Three Gorges.

BROWNE: Yes, you did.

NEMTSOV: I did not mention that.

BROWNE: Yes, you did. Mr. Nemtsov, do not be so quick to lie. Let me get the questions in and show you the documents and you may not tell a lie then which…

JUSTICE EADY: Mr. Shields.

SHIELDS: First we have to establish whether the witness is answering in relation to the *Komsomolskaya Pravda* article or the witness statement, because he is moving from one to the other, before he accuses him of being a liar and making a speech about it.

BROWNE: Mr. Nemtsov, if you had let me put the question, I would have saved you from that last answer, which I suggest was untrue. Please look at your witness statement.

NEMTSOV: "Traveled together to the Three Gorges," yes, what do you mean?

BROWNE: Contrary to what you seem to be telling the jury in your witness statement, you did mention the trip to the Three Gorges.

NEMTSOV: Yes, I mentioned it, but I do not—I did not mention it in the interview. What is the problem?

BROWNE: Let me just ask the questions, Mr. Nemtsov. "Furthermore, Mr. Chernomyrdin, Mr. Berezovsky and I traveled together to the Three Gorges water power plant on the Yangtze River to discuss the issues of possible Russian/Chinese co-operation in respect of this project with Chinese officials." Now, what I suggest is an embellishment and an untruthful embellishment of your evidence this morning is that on this trip to the Three Gorges hydroelectric plant you discussed the chairmanship of Gazprom with Mr. Berezovsky.

NEMTSOV: No, no, no. We discussed not only the construction and participation of Russian companies in the Chinese construction of the Three Gorges, we also discussed Gazprom, of course, together; together with Berezovsky. Together with Berezovsky, we discussed all of these issues.

BROWNE: You say, "Of course," but it is not of course at all, is it? You do not mention it in your witness statement, do you?

NEMTSOV: I do not mention what? I mention that we were in the Three Gorges and in particular that we discussed the problem of cooperation. This is not, you know, if you look more attentively at this sentence, I do not describe all of the statements which are under discussion. I mention only the reason why we visited this station.

BROWNE: You do not say that on this trip, apparently in the company of Mr. Chernomyrdin, you discussed the chairmanship of Gazprom with Mr. Berezovsky, do you?

NEMTSOV: Well, this sentence showed only one, that we discussed one topic, but this is not all a complete description of our discussion.

BROWNE: I suggest that is because you have invented this detail to try to make your story more plausible for your evidence today.

NEMTSOV: Well, what can I say?

BROWNE: The truth, I hope.

NEMTSOV: I hope too. Well, what can I say? I only mention one thing, that we visited the station, and the reason why we decided to go was the participation of Russian businesses in this project. That is it. But this is not a complete description of our discussion throughout this trip. I mentioned only the reason why we went together at that time, that is it. And maybe we discussed other issues, but in this sentence I describe only the reason why we decided to go. Only the reason.

BROWNE: You see, what you have done is to build dishonestly on something that Mr. Berezovsky admits, namely that he and you and Mr. Chernomyrdin went down the Yangtze River. That is what you have done...

NEMTSOV: This is absolutely wrong.

BROWNE: Right.

NEMTSOV: A wrong conclusion, 100 percent. We visited the Three Gorges. We discussed all these topics, including the ones I mentioned previously. But the serious discussions took place in the Russian Embassy in Beijing and the decision was made in the Russian Embassy in Beijing, that is true. The final decision was made in the embassy, not during our trip to the Three Gorges.

BROWNE: That brings me to the fourth of my four matters. You said this morning that Mr. Berezovsky made the threat out on the street; in other words, after you had left the Russian Embassy. Now that again is something you have never said before, is it not?

NEMTSOV: No, no, no. He said that to me after our meeting was over. The meeting was over, we came out together and he said—whether it happened on the street or in the embassy, frankly, I do not remember—I remember what he said and what happened after that, which is absolutely crucial. At the beginning of June and in the middle of June, I had a popularity rating in my country similar to Putin's. After this sentence of Mr. Berezovsky, he demanded that his channel, Channel 1, destroy me. And over three months my popularity dropped from 60 percent to 3 percent. Nothing happened in the economy, nothing happened in the political situation, we were paying enough wages, we paid pensions, we did everything, but he organized a campaign against me. And in three months he achieved his results. And you can look at the public polls from that time—every week we organized public polls—and you can see what happened after his threat. He did his best to destroy me. And there is a special, you know, TV assassin, Mr. Dorenko, five years later who said that "Boris, I have an order from Berezovsky to destroy you. I don't know anything about you, but I have orders...

BROWNE: This is not pleaded. It is not in the witness statement.

JUSTICE EADY: You have asked him about...

BROWNE: All I asked him about was whether the threat was made on the street or in the embassy.

JUSTICE EADY: He says that he does not remember whether it was on the street or the embassy, but he remembers the threat. And what is more, it was put into effect.

BROWNE: That has never been pleaded.

SHIELDS: He has put this in. You cannot just pick and choose, I am afraid, my Lord: "More or less. I told Berezovsky, 'Boris, you ... political career. And then they set this television assassin on my trail ... my rating at that time was the same as Putin's rating today." He has put it in, my Lord. He has put it in.

BROWNE: This was never put to my client. It is not pleaded. What I was asking him about—and I will return to ask him about—is quite simply this. Your suggestion in your witness statement was that the threat had been made at a meeting between yourself, Mr. Berezovsky and Mr. Chernomyrdin in the Russian Embassy in Peking.

NEMTSOV: "Mr. Berezovsky then told me that if I continued to refuse to sign the document he would do everything he could to destroy me as a politician." The most important word is "then." "Then" means after our discussion with Chernomyrdin. "After meeting Mr. Berezovsky he then told me that if I continued to refuse to sign the document he would do everything he could to destroy me as a politician." This happened after our meeting with Chernomyrdin. Well, he did everything he could to destroy me and, unfortunately, he succeeded.

BROWNE: Mr. Nemtsov, you do not say in this witness statement that the threat to destroy you was not made in the Russian Embassy but on the street. And that, I suggest, is another false embellishment of your story.

NEMTSOV: I just said that this word, I mean "destroy," was used after our meeting; that is it.

BROWNE: You do not say "after the meeting?" You say, having set out what happened at this meeting in the Russian Embassy, you describe what everyone said and then you go on still, I suggest, describing the conversation, to say, "Mr. Berezovsky then told me if I continued to refuse to sign the document he would do everything he could to destroy me as a politician." Nothing about anything being said in the street, is there?

NEMTSOV: I just said in my statement that this thing he said was after our meeting. And the word "then" means after.

BROWNE: I want to move now to the question of presidential decrees. You have only referred to one presidential decree, have you not? There is another relevant decree?

NEMTSOV: Well, I mention in this statement two decrees. The decree which I have spoken about in 1997, is devoted to a very concrete case; I mean Gazprom. Decree number 1200, which was signed by Mr. Yeltsin before that. This decree describes the responsibility of the state representative to the shareholders of the company, that they must be appointed. That is why these two decrees gave me the authority to appoint the position in the shareholders' meeting and the state representatives in the shareholders' meeting.

BROWNE: It is clear, is it not, from your witness statement, that you regard as also relevant the presidential decree of 1994, number 1200?

NEMTSOV: I will try to clarify this. I was a chairman of the Collegium of State Representatives in Gazprom. On the other hand, I was in the Ministry of Fuel and Energy at the same time. As a minister of Fuel and Energy I had the authority to appoint state positions at the shareholders' meeting, as a minister of fuel and energy. As a chairman of the Collegium of State Representatives I had the authority to form and to organize our position, I mean the position of the state representative at the shareholders' meeting. That is why these two decrees show that I had dual responsibility over the appointment of Mr. Berezovsky as possible chairman of the board.

BROWNE: Now, as we have agreed, the consent of the Prime Minister was one essential factor, if Mr. Berezovsky was to become chairman of Gazprom.

NEMTSOV: The Prime Minister has to agree, of course.

BROWNE: Has to agree, yes. Members of the jury, do you have it? It is the 1994 decree. This was a decree for the purpose of ensuring the state administration of the economy and increasing the responsibility of managers of state enterprises for the financial condition of enterprises and so on ... In other words, it governs the administration of state-owned bodies like Gazprom.

NEMTSOV: Well, this is a general decree concerning not only Gazprom but all of the shareholders' companies where the state has shares.

BROWNE: We agree that it is applicable therefore to Gazprom. "President Yeltsin had resolved in 1994, to establish that state representatives in the governing bodies of joint stock companies whose shares have been assigned to federal property ..." That would include Gazprom, would it not?

NEMTSOV: Well, there were two documents which regulate Gazprom from the state. The first is this decree and the second is the decree of 1997. You have to look at these two documents together. I am not a lawyer but I understand why we decided to sign a new presidential decree of 1997, because there were some unclear problems in the decree of 1994.

BROWNE: Please, can we agree that when it refers to "joint stock companies whose shares have been assigned to federal property," it is applicable to Gazprom?

JUSTICE EADY: Mr. Browne, it is probably my fault, but there may be some problems with the translation, because the phrase "has been assigned to federal property" does not convey anything to me. What is this to convey?

BROWNE: It means that they are owned by the state.

JUSTICE EADY: All it is supposed to mean is "federal property?"

BROWNE: In essence. That is my understanding. There is no doubt, is there, Mr. Nemtsov, that this refers to a company like Gazprom?

NEMTSOV: Including Gazprom.

BROWNE: Including it, yes. So state representatives in such bodies. I am now going to read on from the comma where I left off: "...shall carry out their activity in the said company's governing bodies in accordance with this decree." And this is the point I wish to make particularly emphatically: "Decisions of the government of the Russian Federation and also federal executive bodies, or of the Russian federal property funds on whose behalf they act in accordance with the legislation of the Russian Federation." So we are agreed, are we not, that the four state representatives on Gazprom were obliged by clause 3 of this decree to carry out their activities in accordance—amongst other things—with decisions of the government of the Russian Federation?

NEMTSOV: You are wrong. You have to get permission from the government and—and also of federal executive bodies, "also of federal executive bodies." I was a minister of Fuel and Energy. At the same time in 1997, I was a chairman of the Collegium of State Representatives, which is part of the administration of the government. And if you want to get permission you have to get support from the minister of Fuel and Energy, Nemtsov, and from the Collegium of State Representatives in Gazprom where I was a chairman.

BROWNE: Yes.

NEMTSOV: That is why, if you want to get permission, you have to get two votes; one vote from the government and a second from the collegium, and the decision from the minister of Fuel and Energy.

BROWNE: Yes.

NEMTSOV: That is what we are talking about in charter number 3.

BROWNE: Now, what the 1994 decree therefore makes essential for state representatives is for them to carry out the decisions of the government; agreed?

NEMTSOV: This is not enough. You have to get a decision from the government, plus the minister of Fuel and Energy, plus the Collegium of State Representatives. Look more carefully at the sentence.

BROWNE: I appreciate, Mr. Nemtsov—of course I do—that how the four state representatives vote has to be decided in accordance with the decision of the collegium—that is clause 4 of the agreement of the presidential decree. But what I am putting to you is that when it comes to what is called clause 3 of the 1994 decree, decisions of the government of the Russian Federation, there could hardly be a decision of the government with which the Prime Minister Mr. Chernomyrdin did not agree. It is as simple as that, is it not?

NEMTSOV: The decision of the government is not enough to appoint Berezovsky as chairman of the board. You have to get a decision not only from the government but from special organizations—the Collegium of State Representatives and the minister of Fuel and Energy. That was what charter number 3 is describing.

BROWNE: Let us see, I think you accept that one of the things that oblige the state representatives to act accordingly is the decision of the government of the Russian Federation. Please look at clause 7 of the 1994 presidential decree.

NEMTSOV: You need a combination of several decisions from several organizations. Some—one of them is the government, another is the Collegium of State Representatives and the minister of Fuel and Energy. You need several groups to be in agreement.

BROWNE: Can we just look at clause 7: violation by public servants. Do you see clause 7? "Violation by public servants appointed to the post of state representatives in the company's governing bodies …" Those are the four individuals you have mentioned. "…Of the established procedure for coordination of draft decisions, or for voting on draft decisions, or the fact of not voting in accordance with the coordination results …" This is the important bit: "…Or contrary to the decisions of the Government of the Russian Federation and the respective federal executive bodies, shall involve disciplinary measures up to and including dismissal from public service."

So if that is what state representatives were confronted with, if they voted against the decision of the government of the Russian Federation, they were hardly likely, were they, to vote against something which Mr. Chernomyrdin, they knew, approved.

NEMTSOV: Fortunately, you are wrong, because it is impossible to give demands to the state representative if we have no common view on the subject. Do you know why nothing happened with the chairman of the board of Gazprom? Because we have a different point of view on the subject. And if you want to explain to state representatives that you have to vote for or against Berezovsky you must first obtain final decisions from all of the organizations: government, state representatives and the minister of Fuel and Oil. If you have no common decision, this is not—you have no chance to demand anything…

BROWNE: Ultimately…

NEMTSOV: …and guarantee something like that, because there is no decision inside the government.

BROWNE: Ultimately, the decision of the government of the Russian Federation, which is referred to in clauses 3 and 7, was that by Mr. Chernomyrdin as Prime Minister, was it not?

NEMTSOV: It is not enough for the government to agree with the appointment of Berezovsky.

BROWNE: Ultimately—I will put the question to you again—the decision of the government of the Russian Federation was the decision of Mr. Chernomyrdin as Prime Minister?

NEMTSOV: Well, you know, our Russian government is an organization of several members. This is a government decision, and the government has to discuss and agree that Mr. Berezovsky should be appointed. I can say that such discussions never happened, fortunately. Chernomyrdin did not make these decisions himself. That is why he talked with me about his decision. He asked me about my opinion, about why I was against it, et cetera…

BROWNE: That is why, Mr. Nemtsov, if, as you had said, Mr. Berezovsky had the signature of Mr. Chernomyrdin, it would not have been necessary for him to go to Peking, would it?

NEMTSOV: Well, I already explained Chernomyrdin's signature.

BROWNE: We have been over that.

NEMTSOV: This is not a signature on the draft. It is a signature on another side of the draft...

BROWNE: We have been over that point three times already.

NEMTSOV: But you asked the same question once again.

BROWNE: No, I did not, I asked a question you have not answered.

JUSTICE EADY: Which question did you want to have answered, Mr. Browne?

BROWNE: The question to which I did not get the answer is why it was that Mr. Berezovsky would have flown to Peking if he had Mr. Chernomyrdin's approval already in writing.

JUSTICE EADY: The answer I think, which the witness is giving—it is for the jury to decide what they think of it in due course—but the answer he is giving is that this was not a signature to the draft—in other words a signature of approval—but was something on the back of the document to signify, as I understand it, that he has read it; is that correct?

NEMTSOV: Absolutely, 100 percent.

BROWNE: And that is a detail that you never mentioned before either, is it?

NEMTSOV: I mentioned this fact, it seems to me, ten times today, maybe more.

BROWNE: Of course today, but never before you went into the witness box today?

NEMTSOV: We have already discussed this subject.

BROWNE: Good. Let us just look and see what must have been going through Mr. Berezovsky's head. He needed, in order to become chairman of Gazprom, to persuade Mr. Chernomyrdin. We agree on that, do we not?

NEMTSOV: No. This is not enough.

BROWNE: That is why he flew to China.

NEMTSOV: This is not enough. He needed, at that time, two people to agree, two signatures: Nemtsov and Chernomyrdin. Two.

BROWNE: But if he did not have Mr. Chernomyrdin's signature then that would be fatal in itself, would it not? We can agree on that. We have agreed on that?

NEMTSOV: He needed support from two individuals.

BROWNE: That is why he flew to China to get Mr. Chernomyrdin's approval. He did not need to threaten you and he did not threaten you, did he?

NEMTSOV: Absolutely wrong.

BROWNE: And you have told this constantly varying story, I suggest, out of loyalty to Mr. Fridman—who has been your lifelong friend—and out of gratitude for the funding that Mr. Fridman and *Alfa* have provided over the years to the political body of which you were formerly the head. That is my suggestion.

NEMTSOV: I am here because Berezovsky threatened me, and the results you know: Putin is the President of the Russian Federation and we have numerous problems with freedom, democracy, censorship, our television, Khodorkovsky's case, all of these cases. That is why I am here. And I can say once again that he played an unbelievably huge role in destroying the liberal democratic government of 1997, including me, and everybody knows about it. Everybody in our country knows about it.

JUSTICE EADY: Mr. Browne, as you rightly said earlier, this is not in the witness statement; it is not pleaded. If you wish at some stage to recall Mr. Berezovsky, I would give permission, but it is a matter for you.

BROWNE: It is really a matter for Mr. Shields.

SHIELDS: With respect to your Lordship, we pleaded to the words complained of, "He made a threat," We did not plead any further than that.

JUSTICE EADY: The witness has now said, "And what is more, the threat was carried out." I am not criticizing you for not pleading it, but since the evidence has come in, if it is continued, Mr. Berezovsky must have an opportunity to deal with it. This particular allegation, about it actually having happened and been carried into effect is a new item. It is not actually relevant to anything in the pleadings, but it is potentially prejudicial. And therefore, if he wishes to do so, Mr. Berezovsky must be allowed an opportunity to answer.

BROWNE: My Lord, I do intend to recall Mr. Berezovsky shortly to deal with the matter. He is now here.

BEREZOVSKY: I want to repeat. I want the presence of some people, including Nemtsov, here because it is important for my statement, for my answering of the questions.

SHIELDS: We are just getting a supplemental statement from Mr. Nemtsov, my Lord.

EXAMINATION BY MR. BROWNE

BROWNE: Mr. Berezovsky, the reason that you have been recalled is that Mr. Nemtsov has made an allegation which is not part of the defendants' pleaded case, which is that not only did you threaten him but that you carried out the threat by way of Mr. Dorenko. Now, could you just tell the jury, who is Mr. Dorenko?

BEREZOVSKY: Dorenko was an ORT anchor during the election campaign of Mr. Putin. Yes, the election campaign, the parliamentary elections where Putin was against—Putin and Yeltsin were running against Luzhkov and Primakov. And as I remember from that time, SPS—I mean Nemtsov's party, attempted to receive privileged status from Mr. Putin as a way of passing through the parliamentary elections.

BROWNE: If this threat over Gazprom took place, it took place in June 1997. Did you, Mr. Berezovsky, after the Gazprom annual general meeting at the end of June 1997, set Mr. Dorenko on Mr. Nemtsov's tail?

BEREZOVSKY: I already mentioned that the structure of ORT—51 percent belonged to the state, 49 percent belonged to our group at that time, and the decision about the general manager of ORT belonged solely to the state, and the nomination of Dorenko as anchor for the program was a decision not made by me. The decision was made by the general manager of ORT, Mr. Ernst. And I want to stress that, and that Mr. Ernst is still the general manager of ORT. Nothing has changed.

BROWNE: Did you give any instructions to Mr. Ernst as to how he was to treat Mr. Nemtsov in June 1997?

BEREZOVSKY: As I told you before, I tried to use my power at ORT for crucial points of the elections. I was not part of any of this—not through Mr. Ernst or through anyone else—concerning these other events, because from my standpoint, the key point was to win the elections against the Communists in 1996—at that time Dorenko was a nonfactor—my focus was to win the elections against Primakov in 1999.

BROWNE: Did you do anything to try to destroy Mr. Nemtsov's political career in the aftermath of the Gazprom annual general meeting?

BEREZOVSKY: As Mr. Nemtsov accurately mentioned several times, we were in the same boat on the democratic side. Perhaps I was more forceful. And that is the reason why I had to leave Russia, because I continued on my way and Nemtsov is still in Russia. And I am forced to ask for political asylum in this country, and I was—I had to leave Russia just because I took a strong position against the Putin regime, when I recognized that he was doing wrong. On the opposite side, Nemtsov is still in Russia and he is still able to travel freely to London, to return back to Russia, he is the absolute opposite of me.

BROWNE: Do you feel hostility towards Mr. Nemtsov at this time?

BEREZOVSKY: No, I was frustrated many times in Nemtsov's office, when people from his party were unable to present clear arguments during our discussions. They were simply unable to debate politics, as successfully as I am, which frustrated them.

BROWNE: Thank you. Please stay there.

JUSTICE EADY: Mr. Shields.

CROSS-EXAMINATION BY MR. SHIELDS

SHIELDS: Thank you, my Lord. About Mr. Dorenko. I am right in thinking that Mr. Dorenko worked for ORT in 1999; is that right?

BEREZOVSKY: Absolutely correct. He joined ORT—he changed jobs several times. He was with ORT, then he was fired from ORT, even when I was—this is a good question—even when I originally had 49 percent of ORT, Dorenko was fired from ORT; you are absolutely correct. And then he was hired again.

SHIELDS: He was a journalist of whom you thought very highly, was he not?

BEREZOVSKY: I respected him a lot, though I should point out that our views on Chechnya were in direct opposition.

SHIELDS: Am I not right that Mr. Putin, after he was elected Prime Minister, was featured regularly on ORT programs, interviewed by Mr. Dorenko?

BEREZOVSKY: This is absolutely wrong. He—Dorenko did interview Putin, this is correct. I do not remember that he interviewed him many times; I remember only one time; maybe two, but I clearly remember one. And I just want to tell you that at the same time Dorenko interviewed his political opponents, including Primakov and Luzhkov.

SHIELDS: I suggest to you that he was interviewed many times on ORT and you are well aware of that?

BEREZOVSKY: No, just a moment. Dorenko appeared many times, it is absolutely correct, because as I mentioned before he was an anchor. But you put to me an absolutely different question, did Dorenko interview Putin a number of times. This is a completely different question. And I gave you an answer.

SHIELDS: I asked you on the second day about your ownership of ORT, and you accepted that you influenced it a lot. You said you are absolutely clear that you sent a message to society that "I tried to influence the policy of ORT." And I said to you: "So is the message you sent society that everyone in Russia knew that you could influence the editorial content of ORT television programs?" And your reply was: "This was absolutely correct." I also asked you whether you had real power through the media, including the power to make or break reputations and to influence the way people voted. And you answered in the affirmative.

BEREZOVSKY: Just a moment. Yes, okay, I will answer your question, but I am just wondering, you did not give me a Bible this time for me to swear that I am speaking the truth. One time is enough?

JUSTICE EADY: You are still under oath from the previous occasion.

BEREZOVSKY: I will repeat what I said before, that I never denied that I had power in ORT, owning over 49 percent. And I also said that the state had 51 percent. My decisions were not the only ones directing ORT. And particularly in the case of Dorenko, as you mentioned, according to the official record, Dorenko was fired from ORT when I owned 49 percent, and then he eventually was rehired. And my position again, as far as Chechnya and other issues, was sometimes opposite to Dorenko, and he continued to present his personal stance on the air. And you are absolutely correct, he is a very influential journalist, primarily because he always maintains an independent point of view.

SHIELDS: I suggest to you that Mr. Dorenko was a journalist who appeared frequently on ORT, that you were close to Mr. Dorenko, and in the case, for example, of the Putin interviews, you had Mr. Dorenko—Mr. Dorenko was effectively following your instructions to boost Mr. Putin's image…

JUSTICE EADY: What period?

SHIELDS: 1999, my Lord. …To boost Mr. Putin's image in the eyes of the public—would that be right or is that wrong?

BEREZOVSKY: That is absolutely wrong. At that time, Mr. Nemtsov was much closer to me than Mr. Dorenko. I will move on. The second point is that I never gave instructions to Dorenko because it is prohibited in accordance with ORT's regulations.

SHIELDS: Would it be right that Mr. Dorenko made scandalous allegations against Mr. Nemtsov on ORT or Russian TV. Can you recall that?

BEREZOVSKY: I should say that I've not seen all of Mr. Dorenko's shows, but again, I will just—I want to be perfectly clear that I never gave any instructions to Dorenko to attack Nemtsov or anyone else. Moreover, if you read President Yeltsin's book, it becomes absolutely clear why he fired Mr. Nemtsov. And you can—I believe we have that passage clearly marked. The president decided to fire him based on facts and not what he had heard reported on television. Moreover, Yeltsin is well known to be someone who never watches TV.

SHIELDS: Did you have any recollection of Mr. Dorenko appearing on Russian television and making allegations in relation to a prostitute having had a relationship with Mr. Nemtsov?

BEREZOVSKY: Yes, I remember that well.

SHIELDS: You played no part in those revelations?

BEREZOVSKY: Not at all.

SHIELDS: So if Mr. Dorenko had told Mr. Nemtsov that that was the case, that would have been a lie, would it?

BEREZOVSKY: It is a question not for me; it is a question for Dorenko.

Tuesday, May 23, 2006

SHIELDS: Good morning, your Lordship. As your Lordship knows, Mr. Potanin was due to give evidence this morning at 10:15 by video link. When I arrived in chambers this morning at 8:40—I was held up on the train—I was informed by Mr. Eardley, who had just received a telephone call from my instructing solicitors, that they had been informed that Mr. Potanin was summoned last night—not to go last night—to go and see the Prime Minister of the Russian Federation today, an engagement which he could not say no to. As a result, he is now unavailable to give his evidence by video link, my Lord. I am having a statement prepared, my Lord, and it should be here momentarily, by Mr. Voronin who is the representative of the defendants who has been here throughout the trial and has communicated in Russian with Mr. Potanin's lawyers. I know that attempts were made—at least so far as I am aware—to get in touch with him to persuade him that he should be present for this court hearing because obviously it is an inconvenience to everyone, my Lord. But as I understand it, the position is that he is at this meeting and not available to give evidence.

JUSTICE EADY: I am sorry about the delay, members of the jury, I am sure it has been very frustrating for you. I am sure it has also been frustrating for the parties; but what has happened is this. Mr. Potanin was called urgently, or at short notice, to a meeting at the White House in Moscow with the Prime Minister for this morning. It was anticipated that that meeting might go on all day. It was suggested that I might adjourn the case until tomorrow.

I declined to do that because I was concerned about time and so I gave until 2 o'clock for him to become available. He in fact did become available and was waiting at the end of the line in Moscow but unfortunately it then emerged that this equipment was not working. For three quarters of an hour people have been trying to make it work and it has not worked. Under those circumstances, rather than waste any further time, I have decided that in view of this case's timeframe we must proceed on the basis of Mr. Potanin's witness statement, which will be read to you.

That is obviously less satisfactory than hearing him give evidence in person. It obviously cannot be cross-examined, but nevertheless it is better than nothing. So under the circumstances, this is the compromise I have decided to make.

So now what will happen is that Mr. Shields will read you that statement and Mr. Browne will read you an extract from a press conference which he will argue to you is relevant weight to be attached to the statement. So that is what is now going to happen. After that, Mr. Shields will begin his closing statement to you. Yes, Mr. Shields.

SHIELDS: Thank you, your Lordship. Members of the jury, this is the statement of Vladimir Olegovich Potanin. It was made in Russian and translated into English and is dated February 21, 2006. (*Witness statement of Mr. Potanin read.*)

BROWNE: Members of the jury, just by way of introduction, you will remember that in what Mr. Shields has just read there was a reference to a meeting with Mr. Chubais in the South of France attended by Mr. Gusinsky, Mr. Berezovsky and Mr. Potanin. Now, as you will see from the document you have just been handed this is a translation into English of the official Kremlin international news broadcast of a press conference which was held by Mr. Potanin on July 31st; in other words six days after the results of the Svyazinvest auction.

Closing Statement by Mr. Shields

SHIELDS: Members of the jury, and my Lord, there were many occasions during the last seven days when anyone watching this case could be forgiven for thinking this was an action brought by Mr. Berezovsky against Vladimir Putin, the President of the Russian Federation. Indeed I suggest it is even possible that a word search of the transcripts taken during the trial will reveal that the name of Putin has been mentioned more than any other.

The claimant will no doubt argue that it is my client's motive in allegedly defaming the claimant, which can only be explained in the context of his relationship with the president. In the course of this speech I will show why that argument simply does not wash. The real reason I will suggest to you, that the claimant wants to focus on the events since 2000, is that he wants to tempt you into a simplistic and emotional decision and thereby divert your minds from the true battleground in this action: not life under Putin, but life under Yeltsin, in the frenzied years of capitalism in the 1990s, when money, power and politics became inextricably entwined.

Now, members of the jury, before I take you back to the 1990s, let me just remind you of the first issue you need to resolve; one which may have become somewhat hidden or blurred, you might think, in the passion of the last few days. It is Mr. Berezovsky's case that the program broadcast on October 28, 2004, on NTV World, contained statements which have defamed him, have damaged his reputation.

The first thing you did as a panel, if you think back to last Monday, was to watch the program without interruption and without your mind being influenced by Mr. Browne or by me. There was a very good reason for that, because only that way can you ask yourself what impression those two sentences—two sentences—of which Mr. Berezovsky complains would have had on a Russian speaking viewer watching the program through without interruption that night.

We now know that the program had not been advertised or previewed. Viewers who turned on that night came to the duel cold; not looking for or expecting anything, I would suggest, other than the normal cut and thrust of such an aptly named program. That, of course, members of the jury, is what they got. In other words, two intelligent men trading their respective positions, egged on by the caustic and occasionally inflammatory remarks of the host Mr. Soloviov.

Let me remind you briefly and for the last time of what was said. Remember this, it is about halfway through the program, and the debate is focusing on *Alfa Bank's* recent libel action against *Kommersant*. Mr. Fridman:

"We definitely feel that we are winners in the legal sense. In the moral sense this seems to be a Pyrrhic victory because we have great respect for *Kommersant*. I believe that *Kommersant* is an epoch in the history of Russian journalism ... are working for *Kommersant*."

"Host:

"And now they will all go into *Alfa's* pocket because you will give them loans and then buy them.

"Fridman: They will not be *Alfa's* pocket because we are not involved in politics, and this is why I believe that this was a Pyrrhic victory, right? ...As *Kommersant* to understand before they publish information that can affect the interests of millions of people they should verify it most carefully. In 1998, during the crisis we were the only bank that did not steal from its investors. We paid back everything."

Now, members of the jury, note, Mr. Vasiliev, in for the attack:

"In 1999, you were trying to buy *Kommersant* together with Chubais. You failed. Come on.

"Fridman: being friends with Chubais is definitely one of the bravest things one could admit in this life. I would like to clarify the situation just mentioned by the respected editor-in-chief. In 1999, everyone knew that Boris Berezovsky was going to buy *Kommersant*.

"Vasiliev: You decided to save it?

"Host: Save Boris Berezovsky?

"Vasiliev: Well, I do not know.

"Fridman: The newspapers ... partners came to us and requested a loan so that they would be able to reacquire this publication and prevent Berezovsky from buying it. I will remind you that in 1999 Berezovsky controlled the public Russian television where Mr. Andreyev Vasiliev is working as head of information programming."

Now, watch this, members of the jury. Talk about cut and thrust. Straight in:

"Now you are a liar again ... well at least you were working.

"Vasiliev: It is a good thing that you are not a journalist, you would be sued at every turn.

"Fridman: And we told them at that moment ... we are ready to offer them a loan. And the question was discussed. Moreover, even Berezovsky called me with regard to this matter. He was very displeased.

"Did he give you a piece of advice?

"No, he threatened as usual. He said that."

Then either Vasiliev or the host:

"And you too?

"Fridman: He even threatened me. He threatened everyone. That is how he works."

Then Mr. Vasiliev picks up and goes forward about not being involved in politics.

"I remember you were ... and behind you all the time Putin was standing at attention while you were signing."

Again on the attack.

So when I say to you, "Look at the impression it would have made on a viewer," you will seek to put yourself in the position of someone watching this program, aptly called *The Duel*, where it is quite clear that both parties are fencing with each other. A few fleeting words, members of the jury, in a program lasting about one hour 20 minutes, including the commercials. But you see, it is very easy when we come to this courtroom to focus on the words in a way which is unreal. They are set out apart in your jury packet, but the reality is that they are not set out apart for the viewer; the viewer is watching the program as a whole.

Now, the claimant says—and invites you to conclude—that any reasonable viewer of that program would have sat back at that exchange I just read out to you, and would have understood the words to mean that Mr. Berezovsky had called Mr. Fridman—senior banker in 1999—and made threats of physical violence, or alternatively threats which were otherwise improper or intimidating towards him in order to stop him assisting rival buyers to take control of the newspaper *Kommersant*, and that this was Mr. Berezovsky's usual way of doing business.

Now, when I opened this case—and I was pretty quick when I opened this case—I said to you that the Russian viewer watching in his living room does not have a pause button. In other words he does not pause it just to get those words, remember what they were. Nor does he have the advantage of having my learned friend Mr. Browne sitting beside him on the sofa, holding a transcript and analyzing each word as if he was construing a legal document.

In fact, as we all know, the impact of television is very, very different. It is transitory. It is fleeting. The message is far more elusive. The reality, we say to you, is this, that those two sentences would have made very little impression on a sensible, reasonable Russian viewer that night in the context of the thrust and parry of the debate, and they certainly would not have purveyed any impression that Mr. Fridman was referring to threats of a physical nature. We say this, that the very worst impression a viewer would have been left with is that Mr. Berezovsky had been displeased that the defendants were prepared to lend money to the shareholders of *Kommersant* to keep the newspaper independent, when he wanted to buy it, and that he has as a consequence threatened the claimant and that Mr. Berezovsky was used to making such threats in business.

Those threats, we will suggest to you, could only have been understood by any viewer to be of a commercial not a physical nature.

Now, the next question you may want to ask yourself at this stage—because, remember, although we are in a courtroom the reason you are here is that you bring your collective common sense to this courtroom, it must not be confused with believing that we are in a theatre—is to ask yourself who would actually watch this program?

We do know that it can only have been seen by those viewers who subscribe to the NTV channel. That is our starting point. We know that the only company which had been identified as selling the cards in England and Wales is Vitex, and that it has sold, I think it was, 99 or 100 cards between August and October 28, 2004. He also told us that there are up to 200 or so cards—old cards—in existence, but he cannot say how many of those would have been renewed when the card was changed by the new German suppliers who came on the scene in February, in September 2004.

Now, the statement in your packet from the suppliers in Germany speaks of about 440 or so cards in existence now, and estimates it would have been 10 to 50 percent greater in October 2004. But no reason is advanced for such an inference.

Now, there clearly can be no certainty as to exactly how many subscribers there were. But there is, I would suggest, something of which we can be pretty well certain, that all or nearly all of those subscribers had access to at least eight other Russian channels if they had purchased package 1.

So, members of the jury, you have to ask yourself this, because we have to bring ourselves back into the land of reality, just how many, or rather just how few—50 or so people—would have turned on *The Duel*, unadvertised that night. It was advertised and said there was going to be a duel, but no one knew who was going to be the duelists.

We of course know that Mr. Berezovsky watched it, and Mr. Voronkov watched it, who works for Mr. Berezovsky, and Mr. Dubov watched it, who worked for Berezovsky, because they knew it was coming on and they wanted to watch their friend Mr. Vasiliev on the program. But how many others?

You may remember evidence to the effect that it was the kind of program that Russian viewers would have watched because they liked to watch Russian programs. Well, is that really right? Because let us look at what might be a typical Russian viewer, Mr. Litvinenko, who gave evidence on behalf of the claimant who had been sent out, as we know, to find viewers. And Mr. Litvinenko, who is maybe one of the 99 or 100 sold by Mr. Burkin, said this:

"Question: In October 2004 did you have a subscription to NTV World?

"Answer: Yes, I did have a satellite dish.

"Question: But I think it is right you did not watch the program.

"Answer: No, I did not, I do not particularly like watching Russian programs."

So cast aside the inference that all Russians in this country, who have subscribed to NTV, are avidly sitting around on Thursday nights watching the duel. It may be, contrary to the scorn poured by my learned friend in opening, that they were content to watch *East Enders* and had become part of this society in which they have chosen to live.

Now, members of the jury, I turn to the aspect of this case which has taken up so much time. It is of course Mr. Berezovsky's case he has not been guilty of making any of the threats as my clients seek to justify, let alone a threat of a physical nature. Indeed, he has been presented to you at times as almost a saintly figure, fighting a crusade against the injustices of the modern Putin regime. But again as I said to you earlier, this case is not about Russia in the 21st century but about Russia in the 1990s, and how the claimant conducts himself in that period that we say alone is relevant.

What we suggest is quite clear. By 1997, Mr. Berezovsky was a man of immense wealth and immense power, and he wielded both in the media and in politics. He had financial interests ranging from car dealerships—every make of car—to control of one of Russia's biggest oil companies, Sibneft. He had bought his way into a substantial position in the media and was fully prepared to use it to further his political ends.

Let me just remind you what he himself said in evidence about this. I am going to read to you some selections from the transcripts. This is when Mr. Browne is asking him questions:

"Question: Now, in November 1994, did you consider the question of going into television?

"Answer: Yes, it was maybe not only television; I also began thinking about going into politics. Because as maybe you know, the reforms were passed with a lot of difficulties and there were many mistakes, and a lot of people who initially supported democracy in Russia started to think in a different way. Because life did not become immediately better; life became worse for the majority of the population, compared with Soviet times. It was very complicated to understand that this was a necessary result of any revolutionary transformation. And many people were disappointed by Yeltsin, by rich people at that time in Russia. And I recognized that there would be a big battle in the new presidential elections between new and old, let us say, between Russian Democracy and Communism. And it is for this reason that I decided to move into television and politics, because I understood that the mass media would play the decisive role in the new elections."

Now, I asked him when I was cross-examining him, about his interference in the media—you might think something which he has subsequently tried to play down. But these are his answers, Day 2:

"Question: Let me just ask you this question: does that mean you would never interfere in any media organization which you own?

"Answer: No—that is not correct. I had a great deal of influence over ORT.

"Question: That is right. So you are quite happy to interfere in ORT, are you not, Mr. Berezovsky?

"Answer: No, no. I stated openly that I was actively managing ORT's policy, even though I had hired a manager. But I own also 49 percent and I made it absolutely clear to society that I was attempting to influence the policy of ORT.

"Question: Thank you. So that is a message you sent to society: everyone in Russia knew that you could influence the editorial content of ORT television programs?

"Answer: That is absolutely correct."

I returned to this again:

"Question: So your desire, as you told us in evidence yesterday, to use the media for political ends was very well satisfied by your interest in ORT?

"Answer: This was my goal in 1994. My goal was not to allow the Communists to take power in Russia and this is the reason why I insisted, in front of the president, that ORT should be privatized. That is absolutely correct.

"Question: So you had real power through the media?

"Answer: Absolutely correct."

Listen to this question and answer:

"Question: You had the power to make or break reputations?

"Answer: Absolutely correct.

"Question: You had the power to influence the way people would vote?

"Answer: This is how ORT used its power. Absolutely correct. You are absolutely correct about how ORT used its influence."

Then I went on:

"Question: Yes. You bought out the other shareholders at ORT so at the end you had effective control. That is right, is it not?

"Answer: We should again, to be precise, agree on a definition because you continue to use the phrase 'effective control,' and I've already stated several times that I had only 49 percent. Do you mean effective control in terms of shares, or as something that is less than 50 percent, or control over management, or all of these. What do you mean in this case by 'effective control?'"

That is Mr. Berezovsky asking me a question:

"Question: Let us put it like this. I want to ask you this in terms of public influence, using it as a means of communication. The state, you say, owns 51 percent?

"Answer: Correct.

"Question: And you own 49 percent?

"Answer: Correct.

"Question: Who decided editorial policy, you or the state?

"Answer: The editorial policy was decided completely by the company itself, and again I want to say that I only used my power to help convince the president to hire a proper general manager because, as I've said, the state had 51 percent and it was the president's job to nominate a general manager. After that the general manager made all the decisions.

"Question: But your interests and the state were one and the same, were they not, in the 1990s?

"Answer: Absolutely correct."

Then I ask him about other newspapers and I said the following:

"Question: Now, Mr. Yeltsin was reelected, as you said in July …"

That is July 1996, members of the jury:

"…And would it be right that you used ORT to support him and to discredit his Communist rival?"

"Answer: You are absolutely correct."

It could not be clearer, could it, members of the jury: whatever line may now be given to you, he used that media power and he was prepared to use it to discredit others.

Now, at the same time, members of the jury, he was building himself a political power base. Beginning in 1994, he started to become part of President Yeltsin's inner circle. He was advisedly told, "You should join the exclusive President's Club." He got to know the president's younger daughter, Tatyana. He was given high office in Mr. Yeltsin's government in 1996, as Deputy Secretary of the Security Council of the Russian Federation. He had, members of the jury, in short become what *Forbes* magazine so aptly described as "Perhaps the most powerful man in Russia," financial backer and adviser to Boris Yeltsin. This then, members of the jury, is the man whose conduct you have to evaluate when you consider his desire to become chairman of Gazprom, the role he played in the telecom auction, and his telephone conversation over *Kommersant* with Mr. Fridman.

But, members of the jury, that power and its use was not just confined to 1997. In 1999, it was revealed in all its glory when Mr. Berezovsky's world came under threat. Mr. Primakov was in power. He was Prime Minister and he was showing dangerous allegiance to the Communists in the Duma. In March, Mr. Berezovsky lost his position as Executive Secretary of the Commonwealth of Independent States. In May, the Communists tried to impeach Mr. Yeltsin, the Communists in the Duma, the Lower Parliament.

The danger to Mr. Berezovsky's capitalism was clear and present. It was necessary to find a suitable replacement and, in the knowledge that the Prime Minister would have a real chance of succeeding the president, Mr. Berezovsky became involved in finding the successor.

Now, you might recall how in Mr. Browne's opening all those days ago he painted this image of Mr. Putin—the former colonel in the KGB and the man who rose to become head of the KGB's successor—as the kind of person no reasonable person would associate with. Well, that obviously did not apply to Mr. Berezovsky at the time. What we now know is this, members of the jury: there could be no doubt that Mr. Berezovsky was one of the inner circle, the closed circle, who chose Mr. Putin, and then used his media power to have him made acceptable to the country. Mr. Berezovsky even went so far as to found a political organization—not a party—to give credibility to Mr. Putin because he had come out of the shadows, he had no known political allegiance. I will just remind you of some of his answers in relation to this so you can get a true feeling of what we say was a man with the power almost to be a king-maker in 1999. I would like to start on Day 2. I am cross-examining:

"Question: In May 2000, you were concerned as to who might succeed Mr. Yeltsin."

Mr. Browne, ever alert, corrects me: "It is 1999."

"Shields: I mean 1999.

"Berezovsky: Correct.

"Question: And it therefore became imperative to find a suitable successor.

"Answer: You see, everybody in Russia who was directly involved in politics understood that Russia was still not at the final stage of democracy, and we all wondered what would be next?

"Question: I asked you this morning, Mr. Berezovsky, I said, 'Your power was such you could almost make presidents.' Do you remember me asking you that question?

"Answer: You put forth the question and I gave you an answer.

"Question: You did. And therefore I suggest that what happened in June, it was very much that you were part of a group who decided that Mr. Putin was the man to become Prime Minister?

"Answer: I do not refute that, that is correct.

"Question: You do not refute that, do you? At that time, Mr. Putin was described by your counsel in his opening that he had been a KGB colonel and that he had become head of the FSB, the body which is successor to the KGB. The impression that I got—I do not know what other people got—from that was that it was being portrayed that he was the kind of man no one would want to do business with because of his background?

"Answer: Is that a question?

"Question: Yes.

"Answer: You see, the problem is that you don't always have a choice between good and bad. At that time we had to choose between bad and worse. And the 'worse' was Primakov, the 'bad' was Putin.

"Question: The bad was Putin?

"Answer: Yes. Just a moment. Let me—I understood the problem with Putin, that he had been in the KGB. I understood this and his mindset. But unfortunately—I don't mean to be impolite, but it really was not how you describe it, that I had 'the power to make presidents.' I never made this choice. And the choice didn't belong to me, but to President Yeltsin, and the main problem was that he had tried many people in the roll of his successor. If you remember, after Chernomyrdin was fired in 1998, he put in Kirienko. I was completely against that. I was against the move. But in spite of being against it, he put him in office. Then three months later he put in another person. My point is that I did not have the power to choose presidents. I did have power, and a considerable amount, but it was restricted to giving recommendations, to explaining my vision for things, and not even directly to Yeltsin, unfortunately.

"Question: I suggest to you that you are understating your power, Mr. Berezovsky. Your power is very important in this case. Is it not right that you went down and saw Mr. Putin on vacation in the South of France?

"Answer: Absolutely correct.

"Question: And you spent the entire day talking with him?

"Answer: Absolutely correct.

"Question: And at the end the day—and these are your own words—'Putin accepted our offer.' That being an…"

And he interrupts me:

"Answer: Absolutely correct."

I go on:

"Question:—offer to become Prime Minister.

"Answer: Absolutely wrong.

"Question: So it was an offer from you to make Mr. Putin Prime Minister?

"Answer: Absolutely wrong.

"Question: Absolutely wrong?

"Answer: Can I correct you? Not an offer from me, an offer from President Yeltsin to take this position. The message was delivered to Putin through me because I had already known him for ten years; that is the point. It was not my offer, it was an offer from President Yeltsin.

"Question: I will show it to you, I am quoting from your words on the television program, 'Our offer.'

"Answer: That is also correct."

Then I go on to the founding of his political body:

"Question: And when Mr. Putin became Prime Minister in June 1999, it would also be right that he had no party?

"Answer: When Putin became Prime Minister, he was not a member of any party.

"Question: He was a political nobody?

"Answer: If head of the FSB is nobody, then he was a nobody.

"Question: Then you, Mr. Berezovsky, decided that the only way to get him to stay in power and help him become president was to create a party which backed him?

"Answer: Unfortunately, according to Russian laws. It is not possible to create a political party, because a political party needs at least one year to form. And that is the reason why I proposed to create not a political party, but a movement of people who would support him.

"Question: Was that called 'Unity,' 'Yedinstvo?'

"Answer: It was at that time—yes, initially—'Interregional Movement Unity.'

"Question: Unity?

"Answer: Then it was shortened to just 'Unity.'

"Question: I can show you the clipping from the TV program, but you say: 'I remember that meeting at the country house ... Putin was there, Yeltsin's daughter Tatyana and her husband. I said that we needed to create a political party that would concentrate the power of the state machine. They said I was crazy.'

"Answer: That translation is not correct because again I proposed to create not a political party, because according to Russian law this is impossible; I created a political movement. In the way that you put the question to me it does matter."

Then I go back to it:

"Question: I may be putting this badly. My suggestion to you is as follows. You set about consolidating Mr. Putin's position as Prime Minister?

"Answer: You are absolutely correct.

"Question: You knew that the person that was prime minister was most likely to become president?

"Answer: You are absolutely correct.

"Question: You created a party called Unity, or financed the party or a movement called Unity, which backed Mr. Putin?

"Answer: Absolutely wrong. I created the idea to do that. And I created the idea for how to consolidate people around Putin. That is correct."

Then finally I mention that he had not just the power to choose the man who was going to become prime minister with a view to that man becoming president; he had the power through the media to ensure that that person featured well in the public eye:

"Question: I am asking you, am I not right that in that period, the end of 1999 [this about Putin] he was supported by ORT, he regularly appeared on an ORT television program hosted by Mr. Dorenko?"

Listen to this answer and contrast it with the answer he gave when he was recalled the other day:

"Answer: You are absolutely correct, compared to Primakov.

"Question: Thank you.

"Answer: You are welcome.

"Question: You put your political muscle and media muscle behind Mr. Putin.

"Answer: You are absolutely correct."

You see, members of the jury, this is the man who you have to judge against those three instances that we put before you where we say he was quite happy to use threats. Because this is the man who in 1997 and in 1999, expected—expected—to get his own way; a man who prides himself on not making a proposal which he knows could be refused.

Now, members of the jury, we have put before you three instances where Mr. Berezovsky's script did not go according to plan.

Let us begin with the sudden proposal that he should become chairman of Gazprom. You will recall I asked him about Gazprom. I do not think it is disputed that Gazprom, even in 1997, was I think Russia's biggest company: it employed several hundred people; it generated something like 8 to 10 percent of the Russian gross national product; it was the subject of the quip that "Gazprom heats and feeds Russia." It was enormous. A big company in a big country.

Now, it would appear that Mr. Berezovsky was not content with being Deputy Secretary of the Security Council of the Russian Federation. Now, unfortunately, even for Mr. Berezovsky, there was an obstacle in his way in this fledgling democracy to becoming chairman of Gazprom and that obstacle was a certain Boris Nemtsov.

Now Mr. Nemtsov's political star was in the ascendant. He had become First Deputy Prime Minister to Mr. Chernomyrdin. He had been appointed minister in charge of fuel and energy. He was, you may recall, chairman of the collegium which supplied four of an eleven-man board. As he told you in evidence, it would need six members of the board to vote in favor of Mr. Berezovsky for the board to appoint him chairman. The collegium supplied four, and he was fairly confident of how at least two other of the votes would go. So frankly, without the support of Mr. Nemtsov, we suggest becoming chairman of Gazprom was not possible.

You recall how much of yesterday's evidence—the cross-examination of Mr. Nemtsov, it went on for hours—was devoted to trying to pick out inconsistencies in his written statement to the court, his oral evidence to the court and what might be called the "steamy" interview in a magazine published under the auspices of *Komsomolskaya Pravda*, a magazine, I think, which Mr. Nemtsov compared to *The Sun*.

What I suggest shone through the interview, the witness statement and his evidence, despite the verbal onslaught, was this: an unerring consistency in the central allegation we make that Mr. Berezovsky wanted to be chairman of Gazprom; that he realized he needed Mr. Nemtsov's support as well as that of Mr. Chernomyrdin and Mr. Viakhirev; that he went to see him with the draft document initialed by those gentlemen. That Mr. Nemtsov was astonished at such a proposal—effectively a bolt out of the blue—that Mr. Berezovsky had suddenly appeared wanting to become chairman of Russia's biggest company. He telephones both those gentlemen: Mr. Chernomyrdin he tells you sits somewhat on the fence; Mr. Viakhirev says he hopes he will make the right decision. To this appointment of Mr. Berezovsky, Mr. Nemtsov will not agree.

Now, Mr. Berezovsky is not a man who likes to be disappointed in his objectives. He flies to China to see Mr. Chernomyrdin and Mr. Nemtsov is there as well because he has co-ordinated that cultural trip to China. Mr. Berezovsky confronts them both in the Russian Embassy in Beijing. He cannot understand why Mr. Chernomyrdin is not agreeing to him becoming chairman. The meeting over, he threatens Mr. Nemtsov with ruin, outside as Mr. Nemtsov told you. Of course Mr. Berezovsky says that this is a litany of lies. All he needs to do is to get the signature of Mr. Viakhirev, the signature of Mr. Chernomyrdin and that is it. He told you—I will not read from the transcript—he does not need to talk to the board. The mechanisms of decision-making in the Russian Government work this way: it works that if the prime minister says "yes," you have it. You might think it is somewhat strange that here is a man, who professes such a respect for democracy, who would dare to ride roughshod over not just the board, who it appears were not even consulted—this the board of directors of the biggest company in Russia—but even so, the minister who was in charge of fuel and gas. I suggest to you that this is actually quite a simple tale, members of the jury. Mr. Berezovsky wanted something. He recognized he needed Mr. Nemtsov's approval and he turned extremely nasty when he did not get it. Because, members of the jury, recall those passages I read to you earlier in the transcript, which may be glossed over now, but they are unequivocal: he was quite happy when it suited him to use ORT to make or break reputations.

One of his problems with Mr. Nemtsov is that whereas he is quite happy to accuse my client or Mr. Aven of being political toadies to Mr. Putin, he cannot do that to Mr. Nemtsov, can he, because Mr. Nemtsov is an opponent of President Putin; he is the one who campaigned against Mr. Putin having a third term. So he has to scratch around for some reason why Mr. Nemtsov is a liar and he gave about three or four reasons but you might think the one which he most focused on was this: Mr. Nemtsov has come to this court because my client and Mr. Aven had been financial supporters of his party. But as he told you, no one by the party rules is allowed to contribute more than 5 percent of this budget. You might think it is a pretty extraordinary state of affairs if, in order to stay close to Mr. Fridman and Mr. Aven, this man, who keeps his business separate from his politics—and whose whole credo is that business should not be part of politics—is prepared to come to court to perjure himself for that reason. There is an inherent logic to the story he tells and I invite you, members of the jury, to accept it.

Now I turn to Svyazinvest and the nationalization or privatization of the telephone company. The auction of this company was clearly a major event in the privatization of Russia's state interests. Formed as it was out of, I think, an amalgamation of 88 telephone companies and the long distance provider, this was seen as a potential source of great income for the government and potential large profits for the winning bidder. Of course, as you know and we all know, it is the essence of an auction that the highest bidder wins. That in a sense is its purity and its charm. We know there were two rival consortiums: one headed by Mr.

Gusinsky; the other led by Mr. Potanin. Mr. Berezovsky says to you that his position was neutral, but you heard from Mr. Fridman when he gave evidence—evidence which I remind you was unchallenged and he was a member of the consortium of Mr. Gusinsky—that as follows, let me just remind you what he said. I asked him:

"Question: Was Mr. Chubais involved in the organization of the auction?

"Answer: Yes, because he was the Deputy Prime Minister at that time. So therefore, as First Deputy Prime Minister—he was involved in the auction, obviously.

"Question: Can you remember any meetings of Mr. Gusinsky's consortium where Mr. Berezovsky may have been present?

"Answer: Yes, I remember a few meetings where Mr. Gusinsky and Mr. Berezovsky, me and other, you know, people, participated and discussed, you know, conditions and terms of the auction.

"Question: If someone asked you whose side Mr. Berezovsky was on, what would your response have been?

"Answer: Mr. Berezovsky obviously was supportive of our side."

That evidence was given by Mr. Fridman and although Mr. Fridman was cross-examined for about four or five hours he was not challenged on that. Obviously if I missed that in the transcript I will be reminded about it by my learned friend, and you will be tomorrow, when he makes his closing speech.

So it is clear, is it not, that Mr. Berezovsky was on a side. We know that he flew down—because he admits that—with the parties to see Mr. Chubais. You will recall I put to him that he was most put out, as Mr. Potanin says in his witness statement, by the attitude being adopted by Mr. Chubais; the attitude being that this was going to be a fair auction, that the higher bidder would win and that there would be no carve-up. Mr. Berezovsky's response to that is he took the view that Mr. Chubais was favoring Mr. Potanin's side because of the Oneximbank connection. Well, it is very hard to favor someone in an auction, members of the jury. The only way you can favor someone in an auction, I suggest to you, is that one party tells the other party what the first party is going to bid. There is actually no other way when you think about it.

So there it is. Mr. Berezovsky is not getting his own way and quite happy to accuse Mr. Chubais of corruption.

Now we come to *Kommersant*. What we are certain about *Kommersant* is this, that in June 1999 Mr. Berezovsky had a fairly powerful stable in the media world: Channel 6, I think it was; he owned a newspaper; he owned or had a large share in ORT—I cannot say he owned it, he had 49 percent—and he was a very powerful figure in the media. He was also in with President Yeltsin, a man of power. Now he wanted to buy *Kommersant*, a newspaper highly regarded in the business world. What he discovered—much to his displeasure—was that my client Mr. Fridman was involved in possible negotiations with one of the other shareholders which could lead to a management buyout. A management buyout, as you realize, could put Mr. Berezovsky's media aspirations in jeopardy. So what happened, we say, is this: he picked up the phone, he called Mr. Fridman, and he made it clear to him that he did not like him showing interest in *Kommersant*, and he told him in no uncertain terms that he should basically leave it alone.

He used the phrase "my vas zamochim." That phrase will no doubt be spoken to you several times in the course of my learned friend's closing speech. Picked out, as he will say, as an example of the fact that my client cannot be telling the truth because it was a phrase used by President Putin and denounced as criminal slang in a newspaper. But you know what my client said about that: it was a vulgar expression, it was argot; that the Russian people would not have been at all surprised when it was used by the president. They would not necessarily have liked it.

The language of the business street is not always attractive. The language of the trading floor is not always attractive. That is the reality of life. Mr. Berezovsky is the kind of man, as I suggest to you, who likes to get his own way. He was no slouch at showing his disfavor and his displeasure. Mr. Aven is Mr. Fridman's partner. Mr. Aven came to this court and told you that shortly after this conversation his partner came in and told him that he had been telephoned by Mr. Berezovsky who had threatened to damage their business interests if they went ahead with the *Kommersant* deal. And you are invited to believe that it was pure invention by Mr. Aven.

Now, you recall, members of the jury, how at the beginning of this speech I said that the claimant's justification for introducing so much material in relation to President Putin—and human rights abuses since he came to office—was that it was said to be an explanation for my client's motive in effect for lying about this conversation. And he has spent many, many hours in front of you seeking to destroy and attack Mr. Fridman's credibility and integrity.

Now, you are going to be the judges of Mr. Fridman. Let me just say something about him now to you. There is no crime in building up a huge business from scratch, which is what he has done in Russia. He is a Russian citizen who lives in that country. He has many, many employees. His bank has thousands of clients. His reputation, or his company's reputation, is such that it seems that BP, one of our biggest companies, is quite happy to enter into a joint agreement, a partnership, with it. So do not be assuaged or swayed by constant references of post-Putin conduct into thinking that anyone who has stayed in Russia—Mr. Fridman or any other individual who has stayed there and run a business—is somehow bad, tainted.

There is nothing wrong in Mr. Fridman being a Russian citizen. There is nothing wrong in Mr. Fridman being in that country where President Putin has been elected by the majority of the Russian people. There is nothing wrong in him carrying out his business, and there is nothing wrong in him not agreeing with my friend seeking to denounce Russian justice. He is fully entitled to stay that he respects the decisions of the Human Rights courts just as he respects the decisions of the Russian courts; he is not present on either occasion. He has not become involved in politics. And you might think that that is not a bad thing because we see what can happen when businessmen become politicians. That is the very corruption that Mr. Nemtsov railed against; something we often rail against in this country: keep business out of politics. And that is what he sought to do over two days in the witness box.

Now, the claimant's case against Mr. Fridman is put in two ways: In fact, they contradict each other. First it is suggested that the reason he has lied about this is because he is terrified of being treated by President Putin in the same way as Mr. Berezovsky, Mr. Gusinsky and Mr. Khodorkovsky, and he wants to show loyalty to Mr. Putin in order to save his skin. As I said to you, he is a businessman. Mr. Berezovsky chose a political route. Mr. Gusinsky chose to oppose President Putin on his television channel. Mr. Khodorkovsky announced that he was leaving business to pursue political ambitions.

Now, it is not for me to judge those gentlemen. But there is nothing about Mr. Fridman which makes him like them, in that he has kept his business interests out of politics. He is not therefore to be said to be at risk from Mr. Putin, or in fear of Mr. Putin, nor can that possibly be a motive for him to come here before you and lie.

Now, the other allegation against him—which is in fact the other side of the coin—is that he is so in with Mr. Putin that he is defending this action—he went on the television channel, accepted the invitation to the duel because it was a good opportunity to tell lies about Mr. Berezovsky, the enemy of Mr. Putin. Well, there can be no basis for that assertion because, as he told you, he has never been alone with Mr. Putin. He has been in a room with other businessmen with Mr. Putin on a number of occasions—and that should not be a surprise; our own Prime Minister frequently has businessmen to Downing Street. There is no crime in that. There is no basis for asserting that he is somehow here because he owes Mr. Putin a favor because he wants to keep in with him.

Now, as against Mr. Aven—because Mr. Aven is a problem, is he not, because he corroborates Mr. Fridman—it is difficult to take any kind of line in relation to him. He was a politician who turned to business. It is put to him that his friendship with Mr. Berezovsky, or his admiration of Mr. Berezovsky, was revealed by that birthday greeting that he put in *Kommersant*. That is no reason therefore for suggesting to Mr. Aven that he wants to stay close to President Putin, because, if he did, the last thing he would do is put a birthday greeting in *Kommersant* to Boris Berezovsky. And equally it was then suggested to him that he does not see much of Berezovsky in London because he is afraid of what Mr. Putin might think. And you remember his answer to that? He is not afraid of that at all. He is quite happy to be public, as he was in the court, that he opposes Mr. Putin having a third term of office. I put Mr. Aven in front of you as being a totally honest witness. He was not the least bit afraid of telling you of his own political stance, in that he opposed a third term. He was a businessman who kept out of politics.

Now, members of the jury, you have three separate instances, each I invite you to test on its own. Each I invite you to test against the man we now know to be Mr. Berezovsky, the kind of man we know to be Mr. Berezovsky. When you test each of those, I want you to ask yourself and look at each of the evidence given by the witnesses we have called.

In Mr. Potanin's case he has not given evidence before you and has not been cross-examined. But you will recall the statement I read to you. And that statement, I would suggest to you, is fairly unequivocal that he was present at meetings with Mr. Gusinsky where Mr. Berezovsky was also present. It was quite clear that Mr. Berezovsky was on the other side, and that Mr. Berezovsky was very disappointed by the stance taken by Mr. Chubais and that the message he conveyed to him by Mr. Berezovsky—the precise words and dates he cannot remember, I have to accept that; but the message was clear: the same message that his business interests would be damaged, his reputation, his image would be tarnished if he went through with his opposition to Mr. Berezovsky's chosen winner. How to render an auction worthless. And who are the losers? Ultimately it is the state, is it not, because it is the state that gains the profits from that privatization? It is the state, the people of Russia who will be the winner, by the highest bid.

So, members of the jury, when you look at those questions, we invite you, if you find that the words complained of were defamatory of Mr. Berezovsky—and you have heard my arguments on that—to find emphatically that they are substantially true, that we have justified them.

Now, you will also see on that list of three questions there is a final question devoted to damages.

Now, we say to you that Mr. Berezovsky is not entitled to a single penny. But there are two circumstances where you might have to consider damages—although obviously my case to you is that you do not have to—but equally it is my duty to address you upon them. The first circumstance is this, that if, contrary to my submissions on the meaning of the words, you decide that they convey the use of physical harm.

Now, even if they do bear that meaning, it is accepted, I think by Mr. Berezovsky in cross-examination, that making threats of any kind is a very serious matter. And if you accept that we have proved one, two, three of the instances I have outlined to you again in my closing speech, you will be entitled, I suggest to you, to reduce any award of damages to nil; because at the end of the day he basically does not have any reputation at all worth compensating. Equally, if you took the view that there were at worst some form of commercial threat or a threat to someone's political future, but we have failed to convince you—the burden being on us—that each of these instances took place, you would be entitled to reduce the damages in the same way as if you had found that one or two of them had been fully justified.

Finally, let me say this. The purpose of an award of damages is to compensate a claimant for the damage to his reputation and any hurt to his feelings. In such circumstances, as you will appreciate, the number of viewers becomes highly relevant. I have submitted to you in the course of this speech that any viewing of this program was of a very modest nature, and its effect on Mr. Berezovsky's reputation minimal. It is quite clear, for example, that Mr. Voronkov was uninfluenced by what he had heard, as was Mr. Berezovsky's other employee.

Let me just remind you about the other witnesses who were called. You will recall that Mr. Litvinenko did not even see the program. His role in July 2005 was to go out and find people who did. He was not very successful. And the claimants seek to diminish part of that failure by reference to viewers who were afraid, they say, to give evidence. You will recall that Mr. Dubov, I think it was, said that no witness needed to be afraid to give evidence in this action.

So, members of the jury, in conclusion what we say is this, that this program at worst contained statements that Mr. Berezovsky made threats of a non-violent nature, that the publication was virtually non-existent, and sadly but truly, any damage to Mr. Berezovsky's reputation was thoroughly deserved. Mr. Berezovsky has come to this court and has had no hesitation in calling Mr. Fridman a liar, of either being a Putin toady who libeled to keep in with Mr. Putin, or so afraid of Mr. Putin that he has defended this action to curry favor and to avoid the fate which has befallen other oligarchs. He has accused Mr. Aven of inventing his evidence out of loyalty to his friends; Mr. Nemtsov of giving perjured evidence on the basis of monies he has received for his party. Not paid to Mr. Nemtsov, but monies given to Mr. Nemtsov's party.

You see, members of the jury, Mr. Berezovsky finds no difficulty in finding something discreditable to say about anyone who has the courage or the temerity to stand up to him. Those witnesses have come to this court and stood up to him. He is used to power. He is used to getting his own way. We invite you through your verdict on this occasion to deny him such an outcome.

Closing Statement by Mr. Browne

BROWNE: Members of the jury, in the seven-odd days of this case, Mr. Shields and I have not agreed on much, but on one thing this afternoon it is clear that we do agree, and you may too, and that is that the key to this case—the key to who is telling the truth—is whether Mr. Fridman is a man you can trust. Is he a man you can trust to tell the truth?

Let us just start by looking to see why the answer to that question must be no. Let us look first at what Mr. Fridman told you—particularly when he was answering his own counsel, Mr. Shields, and then compare it with what was extracted from him in cross-examination. Then, once we have looked at the difference between those two, let us go on and have a look at why it was that Mr. Fridman was simply not willing to tell you the truth. Let us just wind the clock back a few days to Mr. Fridman's initial evidence before it came under the spotlight of the cross-examination.

First of all, we had the pretence that he had nothing to do with politics. Indeed, we have had it again from Mr. Shields only a few moments ago. Mr. Shields was saying that Mr. Fridman had sought to keep business out of politics and always kept his business interests out of politics. That of course is in line with what he told Mr. Shields back last Thursday. Personally, he said, he was not involved in political things. "I am an ordinary businessman," he said, "not a kind of public figure." He told you he had never tried to be politically influential. Secondly, his initial stance was to play down his relationship with Mr. Putin. He said he had never met with Mr. Putin one-on-one. Do you remember him saying he had only met Mr. Putin a couple of times with a group of businessmen. A couple of times. If he went to the Kremlin having received an invitation from Mr. Putin, he went, he said, out of politeness because it would be rude to refuse. His respect for Mr. Putin he said was there, but he did not have any special relationship. Then thirdly, looking at his initial evidence, we had what we now know is the pretence that he was not a public figure or interested in appearances on the media. He told you in no uncertain terms that he was not a public figure. He tried to pretend that participating in the debate with Mr. Vasiliev had been quite a unique case for him. He told you that businessmen should stay out of the media and, do you remember, we had that exchange about chat shows, and he said he tried not to appear on television or chat shows.

So what we have is a picture which is fundamentally untrue. And insofar as it is true, it is not the whole truth. Take for example his membership in the public chamber, the new body set up by Mr. Putin to review government legislation. It is obviously very important to Mr. Putin that that body should be on his side. We all know how annoying it is for a government in power if a reviewing body, such as in our own case the House of Lords, proves difficult about the introduction of legislation. And we know that the public chamber is Mr. Putin's idea. We know, too, that Mr. Fridman, and for that matter Mr. Potanin, was selected by the initial 42 nominees of Mr. Putin. It is an odd system. You will remember the details: Mr. Putin selects 42 and they select another 42 and the 84 select the final 42. And bizarrely, members of the jury, Mr. Fridman is there as a representative of officers' wives. That only emerged in cross-examination. It also emerged in cross-examination that the fact that he was there as the representative of a group called Officer's Wives had caused enormous public protest.

So how does Mr. Fridman deal with that? He has of course to pretend that that protest has all been initiated by his competitors. He ignores the fact, I would ask you to accept, that Officers' Wives was simply a front set up to challenge Soldiers' Mothers—a much better group, which has been campaigning for may years to improve the conditions of young conscripts in the Soviet military.

Now, let us think about what happened, what came to light overnight, between Thursday and Friday. And as you listen to me, think what a misleading picture you would have been left with if by chance Mr. Fridman had left the witness box on Thursday night and if that had been the end of his evidence. You would not have heard the half of it, you would not have heard a quarter of it. Let us just look in the blue file at the *Izvestia* letter, written in late April 1996, on the eve of the Russian presidential election. In effect, President Yeltsin running for re-election against the Communists, and Mr. Fridman and Mr. Potanin, whose names you will see along with Mr. Berezovsky and Mr. Gusinsky, all concerned, very concerned, that the Communists should not get in.

Well, members of the jury, ask yourselves: is this the letter of a man who always tried to stay out of politics, as he asserts, and Mr. Shields again asserts today? A man who never tried to be politically influential? One has only to detect the lie in that to look at the very last paragraph but one. This is an open display of Mr. Fridman and his business colleagues using their political muscle. Just look at the last sentence:

"Those who seek to undermine Russian civil society, gambling on a desire for ideological revenge and social confrontation must understand that Russian entrepreneurs [that is Mr. Fridman and his colleagues] possess the necessary resources and willpower to exert their influence on politicians who are either too unprincipled or too uncompromising."

Well, on Friday, confronted with that letter, Mr. Fridman's tone change, you will recall. And he had to accept, perhaps not surprisingly, that nothing could have been clearer than that letter as an attempt by businessmen—entrepreneurs, if you like—to exert their influence on politicians. What else did we learn for the first time on Friday? We learned that, far from being the shrinking violet for whom the appearance on *The Duel* was a unique occasion, Mr. Fridman, the man who is not, he says, a public figure and never appears on television or chat shows, had gone, in July of 2002, on to breakfast television with his longstanding friend and university contemporary, Mr. Soloviov. And again the tone changes and he is forced to change his story in the light of the transcript.

You will remember—I said it a moment ago—initially he said he had just a couple of meetings with Mr. Putin, never one-on-one. Now, he was forced to admit that he and other businessmen had had regular—"regular" was the word he used—meetings with Mr. Putin over six years beginning in 1999, when Mr. Putin came to power. Not just a couple of times, but sometimes, he said, as often as four times a year. Four times a year: that is a lot of meetings, is it not? Indeed, members of the jury, so close is Mr. Fridman's relationship with Mr. Putin that he was able to tell Russian television viewers about his personal experience of dealing with the president: "I would say, from my [not 'our', but 'my'] personal experience of dealing with the president that despite his way of expressing emotions, which can indeed be singled out, he is a living person and this probably accounts for his being such a popular and successful politician."

Well, there is a pretty hefty dash of sycophancy there, is there not, members of the jury? Then Mr. Soloviov asks, five lines below that: "When you communicate with the president, do you have a sense of his personal attitude to you?"

Mr. Fridman:

"Good question. I would say, as I have seen it, to give the president his due, everybody who communicates with him has a good idea of his attitude to them. I do not know if it is only a feeling on an emotional level."

Well, there you have it from a man who supposedly has never met with the president one-on-one.

If we continue, we see that he is remarkably revealing, too, about his financial support for all the political parties, bar the Communists. You will remember what I put to him based on *Alfa Group*'s website. You will remember that the *Alfa Group* website had posted an article. This is the article which says that Mr. Putin's favorite oligarch is Mr. Fridman: "Like most oligarchs, however, Fridman is a heavy contributor to the United Russia Party, the political entity most closely linked to Putin."

Well, you may think it is extraordinary that when that is put on *Alfa Bank's* website in order to encourage people to believe—who may be investing in *Alfa Bank*—that it is a safe investment because those who run it are so closely tied in to the government of Mr. Putin, that Mr. Fridman should say to you that it was quite untrue. I invite you to reject that evidence and to find that the overwhelming likelihood is, as is mentioned on the program, that *Alfa* support, all the parties but of course not the Communists. Mr. Soloviov:

"So you place a call to the boss [Mr. Nemtsov]?

"I can easily meet them and explain that there is a certain issue and I would like their support on it."

The cynical Mr. Soloviov says:

"Will they ask you for money?"

And Mr. Fridman replies:

"Well, I would say they will ask for support for their activities in some form."

"Some form" doubtless including money. Mr. Soloviov the moderator asks:

"Do you have to spend a lot of money on direct political support to the same parties during election campaigns?"

And Mr. Fridman says:

"I would say that what we spend is normal by Russian standards but can be considered a lot by Western standards."

Well, members of the jury, we did not get much detail about what was paid, but we do know by our own standards what huge sums people pay to political parties these days. And if Mr. Fridman and *Alfa* are paying more then they are very, very sizeable sums indeed. Mr. Shields attempts to laugh it off by saying it is only five percent, but just think, that means 20 people could buy up a political party:

"Moderator: Do you give equal amounts to all parties?

"Answer: Absolutely, not. For example we would never fund the Communists."

He may not say it in specific terms but is he not saying there, in effect: well, yes, amongst the parties we do financially support are United Russia, Mr. Putin's party, the party in government. And just consider how his evidence changes. On Thursday I asked him this question:

"Has *Alfa Bank* or yourself ..."

And I just emphasize that "or yourself," " ...or any company within the *Alfa Group* ever provided money to the Union of Right Forces?" Answer from Mr. Fridman:

"As far as I know, *Alfa Bank* as an entity never provided any money to the Union of Right Forces. What I am aware of is that a few people, including my partner, provided certain financial support to the Union of Right Forces.

Then, curiously, he went on to say that he did not know if Mr. Aven had provided financial support.

Well, note I had asked him: did he support the Union of Right Forces? With the benefit of that transcript, the following day I got Mr. Fridman to agree that he personally had contributed to the Union of Right Forces.

It was, on his own admission, tens of thousands of dollars, which he called a "relatively small amount."

He then also shifted his ground and accepted that it was possible that some part of *Alfa* had subscribed to Putin's party, United Russia.

So there we have it. Thursday, I ask him:

"Has *Alfa Bank* or you provided money to the Union of Right Forces?"

I receive an evasive answer:

"*Alfa Bank* as an entity never provided any money."

When I have the transcript he has to agree that he personally—personally—had contributed to the Union of Right Forces.

Members of the jury, you may think that that money—as money always does when business mingles with politics—buys influence. We see it. He can easily pick up the telephone, get a hold of Mr. Nemtsov and, to use Mr. Fridman's own words: "...explain that there is a certain issue and I would like their support on it."

And Mr. Soloviov knows what that means because he then comes back and says: "Well, will they ask you for money?"

Well, we do not need to be cynical to know that that is exactly what the exchange is going to be.

Throughout that interview—details of which you were never told when Mr. Fridman was questioned by Mr. Shields—Mr. Fridman was positively boasting about the political influence he was able to exert and influence in Russia today.

Members of the jury, that is a good moment, if my Lord agrees, to take a break. Tomorrow I will move on, and the question that I will be asking you to think about is: what is the reason for the difference between the evidence initially given by Mr. Fridman and what subsequently emerged, particularly on Friday of last week?

Wednesday, May 24, 2006

Closing Statement by Mr. Browne (*continued*)

Browne: Members of the jury, when we adjourned last night we were looking at the dramatic difference between what Mr. Fridman initially told you under the tender questioning of Mr. Shields, and what emerged subsequently, particularly on Friday when he was confronted with those documents, the open letter to *Izvestia* and the transcript of the Soloviov television program. I said that the next question I was going to confront was why it was that there was such a difference between Thursday's evidence and Friday's evidence. Well, the first thing of which you can be sure is that the explanation for the difference is not absent-mindedness or forgetfulness, is it? It is something much more sinister. What it is, is that Mr. Fridman was trying to minimize, if not conceal altogether, a very close relationship with Mr. Putin. Just for a moment, contrast that with Mr. Berezovsky's position. Mr. Berezovsky was frank about his initial support for Putin, which was undermined by the manner in which Mr. Putin behaved once he had the reins of power.

I said in my opening to you that Mr. Berezovsky had played a part in actually suggesting Mr. Putin for Prime Minister, but ironically when Mr. Putin took power Mr. Berezovsky realized, at great cost, that he had made a mistake. But Mr. Berezovsky never concealed that initial support for Mr. Putin, nor did I. So when Mr. Shields, like a conjurer, takes the rabbit of the television program on which Mr. Berezovsky appeared out of the hat and waves it about as though it is magic, there is no magic in it at all. The truth is that Mr. Berezovsky has been frank about this all along, frank on television, frank with you, that he was one of those that helped to put Mr. Putin in power. But it has turned out to be at his expense.

Let us go back to Mr. Fridman. Why is Mr. Fridman behaving in this way? I suggest that the answer is clear enough. Both in his evidence in this court in 2006, and in his contribution to the television debate in 2004, he was trying to curry favor with the Kremlin. Now, the libel and the lies have all been under the prime ministership of Mr. Putin. It is only the subject matter of the libel and the lies which happens to relate back to the Yeltsin era. So Mr. Shields' attempts to distinguish between Yeltsin and Putin do not really help. The key factor here is the shadow of Mr. Putin over Mr. Fridman in October 2004, when he goes on television and speaks the libel, and today in this court; because no one wants to be the next Gusinsky, or the next Khodorkovsky, thrown into jail on politically motivated criminal charges, and then see your assets and your shareholders' assets seized by the state. You will remember the chilling gallows humor of Mr. Soloviov on the program. The question posed that all the oligarchs fear, "Do you know Khodorkovsky? You are next."

If you look at the transcript at any time, you will see that the audience bursts into applause, pretty chilling applause, at that question. No one wants a visit from the tax police, as Mr. Fridman confirmed to Mr. Soloviov in 2002, on the breakfast television show. Still less do they want to be confronted with the choice that Mr. Berezovsky had to face: political exile or political prison. So I suggest that the explanation for all of this is to be found in Mr. Fridman's position—toeing the party line means putting the boot into Mr. Berezovsky. And Mr. Berezovsky, his fellow wealthy businessman, is his target for no other reason than that he refuses in exile in this country to be cowed into silence about Mr. Putin's anti-democratic policies and he has thwarted, as you have heard, every effort of the Russian Government to extradite him. The English court has thrown out the charges and the British Government has given him political asylum, which they would never have done if they had thought that there was substance in the suggestion that he was a criminal.

So I have talked about the shadow over Mr. Fridman and Mr. Aven even whilst they were in the witness box in this court. It is not just flimsy barrister's rhetoric; it is based on solid evidence that you have heard from witnesses about life in Russia today. You will remember Mr. Litvinenko who had worked in the KGB for 20 years before obtaining political asylum here in 2001. Well, I imagine it was the first time you had heard direct from the horse's mouth about the operations of the KGB rather than reading it in Len Deighton or John Le Carre. And what he said was pretty chilling. He had been deputy head of the most secret department of the KGB's successor, the FSB. So secret, I think, was the department that he did not tell us what it was. But at any rate, that was his evidence. And he said, and I quote, that he was:

"100 percent certain that minutes of this hearing will be on the table of the Russian Special Intelligence Services."

Well, he said that, of course, as you remember, in the context of an explanation of why people in this country who had watched the program were unwilling to stand up and be counted in this court. But Mr. Fridman knows what is going to be on the table of the Russian Special Intelligence Services and I suggest that he does not want to be asked about his evidence in London by Mr. Putin the next time they have one of their regular meetings at the Kremlin, perhaps to discuss a massive tax demand such as the one confronted by *Alfa* in April 2005 when, as we know, Mr. Fridman had to go and see Mr. Putin over a tax claim for nearly US $1 billion.

We know from the experience with Mr. Potanin yesterday that when the Prime Minister of Russia talks, when he summons a businessman to the Prime Minister's residence at the White House, the businessman drops all previous engagements, even if it is wildly inconvenient, even if the summons comes at 9 o'clock at night and is for a meeting the following morning.

Well, members of the jury, am I making a meal of this? I suggest not. The evidence is all there before you, which enables you to detect just how keenly Mr. Fridman feels he has to curry favor with the Kremlin. The test is to look and see what he revealed about his attitude to the predicament of Mr. Khodorkovsky and Mr. Gusinsky. Did it not strike you, members of the jury, that he was chillingly indifferent to infringements of human rights in Russia today? He simply told you that he did not know whether such concerns had a real foundation.

Well, was that just so much floundering? Was that simply, as I suggest it was, an attempt to evade the question and to avoid telling you what he really thought, and above all what he really knew?

Let us just deal with the two names, Khodorkovsky and Gusinsky. Mr. Fridman told you that they had been found guilty according to the Russian court and he made it clear that he did not want to criticize the Russian court. And he stuck to that position even when I showed you the decision of the court here in London that the prosecution of Mr. Khodorkovsky had indeed been politically motivated and therefore Mr. Khodorkovsky's business associates would not be extradited to Russia. His persistence in refusing to concede that there was anything wrong with the Russian court decision was all the more astonishing when I pointed out to him that in his judgment the senior district judge had said that the public prosecutor had actually reported to Mr. Putin in April 2003, that there were no grounds for taking action against Mr. Khodorkovsky, and then two months later, without there being any new evidence at all coming to light, Mr. Putin had apparently directed a prosecution. But still, Mr. Fridman would not accept that there was anything that was open to criticism in the Russian court behaving in the way they did. Eight years in a Siberian labor camp.

Mr. Gusinsky. Well, again, Mr. Fridman said he was not going to comment. He tried to sidestep my questions on whether the arrest and imprisonment of Mr. Gusinsky was politically motivated. He actually went further and said that he did not think that Mr. Gusinsky had been arrested in order to put pressure on him, pressure on him to surrender NTV and Gazprom.

Well, Mr. Aven was not quite so obstinate or so unconvincing. He accepted that the arrest of Mr. Gusinsky and the surrender of NTV to the state-owned Gazprom were plainly linked, and he had to accept that because I asked him—and you will remember the clipping from *The Moscow Times* which is in the packet, which exhibits the agreement between Mr. Gusinsky and Gazprom—he had to accept it because a government minister, Mr. Lesin, had actually put his signature to the deal.

So we have there the fingerprints of the Putin government all over this agreement, and Mr. Lesin took the rap. It was he who accepted that what had happened was inexcusable.

Mr. Nemtsov, as you know, now an opponent of Mr. Putin, said that everybody knew that Gusinsky was arrested for political reasons. "Everybody knows," he said.

And yet Mr. Fridman, as I have said, had obstinately refused to acknowledge what everybody knew and what I suggest he knew. That, I suggest, was dishonesty. It can only be dishonesty. And it is a total lack of candor, which means that you cannot trust any part of his evidence because whereas Nemtsov said everybody knew, and you have seen the publicity in the papers, Mr. Fridman carried on saying he just did not know whether there was a connection between the imprisonment and the surrender of NTV.

So it is not just a barrister being melodramatic when I say that throughout his evidence Mr. Fridman behaved as though Mr. Putin was in the back of this court watching him and listening to every word he said here.

Let me move now, members of the jury, to the debate on television. What do the words mean? Can I just start by saying one thing that might have struck you as slightly odd, and that is that you have not heard from the witnesses who saw the program what it meant to them. Well, there is a very simply reason for that. The question of what the words meant is entirely up to you. And barristers are not allowed to ask witnesses who have seen a television program or read an article in the newspaper what they thought the words meant. That is out of bounds. And that is why you have not heard that evidence.

If you look at the transcript you will see how Mr. Fridman gratuitously dragged Mr. Berezovsky's name into the debate. In the debate they were of course discussing events in 2004. The trigger for the debate has been the huge award against *Kommersant*. And it is Mr. Fridman who turns the clock back to 1998, and begins to mention Mr. Berezovsky.

You will see that even though Mr. Vasiliev and occasionally Mr. Soloviov interrupt, Mr. Fridman, determined to deal with Mr. Berezovsky, ploughs on his way. You will see that he ploughs on even with Mr. Vasiliev and Mr. Soloviov interrupting. He is unstoppable. He is plainly determined to get this out.

How would the Russian or the Russian-speaking audience have reacted? Well, I suggest you can be confident on the evidence you have heard from the people who watched the broadcast that they would have sat up at once at the mention of the well-known name of Mr. Berezovsky, particularly viewers here where he now lives and who know him as a fellow expatriate.

Mr. Shields would have you believe that this was simply a throw-away remark. But that will not wash, will it, members of the jury, because the fact is Mr. Berezovsky is so well known to Russians and the accusation is so serious it will have inevitably stuck in their minds. And we know that it did. So it is not, as Mr. Shields would have you believe, just a flash in the pan; it is a very significant allegation, a grave charge against a well-known man, which remains in the minds of those who saw it.

Then Mr. Shields says, "Well, the audience does not have a pause button." Well, he ignores, of course, the fact that some people will have recorded it. So that does give them a pause button. And it also means that the program is in circulation, the poison flows through the system: other people who did not initially see the broadcast are provided with the tape and they will see it too.

I said in opening to you—and I will repeat quite shortly because it is important—that what Mr. Fridman said clearly suggested and can only suggest that Mr. Berezovsky had threatened him with violence and, worse still, that that was the way in which Mr. Berezovsky habitually behaved.

Now, the translation has been agreed upon. Let me repeat what I said at the start of the case because I ask you to bear it in mind when considering the question of meaning. When we use the word "threaten," when someone claims that a threat has been made, but the threat is not specified, it must imply that it is a threat of violence. If I come into this court and say I have just been out in The Strand; I met Mr. Nicklin and he threatened me on the pavement, that plainly suggests a threat of violence. It is only when the words are qualified or explained that the implication of violence disappears. If say, "Mr. Nicklin threatened to leave the room if I carried on playing old ABBA records," then the threat is very different. I hope none of you are ABBA fans. But, members of the jury, the threat in those circumstances is immediately diminished. We know at once what the nature of the threat is. It is not a threat of violence, it is simply a statement of what you will do in that certain eventuality.

Now, that is the starting point and that, I suggest, ought to be good enough. But here the implication of violence is strengthened by context. Notice, Mr. Vasiliev says to Mr. Fridman:

"Did Berezovsky give you a piece of advice?"

To which Mr. Fridman responds:

"He threatened as usual. He said that …"

And then he goes on:

"He even threatened me; he threatened everyone. That is how he works."

So it was not advice that Mr. Berezovsky gave Mr. Fridman, according to the latter; it was quite different, it was a threat. Not advice, a threat of something physical; not simply advice to be careful or watch his step.

So that is the first aspect of the context. The second is that Mr. Fridman emphasizes that Mr. Berezovsky had even threatened him. You may ponder why he says "even" him, but he goes on to say that he threatened everyone.

Well, presumably that must mean everybody involved in trying to acquire *Kommersant*, although significantly that is not what is alleged. "He threatened everyone" must relate to *Kommersant*. If he had merely been meaning to say that is how Mr. Berezovsky works, he would have used the present tense, "he threatens everyone." And it is the suggestion that the use of threats on Mr. Berezovsky's part was habitual which I suggest finally underlines that the threats were threats of violence.

Members of the jury, I am going to move now to the supposed justification. In this context the solicitor's correspondence is very important because, as I have stated, and I said to you in my opening, the fact that Mr. Fridman's solicitors never mentioned in any of their letters the points that first emerged when they put in their court defense in June 2005, indicates, does it not, that these matters have been dredged up in the period between the first complaint by Mr. Berezovsky's solicitors in November 2004, and June 2005, in order to get Mr. Fridman out of a hole of his own making.

There is the first letter of complaint, the one of November 18th. There is the response three weeks later on December 9th. In it Mr. Fridman claims that the threat or threats were not of violence but of a purely commercial nature and that Mr. Berezovsky had made a threat to bring commercial pressure to bear, whatever that may mean. It is clear, is it not, from this letter that at that stage Mr. Fridman was in some difficulty? He had claimed on television that he had been threatened with violence, and he had not been, and could not claim that he had been. He could not substantiate his allegation that that was how Mr. Berezovsky habitually behaved because there is no suggestion in this letter to that effect. There is no suggestion in this letter that Mr. Berezovsky has used threats or a threat had been used on any other occasion than the one in relation to *Kommersant*.

So, if you put it colloquially, Mr. Fridman was in a bit of a pickle. And it got worse in the New Year. Turn to the letter of Fridman's solicitors of January 14, 2005. Clearly, at this stage Mr. Fridman's instructions to his lawyers were to play the matter down. In this letter the attempt is made to portray Mr. Berezovsky's complaint as making a molehill into a mountain, to exaggerate the complaint, to make it appear that what was really a typhoon was merely a storm in a teacup. What the solicitors stated was that threats of a commercial nature were relatively commonplace in the context of Russian business and therefore no one would think the worse of Mr. Berezovsky if that allegation had been made against him. It was not, they said, defamatory, indeed they said it was not even capable of being defamatory.

Well, it is a pretty extraordinary letter, not just because it is an attempt to give Mr. Berezovsky the brush-off. If what Mr. Fridman, on instructions to his solicitors, says there is true, then it is very revealing, is it not, about the way in which Mr. Fridman does, and did business? And that comment makes you realize that this letter, written on his instructions, gets him into all sorts of difficulties.

So what does he do? Last Friday when giving testimony he tried to pretend that his solicitors had written the letter without instructions.

He tried to pretend that it was not his personal instruction to say that threats of a commercial nature were common practice or commonplace. But just look. Distinguished firms of solicitors like Herbert Smith do not write letters saying that they have taken their clients' instructions, having waited for the Russian New Year holiday to be over, when they have not. And you can be sure that they accurately set out what those instructions were.

So for Mr. Fridman, to pretend that this letter was written without instructions, simply will not wash. And in any event his account was self-contradictory because what he said was: "No, we talked about that with the lawyers and I told them the whole story, about what had happened with Mr. Berezovsky. We described all the circumstances of the conversation and then asked them to take the necessary steps—I told them that it was a very important matter to me."

In other words, the brush-off. But remember that he concedes that he talked about it with the lawyers and he told them the whole story about what had happened with Mr. Berezovsky.

Well, members of the jury, the lawyers corresponded for another six months before, as I say, in the middle of June, Mr. Fridman had to file his defense document to the court. In opening, I generously spared you all those letters. Mr. Shields has had them put into the packet. But he has not referred to them, and you can take it from me that nowhere in what I think are some nine pages of letters over that six-month period is there a single word alleging that there had been threats by Mr. Berezovsky on any other occasion. So let us just pause and see where that gets us. If Mr. Fridman was telling the truth on the program in October 2004, it is simply inconceivable that these long delayed accounts of other threats, which only emerged in June 2005, are correct. Only on June 16th do the allegations about Gazprom and Svyazinvest emerge for the first time. You may think, looking back over the evidence as a whole, that the very interesting thing about it is that neither Mr. Nemtsov nor Mr. Potanin claim to have told Mr. Fridman about these alleged threats in 1997, before the television debate on October 20th. More significantly still, nor does Mr. Fridman claim that they had told him. It has never been suggested in evidence or by Mr. Shields that these supposed threats in 1997 were what Mr. Fridman was referring to on the program. My suggestion is that Mr. Fridman, having made this allegation of habitual threats, then, as I have said, had to dredge up this evidence subsequently. And it is plain that he simply did not know of these matters at the time he made his utterly false charge of habitually threatening Mr. Berezovsky.

Well, I am going to look with you in a moment at the evidence of Mr. Fridman and Mr. Aven, Mr. Nemtsov and Mr. Potanin. Before we do, it may assist you if I just summarize what we say on behalf of Mr. Berezovsky about these baseless allegations that have been made against him. There is not, as must be obvious to you, a simple explanation: one size fits all; we have to take the witnesses as individuals. But I am going to take Mr. Fridman and Mr. Aven first and take them together. It is quite clear, is it not, that each of them has a deep-seated resentment, perhaps loathing for Mr. Berezovsky, the man, and his politics. Neither of them lost any opportunity to take a crack at Mr. Berezovsky on any subject whether it be relevant to the issues in this action or not. Witnesses in this court are given a lot of rope, and sometimes they hang themselves with it. But, members of the jury, how many times, looking back over the evidence, did Mr. Fridman and Mr. Aven, instead of answering the question, just take the opportunity to take an irrelevant crack at Mr. Berezovsky, to say something hurtful or defamatory about him which had no relevance to the question that I was asking?

Well, that is one thing, their general attitude towards Mr. Berezovsky as displayed by their evidence. The other thing of course that I have already covered is the fact that they are so closely tied into the Kremlin and naturally wish to curry favor in that quarter.

Now, Mr. Nemtsov. In his case the story comes completely apart once you start examining the details. If the motivation for telling an untrue story is something that concerns you, then I do not shrink from suggesting that it has been a sense of loyalty or of obligation or even gratitude to those in the *Alfa* camp—the individuals and the *Alfa* companies—who have been generous financial supporters of his party. We do not know precisely how much, but we know that it was a lot; more than the contributions made in Western countries. What did you make of Mr. Nemtsov, members of the jury? He was a robust, determined politician. Like all politicians he was capable of making speeches. But the witness box is not the place to make speeches. The silent evidence of the photographs, the photographs taken in Mr. Berezovsky's office in April 2004, do not exactly show Mr. Berezovsky threatening Mr. Nemtsov, do they? Or on holiday on Mr. Berezovsky's yacht off the cost of Eilat. Cordial friendly relations. But the fact is that Mr. Nemtsov is as two-faced as a politician can ever be. He laps up the hospitality of a man he does not genuinely believe was guilty of threatening him. He appears to have cordial relations with him, he accepts all of Mr. Berezovsky's generous hospitality but then he goes and digs in the knife, and twists it in the witness box: apparently, if what he says in his evidence and said in his *Pravda* interview was true, out of some misplaced resentment that Mr. Berezovsky was somehow the man who prevented him today being president; prevented him being President Nemtsov in the Kremlin in 2006.

Members of the jury, let me sum him up in a single sentence: a vain man capable of infinite self-deception. Now for Mr. Potanin. Well, Mr. Potanin, you may think, as this trial has turned out, is the man who never was. A witness whose recollection of events nine years ago is so vague that you cannot rely upon it to prove an allegation against Mr. Berezovsky. I will deal with this in more detail in just a moment. But it is apparent, is it not, that his memory is so sketchy that it cannot be relied on, and that in one respect what he recalls now about what happened all of nine years ago is fatally contaminated by his fundamentally mistaken belief about one matter, and that is whether Mr. Berezovsky had a financial interest in the Svyazinvest bid. He says that he did. The defendants on their own case make it clear that Mr. Berezovsky did not. And that is not surprising, because he was, as he told you, outside of business then and in politics as Deputy Secretary of the Security Council.

Why do I call Mr. Potanin "the man who never was?" Well, he is not a witness that I have been able to cross-examine. And my Lord will give you a direction about how you should therefore approach his evidence. But as I say, the story speaks of Mr. Potanin, and why we did not see him speaks volumes about Russian life and the interplay between politics and business today. As I say, 9 o'clock, summoned to see the Prime Minister. The following morning we are told by the defendants, by their in-house counsel, that Mr. Potanin would not be available all day; in other words that the meeting would last all day. But then, presumably, he tells the Prime Minister, "Oh, but I have an urgent appointment to give evidence in London," and the Prime Minister says, "Well, tell me about the case," and Mr. Potanin says: "Well, the defendant is Mr. Berezovsky and I am helping Mr. Fridman with my evidence in that case." You can imagine how the Prime Minister behaves. The all-day meeting ends at about lunchtime and Mr. Potanin is able to give evidence, and only the fact that the defendants could not get the video link to work from this court prevented him from doing so. It puts me at a very serious disadvantage. It puts you at a very serious disadvantage. But you must, with respect, give me the benefit of the doubt in assessing Mr. Potanin's evidence because it has never been tested. I will address you in a moment about why, even on what we currently have, it would be wrong to believe what he says about a threat, if that is what he really said, but you must, as I say, give me the benefit of the doubt. You must not—because it is the defendants who bear the burden of showing that these serious allegations are correct—you must not, we say, proceed on the basis of such immeasurably flimsy evidence.

Well, now let me turn and deal with them in a little more detail bit by bit. Mr. Fridman first of all. The alleged threat to him by Mr. Berezovsky over *Kommersant*, supposedly in June 1999, in other words two years of course after Gazprom and Svyazinvest. I am taking them out of chronological order because this is really the key allegation, and the others you may think are really so much makeweight. Now, Mr. Berezovsky told you that he was not running the negotiations for the purchase of *Kommersant*. He was candid about telling you that, apart from one meeting at the start with Mr. Yakovlev in Amsterdam, all the negotiating had been left to his partner with the unpronounceable name, "Badri," and the negotiations had been conducted with Mr. Yakovlev and Mr. Badri in the United States and California. So it was the other side of the globe to Mr. Berezovsky who was in Russia. If you believe that, and given as I say the distance between Moscow and California, there was no reason for Mr. Berezovsky to ever contact Mr. Fridman and no reason why he should not, as he says, have left it all to Mr. Badri. And besides, members of the jury, if Mr. Berezovsky had somehow wanted to get *Alfa Bank* out of the race for *Kommersant*, is it not much more likely that what he would have done would have been to have had a quiet word with Mr. Aven and persuade him, Mr. Fridman, and *Alfa Bank* to leave the field? After all, Mr. Berezovsky had known Mr. Aven for almost 30 years. They were close personal friends for many years, Mr. Aven told you this. Even now, according to Mr. Aven, the friendship is not completely at an end. So he would not have needed to threaten Mr. Fridman. He need only have picked up the telephone to his old friend Mr. Aven.

Well, the next point—possibly—certainly the only Russian words that I know, I do not know if they will ever come in useful if I ever go as a tourist to Russia, "my vas zamochim." I suspect I would be very ill advised to use them going round St. Petersburg or going round Red Square. We know what they mean. But let us just go back to the beginning. Initially, as we have seen from the correspondence, it was said that the threat that Mr. Berezovsky had uttered had been simply to bring commercial pressure to bear. That is what Herbert Smith say in their first letter in December, and that there had been no threat of violence. They expressly say that. Mr. Fridman does not claim that the phrase "my vas zamochim" was used for at least another nine months. We do not get that until a court document at the end of September 2005.

Now, if the words "my vas zamochim" had been used, they would have plainly suggested violence, and indeed more than mere violence, fatal violence: rubbing out. And as the judge pointed out—and there is no answer to this point—Putin in September 1999, when he used these words, was not saying that if he caught a Chechen on the lavatory he was going to apply commercial pressure to him. And yet, if what is being said by Mr. Fridman and if what was said by Herbert Smith in their letter of September 9th are consistent, that is the ludicrous result that Mr. Fridman arrives at. So he has to wriggle out of that difficulty, and he tries to do so by pretending that the word has changed its meaning, curiously, at some stage from criminal slang "to waste or exterminate" to a business term meaning simply "to apply commercial pressure."

Now, members of the jury, we are back in 1999. The threat is said to have been in June 1999; the threat from Mr. Berezovsky to Mr. Fridman (sic) in which Mr. Berezovsky used the words "my vas zamochim." Mr. Putin uses them three months later. Now, I mention that because one wants to try to form a view as to how they were understood in Russia in 1999. You will dismiss as absurd the suggestion that because Mr. Berezovsky had used these words to Mr. Fridman it somehow triggered Mr. Putin's outburst in September 1999. That was what Mr. Fridman was trying to say at one stage. But all of this is nonsense. Why can you be so confident that it is nonsense? Well, so far as I know none of you speak Russian, but we can be sure what the words meant in 1999 by looking at the reputable newspaper *Vedomosti* on September 28th of that year. *Vedomosti* was so taken aback by what Mr. Putin had said that it actually becomes their quote of the week. They refer to Prime Minister Putin starting to speak like a long-serving convicted criminal of a modest rank. The fact that this language was so stark is emphasized by the fact that, even when he first speaks the words, Mr. Putin hesitates for a moment—as you will see at the top of the page, the first line—and says, "Pardon my language." Then he is feeling obviously slightly ashamed of himself for using such vile language because the following day he apologizes for what, as you will see in the second paragraph, is described by *Vedomosti* as this "unpremeditated use of prison slang," saying he was not yet an experienced public speaker. You will recall he had become Prime Minister the previous month. Then you will see the last paragraph but one: "Primakov, with his educated highbrow vocabulary, can forget all about it; the prime minister's political opponents will have to urgently hire speech-writers from street gangs, or at the very least study the very modest dictionary of Russian prison slang."

Members of the jury, we can be sure, can we not, that this coarse Russian prison slang had not, as Mr. Fridman suggests, changed its meaning into a term used in the business community meaning "to apply commercial pressure."

Now, let us just think about what Mr. Shields' advances as an important part of the support for Mr. Fridman's account: the supposed mention of the alleged threat to Mr. Aven. Well, if that were true, it might be persuasive. But we say it in fact underlines that not only is Mr. Aven not telling the truth, but the need to get Mr. Aven to give you untruthful evidence corroborates that Mr. Fridman's evidence is untrue. Why do I say that? Well, first of all the evidence that Mr. Aven gives that Mr. Fridman—who was in the next-door office to him—had mentioned this right from the beginning, has never been mentioned in any of the solicitor's letters. Very significantly, members of the jury, Mr. Aven was not listed as a witness when the defendants' solicitors were asked in July last year by the court to say who their witnesses were going to be. There is a very important point in the preparation of cases for trial when each sides' solicitors have to answer this question: "So far as you know at this stage, what witnesses of fact do you intend to call at the trial?" The three names given were Fridman, Potanin, and Nemtsov. No mention of Mr. Aven at all.

The claim that Mr. Fridman told Mr. Aven about the alleged threat is nowhere in the correspondence, is nowhere in the court documents, and only emerges for the first time when they put in their witness statements in February this year, 16 months after Mr. Berezovsky first complained. Do you not think, if this evidence were true, it would have been mentioned at the start; mentioned in the correspondence or mentioned in the court documents? Is it not clear from the timing of its emergence that this is another attempt to dredge up an untruthful case to get Mr. Fridman out of the hole he had dug himself into. It is not just the timing, is it, members of the jury, either? The fact is that Mr. Fridman and Mr. Aven then, having cobbled together the story to try to support Mr. Fridman's credibility, failed to get their stories right. As so often happens with liars in the courts, they are exposed by telling stories which differ in the detail. Mr. Fridman, as we know, claims that Mr. Berezovsky used the word, or words, "my vas zamochim." But Mr. Aven, as we know and he accepts, said in the original version of his witness statement in Russian that the word used by Mr. Berezovsky was the ordinary word for destroy, "unichtozhit," a word which carries the range of meanings that "destroy" does in English.

Of course, if "unichtozhit" had been used by Mr. Berezovsky, if Mr. Fridman is not telling the truth about "my vas zamochim," and if it was a commonplace phrase meaning only "to apply commercial pressure"—in other words run-of-the-mill *Alfa Bank* commercial dealings—then there would have been nothing out of the ordinary about this incident and no reason for Mr. Fridman to mention it to Mr. Aven.

So that is why, in a nutshell, Mr. Fridman is forced into saying that his solicitors were at fault in saying that threats of commercial pressure were so commonplace in Russia that no one would think about them twice. He has to disown that letter written on the defendants' instructions because it does not square with there being anything so remarkable about Mr. Berezovsky's supposed threat to Mr. Fridman to have Mr. Fridman mention it to Mr. Aven. Then, finally, members of the jury, is it really credible that if this had all happened Mr. Aven would have gone on socializing with Mr. Berezovsky on his visits to London? The dinners at a swank Chinese restaurant in successive years, in 2003 and 2004, at which Mr. Berezovsky was the host and at which their respective wives were present on one occasion. Mrs. Aven is present in 2003, Mrs. Berezovsky in 2004. Not just business meetings but social occasions.

Let me turn now to Mr. Nemtsov. As I have said a moment ago, in reality the heart of this case is Mr. Fridman and whether you think Mr. Berezovsky threatened Mr. Fridman. The other matters, you may think, are secondary but I am going to deal with them because they are serious allegations and they need dealing with in detail. I have said a bit about Mr. Nemtsov. I am not going to repeat it. But as we look at his evidence, can I just ask you to remember these facts? He continues to have frequent dealings with Mr. Berezovsky even during this litigation. Indeed, on his own account they were discussing affairs in Ukraine as recently as the end of last year, 2005. They are not just discussing politics, as we have seen from the photographs.

Looking at Mr. Nemtsov's relations now, not with Mr. Berezovsky but with Mr. Fridman, Mr. Fridman has known Mr. Nemtsov well since the early 1990s. They are of roughly similar age and Mr. Fridman said on Friday that he would call Mr. Nemtsov a friend. We know from that television transcript that Mr. Fridman acknowledges that at any time he can easily pick up the phone, arrange a meeting and explain that there is an issue on which he needs Mr. Nemtsov's support. You will probably remember how, when he says that on television, Mr. Soloviov says, "And then I expect that Mr. Nemtsov asks you for money." And that is precisely what happened.

I am going to look at Mr. Nemtsov's story in a bit of detail because I have to do so to explain to you why I suggest it is simply not worthy of belief. Mr. Shields said that there was an inherent logic in Mr. Nemtsov's account. I suggest there is not. On the contrary, it is when you look at the logic that you see at once that Mr. Nemtsov is an out-and-out liar. I am going to take a number of matters separately to make that good. First of all, the abandonment by Mr. Nemtsov of his initial account that Mr. Chernomyrdin had actually signed the agreement appointing or approving Mr. Berezovsky to be chairman of Gazprom. In his witness statement, which you do not have, so I will remind you—he said that the agreement had already been signed, but the document only required Mr. Nemtsov's signature to have Mr. Berezovsky's candidature finally approved for consideration by the Gazprom board. So it only required Mr. Nemtsov for Mr. Berezovsky's candidature to be finally approved. And he went on to say that, after being shown the agreement which had already been signed by Mr. Chernomyrdin, he telephoned Mr. Chernomyrdin and Mr. Chernomyrdin confirmed that he had signed the document. Signed the document; not, as he pretended in that piece of pantomime when he held up the clipping from *The Moscow Times*, simply endorsed his signature on the back.

Let us think about Mr. Shields's "inherent logic." On the account that Mr. Nemtsov gave in the witness evidence it makes no sense for Mr. Berezovsky to fly to China in pursuit of Mr. Chernomyrdin. He already has the signature.

Now, the penny must have dropped about the lack of logic in Mr. Nemtsov's story at some stage between February 21st of this year when he saw his witness statement and the interview he gave to the *Pravda* reporter; because the problem for Mr. Nemtsov in changing his story to make it appear, in Mr. Shields's words, that Mr. Chernomyrdin was sitting on the fence, is that it all starts to unravel. The logic brings down the building. You will remember what he said on Friday: no suggestion that Mr. Chernomyrdin signed the agreement as opposed to simply scribbling his signature on the back. What he is saying is that Mr. Chernomyrdin was indecisive. You will remember the words, "Maybe I support it, maybe not." Not, "I have signed the agreement." Now, if Mr. Chernomyrdin had never signed the document nor made up his mind—in other words the revised Nemtsov version—Mr. Berezovsky never got off first base. He had a reason to travel to China but he did not have a reason to threaten Mr. Nemtsov. The whole story collapses. The logic breaks down. There was no need to threaten Mr. Nemtsov because without the support of Mr. Chernomyrdin, which Mr. Berezovsky flew to China to get, Mr. Berezovsky had never reached the point where Mr. Nemtsov was the only obstacle. That is the main point.

There are a group of points about the details. Details are very important. They cannot just be brushed away. The way in which we expose liars in this court is by cross-examination, and liars are exposed because they cannot get the details right. Mr. Shields said this was quite a simple tale. Well, members of the jury, it was not so simple that Mr. Nemtsov could remember the details of an invented account. And when caught, what did he do? He simply blustered that it did not matter.

Well, members of the jury, it does matter. How often did we hear him blustering that it did not matter? Was it up to a dozen? Would not an honest witness, trying to give you a truthful account of what had happened, be very concerned to get the details right? Pause for a moment and contrast this Mr. Nemtsov with Mr. Berezovsky. Mr. Berezovsky realized after he had left the witness box that he had made a minor error, you may think, about Mr. Viakhirev being both chairman and CEO of Gazprom. At the time he made the statement he asked Mr. Shields to correct him. And when he realized he was wrong—after Mr. Shields had failed to correct him—he did not just let it fester; he volunteered the error and went straight back into the witness box to put it right. Let us just think: if you were giving evidence in court and you had muddled the detail to the degree that Mr. Nemtsov did, would you think it did not matter?

I will take them one by one. The order in which he called Viakhirev and Chernomyrdin. Remember, this is a simple tale, says Mr. Shields. All the details vary according to the stage that Mr. Nemtsov describes them. And it really will not do, will it, to say, "Well, when push came to shove he always said that Mr. Berezovsky had threatened him, and all the details do not matter." He was not such a liar that he was caught in anything other than the details. And in all the details he was caught. The order of calling Viakhirev and Chernomyrdin. His witness statement: first Chernomyrdin and then Viakhirev. *Pravda*: Viakhirev and then Chernomyrdin. Order reversed. His evidence-in-chief when questioned by Mr. Shields: Viakhirev, then calling Mr. Chernomyrdin. Cross-examination by me on Monday: now he does not remember at all. Members of the jury, what sort of witness is that? Contradictory, and then saying he just does not recall. If it is true that he does not recall that, can you place any weight on any part of his recollection at all?

Next point of detail. Who was it who told Mr. Nemtsov, "I hope you will make the right decision?" In the witness statement in February he does not suggest either Mr. Viakhirev or Mr. Chernomyrdin spoke those words to him. So the words are an invention for the *Komsomolskaya Pravda* reporter in the sauna when, for the first time, it is said that Mr. Chernomyrdin avoided answering the question whether he supported Mr. Berezovsky for the chairmanship, and told Mr. Nemtsov, "I know you will make the right decision." But Mr. Nemtsov cannot get this right because he told Mr. Shields that it was Mr. Viakhirev who said, "I know you will make the right decision."

Another way in which that witness box has seen liars caught out is gilding the lily. I know you will all know what I mean by that: the embellishment of details to make evidence appear more plausible. Here, the gilding of the lily that goes on is in at least two respects. First of all, the suggestion that the threat was made in the street outside the embassy. The defendants' case in the court documents is that there was a discussion inside, in the Russian Embassy in Peking, and the threat was made there. What Mr. Nemtsov said was that "finally when we stopped our discussion ..." This is obviously in the embassy. "...And we went into the street, Mr. Berezovsky said 'I will destroy you as a politician.'" No threat to use the media; "I will destroy you as a politician."

The important point is that this is completely new. His witness statement says nothing about the discussion in the embassy ending and then their going into the street and then the threat being made. It has never been suggested before. As I said, the case was that it took place at a meeting in the presence of Mr. Chernomyrdin in the embassy. So perhaps that is a way of trying to explain on the defendant's part why there is no support from Mr. Chernomyrdin for what they say.

The claim clearly took Mr. Shields completely by surprise since he never put it—as he should have done if it were his case and he knew it was his case—to Mr. Berezovsky in cross-examination so that he could answer it.

Next, gilding of the lily. The claim that Mr. Nemtsov and Mr. Berezovsky discussed the chairmanship of Gazprom on their trip on the Yangtze River. That is to the Three Gorges dam, which as it happens I think has opened only this weekend. Again, never mentioned before, ever. Again, not put by Mr. Shields to Mr. Berezovsky, and not in Mr. Nemtsov's witness statement even though in that statement he referred to going there to discuss issues of possible Russian/Chinese co-operation in respect to this project, with Chinese officials. So that is what they were discussing, the dam project. It was not, as I suggest, Gazprom; nor is it said that it was Gazprom, still less that a threat was made on that or any other occasion.

Finally, we have the dagger thrust of a previously unmentioned accusation against Mr. Berezovsky, a matter so far outside the defendant's case that it requires Mr. Berezovsky to have to be recalled to deal with it. Can I just remind you how this all arose? Towards the end of Mr. Nemtsov's cross-examination, when it must have been clear to him, as I suggest it was to everyone else in court, that his story of a threat had come completely apart, he attempted to resuscitate it by claiming that not only had Mr. Berezovsky threatened him but Mr. Berezovsky had also carried out the threat.

Now, never mentioned before, never in the court documents, never in his evidence to Mr. Shields; an invention, I suggest, and a last-minute invention. It was not put of course by Mr. Shields to Mr. Berezovsky; an accusation we suggest completely without substance. Mr. Shields must have been taken by surprise yet again by the unending imagination of his witness. And it required Mr. Berezovsky to be recalled. The dry run, you may think—if that is the appropriate language to use about an interview in a sauna bath—but the dry run for Mr. Nemtsov's evidence in his interview with the *Komsomolskaya Pravda* journalist, did make an accusation of this sort, but it has never been part of Mr. Shields' case.

Let me explain why it was pure invention and why it is without substance. It is claimed in melodramatic terms that Mr. Berezovsky set a journalist called Dorenko on Mr. Nemtsov's trail. Now, Mr. Berezovsky accepted in his evidence that on one occasion he did use the media, used ORT, and that was in the vital 1996 election in which all the businessmen—including Mr. Fridman as you have seen from the *Izvestia* letter—were determined to keep the Communists out.

Mr. Shields read a passage to you from the evidence referring to the goal; that the goal was simply the re-election of President Yeltsin in the

1996 elections. And on that occasion, as it happens, Mr. Berezovsky was supported by Mr. Fridman and by *Alfa*, who, as you have heard, at that stage were indeed five percent shareholders in ORT.

Now, it is in that context that all the answers Mr. Shields read to you were given: the context of the use of ORT in the 1996 election. But it is quite wrong to suggest from that that in other political contexts Mr. Berezovsky has abused the media. We know and we can be sure that he has not, from Mr. Fridman's own account. Mr. Berezovsky bought *Kommersant* in 1999 and in 2004 on the broadcast Mr. Fridman himself was praising it as having golden quills for its journalists and being an epoch in Russian journalism. He could not have said that if its proprietor was manipulating the newspaper to do his work. So do not be confused into thinking that because Mr. Berezovsky, as he has candidly said all along, used ORT, along with Mr. Fridman, to promote Mr. Yeltsin in the 1996 election, he has manipulated the media other than that. On Mr. Fridman's own account he has not. Well, I mentioned why it was that Mr. Berezovsky had to go back into the witness box. Mr. Nemtsov then stepped right outside both his witness statement and the court case.

Then, what was this supposed media campaign, orchestrated by Mr. Berezovsky against Mr. Nemtsov? You will remember Mr. Shields went to the back of the court and took instructions and spoke to Mr. Nemtsov, and it amounted to this, as put to Berezovsky: there was one article, on a date which Mr. Nemtsov could not remember, about his having an affair with a prostitute. It was not suggested that that story was invented or untrue.

Now, just think, members of the jury, if the media got hold of a story like that, the Deputy Prime Minister running around with a prostitute, whether it is the media here or the media in Russia, they are bound to run with it. We know that from very recent experience; not of course with a prostitute, but we know that from our own dear Deputy Prime Minister. The media does not have to be told to run with this story; if they get it they will publish it. And it would be wrong in a democracy for them to sit on it. So that is all Mr. Nemtsov's supposed media campaign amounts to. Mr. Berezovsky remembered the article but was emphatic that he played no part in the revelations. Members of the jury, there is not the slightest reason to think that he did. And you should reject the suggestion made by Mr. Nemtsov as yet another part of the embellishment of his story and the attempt to keep it going by the introduction of untrue details which previously had never been mentioned.

Now, let me direct your attention to this key meeting in France; the meeting, incidentally, that was referred to by Mr. Potanin some six days after it had happened rather than in the press conference that we looked at last night; whereas in this witness statement of course in 2006 he is talking about events back in July 1997: a lapse of nearly nine years. The auction was due on July 25th, a Friday. The meeting in France was over Wednesday, July 23rd, the evening, and the morning of Thursday 24th. In other words the day before and two days before the bids were going to be looked at. Mr. Chubais, the Deputy Prime Minister, was on holiday in the South of France. Mr. Potanin, Mr. Gusinsky and Mr. Berezovsky flew together to see him in the South of France. Mr. Berezovsky told you that Mr. Gusinsky and Mr. Potanin had invited Mr. Berezovsky. He of course was then Deputy Secretary of the Security Council and was temporarily out of the business arena; his affairs were in the hands of trustees; he was in the government. But naturally, being in the government, he was concerned with the result of the auction not with the result in what he called a "new war breaking out," a new war between businessmen.

Now, Mr. Shields suggests that Mr. Berezovsky's account of what happened involves Mr. Berezovsky suggesting that the meeting was a carve-up and Mr. Chubais corrupt. And Mr. Berezovsky said that simply was not so. We know it is not so because we have Mr. Potanin's account just a matter of days after the meeting. Mr. Potanin refutes Mr. Shields' suggestion that there was a sinister carve-up going on at this meeting in the South of France; he confirms that the visit took place; he says it is a more complex situation than has been described and states that it would be an absurd situation for the businessmen to not try to come to an agreement. So there was no improper carve-up going on here, still less under the nose of a corrupt Deputy Prime Minister, Anatoly Chubais. All groups always try to reach some sort of a compromise, and if a compromise cannot be found then the competition begins.

You will remember that Gusinsky had a strong claim on Svyazinvest because he was its creator, the man who turned 88 individual small telephone companies into one large one. "In this case there was a need to ensure that the state was committed to playing by the rules at its announcements, that would have fair competition at the auction. When we realized that no compromises could be achieved and the government was firmly committed to holding the auction in this format, attempts were abandoned to reach a compromise."

Then these important words: "I see nothing odd, nothing odd, about the fact of business people entering negotiations in order to form alliances in respect to certain objects. In this case, an agreement was not reached."

That is Mr. Potanin on July 31st, a week after the meeting on the 24th. And what he said at the time is completely inconsistent, is it not, with his rewritten version of history later, or at any rate Mr. Shields' rewritten version of history, which involves Mr. Berezovsky trying to take part in a corrupt carve-up and, when the carve-up fails, threatening Mr. Potanin. Just contrast "nothing odd about what was going on," said Mr. Potanin, with what he says now.

Today it is clear, you will see, now thankfully you have the witness statement, that Mr. Potanin's memory, which is sketchy at best, is completely contaminated by his mistaken belief that Mr. Berezovsky had a financial interest in Mr. Gusinsky's consortium, the one that was competing against Mr. Potanin; because if you look at the witness statement, Mr. Potanin says this:

"As I understood it then, Mr. Berezovsky was assisting Mr. Gusinsky in connection with the auction as he had a financial interest in the auction being won by the consortium of Mr. Gusinsky."

Well, that is completely wrong. We know it is wrong for two reasons. Firstly, Mr. Berezovsky was out of the government, he was the Deputy Secretary of the Security Council, and the second reason that we know it is wrong is that it is accepted by Mr. Fridman and *Alfa Bank* in their own defense court document in this case that Mr. Berezovsky was, and I quote, "not a financial party to the Gusinsky consortium."

So Mr. Potanin has got it wrong. He has got it all wrong. Mr. Potanin's evidence, I suggest—even if it were not at odds, at total odds, with what he said at the time of the press conference—is so lacking in detail when you get to see the statement on paper in front of you, that you cannot possibly be confident that in the account that he gives you now, nine years later and without seeing him give evidence and be cross-examined, Mr. Berezovsky made the threat he claims. Remember, the defendants have to prove it; Mr. Berezovsky does not have to disprove it.

You cannot, I suggest, be satisfied that Mr. Berezovsky crossed the line from what may well have been a strong advocacy of Mr. Gusinsky's moral claim to a share of Svyazinvest because he was its creator, to making a threat.

Now, if there is one thing we have learned from this case, it is the importance of words. Without Mr. Potanin telling you what Mr. Berezovsky said, you cannot begin to judge whether they were a threat. That is why it is important to look and see if Mr. Potanin can tell you what the words were, which were spoken by Mr. Berezovsky. And the short answer to that is that he cannot. That is why I say this witness statement, upon examination, does not add up to a row of beans. All that he says is that he had an understanding, formed over various meetings—in other words not simply the meeting in the South of France but other meetings—the details of which he is completely unable to tell us; he had formed an understanding over various meetings of what he thought was Mr. Berezovsky's opinion.

The wording is so extraordinary, so vague, so unspecific, that one cannot, I suggest, attach any weight to it at all. "During the course of the meetings ..." "...during the course of spring and early summer 1997, I met with Mr. Gusinsky on a number of occasions..." "I am not able now to recall the location and date of such meetings; however, I do recall that Mr. Berezovsky was present at a number of these meetings." Terribly, terribly vague, and sketchy to the extreme. It is almost as though Mr. Potanin is unwilling to provide any details in case he is cross-examined about them and caught in a lie. Alternatively, one just does not know as I have not had the opportunity to cross-examine him—it may be that he just does not remember, as he claims. Well, if his memory is so defective nine years later, you have to go back to what he said at the time seven days after the meeting in the South of France, when he said, "There is nothing odd about it."

"During the course of the meetings to discuss the auction I formed an understanding that if the companies associated with me were to participate in the auction then in Mr. Berezovsky's opinion I would be going against his interests and Mr. Berezovsky would use his political power and media resources to inflict harm on my image as a businessman, which would affect my capacity to conduct business." Well, this is not a case where it is suggested that Mr. Berezovsky made a threat and carried it out. Indeed, we are not told what Mr. Berezovsky said at any of these meetings, so that you can judge whether it really was a threat. The wording is extraordinary: "I formed an understanding about Mr. Berezovsky's opinion ..." It is language that really is wholly inappropriate for a witness who is trying to establish that he was threatened, and seriously threatened. You will see, "I am not able ... to recall the exact meetings on which he made such statements nor the precise words which were used." Well, is that not the end of it, members of the jury? If he cannot recall the precise words then you cannot tell whether they were a threat. At least Mr. Nemtsov claimed to be able to recall the precise words; Mr. Potanin cannot.

And Mr. Potanin—and this is in another document that you do not have, but take it from me it is in a court document—the defendants have stated in a court document that Mr. Potanin cannot recall the precise number of meetings that took place between him and Mr. Berezovsky, or their dates, or their location, apart from the French one—because he has been asked this specifically—and is he not able to recall even the precise words used at the meeting in France, other than the fact that he wants to make it clear that Mr. Berezovsky had not made threats of a physical nature.

Now you have seen this statement, you can see that it is not worth the paper it is written on. It is hopelessly insufficient to prove this serious charge of a threat, even before you take account of my inability to cross-examine Mr. Potanin and what I say is the benefit of the doubt that you must give me on that account, and it is hopelessly insufficient even before you look at the totally inconsistent account that he gave at the press conference when questioned by the Voice of America journalist.

There was not, as Mr. Shields suggests, a carve-up. Mr. Potanin made that clear. There was nothing odd about what took place. The point of the meeting is as he described. So if there was no carve-up, then Mr. Shields' case collapses, that it was resentment on Mr. Berezovsky's part that there was no carve-up, and so he threatened Mr. Potanin. No carve-up, no threat, not worth the paper it is written on.

So, members of the jury, remorselessly we reach the stage of damages, question 3 on your question paper. The audience in England and Wales for this broadcast on NTV may, I accept, have been relatively small compared with the number of people who read a tabloid newspaper. But for Mr. Berezovsky it was the single audience—small though it was—that mattered: namely, the Russians and the Russian speakers in England where he has made his home. How they perceive him is naturally of the greatest possible importance to him. You would not expect anything different.

Now that Mr. Fridman of all people should have chosen to make these remarks is especially damaging because people know—Mr. Fridman has said this—that he and Mr. Berezovsky have done business together in the past. If they know that and then they hear this allegation from Mr. Fridman, they will assume that he speaks from direct experience of having business dealings with Mr. Berezovsky and that he therefore is in a position to know and to tell the truth. Well, they would be right about the first; they would not be right to assume that he told the truth. Of course if the world ends up believing this about Mr. Berezovsky, that he is a man that goes through life threatening people with violence, that is going to suit Mr. Putin very nicely, is it not? Because it is going to enable him to undermine Mr. Berezovsky's public credibility when he protests at human rights abuses.

You have seen the solicitors' correspondence. I can go over it briefly; I will not ask you to look it up. It shows that all Mr. Berezovsky wanted at the beginning was quite simply an apology. But so far as Mr. Fridman was concerned, "sorry" proved to be the hardest word. An apology was obstinately refused. The solicitors engaged by Mr. Fridman and *Alfa Bank* appeared to regard the complaint with contempt, as having no weight or substance at all, a song and dance about nothing. And since an apology was refused, Mr. Berezovsky's only option was to begin an action for damages.

You may not know this but the English court—unlike some foreign courts—cannot order a defendant to apologize. So when a defendant says, "I am not going to apologize. That is that. You are making a lot of fuss about nothing," the claimant then has only one choice—to bring an action for damages—for money, compensation—in order to achieve vindication. I will explain in a moment what I mean by vindication. It is in that way that the defendants have to prove that their defamatory allegations are true. As I have said already—but I repeat it because it is so fundamental—it is not for Mr. Berezovsky to prove that they are untrue.

Can I now, as I come towards the end, just rattle through—I will do it as quickly as I can, but I may be another ten minutes or so—the relevant considerations in assessing damages?

First of all, the gravity of the libel. Not just a suggestion of using threats, which would be bad enough, but a suggestion of using threats with violence; and not just the suggestion of using threatening violence on one occasion but of doing so habitually, making it a way of life.

The second factor, the scale of publication. You are going to have to form a rough estimate of the number of people who watched the program. Of course, not all the potential subscribers would have watched at the same time, but it was a peak viewing time, and you know from the evidence that you have heard that it is likely that it was being watched by more than one individual. In other words, that the subscriber had his friends or family in to watch the program.

All the witnesses agreed about its popularity and even Mr. Fridman accepted that it was very well known. Mr. Voronkov said he tuned in on a regular basis. It is true that Mr. Litvinenko said that he did not particularly like watching Russian television, but the evidence otherwise was consistent that people naturally felt homesick for Russia, were interested in continuing political news and debate from Russia and NTV's program *The Duel* was just the kind of thing that they would watch. I cannot do any better than to repeat Mr. Voronkov's words that it was a primetime program which is of significant interest to the Russian-speaking audience. Not at least of course because Mr. Soloviov is so well known. He was clearly a very, very well-known and popular interviewer and talkshow host.

Now, let us just rattle through the evidence that we have heard of who watched it. There were Mr. and Mrs. Voronkov and Mr. Dubov. Mr. Shields cannot brush them aside simply because they are employees. The way in which an employer is viewed by his employees is naturally very important to him. It is perhaps the most insidious quarter in which an employer's reputation can be undermined. So Mr. Voronkov and Mr. Dubov and Mrs. Voronkov are important so far as Mr. Berezovsky is concerned. There is potentially a large audience. The figures from the Home Office show the number of Russians settling in the UK. The figure has doubled between 2002 and 2003: settlement now appears to be at the rate of over 4,000 a year. There are two listing magazines—Russian London Info and Seven Plus Seven, the magazine published in Germany but sold here.

So you have a picture which emerges of a substantial expatriate Russian community eager to keep up with affairs in their homeland, and what better way to do that than through NTV and the very popular Mr. Soloviov and *The Duel*.

The third factor: the injury to Mr. Berezovsky's feelings at being treated like this, including being put through a public trial when a simple apology would have sufficed. He told you, when he was cross-examined by Mr. Shields, that watching the program with his wife he was shocked and angry. It must, you would think, contribute to his anger, his embarrassment and his distress that his wife was alongside him as he watched it, and Mr. Voronkov told you that the following day he was outraged and upset. That outrage and upset has been immeasurably aggravated by the conduct of this trial. It has been a personal ordeal. It has added to the damage to his reputation as Mr. Fridman and his witnesses claim every opportunity they can to blacken his name: he is not just a threatening bully but an out and out liar.

I say "Mr. Fridman and his witnesses," just remember for example Mr. Fridman making an untrue allegation—something Mr. Shields did not dignify even to mention in his closing speech—the claim that Mr. Berezovsky had even threatened Mr. Soloviov. Well, not only was that a completely new allegation never made before, we can be sure it is totally untrue: an invention from the witness box to try to smear Mr. Berezovsky's name in your estimation. If—and it is a big "if"—Mr. Fridman's solicitors sitting there had thought for one moment that it was true and they could prove it, it would have been part of his case. If Mr. Shields had known about it at the time he was cross-examining Mr.

Berezovsky it would have been part of his duty as a barrister to put it to Mr. Berezovsky so that he could answer the charge.

If it had been true and not just a spiteful invention in the witness box by Mr. Fridman, Mr. Fridman could have called on his longtime close friend of 15 years, going back to university days, Mr. Soloviov to give evidence about it. Mr. Soloviov could have come to London like the other witnesses. We know from Mr. Fridman that he remains in very good health and if there was any truth to it, you can bet that he could have given evidence to support him. It is an indication of the absolute desperation that Mr. Fridman and *Alfa Bank* have been driven to in their efforts to justify this allegation: making it up as they go along, but in a way that could not be more calculated to cause distress to Mr. Berezovsky as he sits in this court having to listen to it and the damage to his reputation. And Mr. Aven behaved—taking his lead from Mr. Fridman—just as disgracefully. He made in the course of his evidence a completely new accusation about Mr. Berezovsky having threatened an unidentified finance minister. Again, never mentioned before, never put by Mr. Shields to Mr. Berezovsky. Indeed, you can test how absurd it was—an insult to your intelligence you may think—to make the allegation when he could not tell you the name of the minister who was threatened, the occasion, the date, or what was said.

These are witnesses who are prepared, I repeat, are prepared to make it up as they go along, thinking that they can come to London, stand before a London jury and that what they say will be convincing if they say it firmly and strongly enough.

The next matter is the thoroughly insulting way in which Mr. Fridman has throughout treated Mr. Berezovsky's complaint. He and his solicitors have attempted to brush it off, to treat Mr. Berezovsky as a man with no basis for a complaint. Indeed, it was almost as though he, Mr. Fridman, had the complaint not Mr. Berezovsky. Do you remember how he grumbled when I cross-examined him about having been taken away from his office for two whole days for what he called a relatively small matter? I asked him in riposte: could he not see it from Mr. Berezovsky's point of view? To which I received the arrogant answer, "I do not know what his point is." He has gone on the counterattack. He has accused Mr. Berezovsky quite unjustifiably of using this court as a tribute to promote his personal and political faith.

You may think that Mr. Fridman does not need to worry about all of this and that is the reason for his arrogance, because Mr. Berezovsky is in exile and the only possible downside is an award of damages which will be, for Mr. Fridman and *Alfa Bank*, infinitesimal compared to their assets. So what happens? He jets in and out of London for just long enough for him to give evidence and then he departs, showing no interest in this case and no sympathy whatsoever for Mr. Berezovsky's predicament of which he has been the cause.

Finally, Mr. Berezovsky's entitlement to vindication. I said I would tell you what is meant by vindication. It is this: the amount of damages that you fix must be large enough to show the world that Mr. Fridman's allegation is completely false, that it is an out and out lie. It must be a figure large enough for Mr. Berezovsky to be able to point to if anyone were to say to him, "Well, that is what Mr. Fridman said, that you were a man who habitually threatened people with violence." He has to be able to say to such a doubter, to someone who thinks there is no smoke without fire, "Well that is what Mr. Fridman said about me, but just look at the opinion of a London jury. They awarded me X amount of damages and that sum shows how untrue Mr. Fridman's allegations were." The precise amount of that sum is a matter for you. I am not going to say anything about it, other than that it should not be as much as 6.5 million—those are Moscow rates not London rates—but it obviously has to be substantial to form the function of a vindication.

Now just looking at the questions. Number 1: "Are the words complained of in the program defamatory of Mr. Berezovsky?" I do not expect you will hesitate very long about that. Even in Mr. Shields' case they are plainly defamatory in that they suggest the threat—it goes further than that: it is threats of violence and habitual. "Have the defendants proved to you . . ." I emphasize those words: "Have the defendants proved to you . . ." It is not for Mr. Berezovsky: ". . . on the balance of probability that the meaning you find those words to bear is substantially true?" Well, for all the detailed reasons I have given the answer to that is "no," and then you come to the damages. It is at that point that you have to take account of what is necessary for Mr. Berezovsky to have his reputation vindicated by you.

Summation

Justice Eady: Members of the jury, all that now remains is for me to sum the case up to you, and for you then to retire to consider your verdicts or to answer the questions which you have been posed. Although this case may be thought to be relatively straightforward as libel actions go, there are a number of preliminary matters which I should go through and explain to you. Many of them you will know already so I hope you will bear with me.

I need to say something first of all about our respective functions, yours and mine, because we try the case together but have separate roles to perform. My function at this stage is twofold. First of all, I have to give any necessary directions on the law, and that of course is my province alone; you accept the law from me. Secondly, I have to remind you of some of the evidence—not all of it, of course—but some of the salient points of the evidence. And all I am attempting to do when I do that is to assist you by reminding you of the salient points and trying to relate that to the issue that you have to determine; in other words to your three questions which you were given yesterday.

That brings me to your role, because just as the law is exclusively my province, so the facts are entirely within your province. It is for you and you alone to decide what happened, what you make of the witnesses and what you find credible and what you do not. Therefore, when I am attempting to help your task by reminding you of the evidence, please remember that if I leave something out which seemed to you, at the time the evidence was given, to be of significance, then you give it the weight you think right. By the same token, if I spend time on something which appears to you not to have very much bearing on the case, again you are free to ignore it because it is your view of the facts that matters, not mine. If at any stage I should give you the impression that I have formed a personal view of the facts, including for example the meaning of the words or that I have formed an opinion of one of the witnesses or something of that kind, then that is something again you are entitled to ignore. It does not matter what I think of the facts; it is only your conclusions that count.

I do not know how many of you are familiar with the political and constitutional affairs of Russia, but it does not matter because we all have to try this case on the evidence that we have seen or heard in court and leave behind any general reading which we may have done about such matters. It is not for us to pronounce on the affairs of another country; we are concerned only to focus on the issues which arise in this case, which are, as you can see from your sheet of questions, relatively narrow. But of course, the political matters you have heard about—some of them highly controversial—are there as important background to what you need to decide. Everything takes place against that political background. But that is what it is, and remains: background only.

It is important for you to bear in mind in this context that the standard of proof is not as high as in a criminal court. Whenever the defendants have to establish facts in this case—or for that matter the claimant has to establish facts—that does not have to be proved so that you are sure, or certain, or as it is sometimes put in criminal cases "sure beyond reasonable doubt." It is only necessary for such facts to be proved on the balance of probabilities: has it been shown to be more probably or more likely than not? The issues in this case can be stated very straightforwardly. First of all, do you think that the words spoken by Mr. Fridman on the television program were defamatory of Mr. Berezovsky? I will say a bit more about what defamatory means in a moment. In other words, did Mr. Fridman's remarks reflect adversely on him in the eyes of reasonable viewers of the television program? If not, that would be the end of the case. Two, if you conclude that those remarks were defamatory of Mr. Berezovsky and reflect adversely upon him, have the defendants proved on the balance of probabilities that those words or those allegations were substantially true? If you think the allegations made by Mr. Fridman were substantially true on the balance of probabilities, that again would be the end of the case. Thirdly, if the defendants have failed to prove that the sting of the libel—the real thrust of the libel—is true, then you will need to consider what sum of money should be paid to Mr. Berezovsky in order to reflect that and to compensate him.

Let me say a few words in general about the purpose of a libel action. The purpose of any libel action is to vindicate the claimant's reputation. That is a term that Mr. Browne has used to you already this morning. What it means is to put right any injury that may have been done to that reputation by the communication of a defamatory allegation. What does defamatory mean? It is always for the jury to decide whether what was said or written is defamatory or not. There are an infinite number of ways in which you can defame a person. All it means is that something has been published about the claimant—in this case, Mr. Berezovsky—which reflects adversely on his or her reputation, something that causes those who read the words or see the program in question to think worse of that person.

Sometimes there may be considerable doubt about what the implications are in a particular passage in a newspaper article, and the jury, as ordinary fair-minded readers, will then have to consider carefully, in the context, whether what has been said actually does reflect on the claimant or not, and if so in what way precisely. Sometimes, on the other hand, the meaning may be more straightforward. But it is for you and for you alone to decide what the words mean, and so far as there is any dispute about them; as there is to some extent in this case. It is also for you to decide whether the words are defamatory, whether they would make reasonable viewers of this Russian program think worse of Mr. Berezovsky.

The defendants of course do not accept—as Mr. Shields has made clear to you—that anyone who heard those words on the program would think worse of Mr. Berezovsky. As I say, that is your decision. You know what Mr. Berezovsky suggests, through Mr. Browne, that the words mean. He complains that the real sting of the article is that he threatened violence to Mr. Fridman and that this is moreover his usual way of doing business. It is for you to decide if that is what those words convey. You are not bound in any way by what Mr. Shields says or Mr. Browne says about meaning, or Mr. Berezovsky or Mr. Fridman. You are free to come to your own conclusions.

What if you decide that the words did not necessarily mean that he threatened violence, but rather that he threatened Mr. Fridman in some less specific way, perhaps commercial pressure? Then it will be for you to decide whether or not reasonable viewers would nevertheless be inclined to think worse of him. You may remember that at one stage it was suggested in that letter by the defendants' solicitors at the outset of the dispute, that threats of commercial pressure are so frequent in Russia that nobody would think worse of them. That again is a consideration for to you bear in mind when you come to your decision about it. If you decide that Mr. Fridman's words did convey to ordinary reasonable viewers of the program—naturally they would be Russian speakers—that Mr. Berezovsky threatened violence then there is no attempt to prove that that was true. If you think that is what it means, the defendants do not seek to defend it by saying that he did threaten violence, still less do they say that threats of violence are his usual way of business.

What the defendants do allege to be true is that Mr. Berezovsky threatened commercial harm of some kind. If you decide that the words spoken by Mr. Fridman would convey the allegation that he threatened violence then obviously Mr. Berezovsky would be entitled to win the case, because there would be no defense. But if you were to come to the conclusion nevertheless that he did threaten people with commercial consequences, commercial damage of some kind, then that would be something you would be entitled to take into account when deciding the appropriate amount of damages. In other words, if you think that the words mean that he threatened violence, then you might very well award a greater sum to a man who was completely innocent than to a man who you thought was guilty of threats of commercial violence.

These are various possibilities, various hypotheses, because I obviously do not know what you think of the words and what you think of the evidence. But I have to address these various possible scenarios. If you think that the words mean "commercial pressure" only, and not threats of violence, then if you decide that is defamatory it will be for you to decide whether the defendants have proved that the guts of that allegation was true.

Let us just have a look at the words complained of. You will remember of course that they are extracted and they are part of a much longer program, and you saw the whole of the program at the outset of this case with the benefit of subtitles to help you. But the essential complaint is of this relatively short passage in the program. I am just going to go through these words with you but do remember they come in context and very often context is important for construing the significance of words. There is a certain amount of cut and thrust here, which gives you the flavor of the program but is not, you may think, directly relevant to the point at issue.

Mr. Vasiliev says:

"It is good thing that you are not a journalist, you would be sued at every turn."

And Mr. Fridman says: "And we told them at that moment that if they want to buy shares in order to keep the newspaper [that is *Kommersant* of course] really independent we are ready to offer them a loan. And the question was discussed. Moreover, even Berezovsky called me with regard to this matter. He was very displeased."

Vasiliev said:

"Did he give you a piece of advice?

"Fridman: No, he threatened as usual, he said that …

"Vasiliev: And you too?

"Fridman: He even threatened me. He threatened everybody; that is how he works."

So you see there the two particular phrases that are relied upon by the claimant, "as usual" and "that is how he works. He threatened everybody" as suggesting that this was a general allegation going beyond the specific allegation of having threatened Mr. Fridman himself.

So you will decide what you think those words mean and would convey to the reasonable viewer.

Now, there has been quite a lot of evidence about the extent of the broadcast in this jurisdiction. I will come back to that later. The burden is on the claimant to prove on the balance of probabilities that some people in this jurisdiction received and saw and understood the broadcast complained of. But as such, that is no longer a live issue because it is not challenged that some people at least did see the program. The defendants nevertheless maintain that the numbers who viewed the program were not very significant, in this jurisdiction, and that the number of viewers in this country were not such as to do any material harm to Mr. Berezovsky's reputation or to cause any significant hurt to his feelings. And that will be for you to judge in the light of the evidence.

The claimant seeks to prove the extent of the number of viewers in two ways. First, witnesses have been called who say they actually watched the program. Secondly, you heard evidence about people who saw the program but did not come to court, some of who were apparently unwilling to do so and thus be publicly associated with Mr. Berezovsky or his point of view. Thirdly, you are invited to draw an inference from the number of subscriptions to NTV and other channels that the likelihood is that some of them did indeed see the program. In the nature of things, of course one cannot give precise numbers. It is a matter of simply assessing the likelihood as best you can. I will return to that later where it belongs in the context of damages.

Now I am going to turn shortly to this defense of justification, as it is called, which is the matter to which the second question on your sheet relates. I need to say a little bit more about that in general terms. Justification, in the context of a libel action, means really the same as "truth." It could be called the defense of truth. If that defense succeeds, then the claim will fail. You can publish allegations about people that are as defamatory as you like, provided you can prove them to be substantially true. You may decide in due course in the course of your deliberations that that is the central issue in this case. Certainly, a defendant does not have to prove that every word that was spoken or written about the claimant was literally true. The way of approaching this is to ask yourselves: if there are some inaccuracies, do they make any significant difference? Just look at the guts of the allegation about the threats and ask yourselves whether it is substantially true. I will come to the evidence shortly but just a few words of introduction. You may think here that someone must be lying. This is not one of those cases where there is room for misunderstanding or different interpretations of what took place. There are often examples of such cases in these courts, for example, who saw what in an automobile accident, or something of that sort; people see things from different angles, have a different impression of events, and so on. But here you may come to the conclusion that either Mr. Berezovsky did threaten one or more of these or he did not. If you decide that he has threatened one or two, but not all three, then that would be for you to decide how that impacts upon the case. In such circumstances, would the defendants have shown nevertheless that the words were substantially true?

If you say of somebody—to go away from the facts of this case for a moment—"He is a burglar; he burgled A, B, C and D," and you only succeed in proving A, or A and B, has the sting of the libel nevertheless been made out? It is simply a matter of assessment, common sense and judgment, for you to decide. So you will consider each of these three allegations separately and come to individual conclusions on them and then decide how it impacts on the case. They are not a job lot or a package to which the answer is "yes" or "no" in every case. It is a question of assessing each individual situation.

When you retire to consider your verdict, which may be late this afternoon or it may be early tomorrow morning, I am not sure, there is no pressure of time on you. If I were to send you out to begin your consideration this afternoon—I do not know whether I shall or not—that does not mean that you are pressed to reach a verdict today. Of course not. You can come back tomorrow and carry on, and if necessary you can come back on Friday and carry on. It is not like the old days where you would have to be closeted away with one another in a hotel overnight or anything of that sort. All that stopped about twelve years ago. So I shall release you at the end of the day in the usual way and ask you to carry on your deliberations the next morning at the usual time. So there is no pressure of any kind about that.

Members of the jury, let me summarize briefly at the outset each side's case on this defense of justification or truth. It is a classic jury case in the sense it turns on which of the conflicting accounts is to be believed, and here there are three incidents relied upon by the defendants in support of the proposition that Mr. Berezovsky uses threats in business. There is the alleged telephone conversation in the summer of 1999, with Mr. Fridman himself in the context of the proposed acquisition of a newspaper business, *Kommersant.* Mr. Berezovsky says no such call took place and in any event he would never have used the criminal slang expression that Mr. Fridman now attributes to him. You remember the one which Mr. Putin used in 1999, when saying that he would "waste the Chechens" or words to that effect. Then there are the two incidents alleged to have taken place in 1997. He is supposed to have threatened Mr. Nemtsov in China in connection with his bid to become chairman of Gazprom. Again, it is a straight conflict: Mr. Nemtsov says he did, and Mr. Berezovsky says he held no conversation with him on that subject. In fact, Mr. Berezovsky says he went to China to persuade the man who had the power to make the decision, Mr. Chernomyrdin. He wanted to see the organ grinder and saw no point in trying to persuade someone lower down the pecking order. Thirdly, there is the allegation relating to the auction of a share in Svyazinvest. There had apparently been many regional telephone companies and they had been amalgamated into one public body, and it was 25 percent of that was being made available for bids. There was to be an auction with sealed bids under the supervision of Mr. Chubais, and this time he is supposed to have threatened Mr. Potanin. You have his statement now and will look at that later. Again it is in each case for you to make up your minds which version you prefer.

Before dealing with the three separate incidents, let me just set the scene by reminding you of the evidence given by each of the main protagonists by Mr. Berezovsky and Mr. Fridman about their lives because that is potentially important background for you, and you have to decide whose evidence you prefer.

Mr. Berezovsky was born in Moscow in 1946. He went to school and university there. For 28 years he was in the field of applied mathematics at the Institute of Control Sciences and the Academy of Science of the Soviet Union. He got a PhD, and ultimately became a professor with his own laboratory. This produced computer-aided design systems. He became a correspondent member of the Academy of Sciences just about the time that the Soviet Union collapsed in 1989. He had written more than 100 articles in his field of expertise, which apparently is called multi-criteria optimization. He has also written two books and addressed conferences in his field all over the world.

He has been resident in England now since October 2001, when he applied for political asylum. He was eventually granted political asylum because it was decided in this country in court that there was a well-founded fear of political persecution if he were to return to Russia. There was an attempt to extradite him to Russia on criminal charges, but that attempt was unsuccessful because it was concluded that the charges were politically motivated and there was no evidence of any criminal activity. Eventually, a couple of years later, the Higher Russian Arbitration Court in Moscow came to the same conclusion. He was meanwhile granted political asylum in Britain in September 2003.

He told you that he started up his own company shortly before the collapse of Communism in April 1989, because he sensed that there was a new era dawning, with commercial opportunities. His company was called LogoVAZ, which derived the first part of its name from an Italian company with whom he was in a joint venture, and the second part from the original Russian car manufacturing company called AvtoVAZ. He saw opportunities of developing the market in automobiles because, as he told you, every Russian had two dreams, namely to own a car and to own an apartment. Therefore LogoVAZ increased its area of activity from developing software to selling cars and, importantly, providing workshops for repairs. He signed contracts with Mercedes, Volvo, General Motors, Honda and Daewoo, among others. And in short order, LogoVAZ became the number one automobile company, not only through buying and selling cars, but also because it had managed to develop the infrastructure to provide for repairs.

In November 1994, he considered developing his commercial activities into the media and becoming active in politics. He detected that a lot of people who had initially supported democracy in Russia were after a few years disappointed because things seemed to be getting worse for the majority of the population rather than better. He foresaw there was to be a big battle for president between, as he put it, new and old, or in his terms, "Democracy versus Communism." He realized that the mass media would play a significant part in the forthcoming elections. Eventually he was introduced by Mr. Aven—who, as you know, is a witness in this case, and is now the chairman of *Alfa Bank*—to Mr. Yumashev, who later became the head of Boris Yeltsin's administration. He purchased shares in the newly privatized television station ORT. A consortium of leading businessmen bought shares in ORT, of which 51 percent remained under state control and 49 percent went into private hands. Other businessmen involved at this stage were Mr. Fridman himself and Mr. Potanin. And gradually others sold their interest to Mr. Berezovsky and he correspondingly controlled a greater share.

Mr. Yeltsin's second term started in 1996, having been first elected in 1990. And Mr. Berezovsky was proposed by Mr. Rybkin, who was the Secretary of the Security Council of Russia, to become his deputy. The purpose was primarily for him to concentrate on helping to build peace in Chechnya after the first Chechen war. He held that position for little more than one year, and helped to broker a peace agreement between Russia and Chechnya on May 12, 1997. At that time, one of the first deputy prime ministers—as you know, they have more than one first deputy—one of the First Deputy Prime Ministers in Russia was Mr. Nemtsov, who of course you have also heard from. And Mr. Berezovsky and Mr. Nemtsov were involved in negotiations following the settlement with Chechnya with a view to transporting Azerbaijani oil through Chechnya to a Russian port on the Black Sea. This was apparently with a view to assisting economic recovery after the war.

Mr. Berezovsky maintains that he has always remained on friendly terms with Mr. Nemtsov, including after he left to live in Great Britain. You heard of visits to London where Mr. Berezovsky entertained Mr. Nemtsov and others in his office and his home. You have also seen some photographs of apparently relaxed circumstances. He said that he has visited him at his home in Surrey and also met him on social occasions in Israel.

After he ceased to be Deputy Secretary of the Security Council he took up another post a little later in April 1998. As you know, there were 15 new countries after the Soviet Union collapsed. The three Baltic republics of Estonia, Latvia and Lithuania all moved as it were into the Western camp straight away. But all the rest created what was called the Commonwealth of Independent States, or CIS, and Mr. Berezovsky was elected in February 1998 as the executive secretary of that organization. Mr. Yeltsin was the chairman and Mr. Berezovsky the executive secretary. The 12 members of the CIS had elected him unanimously.

When he was in political office he told us that he turned over all his activities to his partners and did not participate in business during those periods. In April 1999, he ceased to be the executive secretary, and later that year stood for the Russian parliament, the Duma. He was elected as a member in December 1999 to represent a constituency in the Caucasus. As it so happens, Mr. Yeltsin resigned as president in the same month, December 1999, and on December 31, 1999, Mr. Putin became president. Mr. Berezovsky had known Mr. Putin by this time for some ten years. He had become Prime Minister of Russia a few months earlier in August 1999. This was an appointment by Mr. Yeltsin, which at Mr. Yeltsin's request Mr. Berezovsky conveyed personally to Mr. Putin while he was on holiday.

Mr. Putin's background was as a colonel in the KGB and subsequently as Deputy Mayor of St. Petersburg. He apparently had got on well with Mr. Putin at one time and traveled with him abroad on skiing holidays. Mr. Berezovsky had supported Mr. Putin's appointment as Prime Minister in 1999 and was also willing to support him as president later in the same year. As he told you, in those days his prime concern was to prevent the return of Communism. And as he put it, they did not have a choice between good and bad in Russia, only between bad and worse. Mr. Primakov was proposing to return to Communism, and Mr. Putin was seen at that stage by Mr. Berezovsky as supporting democracy. His main objective was to see that Mr. Putin was elected as president rather than Mr. Primakov. At that time Mr. Putin did not even have a party around him, and Mr. Berezovsky was one of those who initiated a political movement to give him a base. This became known as "Yedinstvo," or "Unity."

At that time, there were no particular policies in view, except in general terms; it was perceived simply as a question of Democracy versus Communism. Even before Mr. Putin became president in October 1999 he started the second Chechen war and Mr. Berezovsky fundamentally disagreed with this and advised Mr. Putin that it was impossible to find a military solution. Later, after he became president, Mr. Putin began to initiate laws, which in Mr. Berezovsky's view would work against democracy. In particular, he took the power to fire the elected government. That was in March 2000. Mr. Berezovsky told Mr. Putin that he would take a public position opposing him in respect of some of his policies. He wrote an open letter to Mr. Putin dated May 31, 2000, which was published in the *Kommersant* newspaper on the same day.

Another problem so far as Mr. Berezovsky was concerned is that Mr. Gusinsky was put in prison between June 10-13, 2000. And in his view this had been done purely for political reasons. Mr. Berezovsky told us that Mr. Putin's aim was to obtain control of one of the television companies, NTV, which was at that time under the control of Mr. Gusinsky. He said that Mr. Gusinsky had for the first time in Russian history created an independent mass-media vehicle, and he thinks that this was part of the reason he had been thrown into prison. Mr. Gusinsky was forced to surrender NTV to Gazprom, the state-owned energy company.

Gradually Mr. Berezovsky realized, as he put it, that the Russian Duma had become, in his words, a puppet of Mr. Putin, and he therefore resigned from parliament in July 2000, less than a year after being elected. He announced publicly that he was going to provide a focus for real opposition to the existing government. He further incurred the disfavor of Mr. Putin in August 2000 by the coverage in the *Kommersant* newspaper of the Kursk tragedy when those Russian submariners lost their lives in the Northern Sea off the coast of Russia. ORT, the television station Mr. Berezovsky had to a large extent controlled from the mid 90s, had broadcast interviews at that time with wives and sisters of those who had sunk on the submarine. Mr. Putin called in Mr. Berezovsky and was very angry with him. That was the last meeting they ever had. He said that it was his wish to control and manage the television channels and told Mr. Berezovsky to return the shares in ORT to the state.

This was of course some two months after Mr. Gusinsky had been forced to hand over NTV. Shortly afterwards in October 2000, when Mr. Berezovsky was traveling in France, he heard about an announcement from the Russian public prosecutor that he was to be prosecuted for various alleged crimes, and he did not return to Russia. In December 2000, Mr. Berezovsky's friend and business partner, Mr. Glushkov, was arrested and put in jail also. He was, as it turned out, to spend three and a half years in jail despite the fact that he was in a poor state of health.

Mr. Abramovich, Mr. Berezovsky's former partner from the oil business, conveyed a message to Mr. Berezovsky that if he were to release his shares in ORT, Mr. Glushkov would be released. Mr. Berezovsky, under that particular pressure, sold his shares to Mr. Abramovich. But the bargain was not kept and Mr. Glushkov remained in prison. Mr. Abramovich had told Mr. Berezovsky that he was acting on Mr. Putin's instructions.

As I have said, Mr. Berezovsky was granted political asylum in September 2003. Just over a year later the broadcast took place on October 28, 2004, which forms the subject of these proceedings. Mr. Berezovsky said the program is very popular and that the anchorman Mr. Soloviov is a well-known and popular journalist in Russia. He had been told shortly in advance by Mr. Vasiliev that he was to participate in the program and therefore he watched it. The context of the program, as you know, was that on October 20, 2004, a week before the broadcast, a Moscow court had awarded *Alfa Bank* something like $11 million in libel damages—or the equivalent in roubles of course.

This was something of a talking point in Russia for those interested in Russian affairs, and it of course formed the subject matter of the program. Mr. Berezovsky's view was that the award of damages was quite ridiculous and that 88 percent of it was supposed to be compensation for injury to the bank's reputation. His understanding of Russian law—although this does not matter very much—was that a company could not obtain damages for injury to reputation. Only 12 percent of the damages were supposed to represent actual financial loss which could be proved by the bank. Later on, as we now know, the damages were substantially reduced by the Russian court on appeal to something like 10 percent of what had been originaly awarded. But at this stage people are obviously interested in the huge sum of damages which had just been awarded the week previously.

When Mr. Berezovsky watched the program he said he was very surprised by what Mr. Fridman had said, because "I was surprised because I did not have any particular problem with Fridman before." He went on to say: "I certainly understood that they were all trying to be nice to Putin, but not on this level." He had been in business relations with Mr. Fridman previously when they had both taken a share in ORT, and when he heard this said, "At first I was more disappointed than shocked."

After he discussed the matter with his partner and close colleagues he decided that he did not have a choice but to take the matter to court. He was shown the letter of complaint from his solicitors and he eventually confirmed that if he had been offered the public apology he was seeking he would not have resorted to court proceedings.

Mr. Berezovsky explained that NTV tended to be regarded as appealing to what he called the "more intellectual" part of society, rather than ORT, for example, and the other state channel. He also said that Russians living abroad tended to prefer to watch NTV to the other Russian channels. He said it was part of the Russian tradition when people move abroad to follow closely events at home, to keep in touch. He was asked how widely he was known among the Russian community in England, and he said that because he was involved in almost all the important political events in Russia in the previous decade most people would know of him. And he described how sometimes people would come up to him in the street and shake his hand.

So that sets the scene so far as Mr. Berezovsky is concerned. It is right I should now correspondingly give you an introductory account of Mr. Fridman and his background, just as I have in the case of Mr.

Berezovsky. Of course, what ultimately matters is your decision about the specific allegations in the case and the evidence from both sides in respect of them, but you need to know something about each of the main protagonists.

Mr. Fridman explained that he is the Chairman of the Board of *Alfa Bank* and one of the co-founders of the *Alfa Group* Consortium. It is now one of the leading financial industrial groups in Russia, and has a considerable participation in the oil and gas industries. He was born in April 1964, and is thus some 18 years younger than Mr. Berezovsky. He was born in Lvov in the western part of the Ukraine, and now lives in Moscow. His background is that he went to university in 1981, and studied at the Moscow Institute of Steel and Alloys. After he graduated in 1986, he became a metallurgical engineer in the Moscow region. He started up a business towards the end of the 1980s before the final fall of Communism, which involved hiring students to clean windows and trading in consumer goods.

One of his first businesses was to implement new technology in the photo industry in the Soviet Union. And then he traded in computers, copiers and fax machines. They also began to import goods from other countries and then invested in the banking business. The *Alfa Bank* was established in 1991, and is now the largest privately owned bank in Russia. He explained that it is currently in partnership with BP in a joint venture concerned with oil and gas. *Alfa Bank* has also heavily invested in the telecommunications industry.

Mr. Aven had been a member of the first democratic government back in 1991 under Mr. Gaidar as Prime Minister, and of course Mr. Yeltsin as president. When he resigned in 1992, he went into private business. They met each other in 1993, and began to work together from then onwards. It was Mr. Aven who introduced Mr. Fridman to Mr. Berezovsky. Mr. Aven had known him since the 1970s. As I have already said, Mr. Fridman and *Alfa Bank* were involved with Mr. Berezovsky in the ORT television project and eventually sold out their interest to him.

Mr. Fridman denied that he was a tool of Kremlin policy and said that he tries to avoid becoming involved in politics and is primarily concerned with being a businessman. Nevertheless he accepted that it was: "Normal practice to be in contact with political authorities because we are doing business which obviously touched the interests of the state as a whole. It is absolutely logical to be in contact." Also, he accepted that he was a member of the public chamber, and had been elected as a representative of the body known as Officers' Wives. The public chamber, as you know, is a recent creation in the Russian constitution. It is a kind of revising body.

It was put to him by Mr. Browne that the public chamber has 126 members, of whom the first 42 are nominated by President Putin. In turn, those 42 nominees select the next 42 from names advanced by various organizations, of which Officers' Wives is one. The 84 then select the final 42. Thus, as Mr. Browne put it, the public chamber would have the stamp that President Putin put upon it because he selects the first group of 42. I think Mr. Fridman accepted that that was broadly speaking correct. He said, I think, he "impacts" on the 42. He accepted that he had been an adviser to President Yeltsin although he would not accept that he had met Mr. Yeltsin, or for that matter Mr. Putin, one-on-one. He had nevertheless attended various meetings at the Kremlin with Mr. Putin.

As you will recall, various postings on the *Alfa Bank* website were put to Mr. Fridman by Mr. Browne in cross-examination on the basis that he was using the website to promote *Alfa Bank* by telling people how closely linked he was to President Putin. You have some of those documents in your file, members of the jury. He denied that this was so. And his attention was drawn in particular to an article in *Institutional Investor* on September 1, 2003. It was put to him that the article was on the website because potential foreign investors would think to themselves: *Alfa Bank* is the bank for me because they are a safe investment in Russia; they are closely tied to President Putin.

There is one particular passage to which your attention is drawn: "The presidential elections are looming ahead. Have you already decided which of the candidates you are going to support or is it the money issue, you have decided when you have to financially commit yourself.

"Mr. Fridman: I think this question is largely rhetorical at the moment.

"Moderator: I mean the one who guarantees stability; his name is already known.

"Mr. Fridman: Well, yes, of course and this is pretty obvious, I guess.

"Moderator: However, the person we are now talking about, Vladimir Vladimirovich Putin, allowed himself to address the oligarchs with this phrase, 'You will have a lot of dust to swallow,' and in general he often demonstrates his emotional rejection of the mere existence of the oligarchs as a cluster, to borrow your term. Have you ever felt the impact of his attitude?

"Fridman: You know, due to the specifics of my job I am used to taking emotional outbursts rather philosophically. I would say from my personal experience of dealing with the president I see that, despite his way of expressing emotions, which can indeed be singled out, he is a living person, and this probably accounts for his being such a popular and successful politician. He remains a rational, well-balanced, and serious man. I believe that what is important is not how a politician expresses their emotions but rather whether or not they understand the necessity and possibility of interacting with the entrepreneurial community, and I have no concerns in this department.

"Moderator: "When you communicate with the president, do you have a sense of his personal attitude to you?

"Fridman: "Good question. I would say, as I have seen it, to give the president his due, everybody who communicates with him has a good idea of his attitude to them. I do not know if it is only a feeling on an emotional level."

It was suggested that Mr. Fridman's website—and you will obviously have a chance to consider this as much as you wish when you retire, members of the jury, to consider these documents and see whether you find this persuasive or not. But it was suggested that Mr. Fridman's website was drawing a contrast between *Alfa Bank* and Mr. Khodorkovsky, who you will remember was thrown into jail for 18 months and then given an eight-year prison sentence. It was put to Mr. Fridman that this was a blatantly motivated prosecution and that his website was intended to show potential investors that *Alfa Bank* was unlikely to fall into that trap, crossing the line between politics and business.

Mr. Fridman would not accept that Mr. Khodorkovsky had been thrown into jail for political reasons, and gave the explanation that he, Mr. Fridman, was not qualified as a lawyer. Mr. Browne returned to this theme and put to Mr. Fridman that President Putin directed the prosecution of Mr. Khodorkovsky. His answer was this: "I of course would like to say that I respect the judgment of the British lawyers and British judge about that … and as I am not a professional lawyer, I could not make my own judgment from the legal point of view whether it was politically motivated or for some other reason."

He was being cross-examined about the findings of the magistrate or district judge in relation to the extradition of two people closely linked, called Mr. Maruyev and Ms. Chernyshova, in the course of which he had to consider the circumstances of Mr. Khodorkovsky. The magistrate's attention was drawn to the fact that Mr. Putin caused the prosecution to be launched in June 2003, despite the fact that the prosecutor had advised that there were no grounds for action against Mr. Khodorkovsky. Mr. Fridman's response again was this: "Again, with all my respect for the opinion of the British judge, it is a completely contradictory opinion to the Russian court. How can I decide whose opinion is more professional. I am not a lawyer." He added: "I think that I have a responsibility to my partners, to my shareholders, to my clients, creditors and so forth, and so I will repeat my formal position, I am not a lawyer. I am unable to make a fair and professional judgment about the merit of this court case." He continued: "My business interests require actually not to get involved in political life, because I think for business purposes it is not useful to get deeply involved in political issues."

So that was Mr. Fridman's stance in relation to this letter explaining how he treads a line keeping out of politics and concentrating on business. He was not prepared to be drawn on matters of political prosecutions. Reference was made to the interview with Mr. Kandell. He was the journalist conducting that particular interview. In that article, Mr. Fridman was described as Russia's third richest man, who has emerged as President Vladimir Putin's favorite oligarch. But Mr. Fridman would not accept that characterization. He was asked if he had been a heavy contributor to the United Russia Party, as Mr. Kandell's article suggested. But he denied this. Mr. Kandell also alleged: "Fridman leaves no doubt that he would support Putin and the United Russia Party."

Mr. Fridman said however that that was just wrong information. He denied ever having been a contributor to the United Russia Party, and he was unable to explain why Mr. Kandell had that impression or why the article was on the *Alfa Bank* website: "Like most oligarchs, however, Fridman is a heavy contributor to the United Russia Party, the political entity most closely linked to Putin, who remains highly popular and heavily favored to win a second term. Fridman leaves no doubt that he will support Putin and the United Russia Party ... Fridman ... points out that threats to businesses and their owners were commonplace during the Yeltsin era. Business-related murders have dropped to about a score a year. Heavily armed private security squads have almost disappeared ..."

So all of that is there, members of the jury, for you to consider, but you see it was put to him because it was being suggested that he was seeking publicly to be linked to Mr. Putin for business purposes, and he denied that. He said that so far as that was described by Mr. Kandell, he had got it wrong and he could not explain why it was on the *Alfa Bank* website. He was the chairman and did not have control over the website, and he did not know it was there. He accepted that he attended the meeting on July 28, 2001 in the Kremlin, but would not accept the description that Mr. Nemtsov had organized this meeting in order for Mr. Putin to call a truce against big business. He said: "I was just attending because I received an invitation from Mr. Putin."

He was asked about the fact that Mr. Gusinsky had been arrested and held in jail until he surrendered NTV in July 2000. Again he responded: "I am not a lawyer." He did not accept that he was going so far as to say that the Russian criminal justice system was properly employed against Mr. Gusinsky. He maintained his neutrality. He added, "I did not say that, I said, you know, it was a legal decision. I would like to comment; I do not have any professional ability to make fair and serious judgments about whether it was politically motivated or legally motivated." He knew that Mr. Gusinsky relinquished his NTV interests after being thrown into prison but he did not wish to comment on the legality of that. He was asked if he knew about the judgment of the European Court of Human Rights in relation to the treatment of Mr. Gusinsky. He said he had heard about it but forgotten. He was asked whether he knew of the finding that Mr. Gusinsky's human rights had been breached, but he said he knew little about it.

The only relevance of this material, members of the jury, is to enable you to take all of that material into account when deciding whether or not Mr. Fridman's motivation for attacking Mr. Berezovsky on the program was that he was, as it were, jumping on Mr. Putin's anti-Berezovsky bandwagon. He denies that was so, and it is for you to decide whether that has any plausibility: is he an uncritical supporter of the Putin line?

We are not concerned with the rights and wrongs of Russian politics, as I mentioned earlier, but it comes into this case in part because it is attributed to Mr. Fridman as a motive for what he said about Mr. Berezovsky. So it is against that background that I must now remind you about the evidence of the particular incident, or non-incident, depending on your point of view, which forms the primary subject matter of this dispute, and that is the bid for *Kommersant* in 1999. Here the conflict is between the evidence of Mr. Berezovsky on the one side and Mr. Fridman on the other. And to some extent also the evidence of Mr. Peter Aven is relevant, and I must remind you of that. As you know, Mr. Browne's case is that Mr. Fridman was lying on the television program and that no threat was uttered to him by Mr. Berezovsky in connection with *Kommersant*. We know that *Alfa Bank* was interested to an extent in the acquisition of *Kommersant* at that time.

Mr. Browne suggested at one stage that this was because if *Alfa Bank* made a loan to shareholders or managers who were interested in a management buy-out of the newspaper, the likelihood was that they would be unable to afford the repayments and therefore the newspaper would ultimately fall into the hands of *Alfa Bank*. This was denied both by Mr. Fridman and by Mr. Aven. They said their sole interest in the matter was to protect the independence of *Kommersant*. Mr. Fridman's case was that if this happened he would be obliged to dispose of the asset if it fell into his hands in those circumstances. He and Mr. Aven had both stated that their only interest in supporting a possible management buy-out was that it would help to maintain the independence of *Kommersant*, that is to say from any powerful individual such as Mr. Berezovsky.

To be fair to Mr. Berezovsky in this context, you will remember that no one has suggested that over the five or six years when *Kommersant* was in fact under his control, for the most part when he was living in

England, he had in any way undermined or compromised the independence of that newspaper. Indeed, as you know, on the program itself on October 28, 2004, Mr. Fridman himself acknowledged his respect for that newspaper, which he described as "an epoch in Russian journalism."

That is just part of the background. We are concerned of course in this case with perceptions as they were in the summer of 1999, and it was to protect its independence, say Mr. Fridman and Mr. Aven, that *Alfa Bank* took an interest. Mr. Berezovsky says that he had no telephone conversation with Mr. Fridman at all on the subject of *Kommersant*. What was proposed was that he would be acquiring the shares of Mr. Yakovlev and he left the negotiations in that respect largely to his colleague and partner, who we have been referring to as Mr. Badri. Mr. Berezovsky's personal involvement was confined to a meeting with Mr. Yakovlev at the outset in Amsterdam. Mr. Yakovlev was thereafter based mainly in the United States, and it was there that Mr. Badri had dealings with him.

So what could Mr. Fridman's motive be for lying in this instance. As you know, Mr. Browne put it to him that it was really to toe the current line; that is to say to toe the line of the Russian government in 2004, namely that Mr. Berezovsky was *persona non grata*. And it was to curry favor with Mr. Putin. You will decide what you make of that. You have heard Mr. Fridman and Mr. Aven giving evidence and you will make your assessment. Mr. Browne suggests—and you will consider this in the context of the transcript—that Mr. Fridman took the opportunity while participating in that debate just to drag in the name of Mr. Berezovsky in order to disparage him. He says it had nothing to do with the thrust of the argument between him and Mr. Vasiliev. Again you will consider the context of the program. We have not been through it with you *in toto* because that would be tedious. You saw it once and it is entirely up to you how much you go through and consider it in your own deliberations.

Also, Mr. Fridman denied that he is a toady of Mr. Putin. In this context you will need to bear in mind the items that Mr. Browne put to him from the website. I have already referred to them. He suggests that this does confirm that he takes every opportunity to give the impression that he is close to Mr. Putin and that this closeness would be advantageous to foreign investors in particular. And I have referred to the interview with Mr. Kandell.

It is now necessary to consider the nature of Mr. Fridman's case and the way Mr. Aven's evidence has developed. You were shown this morning some of the solicitors' letters. In particular there is the one of December 9, 2004, and there is the one of January 14th from the defendants' solicitors. That may be of some significance. So it is for you to consider what you think of it. I will just go through it with you now:

"We refer to your letter of December 23rd on which you have now had an opportunity to take our clients' instructions following the Russian New Year holiday. We have made our clients' position clear. Mr. Fridman's statements referred to threats of a commercial nature, and this is how the audience of the broadcast would have understood them. We note that in your letter you seek to characterize threats of this nature as improper. We understand that, in the context of Russian business, threats to exert commercial pressure are relatively commonplace. We are instructed that this was particularly true at the period in question. Accordingly, the statement that your client made threats of a commercial nature in 1999 are not capable of being defamatory of him; in other words no one could possibly think worse of him."

Now, there is something of an issue you have to consider here because Mr. Fridman said in evidence in this court that that letter was at least to some extent written without his instructions, despite what is said in the opening line. And he does not accept that it was his case, personally, that threats to exert commercial pressure are relatively commonplace. So you will consider that.

Mr. Fridman added in court, in the course of his evidence, that he was not saying that it was commonplace for threats, commercial threats, to be made in business in Russia, but it was just commonplace for Mr. Berezovsky. The first time it was suggested that there was any other example of Mr. Berezovsky threatening anybody else apart from Mr. Fridman was on June 16th last year. In other words, about six months later. It was then that Mr. Fridman's defense had to be served, identifying the nature of this case. It is unclear of course exactly to what Mr. Fridman was referring on the program on October 28, 2004. He did not tell us in court that he was at that stage referring either to Mr.

Potanin or to Mr. Nemtsov when he made the allegation of habitual threats on Mr. Berezovsky's part.

At all events, no examples were given of any other threats whether to them or to anybody else throughout the correspondence up to the date of the defense in June. That came later. We heard from Mr. Aven in the course of the trial to the effect that Mr. Fridman had told him immediately afterwards of Mr. Berezovsky's threat over the telephone, back in the summer of 1999. But no mention of that had been made in the correspondence either. And of course it is perfectly true to say that when you plead your case—as we call it—setting out your case in the legal document, the defense, you do not plead your evidence, you plead the nature of your case. So it would not be necessary at that stage to set out or identify your witnesses.

The point is made that nothing was said to the effect that, by way of negotiation or discussion with the solicitors, well, not only did he threaten Mr. Fridman but he has a witness to the conversation immediately after it took place. So you will consider those matters and whether you think them of any significance. In July, in accordance with the modern practice, the defendants were required to identify the witnesses they were proposing to call at this trial. Mr. Browne has pointed out that Mr. Aven's name was not mentioned at that stage, despite the fact that he has long been a close colleague of Mr. Fridman and was at one time even in the next-door office.

Now it is perfectly true that when parties are called upon to identify their witnesses at such an early stage it is not binding on them in the sense that they are confined to those witnesses; it is open to them to call others. What is said here is that it is perhaps a little surprising that if Mr. Aven was such a key witness to the critical threat made by Mr. Berezovsky that he was not up front as a key witness early on. If that is of any significance, members of the jury, it is for you to decide. Eventually Mr. Aven's statement was served in February this year. At that stage Mr. Berezovsky was notified for the first time that the alleged threat had been reported. But Mr. Aven did not say that he was told anything about Mr. Berezovsky having used the striking phrase from criminal slang, which is something like this: "my vas zamochim." Indeed, that phrase did not surface even in the defense in June 2005. It was introduced for the first time apparently in another supplementary court document on September 23, 2005, when Mr. Fridman was asked to be a bit more specific. And it was then that Mr. Fridman attributed to Mr. Berezovsky the criminal phrase which had apparently been so notoriously used by Mr. Putin in relation to the Chechens in 1999, for which he was forced to apologize. The reference to that is in the magazine *Vedomosti*, dated September 28, 1999. So in other words, Mr. Putin used the phrase a few weeks after Mr. Berezovsky is now alleged by Mr. Fridman to have used it on him.

Mr. Browne invites you to consider why Mr. Aven was not told of that phrase and why it only came to light some months after the defense was served. You will recall that at one stage during the course of his evidence Mr. Fridman suggested that Mr. Putin had picked up this vulgar criminal slang from Mr. Berezovsky in one of his meetings, because Mr. Putin used it after Mr. Berezovsky. Once again you are also asked to bear in mind the longstanding friendship between Mr. Aven and Mr. Berezovsky and the apparently continuing cordial relations even after Mr. Berezovsky sought asylum in England. He was entertained by Mr. Berezovsky twice in London, in a Chinese restaurant—I do not know whether you made a note for future reference, but I am not going to repeat it—in 2003 and 2004. Again Mr. Browne asked you to consider whether those friendly meetings were consistent with Mr. Berezovsky having threatened to destroy Mr. Fridman, since Mr. Fridman's business, *Alfa Bank*, was also Mr. Aven's business, and if Mr. Berezovsky had threatened to destroy Mr. Aven's business, how likely would it be that they would continue a social relationship?

Those are the arguments you will consider, members of the jury, in relation to that.

I now come to the other two incidents dating back to 1997, which were raised last summer. There is no particular order but I will deal first with Mr. Berezovsky's bid to become chairman of Gazprom in the summer of 1997. Here there is effectively a straight conflict of evidence between Mr. Berezovsky on the one hand and Mr. Nemtsov on the other. Mr. Berezovsky's case in short is that he flew to Beijing that summer in order to speak to Mr. Chernomyrdin, the then Prime Minister, because as everybody agrees he was at least an essential key to the process. Without his approval, Mr. Berezovsky could not become chairman. His attitude, he told you, was that if Mr. Chernomyrdin gave his support, everything else would fall into place. Whether he is right about that is another question. But that was his attitude when he flew to China. It was unlikely that Mr. Nemtsov, he thought, being one of the Deputy Prime Ministers and the minister for fuel and energy at the time, would refuse to give his consent if Mr. Chernomyrdin gave his. On the other hand, it is Mr. Nemtsov's evidence that whatever Mr. Berezovsky's purpose in flying to Beijing was, he discussed his proposal to become chairman with Mr. Nemtsov and what is more threatened him that he would damage his political career unless he fell into line.

Mr. Berezovsky says that simply never happened. He directed his attention to Mr. Chernomyrdin only. He agrees that he went with Mr. Nemtsov and Mr. Chernomyrdin but denies speaking on the subject of the chairmanship of Gazprom with Mr. Nemtsov on that trip. He also denies any threats, and his case simply is that Mr. Nemtsov is lying about this. In this instance, of course, the motive that Mr. Browne put to Mr. Nemtsov is not that he was giving evidence in this case to butter up Mr. Putin; far from it: everybody recognizes that Mr. Nemtsov is politically opposed to Mr. Putin, who runs what he described to you in his words as a "KGB government." The motive that Mr. Browne put to Mr. Nemtsov is that he was supporting Mr. Fridman out of loyalty to Mr. Fridman, and not least because of financial support that he has received from various people in the past for his political movement, the SPS, from *Alfa Bank*.

In particular, Mr. Fridman accepted that he personally had contributed money to Mr. Nemtsov's political movement, although he was a little vague on how much. He accepted at various points in his evidence that it would be measured in dozens of thousands of dollars rather than hundreds of thousands of dollars, and that it was probably less than $100,000. Consider what you think about that motive put by Mr. Browne, and more generally assess Mr. Nemtsov's evidence as he gave it from the witness box. In this context there is one passage you were referred to in the course of evidence—you might like just to have it in mind in case you think it relevant. Mr. Fridman says this:

"The world pictured by the mass media is in my opinion very far from reality. Therefore, talking about the deputies, I can say that of course I know many of the deputies. But in principle perhaps if I wanted to I could have established closer relations with them. But this is not my goal, not because I am a person of such high morals—although I do hope I do not lack a sense of morals—but mainly because I do not really need those connections. I believe that if there are issues that do need the support of the deputies, one can find a much easier way.

"Moderator: How so?

"Mr. Fridman: First the issues that need the support of the deputies are as a rule issues to be dealt with from the standpoint of an ideology, of a political force, for example SPS or Yabloko."

SPS of course, as you know, is or was the movement chaired by Mr. Nemtsov.

"Moderator: So you place a call to the boss?

"Mr. Fridman: I can easily meet them and explain that there is a certain issue and I would like their support on that.

"Moderator: Will they ask you for money?

"Mr. Fridman: Well, I would say they will ask for support for their activities in some form."

Then a little later on, just by the lower punch hole, the moderator says:

"Do you have to spend a lot of money on direct political support to the same parties during election campaigns?

"Mr. Fridman: I would say that what we spend is normal by Russian standards but can be considered a lot by Western standards. The amount of individual and collective assistance one receives from one company is much less than here, but the total number of participants in the funding is gigantic. Here, due to the structure of our company …"

And a little lower:

"Do you give equal amounts to all the parties?

"Fridman: No, absolutely, not. For example we would never fund the Communists."

So there was the discussion about political funding. And Mr. Browne suggests that, to put it crudely, Mr. Fridman was calling in a debt from Mr. Nemtsov in asking him to support him in this case.

It is very important that you weigh the witnesses—Mr. Fridman and Mr. Nemtsov—and come to your own conclusions about that, test that allegation against the impression that they made upon you. As I said earlier, this is a classic jury case. One of the main reasons why juries are retained in some libel actions—just as they are in criminal cases—is because juries are thought to bring fresh minds to the judicial process and to be able to apply their own experience of day-to-day life and their own judgment of people. And you can all pool your common sense and your experience of people and come to a conclusion. And particularly that is valuable when you are assessing the personalities of witnesses giving evidence.

Now, as I have said, Mr. Berezovsky's case on this matter is that he went to see Mr. Chernomyrdin and he was only interested in persuading him at that stage. He did not consider that he needed to discuss it with Mr. Nemtsov. Mr. Nemtsov says that he had two roles at that time which were material: one as minister for fuel and power and the other as chairman of the collegium of state representatives in relation to Gazprom. He pointed out that Gazprom was the third largest company in the world and the largest gas corporation in the world; it was capitalized at something like 300 billion dollars. And he was against the idea that Mr. Berezovsky should become chairman. At that time the chairman was Mr. Kazakov and the chief executive officer was Mr. Viakhirev. Mr. Viakhirev was also deputy chairman. You remember at one stage Mr. Berezovsky's recollection was that Mr. Viakhirev was chairman and also chief executive, but he came back to correct that to say that he was chief executive and deputy chairman.

Mr. Berezovsky's aim and suggestion at this stage was that he should become chairman, and that Mr. Viakhirev would then concentrate on the duties of chief executive. And although Mr. Berezovsky had no direct experience in the gas industry, he had a good deal of experience in recent years in the oil industry, through Sibneft.

On the question of whether or not Mr. Nemtsov would fall into line if Mr. Berezovsky had succeeded in persuading Mr. Chernomyrdin, you will remember that Mr. Shields challenged Mr. Berezovsky in cross-examination at one point by saying to him that he would have the opportunity of putting to Mr. Nemtsov when he came to court that he was "Mr. Chernomyrdin's poodle." You will remember that Mr. Berezovsky chuckled at this point and said that that was exactly the reputation Mr. Nemtsov had at the time in Russia, not least of all because of his hairstyle, which apparently is thought to be rather like a poodle.

Be that as it may, it was far from Mr. Nemtsov's perception of his relations with Mr. Chernomyrdin, whom he regarded as an indecisive Prime Minister by contrast with himself. He told you he was firm about it; he was 100 percent against Mr. Berezovsky becoming chairman and there was no way that he would be swayed against that view. In court, Mr. Nemtsov's evidence about the threat is that it came after he and Mr. Berezovsky had left the Russian Embassy in Beijing and were out on the street. At this stage he said something to the effect that he would see to it that Mr. Nemtsov's political career was ruined.

Mr. Berezovsky denied he said anything of the sort, and of course it is his case that if he had done so, it would hardly be consistent with the continuing cordial relationships between them, the exchange of the hospitality, and the relaxed photographs you have seen.

There are a number of specific points that Mr. Browne has made about Mr. Nemtsov's evidence in inviting you to disbelieve his account. It is right that I should remind you of those so that you can give them full consideration in due course. Some of you may think they have a greater force than others, but it is a matter for you whether they have any force at all. He suggests that Mr. Nemtsov's was something of a shifting story. I will mention his points in no particular order of priority. First, in his witness statement he gives an account of the first discussion which took place between him and Mr. Berezovsky on the subject of Gazprom in Mr. Nemtsov's office in the White House in Moscow. Mr. Berezovsky gave the impression that he had, or was likely to obtain the support of both Mr. Viakhirev and Mr. Chernomyrdin. Mr. Nemtsov therefore telephoned both these people in order to see whether this was in fact the case. In his witness statement he says that he telephoned Mr. Chernomyrdin first, although he changed the order when he gave evidence. Mr. Nemtsov says the order of events is of no significance; what matters is that he made the calls.

The second point is that he gave evidence to the effect that someone had said to him that he had offered his support to Mr. Berezovsky, but, "I hope you make the right decision." That was not in his witness statement. What appeared in his witness statement—which of course you have, on which he was cross-examined—was that Mr. Viakhirev said to him, "I hope you do something to prevent this appointment."

That wording is obviously different; whether it is significantly different is a matter for you. Your attention in this respect was drawn also to an extract from *Komsomolskaya Pravda*, which you have. You remember that sauna interview that Mr. Nemtsov gave, where someone else did say, according to the account Mr. Nemtsov was then given—"I hope you make the right decision."

This incident was attributed to Mr. Chernomyrdin rather than Mr. Viakhirev. In court, by contrast with the account in *Pravda*, Mr. Nemtsov told us that Mr. Chernomyrdin was simply indecisive, i.e., not that he was hinting that Mr. Nemtsov should prevent Mr. Berezovsky's appointment. So you may think there is a difference, or at any rate a difference of emphasis between what he said to *Pravda* and what he said in court.

Those are said by Mr. Browne to be inconsistencies, which he submits to you are significant, whereas Mr. Nemtsov explained that *Pravda* by saying this was adopting simply an informal style of journalism, for which it is well known, and his account in *Pravda* is not to be taken as authoritatively as his evidence in court.

The third point which Mr. Browne takes is that the discussion of the chairmanship of Gazprom was said to have been discussed on the trip to the Three Gorges hydroelectric station in China, whereas there was no mention of this discussion in Mr. Nemtsov's witness statement, which you can check. Mr. Browne therefore describes that as an embellishment in court. Mr. Nemtsov says simply that he did not include everything in his witness statement. His witness statement simply describes a discussion between himself, Mr. Chernomyrdin, and Mr. Berezovsky in the Beijing embassy. Mr. Berezovsky's evidence is that such a discussion did take place, but it was only between him and Mr. Chernomyrdin.

A fourth point taken by Mr. Browne is that it was only in court for the first time that Mr. Nemtsov referred to a conversation with Mr. Berezovsky in the street when they were alone; i.e, not in the Russian Embassy. Mr. Nemtsov's reply to that was: "Well, I did say then." You will see that in his witness statement. In other words, he is suggesting that the fact that he refers to the threat having taken place after the discussion is consistent with it having taken place later out on the street.

Mr. Browne suggests that the meaning of the witness statement was that it was a continuing part of the discussion, for which Mr.

Chernomyrdin was present in the embassy. It is a different account, and according to Mr. Berezovsky, both are false. Again, you will make up your minds.

A very significant new departure which Mr. Browne relies upon is that for the first time Mr. Nemtsov suggests not only did Mr. Berezovsky actually threaten him in relation to his future political career, but he carried out the threats in practice by arranging for a journalist or journalists to damage Mr. Nemtsov's reputation. It was suggested, as you know, in *Komsomolskaya Pravda* that it might very well have been the case that Mr. Nemtsov would now be President of Russia. Whether you take that seriously or not is another question, but that was put forward as a possibility. And Mr. Nemtsov certainly told us in court—again, for the first time—that his reputation was significantly damaged in the period of 1998 and thereabouts, and he apparently blames Mr. Berezovsky for that.

So let us be quite clear about this: it was never alleged in the formal documents in the case, it was not part of the defendants' case, nor was it in any witness statement. Accordingly, it was never put to Mr. Berezovsky in the witness box, because if it is part of your case it is your duty to put it to the other side when they are being cross-examined. That is entirely, of course, consistent with it not being in accordance with Mr. Shields' instructions from his clients. So it was a new factor introduced into this case. Once it is said, it cannot be unsaid. One cannot just pretend it was not said. That is why I gave permission for Mr. Berezovsky, if he wished to take the opportunity, to go back into the witness box to deal with these allegations, which were potentially very serious, and made for the first time in court.

We generally nowadays in litigation have a culture against ambush and surprises, and people are entitled to be notified in advance of the case they have to meet. I am not criticizing anybody for that, because it was introduced by Mr. Nemtsov, and I am not suggesting for a moment that the defendants or their legal advisers knew of it. But that is how it came about. On Monday afternoon Mr. Berezovsky decided to go back into the witness box, briefly, and he denied that he had anything to do with blackening Mr. Nemtsov's reputation in late 1997/8, et cetera. In particular, he had nothing to do with making allegations about his relationship with a prostitute. It is in this context that Mr. Browne relies particularly, as I understand it, on the continuing friendly relations between the two men.

As you heard, there were visits to Mr. Berezovsky's office, to his home in Surrey, similar in a way to the meetings with Mr. Aven. You have seen photographs of those visits, and also of both of them in their trunks on Mr. Berezovsky's yacht. You need to consider whether, if Mr. Berezovsky had set out to destroy Mr. Nemtsov's political career, and his chances of becoming president, he would have been quite so friendly.

Mr. Browne asks you to consider those and also the continuing, and apparently frequent discussions which the two men had over the telephone at the end of 2004, in connection with the Orange Revolution in Ukraine. And you will know that Mr. Nemtsov is now currently still an economic adviser to the President of Ukraine. Mr. Nemtsov suggested as I understand it, to explain this apparent inconsistency, that this was all water under the bridge now; the damage was done, they have what he called a "KGB Government" in Russia. Neither of them can do anything about it, and they might as well bury the hatchet.

That was my understanding of his account of the apparent inconsistency. So you will no doubt consider each of those points of view, and give them such weight as you think right.

Finally, there was a point on the draft appointment deed for Mr. Berezovsky. Originally Mr. Nemtsov said that the document was signed both by Mr. Viakhirev and by Mr. Chernomyrdin. If that were so, queried Mr. Browne, why on earth would Mr. Berezovsky need to go to China in order to persuade Mr. Chernomyrdin? He suggests that Mr. Nemtsov has backtracked on this because he now says in the court that the document was not actually signed in the sense of giving authority for the appointment of Mr. Berezovsky, or approval, but was rather signed simply on the back of the document as an indication that Mr. Chernomyrdin had read it, rather than approving its contents. So you will consider that point, and whether you think it has any force either way.

The third incident relied upon related to Svyazinvest. That again is the summer of 1997. This time you will remember that Mr. Berezovsky was Deputy Secretary to the Security Council of the Federation. It was proposed to privatize part of the telecommunications industry, and Mr.

Berezovsky was not directly involved. There were two consortia bidding for the relevant shares. There was the Gusinsky consortium, which included Mr. Fridman and *Alfa Bank*, and also a Spanish company called Telefonica. The competing consortium was that of Mr. Potanin, who also had some involvement on the part of Mr. George Soros. He has a reputation of course as a financial speculator, and came to most people's attention perhaps during the Black Wednesday crisis of 1992.

The person in charge of overseeing the auction was one of the First Deputy Prime Ministers at the time, Mr. Chubais. He had responsibility for privatization projects in Russia at that time. Mr. Berezovsky's evidence was that he had attended one meeting between Mr. Gusinsky and Mr. Potanin, so far as he could recall, at which the auction was discussed. He had attended at the request of Mr. Yumashev, who at the time was head of President Yeltsin's administration, and he was then invited by both Mr. Gusinsky and Mr. Potanin to meet Mr. Chubais, who happened to be in the south of France at the time. It was put to Mr. Berezovsky on behalf of the defendants that he wanted Mr. Gusinsky to win the auction. He denied this claim; he said that his reason for meeting Mr. Chubais was to try to prevent war breaking out. That is why he was invited on the president's behalf to become involved. He did begin to have doubts as to Mr. Chubais's independence; he was not sure how objective he was at that time. Mr. Yumashev had told him of his own doubts as to his integrity, and Mr. Berezovsky had no hard evidence as to any corruption, but was beginning to have his doubts also.

Mr. Berezovsky denied absolutely that he had threatened Mr. Potanin, that he would use his political power and media resources to inflict harm on him as a businessman. That was how it was put to him in cross-examination. His response was: "It is a lie." The result of the auction apparently was that Mr. Potanin's group won, with a bid of about $1.8 billion, or just over, just ahead of Mr. Gusinsky's bid of $1.7 billion or thereabouts. He suspected that someone might have revealed the information that the result of the auction was not truly fair, because the two outcomes were suspiciously close. He told Mr. Chubais apparently that he was not a proper arbitrator to run the auction in that case, because it was well known that he had an active business relationship with Mr. Potanin. He said after the auction was over that he went to Mr. Kokh, who at that time had responsibility as Minister for Privatization. He was a friend of Mr. Chubais, and had been nominated by him for that position. He went to see him in his office after the auction, and remembered very well that it was a morning meeting at which Mr. Kokh appeared to be somewhat drunk. Mr. Kokh apparently said to him at that stage, "Boris, I am Onexim. I am Onexim," meaning that he was one of the parties involved in bidding at the auction. Mr. Berezovsky was absolutely shocked. He reported back to Mr. Chubais, and Mr. Chubais reassured him that it was impossible; it could not be. Mr. Berezovsky said, "You are lying. I have just come from Kokh." And Mr. Berezovsky suspected that there might have been a spy from Mr. Potanin's camp in the Gusinsky consortium, and that is how the evidence leaked out.

There is no evidence one way or the other about that, it is not our business to decide. But we are concerned with Mr. Berezovsky's state of mind at that time, and what he believed or suspected. The central point remains that he strongly denied having threatened Mr. Potanin.

Now the evidence of Mr. Potanin you now have, members of the jury, and you will no doubt wish to read it at your leisure when you retire in due course. He says here—this is the case that the defendants rely upon, although of course it was not cross-examined to you for reasons you know about. But at any rate, it is evidence in the case upon which the defendants rely. "As I understood it then, Mr. Berezovsky was assisting Mr. Gusinsky in connection with the Svyazinvest auction, as he had a financial interest in the auction being won by the consortium that Mr. Gusinsky instructed."

As you know, that is hotly disputed by Mr. Berezovsky, and it was not put to him in cross-examination that he did have a financial interest. So for our purpose we can proceed on the basis that he did not.

"During the course of the meetings to discuss the auction I formed an understanding that if the companies associated with me were to participate in the auction then in Mr. Berezovsky's opinion I would be going against his interests and Mr. Berezovsky would use his political power and media resources to inflict harm on my image as a businessman, which would affect my capacity to conduct business.

"I am not able to recall the exact meetings on which he made such statements, nor the precise words which were used. However I am certain that such promises to exert commercial pressure were made, and I am equally certain of their content. I would like to make it clear that at no time has Mr. Berezovsky made threats against me of a physical nature. I was aware that Mr. Berezovsky's capabilities were serious, and that he was capable of carrying out such actions."

Well, members of the jury, those are the two competing accounts. Although it has not been cross-examined to, because Mr. Potanin was not, unfortunately, available to us yesterday, it remains evidence in the case, but you must do your best to attach to it the weight you think right in the context of the statement as a whole, and in the light also of Mr. Berezovsky's evidence and the submissions you have heard from counsel on both sides about the role of Mr. Potanin.

I said earlier, members of the jury, that I would return to the subject of the scope of the audience, in the context of damages. I am going to come to damages shortly in more general terms, but let me remind you of the evidence about the extent of the broadcast in this jurisdiction, which now really is only of relevance for you to take into account on damages. It is not possible of course to prove exactly how many people have seen a television program. It will generally be a question of making an informed guess on such evidence as is available. Obviously it is not Mr. Berezovsky's case that the numbers who saw this program in this jurisdiction were in any way comparable to an audience for BBC *Question Time*, or an edition of *Panorama*. It is his case that it would have been seen probably at most by hundreds, rather than thousands of people. There is no magic number. Even if it was seen by very few people in England and Wales, that would still be enough to establish a claim, assuming of course you think the allegation is defamatory of Mr. Berezovsky. On the other hand, the number of people may be relevant in arriving at a suitable figure for compensation. I shall come to that matter later, but it is common sense that the number of people who have heard defamatory allegations is one factor in determining the appropriate amount of damages. If a defamatory program has been seen only by a very few people, that can be reflected by the jury in the amount it decides to award.

Sometimes of course defamatory words can be published to only one person, with very grave consequences, so it is a question of balance. The number of people who receive the information is only one factor. You have to measure it also against the gravity and the potential seriousness of the impact on those people. If you say to a husband or wife that his or her partner is off down the road on holiday with someone else, that would be an audience of one, but of course the consequences could be devastating. It depends entirely on the circumstances.

It is important to remember that we are not concerned with the broadcast of the program in Russia itself, or in the Baltic States, or in any other Russian-speaking country. We are concerned only with the broadcasting received by Russian speakers in this jurisdiction, England and Wales. Correspondingly, however artificial as it may be, you will be concerned if you find the words to be defamatory of Mr. Berezovsky, with compensating him for injury to his reputation within this jurisdiction, among the Russian community presumably in this country and others who know him. And so far as he suffered hurt feelings, then the element that is attributable to that limited audience. As I say, to that extent it is an artificial exercise, but that is the theory of what has to be achieved.

Let me now turn to the evidence relating to publication. It falls into various categories. Some of the evidence is from people who actually saw the program themselves. Some of the evidence is about other people who saw the program, but who for one reason or another were reluctant to come forward and give evidence in this case. Another category is the number of subscriptions to NTV. Naturally, not everybody who had a subscription would be watching that program on that evening. What that evidence does is to give in general terms an idea of the number of people who would have had ready access to the program, and might have been interested in it.

You also had evidence from Mr. Vladimir Voronkov, who runs Mr. Berezovsky's office in London, and who has worked for him for about 10 years. He was formerly a journalist. He explained that you can obtain access to the NTV channel either by applying to a local dealer who would install the necessary equipment, satellite dish, and receiver, or you can call NTV World direct and obtain a card for use in your existing equipment. Mr. Voronkov saw the program himself. He also explained the program guide, which informs Russian speakers of the programs available on the relevant day. Mr. Voronkov said the program is quite popular with Russian speakers interested in current affairs, particularly because the participants are able to express their views openly and to confront each other by way of a relatively interesting dialogue. He said it was more or less on a par with the English program *Question Time*. Also it was dealing with a subject, the Russian banking crisis, in which many people were interested because of the impact on their own finances or the finances of their relatives or families in Russia. He said that his wife also watched the program. He said that they watched the program regularly on Thursdays, and he described it as a primetime program which is of primary interest to the Russian-speaking audience.

There was evidence also from Mr. Yuli Dubov, who was formerly the general manager of LogoVAZ between March 1995 and October 1999, and who subsequently became chairman of the board of *Kommersant* while he and Mr. Berezovsky were in England from about 2001 or 2002 to 2005. He too saw the program because he had had a phone call from Mr. Vasiliev, who told him that he would be appearing in the debate. He also said that other people in the Russian community in England had told him they had watched the program, including his dentist and people he met at church. People he asked to come and give evidence simply to the effect that they had actually seen the program were unwilling, because they did not wish to publicly be associated with Mr. Berezovsky, still having close connections with Russia. He told us for example that his dentist was unwilling to help because he is still a regular visitor to Moscow, and did not wish to be seen to be publicly associated with Mr. Berezovsky because of possible repercussions.

He asked Mr. Alexander Litvinenko to assist by trying to find people who had actually watched the program and were willing to give evidence in court to say so. We have heard also from Mr. Litvinenko himself, a former Lieutenant Colonel in the KGB. He did not see the program, but he did make inquiries to see if he could find witnesses. He said some people were scared when he asked the question, and they were reluctant to come forward and identify themselves, even to the extent of saying they had seen the program. He said, "I am 100 percent certain the minutes of this hearing will be on the table of the Russian Special Intelligence Service. People do not want their names finding their way into that organization." He referred in particular to one lady who was a friend of his wife, who at first agreed to go to the solicitors and provide a statement. And then he said, "...the next morning, after she had left, I found a note from her. I can produce this note. The note said: 'Sasha, I am sorry but I am too scared.'"

Members of the jury, none of this reflects on the defendants. Of course it is nothing to do with Mr. Fridman; nobody is suggesting that he has anything to do with those fears. But the explanation was given, and it is for you to make up your minds about it, because otherwise the position would be simply that there were 25 people, or whatever it is who saw the program, and it would be said: well, there is no reason to assume anybody else saw it, because they have not been able to come up with anybody. It is not quite that straightforward. Here there were people who had seen it, but were unwilling to come forward. So it is relevant to the extent of the broadcast. It is for you to assess the evidence and give it such weight, if any, as you think right.

I will just say a little about the subject of damages. Of course that only becomes relevant if you hold that Mr. Berezovsky has been defamed, and that the words were not substantially true. But I have to address it as the counsel has also addressed it. Before I start on the subject of damages, three little points to tidy up from what I have said to you already.

The first point is this: I did not mention it because it almost seemed to me to go without saying because everyone seems to accept this, that it was of course the case in the mid-1990s to late 1990s, that Mr. Berezovsky's substantial interests in the media were such that he was in a position to wield considerable influence in Russia and to affect public opinion and thinking. And that, because of his various positions in high office from time to time and contacts with the government administration, he was in a position to wield significant political influence and power for a time until, as we know, he fell out with Mr. Putin. So I hardly needed to say that because I think you recognized that.

Another point I was going to mention was this: you heard Mr. Browne this morning in a sort of advocate's flourish refer in the context of Mr. Potanin to the fact that he had not come here yesterday and rather speculated about how he spent yesterday with the Prime Minister and what may have passed between them. I am sure you recognize that was an advocate's flourish and we have no evidence at all about whether the Prime Minister was interested in releasing him for these proceedings or not. That is something which I think one might call poetic license, as it was intended to be.

Thirdly this: in the context again of Mr. Potanin's evidence, we have not heard from him in person so Mr. Browne was inviting you also to take into account—it was referred to only this morning—that he made some observations at a press conference. He said: "...groups always try to reach some sort of compromise and they enter into competition when no compromise is found. ...In this case, there was a need to make sure the state was committed to playing by the rules and it has announced itself that it is to have fair competition at the auction. When we realized no compromises could be achieved and the government was firmly committed to holding the auction in this form attempts were abandoned to reach a compromise."

This was the passage he specifically asked you to take into account: "I see nothing odd about the fact of business people entering negotiations in order to form alliances with respect to certain objects ... In this case an agreement was not reached."

So you are invited to set that alongside his statement in coming to an overall assessment of its worth.

Now, members of the jury, damages. If you decide that Mr. Berezovsky was libeled in this country and that there is no defense of truth, you will come to your question 3, the stage of deciding on the remedy to which he is entitled. As you have been told, it is not possible to order an apology. The only remedy which the law affords is that of damages. It will be another of your tasks if you get to that stage to fix the fair and just award of damages taking all the surrounding circumstances into account.

The purpose of libel damages is threefold. First it is to compensate for any distress and hurt feelings you may have found to have been occasioned to the relevant claimant. Not everybody is the same, some people have thicker skins than others of course, and that is a factor that needs to be considered. It is very much a question of your own assessment of the individual concerned.

The next factor is that of providing some rough and ready compensation for any actual loss of or injury to reputation, assuming that you come to the conclusion that the reputation was in fact injured. Thirdly, the damages serve as an outward and visible sign of vindication.

Let me just say a word about that. If people have read or heard about a libel and as a result they really do think worse of the claimant because they think perhaps he or she has done what was alleged against them, or perhaps because they have just put a mental question-mark temporarily against the person without necessarily coming to a conclusion, then it may be that such a person will need to be persuaded that the allegation was wrong. That can only really be achieved under our system either by an unqualified apology or, if that is not forthcoming, by the award of damages by a jury. It needs to be such as to achieve such vindication or, to use another phrase, restoration of reputation as the jury thinks the claimant is entitled to. It needs therefore to be proportionate to the level of gravity by which the jury actually assesses the libel in question.

That word "proportionate" is a key note on the question of damages, members of the jury. Let us say that someone has been accused in a television expose of murder or of being a serial rapist and there has been some mistake of identity. Any of the no doubt hundreds of thousands of viewers might not be very impressed if afterwards they were to read of an award of, say, £500 or even £5000. They might say to themselves, "That does not seem very convincing, maybe there was something in this after all." On the other hand, if the libel itself was more at the trivial end and the claimant has been accused merely of some social ineptitude, or being a bit mean about buying his round of drinks, or perhaps a bit the worse for wear at a party, then no doubt vindication or restoration of reputation could be achieved by a much more modest award. As always, it depends on the circumstances.

To say of a person that they were drunk not at a party, but say while driving someone's child home from school, would be thought by most people to be a much more serious allegation requiring a correspondingly greater or more generous sum by way of vindication. Circumstances that need to be taken into account in general terms are: how serious are the allegations; to how many people were they distributed; did anyone actually take any notice of them or were they likely to be dismissed; did the libel affect the claimant's social or professional life in some way; if there were any adverse effects for how long did they last; has the defendant done anything to make amends or mitigate the effect of what was said originally; has there, for example, been an apology and, if so, how far has it gone to correct any false impression or assuage the claimant's hurt feelings? Obviously, that does not apply in this case.

An important factor in the present case is that we are only concerned with those people who saw the program if you conclude there were such people in England and Wales—there obviously were some—we are not concerned with publication outside the jurisdiction as I have already said. You are also entitled to take into account damages, if you think it relevant the conduct of the defendants so far as this litigation is concerned. Has that in any way added insult to injury? Obviously in this case the defendants have never withdrawn the allegations. They have repeated them and asserted publicly that they were true. Obviously this has the effect of rubbing salt in the wound and would tend to aggravate or increase any award of damages. On the other hand, if you genuinely believe that you have done nothing wrong and that you have said nothing false or misleading, the absence of an apology may be more readily understood. Nevertheless, you have to take into account of course as one of the factors the public repetition of the allegations.

When I say that there are three purposes to be served by libel damages, all I mean is that these are all factors that need to be taken into account in satisfying yourselves that you have arrived at an appropriate figure. I most certainly do not mean that you should fix on a separate sum for each of these elements and then add them altogether. You only need to arrive at a global figure such as you think appropriate for Mr. Berezovsky himself if you think there has been libel. It needs to be in proportion to what happened overall but in making the assessment each one of those factors needs to be borne in mind. Here we are concerned with allegations some of which would probably be classified when it comes to assessing the appropriate compensation as falling somewhere in the middle but towards the top end of the scale of gravity. Of course it depends what you think Mr. Fridman's words actually meant. If you think he was accusing Mr. Berezovsky of threatening violence that would be getting towards the top of the scale. On the other hand, if a reasonable viewer would conclude that he was being accused of threatening commercial pressure only, i.e., not physical violence, you may come to the conclusion that it is somewhat lower down the scale of gravity. As always it is a matter for your own good judgment and assessment.

One has to fit the damages to the relative seriousness of what is alleged against the particular claimant. You just apply your own experience of life and, as I said earlier, that is one of the reasons you are here of course, because society trusts a jury of twelve—or in this case eleven—to apply its collective common sense to the situation at hand. Another way of putting it is to say: keep a sense of proportion. Remember as a matter of principle that the exercise is one of compensating the claimant, not punishing the defendants. This is not a criminal court where defendants are to be punished. Also, the parties' relative wealth is irrelevant. It makes no difference that the defendants are wealthy, nor yet does it make any difference that Mr. Berezovsky is himself very wealthy, because the issue is compensating proportionately for what was actually published.

If you were fining somebody in a criminal case their means might very well be relevant but that is irrelevant to our exercise. What matters is fair compensation, if compensation is called for, and that is for you to decide, particularly having regard to your own experience of the value of money. It is real money we are talking about. Actual money has to change hands as a result of any award you make, so bear in mind your own day-to-day experience of investments, holidays, homes, cars, whatever it is. It is real money we are talking about.

Some years ago the European Court of Human Rights held in relation to a jury award in this country that English libel law was a bit unsatisfactory in the sense that it was a bit unpredictable as what the award should be. It was a bit arbitrary apparently, and that was a case where a jury had awarded £1.5 million to a claimant. As a result of that ruling of the European Court of Human Rights in 1995, English courts set about bringing themselves into line with the principles of the Human Rights Convention. At that time we did not even have the Human Rights Act in force, but it did not matter: we were always applying it anyway.

The practical consequence is that we work to a ceiling of damages; a rather arbitrary ceiling but nevertheless people knew better where they stood, and the ceiling was fixed at about £200,000 by reference to comparisons with personal injury damages. Allowing for inflation, you might say that the ceiling is now about £215,000. What that means is that that highest level of damages is reserved for the highest level of libel, the most serious level of libel. When a jury is assessing the gravity of the libel in their particular case, it is sensible to have that scale in mind leaving room for less serious libels lower down the scale. So bear in mind that scale when working to achieve consistency and predictability to some extent.

When you retire to consider, or begin to consider, your verdicts, I suggest if you have not done so already, you should appoint one of your number to act as your spokesperson and to chair your discussions. Take any notes and your packets, take your list of questions. You realize of course that—it is obvious—that the answer to the first two questions will be either "yes" or "no," and the answer to the third question will be the sum of money if you reach that stage and your spokesperson will announce those results.

I must mention one matter to you at this stage. You may have heard of majority verdicts and it is true that in some circumstances a judge can accept a majority verdict both in criminal and civil cases. Those circumstances have not arisen in this case. If they do, you will be invited back into court and given further guidance. For the present, what I must ask you to attempt to do is to reach decisions that are unanimous on your questions. That is to say, verdicts upon which all eleven of you are agreed.

Friday, May 26, 2006

JUSTICE EADY: Mr. Shields, Mr. Browne what I propose to do now is to invite the jury back into court and the associate will ask the foreman to stand and whether they have reached a verdict. Assuming for the moment the answer is no, I will then give a majority direction.

THE ASSOCIATE: Would the foreperson please stand. Madam foreperson, will you please answer my question yes or no. Has the jury reached a verdict upon which they are all agreed?

THE FOREPERSON OF THE JURY: No.

JUSTICE EADY: Do sit down. Members of the jury, at this stage the point has arrived at which I would be able to accept a majority verdict, but let me explain what that means. It means a verdict, or that is to say answers to your three questions, on which at least ten of you are agreed. Of course there are only 11 of you but at least ten of you would have to agree. What I am going to ask you to do again, for a while at any rate, is to continue your deliberations and attempt to reach a unanimous verdict, but if you are able to reach a majority verdict, in the sense which I have described, I would be able to accept that; that is to say an answer to the questions on which at least ten of you are agreed. I am going to ask you to return to your rooms again, thank you very much.

(The jury retired to consider their deliberations, and then returned to the court to deliver a verdict at 3:07 pm.)

THE ASSOCIATE: Would the foreperson please stand. Madam foreperson, has the jury reached a verdict upon which they are all agreed?

THE FOREPERSON OF THE JURY: No.

THE ASSOCIATE: Have you reached a verdict upon which at least ten to one are agreed?

THE FOREPERSON OF THE JURY: Yes.

THE ASSOCIATE: In respect of the first question, are the words complained of in the program defamatory of Mr. Berezovsky?

THE FOREPERSON OF THE JURY: Yes.

THE ASSOCIATE: That is the majority of 10 to 1?

THE FOREPERSON OF THE JURY: Yes.

THE ASSOCIATE: Question 2. If so, have the defendants proved to you that on the balance of probabilities of the meaning you find the words to bear to be substantially true?

JUSTICE EADY: You are agreed on the answer to the second question are you?

THE FOREPERSON OF THE JURY: Yes.

JUSTICE EADY: When you are confident about it please announce it. Pause for a moment. I think you better retire to your room again and make sure that you have the answers when you come back, because we do not want any possibility of confusion. So unless you can be confident of giving the right answer now, I think you better retire again.

THE FOREPERSON OF THE JURY: I am fine.

JUSTICE EADY: You are all right. Thank you. Could you give the answer to the second question.

THE FOREPERSON OF THE JURY: No.

THE ASSOCIATE: Question 3. If not, what sum do you award Mr. Berezovsky in damages?

THE FOREPERSON OF THE JURY: £50,000.

THE ASSOCIATE: £50,000. Thank you.

JUSTICE EADY: Thank you very much. Yes, Mr. Browne.

BROWNE: My Lord, in those circumstances I would ask for judgment for Mr. Berezovsky for £50,000 and for an injunction as sought in the particulars of the claim which your Lordship has in the trial packet.

JUSTICE EADY: Then you are entitled to judgment in the sum of £50,000, Mr. Browne, and an injunction in the terms prayed.

BROWNE: My Lord, coming to costs. As your Lordship and the jury know, it was made clear at the start that Mr. Berezovsky had originally requested a public apology. Your Lordship has the original letter before the action of November 18th. On November 25th last year an offer without prejudice save as to costs was made, which I will ask my instructing solicitors to hand up, together with the rejection of it by Herbert Smith's letter of December12th. As your Lordship sees, it was written after the date the trial had been fixed and in an attempt to save the incurring of further costs. It reads: "What our client has been seeking since he first made claim against Mr. Fridman's allegation in his letter of claim dated November 18, 2004 is a public apology. If your clients would be prepared to give such an apology and withdraw the allegations, we would suggest now that proceedings are on foot, in the form of a statement to be read in open court and agree to pay our clients costs, our client would be prepared to forego his claim to any damages."

JUSTICE EADY: So the offer expired 21 days after November 25th?

BROWNE: Yes. On the 12th. The material date is December 12th, which, as it happens, was also the date of Herbert Smith's letter rejecting it without qualification. Your Lordship will see: "Our clients at Herbert Smith are not in a position to consider settling this case on the terms proposed by your client due to the lack of information available to them at the present time. [By that it appears they mean the lack of information relating to substantial publication]. It would plainly be premature for our client to make such a concession in the absence of any evidence from your client to support his case that substantial publication occurred in the jurisdiction." Then they simply say they would be prepared to walk away. In those circumstances my submission is, having regard to the terms of the letter before action, we are entitled to indemnity costs from the start. So far as the subsequent offer is concerned, if I am wrong in my first submission, I must surely be entitled to indemnity costs from December 12th last year.

JUSTICE EADY: Mr. Browne, it seems to me you are entitled to your costs of the action, but only from December 12th at the indemnity rate, and you are entitled also to interest at 10 percent above base rate on those costs.

JUSTICE EADY: That disposes of that; there was something else you wanted to raise.

BROWNE: My Lord, could I also ask for an interim payment in relation to costs. I do not have to burden, your Lordship will be able to work out broadly what the costs concerned are, I am not going to give any figures. Your Lordship is quite experienced enough to guess what they must be and to order an appropriate portion of them as an interim payment.

JUSTICE EADY: I would be inclined to say £50,000 on account within 21 days.

SHIELDS: I am obliged, your Lordship.

JUSTICE EADY: That disposes of all matters?

BROWNE: And, my Lord, the damages in the same period to be paid, payment of the damages within the same period.

JUSTICE EADY: Yes. Well Mr. Shields, I will give you a stay of execution if you go to the Court of Appeal within 21 days seeking permission. I will give you a stay of execution until that matter is determined. If permission is granted, then until the appeal is disposed of; that applies both to damages and costs. All that remains, members of the jury, is for me to say a few words to you. I think you will all appreciate how inconvenient jury service can be to people sometimes and you have certainly had a very stressful period, particularly over the last two or three days. It is a valuable and important public service that you perform and may I take this opportunity for thanking you all for your assistance in this case, thank you very much, it is much appreciated and I am sure by the parties. That disposes of all matters, thank you.

APPENDICES

Appendix 1

NTV TV Channel
Program *The Duel*

October 28, 2004, 10:35 pm
Host — *Vladimir Soloviov*

Round One

HOST: The conflict between *Kommersant* and *Alfa Bank* is not over yet. Journalists were not satisfied with the Arbitration Court ruling that forces *Kommersant* to pay $10 million in compensation for damage caused to the bank's reputation. And the reason is not just the excessively high amount awarded by the court, but the principle of the decision. *Kommersant* does not just intend to appeal the verdict, but to file a libel countersuit.

— Good Evening. This is Vladimir Soloviov's talk show *The Duel.*

MIKHAIL FRIDMAN: As plaintiffs, we are quite satisfied with the court ruling. However our opponents have voiced publicly two very serious allegations against us. They accuse us first of carrying out the Kremlin's orders, and secondly they say that we are stifling the independent free press. Both allegations are strong reasons for meeting them and answering questions face to face.

ANDREI VASILIEV: I accept Mikhail Fridman's challenge because I want finally to understand why *Alfa Bank* wants to extort almost $11 million from *Kommersant.* I absolutely could not fathom this from their claim, even less from the case, and viewers I believe might be interested in seeing how *Alfa Bank* acquires its extra millions.

— Mikhail Fridman is called to the platform. Andrei Vasiliev is called to the platform. Gentlemen, Vladimir Soloviov.

HOST: Gentlemen, are you ready to duel? Allow me to introduce our jury. Publisher Vladimir Grigoriev, Academician Yevgeny Velikhov, Honored Athlete Ilya Averbukh, President of the National Association of the Teleradiobroadcasters Eduard Sagalayev. As you know, during the duel, our viewers will be casting their votes for you, and their choice eventually determines the winner.

— To vote for Mikhail Fridman, Call 995-81-01. To vote for Andrei Vasiliev, call 955-81-02. Round one!

HOST: Andrei, as a slight compensation for the $11 million, you have the right to ask the first question.

ANDREI VASILIEV: Very slight. Well, the question is not about me. On July 7th or 8th this bank—in order to scare their primary investors—introduced a so-called "compensation." That is, in order to withdraw your deposit you have to pay 10% of the amount. Of course, this is illegal. This contradicts Article 837 of the Civil Code because deposits must be returned on demand. Isn't that so? That is until the first lawsuit. Nevertheless, you have earned 90 … 99 million rubles like this. And almost no one sued you. Why is that, do you think? Are people afraid of you?

MIKHAIL FRIDMAN: Andrei what you just said … sorry, but intentionally or unintentionally you have misinformed the public. We have introduced a charge, which by law we have the right to introduce under current law, on investments that have been deposited for, let's say, three months. But due to the panic created by your article, among other things, people wanted to withdraw early. Corporate entities do not have the right to do this, although individuals do, according to the Civil Code. But the Civil Code does not preclude the possibility that a bank, which relies on this money for a certain period, might introduce a fee for its early withdrawal. We have introduced a fee for its early withdrawal and we believe it to be legal and, as you correctly pointed out, hardly any clients went to court because our legal position in this sense was quite strong. But, I want to point out to you that just two weeks ago we announced that we would refund all the fees taken from our clients. Not because they sued us, but because we have introduced this measure to avoid more panic, not because we wanted to make money.

ANDREI VASILIEV: You have still made 99 million. Whether you will actually give it back or not—we don't know yet. But, there was a comment from one of your employees that you are going to win the lawsuit …

HOST: I am sure he has been fired by now.

ANDREI VASILIEV: No … we will win the lawsuit against *Kommersant*, and then we'll give it back. I mean, you want to hand over the money that was placed with, I mean give it back to the clients …

MIKHAIL FRIDMAN: We have already given the money back …

ANDREI VASILIEV: I didn't interrupt you.

MIKHAIL FRIDMAN: I'm simply explaining to you that we have returned the money already.

ANDREI VASILIEV: So, you … So, this is your procedure, to return what you should return, with other people's money?

MIKHAIL FRIDMAN: This money is already in our clients' accounts. This is the first point.

ANDREI VASILIEV: But your statement that after the first …

MIKHAIL FRIDMAN: Second, in principle, a bank makes money on taking other people's money, investing it, making a certain profit and …

ANDREI VASILIEV: I know that. You took the money? You must return it immediately. It says so in black and white …

MIKHAIL FRIDMAN: Not only are you no banking expert, you are no legal expert either. Well, I assure you that as far as I understand it, we acted fully in accordance with the law.

ANDREI VASILIEV: May I just quote a classic?

HOST: Karl Marx?

ANDREI VASILIEV: Peter Aven. An interview …

HOST: Classics!

ANDREI VASILIEV: … to the *Argumenty i Fakty* weekly on October 12th. The title is "Poverty Is Not Our Problem." I quote: "Poverty is marked by God. The rich are more moral than the poor because they can afford much more."

MIKHAIL FRIDMAN: First, I …

ANDREI VASILIEV: I see that you have already answered my question.

MIKHAIL FRIDMAN: I am not my brother's keeper, so to say. This is one. Second, now we are discussing a different question.

HOST: So the sentence did not originate with a reliable historical character.

MIKHAIL FRIDMAN: Yes. As for …

ANDREI VASILIEV: But you would not call him a minor author, right?

HOST: He … I believe would rank a bit higher … than Fridman.

MIKHAIL FRIDMAN: Quite right. As a matter of fact, that interview was given on an entirely different subject. On the subject of Protestant values—and why are the Western countries so successful—it's because they believe that riches are a gift from God …

ANDREI VASILIEV: I have not distorted the interview.

MIKHAIL FRIDMAN: You have distorted the interview, because what it says is "Richness is marked by God," not poverty is marked by god.

ANDREI VASILIEV: Then I am sorry.

MIKHAIL FRIDMAN: Exactly. *(Applause.)* And here lies the deep divide between Protestant ethics, Protestant ethics and, say, the ethics we find in our country.

HOST: And now—your question, because you have not had a chance yet to ask a question.

MIKHAIL FRIDMAN: Andrei, whether you agree or not, at least the court has ruled—and now the question is not how much you should pay us, but the fact that the story you published contained many inaccuracies, to put it mildly, or false information, to put it simply. So tell me, did you hold an internal investigation as to what happened? How did this story get published? Who wrote it? What was the motive for publishing the inaccurate information that appeared on the pages of your newspaper?

ANDREI VASILIEV: Thanks for not asking who paid us for that story. Well, where did it come from? The Vice President of *Alfa Bank* Alexander Gafin was a guest on the *Silver Rain* Radio show on June 6th, on which he said, among other things: we expect a certain outflow of deposits. Moreover, on *Ekho Moskvy* on the 6th a host said—sorry, they are colleagues, so I will quote so as not to make another mistake, OK? There were earlier reports that starting today, to withdraw your deposit from *Alfa Bank*, you had to get on a waiting list. Now, *Noviye Izvestia*, again a day before the *Kommersant* story: A number of small and medium-sized banks—partners of *Alfa Bank*—closed their credit lines to *Alfa Bank*; and the *Gazeta* daily on the fifth wrote that *Alfa Bank* allegedly is experiencing problems due to overlending. These are, actually, defense exhibits, they are all admitted and filed with the court, and there are over 80 items. Well, naturally, the judge could not read the entirety of this large volume of material. What should our journalists do, when they receive so much information? And moreover, there was a press release from your bank's Vice President, Kristyuk, who was desperately calling on clients not to worry. What should we do, our journalists?

HOST: Your question was about something else.

MIKHAIL FRIDMAN: Yes, I asked whether you investigated the matter.

ANDREI VASILIEV: Yes, I am telling you the results of the investigation.

MIKHAIL FRIDMAN: How the inaccurate information got into it?

ANDREI VASILIEV: It was accurate.

MIKHAIL FRIDMAN: It is absolutely inaccurate.

ANDREI VASILIEV: Journalists saw quotes from people, saw ATMs that weren't operating, saw closed branches—not all branches, I repeat.

MIKHAIL FRIDMAN: This is a lie. Not a single office was closed on that day.

ANDREI VASILIEV: This is why as early as on the sixth you ordered six additional cars that transport cash—what are they called?

HOST: Cash-in-transit vehicles.

ANDREI VASILIEV: Yes, cash-in-transit. Yes, one vehicle was working through the night of the sixth, four vehicles were working the entire day on the seventh, and one more … does that mean that you had anticipated our story in *Kommersant*? Or had you heard what was on the radio, in the newspapers etc., on the sixth.

MIKHAIL FRIDMAN: Well, Andrei, we are not discussing what was on the radio and in the newspapers. We are discussing what was written in the *Kommersant* article, and that was a blatant lie. You wrote …

ANDREI VASILIEV: … and this is why you ordered these vehicles one day before the story was published?

MIKHAIL FRIDMAN: We ordered the vehicles because the market was in an uproar. *Guta Bank* declared itself bankrupt the day before your article was published, and there was massive pressure on our private banks—including the *Bank of Moscow, Rosbank*—from their clients.

ANDREI VASILIEV: And that's what we wrote about.

MIKHAIL FRIDMAN: You wrote lies that we had closed some branches, that we would limit—it says so in your article—cash payments.

ANDREI VASILIEV: That's right.

MIKHAIL FRIDMAN: It's lies.

ANDREI VASILIEV: Well, the 10% commission is a limitation.

MIKHAIL FRIDMAN: No, this is not a limitation; this is … we're only talking here about deposits. We insist that we were perfectly within our legal rights, and we did not introduce any additional restrictions.

ANDREI VASILIEV: The rich can afford anything.

MIKHAIL FRIDMAN: So, let me continue, you did not carry out an investigation, but we did. And we know very well how this article appeared.

HOST: Tell us, don't keep us in suspense.

MIKHAIL FRIDMAN: Unfortunately, I can't do that publicly, but I can tell you …

HOST: Will you sell it to Vasiliev?

MIKHAIL FRIDMAN: Free of charge.

HOST: So for $11 million, you'll give it to him …

MIKHAIL FRIDMAN: Yes.

ANDREI VASILIEV: So you intentionally organized this story in front of your branches to fool our reporters, and this is how the story came about, right?

HOST: Excuse me, both of you, I think, speak wonderfully, it reminds me of that trial that already took place and was lost. So, please explain to me so that the story's story is clear; the judge issued a verdict but you are saying that he's a Kremlin henchman and is shutting you down in order to destroy press freedoms in Russia.

ANDREI VASILIEV: I said that?

HOST: Well, in your interview … It says precisely this; they decided to assist the Kremlin, to demonstrate their loyalty to the Kremlin.

ANDREI VASILIEV: I repeat, and I repeated this numerous places, that this information, I don't know this for sure.

MIKHAIL FRIDMAN: This information, as they say, is an insult to my intelligence. One of my most important qualities as a person who earns his money, I believe, is the opportunity to choose; freedom of choice. I am doing this because I believe deeply that I am doing the right thing. I believe that the free and independent press and the unobjective and untruthful press are two different things. I believe that the press—and the most respected business newspaper in this country—must bear a heavy responsibility for what it publishes. Were you thinking, when you were writing your story, about what might have happened if we—God forbid—were not able to raise the money for withdrawals demanded by our clients? We had one billion dollars. I think that we were the only bank in this country that had this fundraising ability.

HOST: The only privately owned bank.

MIKHAIL FRIDMAN: Privately owned bank, I beg your pardon. What if our bank had suspended payments? Did you know about the one million individual clients, our 100,000 corporate investors? Let me tell you a story. I had a visit from the head of *Guta Bank*, Artyom Kuznetsov, a well-known Moscow businessman …

ANDREI VASILIEV: I had a visit from him too.

MIKHAIL FRIDMAN: Well, we sat with him and he was telling me. On the 6th they announced that they were stopping payments. They issued a press release and sent it out to the media. That happened at two p.m. He said: "I had prepared myself next morning, on the 7th, to open a newspaper and read all the mud that would be thrown at me. I opened *Kommersant* because all decent people open *Kommersant* first thing in the morning, like I did, for example, and read it.

HOST: Soon they won't be able to.

MIKHAIL FRIDMAN: We'll discuss this separately.

ANDREI VASILIEV: Freedom of speech …

MIKHAIL FRIDMAN: I read the article, the editorial. And he says, "I could not believe my eyes. The article was not about us, but about you. Because it says in very small print that *Guta Bank* had stopped payments, but the main story was about the problems of *Alfa Bank*. During that hour, I got phone calls from perhaps 200 people. I know very well the price of a story published in *Gazeta* or in other well respected newspapers, and the price of a story in *Kommersant.*

ANDREI VASILIEV: So you would claim less money from *Gazeta* for this?

MIKHAIL FRIDMAN: Definitely. Because you are its leader. We never doubted this. And we value your outstanding contribution.

HOST: And will you continue to acknowledge it?

MIKHAIL FRIDMAN: Yes we hold it in high esteem for its qualities. That's perfectly true.

ANDREI VASILIEV: We value your high esteem. Thank you.

MIKHAIL FRIDMAN: As for the numbers, Andrei, believe me, this just does not sound very solid. When you talk about numbers—it is the same as if I were to start telling you about journalism.

ANDREI VASILIEV: I will give you these documents during the break.

MIKHAIL FRIDMAN: You can give them to me whenever you want.

ANDREI VASILIEV: Not whenever you want. I have each word confirmed by your documents not mine.

HOST: This is not the Kremlin agent. Then why were you going after *Kommersant*?

MIKHAIL FRIDMAN: We believe that people should be held accountable for prosperity and the economic conditions of our clients. Not just us, but also the people who subject this prosperity and stability to a jolt. I believe that *Kommersant* must realize the extent of its responsibility for what it publishes.

HOST: That is, the 10 million dollars to you for moral damages?

MIKHAIL FRIDMAN: Is it I who should call you, ask questions and find out the facts?

HOST: That is what real free journalism is—pick up a phone and call.

ANDREI VASILIEV: So what shall I be liable for this time?

MIKHAIL FRIDMAN: No, you should ask questions. Is this true or not?

ANDREI VASILIEV: We did ask.

MIKHAIL FRIDMAN: No, Andrei. You and I have known each other for many years. Moreover, the bank has given *Kommersant* loans starting in '96; millions of dollars; handled accounts of the *Kommersant* staff. And the moment you published this story—and we've known each other for years. We shake hands when we meet. And then, for some reason, you could not take a second to pick up a phone and tell me. Folks, you really do have issues. No one, not a single person called.

ANDREI VASILIEV: Yes, they did.

MIKHAIL FRIDMAN: Look, we helped you.

ANDREI VASILIEV: The article had a quote from Mr. Gafin; it is printed in full.

HOST: I am particularly concerned about this $10 million precedent.

ANDREI VASILIEV: I cannot begin to tell you how much I am concerned about it. The rich are healthier than the poor because they can allow themselves more, right.

HOST: That is, you can afford to pay $10 million? Am I revealing a terrible secret here? You both are not poor?

ANDREI VASILIEV: At the moment.

MIKHAIL FRIDMAN: Perhaps I could say a few words about this $10 million amount. Well, first of all this amount was calculated very carefully by people even more professionally qualified than the editor-in-chief of *Kommersant.*

HOST: You are breaking my heart; no one is more professional.

MIKHAIL FRIDMAN: Practically no one, but we managed to find someone. And they did some research and analysis and calculated this amount as the amount of damages caused to us, both material and moral. We do not see this amount as a revenue source. We are actually quite a large organization and we definitely do not have any bloodthirsty intentions to strip you of $11 million and pocket it, so to speak.

HOST: But if you take it, you'll be called bloodthirsty anyway.

MIKHAIL FRIDMAN: If we take it—we will certainly collect it. Because we believe that in order to make journalism more responsible …

HOST: You need to destroy them.

MIKHAIL FRIDMAN: Absolutely not. I am convinced that they will not be destroyed completely; this will not bankrupt them. Incidentally, if they do have financial problems, we are always ready to help them out.

HOST: Funny.

ANDREI VASILIEV: The authorities were quick to pay the compensation—that was a compensation for the damages too—in the amount of 46.1 million rubles. It was paid to all the victims of the "Nord-Ost" hostage crisis. So if we divide this amount by the amount that *Alfa Bank* claimed from us, the result is that the story published by *Kommersant* caused *Alfa Bank* damages that are 6.8 times higher than "Nord-Ost." Do you really think that your tragedy was that great?

MIKHAIL FRIDMAN: We definitely do not think that we suffered a tragedy like that of "Nord-Ost."

ANDREI VASILIEV: 6.8 times the tragedy.

MIKHAIL FRIDMAN: Yes, this is sacrilege, but on the other hand I am sure …

ANDREI VASILIEV: And for you the amount is sacrilege, yes?

MIKHAIL FRIDMAN: Yes, but on the other hand I am sure that everybody present here does not quite agree with that material evaluation of the "Nord-Ost" tragedy.

HOST: We'll talk about this during our jousts two and three. So many numbers. It's a good thing that I did not leave my calculator at home, please sit down. And I'll look over your numbers.

YEVGENY VELIKHOV: I think we have to look at the facts. The unscrupulous and inaccurate publication is a fact. Therefore, a punishment should follow and I believe that the amount—in my modest experience—I do not run a business, any bank, by the losses sustained by the Kurchatov Research Institute as a scientific organization in investments etc., because an unscrupulous press is on a similar scale, and therefore $10 million is a reasonable sum.

VLADIMIR GRIGORIEV: I'm not totally in agreement. There were market problems for sure, there were lines at ATMs, but the other thing is that in this round we should give Mikhail Fridman his due. He was ironic but logical. Andrei Vasiliev on the *Kommersant* side was perhaps not quite ready for that format. Because he was obviously losing to his opponent. But I am still not totally sure that *Alfa Bank* is right.

EDUARD SAGALAYEV: Honestly, I am disappointed because I was expecting Andrei to have a more articulate and strong stance. Fridman is more conclusive and more precise. And the most important thing—when he said that, "Andrei, you are the leader," he demonstrated that in this situation he is a more broadminded person. Although in this instance, I believe that a fine like that for a newspaper—even if it lied—is a terrifying precedent. But Fridman is the winner, of course. That's obvious.

ILYA AVERBUKH: I think he is the winner too, without a doubt. And I think that Andrei's big mistake was to try and play on Fridman's turf. Because those questions that he asked were clearly provocative to Fridman and Fridman gave the right answers. The only proof he presented was to say that other newspapers were writing about this too.

EDUARD SAGALAYEV: I hope that Andrei will begin to concentrate. Because he is a figher after all.

ILYA AVERBUKH: I too think that Mikhail Fridman won.

— The winner in our duel is determined by the viewers. Call the numbers on our screen, and you can vote for the participant you support.

Fridman, Mikhail Maratovich. Born April 21, 1964, in Lvov. Graduated from the Moscow Steel Alloy Institute in 1986. Worked as a design engineer in the Elektrostal Plant. In 1988 originated the *Courier* co-operative. In 1989 created a firm called *Alfa-photo*. In 1990 the *Alfa Capital* company. Since 1991, Chairman of the Board of directors of *Alfa Bank*. Since 1996—Chairman of the Board of directors of the *Alfa Group* Consortium. Since 2003—Chairman of the Board of directors of the combined *TNK-BP* company. Leading businessmen and professional managers in Russia and in Europe. Likes to travel. Prefers exotic routes. Enjoys theatre and cinema. His personal collection contains over 3,000 examples of cinema art.

HOST: John Law—the future great financier and inventor of paper money—displayed a talent for mathematics and commerce in his youth. These qualities were surprisingly combined with his skill at cards and dueling. In April 1694 in London, Law killed his opponent in a duel and was sentenced to death. Without waiting for the hangman to call he escaped from prison with the help of friends and went into hiding in France. These things progressed brilliantly. Law established the General Bank and the India Company. The young Scot enjoyed such trust and support from crowned persons that he became the controller general of France's finances.

— During the second round the seconds join the battle. They can provide the duelists with serious support. So can you with your phone calls.

Round Two

HOST: Something is rotten in our kingdom of non-Denmark. Because we have a banker talking about matters of the soul, and our journalists—about financial matters. Questions from Mr. Vasiliev's side. Yes, please.

— Pavel Astakhov, a lawyer. Mikhail Maratovich, you are certainly right to say that a banker must be accurate with his figures. Just as a journalist, covering a story, should always receive accurate information and documentary support. All the information that Andrei Vasiliev presented here was absolutely accurate, I assure you. Here are the documents issued by your bank, *Alfa Bank*. But this is not the question. The question is something else. You said that your clients became nervous after they read the story in *Kommersant*, and started withdrawing their money. But there was an instance when one of *Kommersant's* readers, after reading the article, made a demand deposit in the amount of 266,131,450 USD. Is this correct?

HOST: And his name is?

MIKHAIL FRIDMAN: This is correct.

PAVEL ASTAKHOV: Therefore, Mikhail Maratovich Fridman, upon reading the *Kommersant* article, deposited money instead of withdrawing it. And this is not the question either. You have answered it already. But you said at the beginning that you are satisfied by the court decision. Yes, the decision was made. It is indeed in your favor, although it is viewed differently by different people, of course, and it looks rather strange. So tell us please, do you feel like the victor in this trial?

MIKHAIL FRIDMAN: As for the arguments that you have in that folder of yours, I don't know whether you represent *Kommersant* or not; if not, I advise them to hire you, and you will certainly be able to present all these arguments to the court and defend their interests better than it was done by their present lawyers during the first trial. As for this strange client who deposited money, yes, indeed, we the shareholders, not just I alone, but also my colleagues, my partners, were forced to deposit our personal funds, take them from other businesses. Fortunately we had these funds available, and we transferred them so as to avoid catastrophic consequences, not just for *Alfa Bank* and its clients, but, I believe, for the entire country.

PAVEL ASTAKHOV: All this is understood, Mikhail Maratovich. This is your business. Your business, this is understood absolutely. I am interested most in this question: do you feel yourself to be the winner?

MIKHAIL FRIDMAN: We definitely feel that we are winners in a legal sense. In the moral sense this seems to me a Pyrrhic victory. Because we have great respect for *Kommersant*. I believe that *Kommersant* is an epoch in the history of Russian journalism. I believe that the best, the golden quills of Russian journalism—such as Paniushkin, Kolesnikov, Natasha Gevorkian—are working for *Kommersant* …

HOST: And now they will all go into *Alfa's* pockets because you will give them loans and buy them …

MIKHAIL FRIDMAN: They will not be in *Alfa's* pockets because we are not involved in politics. And this is why I believe that this is a Pyrrhic victory. But I believe that it is very important for journalists, and most of all for editors, people responsible for publishing such an influential newspaper as *Kommersant*, to understand that before they publish information that may affect the interests of millions of people, they should verify their information extremely carefully. In 1998, during the crisis, we were the only bank that did not steal anything from its investors. We paid back everything.

ANDREI VASILIEV: In '99 you attempted to buy *Kommersant* together with Chubais. You failed … Come on!

MIKHAIL FRIDMAN: We never tried to buy *Kommersant*.

HOST: And why would he need Chubais? You are friends with Chubais!

MIKHAIL FRIDMAN: Being friends with Chubais is definitely one of the gravest sins that one can commit in this life. I'd like to clarify the situation just mentioned by the respected editor in chief. In '99, when everyone knew that Boris Berezovsky was going to buy *Kommersant* …

Andrei Vasiliev: You decided to save it?

Host: Save Boris Berezovsky?

Mikhail Fridman: … the newspaper founder, Yakovlev. The *Kommersant* shareholders, Yakovlev's partners, came to us and requested a loan so that they would be able to reacquire this publication. And prevent Berezovsky from buying it. I will remind you that in '99 Berezovsky controlled the Public Russian Television where Mr. Andrei Vasiliev was working as the head of information programming.

Andrei Vasiliev: Now you are lying again. I was not working there in '99. I quit in '98.

Host: Well, at least you are working.

Andrei Vasiliev: It is good that you are not a journalist. You would be sued at every turn.

Mikhail Fridman: And we told them that if they wanted to buy shares in order to keep the newspaper truly independent, we were ready to give them a loan. And the question was discussed. Moreover, even Berezovsky called me with regard to this matter. He was very displeased.

Andrei Vasiliev: Did he give you a piece of advice?

Mikhail Fridman: No. He threatened, as usual. He said that …

Andrei Vasiliev: And you too?

Mikhail Fridman: He even threatened me. He threatened everyone. That's how he works.

Andrei Vasiliev: About not being involved in politics. I remember you were signing the TNK-BP agreement in London and behind you all the time Putin was standing at attention, while you were signing. And just after that, incidentally, Berezovsky received political asylum. Before that he was refused, and after that he was granted it. Now, I do not know if there is a connection, really …

Host: Fridman interceded on Berezovsky's behalf, and he got it …

Andrei Vasiliev: … with how it was signed. I know how Mr. Fridman was sitting …

Host: Bad boy this Fridman.

Andrei Vasiliev: I saw how Mr. Fridman was sitting, and Putin was standing at attention … the entire country saw it.

Host: Questions to Mr. Fridman.

Andrei Makarevich: I am Andrei Makarevich.

Andrei Vasiliev: I am Andrei Vasiliev.

Andrei Makarevich: For a long time I naïvely believed that the press exists to supply us with fresh and objective information. Until recently I clearly divided all the press into the "yellow" press that would stoop to anything, and the respectable analytical press, that was less numerous. Today I feel that this borderline is barely visible. In my own experience, I have often times woken in the morning in a very good mood, opened up a newspaper, and then read some outrageous fabrication about myself, realizing that hundreds of thousands are reading the same stuff at this very moment. And you realize that you cannot do anything about it. Because no explanation, no correction at the bottom of the last page will change anything. Silver spoons are found, but a nasty aftertaste remains. I want to ask this question. If the concept of conscience is not applicable to our journalism any more, at least a sense of responsibility—how is it measured?

ANDREI VASILIEV: Andrei, if you mean that review about your anniversary concert …

ANDREI MAKAREVICH: Andrei, please, if you think … you think me petty, I have gotten much worse reviews …

ANDREI VASILIEV: I did not interrupt you, Andrei, we are both civilized … OK, you are, you are a civilized person.

ANDREI MAKAREVICH: Believe me, this is not about me, I had about 300 negative articles.

ANDREI VASILIEV: Then give me an example about a lack of conscience. Please give an example, Andrei, really.

ANDREI MAKAREVICH: Well, we all know what I mean.

HOST: The one worth $10 million, for example.

ANDREI VASILIEV: I believe that our journalists—whether you like it or not, although I might not like it either—should write the truth. If thousands of people had been running around Moscow with their eyes popping out, standing in lines at the branches, and our reporters had not written about it, I would have sustained losses that far exceed $11 million. For sure. Because our newspaper would have stopped being a real newspaper forever. And Mr. Fridman would stop reading it first thing in the morning.

MIKHAIL FRIDMAN: That's a lie.

ANDREI MAKAREVICH: Andrei, you understand perfectly well that if we start speaking about information in general—all the information that we have is what you deem necessary to print.

ANDREI VASILIEV: I asked for an example.

MIKHAIL FRIDMAN: A lie.

ANDREI MAKAREVICH: Everything else is a rumor. And if you too—as it turns out—use rumors, than what kind of true information is there, anyway?

ANDREI VASILIEV: What rumors? What rumors?

MIKHAIL FRIDMAN: Listen, I am not going to debate the court verdict for a second time.

ANDREI VASILIEV: But what rumors! Go out on the streets, and you will run into people who were waiting in lines on the 6th, staring into the empty ATMs. And how are you going to look them in the eye?

MIKHAIL FRIDMAN: You are lying brazenly at this very moment. Besides, if you lie publicly, I will sue you again. And I am afraid that you will lose even more money. So I advise you to consider carefully, carefully before you speak.

ANDREI VASILIEV: … Just don't throw me in the briar patch …

HOST: A question was asked, what is the answer? Do I understand it correctly? What is the measure of responsibility? That was the question.

ANDREI VASILIEV: Yes. There is a measure of responsibility when you publish a correction, for example. Which we do incidentally, when …

MIKHAIL FRIDMAN: In very small print at the bottom of the last page.

ANDREI VASILIEV: And there is a measure of responsibility, for example, which is $11 million, and there is a measure of responsibility when you lose your readers' trust. This is worse than bankruptcy for us, worse than this 11 million.

HOST: I see. Are you satisfied?

ANDREI MAKAREVICH: A final question. You use the term "free press" very frequently. Don't you feel that today our press is as free as a semi-conductor; it's a one-way freedom, if it needs to throw mud at someone or something. But when it needs to find a kind of word or an objective word, you only do it for money.

ANDREI VASILIEV: Andrei, for things like that you actually can be caught, you can be sued, but you did not say *Kommersant* specifically, so I won't be able …

ANDREI MAKAREVICH: I am talking about the press.

ANDREI VASILIEV: I believe it is much harder to be an objective press, than, say, a corrupt press, because the latter takes stuff from both sides, and no one is angry about it. Yes, when the press is objective, every day … each and every day we can and we risk displeasing our readers, and our owners. And the authorities.

HOST: Are the authorities often displeased?

ANDREI VASILIEV: Very often.

HOST: And in all my days of reading *Kommersant* I never heard a bad word in his address.

ANDREI VASILIEV: Are you sure you were reading *Kommersant*, Volodya?

HOST: All the time.

ANDREI VASILIEV: Are you sure you are not confusing it? There is a *Communist* newspaper …

HOST: No, no. Incidentally, is the *Communist* published with Boris Abramovich's money too? Mr. Geraschenko has a question, please.

— Geraschenko, a former employee of the country's Central Bank.

HOST: Spoken modestly.

VIKTOR GERASCHENKO: Mikhail Markovich, I always respected your bank and your group, and I can confirm your words that your bank was the only one of those so-called "big seven" to come out of the '98 crisis honorably. And the fact that your institution strives to attract private funds to develop its financial activity is quite understandable. Buy why did private funds deposited in your bank drop 1.5 billion rubles between January 1, 2004, and April 1st, 2004? There was no crisis at that moment.

MIKHAIL FRIDMAN: Because of *Kommersant.* I'll explain in a moment. I'll explain it to you in more professional terms than ...

VIKTOR GERASCHENKO: Everybody else may leave, that's what you mean?

MIKHAIL FRIDMAN: No, no, no. It's just that our policy is rather conservative and we offer noticeably lower interest rates on deposits than many other commercial banks. Therefore part of the time deposits flowed out to the banks with higher yields on deposits. In principle we plan our profits not from deposits but from client services; this is our strategy. Therefore our time deposits went down, while the amount of demand deposits rose significantly.

VIKTOR GERASCHENKO: Then what right did you have to introduce this 10% commission?

MIKHAIL FRIDMAN: I've said already, it's understandable ...

VIKTOR GERASCHENKO: This is not stated anywhere, you were in breach of your deposit agreement with investors.

MIKHAIL FRIDMAN: I can show you our deposit agreement; it says that the bank has the right to introduce a penalty in case of early withdrawal. And all these agreements are signed by our clients. Consequently, we had complete legal right to introduce this commission. But our goal was not to make money on this, but to stop the panic. Incidentally, this worked very well. I think that being a banker you understand perfectly well that this story in *Kommersant* which we are discussing here led to the withdrawal of many private deposits on that day. $800 million just evaporated. And it was useless to claim: "folks, we are in great shape, don't you worry," because the more you say that, the less they believe you.

ANDREI VASILIEV: That's sympathetic, Mikhail.

MIKHAIL FRIDMAN: Yes.

ANDREI VASILIEV: The more you say, the less you're believed, really.

MIKHAIL FRIDMAN: Very true.

ANDREI VASILIEV: Serious people, corporate clients, they all read *Kommersant* like its the alphabet, like their mother tongue.

MIKHAIL FRIDMAN: Very true

ANDREI VASILIEV: And holding this newspaper they rushed to withdraw their money from you. Some partners that you have, some corporate clients.

MIKHAIL FRIDMAN: Very true. This is our country; we don't have another. And we don't have other writers either. Did I answer your question?

— Not completely satisfactorily.

HOST: A question from Mr. Fridman's side.

YURI BASHMET: I am Yuri Bashmet. I want to say that the *Kommersant* newspaper employs people who are not professional. I am speaking now only about music. They have a department where a person works without a higher education, a person who confuses composers' names, a person who doesn't know musical terms. But this person is the critic responsible for reviews published by *Kommersant*. Now, of course, Andrei will claim that this is about a review of one of my concerts. But the fact is that this country lost Rostropovich, although he is alive and well and in perfect shape, because of such a press. He announced that he won't play in Moscow. And I've been listening to talk of freedom of speech. We don't need that. I believe that these two concepts should not be confused. I am for freedom of speech, too. But not for the freedom of insolence. We have Spivakov, we have Gutman, we have Petrov, and I, your humble servant. It works. Audiences give us standing ovations.

ANDREI VASILIEV: What is your question, Yuri? How long will it take? You are not playing cello.

YURI BASHMET: Keep quiet. Or our conversation will end with you know what.

HOST: That is, you'll punch his façade?

YURI BASHMET: Yes, I'll call my big brother Klichko now.

HOST: Your two big brothers.

YURI BASHMET: But the point is that right now I am in a very good mood actually, and you know why? I am happy that a person has finally been punished for this. Although it means nothing to him because it's not his money. Still, justice has prevailed, and I am happy now. And I think that if all the incompetent press—just in the field of music—were gathered together now, even the person who finances it would not have enough money to pay. You see. Finally the door cracked open and you got kicked in the ass. I am happy.

ANDREI VASILIEV: As I understand it, I put a question mark here?

HOST: What is your question? Would Berezovsky go broke if all insulted musicians filed lawsuits?

YURI BASHMET: No. The question is: who is Vasiliev working for, and who is paying him for trying to destroy the State? This is anti-government activity. What is your work? You know what it is? When a girl or a boy comes to a concert hall and listens to Natalia Gutman, who has dedicated her entire life to cello? And your illiterate journalist, without an education, writes that she is bad? Well, let's just say it. Do you understand what this means? You are a saboteur.

ANDREI VASILIEV: Is that the question?

HOST: The question is: are you a saboteur?

ANDREI VASILIEV: I'm not a saboteur. I'm a user.

MIKHAIL FRIDMAN: May I clarify the question.

YURI BASHMET: The question was: Who are you working for? Who hired you to destroy the State?

ANDREI VASILIEV: All right. I am sick and tired of all this irresponsible talk about who I am working for, who pays me.

YURI BASHMET: Incidentally, you are the editor-in-chief.

ANDREI VASILIEV: Our figures, not those from *Alfa Bank*, show that in the year 2003 we earned 157 million 439 thousand rubles, not counting affiliated enterprises, from which we paid 50 million 400 thousand in taxes on those earnings. This money, part of this money goes to my payroll, journalists' payroll, and janitors' payroll. Et cetera. Who pays me? I've had enough of the question, "who pays me?" It's been a very long time since anyone has paid me. Incidentally, Mikhail most likely understands this very well—that we are making a profit.

HOST: And these illiterate people who insulted Bashmet, Spivakov and many others? Are they on the payroll too?

ANDREI VASILIEV: Yes, indeed, there was a case like this, and more than one. There have been several reviews where the reviewer liked how he plays cello, but not how he conducts. And our critics have the right to personal opinion. And if I tell them: do not write that you did not like it because …

We are going on a break.

HOST: A break. I see. Before this, incidentally, the critic worked as a lathe operator? A doctor? A musician? A girl … musical? Of course. Well, all right.

MIKHAIL FRIDMAN: Just in case, let me explain that Mr. Bashmet was playing alto.

HOST: That much we know. That you don't need to explain.

MIKHAIL FRIDMAN: It is Rostropovich who plays cello.

ILYA AVERBUKH: As far as I am concerned, Fridman won this round again. I did not like the way Andrei Vasiliev behaved. There was a certain boldness in his behavior, even insolence at times.

EDUARD SAGALAYEV: I think that Fridman was also rude.

ILYA AVERBUKH: Well, maybe, although he did finally decide to wake up after completely losing the first round. But he gives no facts. You can't talk to Bashmet like that; you can't say that he plays cello when he actually plays alto.

EDUARD SAGALAYEV: This is true. Although for the sake of fairness, I must say that first, this was a bloody round. Second, they went to the core, to the essence, to the core of the problem. The issue is: if we actually have a free, truly independent press, does it have the right to make mistakes. And I certainly believe that—yes, it has this right to make mistakes, and to question this as Fridman's seconds do …

ILYA AVERBUKH: Nevertheless Andrei Vasiliev's defense is rather weak …

EDUARD SAGALAYEV: But certainly it does not have the right to malicious … slander. For the sake of objectivity, although I am not happy, I have to admit that Fridman wins. Fridman wins on points. Not by a knockout yet.

VLADIMIR GRIGORIEV: Although Andrei looks superficial, still I would like to side with him after this round. Both Yuri Bashmet, whom I respect deeply, and Andrei Makarevich, whom I admire, touched upon a purely professional side, without realizing what is it that Andrei does as editor-in-chief, as head of the publication. And Fridman noted that quite correctly. They have created the best newspaper in this country. Tens of thousands start their day with this newspaper, and for a number of years they had the best culture section. And to pick up on some particulars, to speak … to merge them with others is a completely wrong assessment.

YEVGENY VELIKHOV: The point is not respect for this newspaper; the point is a specific case of misinformation, which no one has yet refuted. It did happen. And damage was caused by this misinformation. So for me this is a very positive result, because I was skeptical about the possibility of suing the press. Now I am going to consider this as a possibility.

— We remind you that the duelist who receives more viewer votes will be declared the winner. Call us, the numbers are on the screen.

Vasiliev, Andrei Vitalievich was born July 20, 1957 in Moscow. Studied for 13 years at the Moscow State Institution of Chemical Engineering. Began his journalistic career in 1979 with *Moscow Komsomolets*. Worked on various papers. In 1989 became head of the pre-publishing department of *Kommersant*. Then deputy editor-in-chief and editor-in-chief of *Kommersant-Vlast*. Worked for a time in television. Held management positions at ORT. In 1999 returned to *Kommersant* as editor-in-chief of the paper and editor-in-chief of the combined editorial office of *Kommersant* publishers. Since 2001, director general. In his free time likes billiards and downhill skiing. Has appeared in small film roles. Also has stage experience. Married, he has a son and a daughter.

HOST: The famous Count Fyodor Tolstoy was playing cards with a friend of Pushkin's, Pavel Naschekin. When it came time to settle up, Tolstoy decided that Naschekin had lost 20,000 to him. He refused to pay. The count then placed a pistol on the table and declared: "It is loaded. Will you pay or not?" Naschekin took his watch and wallet from his pocket and said: "the watch may be worth 500 rubles, the wallet has 20 in it. This is all you'll get if you kill me. To conceal the crime you will have to pay the police several thousand. So what is the sense of killing me?" "Fine fellow," Tolstoy replied and held out his hand to Naschekin. They were lifelong friends.

— During the third and final round the duelist will face questions from Vladimir Soloviov's questions.

Round Three

HOST: Andrei, we always associate you with the free press, free journalism. Can you explain to me what freedom of speech is?

ANDREI VASILIEV: Actually there is no such concept. And there should not be. We have to be responsible for our words.

HOST: Yes.

ANDREI VASILIEV: Just like a civil servant must be responsible for his words. We should not confuse responsibility and control with these words.

HOST: Yes.

ANDREI VASILIEV: I cannot send Andrei Makarevich's friend to cover Andrei Makarevich's concert. I cannot send Yuri Bashmet's girlfriend to cover Bashmet's concert. I cannot send to a bank—for example, to your bank—an ex-employee of *Alfa Bank*.

HOST: That is, if you say that journalism must be responsible, than this lawsuit, the fact of this lawsuit does not surprise you?

ANDREI VASILIEV: Of course it does not.

HOST: Were you expecting *Alfa Bank* to sue you?

ANDREI VASILIEV: Well, you know, we have quite a lot ... This is a routine thing for us.

HOST: That is, you are sued all the time?

ANDREI VASILIEV: Yes, well, some we win, others ...

HOST: Then please explain why do you see a Kremlin plot behind this particular lawsuit?

ANDREI VASILIEV: Who told you that I saw this anyway?

HOST: Sorry, you did.

ANDREI VASILIEV: No, I said that according to my sources, unconfirmed, Mr. Fridman decided to trade his loyalty to the Kremlin. That is what I said. I did not say that this was a Kremlin plot. I did not say that the Kremlin gave him orders about this. Absolutely not. But I did say that other thing. I believed that this was Fridman's initiative.

HOST: Fridman himself?

ANDREI VASILIEV: Yes, and I can confirm it. I assumed it was Fridman himself.

HOST: Right, Mikhail tell me please.

MIKHAIL FRIDMAN: According to my sources, Mr. Vasiliev is lying.

HOST: Please clarify: what was the time period between the publication of the article and the court ruling?

MIKHAIL FRIDMAN: Well, let's count, between the 6th of July and today.

HOST: That is, a bit over three months.

MIKHAIL FRIDMAN: Yes.

HOST: This is usual practice in Russia—you file a suit, and suddenly boom-bam, in just three and a half months you have a decision?

MIKHAIL FRIDMAN: This is completely standard practice when hearing cases in the Moscow Arbitration Court.

HOST: And it is regular practice for the court to look at a piece of paper with a $10 million claim for moral damages—and say yes, indeed, this is completely in line.

MIKHAIL FRIDMAN: Yes, certainly this sets a precedent. But in principle we have already created similar precedents in respect to other publications. Simply those other publications were of a much smaller size than *Kommersant,* although the amounts we claimed from them were quite substantial in their terms. Besides, we regularly sue foreign publications that reprint stories of this kind that appear in newspapers here. And when we go to court there ...

HOST: I can imagine newspaper headlines tomorrow; "*Alfa Bank* Secret Revenue Source."

MIKHAIL FRIDMAN: Yes. The first …

ANDREI VASILIEV: The secret revealed.

MIKHAIL FRIDMAN: And the first thing they ask in any foreign court is: "did you sue the publication that was reprinted by the Western press, back in your own country, in Russia?"

HOST: And you say, now, "yes."

MIKHAIL FRIDMAN: We have to do this because otherwise they will say: "well, you did not sue your own press." Although we try to explain to them that if …

HOST: That is, otherwise you would not sue them? But just because they are being reprinted?

MIKHAIL FRIDMAN: Of course, we are not their enemies. We simply believe that, among other things, we have to fight for the independent press to be responsible, as Mr. Vasiliev suggests. I believe that in general many concepts that normal people hold sacred are discredited here. When we say "democracy," for people here democracy is a dirty word. When we say free and independent press, a normal Russian citizen believes that this means corrupt, kept journalism.

HOST: And when we talk of a "free and independent court," what does a common Russian citizen think then?

MIKHAIL FRIDMAN: He doesn't think very highly of it probably, unfortunately.

HOST: Interesting. Mr. Vasiliev has started this topic, but then suddenly stopped. The "Nord-Ost," the "Transvaal Park," the Metro, which everyone is silent about. Not a single claim for moral damages, if I understand it correctly, was awarded. Several years passed, but as it turns out, this is quite a regular practice for one of the country's largest, excuse me, oligarchical structures, to pick up 10 million dollars just like that?

MIKHAIL FRIDMAN: Definitely, it is very hard to watch victims in court who cannot defend their rights. Of course, our lawyers are perhaps more forceful and professional than the lawyers who defended the rights of those people. But unfortunately we have no other writers, as you quite correctly stated. This is the only court we have. We do not have anything else.

HOST: The court that loves rich corporations and does not like victims.

ANDREI VASILIEV: Please ask Mr. Fridman. A Mr. Renov, Eduard Nikolayevich, until '98 he was a vice president of the Tyumen Oil Company. Then he left the company and became a Deputy Minister of Justice. And now—by some strange coincidence—is the Deputy Head of the Supreme Arbitration Court. When he took us to court, did he not count on this man?

HOST: This is normal. Andrei, tell me please, what would make you fire a staffer who you do not like? What if, for example, such insignificant musicians as Makarevich, Spivakov, Bashmet, Rostropovich are telling you that this person is incompetent? And you reply—no, I have a better understanding of the situation, she is very professional; they are taking offense for no reason?

ANDREI VASILIEV: These journalists are invited all the time to attend classical music concerts. Yuri Bashmet invites them too, and he is highly offended when we do not come.

HOST: So your criterion is—who is invited?

ANDREI VASILIEV: No, she is invited personally. Why did she not come? Well, why invite her then?

HOST: You are covering the banking sphere—a very specific one, a very difficult area, where every word brings consequences where people file lawsuits or suffer heart attacks after reading something. Because on that day I was working at the *Silver Rain* Radio studio, and people were hysterical. They believed that '98 was back, that their life was over. Well, in this sphere—who among bankers is in your reference group, who are the people you consult to find out how professional a particular journalist is who covers this sphere?

ANDREI VASILIEV: I probably would not discuss the professional qualifications of a journalist with a banker, this is not a banker's area. Some subjects I do discuss with the bankers that I know personally, such as our angle of the coverage.

HOST: And with whom were you discussing the angle of the *Alfa Bank* coverage, because you suddenly allowed such a potentially explosive story to appear without discussing the issue?

ANDREI VASILIEV: When it rains, I do not discuss it with the State Weather Control Center, I can see that it's raining.

HOST: And they reach for the umbrella?

ANDREI VASILIEV: And I tell my readers to take their umbrellas. When I see people waiting in likes at the *Alfa Bank* branches, I do not need to ask permission to cover the story.

HOST: So you personally saw lines at *Alfa Bank* branches?

ANDREI VASILIEV: What, do you mean personally? It's not my job. I'm not editor-in-chief, I'm the director general. I got about 15 phone calls from close friends who told me: we are calling from a line at *Alfa Bank*, should we withdraw our money or not?

HOST: Write about this. Were there any bankers among them?

ANDREI VASILIEV: What have bankers got to do with this?

HOST: As our grandfather Lenin and lawyers used to say—*qui bono*, who benefits? What Fridman was hinting at, Mikhail, and say, for example, that now that *Alfa* will sue the *Kommersan*t daily, but say, a Duma Deputy Pupkin. Say, Deputy Pupkin does not appreciate that he was called Gubkin. He believes that he sustained terrible moral damage. And now there is a definite precedent. He sues *Kommersant*, and eventually *Kommersant* will be shut down, because there will be—maybe not more than 450—but still quite a few Gubkins. So it turns out that you have opened that very door through which—in the case of an absolutely imperfect court system—enters people with faces like that, fists like that, and absolutely no intellect whatsoever. And they can say that *Kommersant* is oppositional, which is true, and you are unpleasant, which is true, that you are malicious, which perhaps is also true, but we are indisputably the best—or was the best. Because after all these lawsuits one can eventually forget about its existence. So by this token the freedom-loving fighter for the interest of journalism at large, Fridman, will turn into a gravedigger for the free press.

MIKHAIL FRIDMAN: I definitely believe that the precedent that we created is rather dangerous. Because indeed many might be tempted to repeat this situation and demand—perhaps without sufficient reasons—large compensation. I presume that without sufficient reasons the Arbitration Court will not side with such plaintiffs. If *Kommersant* needs help, and we—for example—will be convinced that they have a just case and that their publications are fair—this is a subjective thing—then we are ready to help them. But in the given situation ... Why did I come here at all? Some advised me against coming here. People do not like oligarchs, and I am not a public person, usually I do not appear publicly ...

ANDREI VASILIEV: Neither am I a public person, and I was advised against.

MIKHAIL FRIDMAN: I believe that I am doing the right thing ...

HOST: Well, I was advised against coming here too. *(Applause.)*

MIKHAIL FRIDMAN: I believe that an independent press is the key element to the very existence of private business in our country.

HOST: Good. Independent press—what is that?

MIKHAIL FRIDMAN: An independent press is an objective press. It automatically becomes popular and independent because it pays its own bills, it does not need owners. Shall we say, it does not need donors, it needs shareholders ...

HOST: According to that definition, *Kommersant* is unquestionably independent? Andrei, please explain to me, you keep hinting that the Kremlin does not like *Kommersant* ...

ANDREI VASILIEV: Not the Kremlin. What's the Kremlin got to do with it?

HOST: There is this feeling. That it is oppositional, it is annoying …

ANDREI VASILIEV: First, our Kremlin has no reason to love *Kommersant.* This is true. On the other hand, saying that we have certain problems with the Kremlin … I don't have them. Except regular working ones.

HOST: Working ones—what are those? I ask Putin to come in for an interview, and he doesn't?

ANDREI VASILIEV: I requested a couple of times, yes. And he didn't. Well. *(Applause.)* This is normal. On the other hand, the fact that when it becomes profitable in society to win points with the Kremlin by harming *Kommersant* …

HOST: Why?

ANDREI VASILIEV: That's a symptom of the society.

HOST: If I understand it correctly, the president likes what your Kremlin correspondent writes?

ANDREI VASILIEV: Ask him. I don't feel free to ask because … Bashmet does not like it, the president does not like it …

HOST: I know the president's last name, it is not Bashmet. Do you personally believe that you are so disliked by the Kremlin, that the Kremlin could not find a simpler way than to take Fridman—who is regularly accused, incidentally, or to whom they say: "Do you know Khodorkovsky? You are next." *(Applause.)*

ANDREI VASILIEV: Well?

HOST: So he tried to leave the line. Is this the logic?

ANDREI VASILIEV: I cannot understand it. We have had normal relations with *Alfa Bank,* really constructive relations for many years. Yes? Well, we have been on friendly terms with Mr. Fridman …

HOST: Bottoms up!

ANDREI VASILIEV: What is more … Mr. Fridman knows for sure, of course, that the lines we were writing about, that it was true …

HOST: No—no—no …

ANDREI VASILIEV: And suddenly such a situation comes up, such a collision. I never said that he received orders. I had a feeling …

HOST: Based on unconfirmed sources.

ANDREI VASILIEV: Yes, I personally had this feeling. I have the right—unlike *Kommersant*—to work with unconfirmed sources. I am not writing stories for it.

HOST: Do you understand any of that?

MIKHAIL FRIDMAN: No. I want to say that if Mr. Vasiliev thinks that I was just mildly annoyed when together with my partners I had to raise one billion dollars in two days in order to stop, so to say …

HOST: Tell me, how does one do this? Because this is very common—I head out in the morning and begin to think: where can I raise a billion dollars?

ANDREI VASILIEV: Because of one story in *Kommersant* he had to look for a billion dollars? Is this plausible? Is this plausible at all?

MIKHAIL FRIDMAN: Yes, certainly.

HOST: I cannot picture how one can start looking and find a billion dollars in a couple days.

ANDREI VASILIEV: Then picture what the *Kommersant* newspaper is.

MIKHAIL FRIDMAN: I can picture very well what the *Kommersant* newspaper is. Because while I was driving in the car and reading this article ... I got into the car and read the story. And I got about 40 phone calls.

HOST: Stop. You said almost 200 at the beginning.

MIKHAIL FRIDMAN: During the day. This was while I was still in the car.

ANDREI VASILIEV: List these people.

— Break.

HOST: Well, while Fridman is recalling and putting together a list of people that he will show us I hope sooner or later, sit down, please. The last thing left is for you to hear the opinions of our most respected jurors.

— Just a few minutes left to the end of the program. But you still can affect its results. Please vote.

MIKHAIL FRIDMAN: I believe that *Kommersant* must realize the extent of its responsibility for what it publishes.

ANDREI VASILIEV: I believe that our journalists—whether you like it or not, although I might not like it either—must write the truth.

MIKHAIL FRIDMAN: ... the free and independent press and the subjective and false press are two different things.

ANDREI VASILIEV: ... When it rains, I do not discuss it with the State Weather Control Center, I can see that it's raining.

MIKHAIL FRIDMAN: ... if you lie publicly, I will sue you again. And I am afraid that you will lose more money.

ANDREI VASILIEV: The more you say, the less one believes you, really.

MIKHAIL FRIDMAN: ... the story you published contained many inaccuracies, to put it mildly, or false information, to put it simply.

ANDREI VASILIEV: Do you really think that your tragedy was that great?

— Here comes the peak moment of our duel. The jurors are about to announce their verdict, and we will count the viewers' votes.

HOST: Well, you are used to this by now, so hear the verdict, but your supreme judge is the people. So, Mr. Grigoriev.

VLADIMIR GRIGORIEV: You know, when late in the '80s—early in the '90s the "White" movement's memoirs and documents began to appear in publication, it became clear basically that it was not the Red Army that had won, but the "White" movement that was torn to pieces by internal conflicts and ambitions. Knowing both opponents quite well, I can say that they both represent the same movement. The *Alfa Group* has created a fantastic school of innovative managers, and *Kommersant* has created a fantastic school of new innovative journalism. But summing up all three rounds, of course I have to award victory to Mikhail Fridman for being bright, metaphoric, and arguing well. But I also would like to quote Mikhail Fridman that as the court ruling goes, this is a Pyrrhic victory.

HOST: Academician Velikhov?

YEVGENY VELIKHOV: I am not siding with any camp here; I have no connection—either personal, or corporate—with *Alfa Bank* or with *Kommersant*. But I have to say that the first round looked indeed—if false information was indeed disseminated, this should be punished accordingly. The second joust revealed that this goes far beyond the limits of economic cases—here you have the case of musicians, I have had the same experience, when stress is caused to millions of people by unscrupulous information. It is important to me that a case of unscrupulous information was finally punished properly. I hope that after this the media in general, who have objective reasons to always choose negative information, will start being more responsible.

HOST: Thank you. Mr. Averbukh.

ILYA AVERBUKH: I will agree with the previous speakers. Of course, today's winner is Mikhail Fridman, and he wins first of all because of his thoughtfulness and sound arguments. We—people in creative professions—suffer much from a press that confuses democracy with disorder. This is why Mikhail Fridman wins.

HOST: Mr. Sagalayev.

EDUARD SAGALAYEV: On my way here I opened the *Kommersant* newspaper and read about what to expect here, at this show. In the section that I trust most of all—the Horoscopes. About Libra—I am a Libra—it says: that you are heading for a trap in relationships, because I am actually by definition on the side of the press, I am a journalist. And it really hurts me that at today's show a blow was dealt—maybe not a crushing blow, but a blow nonetheless, to *Kommersant's* reputation, and I respect this newspaper very much and I want to say that the people who cover television there, for example, are absolutely professional. I am very sorry that we are witnessing a confrontation here—shall we say—between the capitalist press and the capital. Yes, being objective, I think that another winner here is *NTV*, because this was a sound and meaningful program, and if *NTV* continues these discussions of what a free press is in modern Russian society, what are its possibilities, what are restrictions to its activities, then I—I will be very satisfied, and satisfied by today's program, too. Thank you.

HOST: Well, you have heard the opinion of our respected jurors, but the people name the real winner.

— Viewers, as well as the jurors, award victory to Mikhail Fridman.

Appendix 2

The "Evolving Oligarch"

Institutional Investor

September 1, 2003

Mikhail Fridman's headquarters in Moscow has the look and feel of an old-time Hollywood mogul's lair: The ceiling vaults 20 feet, colossal abstract paintings hang on the walls, designer chairs induce soothing comfort, and a broad staircase leads to a very private alcove. In this opulent setting Fridman is summarizing a few of the basic tenets behind his improbable rise from window cleaner to billionaire oligarch in barely a dozen years.

Rule No. 1: Only make investments that offer potentially huge returns. "When we began, we never thought of investing in … " — here Fridman pauses, straining to locate objects of insignificance amid all this splendor — " … in cups or ashtrays, for example. We looked for really big businesses, like banking and oil."

Rule No. 2: Foreign investors are welcome, but only after Russian insiders have won the most lucrative battles for assets (see box, page 126). A case in point is the recent merger of Fridman's oil company with BP, which didn't take place until the British petroleum giant had been forced to forgo several years of profits in an earlier investment in the same property.

Rule No. 3: Don't expect reforms to change Russian capitalism's robber baron mentality anytime soon. "It's not that I object to reforms, but businessmen can't wait around for the government to act," he says.

Rule No. 4: "Eventually, everything we own is for sale — probably to foreign investors," says Fridman.

And rule No. 5: No matter how much wealth you amass, stick to business and leave politics to the professionals. Mikhail Khodorkovsky, Russia's richest oligarch, appears to have gotten himself into deep trouble by breaching that barrier (see page 9). After hinting at presidential ambitions, he and his Yukos Oil Co. recently came under criminal investigation. On the other hand, the more prudent Fridman — a tall, burly 39-year-old with an impish grin who is Russia's third-richest man — has emerged as President Vladimir Putin's favorite oligarch; he even got the Russian leader to show up for the June signing ceremony in London of the merger of his company, Tyumen Oil Co., or TNK, with BP.

That $6.15 billion deal, which covers oil and gas production, has made Fridman a household name in Russia. But he was already super rich from investments in oil, telecommunications, banking, food distribution and commodities trading funneled through his *Alfa Group* Consortium. That financial-industrial conglomerate was cobbled from the profits of a motley assortment of capitalist ventures — from nightclubs to laboratory-animal breeding — undertaken by Fridman as a university student and young factory engineer in the waning days of the Soviet era.

It's the kind of incredibly swift rags-to-riches story that has induced investors to become bullish on Russia once again. Memories of the devastating financial crisis are fading. In the first six months of 2003, share prices on the local bourse, the Russian Trading System stock exchange, climbed about a third. Russian corporate bond issuance reached $3.5 billion in the same period, easily topping the total for all of 2002. And, fueled by oil exports, GDP grew by 4.3 percent in 2002 and surged at a more than 7 percent annual rate in the first half of this year.

Although most of Fridman's *Alfa Group* investments are privately held, the publicly traded shares in the two telecoms controlled by the group — fixed-line operator Golden Telecom and wireless operator JSC Vimpel-Communications, both with clients mainly in Moscow and St. Petersburg — have easily outperformed the local stock market. Golden Telecom (Nasdaq symbol: GLDN) soared from a 52-week low of 10.15 last October to 30.55 in July. VimpelCom (NYSE symbol: VIP) rose from a 52-week low of 20.62 in July 2002 to 49.02 a year later.

Business oligarchs like Fridman continue to power the Russian economy — and to hold the fate of minority shareholders in their hands. According to a December 2001 study by Brunswick UBS Warburg, a Moscow-based investment bank, eight financial-industrial groups control the 64 largest private companies in Russia. Among the prominent oligarchs cited in the study alongside Fridman and Khodorkovsky were Roman Abramovich (Russia's second-richest man, who is merging his oil operations with Khodorkovsky's), Oleg Deripaska (who owns the largest aluminum producer in the country) and Vladimir Potanin (who used part of his oil proceeds to corner Russia's nickel output). Critics contend that this concentration of wealth creates barriers to competition, makes it more difficult for new businesses to get started and offers portfolio investors very limited choices on the local equity markets. The big financial-industrial groups "aren't acting very differently from monopolies anywhere else," says Christof Ruehl, chief economist at the World Bank's Moscow office."

Both the World Bank and the International Monetary Fund are urging Moscow to press ahead with structural reforms that would diversify the economy beyond its heavy dependence on oil and other natural-resource exports. With most banks linked to the big financial-industrial groups, credit is virtually unavailable for other businesses. "Sounder financial institutions and stronger financial intermediation will be key to improving the climate for private sector activity, particularly for small and medium-size enterprises," asserted an IMF report in May. According to a World Bank study released last year, such businesses account for only 12 percent of Russia's GDP, compared with more than 50 percent in the U.S. and much of the European Union.

Defenders of the Russian capitalist model argue not only that it isn't broken but that it doesn't need fixing. Only China's economy is expanding faster, they note. Besides, say the optimists, oligarchs have moderated their hard-boiled approach to business. But skeptics remain. "With Russia's kind of growth, it's hard to convince people that business and banking reforms are urgent," says Stephen Jennings, chief executive officer of Renaissance Capital, a leading Moscow-based investment bank.

Fridman is often cited as a paragon of the evolving oligarch. "He played some rough games earlier in his career," says Marshall Goldman, a Harvard University economics professor whose recent book, *The Piratization of Russia: Russian Reform Goes Awry*, offers a scathing vision of buccaneer capitalism. "But nowadays he looks like one of the more enlightened entrepreneurs." Nothing better illustrates Fridman's progress from notoriety to celebrity than his dealings with his new partner, U.K. oil giant BP. Even though BP once sued Fridman for seizing valuable petroleum fields for which the British company had paid close to a half-billion dollars, this past June BP signed a deal to pay $6.15 billion — the largest foreign investment in post-Communist Russia's history — for half of Fridman's TNK, which controls the same oil fields. Between these two bookends is a rough-and-tumble saga about "learning to do business in Russia — the hard way," says Robert Dudley, the BP vice president who has been named chief executive officer of the joint venture, TNK-BP.

It all began in 1997, when BP spent $471 million for a 10 percent share in Sidanco Oil Co., which owned rich deposits in western Siberia and was controlled by oligarch Potanin. Potanin plunged Sidanco deeply into debt, and Fridman, the rival oil tycoon running *Alfa Group*, swiftly moved to take over the Sidanco subsidiaries that held the largest petroleum fields. In 1999, Fridman had a Siberian court declare the Sidanco units bankrupt and then purchased them cheaply for his own company, TNK.

"Legally, we acted properly," says Fridman. "True, our bankruptcy laws can be contradictory — even our judges don't always understand them."

Fridman says that BP was an unfortunate bystander in his battle with Potanin, but he insists that the British company refused to listen to his explanations and instead took legal and political action against him. Besides fighting TNK and Fridman in Russian courts, BP sought to regain the oil fields by appealing directly to Putin and then prevailing upon British Prime Minister Tony Blair to make a written plea to the Russian leader. In Washington, BP lobbyists stalled a $500 million loan that TNK was seeking from the Export-Import Bank of the United States. But all this global clout didn't mean much in Moscow or Siberia. "BP is a big, influential company in the world," says Fridman. "On the other hand, in Russia we are stronger."

So why did these bitter foes become partners? BP was driven by the need for new reserves. With oil fields in Alaska and the North Sea depleting, Russia offered the most promising venue outside of the Middle East. And in Siberia, Fridman controlled some of the most attractive fields, including the Sidanco properties. BP dropped its legal and political actions against Fridman and began exploring the possibility of going into business with him. Not wishing to be gored again, BP first tested Fridman's reliability by purchasing an additional 15 percent of shares in Sidanco in 2001. According to BP's Dudley, there were no hitches in co-managing Sidanco with TNK or getting Fridman to agree on a long-term company strategy. Convinced it could work with the oligarch, BP signed the deal with TNK earlier this year, creating the third-largest oil company in Russia, with assets of about $14 billion and production of some 1.2 million barrels a day.

"Sometimes you can build mutual trust through adversity," says Dudley. Still, BP must have wondered again about its new Russian partner's trustworthiness when a few weeks later, on the eve of the June 26 signing ceremony in London that would be attended by both Blair and Putin, an awkward hitch developed. It seemed that TNK had purchased an interest in another Russian oil company, Slavneft, last December, adding about $600 million in debt to TNK's books. Apparently not informed about this extra burden, BP balked at paying the previously agreed-upon $6.75 billion for half of TNK and signed the final accord only after all-night negotiations reduced that figure to $6.15 billion. BP says that it may yet include the Slavneft stake in the joint venture but that it will insist upon some rigorous due diligence before deciding.

Though BP was paying a second time for access to the same reserves it had bought in 1997, it still got its Russian oil cheaply. According to a Renaissance Capital analysis, BP purchased TNK's reserves at about one third the price per barrel that it would have paid for oil in countries with more reliable track records. Dudley concurs: "BP believes it paid a fair price, because the risks are clearly there."

For Fridman, the deal was a no-brainer. With BP's technical and marketing prowess, he says, "the company's performance will improve, and our shares will rise many times if we decide to sell them in the future." Some analysts view Fridman as the clear winner. "He took a global operator like BP and made them play to his terms," says James Fenkner, chief strategist at Troika Dialog, a Moscow-based brokerage. Adds William Browder, chief executive officer of Hermitage Capital Management, a Moscow-based fund, "Fridman was one of the first oligarchs to figure out that his assets would become even more valuable if he brought in foreign investors."

But Fridman isn't gloating. He still has to contend with a $1.5 billion racketeering suit filed against him and his Russian partners in U.S. District Court for the Northern District of New York last year by Canada's Norex Petroleum, another minority shareholder in Sidanco's oil units. "We're demanding the return of the oil and other assets taken from us by TNK and *Alfa Group*," says Norex president Phil Murray. Fridman responds that Norex is hoping for an out-of-court settlement. "But we are not prepared to bargain with them, because it's a question of our reputation," he says. "They are accusing us of terrible crimes."

A smooth partnership with BP would go a long way toward enhancing Fridman's reputation. Under the agreement BP's Dudley will be in charge of the joint venture's day-to-day management, while Fridman as chairman of the board will seek to smooth out any political road bumps and arrange further acquisitions. "One of the strengths of Russian partners is that they know the landscape and what new opportunities are out there," says Dudley.

In his meteoric career Fridman has certainly demonstrated a nose for new business opportunities. Born in the Ukrainian city of Lvov, he came to Moscow in the 1980s to study metallurgical engineering. While still at university he earned money as a private window washer and as co-owner of a discotheque — activities that were officially illegal in the Soviet Union. Later, though employed as an engineer in a state electrical-machinery factory, Fridman found time to start a private courier service, an apartment rental agency for foreigners, a company that imported cigarettes and perfumes and another that sold used computers. He even bred white mice for laboratories. Fridman says his business mentor was his grandmother, who owned a kitchenware shop back in Lvov. "When I first got started, I went to her for advice," he recalls. "She told me, 'Never have dealings with the Reds.'"

When Communism collapsed in 1991, Fridman was ready for the new, capitalist era. With the profits from his sundry businesses, he paid the required $100,000 fee to establish a bank — *Alfa Bank* — that would become the core of his *Alfa Group* Consortium, which has holdings in oil, telecommunications and supermarkets, among other ventures. Fridman's *Alfa Group* has often acted in partnership with Access/Renova Group, a New York based investment firm owned by Russian emigres Victor Vekselberg and Len Blavatnik. *Alfa* and Access/Renova each owned half of TNK and now hold equal 25 percent shares in TNK-BP.

The sale of state companies to the new private sector was marred by bribery, phony loans-for-shares schemes and the hiring of private paramilitary forces to seize disputed properties. In 1995 alone more than 400 businessmen and their political associates were murdered by rivals. "It was no different from the Wild West in the U.S. 150 years ago," says Fridman.

Fridman emerged from these capitalist wars with a mega-fortune, thanks in large measure to his being part of a group of seven entrepreneurs who helped finance Boris Yeltsin's 1996 presidential election campaign. Grateful for his unexpected victory, Yeltsin allowed these men to acquire for a pittance some of the state's most valuable natural-resource and industrial enterprises. When Putin ran for president three years ago, he vowed that "oligarchs will cease to exist as a class."

But aside from Boris Berezovsky and Vladimir Gusinsky — who were forced abroad after clashing with Putin — the new president allowed the oligarchs free rein until recently. In fact, there are now 17 known Russian billionaires. But with parliamentary elections in December and his own re-election campaign pending next March, Putin appears to have turned up the heat on some of the oligarchs, who as a group are deeply resented by many voters. Khodorkovsky, the Yukos oil tycoon, has been the main focus of this campaign. In early July Russian police arrested Platon Lebedev, a close Khodorkovsky associate at Yukos, and accused him of stealing state property during the 1994 privatization of a fertilizer plant. Since then police investigators have searched Yukos offices, presumably for damaging evidence against Khodorkovsky. The incidents come several months after hints by Khodorkovsky that he might someday run for president and after he announced his financial support for several political parties that oppose Putin.

Like most oligarchs, however, Fridman is a heavy contributor to the United Russia Party, the political entity most closely linked to Putin, who remains highly popular and heavily favored to win a second term. Fridman leaves no doubt that he will support Putin and the United Russia Party. "Under Putin the right of business to exist is no longer in question," says Fridman, who points out that threats to businesses and their owners were commonplace during the Yeltsin era. Business-related murders have dropped to about a score a year. Heavily armed private security squads have almost disappeared. Nowadays, Fridman rarely deploys more than a couple of visible bodyguards and feels safe enough to indulge his passion for jazz at Moscow clubs on sudden whims (though apparently he worries enough about his family's safety to install his wife and two young daughters in Paris, where he visits them on weekends). The tycoons' new image is reflected in their clothing: Gangsta-rap leather jackets are out; Armani suits are in. Even more startling, oligarchs have become cultural philanthropists, and Fridman is among the most generous, contributing hundreds of thousands of dollars each year to the arts, especially the Bolshoi Theatre (see box at left).

Most of Fridman's philanthropy falls under the auspices of *Alfa Bank*, the enterprise he uses to project his more modern, sophisticated business side. With a net income of $105 million on assets of $4.12 billion at the end of last year (compared with $85 million in net income on $2.7 billion in assets in 2001), *Alfa* is the largest private bank in Russia. But it still holds less than 5 percent of a market dominated by state-owned Sberbank, which last year had $33 billion in assets, 40 percent of total bank deposits and 30 percent of all loans.

Alfa Bank CEO Peter Aven points out that the state bank can offer lower interest rates on loans than his bank because of its near-monopoly on the savings accounts of pensioners, military personnel and just about anybody living outside the major cities. "Sberbank's presence destroys the possibility of fair competition," Aven says.

Nonetheless, *Alfa*, which made its mark in corporate lending, is moving relentlessly into the less-profitable retail sector. "We want *Alfa* to be more 'sellable' — and at the highest possible price — should we decide to sell it someday," says Aven, who believes that if *Alfa* becomes a stronger universal bank, it will increase its allure to potential buyers abroad. This year it is launching 25 *Alfa* Express outlets in Moscow — highly automated, minimally staffed branches that appeal to upscale clients. But for now *Alfa* arouses little interest among foreign buyers. Says a Moscow representative of a large Western bank, "No private bank has a significant enough market share to make it worth buying."

Alfa currently has a B credit rating from Standard & Poor's, placing it near the top of Russia's private banks. But *Alfa* has inevitably been tainted by the weaknesses of the Russian banking system. According to an April report by S&P, up to 75 percent, or $43 billion, of all corporate loans by Russian banks are "problematic" and "face a high degree of risk." Moreover, the bulk of these loans were made to the oligarchs who own them. "Many private banks exist to serve their financial-industrial groups," says Ekaterina Trofimova, the S&P analyst who wrote the report. There is a near-absence of credits for small and medium-size enterprises, or SMEs, which play a much smaller role in Russia than in Eastern Europe.

Fridman acknowledges *Alfa's* fondness for related-company loans. And though he concedes that more SMEs would create a healthier, more balanced Russian economy, he makes no excuses for virtually ignoring smaller enterprises (they receive less than 10 percent of *Alfa's* commercial loans). "If we continue to loan to our group companies, it's because they are fast-growing, profitable businesses that are much safer clients," he says. He also dismisses criticism by credit rating agencies that *Alfa Bank* should reduce its exposure to related companies in favor of less-risky government bonds. That advice, he points out, would have been disastrous in the 1998 financial crisis, when the government defaulted on many of its debts. Thanks to holdings worth hundreds of millions of dollars in oil producer TNK, a related company, *Alfa Bank* was able to weather the storm and distinguish itself as one of the few banks that continued to allow withdrawals by its customers.

Over the past three years, *Alfa* has in fact reduced its loans to related companies to about 15 percent of its portfolio, a low share compared with other Russian private banks. "*Alfa* has improved in this respect more than almost any other bank," says Trofimova, "but it continues to abuse its balance sheet by taking on too much credit risk from its group companies." As a glaring example, she cites the use of *Alfa Bank* loans to finance *Alfa Group's* acquisition of a controlling 48 percent stake in Golden Telecom, a fixed-line telecom operator that targets mainly corporate clients in the major Russian cities. With a current $749 million market capitalization, Golden Telecom had $29.8 million in net income on revenues of $199 million last year, compared with a loss of $39 million from $140 million in revenues in 2001.

For Fridman, though, Golden Telecom is a fine example of the synergy between the bank and the rest of *Alfa Group*. "Banking isn't so profitable as our other investments, but when we make loans, we become aware of new business opportunities," he says. "That's how we got into the telecom sector." Besides Golden Telecom, *Alfa* has a 25 percent stake in JSC Vimpel-Communications, the second-largest cellular phone company in Russia, with a market capitalization of $2.1 billion and net income of $130 million from $768 million in revenues last year, compared with net income of $47 million from $423 million in revenues in 2001.

Rounding out *Alfa Group's* holdings are commodities trader *Alfa-Eco Group* ($13.8 million in net income in 2002) and supermarket chain Trade House Perekriostok (net income of $7.9 million in 2002 on revenues of $305 million). But all these businesses — banking, telecoms, commodities and retail

— are dwarfed by Alfa Group's oil holdings in TNK and Sidanco, which accounted for more than 80 percent of the group's net income of $800 million last year (virtually unchanged from $797 million in 2001) on total assets of $6.84 billion, despite the huge run-up in oil prices.

Though Fridman prefers to run his varied conglomerate wearing banker's pinstripes, ensconced in *Alfa Bank's* elegant Moscow headquarters, the bulk of his fortune comes from the rough oil trade in the Siberian wilds. According to *Forbes* magazine, he has a personal worth of $4.3 billion, behind only Khodorkovsky and Abramovich, who agreed to merge their oil companies, Yukos and Sibneft, after the TNK-BP deal was announced.

Fridman views himself as an investor more than an oilman or a business manager. He intends to funnel most of the proceeds from any enterprise he sells back into Russia's bountiful oil and gas fields. "He needs businesses of the scale that only natural resources can provide," says Renaissance Capital's Jennings, meaning that no other businesses can provide the huge returns that Fridman insists upon.

Those are also likely to be the businesses that will continue to arouse the greatest interest among foreign investors — and pose the biggest risks. Recently, progress has been made in improving transparency, strengthening minority shareholders' rights and ensuring better corporate governance. The quality of corporate management has improved, according to some investment bankers and fund managers. Businesses are less likely to be stripped of cash and assets without any concern for minority shareholders. But perversely, corporate scandals in the U.S. have somewhat reduced the pressure for further business reforms in Russia. Nowadays it's fashionable in Moscow to drolly point out that cases like WorldCom's Bernard Ebbers and Enron Corp.'s Kenneth Lay aren't unique to the U.S. "We still have some Siberian provinces that resemble Texas," says Timerbulat Karimov, an oil and gas analyst at Aton Capital Group, a Moscow brokerage firm. "We even have our own Kenny Boys."

Fridman couldn't agree more. "Even in Western countries businesspeople don't always follow the letter of the law," he says. "No matter how much legislation is passed here, it still is going to take years for Russian businessmen to behave in ways that foreigners consider normal."

Fridman on BP, investing and guns

Observers of Russia's coarse capitalism tend to name Mikhail Fridman as their favorite oligarch. "A very disciplined investor" and "a guy with an understanding of business that few people here have" are some of the more positive comments he elicits. "At least he's not linked to any awful stories of violence" goes the more grudging sort of comment. In an hourlong interview at his Moscow headquarters with *Institutional Investor* Contributing Editor Jonathan Kandell, Fridman spoke with his well-known mix of charm, candor and gallows humor about what investors can expect from Russia nowadays — and about his own business plans.

INSTITUTIONAL INVESTOR: What has to be done in the Russian business world to change the perception abroad that investing here is still too risky for minority shareholders?

MIKHAIL FRIDMAN: We understand the need for more transparency, international accounting standards and better corporate governance if we want access to capital markets. But the biggest problem for foreign investors is a lack of experience and understanding of the business climate here.

INSTITUTIONAL INVESTOR: Should foreigners wait until Russian insiders have divided up the spoils before investing in the country?

MIKHAIL FRIDMAN: It is very risky to participate in the privatization of a company at its earliest stages. This isn't like investing in U.S. Treasury notes. People have to be ready for a fight, though hopefully they can do it in the courts nowadays instead of with guns [laughter].

INSTITUTIONAL INVESTOR: BP at one point accused you of illegally seizing its oil reserves. How were you able to overcome all that bitterness and get BP to agree to a merger?

MIKHAIL FRIDMAN: We both had to demonstrate flexibility and a deeper understanding of the other side's motivations. Legally, we acted properly, and I think they now recognize this. As far as ethical considerations, that's another matter. From BP's point of view, our behavior was unreasonable.

INSTITUTIONAL INVESTOR: Under the merger there is an equal partnership between BP and your Tyumen Oil Co., but who has the ultimate say in case of disagreements?

MIKHAIL FRIDMAN: President [Vladimir] Putin asked us the same question. The answer is, we have an informal but clear understanding of each side's sphere of responsibility. Everything concerning technical issues will be in the hands of BP. Of course, our decisions will prevail in everything concerning Russian issues. The biggest potential conflict could arise in strategies abroad. For example, Tyumen wants a presence in Eastern Europe, and that might put us in competition with BP operations in those countries.

INSTITUTIONAL INVESTOR: What are your strategies for your telecommunications companies?

MIKHAIL FRIDMAN: We don't intend to keep anything until we die. But it is a matter of deciding when it is best to sell. In the case of selling one half of TNK to BP, it made sense because it would improve the company's performance and value. In telecommunications it makes no sense to sell at this point because we are in the early stages of a very fast-growing market.

INSTITUTIONAL INVESTOR: Is *Alfa Bank* for sale as well?

MIKHAIL FRIDMAN: Eventually, we will sell or merge with a foreign partner. But it's premature for now because Western banks aren't very active in Russia yet, and we wouldn't get a good enough price.

INSTITUTIONAL INVESTOR: Where do you think you will make future investments?

MIKHAIL FRIDMAN: Energy is still the most promising business in Russia. The oil market has more or less been divided up. But we are just at the beginning stages of the natural-gas market. Sooner or later the reform of the gas market will be carried out, and we want to participate.

Views on the Russian economy seem to be polarized, with many investment banks extolling its high growth while organizations like the International Monetary Fund and World Bank warn of serious problems ahead.

That reminds me of what Tolstoy wrote in *Anna Karenina*: "Happy families are all alike; every unhappy family is unhappy in its own way." We are a country of many unhappy families, and there is no one cure for our troubles. But to really know what Russia needs, you have to live here for many years not just be a foreign expert on a short stay. Outsiders ask how we can live with so much turbulence. But we have adapted, and things are getting better. We are ready for whatever comes.

INSTITUTIONAL INVESTOR: You are only in your 30s and already a multibillionaire. Where do you want to be 20 years from now?

MIKHAIL FRIDMAN: My goal is to lead as interesting a life as possible. I still prefer spending time at the office to going on vacation. As long as I feel that way, I'll keep doing the same thing.

Ballet school

Becoming a major patron of the opera has always lent a patina of class to new money, no matter how outrageously that money was acquired. Jay Gould and J. P. Morgan, robber barons of America's Gilded Age, contributed heavily to New York's newborn Metropolitan Opera. Now, more than a century later, Mikhail Fridman and Russia's other maligned oligarchs are making generous donations to the Bolshoi Theatre, home to Moscow's legendary opera and ballet companies.

Representatives of a dozen private enterprises, including Fridman's *Alfa Bank*, each pony up $250,000 a year to sit on the Bolshoi's board of trustees. Though Fridman neither likes opera nor attends performances, he knows that such contributions can enhance his public image. "Russia has always been proud of the Bolshoi," says Alexander Gafin, the *Alfa Bank* vice president who sits on the theater's board of trustees.

The injection of private philanthropy comes not a moment too soon for the Bolshoi. Built in 1856, the former cultural jewel box of czarist and Soviet Russia has deteriorated so seriously that the theater itself poses a safety threat. "If renovation is put off any longer, there will be nothing left to renovate," Tamara Nosenko, a Moscow representative of the United Nations Educational, Scientific and Cultural Organization, warned in a June press conference. The rot isn't evident from the orchestra and dress circle seats, where tuxedoed and gowned season ticket holders can gaze around at all that luxurious red velvet and gilded plaster. But with rescue efforts barely under way, a peek behind the scenes reveals a drearier reality. Stage machinery hasn't been replaced since the start of the 20th century. Paint peels from corridor walls; floors creak; musicians squint at tattered score sheets. It's easy to imagine a Phantom lurking in those dark, musty stairwells and basement chambers.

The Bolshoi was kept afloat as a cultural showcase during the Communist era, but the 1991 collapse of the Soviet regime plunged the theater into crisis. Budgets were cut, and administrators had no idea how to find new, private sources of financing. "They knew nothing of fundraising, nothing of market forces like what productions would draw audiences and how much customers should be charged," says Anatoly Iksanov, who took over as the Bolshoi's general director three years ago.

The capitalist underpinnings of the new cultural era were no mystery to Iksanov. In 1991 he was studying theater management in the U.S. on a Ford Foundation grant. Returning to Russia, he wrote a book on American fundraising techniques that gained him an invitation to head the Bolshoi. Because his budget precluded hiring a large staff to canvass widely for donations, Iksanov decided to seek the bulk of private contributions from a small number of big banks and businesses. Today 60 percent of the Bolshoi's annual budget is covered by state subsidies, and the rest comes from philanthropy, ticket sales and the rental of the theater for social and corporate galas. The state-to-private funding ratio is on a par with Western European opera houses, though the Bolshoi's $35 million annual budget is only a fraction of the expenditures at London's Royal Opera House at Covent Garden or the Met in New York.

The transition away from state control wasn't smooth for the artists. When Alexandra Dursenieva, a leading mezzo-soprano, joined the Bolshoi in 1994, the organization was ripped apart by dissension between state-coddled veterans and reform-minded newcomers. "Big-name old-timers were being pushed out," she recalls. "I performed often abroad, so I could see how far behind the Bolshoi had fallen." But lately, she adds, there is more money for musicians, singers, sets and new productions. "Famous foreign artists are invited to perform here," she says. "We are moving forward in long strides, and all those bad years seem worthwhile now."

To extend opera's reach to a broader audience, Iksanov is looking into the possibility of radio broadcasts. Well aware that Texaco (now ChevronTexaco Corp.) sponsored Metropolitan Opera broadcasts on Saturday afternoons for more than six decades, he is hoping that a similar arrangement with a big petroleum producer could benefit the Bolshoi. Fridman's recent deal to merge his oil company with BP presents such an opportunity. "Maybe through *Alfa* we can get BP to join our board," says the Bolshoi director, who adds that he hasn't yet broached the subject with Gafin, Fridman's representative on the Bolshoi board.

Over the past few years, the Bolshoi has rid itself of a mediocre repertoire of state-imposed operas and ballets heavily laden with Marxist ideology. But the struggle for artistic independence hasn't ended with the new age of private philanthropy. "We make it clear to trustees and other private donors that they cannot interfere in the artistic field," says Iksanov. Instead, he tries to keep them focused on their areas of expertise as business managers, bankers and lawyers: determining how spending can be cut and income targets met or how to best take advantage of the Bolshoi brand in marketing consumer products. "But there is always some big donor who will ask that his favorite opera or ballet be produced," says Iksanov, "and we have to insist that what goes on stage is up to us."

The most talked-about opera of the recently ended season was not any oligarch's first choice: Imaginatively staged and sung in its original English for the first time in Russia, *The Rake's Progress* by Igor Stravinsky told the story of a dreamy young man who unexpectedly gains a fortune but loses his moral bearings. Not the kind of allegory that's likely to enthrall Russia's new magnates.

Appendix 3

Discussion with Mikhail Fridman, Chairman of the Board of Directors of *Alfa Bank*

Recorded by S. Krysanov, transcribed by S. Yemetz

TVC TV Channel, *Breakfast with Soloviov*,

July 28, 2002

Moderator — *Vladimir Soloviov*

Moderator: How does the president treat oligarchs, whether or not oligarchs can appoint the cabinet, how do the oligarchs treat each other? These are the topics we are going to cover in our talk with Mikhail Fridman, one of the most influential people in Russian industry. Good morning, Mikhail.

Mikhail Fridman, Chairman of the board of directors of *Alfa Bank*: Good morning.

Moderator: To what extent does the present day government, the ministers and the president, in particular, depend on the captains of industry, on the oligarchs? If, for example, the oligarchs say, well, we don't really care for Mikhail Mikhailovich Kasyanov, we want a different prime minister; will the president have to listen to their demands?

Mikhail Fridman: No, I think this is a primitive way of thinking. It is undoubtedly, a) harmful and secondly, this does not exist anymore. There were instances of such dependence in the past; however, even then not all of the oligarchs as a class were involved, only some of them, I would say, only certain characters.

There exists a much more fine-tuned mechanism. I am convinced that if all the representatives of Russian business do indeed decide that this or that official is bad at his job, it may happen spontaneously, rather than in any organized way. Yes, look at him, he is bad, incompetent, accepts bribes, I don't know, and (if) people do indeed go on talking about it long enough, again, not in any organized way but because of their own views of the matter, then after some time this person is likely to disappear, because that will be a fairly objective reflection of public opinion.

Moderator: What kind of a systemic mistake did Mssrs Berezovsky and Gusinsky make? Where did they cross the line between themselves and the state, for the state to start spitting fire on those who come too close?

Mikhail Fridman: If one starts analyzing, their mistake was in their, as I see it, lack of knowledge of Russian history, of history in general. Russian history, by the way, is very rich in similar examples. For instance, there was Menshikov, Osterman, if you remember, a man who was very close to the throne, Biron, and so on. All of them moved through life in a similar way; that is, they aimed to reach a high degree of closeness to the power, gain clout.

MODERATOR: What is the degree of your own influence on Russian politics?

MIKHAIL FRIDMAN: I have little personal influence. If, for example, we are talking about the oil or banking business, then we are actively involved in those, yes. And our company is a leader in those areas. Apparently, when those issues are discussed, my own opinion and the opinion of my colleagues, the people I am working with, has certain weight.

MODERATOR: However, we do know that there are two groups inside the Kremlin. The first is referred to as the "old team," the "family," and is linked to the name of Voloshin. The second consists of the "Chekists," ex-KGB people, in all their richness and variety. The general opinion is, many people are somehow connected to you, and they are in the second group, not Voloshin's group.

MIKHAIL FRIDMAN: In the KGB group?

MODERATOR: Yes, in the KGB group.

MIKHAIL FRIDMAN: I certainly know that different groups do exist. I think the mass media pictures everything in a somewhat cartoonish way, because the real mechanism is far more complicated, more fine-tuned, more balanced; it is not strictly a matter of teams, there is a certain polyphony there.

We subscribe and have subscribed for all the years of our business existence to the concept of the non-association of our business and ourselves to any political figures or public officials. In principle, as we view the government as something heaven-born, so to speak, we do not try and maintain a loyal and friendly relationship with the representatives of the government, with any of its branches.

At the same time we do try and deliberately maintain our distance, so that we are never associated with any individual public official or any individual politician.

MODERATOR: But there are certain names directly linked to yours. They are even called "*Alfa's* people." You are sure to know the names very well. For example, Mr. Surkov.

MIKHAIL FRIDMAN: This collective name is in a way justified. It simply means that these people worked with us before they went to the Kremlin. Besides, speaking about Vladislav Yurievich Surkov, I do not deny that we have known each other for many years, just like you and I. We attended the same college, the Moscow Institute for Steel and Alloys, which trains, as we can see, broad specialists.

MODERATOR: The broadest of specialists.

MIKHAIL FRIDMAN: Which is why, as we used to attend the same lectures, I have known him for more than twenty years now. We are on good terms.

MODERATOR: He comes to you for advice?

MIKHAIL FRIDMAN: No, I think, as for the issues he is tackling in the Kremlin, he is particularly ... Well, when we meet, I don't know if this qualifies as giving advice, we simply talk about general political topics, make projections, assessments, and so on.

MODERATOR: Does he fall into the category of the people you find acceptable?

MIKHAIL FRIDMAN: Yes, absolutely.

MODERATOR: That means you speak the same language?

MIKHAIL FRIDMAN: Of course, we belong to the same group, the same generation, so to speak.

MODERATOR: Who else is close to you in the government?

MIKHAIL FRIDMAN: There are several other people who went to the Kremlin from our structure. Abramov, Alexander Sergeyevich, Popov, and some others I know.

MODERATOR: Why do people leave your bank, a place where they get good salaries, where they get to do what they like, to take jobs in the government, where remuneration is not comparable to what they used to earn in the business world.

MIKHAIL FRIDMAN: Well, I agree with you that it does seem strange, even though this move is a wise and justified thing. By the way, this happens not only in Russia, it happens in all countries of the world, in America, for instance. A governmental job means a financial loss, true, but at the same time it means a gain in terms of one's reputation, public recognition, private ambitions, and so on.

Besides, the scale of the problems that people in the government are dealing with is much more impressive. And this explains why people are willing to work for less money in a governmental structure, especially when one's needs are well provided for. I mean, when one has already earned enough to live a decent life.

It is certainly very odd when someone works in a public office and proudly insists on turning down any job offer that could bring them better money. However, if someone worked long enough in business, and earned good money, (then he) feels free, has a good car and a dacha ...

MODERATOR: Why not lend a helping hand to the society then, right?

MIKHAIL FRIDMAN: Yes. I once met a former finance minister Rubin, who went to work at City Bank after his resignation.

MODERATOR: Not the Russian finance minister.

MIKHAIL FRIDMAN: Yes, yes, yes, quite right. At the entrance they have a gallery of all the American finance ministers, starting with the first one. About 50 or 70 of them. He says, I am going to be up there, too … And there are dates everywhere, that is, the terms of office … He says, I have been Minister of Finance for 8 years, the longest of all, and you know why? I am the richest finance minister in the whole of American history. He came to the office when he was a multimillionaire, so it was not difficult for him to work there.

MODERATOR: Well, I don't think you are trying to compare Rubin's income to the income of Mr. Surkov, are you?

MIKHAIL FRIDMAN: No, of course not. But his level of income is quite sufficient for Russia.

MODERATOR: However, there is a reverse tendency, as far as I understand. Aren't there many former public officials who are now working at *Alfa*?

MIKHAIL FRIDMAN: Yes, certainly, there are: Sysuev, Aven, if anyone remembers that he used to be a public official, and others. But I believe it is a totally normal transition.

Rubin, who I mentioned before, is exactly this kind of example. He had worked at Goldman Sachs, then he was a finance minister, and now he heads the City Group.

MODERATOR: And how does such a move take place, when people go from you to the Kremlin? Do they phone you and say, look, Mikhail, I got this job offer, I want your advice.

MIKHAIL FRIDMAN: Well, something like that. Sometimes I get a phone call from someone who made the offer who says, look, I would like to hire so and so, what do you think? It is a rhetorical question, in principle, because if they have already reached an agreement, then …

MODERATOR: Then no way.

MIKHAIL FRIDMAN: No, I am OK with that. I do not think we gain anything, because we lose a qualified professional, as a rule.

On the other hand, I do believe that the people who move up the career ladder are really worthy and efficient. In the same sense that their performance in a government office has an indirect positive impact on us, too.

If there are simple and comprehensible rules of the game, we are, so to say, arrogantly confident that there are equal terms for all participants. That is we are sure we are not going to come in last if everything else is equal.

However, we would not want to be discriminated in this way. And therefore we certainly must maintain our relationship with the government to avoid (this) …

MODERATOR: The relationship with the government is of a material character. So, can someone from the government phone you and say, look, Mikhail Mikhailovich, there is a need to support the fund of the poor and crippled?

MIKHAIL FRIDMAN: Yes, of course.

MODERATOR: Does it happen on a regular basis?

MIKHAIL FRIDMAN: Often enough.

MODERATOR: Do you write it off as a business expense?

MIKHAIL FRIDMAN: I am no accountant, I do not know.

MODERATOR: The Kremlin charity?

MIKHAIL FRIDMAN: Why necessarily the Kremlin? This happens at every level. This happens on the regional level, too. We receive stacks of mail every day. Sponsorship, help, charity and so on.

MODERATOR: Has Putin ever phoned?

MIKHAIL FRIDMAN: Well, not in connection with something like this, never.

MODERATOR: And not in relation to the human resources issue, either?

MIKHAIL FRIDMAN: No, no.

MODERATOR: Has Voloshin ever phoned?

MIKHAIL FRIDMAN: Well, Voloshin has phoned, in relation to the human resources issue, for example.

MODERATOR: How do you get in contact with the people who start receiving such phone calls? I mean, when does the government start soliciting a businessman?

MIKHAIL FRIDMAN: Well, simply to discuss certain issues. I don't truly know which criteria they use to invite us in. There is a kind of publicly recognized group.

Our capital at that time was not comparable with what we have now, but in principle we were, even back then, recognizable as a force. Many now well-known public figures were there.

Since then I have been a fairly regular participant in these powwows. Some of the people left for certain objective reasons. New ones have appeared.

MODERATOR: A powwow—is that a slip of the tongue or your real attitude?

MIKHAIL FRIDMAN: No, it is only an ironic comment.

MODERATOR: Mikhail, when you meet at Kasyanov's, it is usually Mr. … who delivers the ironic speeches, Mrssrs Mordashov and Deripaska fight for their absolutely transparent interests. But your name is left out of the chronicles. Do you keep silent there or are you dealing with such specific technical issues that no one really sees you?

MIKHAIL FRIDMAN: No, I would say I do not really like speaking in front of these kinds of audiences. It is usually clear what people generally think about different issues, so one should be either a brilliant speaker, who enjoys the process of public speaking, or they should deal with the purely technical issues. Well, I often have none of the latter. Once they started talking about banks, so I said a few words about the insurance business, as I know a little about that. They listened to me about this.

MODERATOR: What are the relations inside your community, because, for example, recently Mr. Deripaska and Mr. Kobo agreed not to use force against each other, and this is practically the news of the day in Russia.

MIKHAIL FRIDMAN: If one describes this global kind of relationship, then it is, in my opinion, based on two fundamental principles. First, you are no one's friend, so to speak, because all of us are competitors to some degree. Second, all of us are of the same blood, all of us do the same thing, belong to the same social cluster, think in much the same way.

MODERATOR: That means you can be united into one Falange only if there is a real threat of extinguishing you as a cluster?

MIKHAIL FRIDMAN: Well, or let's say, there is a public challenge against this social group. Certainly, this can easily be a uniting force. In that sense the people are quite responsible.

MODERATOR: But you do greet each other, don't you?

MIKHAIL FRIDMAN: Of course.

MODERATOR: Keeping up the appearance of decency?

MIKHAIL FRIDMAN: I would say, everything is very individual there and there are certainly people who are on much better terms with one another.

MODERATOR: Are there any individuals in your social cluster you find repulsive?

MIKHAIL FRIDMAN: Of course. I would hope this bears no relation to their commercial success. It is more about their morality, psychology, etc. I certainly would not want to name any names, although I can add that there are others that I find very nice.

MODERATOR: Whom do you find nice?

MIKHAIL FRIDMAN: I, for example, like Mr. Yevtushenkov, Vladimir Petrovich, a prominent businessman. We belong to different age groups and are of very different … Nevertheless, we maintain a warm and friendly relationship. By the way, I like Mr. Kogan very much. Volodya Kogan. He is charming. We do not see each other much, due to the geographic distances. However, we are on rather friendly terms. And so on. There are others. I find Mr. Vakselberg very nice; he is the head of SUAL and my partner in the Tyumen Oil Company, also Oleg Kiselyov …

MODERATOR: There was much talk about your very complicated relationship with Mr. Kiselyov, is that correct? You used to work together, is that true?

MIKHAIL FRIDMAN: Well, we started out working together. Everything goes back to the old days, as we all know. I can remind you that Oleg Kiselyov graduated from the same college as I did, then he was the director of the student hostel, the one we lived in. I forgot, did you stay there as well?

MODERATOR: No, I am a Muscovite.

MIKHAIL FRIDMAN: So, he was the boss in the hostel and my senior, both in age and in position.

MODERATOR: But you split your business without much of a fight, is that correct?

MIKHAIL FRIDMAN: It seems to me, yes. Now, at any rate, we have a very good relationship. When people go their own ways, there certainly are reasons for their being unhappy with each other, what with them splitting. It is a question of the degree of their unhappiness. I believe that in our case this degree was quite acceptable and within the limits of any relationship between two normal people.

MODERATOR: Obviously your company has to take part in the regional elections. And I think it often happens that your personal political views come into conflict with your company's interests. One should support those who will guarantee stability, not necessarily a pro-market person.

MIKHAIL FRIDMAN: I would say that any open non-supporter of a market economy will never receive our votes, because he will eventually become a threat to us. If we elect someone as a citizen and an individual we would most likely support a more liberal type of politician.

Here, as you have correctly pointed out, people mainly support those who will provide stability and continuity, and besides, those who stand a real chance to be elected. See, we are dealing with …

MODERATOR: This means, "The Carp Who was an Idealist"—is that about us?

MIKHAIL FRIDMAN: We are in the type of business that prevents us from idealizing the surrounding reality. It is dangerous from a business point of view.

What is undoubtedly uniting us is the axiom about the non-use of violence. Yes? At least at the verbal level, the declarative level. I am convinced that no businessman of any kind of internal gathering, any kind of private meeting, would openly call for the use of violence against one another.

MODERATOR: You mean you are past this stage?

Mikhail Fridman: I am not saying that they have stopped using violence. But one will never openly admit it.

Moderator: In a number of areas your interests directly conflict with the interests of other oligarchs. How do you settle your conflicts, do you phone each other before the elections, are you trying to agree about who to support?

Mikhail Fridman: You know, I would say this. There is much talk about our active involvement in the regional elections, but this is a big exaggeration. I would say that there are some organizations that are indeed active.

We as a bank assume a very passive role and try to be loyal to all the candidates, because, as I said before, it is most important for us to be left alone, so that we do not have to deal with the tax police all the time, etc.

Moderator: Well, OK. Let's say that someone is running for a government position in the Krasnoyarsk region.

Mikhail Fridman: Yes. We would not participate in any way. Not at all. There are, of course, different forces there: Rossisiki Alumini, Norilski Nikel. As far as I understand, the way it happens, sometimes people get together and try to agree about something.

Moderator: Has Mr. Potanin already talked to Mr. Deripaska about that?

Mikhail Fridman: I don't think they have talked even about this situation, because it is very hard for them to agree on anything.

Moderator: The name of Mr. Raikov is directly linked to the group, the consortium, also all of the deputy corps, a number of SPS people, about 80 deputies, almost one third of all the senators, plus a number of the regions. Did you know anything about this?

Mikhail Fridman: The world pictured by the mass media is, in my opinion, very far from reality. Therefore, talking about the deputies, I can say that, of course, I know many of the deputies, but in principle, perhaps, if I wanted to, I could have established more close relations with them.

But this is not my goal; not because I am a person of such high morals, although I do hope that I don't lack any sense of morality, but mainly because I do not really need them. I believe that if there are issues that do need the support of the deputies, one can choose a much easier way.

Moderator: How so?

Mikhail Fridman: First, the issues that need the support of the deputies are, as a rule, issues to be dealt with from the standpoint of an ideology of a political force, for example, SPS or Yabloko.

Moderator: So, you place a call to the boss?

Mikhail Fridman: I can easily meet them and explain that there is a certain issue, and I would like their support on that.

MODERATOR: Will they ask you for money?

MIKHAIL FRIDMAN: Well, I would say, they will ask for support for their activities in some form.

MODERATOR: Political services?

MIKHAIL FRIDMAN: Well, I don't know—please support so and so in whatever region. I think this is quite normal.

MODERATOR: So, the ever present union of the sword and the plough?

MIKHAIL FRIDMAN: Yes, I would say, if we are talking about the liberals, for example, SPS, I am absolutely convinced that if our requests to Nemtsov do not go together with the ideology of his organization, then ...

MODERATOR: They will turn you down?

MIKHAIL FRIDMAN: Yes, they will turn us down, despite all our mutual sympathies, assistance, support, etc, I am sure of that. They are very firm in their principles.

MODERATOR: Do you have to spend a lot of money on direct political support to the same parties during election campaigns?

MIKHAIL FRIDMAN: See, I would say that what we spend is normal by Russian standards but might be considered a lot by western standards. Because western society is much more diversified. The amount of individual and collective assistance one receives from one company is much less than here, but the total number of participants in the funding is gigantic. Here, due to the structure of our economy ...

MODERATOR: Those who are prepared to shoulder the burden are fewer in numbers.

MIKHAIL FRIDMAN: Yes, absolutely. Therefore, one's specific load is much higher.

MODERATOR: Do you give equal amounts to all the parties?

MIKHAIL FRIDMAN: No, absolutely not. For example, we would never fund the Communists.

MODERATOR: The Fatherland—All-Russia?

MIKHAIL FRIDMAN: We were helping The Fatherland—All-Russia party because we live in Moscow, together with Luzhkov ...

MODERATOR: What about the LDPR?

MIKHAIL FRIDMAN: No. No way. This is like talking about violence; it is beyond good and evil. And we are certainly helping the liberal parties, absolutely voluntarily.

MODERATOR: The presidential elections are looming ahead. Have you already decided which of the candidates you are going to support, or is it a money issue, you have to decide when you have to financially commit yourself?

MIKHAIL FRIDMAN: I think this question is largely rhetorical at the moment …

MODERATOR: I mean the one who guarantees stability, his name is already known.

MIKHAIL FRIDMAN: Well, yes, of course. And this is pretty obvious, I guess.

MODERATOR: However, the person we are now talking about, Vladimir Vladimirovich Putin, allowed himself to address the oligarchs with the phrase: "you'll have a lot of dust to swallow." And in general, he often demonstrates his emotional rejection of the mere existence of the oligarchs as a cluster, to borrow your term. Have you ever felt the impact of his attitude?

MIKHAIL FRIDMAN: You know, due to the specifics of my job, I am used to taking emotional outbursts rather philosophically.

I would say, from my personal experience of dealing with the president, I see that despite his way of sometimes displaying emotions, which can indeed be pointed out, he is a real person, and this probably accounts for his being such a popular and successful politician.

He remains a rational, well-balanced, and serious man. I believe that it is not a matter of emotions displayed by our politicians, but rather whether or not they understand the necessity and possibility of interacting with the entrepreneurial community. And I have no questions in this department.

MODERATOR: When you communicate with the president, do you have a sense of his personal attitude towards you?

MIKHAIL FRIDMAN: Good question. I would say, I see it, to give the president his due, everybody who communicates with him senses a very positive attitude. I do not know if it is only a feeling, but it is at least there on an emotional level.

MODERATOR: As we know, since the times of Ostap Bender, people in Russia have believed that one cannot build a fortune and stay an honest person?

MIKHAIL FRIDMAN: The issue of an honest or dishonest way of earning money can be defined by public attitude. If we assume that everything that has happened here in the last 12, 13, 15 years is a crime, then in that sense I am as much a representative of my times as anybody else.

I certainly think that for me, as well as for others, the main source of making money in the last decade has been the revolutionary situation in our society, primarily in the economy. The privatization, small businesses, and so on. In that sense the life of the public collective consciousness has been, in a way, criminal. I am, however, a rather loyal citizen.

MODERATOR: Mikhail, do I really hear notes of regret, or is it just my imagination?

MIKHAIL FRIDMAN: No, what you hear is, rather, a note of compassion for the people, because their attitude to the process of making money largely reflects their own failures, disappointments, which is something very natural, considering that most of our Soviet people entered the era of the primary accumulation of capital without any skills, knowledge, or experience.

And they have lost a lot, quite naturally. In both a relative and absolute sense; having lost their life savings and slipping down the social ladder. Large social groups of people, the intelligentsia, etc.

I cannot say I am happy about it. My explanations do not really satisfy them, either. They are disappointed, angry, and so on. Nevertheless, this is in a way a social situation one must reckon with.

MODERATOR: How many people work in the affiliated structures?

MIKHAIL FRIDMAN: Hundreds of thousands, it seems to me.

MODERATOR: Do you pay them salaries?

MIKHAIL FRIDMAN: Yes, in that sense I think our affiliated structures have no problems.

MODERATOR: We know that you take a company, buy it out, come in with a western type of management and approach to finances, bring it to a new level in terms of quality, and then sell it. This is how you make your money in different branches. There are persistent rumors that very soon *Alfa Bank* will be part of a western structure, CitiCorp. How true are these rumors?

MIKHAIL FRIDMAN: Well, I would say that it is, unfortunately, an absolute lie. Unfortunately, because it seems to me that if such organizations as CitiCorp or Deutsche Bank, or any others come to Russia and become owners or co-owners of big Russian companies, then consumers, i.e, our clients, would benefit from that.

MODERATOR: Does this mean that you are ready to sell *Alfa*?

MIKHAIL FRIDMAN: I would say, speaking as an individual—it would not be a good thing, because I would have no job, no office to go to. I do have certain nostalgic feelings about this. Luckily, I think this is not going to happen for at least the next five years.

As for my feelings as a businessman, if a bank or any other organization comes with an offer that seems rational and effective, if the people who bring this proposal seem serious and professional, then, I think, one should be rational about it, regardless of one's personal emotions.

Appendix 4

Birthdays
Today Boris Berezovsky is 60 years old

Kommersant, January 23, 2006

Peter Aven, President of *Alfa Bank* congratulates Boris Berezovsky:

"Borya, many happy returns of the day! You are having a fantastic, interesting life, so rich in extraordinary events. It was impossible to forecast anything like this 30 years ago, when we first met. And indeed you are happy. I suppose I have never met a person who is as happy as you are (though not everyone believes it is true). In spite of the fact that we have almost never agreed on anything (and still do not) I wish you all the best, I wish you love (I remember you tried to convince me once that unlike all other ordinary people you fall in love "in earnest" once every half a year), I wish you health and happiness, the latter, as I've already said, is always with you, it simply cannot abandon you."

Reported by Oksana Alexeyeva (*Kommersant*)

Appendix 5

Boris Berezovsky and Boris Nemtsov.
Berezovsky's yacht, 2004.
Eilat, Israel.

Appendix 6

Defendant
Vladimir Potanin
First "VP1"
February 21, 2006

In the High Court of Justice Queen's Bench Division

Case No. HQ05X00865

BETWEEN:
BORIS BEREZOVSKY
CLAIMANT

and

1. MIKHAIL FRIDMAN
2. *ALFA BANK*
DEFENDANTS

WITNESS STATEMENT OF VLADIMIR POTANIN

I, *Vladimir Olegovich Potanin,* of 9, ulitsa Bolyshaya Yakimanka, Moscow, testify as follows

Introduction

1. I am the Chairman of the Board of Directors and the President of the CJSC Holding Company INTERROS ("INTERROS"). INTERROS is one of the biggest private investment companies in Russia. INTERROS operates in the majority of Russian regions, and in European, Asian and North American countries. I am a member of the Management Board of the Russian Union of Industrialists and Entrepreneurs, Chairman of the National Council on Corporate Governance, a member of the Public Chamber of the Russian Federation and Chairman of the Commission on issues of development of charity, philanthropy and volunteer work of the Public Chamber of the Russian Federation. I was also a member of the Russian Federation Government during Boris Yeltsin's presidency. I acted as First Deputy Chairman of the Russian Federation Government between 14 August 1996 and 17 March 1997, in charge of economic issues.

Save where I state to the contrary, the facts and the matters contained in this witness statement are within my own knowledge. Where the facts are not within my own knowledge, I have identified my sources of information and/or belief.

2. This witness statement is made on the part of Mr. Mikhail Fridman and OJSC *ALFA BANK*. I am aware that Mr. Boris Berezovsky has brought proceedings against Mr. Fridman in the English court for defamation *(slander)*. I understand that these proceedings relate to a statement made by Mr. Fridman in the television program 'To the Barrier,' broadcast 28 October 2004 (NTV television channel, OJSC Television Company NTV).

My relationship with the parties to the proceedings

3. I have known Mr. Fridman for approximately 15 years. We are business acquaintances. The companies associated with myself and the companies associated with Mr. Fridman have been and continue to be competitors on the Russian market. In relation to the oil company Sidanko, I would note that there was a protracted high-profile corporate conflict between our companies, which was resolved in 2001. I currently hold a minority interest in the Kovykta gas condensate deposit development project, in which Fridman also holds an interest. We also participate in the work of the Russian Union of Industrialists and Entrepreneurs and the Public Chamber.

4. I have known Mr. Berezovsky for approximately 10 years. We are business acquaintances, although we did not work on any joint projects. We were in contact through the state service, as we partly worked in the Russian government at the same time. The last time I was in contact with Mr. Berezovsky was when I met him by chance around 3 or 4 years ago at the Nice airport.

5. In the 1990s Mr. Berezovsky was an extremely powerful individual. Mr. Berezovsky owned a large number of mass media outlets.

Auction for the sale of a block of shares in the Open Joint Stock Company Svyazinvest

6. In July 1997, the state authorities put up a cash auction without investment conditions for a 25% plus one share stake in OJSC Svyazinvest. Importantly, the auction was declared open to all, i.e., both residents and non-residents were permitted to take part.

7. I was interested in the forthcoming auction for the sale of shares in OJSC Svyazinvest, as I believed telecoms to be an upcoming industry.

8. I learned from the parties to the proceedings that a consortium had been put together to participate in the auction, and that this consortium in-

cluded, amongst others, structures of Mr. Gusinsky and Mr. Fridman, the Spanish telecommunications company Telefonica, and Credit Suisse First Boston, the international investment bank.

9. The Renaissance Capital investment company learned of my interest in taking part in the auction for the sale of the OJSC Svyazinvest shares, and proposed that I take part in the consortium for participation in the deal, the structuring of which was dealt with by Renaissance Capital. As a result, the Mustcom Ltd consortium was formed, and comprised the investment company Renaissance International Ltd, the Deutsche Morgan Grenfell investment bank, Morgan-Stanley Asset Management, George Soros' Quantum Fund and a company representing, inter alia, my interests (the "Consortium").

Meetings with Mr. Gusinsky and threats made by Mr. Berezovsky

10. During the course of spring and early summer of 1997 I met with Mr. Gusinsky on a number of occasions to discuss our respective intentions with regard to OJSC Svyazinvest. I am not able now to recall the location and date of such meetings, which took place over 8 years ago. However, I do recall that Mr. Berezovsky was present at a number of these meetings. I understand that Mr. Berezovsky accepts that he was present on "at least two occasions" when I met with Mr. Gusinsky to discuss the OJSC Svyazinvest auction.

11. OJSC Svyazinvest's privatization was being overseen by Mr. Anatoly Chubais, who was then Deputy Chairman of the Russian Federation Government. As I recall, one meeting involving Mr. Chubais on the issue took place in July in the South of France shortly before the auction. Mr. Gusinsky and Mr. Berezovsky invited me to join them in France to meet Mr. Chubais to discuss that the OJSC Svyazinvest auction would be completely open and fair, and that no exceptions would be made for anyone, including those present at the meeting. I was pleased by the results of the meeting, although Mr. Gusinsky and Mr. Berezovsky did not conceal their dissatisfaction.

12. As I understood it then, Mr. Berezovsky was assisting Mr. Gusinsky in connection with the OJSC Svyazinvest auction, as he had a financial interest in the auction being won by the consortium of Mr. Gusinsky.

13. During the course of the meetings to discuss the OJSC Svyazinvest auction, I came to understand that if the companies associated with me were to participate in the auction, then in Mr. Berezovsky's opinion, I would be going against his interests and Mr. Berezovsky would use his political power and media resources to inflict harm on my image as a businessman, which would affect my capacity to conduct business. I am not able to recall the exact meetings on which he made such statements, nor the precise words which were used. However, I am certain that such promises to exert commercial

pressure were made and am equally certain that such promises to exert commercial pressure were made and am equally certain of their content. I would like to make it clear that at no time has Mr. Berezovsky made threats against me of a physical nature.

14. I was aware that Mr. Berezovsky's capabilities were serious and that Mr. Berezovsky was capable of carrying out such actions. However, based on my general attitude toward life and views on business principles, I decided to participate in the auction in the Consortium created by Renaissance Capital. The Consortium won the auction, having offered US$1.875 billion.

The sale of the *Kommersant* newspaper

15. At the end of the 1990s, the idea arose amongst the business community for the establishment, by several well-known businessmen including myself and Mr. Fridman, of a national business newspaper which might take up an objective position on business issues. The acquisition of the *Kommersant* newspaper was one of the alternatives to implementing this project that was discussed. However, this project was not carried out.

Statement of Truth

17. I believe that the facts stated within this Witness Statement are true.

Signed: … … … … … … … … … ..

VLADIMIR POTANIN

Dated this 21 day of February 2006

Appendix 7

Press Conference Regarding the Results of the Auction of 25% of Svyazinvest Shares National Hotel, 13:00, July 31, 1997

Thursday, July 31, 1997

Prepared by the Federal News Service Moscow Bureau

MODERATOR: Good afternoon, dear colleagues. Let me introduce the participants in today's press conference. They are UNEXIMbank President Potanin, Vladimir Olegovich; Chairman of the Russian Federal Property Fund Lipkin, Igor Borisovich; Director General of the joint-stock company Svyazinvest Ismailov; and Chairman of the State Committee of the Russian Federation for Communications and Informatization Krupnov, Alexander Yefimovich.

LIPKIN: I will allow myself to be the first speaker. I am pleased that the first part of the sale of Svyazinvest shares has been completed. It gives me great pleasure to repeat that the purchase and sale contract have been signed. It also gives me great pleasure to report to you that it has been signed in a timely manner. The deadline runs out on July 31, three days after the signing of the protocol.

Let me convey the original of the contract to the buyers' representative, Mr. Potanin, and I will give copies of the documents to the corresponding persons.

I am handing copies of the document to Mr. Krupnov and to Mr. Ismailov, the leads in this process.

POTANIN: At long last we have gotten what we dreamed of. 25 percent of Svyazinvest is now settled in a tidy little document. As the documents are in my hands I would like to briefly comment on what we are going to do with them and with all the work that has been completed on Svyazinvest.

First of all, Vladimir Borisovich Bulgak has suggested that this is not a strategic investment for us and that we are not a strategic partner of the sector as a whole, and Svyazinvest in particular. Let me just say that our bank and the entire consortium, which took part in the Svyazinvest auction, regard this as solely a strategic investment. This means, among other things, that the structure of the deal preserves these shares as property of the consortium for two years and accordingly, at least for two years these shares cannot be sold, and over at least the next two years we will work in a concerted manner with Svyazinvest to resolve any problems.

As for our bank, this is a strategic investment and it goes beyond the initial two-year period I referred to. Although the contract was signed only yesterday and it has been presented to the public only today, we have already begun consultations with Mr. Krupnov and Mr. Ismailov on further work. I think the agreements, which will soon be reached, will be fixed in a single agreement with the shareholders. Then any further work to increase capitalization of Svyazinvest will enter a normal working phase.

All members of the consortium who took part in the transaction have expressed their satisfaction with its completion, with its results, and are fully resolved, jointly with the sector and the issuer, to work on further capitalization of the company.

MODERATOR: Are there any questions?

Q: *CNN*. What percentage does UNEXIMbank have in the consortium?

POTANIN: In order to give you a more precise answer to this question I will have to explain the actual structure of the transaction.

In order to buy the Svyazinvest shares we set up a special legal entity in which all the interests of the investors were reflected, all the participants.

The structure of this legal entity is such that one part of the investment stems directly from receiving a share of the Svyazinvest package, one part is a derivative of the shares of this company, and one part is a credit.

If we combine the direct outlay of UNEXIMbank and its partners, the Russian organizations, in the credits that were granted to the special legal entity, we end up with a controlling interest in excess of 50 percent. But the voting control as a result of the transaction will depend on the size of the investment made by each participant. Thus, the deciding role in the successful completion of this transaction was played by Mr. Soros, who very optimistically, together with us, assessed the prospects of Svyazinvest and invested almost a billion dollars in this transaction.

Part of this money, as I said, will be spent—*(audio break)*—Svyazinvest and a part will go to this special legal entity. Therefore, considering the credit, the share of the Russian participants exceeds 50 percent.

Q: Could you speak in more detail about the role of Mr. Soros? *(Off mike.)*

POTANIN: Let me start by saying that the practice of attracting a wide circle of investors, both financial and strategic, is fairly common. We did not invent it. Let me cite one example. Leading Russian banks and oil companies *(break in tape)* ... for example, LUKoil used a special legal entity to issue Eurobonds worth $125 million. UNEXIMbank used a legal entity called Unitsim ... International Finance to issue $250 million worth of Eurobonds. *Alfa Group* used a special legal entity, *Alfa* Russia Finance, SBS-Agro also used a special entity with a similar name. Such precedents exist throughout the world. For example, such well-known companies as BASF and Olivetti used special legal entities to promote their debt obligations in the market, and the best-known telecommunications deal was struck when 30 percent was purchased of the analogue of Svyazinvest. At that time, Deutsche Telecom and its partners formed a similar legal entity to implement this deal. Accordingly, a primary investor always emerges in each such deal. In this deal it was Mr. Soros.

I did not personally discuss the details of the deal with George Soros, but as a result of my work with his financial representatives, an understanding was reached, and as an investor he began to change his attitude towards the Russian economy and to the Russian investment climate, as he said in a recent interview.

This was why he agreed to view his participation in this consortium not as a short-term investment, but as a longer-term investment, for at least two years. I have only one explanation for this—the growth of his confidence in the investment climate in Russia. For this reason he accepted the risks for a longer period of time. I think this will have a great deal of impact on the overall investment climate.

I will also note that besides Soros, Deutsche Morgan Grenfell and Morgan Stanley Asset Management also took part in the auction. The participation of such reputable investment organizations strengthened the prestige of the consortium and the transaction.

I must note that the revamped MFK-Renaissance team did a tremendous amount of work on this transaction. Along with the financial participation of Soros, 1.5 billion dollars of the stated 1.875 million was thanks to the work of this team.

Q: Am I right in understanding that the Soros shares will not be sold for two years?

POTANIN: Yes, the shares of Soros and of the other investors will not be sold for two years in accordance with the structure of the transaction.

Q: *(off mike)* the Most group did not take part. Third, *(off mike.)*

POTANIN: It is difficult for me to comment on the first two statements. You see, the terms of the tender were announced widely. In fact, it was the first time that everything was known about the tender, everything in detail.

As for the non-participation of the Most group. I believe that quite the opposite was declared. More than that, I must say that the work of the Most group and *Alfa Bank*, together with Spanish Telefonica and Credit Suisse,—*(inaudible)*—was carried out on a very professional level. The consortium, I believe, worked very professionally. I believe we were worthy competitors in this tender.

I do not understand, therefore, why the Most group and Mr. Kostikov are distancing themselves from this work.

As for "bandit methods." If this is meant to be a statement about us, we never gave any pretext for such charges.

Q: *ROSIKA.* Does it seem like Russia's major assets are now being priced more accurately? That the tender showed that we are now more properly valuing our assets? And my second question. You made provisions for an audit. Will Russian auditing firms be invited to take part in the project, or will you commission only foreign companies?

LIPKIN: I believe you answered your question yourself. I have nothing to add except that we are now reaping the results of our target-oriented work. Indeed, the price of our shares is growing. But we are not selling our fixed assets, as you implied. We are selling securities. The fixed assets will be managed by those people who, by right of the shareholders, will manage them properly.

I believe that the work conducted in Russia over the past 5 and a half years is now resulting in a growth of the value of the shares of our enterprises—*(audio break)*—

KRUPNOV: ... We chose an auditor with an international reputation. That is PricewaterhouseCoopers. We set up a joint venture, Auditsvyaz. At annual meetings of regional companies we will have two audits, one domestic and one foreign, and beginning with the results of the work in 1996, 32 companies will have standard international audits.

LIPKIN: That adds to your question and answer as to how the share prices will grow. The prices will grow depending on the joint actions of the companies.

Q: *(off mike.)*

POTANIN: There are precedents in world practice when, after tenders to sell certain objects, the opposing sides have pooled their efforts because it turns out that one consortium lacks one thing and the other a different thing. One example from Russian practice. In the fall of last year there was a tender to assist in the sale of the shares of RAO UES. Two consortiums were bidding, but eventually they joined forces. Many international names were involved. So, such precedents have happened before.

The structure of the Svyazinvest deal envisaged such a possibility. But up until now, because of the—should I say—emotional atmosphere in the wake of the auction, such negotiations have not yet been held.

As for derivative securities, I think that the program to issue such securities will be developed by the consortium. I don't think it can be implemented earlier than within six or nine months, after the necessary measures are taken to audit the company, to arrange depository services, and to determine regional and tariff policies. After that, derivative securities can be issued. It is premature to speak about the exact kind of securities that we will issue. This will be an element of our forthcoming work, one of the areas that we are prepared to reactivate in Svyazinvest.

Q: *Voice of America.* I have a question for Mr. Potanin and then a technical question for whoever cares to answer it. Mr.Potanin, Mr. Kostikov has just announced that Gusinsky is suing you. Your reaction to the suit and, most important, can you confirm that there was a meeting in France where Gusinsky *(inaudible)* tried to agree that Svyazinvest shares should be sold at the starting price? And a technical question. Yesterday Mr. Seleznyov and Mr. Kostikov today said nearly the same thing, that this strategic sector might be monopolized. Therefore one should give thought not only to budget revenues. Does Svyazinvest include … *(audio break)*

POTANIN: … material resources are tied to participation in Svyazinvest. I hope that it is not as large as in respect to Svyazinvest.

As for the visit to France, I can confirm that the visit did take place. The agreements were much more complex than they have been described. It is an absurd situation when businessmen do not try to come to an agreement. Groups always try to reach a compromise. They then enter into competition when no compromise can be found. In this case, there was a need to make sure that the state was committed to playing by the rules that it had announced, that is, to make sure that there would be fair competition during the auction. When we realized that no compromises could be achieved, and that the government was firmly committed to holding the auction in this form, attempts were abandoned to reach a compromise. I see nothing odd about the fact of business people entering negotiations in order to form alliances with respect to certain matters. In this case, an agreement was not reached.

KRUPNOV: About 100 enterprises in Russia, which ensure the transmission of television signals, are government-owned, unitary enterprises. They are not joint-stock companies. Some time ago the president signed decrees which state that the government should keep a controlling stake in the field of communications. So we do not lose control.

Q: Could you comment on media reports that *(break in tape)* …

POTANIN: I would urge you to draw a distinction between personal relationships and *(break in tape)* … I have tried to keep these two types of relationships separate and I urge everyone else to do the same.

As for having my people in the government. Do you mean only the parliament, or do you include the presidential administration?

Q: All of it.

POTANIN: We do have one man whom we delegated last year. He is Boris Abramovich Berezovsky. He is not our full-time representative because he has been promoted by several banks. There was one other person, but in March of last year he was sent back to reinforce the business community. So, we have no one else.

Q: *Megapolis Continent.* According to the rules of auctions, the winning financial group must include a professional operator and you don't yet seem to have one. This suggests that the buyer, that is, your group, is eventually committed not to the development of production, but to speculation in the exchange. The name of the world famous speculator George Soros is behind you and this seems to directly confirm what I have just said. The activities of Soros have come in for mixed assessments in Russia. So, will the holding develop and to what extent will such development correspond to the interests of Russia's national security?

POTANIN: There is considerable substance in that part of your question which deals with the existence of an operator, indeed, the existence of an operator in such a consortium is a plus, and the consortium set up on the initiative of the *Alfa Group*, the Most group, and the other participants in the consortium had such a plus.

Our consortium, it is true, does not have an operator, and from this point of view this appears to be a shortcoming. On the other hand, since the question of deciding on an operator can be solved at a later stage, this is not such a serious shortcoming that it would prevent us from working with Svyazinvest. More than that, our consultations with a number of professional operators in the communications market tell us that in the coming few months there is really no need to settle on an operator. It is first necessary to introduce an order that will make it possible to create the groundwork for deciding on such an operator.

Naturally we have plans to install an operator. But, and this is a very important point, by having control over the consortium that we set up, we have the possibility to jointly, with the issuer and the industry, arrive at a decision on what role an operator should fill, on how his image and background will work with the consortium, along with the issues of economic security that you mentioned.

As you can see, we retained the freedom of action in our choice of an operator. This is an important advantage.

As for the attitude of the special services, I think they themselves can state their attitude to any investor or to the origin of any monies. As I have already said, I respected the decision of Mr. Soros to invest such a large sum in our country's economy.

LIPKIN: I would like to continue, if I may. This is the second time that I have heard this phrase, that in accordance with the logic of the auction there must be an operator. The statute on auctions has long been known. The legislation on privatization sets very clear-cut and precise demands made of the buyer. There is nothing in it that requires an operator. I do not understand where you are getting this information.

Secondly, I would like to stress that there are demands made of the participation of foreigners, demands that are made by the seller after the auction. All these demands will be observed.

Q: *NHK.* Mr. Chubais said recently that the auction would be conducted according to strict rules. Did you have any preliminary arrangement with him? What *(off mike.)*

POTANIN: All the information that I have on this matter I presented yesterday in my answers to the questions put forth by *Interfax.* As I said today, a very complex compromise was discussed, a compromise that businessmen always strive to reach, a reasonable compromise. I do not want to discuss the details because any new information will only result in stirring up the situation even more. I would hope that the situation would normalize so that we can continue to work calmly with this transaction. We do not want the investors to worry.

I would like to make an appeal to you. If we, businessmen, do not have the brains to refrain from mutual mud slinging and the creation of problems for one another, please restrain us from time to time, and do not report on it in quite such detail.

Q: Did you have any contacts with the Spanish firm Telefonica and *(inaudible)*

POTANIN: We have not had any contact with them so far. As for attracting an operator, as I said, we will consider this together with the minister, with Mr. Ismailov, and I think that the Spanish telephone group will be among those with whom we negotiate.

Q: The journal *Foreign Economic Ties.* I have a question for Mr. Potanin. Is it a coincidence that press conferences are being held simultaneously here and at the Slavyanskaya Hotel?

POTANIN: I think it is a coincidence.

Q: Next question then. What brings you together or divides you from these two banks?

POTANIN: You mean MOST bank? You may find it odd, but there is much more that we have in common. What divides us is the Svyazinvest auction. We are jointly involved in credit and debit cards. And we have a common vision of the country's economic development. We have similar political orientations with the leadership of MOST, including Vladimir Alexandrovich Gusinsky. We have cooperated from time to time. And I hope that after this difficult, emotional period is behind us, we will be able to return to a normal dialogue, which will allow us all to become even richer.

Q: Did your tenure in a government post influence the financial structure?

POTANIN: I wasn't allowed into the top posts.

Q: You wanted to be premier?

POTANIN: No.

Q: *(off mike.)*

ISMAILOV: As for holding the meeting, in accordance with the terms, when the shares are transferred to our partner, we will announce the date of the meeting in accordance with the charter of the joint-stock company.

LIPKIN: That is, after the entire stake is paid for. In two and a half months' time.

Q: *(off mike.)*

ISMAILOV: The press has reported that the second auction (24 percent) will be open only to Russian bidders.

POTANIN: We are not considering this possibility because it is a strategic investment for us. Naturally, the next auction of 24 percent is of great interest to us. And everything will depend on whether we can organize our activities in such a way as to have the necessary assets at the necessary time. Basically, we have already made a sizable investment and we need to match our wishes with our resources.

Q: *(off mike.)*

POTANIN: The way the relationships are shaping up within the consortium, the biggest shareholders will be UNEXIMbank and Soros.

Q: *(off mike.)*

POTANIN: I have already answered this question. It will be a little less than 50 percent. That's including foreign participation.

Q: What percentage will Soros own?

POTANIN: I can't tell you exactly, but as I have already said, if Russian capital controls more than half and foreign capital less than half, the better part of the foreign capital will be controlled by Mr. Soros, and the better part of the Russian capital by UNEXIMbank.

Q: *(off mike.)*

POTANIN: I tried to answer this question. The answer is that we expect to take part, but we must weigh our financial resources.

Q: *(off mike.)*

POTANIN: Mr. Soros's sum has been reported. All the other foreign participants contributed between 100 and 200 million dollars. I don't think it is appropriate to name specific figures, and the other shares belong to the group MFK-Renaissance and UNEXIMbank.

And you wanted more details about the MUSTCOM Company. It is accepted international practice to set up a special legal entity to accomplish such tasks. I have cited examples and let me stress that this is done because people might be pursuing different goals. Some want to buy shares, some want to acquire derivative securities, some just want to credit a deal. All these elements are represented in our investment.

So, in order to marry the interests of different investors, a special legal entity is created.

Q: *(off mike.)*

POTANIN: Nemtsov backed our victory in the auction, but the amount of money earmarked for the budget was larger than expected. The organizers of the tender expected about 1.5 billion. But eventually the sum exceeded expectations and I understand that Nemtsov, Chubais, and other government members, including the prime minister, have expressed their satisfaction with the sum, the result, but not with the name of the specific winner. As for the signing of the contract, it was never planned that I would sign it. You see, the legal entity that was established in Cyprus has its own director, has people with the power of attorney to sign such documents. The people who worked on the structure of the transaction, who have the appropriate authority from the investors and the appropriate authority from MUSTCOM, should sign the document.

Therefore the circle of persons empowered to sign such transactions does not include me. It is a practice that such contracts are signed not on the level of the holding, but on the level of the structures that invested money in the holding. Therefore this was nothing more than a technical matter.

The right of signature belonged to Mr. Roshevkin and to Mr. Smolyaninov. I believe this exhausts the list of persons with this right on behalf of MUSTCOM.

Q: *RIA Novosti (off mike.)*

POTANIN: Concerning Rosneft. We are now studying this question. The answer to this question boils down roughly to the same as in respect to the 24 percent of Svyazinvest. In other words, since our strategic investments in the oil sphere are well known, Rosneft is attractive to us. But the sum of the investment is so large that we will have to adopt a special decision in order to go forward. We will be very carefully weighing our financial possibilities and, most importantly, our organizational possibilities.

We would not want our strategic investments to suffer from the insufficient attention of our brightest intellectual forces in the group.

As for your question about the tax consequences of such a transaction, I don't think the Russian budget will suffer. The participation of our group, through the Cyprus-registered company MFK-Kipr, was set up specifically for this purpose. We obtained a license from the Central Bank, along with permission to export capital to set up this company. We set it up specifically to be able to take part in such a transaction.

Since we have consolidated accounts, I mean with the bank MFK-Renaissance and MFK-Kipr, this structure is absolutely transparent, both to the Central Bank and to our tax organizations.

Registration in an offshore zone allows us to save on taxes, not Russian taxes, but on the taxes of the country of record. And the most well-known international corporations make use of this. Since tax laws are relatively lenient in Cyprus, the company will pay very few local taxes. Everything that is to be paid in Russia will be paid. Because, as I said, the balance sheet is a consolidated one. Everything that we receive as a profit from the Russian organization will be paid to the Russian tax organizations.

Q: Were you invited to the Prosecutor's Office as a witness? How will you square your need to make maximum profit with your other obligations since obviously you will be hiking tariffs?

LIPKIN: The contract includes a time frame.

POTANIN: Payment under the contract must be made within 75 days after its signing. The payment is to be made in two sums. This will be done. In other words, the final payment will be made 75 days from today.

LIPKIN: Not later than October 13, 1997, and the first payment no later than August 14, 1997.

POTANIN: Please, don't upset me. I don't like to speak about money when it comes to giving it away.

As to being summoned as a witness, I have not yet been summoned.

And you also asked about tariffs.

LIPKIN: As we have said already, an end should be put to cross subsidizing. Tariffs related to economic structures, budget structures, and the population should be leveled out. This is the first point.

The second point concerns the following factor. Today in Russia all tariffs for local communications services are much lower than production costs. In Moscow the cost of a telephone to the city telephone company is 35,000 rubles a month, but subscribers, me included, pay only 20,000 rubles. This is not equitable. That is why the task set by the government is to raise tariffs in the short term, to at least 80 percent of cost.

By creating an equitable structure we create a base for the successful development of communication networks. At the same time we will be assisting the budget. Last year communications generated 10 trillion rubles of revenue. As a result of our development, the country will generate more taxes from communications. This is the practice worldwide.

Q: What do you mean when you say equitable?

LIPKIN: I am not talking about fairness. I am simply stating that the costs exceed the payments received.

Q: Will you raise telephone charges, that is what I am asking.

LIPKIN: There is a law set up for veterans—*(inaudible)*—

Q: On what terms will you be setting up your operator?

KRUPNOV: On what terms? It is very difficult to give an answer to this now. We have not yet even decided on how we will conduct our talks with an operator. At this press conference we have returned to this question twice. I will say once again that the process of choosing an operator, at what stage to call him in and what work should precede this decision, is a matter that we will discuss in the future. This work has just begun. And it is hard for me to predict what the terms will be.

Q: But from a professional point of view. Can you tell me who might be a candidate for such a position?

ISMAILOV: First of all, the shares have been sold to a holding company and not to the operator who will offer communication services. Communication services are delivered by subsidiary regional joint-stock companies. Operators have to be brought in at the bottom level and not at the level of the holding.

Secondly. Today many regional companies work with foreign operators in transborder communications, in international communications. This is routine procedure and we also will work in this way.

Q: *(off mike.)*

ISMAILOV: We are preparing several regional companies for a secondary issue. A draft government decree has been prepared to this effect. And we believe that starting in 1998, we will build on our own resources and by agreement with our new partners we will be able to launch secondary issues on a large scale.

POTANIN: It remains for me to confirm this information. We are considering the option of taking part in additional issues of shares by subsidiary companies, meaning to restore the proportional share of Svyazinvest. We believe that this will be a key source for attracting investment to regional companies.

Q: *Mayak*. I have a question in connection with a statement by Dorenko, who made an accusation against your bank in one of his newscasts. He said it carried out a transaction which made it possible to transfer 42 million dollars abroad. As I understand it, this was organized by your bank for the Cherepovets Azot factory. And in connection with this, my question is, can you guarantee that your group will not recommend a shady partner?

POTANIN: I understand your question. To transfer money abroad or to engage in illegal transactions, luckily, for all of us, is no longer possible. The bank structures have become too transparent and the Central Bank is doing an excellent job of monitoring this process, which makes it virtually impossible to conceal any such transactions. As an example, UNEXIM-MFK group, I am afraid, has been inspected more than 30 times over the last year and a half. I am not complaining. This is standard procedure. What I mean to say is that banks are under such close scrutiny that one can hardly hide anything.

Besides, as you already know, UNEXIMbank has a subsidiary in Switzerland and we submit consolidated reports to the Swiss authorities. That is, we report for the subsidiary bank and for the mother bank, that is, UNEXIMbank in Moscow. And they are extremely thorough; they ask many more questions than the Central Bank here, so in a certain sense, the legality of the transaction is even more closely monitored. Even if we wanted to, not a single bank could manage an illegal transaction.

As for Cherepovets, this is a question outside our current discussion, so I will not divert attention to it. But very briefly, participation in the Cherepovets deal was simply a financial investment. That is, we were financial agents on behalf of a group of banks. There were other respectable Russian participants. The roles were distributed. We played the role of financial agent. Other participants were in charge of managing the plant, and so on. The management of the company that was chosen was not up to scratch. So, we decided to replace the manager and to sell the company as a financial asset. It took a year to select a managing company which had the capacity to buy out the stake and to assume responsibility for all the problems at the plant. As a financial investor, we were not part of the solution of the complex problems facing the plant, which were correctly pointed out. So, our task was to pick a new partner.

It was a very painstaking process because of the objective difficulties faced by the plant. That work was completed about a year ago and eight months ago, I believe. The stake was sold and Cherepovets now has a new owner, which hopefully will implement the investment program. Let us keep our fingers crossed that it will forge normal relationships with the management and with Mr. Lipkin.

Q: What will the impact be of the argument over the deal on future Western investments in the country?

POTANIN: Any scandal has a negative impact on investment. This is an axiom. Money, especially big money from serious investors, requires quiet and respect and not scandal.

Q: But the prices are rising.

POTANIN: Yes, prices are rising.

Q: As Mr. *(inaudible)* rightly pointed out, the new owner of Svyazinvest will have to make agreements locally. Do you allow for the possibility that Svyazinvest representatives will get seats on the board of directors of subsidiary companies? For example, do you foresee representatives of UNEXIMbank attempting this in the regions, and locally where they have the time and resources to interact with the local administrations in order to allow (inaudible) … ?

ISMAILOV: Let me repeat that the company has bought shares of Svyazinvest and not shares of the regional companies. So, owning shares of the holding it cannot exert direct influence on the regional companies. Svyazinvest today has representatives and workers in every region who are promoting a policy necessary to manage the regional companies.

As for possible versions of relationships with the company, that will be determined not by emotions, but by what is necessary for the development of communications in Russia.

Q: *Dow Jones*, USA. You have said that on the eve of the auction you tried to make a compromise with the other participant. Do you believe that these attempts are in line with anti-monopoly declarations and could you name other tenders that were preceded by such attempts?

POTANIN: I don't know if you have ever witnessed business people anywhere in the world who in making a deal did not seek to promote their own interests? So, inasmuch as interests are in harmony, compromises are possible. Beyond a certain line it is called an insider deal. This is the line that one should not cross. I do not want to dwell on this issue, but the very fact of the numerous scandals connected with other recent auctions demonstrates the absence of such collusion.

The matter is not only in the anti-monopoly legislation that regulates other questions. Here, I believe, the matter is more about business ethics.

LIPKIN: I would like to add that the legislation on privatization does much to minimize the possibilities for such collusion. This legislation restricts only what should be restricted.

Q: How long did you cooperate with Mr. Soros and how?

POTANIN: Mr. Soros is one of the largest clients of Renaissance-Capital, as far as I know, and the talks with him, just as with the other investors, were conducted by MFK-Renaissance-Capital. I have already emphasized the significant role played by them in completing this transaction. They carried out the entire technical aspect of the transaction, conducted technical talks with the investors, including with Soros.

Q: Do you have a personal relationship with Soros, did you have any meetings, did you conduct any of the talks?

POTANIN: I have not yet met Mr. Soros.

Q: *(off mike.)*

LIPKIN: The protocol was signed on July 25. On July 28 it was approved. I will be happy to hand out copies of the protocol. The consent of the anti-monopoly committee should be received in the course of 8 weeks, and it should be no later than the date of the final payment. If we are denied this consent, we will have to return the money and the transaction will be called off. This is contained in the Regulations.

POTANIN: So, we have covered the anti-monopoly proposition. As for the number of seats, the situation is as follows. As far as I understand, the composition under the Charter is 9 people, and 25 percent gives us the opportunity to put forth at least two of our people.

Q: And what about the management?

POTANIN: Strictly speaking, management is in charge of day-to-day affairs, so Mr. Ismailov and I will be discussing all these activities. And if the company needs specialists to strengthen any aspect of its activities, we will look for them jointly. But we have no right to appoint our man to the management team, we do not insist on this.

Q: I have a question for Mr. Potanin. Don't you get the feeling that the other participants in that Paris meeting are suspicious? After all, there was an initial agreement. How do you account for the intense emotion that has accompanied this deal?

POTANIN: I wouldn't care to attribute the intense emotions to any specific cause. The emotion is there and I hope the emotions soon will subside. As for feelings, the entire episode can hardly prompt any positive feelings. And it doesn't.

Q: Could the other side have emerged from the meeting feeling that an agreement had been reached?

POTANIN: You know, Mr. Chubais so firmly stated the government's position, citing the position of Viktor Chernomyrdin, the position of the president, that it seems to me that neither myself, nor my partners could have had any lingering illusions.

Q: *Obozrevatel.* Your partner George Soros has been accused of violating Russian security information.

Don't you think that because the main fund is Soros's charitable fund, and since they are headed by the same man, you might get into trouble with the security branches in Russia who could accuse you of threatening Russian security?

POTANIN: I don't expect to run into any problems with the "security branches" because they have been familiar with Mr. Soros and his investments for a very long time, and I have never received any official warning that they have any concerns with him. And honestly, I have never seen any official documents to that fact. My experience of cooperation—indirect cooperation with Mr. Soros—is somewhat different. I know of one instance when the government received credits in the intervening period between certain transactions; for example, the issue of Eurobonds in which our bank and the Soros Fund took part. So, I would suggest that he has a friendly attitude towards us and in some cases a somewhat non-commercial approach. That is, the interest he charged on the loans was much lower than could have been charged in such a situation.

So, I am inclined to think—at least I have witnessed episodes that attest to Soros's favorable attitude to the country. By the way, in his recent interview, Mr. Soros said that with the advent of Nemtsov and the new team, the renewed government, he had substantially revised his attitude to Russia as a destination for investments and is now much more optimistic. That's touching on what changed with the advent of Chubais and Nemtsov. A lot has changed for the better.

MODERATOR: Final question, please.

Q: *(off mike.)*

POTANIN: Paeans to George Soros at this press conference. The bank has no interests, either strategic or tactical. The operation that received such coverage was a routine financial operation with debt instruments or bonds that we carried out. As for Soros, I repeat, different people have different views of the activities of an investor or a politician.

In terms of Soros's activities, I have witnessed examples that would characterize him, to use your terminology, as a philanthropist rather than as a speculator. Incidentally, the word speculator in other languages does not sound as ominous as in the Russian language. Therefore, I would say that he is a businessman who develops a relationship with a country in such a way so as to get most favored treatment there. That is from where he proceeds.

LIPKIN: Unfortunately, I have no personal opinion of Soros. I have not concluded any transactions with him. Therefore, there is nothing that I can tell you.

Appendix 8

Carter-Ruck
Solicitors
International Press Centre
78 Shoe Lane
London EC4A 3JB
November 18, 2004

Mikhail Fridman
Chairman
Alfa Bank
107078 Moscow
Kalantchevskaya str. 27
Russia

and at

107078 Moscow
Masha Poryvayeva Str. 9
Russia

Dear Sir

Boris Berezovsky and NTV

We have been consulted by our client, Mr. Boris Berezovsky who, as you know, is resident in this country where he was granted refugee status in September last year.

It is a matter of serious concern to our client that, in a programme broadcast in this country by NTV on 28 October, you alleged that he had called up and "threatened" you while you were discussing with *Kommersant* shareholders the possibility of your bank lending money to them in order to prevent him from taking control of the publication. In context the specific Russian word you used "ugrozhal" meant and would have been understood by Russian-speaking viewers to mean that you were accusing our client of threatening you with violence. Further you went on to allege that this was Mr. Berezovsky's usual approach.

Our client denies that he ever threatened you with violence—indeed he denies even speaking with you at the time concerning his acquisition of

Kommersant—and is deeply offended that you have chosen to make this false accusation against him.

Whilst we do not presently have precise viewing figures for NTV in this country, our understanding is that there are several hundred subscribers, and the programme on which you appeared is popular. Our client's reputation amongst the Russian community in this country, likely to form the bulk of the audience, is important to him, and he is not prepared to allow your allegation to pass unchallenged.

Accordingly, the purpose of this letter is to invite you to agree at the earliest opportunity to issue to our client a public apology, withdrawing the allegation you have made, which we would then propose to invite NTV to broadcast to its subscribers in this country. Our client will also require that you reimburse the legal costs which it has been necessary for him to incur. Our client will review his entitlement to seek damages for libel in the light of your response to this letter.

We should make clear that in the absence of prompt and satisfactory proposals from you, we have instructions to commence proceedings for libel in this country, naming both you and *Alfa Bank* as defendants. We trust, accordingly, that we shall hear from you within ten days of the date of this letter. In the meantime, we should make it clear that all our client's rights are reserved.

Yours faithfully

Carter-Ruck

Appendix 9

Herbert Smith
Exchange House
Primrose Street
London EC2A 2HS
T +44 (0)20 7274 8000
F +44 (0)20 7374 0888

Carter-Ruck
International Press Center
76 Shoe Lane
London
EC4A 3JB

By fax and by post
Boris Berezovsky
December 9, 2004

Dear Sirs

We have been instructed by Mr. Mikhail Fridman and *Alfa Bank* in respect of the complaint of your client, Mr. Berezovsky, set out in your letter to Mr. Fridman dated 18 November 2004. We have now had an opportunity to investigate this complaint with our other clients.

Our clients deny any liability to your client in respect of the statements made by Mr. Fridman in course of the NTV television programme "To the Barrier" broadcast on 28 October 2004 ("the Programme").

We note that you have not provided a transcript of the Programme or the part of the Programme in respect of which your client complains. The Programme consisted of a lengthy debate between Mr. Fridman and Andrei Vasiliev, general director of the publishing house *Kommersant*, and was chaired by Vladimir Soloviov. The subject of the debate was the *Alfa Bank's* recent successful libel action against *Kommersant*. In the course of the debate Mr. Fridman referred to the fact that in 1999 he had discussed with the then shareholders of *Kommersant* the prospect of *Alfa Bank* loaning them money. He further states that your client called him in respect of these discussions and threatened him.

Mr. Fridman informs us that your client did telephone him at the relevant time and made threats that he would use his influence by virtue of his owner ship of certain media entities to bring commercial pressure to bear upon Mr. Fridman and *Alfa Bank* if *Alfa Bank* loaned money to then share holders of *Kommersant*. It was threats of this nature that Mr. Fridman was referring to when he used the term "ugrozhal" and not threats of violence as you suggest in your letter. In context, the viewers of the Programme in this country would have clearly understood the use of the word "ugrozhal" and these terms.

Accordingly, our clients deny publishing any statements that are capable of being defamatory of your client.

We trust that this clarifies the position.

Yours faithfully

[signature of Herbert Smith]

Appendix 10

Carter-Ruck
Solicitors
International Press Centre
76 Shoe Lane
London EC4A 3JB

Tel 020 7353 5005
Fax 020 7353 5553
Date: December 23, 2004

BY FAX AND POST: 020 7374 0888

Herbert Smith
DX 28
London

Dear Sir

Boris Berezovsky, Mikhail Fridman and *Alfa Bank*

We thank you for you letter of 9 December.

Whether viewers of the programme would have understood your client to be alleging that our client had threatened him with violence or that he had made other improper threats (as you assert in your letter) Mr. Fridman's words, spoken in his capacity as Chairman of *Alfa Bank*, are defamatory of Mr. Berezovsky. There is also a direct conflict of evidence between our respective clients; as we have made clear, Mr. Berezovsky denies ever discussing the matter with your client. If, as it appears, your clients are not prepared to apologize, we must ask you to confirm that you have instructions on behalf of Mr. Fridman and *Alfa Bank* to accept service of proceedings in this country.

Yours faithfully

Carter-Ruck

APPENDIX 11

Herbert Smith
Exchange House
Primrose Street London EC2A 2HS
T +44 (0)20 7374 8000
F +44 (0)20 7374 0888
D +44 (0)20 7466 +44 (0)20 7466 2024

Carter-Ruck
International Press Centre
76 Shoe Lane
London EC4A 3JB
January 14, 2005

By fax and by post

Boris Berezovsky

Dear Sirs

We refer to your letter of 23 December 2004, on which we have now had an opportunity to take our clients' instructions following the Russian New Year holiday.

We have made our clients' position clear; Mr. Fridman's statements referred to threats of a commercial nature, and this is how they would have been understood by the audience of the broadcast.

We note that in your letter you seek to characterize threats of this nature as "improper." We understand that in the context of Russian business, threats to exert commercial pressure are relatively commonplace. We are instructed that this was particularly true of the period in question. Accordingly, statements that your client made threats of a commercial nature in 1999 are not capable of being defamatory of him.

Yours faithfully

[signature of Herbert Smith]

Appendix 12

Herbert Smith
Exchange House
Primrose Street
London EC2A 2HS
T +44 (0)20 7374 8000
F +44 (0)20 7374 0888
D +44 (0)20 7466 +44 (0)30 7466 2024

Carter-Ruck
International Press Centre
76 Shoe Lane
London EC4A 3JB
January 28, 2005
By fax and by post

Boris Berezovsky

Dear Sirs

We refer to your letter of today's date.

We are taking our client's instructions in respect of the service of proceedings. We should be grateful if you would confirm by return that you will not make any application to the court for permission to serve out the jurisdiction until we have responded to your letter, on the basis that we respond before 5 pm on Wednesday, 2 February 2005.

Yours faithfully

[signature]

Appendix 13

Herbert Smith
Exchange House
Primrose Street
London EC2A 2HS
T +44 (0)20 7374 8000
F +44 (0)20 7374 0888
D +44 (0)20 7466 +44 (0)30 7466 2024

Carter-Ruck
International Press Centre
76 Shoe Lane
London EC4A 3JB
February 3, 2005
By fax and by post
Boris Berezovsky

Dear Sirs

We refer to your January 28, 2005.

We have not been instructed to accept service of proceedings on behalf of *Alfa Bank* or Mr. Fridman. Accordingly, should your client wish to issue proceedings against our clients, we will be obliged to apply to the court for leave to serve the claim from out of the jurisdiction in accordance with CPR 6.20.

Should your client apply for leave, we should be grateful if you would give us prior notice, and we invite you to provide to us a copy of the witness statement prepared in support of your application. We have reviewed the Court of Appeal's judgment in Dow Jones and Co Inc. v. Yousef Abdul Latif Jameel [2005] EWCA Civ 75 and would expect such a witness statement to contain full particulars of your client's case, including, inter alia, the following:

1. Confirmation that your client is a full time resident in this country;
2. Confirmation that your client is not able to return to Russia, or bring proceedings in that forum;
3. Full details of the case that your client intends to bring, including the words that your client complains of, and the meaning that he intends to ascribe to those words;

4. Full details of the publications of the purportedly defamatory statements in this country, including details as to the extent of the distribution of the publication;

5. The names of any publishers in this country that you are able to identify;

6. Whether it is your case that these publications understood the words complained of to have the same meaning that which your client alleges.

Yours faithfully

[signature]

Appendix 14

Herbert Smith
Exchange House
Primrose Street
London EC2A 2HS
T +44 (0)20 7374 8000
F +44 (0)20 7374 0888
D +44 (0)20 7466 +44 (0)30 7466 2024

Carter-Ruck
International Press Centre
76 Shoe Lane
London EC4A 3JB
April 6, 2005
By fax and by post
Boris Berezovsky

Dear Sirs

We refer to your letter of 30 March 2005. We are taking our clients' instructions, and will respond to your letter shortly.

Yours faithfully
[signature]

APPENDIX 15

Herbert Smith
Exchange House
Primrose Street
London EC2A 2HS
T +44 (0)20 7374 8000
F +44 (0)20 7374 0888
D +44 (0)20 7466 +44 (0)30 7466 2024

Carter-Ruck
International Press Centre
76 Shoe Lane
London EC4A 3JB
April 26, 2005

By fax and by post

Boris Berezovsky

Dear Sirs

We refer to your letters to Mr. Simon Roache of *Alfa Capital Markets* dated 24 March, 11 April, and 20 April 2005.

We note that you have purported to effect service of proceedings on *Alfa Bank* by serving proceedings on *Alfa Capital Markets* at its offices in London. Whilst it is clear that *Alfa Capital Markets* is neither a branch nor place of business of *Alfa Bank*, we see little purpose in applying to the Court to set aside the Claim Form. Accordingly, we have filed an Acknowledgment of Service as Court, but on the basis that *Alfa Bank* makes no admission as to any presence within the jurisdiction. We enclose a sealed copy of the Acknowledgment of Service for your information. You will note that we have included the correct address of *Alfa Bank* in the document.

Yours faithfully
[signature]

Appendix 16

Herbert Smith
Exchange House
Primrose Street
London EC2A 2HS
T +44 (0)20 7374 8000
F +44 (0)20 7374 0888
D +44 (0)20 7466 +44 (0)30 7466 2024

Carter-Ruck
International Press Centre
76 Shoe Lane
London EC4A 3JB

By fax and by post

May 2, 2005

Without Prejudice

Boris Berezovsky

Dear Sirs

We refer to your letters of 30 March 2005 and 4 April 2005, together with our letter of 6 April 2005.

Thank you for providing to us a copy of the Order of Master Turner, together with the First Witness Statement of Andrew Stephenson in support of your client's application to serve proceedings on Mr. Fridman out of the jurisdiction. We note that in your letter of 30 March 2005 you enquired whether Mr. Fridman was prepared to instruct us to accept service of proceedings on his behalf in order that your client avoid the expense and delay of serving in Russia.

On the basis that your client agrees to an extension of time for the service of *Alfa Bank's* Defense of up to 28 days, Mr. Fridman would be amenable to the proposal that he instructed us to accept service of proceedings on his behalf. Given that the Amended Claim Forum and Amended Particulars of Claim were delivered to Alfa Capital Markets on 20 April 2005, and an Acknowledgment of Service has been filed, we calculated the final date for service of *Alfa Bank's* Defense to be Thursday, 16 June 2005. We would propose that a single Defense be served on behalf of both of our clients on this date.

We should be grateful if you would confirm your client's agreement to this extension of time, in which case we will set out our client's position with regard to service in open correspondence.

Yours faithfully
[signature]

Appendix 17

Herbert Smith
Exchange House
Primrose Street
London EC2A 2HS
T +44 (0)20 7374 8000
F +44 (0)20 7374 0888
D +44 (0)20 7466 +44 (0)30 7466 2024

Carter-Ruck
International Press Centre
76 Shoe Lane
London EC4A 3JB
May 9, 2005
By fax and by post

Dear Sirs

Boris Berezovsky -v- (1) Mikhail Fridman (2) *Alfa Bank*: Claim No. HQ05X00815

We refer to your letter of 4 May 2005 enclosing an Amended Claim Forum and Amended Particulars of Claim in respect of Mr. Mikhail Fridman. We enclose a stamped copy of our client's Acknowledgment of Service which was filed at Court earlier today.

We also enclose a copy of our letter of today to the Court Manager notifying the Court that we have agreed an extension of time for the service of our clients' Defense until 16 June 2005.

Yours faithfully
[signature]

Appendix 18

Herbert Smith
Exchange House
Primrose Street
London EC2A 2HS
T +44 (0)20 7374 8000
F +44 (0)20 7374 0888
D +44 (0)20 7466 +44 (0)30 7466 2024

The Court Manager
Queen's Bench Division
Royal Courts of Justice
Strand
London
WC2A 2LL
May 9, 2005

Dear Sir

Boris Berezovsky -v- (1) Mikhail Fridman (2) Alpha Bank: Claim No. HQ05X00815

We act on behalf of the Defendants in the above matter.

The Claimant's solicitors, Carter-Ruck, served an Amended Claims Forum and Amended Particulars of Claim on the Second Defendant on 20 April 2005, and served an Amended Claim Forum and Amended Particulars Claim on the First Defendant on 5 May 2005. We acknowledge service of these proceedings on 25 April and 9 May 2005 respectively. We have agreed with Carter-Ruck an extension of time for the service of our clients' Defense of up to 28 days under CPR 15.5. Accordingly, we should be grateful if you would record on the court file that the agreed final date for service of our clients' Defense is Thursday, 16 June 2005.

Should you have any questions in respect of the contents of this letter, or the matter generally, please do not hesitate to contact Jonathan Cary of this office.

Yours faithfully
[signature]

cc Carter-Ruck

Appendix 19

Herbert Smith
Exchange House
Primrose Street
London EC2A 2HS
T +44 (0)20 7374 8000
F +44 (0)20 7374 0888
D +44 (0)20 7466 +44 (0)30 7466 2024

Carter-Ruck
International Press Centre
76 Shoe Lane
London EC4A 3JB

June 16, 2005

By fax and by courier

Boris Berezovsky

Dear Sirs

We enclose by way of service our clients' Defense.

We also enclose a request for further information and clarification of your client's Amended Particulars of Claim made pursuant to CPR 18. We ask that you provide a response to this request before 8 July 2005.

Kindly acknowledge receipt.

Yours faithfully
[signature]

INDEX